Truth

Engagements Across Philosophical Traditions

"There are no longer two dialogues – analytic and continental. It is all one now, and more complicated than ever. This collection is an indispensable point of entry to the new conversations."

Barry Allen, McMaster University

"It is virtually impossible to imagine a more useful collection of texts on this thorny philosophical topic. There is no pretense that herein lies the truth about truth, but there is the realization of a set of complex issues illuminated from radically diverse, yet often surprisingly overlapping, perspectives."

Vincent Colapietro, Pennsylvania State University

"While there are many collections concerning debates about truth, this book is unique. It not only provides a paradigm for doing philosophy in a pluralistic manner; it also shows how fruitful it can be."

James Bohman, St. Louis University

"This carefully crafted anthology on what Medina and Wood call 'the normative turn' in the debate on truth provides a welcome opportunity to put into practice a philosophical pluralism that is too often absent from the classroom."

Robert Bernasconi, University of Memphis

"This is a remarkable anthology of diverse readings on one of the central philosophical topics. Not many books nestle texts by Heidegger, Levinas, and Catherine Elgin next to one another. Still fewer try to help readers see how thinkers like these offer conflicting, but mutually illuminating, approaches to the same subject matter. This volume promises to help bridge the regrettable rift between 'continental' and 'analytic' ways of doing philosophy, and that is something to be celebrated."

Harvey Cormier, Stony Brook University

BLACKWELL READINGS IN CONTINENTAL PHILOSOPHY

Series Editor: Simon Critchley, University of Essex

Each volume in this series provides a detailed introduction to and overview of a central philosophical topic in the Continental tradition. In contrast to the author-based model that has hitherto dominated the reception of the Continental philosophical tradition in the English-speaking world, this series presents the central issues of that tradition, topics that should be of interest to anyone concerned with philosophy. Cutting across the stagnant ideological boundaries that mark the analytic/Continental divide, the series will initiate discussions that reflect the growing dissatisfaction with the organization of the English-speaking philosophical world. Edited by a distinguished international forum of philosophers, each volume provides a critical overview of a distinct topic in Continental philosophy through a mix of both classic and newly commissioned essays from both philosophical traditions.

Truth

Engagements Across
Philosophical Traditions

Edited by

José Medina and David Wood

Blackwell
Publishing

BLACKWELL PUBLISHING
350 Main Street, Malden, MA 02148-5020, USA
108 Cowley Road, Oxford OX4 1JF, UK
550 Swanston Street, Carlton, Victoria 3053, Australia

First published 2005 by Blackwell Publishing Ltd

Library of Congress Cataloging-in-Publication Data

Truth: engagements across philosophical traditions / edited by José Medina and
David Wood.
     p.   cm. – (Blackwell readings in Continental philosophy)
  Includes bibliographical references and index.
  ISBN 1-4051-1549-1 (alk. paper) – ISBN 1-4051-1550-5 (pbk. :
  alk. paper)   1. Truth.   I. Medina, José, 1968–   II. Wood, David (David C.)
  III. Title.   IV. Series.

BC171.T75 2005
121 – dc22

                                                              2004016923

A catalogue record for this title is available from the British Library.

Set in 10.5 on 12.5 pt Bembo
by SNP Best-set Typesetter Ltd, Hong Kong
Printed and bound in the United Kingdom
by MPG Books Ltd, Bodmin, Cornwall

The publisher's policy is to use permanent paper from mills that operate a sus-
tainable forestry policy, and which has been manufactured from pulp processed
using acid-free and elementary chlorine-free practices. Furthermore, the publisher
ensures that the text paper and cover board used have met acceptable environ-
mental accreditation standards.

For further information on
Blackwell Publishing, visit our website:
www.blackwellpublishing.com

CONTENTS

PREFACE

This editorial project could not have been carried out without the enthusiastic support of Jeff Dean at Blackwell, for whose constant help and encouragement we are most grateful. We are also indebted to all our colleagues and graduate students at Vanderbilt University who have stimulated our conversation and provided the ideal atmosphere for crossing boundaries and maintaining a dialogue across philosophical traditions. We are particularly grateful to those graduates and undergraduates to whom we experimentally introduced some of these ideas in topic-oriented courses: Medina, "Truth and Interpretation," Fall 2000; Wood, "The Paradoxes of Truth," Spring 2003. Special thanks go to our editorial assistant Aaron Simmons who has worked tirelessly and patiently with us on this project and (with Chad Maxson) prepared the index.

We have shared equal responsibility in the development of this project from its inception to its completion. All the selections and introductory essays are the product of our collaborative work over the last four years. For the record, although we share responsibility for each of the sections, José Medina is the primary author of the introductions to sections 1, 2, and 3, and David Wood of those to sections 4, 5, and 6. We co-wrote the General Introduction and the concluding Supplement.

ACKNOWLEDGMENTS

The editors and publisher gratefully acknowledge the permission granted to reproduce the copyright material in this book:

1. Friedrich Nietzsche, "On Truth and Lies in a Nonmoral Sense," pp. 79–91 in *Philosophy and Truth: Selections from Nietzsche's Notebooks of the Early 1870s*, ed. and trans. Daniel Breazeale (Atlantic Highlands, NJ: Humanities Press, 1979). © by Daniel Breazeale. Reprinted with permission.

1b. Friedrich Nietzsche, *The Will to Power*, trans. Walter Kaufmann and R. J. Hollingdale (New York: Vintage Books, 1968), pp. 289, 292. Reprinted by permission of the publisher.

1c. Friedrich Nietzsche, *Beyond Good and Evil*, trans. Helen Zimmern (Edinburgh and London: T. N. Foulis, 1909), pp. 5–6.

1d. Friedrich Nietzsche, *Twilight of the Idols*, trans. R. J. Hollingdale (London: Penguin, 1968), p. 41. Reprinted by permission of Penguin Books Ltd.

2. William James, "Pragmatism's Conception of Truth," in *Pragmatism: A New Name for Some Old Ways of Thinking* (London: Longman, 1907), pp. 197–236.

3. Søren Kierkegaard, excerpts from *Concluding Unscientific Postscript to* Philosophical Fragments, Vol. 1: Text, ed. and trans. Howard V. Hong and Edna. H. Hong (Princeton: Princeton University Press, 1992), pp. 72–82, 85–6, 91–2, 106–8, 189–94, 198–200, 202–5. © 1992 by Princeton University Press. Reprinted by permission of Princeton University Press.

4. Ludwig Wittgenstein, *On Certainty*, ed. G. E. M. Anscombe and G. H. von Wright, trans. Denis Paul and G. E. M. Anscombe (Oxford: Basil Blackwell, 1969), pp. 15–18, 20–3, 27–8 (§ 94–117, 137–62, 191–206). Reprinted by permission of Blackwell Publishing.

4b. Ludwig Wittgenstein, *Culture and Value: A Selection from the Posthumous Remains*, edited by G. H von Wright in collaboration with Heikki Nyman (second edition of the text by Alois Pichler, translated by Peter Winch) (Oxford: Blackwell, 1998), pp. 41, 64. This book was originally published as *Vermischte Bemerkungen* in 1977 (revised second edition 1994). Reprinted by permission of Blackwell Publishing.

5. Donald Davidson, *Inquiries Into Truth and Interpretation* (Oxford: Clarendon Press: 1984), pp. 22–36. Reprinted by permission of Oxford University Press.

6. Hilary Putnam, excerpts from "The Face of Cognition," in *The Threefold Cord: Mind, Body, and World* (New York: Columbia University Press, 1999), pp. 49–59, 64–70. Reprinted by permission of Columbia University Press.

7. Richard Rorty, "Representation, Social Practise, and Truth," from *Philosophical Studies* 54 (1988), pp. 215–28. Reprinted with kind permission of Kluwer Academic Publishers and the author.

8. Jürgen Habermas, "Richard Rorty's Pragmatic Turn," in *Rorty and His Critics*, ed. Robert Brandom (Oxford: Blackwell: 2000), p. 32 (excerpt), 37–55. Reprinted by permission of Blackwell Publishing.

9. John McDowell, "Towards Rehabilitating Objectivity," in *Rorty and His Critics*, ed. Robert Brandom (Oxford: Blackwell, 2000), pp. 109–23. Reprinted by permission of Blackwell Publishing.

10. Paul Feyerabend, "Notes on Relativism," in *Farewell to Reason* (London and New York: Verso, 1987), pp. 49–62. Reprinted by permission of the publisher.

11. Gianni Vattimo, "The Truth of Hermeneutics," © 1991 from *Questioning Foundations*, ed. Hugh Silverman (London: Routledge, 1991), pp. 11–28, 255–6 (notes). Reprinted by permission of Routledge/Taylor & Francis Books, Inc.

11b. Gianni Vattimo, excerpts from *The Adventure of Difference: Philosophy after Nietzsche and Heidegger*, trans. Cyprian Blamires (Baltimore: Johns Hopkins University Press, 1993), pp. 40, 41, 50, 52, 54, 58. Reprinted by permission of Polity Press.

12. Joseph Margolis, excerpts from "Relativism and Cultural Relativity," in *What, After All, Is a Work of Art?: Lectures in the Philosophy of Art* (University Park, PA: Pennsylvania State University Press, 1999), pp. 41–65. © 1999 by The Pennsylvania State University. Reprinted by permission of the publisher.

13. Maurice Merleau-Ponty, "An Unpublished Text" by Maurice Merleau-Ponty: A Prospectus of His Work, trans. Arleen B. Dallery, in *Primacy of Perception*, ed. James M. Edie (Evanston, IL: Northwestern University Press, 1964), pp. 3–11. Reprinted by permission of Éditions Gallimard and Northwestern University Press.

13b. Maurice Merleau-Ponty, excerpts from "Cézanne's Doubt," in *Sense and Non-Sense*, trans. Hubert L. Dreyfus and Patricia Allen Dreyfus (Evanston, IL: Northwestern University Press, 1964), pp. 13–16. Reprinted by permission of Éditions Gallimard and Northwestern University Press.

13c. Maurice Merleau-Ponty, excerpts from "Reflection and Interrogation," in *The Visible and the Invisible*, ed. Claude Lefort, trans. Alphonso Lingis (Evanston, IL:

Northwestern University Press, 1968), pp. 41–3, 49. Reprinted by permission of
Éditions Gallimard and Northwestern University Press.

14. Jacques Derrida, *Of Grammatology*, trans. Gayatri Chakravorty Spivak (Baltimore
and London: The Johns Hopkins University Press, 1976), pp 6–26, 323–5 (notes).
© 1997 by The Johns Hopkins University Press. Reprinted with the permission
of The Johns Hopkins University Press.

15. Edmund Husserl, *Logical Investigations*, Vol. I, trans. J. N. Findlay (London:
Routledge & Kegan Paul, 1970), pp. 760–70. Reprinted by permission of
Taylor & Francis Books Ltd.

15b. Edmund Husserl, excerpt from *Logical Investigations*, trans. J. N. Findlay (London:
Routledge & Kegan Paul, 1970), pp. 144–5. Reprinted by permission of Taylor
& Francis Books Ltd.

16. Martin Heidegger, "On the Essence of Truth," trans. John Sallis, in *Basic Writings*
(revised and expanded edition) ed. David Farrell Krell (London: Routledge &
Kegan Paul, 1993), pp. 117–41. English translation © 1977, 1993 by HarperCollins
Publishers, Inc. General introduction and introductions to each selection © 1997,
1993 by David Farrell Krell. Reprinted with permission of HarperCollins Publishers, Inc. and Taylor and Francis Ltd.

16b. Martin Heidegger, excerpts from "The Origin of the Work of Art," in *Poetry,
Language, Thought*, trans. and ed. Albert Hofstadter (New York: Harper & Row,
1971), pp. 35–6, 38, 41–5, 62, 71. © 1971 by Martin Heidegger. Reprinted by
permission of HarperCollins Publishers, Inc.

17. Emmanuel Levinas, "Truth of Disclosure and Truth of Testimony," trans. Iain
MacDonald, in *Basic Philosophical Writings*, eds. Adriaan T. Peperzak, Simon
Critchley, and Robert Bernasconi (Bloomington and Indianapolis: Indiana
University Press, 1996), pp. 98–107, 184–5 (notes). Reprinted by permission of
Flammarion.

18. Catherine Z. Elgin, "Word Giving, Word Taking," in *Fact and Value: Essays for Judith
Jarvis Thomson*, ed. Alex Byrne, Robert Stalnaker, Ralph Wedgwood (Cambridge,
Mass.: MIT Press, 2001), pp. 97–116. © 2001 by MIT Press. Reprinted by per-
mission of MIT Press.

19. Hannah Arendt, "Truth and Politics," in *The Portable Hannah Arendt* (London:
Penguin, 2000), pp. 545–75 (excerpts). Originally published in *Between Past and
Future* in *The New Yorker*, February 25, 1967.

20. Michel Foucault, "The Discourse on Language," trans. Rupert Sawyer in *Social
Science Information* (April 1971), pp. 7–30. © 1971 by Sage Publications Ltd and
Foundation of the Maison des Science de l'Homme. Reprinted by permission of
Sage Publications Ltd.

20b. Michel Foucault, excerpt from *Power/Knowledge: Selected Interviews and Other
Writings 1972–77*, edited by Colin Gordon (Brighton: Harvester Press, 1980),
pp. 131–3. Reprinted by permission of Pearson Education Ltd.

21. Linda Martín Alcoff, "Reclaiming Truth," a slightly revised version of an article which appeared under this title in *The Hedgehog Review: Critical Reflections on Contemporary Culture*, vol. 3, no. 3 (Fall 2001), pp. 26–41. Reprinted by permission of The Hedgehog Review.

22b. Slavoj Žižek, excerpt from *For They Know Not What They Do: Enjoyment as a Political Factor* (London and New York: Verso, 1991), p. 196. Reprinted by permission of the publisher.

22c. Judith Butler, excerpt (© 1993) from *Bodies That Matter: On the Discursive Limits of "Sex,"* (New York and London: Routledge, 1993), p. 207. Reprinted by permission of Routledge/Taylor & Francis Books, Inc. and the author.

22d. Luce Irigaray, "The Power of Discourse and the Subordination of the Feminine," from *This Sex Which Is Not One*, trans. Catherine Porter with Carolyn Burke (New York: Cornell University Press, 1985), selections from pp. 68, 69, 74, 75, 76, 79, 80, 85. Reprinted by permission of the publisher.

22e. Luce Irigaray, "Veiled Lips," in *Marine Lover of Friedrich Nietzsche*, trans. Gillian C. Gill (New York: Columbia University Press, 1991), p. 86. Reprinted by permission of Columbia University Press.

22f. Jean Baudrillard, *Simulacra and Simulacrum*, trans. Shiela Faria Glaser (Ann Arbor: University of Michigan, 1984), selections from pp. 1–7, 12, 27. Reprinted by permission of the University of Michigan Press.

22g. Gilles Deleuze, *Cinema 2. The Time-Image*, trans. H. Tomlinson and R. Galeta (Minneapolis: University of Minneapolis Press, 1989), selections from pp. 129–47. Reprinted by permission of the University of Minnesota Press and Athlone Press.

Every effort has been made to trace copyright holders and to obtain their permission for the use of copyright material. The publisher apologizes for any errors or omissions in the above list and would be grateful if notified of any corrections that should be incorporated in future reprints or editions of this book.

GENERAL INTRODUCTION

José Medina and David Wood

There is no topic more central to philosophy than truth. Throughout the history of philosophy, truth has remained one of the most fundamental philosophical notions, and it continues to occupy a special place. But the philosophical debate on truth has taken a new and distinctive turn in contemporary philosophy: *a normative turn*. This new direction will be examined in this volume through a series of conversations among philosophers from different traditions and schools. What unifies these conversations and the different philosophical issues discussed in them is the normativity of truth. The question of the normative power of truth was brought to center-stage of philosophical debates on truth by philosophers such as Nietzsche and James who asked radical questions about the value of truth as a norm that guides our practices. Therefore, it is fitting that the series of conversations on truth contained in this volume open with a dialogue between Nietzsche and James. This dialogue will frame the constellation of questions concerning the normativity of truth that constitutes the focus of the book.

Study of the question of truth is certainly valuable for its own sake, but it also affords two additional benefits. In the first place, the philosophical debate on truth provides an excellent *point of access* to a wide set of fundamental issues in metaphysics, epistemology, philosophy of language, philosophy of mind, ethics, political philosophy, and aesthetics. The debate on truth covers questions concerning objectivity, reality, knowledge, communication, standards of correctness, identity, authenticity, freedom, and creativity (among others). Readers of this volume will become familiar with these central questions while mastering the multifaceted debate on truth. In the second place, the philosophical discussion of truth can be a *bridge* between philosophical traditions and schools of thought. And this is exactly how we use it in this volume. The prodigious capacity of this theme to cross (and sometimes question, even destabilize) boundaries and to put in communication unlikely conversation partners has been precisely the inspiration and motivation for the development of this editorial project; and it is reflected in its methodology, which we explain below. Readers of this volume will become familiar not only with some of the most central positions in the debate on truth, but also with their interconnections, their similarities and differences, and the complicated and multiplying pathways that can be created among them. However, this volume does not purport to be an exhaustive sampler of all the philosophical positions in the debate on truth.[1] Being exhaustive has been sacrificed for the sake of being focused and effective. Although all the major trends in the literature are considered, not all the major players in the contemporary discussion of truth are represented in our selections. In order to retain a sharp focus and to be able to make a distinctive contribution to the literature on truth, we have been highly selective. Our introductions and lists of suggested readings, however, broaden our selections and gesture toward a wider spectrum of philosophical views. We also offer as a *supplement* (Part VII), an inconclusive conclusion that addresses some of our exclusions, while insinuating the impossibility of closure in the philosophical conversation on truth.

We have created these dialogues across different philosophical traditions and schools of thought in different ways. In some (exceptional) cases we piggy-backed on existing dialogues (such as the one between Rorty and his critics) and have expanded them by adding new interlocutors who address the same problems, arguments, and objections. But for the most part, we have created the dialogue ourselves, though — we hope — not arbitrarily or artificially. As the specific introductions make clear, the texts we have juxtaposed constitute converging (even while dissenting) discussions of truth that have strong methodological and thematic affinities. We want to highlight two important features of these dialogues on truth: their *intersectedness* and their *openness*. On the one hand, while the different conversations gathered in this volume appear to be compartmentalized in independent sections, they intersect in complex and rich ways. There are many paths that readers can travel across the texts we have selected. In the brief introductions we have appended to each section, we have highlighted some of these paths, calling readers' attention to productive interrelations and possible conversations to explore. On the other hand, the dialogue among the texts of each section stands on its own feet and even seems to have a certain (though not final) closure. Each conversation on truth is presented as a complete whole, yet it is at the same time left *open*, with loose ends and unthematized issues to be taken up by other conversations. The relation of each dialogue to the others can be seen in two ways: as resulting from an exuberant completeness — that is, from an overflow, from an *excess* — or, alternatively, as resulting from a lack of completeness or an *absence*, from the necessity of being continued, *supplemented*, by other dialogues that take up the things that were not talked about or were only touched upon. Each of these dialogues says too much, calling for a more explicit articulation or an extended discussion of its content in other dialogues. But each dialogue also says too little, becoming an invitation to further elaborations in other dialogues. This invitation to further dialogue can be reiterated indefinitely, as Derrida's logic of the supplement indicates. This logic is dialogically and performatively enacted in our volume by providing a *supplement* to the six dialogues on truth — a supplement which in turn, far from providing closure, invites other supplements, other conversations, and indeed an indefinite conversational chain.

The intersectional and open nature of the dialogues on truth of this volume reflects the actual dynamics and methodology underlying the collaboration of the editors. Our conversational methodology is no editorial trick or tool; it reflects the way this volume came together. This editorial project is the product of our ongoing (and constantly challenging) discussions about truth over four years. The conversational methodology underlying the production of this volume is reflected in the organization of the different sections. The following overview of the volume tries to make clear: (a) what unifies the dialogues on truth to be found in the different sections; and (b) what is distinctive about the kind of conversation that the volume as a whole aims to facilitate in the philosophical debate on truth.

The central focus of this book is *the normativity of truth*. Different schools of thought have emphasized the normative power of truth while offering different conceptualizations of it. The normativity of truth does not just mean that truth claims are simultaneously value judgments. It means that "truth" is a space with its own ends, ends that are inseparable from other ends such as freedom and justice. "Truth" designates a normative space, a constellation of desiderata or principles that regulate discourse and agency and what can be disclosed in and through them. In this volume we explore the *ethical, political*, and *historical questions* opened up by different conceptualizations of truth as a normative framework (a regime or complex network of norms) embedded in discursive practices. In what follows we explain how the normativity of truth unifies the different sections by providing the overlapping and criss-crossing dialectical threads that run through the volume.

Why do we value truth? This is the central question that we pose in Part I. We seem to take for granted all kinds of *prima facie* obligations with respect to truth. Other things being equal, we assume that in communication one ought to tell the truth and accept the truth, in inquiry one ought to seek the truth, in life one ought to honor the truth, etc. Truth appears to be one of our highest values. But what is the source of this value? This is the radical question that both Nietzsche and James raised while inviting us to "revalue our highest values." Through a conversation between Nietzsche and James we start with the debate between a nihilistic and a pragmatist account of the value of truth. Nietzsche developed a genealogical account of "the will to truth" in order to show that truth had been put at the service of an ideology or constellation of values, and that the positing of truth as our highest (unquestionable) value was a way of warding off critical scrutiny. In a different way James also insisted that, far from being independent of our valuations, our attitude towards truth is both informed by what we value and a determining factor of what we value. According to James, truth is a "species of good," a practical value: we value truths for their "agreeable consequences," for their action-guiding role. Rejecting the traditional notion of truth as formal *adequatio* (or passive copying), James emphasizes the relation of truth to agency and its ethical dimension. By calling attention to the normative aspects of truth, Nietzsche and James helped to bring the debate on truth into sharper focus, and they set the agenda of this debate in the twentieth century. The different questions raised by Nietzsche and James in their critical examination of the value of truth are explored and developed in the subsequent Parts of the volume.

From within our discursive practices, truth appears as a value that structures how we speak and act, determining (or at least constraining) what can find a place in those practices and how it is to be assessed. In Part II we propose a dialogue around the following question: *Is the normative space of truth something objective, fixed, and homogeneous?* Metaphysical realism gives an affirmative answer to this question. According to this view, truth is an objective and unchangeable relation between our beliefs and the facts. This relation of correspondence has a formally homogeneous structure: that of an isomorphism between our mental representations and mind-independent states of affairs. Kierkegaard's existentialism can be understood as a response to the objectivism and metaphysical realism of correspondence theories of truth. Kierkegaard argues that there is a fundamental difference between the objective perspective on communication (which focuses on what is said) and the subjective perspective (which looks at how it is said). He ties truth to subjectivity, to what he calls indirect communication, and (performatively) to the emancipation of the other. This subjectivist view of truth from the immanent perspective of truth-seekers gives rise to an interesting *pluralism* with respect to truth. A different kind of pluralism is developed in the later Wittgenstein's view of truth as a context-dependent normative notion. On this view, truth talk acquires a rather different normative significance in different "language games." For Wittgenstein, both what can be considered a truth-candidate and how truth-candidates are to be assessed varies from context to context. This view suggests that the limits of intelligibility are to be drawn contextually in a piecemeal fashion. Some have argued that these limits are always being pushed further and remain forever elusive. This is suggested by Davidson's account of interpretation in terms of Tarskian theories of truth for particular languages. Davidson develops an internalism that explains truth "in terms of the language I know" and undermines realist accounts of truth as an external relation between language and reality. A very different kind of neopragmatism can be found in Putnam, who, while rejecting traditional forms of realism and antirealism, wants to preserve basic realist intuitions in a pluralist view of truth that underscores the many ways in which our claims can relate to reality.

In Part III we ask: *What is the normative force of truth talk within communities/practices and between communities/practices?* In this section we include texts that discuss how we are compelled to form consensus as well as to interrupt it for the sake of truth, representing different perspectives on the complex relations between truth, agreement, and community. The normativity of truth has been depicted both as a community-forming force and as a community-transcending force. Some philosophers have emphasized the unifying power of truth and have linked truth to consensus. Consensus theories of truth range from those that are perspectival and relativized to traditions (Feyerabend, Rorty) to those that are universalistic (the early Habermas). The discussion of the relationship between truth and consensus in Part III begins with a conversation between Rorty and two of his critics: Habermas and McDowell. Habermas objects that Rorty's consensus theory of truth leaves out the *unconditionality* of truth claims, which is a formal presupposition of the pragmatics of communication. On the other hand, McDowell argues that there is more to the *objectivity* of truth than allegiance to the standards of a community (whether actual or ideal, particular or universal): our inquiries are normatively beholden to their subject matters and, therefore, our truth claims are answerable to the world, and not just to the community of researchers they address. Feyerabend joins this conversation as a relativistic voice that calls into question community-transcendent claims of objectivity. Arguing against scientistic views, Feyerabend calls our attention to the social processes of manufacturing truths through consensus in scientific communities. He offers a spirited defense of relativism and criticizes any transcendent notion of truth as illusory. This analysis suggests that truth talk can operate as a mechanism of inclusion and exclusion which empowers some and disempowers others. The issue of how any order of truth is grounded in a set of normative exclusions will be discussed later (cf. Parts VI and VII).

Part IV is centered around the question of *whether truth can be thought of in a non-propositional (or pre-propositional) way*, whether we might *need* to think of truth like this, and how best to understand the pre-propositional. We give voice to a number of apparently different accounts of such truth, drawing on language itself, on the intentional structures of art, on our perceptual engagement with the world, and on our culturally embedded "dwelling." And in fact this theme is taken up by essays in other sections, when they write of "forms of life," "embodiment," the world of "simulacra," or "the *experience* of truth." What is denied is not that truth is importantly propositional, but that it is *only* propositional. Indeed if, as it is claimed, propositional truth is intimately bound up with these structuring or background conditions, truth *cannot* just be propositional. If there is some measure of agreement here in the material we have selected, it also shares the need to avoid what we could call a new foundationalism, one that would credit some mystically inchoate and wordless dimension with a determinate founding privilege. Much of the fascination comes from seeing how these thinkers wrestle with that temptation. The contributors in this section sketch distinctive portraits of the place of language, and the truth claims it makes possible, in the broader world of experience and social and cultural practices. Each of them is struggling with a philosophical tradition that has resisted pre-propositional truth, and each makes a persuasive case for resisting it no more.

The conversation in Part V is centered on the issue of *disclosure and testimony*. This conversation is traversed by both a contrast and a continuity. The contrast is that articulated by Levinas, when he opposes disclosure (having to do with *being*, in an ethically neutral way) to the fundamentally ethical dimension of testimony. The continuity or convergence is apparent in our beginning the conversation with Husserl's search for "self-evidence." For what self-evidence, disclosure, testimony, and witnessing have in common is the claim to being fundamental forms of *attestation*, fundamental in the sense of not being derivative from anything else, supplying, if you like, basic *shapes* of truth. The nest of questions raised here include: *Does this opposition between the ontological and the ethical really stand up?* (Husserl sees validation through self-evidence as tied to my being able to be *responsible* for what I say; Heidegger sees disclosedness as a condition for personal and collective authenticity; Levinas seems unable to shake off various ontological assumptions.) Or again: *Where is the dimension of obligation in testimony properly located?* (Do I have an obligation to believe your testimony? Or do you have a duty to speak the truth in a way I can rely on?) *Do these issues really bear on truth in a deep and important way, or only in some loose and allusive way?* Might it not be that the normativity of truth is at stake here as never before in these discussions? We open up this conversation to some current work in moral psychology, which fruitfully engages with the interplay of ethical and epistemological questions in such areas as trust, truth, and truthfulness. And we frame the whole discussion by the challenge thrown down by Vattimo in Part IV (p. 181): *Is not the very idea of testimony anachronistic, a throwback to a "pre-critical" sense of the subject?*

Part VI is concerned with two sorts of questions: constitutive and regulative questions about the *internal* and *external* connections between *truth and power*. The constitutive questions have to do with ways in which truth, in the shape of regimes of truth (discourses, codes, practices), is intrinsically an operation of power – framing, classifying, distributing, excluding, etc. At this level, truth could not simply be said to *serve* power, it would *be* power (or *a* power) itself. This line of thought is most clearly developed by Nietzsche and Foucault. In the external or regulative sense, truth would *serve* power. Here the questions have to do with what value truth has in political life, whether different kinds of truth are more or less susceptible to manipulation, what value there might still be in *impartial* institutions. And this very distinction (between internal/constitutive, external/regulative relations between truth and power) is itself being challenged by our discussants, many of whom highlight precisely the ways in which rigid dichotomies reflect absolutist, agent-neutral, and hence impoverished views of truth. If there is some measure of agreement about the socially embedded nature of "regimes of truth," the question of whether truth can continue to have a critical reflective edge becomes more urgent. We do not need to assume some privileged philosophical truth to fear a collapse of "truth" into discursive practices serving special interests.

Reflecting the problematic of "closure" and completeness alluded to by many contemporary discussions of truth, we have added to this volume a concluding *Supplement*. Here we give voice to various ways in which some of the most arresting contemporary thinkers destabilize the traditional metaphysics of truth, particularly the assured operation of fundamental oppositions, and the classical alliance between True/False and Reality/Appearance. When Baudrillard writes cryptically that "The simulacrum is never what hides the truth – it is truth that hides the fact that there is none," and when Deleuze promotes the forger as the artist of truth, should we treat these pronouncements as the tremors that precede a conceptual earthquake? Or is someone just playing too loudly in the basement?

Note

1   There are two excellent anthologies on truth already currently available: *Truth*, ed. Simon Blackburn and Keith Simmons (Oxford University Press, 1999), which focuses more narrowly on deflationary and minimalist views of truth; and *The Nature of Truth*, ed. Michael Lynch (MIT Press, 2001), a very broad sampler representing many traditions, but without any attempt to construct a dialogue between them.

PART I

THE VALUE OF TRUTH:
"REVALUING OUR HIGHEST VALUES"

INTRODUCTION

Nietzsche and James are responsible for posing the hardest and most crucial questions that subsequent philosophical debates on truth will have to answer. Their radical critical questions concern the very *value* of truth, which is commonly taken for granted both in philosophy and in ordinary life when we assume that it is our obligation to seek the truth, to tell the truth, to acknowledge the truth, etc. The questions Nietzsche and James pose call for more than the aseptic tasks of analysis and theory building. In their hands the discussion of truth becomes a critical endeavor: it becomes, in Nietzsche's words, the critical enterprise of "revaluing our highest values". The Nietzschean and Jamesian critical questioning of the value of truth opens up a set of issues and concerns that can be grouped under three headings relating to different aspects of truth: the *normativity*, the *performativity*, and the *relativity* of truth.

The brief discussion that follows tries to bring to the fore the similarities and differences between Nietzsche's and James's elucidations of these aspects. We try to make explicit both the convergence and the divergence between their views of truth. For although Nietzsche and James are of one mind in posing very similar questions and in setting the agenda for the philosophical debate on truth around the same themes, there are substantive disagreements between them stemming from the crucial differences in the philosophical orientations underlying the positions they defend. So by juxtaposing these texts we hope to create a dialogue between Nietzsche and James, as well as a dialogue with a common interlocutor, namely, *absolutism*, the view of truth as an absolute, unquestionable value. In this twofold dialogue Nietzsche and James appear both as dissenting voices and as kindred voices fighting against a common enemy.

There are other voices that, being both distinctive and akin, can naturally join Nietzsche and James in their critical enterprise of "revaluing our highest values": Marx, Freud, Husserl, F. C. S. Schiller, and Dewey, to name a few critical philosophers who are, roughly, their contemporaries (see *Suggested Readings*).

Why should we value truth rather than falsity? Why should we hold people responsible for respecting the truth and complying with it? Why should we do so ourselves? These questions raised by Nietzsche and James make us critically conscious of a crucial aspect of the concept of truth that traditionally had been either assumed or denied in philosophy:[1] namely, *the normativity of truth*. As Allen (1993) has pointed out, Nietzsche and James warn us that we should be suspicious when it is built into the very notion of something that that thing is valuable. They both encourage a skeptical attitude towards any alleged *built-in normativity*. Nietzsche denounces the virtues associated with truth (such as honesty) as "occult qualities" that explain nothing and are supported by nothing. On the other hand, James criticizes the appeal to truth as "an end in itself," which turns truth into an arbitrary stopping point of explanation and justification. In this way Nietzsche and James both warn us to beware of those properties that are said to have intrinsic value, a value that cannot be called into question; for making a value absolute and self-evident is the best way of protecting it while hiding a dogmatic attitude towards it. Rejecting the absolutist conception of truth, Nietzsche and James argue that truths are desired for their consequences, for the impact they can have on our life-experiences and practices. So, in a general sense, both Nietzsche and James can be characterized as consequentialists, but their *alethic consequentialism* could not be more different. For, although they both tie the value of truth to its practical consequences, they assess these consequences, and hence truth's value, in very different ways.

Nietzsche's alethic consequentialism brings with it a *skeptical* and *deconstructive* approach. He draws a contrast between "the will to truth" and "the will to falsehood," which he characterizes as being at the service of two opposed goals: the preservation of the herd and the preservation of the individual, respectively. His genealogical account tries to show that there is nothing natural about the will to truth, that rather than being a human tendency that arises naturally and spontaneously, it is a duty that society imposes on us: "the duty to lie according to a fixed convention" (p. 17 below). Moreover, he calls attention to the "petty benefits" and the "high costs" associated with the will to truth: it can give us repose, security, and consistency, but at the price of "petrification" and "forgetfulness." The socially enforced will to truth coagulates the prodigious dynamism and diversity of which our life and thought are capable; and it makes us *forget* all those other ways of thinking and acting that are not in conformity with the herd, thus making us lose our creativity and originality. Nietzsche contends that we must overcome the herd mentality and transcend the will to truth. This liberation is the emancipatory goal that, on his view, the critical activity of "revaluing our highest values" should have.

James arrives at very different conclusions in his critical examination of the normativity of truth. Rather than aiming at a nihilistic view through a deconstructive genealogy, he develops a *reconstructive* account whose goal is the rehabilitation of the value of truth on pragmatic grounds. Following Schiller and Dewey in viewing truth as "a species of the good" (i.e. the good in the way of belief), James characterizes truth as what is "expedient in the way of our thinking" (p. 33 below). Denouncing the idealizations and abstractions of rationalism which have led philosophers to despise "the muddy particulars of experience" (p. 36 below), he wants to explain "the cash-value of truth" in experiential terms. His empiricist and pragmatist view tries to bring the concept of truth back to the world of concrete experience and praxis (to the *life-world*) in which it functions. It is important to note that in his experiential and pragmatic justification of the value of truth, James depicts our obligation towards truth as "tremendously conditioned" – that is, as "part of our general obligation to do what pays" (p. 36 below). On James's view, truths are reliable guides in our life and practice. As he puts it, the value of true ideas lies in their "useful leading": they lead to consistency, stability, and solidarity, and away from "eccentricity and isolation."

This is, of course, where James and Nietzsche part company. For although they offer converging accounts of the practical consequences of truth, where James sees only valuable benefits, Nietzsche sees "high costs" that outweigh "petty benefits." Far from assessing eccentricity and isolation negatively, as James does, Nietzsche considers them the source of the creativity and originality that are at the core of human existence. We would like to suggest, however, that within a Nietzschean perspective there is still room to reinstate the value of truth in a new sense: namely, by focusing on the *disruptive, subversive,* and ultimately *affirmative* potential of truth, which neither Nietzsche nor James considers explicitly in these selections. As a wolf in sheep's clothing, the will to truth can be subverted and put at the service of the life-affirming power of creativity. The valorization of these disruptive truths, truths that break agreement and interrupt the social life of the community, is indeed compatible with Nietzsche's critique of the herd mentality. But it is important to note that this disruptive dimension of truth does not merely stand in opposition to standard norms: it is more than a simple (masked) negation of the will to truth that accepts established conventions; it is a subversion of this conformist will that displaces it, destabilizes it, and opens up the possibility of a new affirmation. This Nietzschean valorization of an orientation towards truth that embraces disruption, subversion, and affirmation may be more urgent than ever as modern democracies enter into a new phase.[2] We will revisit this issue in part VII.

A second set of questions raised by the critical discussions of Nietzsche and James concerns *the performativity of truth*. Both Nietzsche and James call attention to the things we do, the actions we perform, with the truth (telling it, hiding it, twisting it, confessing it, etc.). The performative dimension of truth has two different senses: an *instrumental* and a *constitutive* sense (which will be the focus of Part V below). In its instrumental sense, the performative power of truth consists in the consequences it can bring about. In a constitutive sense, truths themselves (and not just their consequences) have a performative character, because they are produced by our alethic discursive acts: they are formed and enacted, constituted and performed, in discursive practices. (This could not be otherwise, for, as James puts it, "All human thinking gets discursified [. . .] by means of social intercourse" (p. 31 below).

Both Nietzsche and James emphasize that truths are not just there, inert and given; they have to be produced. In his critique of the copy theory of truth, James argues that true ideas and thoughts are not mere copies, but symbols, and that therefore they involve more than a passive mirroring: they require an active making. In a similar vein, Nietzsche argues that truths have to be manufactured linguistically. He describes the discursive production of truth as the making of an illusion, for it requires the *forgetfulness* of its own genesis in discursive practices: to believe in the truth, according to Nietzsche, we have to forget how things have been *made* true. Both Nietzsche and James describe truths as symbolic *events* or *processes*, insisting that ideas and thoughts are not veridical in themselves (veridicality is never an intrinsic quality), but that they have to be *made* true. In this sense the focus of their discussions is on making true, rather than on being true (see also Parts II and III below).

The performative character of truth brings to the fore the crucial dependence of truth on our practices and interests (which will be explored and discussed in different ways in all subsequent parts of this book). And this brings us to the last aspect of truth that Nietzsche and James call our attention to: namely, its *relativity*. Both Nietzsche and James reject any philosophical view of truth as an *absolute* property. Emphasizing the holistic and dynamic nature of truth, James describes truths as relative in a twofold sense: truths are relative to the always changeable reality we cope with in our experiences and practices; and they are also relative to the always changeable frameworks or belief systems in which they are inscribed. On the other hand, Nietzsche argues that there are always contingent and arbitrary, "anthropomorphic" elements[3] in any alleged truth which get forgotten: "truths are illusions that we have forgotten are illusions" (p. 17 below). The absolute perspective on truth is an ideological cover-up that makes us oblivious to this forgetfulness and to the illusory nature of truths, which are presented as absolute and final realities. However, although both Nietzsche and James call into question any sharp boundary between what is true and what passes for true in our practices, James does not share the skepticism and thoroughgoing relativism of Nietzsche. James is certainly a pluralist, but is he also a relativist?[4] He defends the diversification of truth according to plural practices and plural interests, arguing that we should always talk about truths in the plural, for they are realized *in rebus*. But no matter how diverse human practical interests may be, James contends that there is always the possibility of convergence provided by the general interests of mankind – that is, by the interests that relate to adaptation and the survival of the species. These general interests constitute the ground for what James calls our "general obligation to do what pays," which is what brings us all together as truth-seekers. On this naturalistic perspective, truth is viewed as what proves to be reliable and adaptive in the long run. Given this neo-Darwinian naturalism, it is doubtful that James should be considered a radical relativist. Although he calls attention to the relativistic elements in our assessments of truth, his empiricist and pragmatic relativism in conjunction with his naturalism make room for a strong notion of objectivity. By contrast, Nietzsche's life-affirming relativism eschews this notion, emphasizing that there is only an aesthetic relation between different spheres of discourse and their different truths. He remarks that, unlike the enslaved "*rational* man," the "liberated *intuitive* man" is bound only by aesthetic criteria. This relativism is quite alien to James's pragmatic view of truth (although they are both based on a critique of rationalism). The issue of objectivity and relativism will be revisited in Part III.

Notes

1   In many discussions of truth in the history of philosophy its normative dimension was simply ignored, but in many others it was considered and denied. The latter is the case in so-called *decriptivist* views of truth. Relying on a strong separation between the factual and the normative, these views treat "true" as a purely descriptive predicate. Although the fact–value distinction has come under heavy attack on various fronts, descriptivism still survives in naturalist approaches defended in the contemporary literature (see e.g. Field 1994).

2   Nietzsche's "disruptive" impact on twentieth-century French and German philosophy has been extraordinary, and particularly on many of the figures selected in this volume. The best-known treatments of Nietzsche – including books by Deleuze, Derrida, Foucault, Irigaray, and Heidegger – are listed here: Gilles Deleuze, *Nietzsche and Philosophy*, trans. Hugh Tomlinson (New York: Columbia University Press, 1983); Jacques Derrida, *The Ear of the Other: Otobiography*, trans. Peggy Kamuf (New York: Schocken Books, 1985); Jacques Derrida, *Spurs: Nietzsche's Styles*, trans. Barbara Harlow (Chicago: University of Chicago Press, 1979); Michel Foucault, "Nietzsche, Genealogy, History," in *The Foucault Reader* (New York: Random House, 1984), pp. 76–100; Martin Heidegger, *Nietzsche*, vol. 1: *The Will to Power as Art*, trans. David F. Krell (New York: Harper & Row, 1979); vol. 2: *The Eternal Recurrence of the Same*, trans. David F. Krell (San Francisco: Harper & Row, 1984); vol. 3: *Will to Power as Knowledge and as Metaphysics*, trans. Joan Stambaugh and Frank Capuzzi (San Francisco: Harper & Row, 1986); vol. 4: *Nihilism*, trans. David F. Krell (New York: Harper & Row, 1982); Martin Heidegger, *What is Called Thinking?* (New York: Harper & Row, 1976); Luce Irigaray, *Marine Lover of Friedrich Nietzsche*, trans. Gillian C. Gill (New York: Columbia University Press, 1991); Karl Jaspers, *Nietzsche: An Introduction to the*

Understanding of His Philosophical Activity, trans. Charles F. Wallraff and Frederick J. Schmitz (South Bend, IN: Regentry/Gateway, Inc., 1979); Carl G. Jung, *Nietzsche's "Zarathustra,"* ed. James L. Jarrett (Princeton: Princeton University Press, 1988); Pierre Klossowski, *Nietzsche and the Vicious Circle* (London: Athlone, 1993); Sarah Kofman, *Nietzsche and Metaphor*, trans. Duncan Large (Stanford, CA: Stanford University Press, 1993).

3   On Nietzsche's view, these elements are unavoidable given the fact that human symbolization is always based on contingent and optional metaphors.

4   F. C. S. Schiller, who had a great influence on James, thought that pragmatism vindicates the Protagorean dictum "Man is the measure of all things," of which he said: "Fairly interpreted, this is the truest and most important thing that any thinker has ever propounded" (*Humanism* (London: Macmillan, 1912), p. xxi). An analysis and defense of Protagoras's dictum will be offered by Feyerabend in Part III.

1

ON TRUTH AND LIES IN A NONMORAL SENSE[1]
and Other Readings

Friedrich Nietzsche

1

Once upon a time, in some out of the way corner of that universe which is dispersed into numberless twinkling solar systems, there was a star upon which clever beasts invented knowing. That was the most arrogant and mendacious minute of "world history," but nevertheless, it was only a minute. After nature had drawn a few breaths, the star cooled and congealed, and the clever beasts had to die. – One might invent such a fable, and yet he still would not have adequately illustrated how miserable, how shadowy and transient, how aimless and arbitrary the human intellect looks within nature. There were eternities during which it did not exist. And when it is all other with the human intellect, nothing will have happened. For this intellect has no additional mission which would lead it beyond human life. Rather, it is human, and only its possessor and begetter takes it so solemnly – as though the world's axis turned within it. But if we could communicate with the gnat, we would learn that he like-wise flies through the air with the same solemnity,[2] that he feels the flying center of the universe within himself. There is nothing so reprehensible and unimportant in nature that it would not immediately swell up like a balloon at the slightest puff of this power of knowing. And just as every porter wants to have an admirer, so even the proudest of men, the philosopher, supposes that he sees on all sides the eyes of the universe telescopically focused upon his action and thought.

Friedrich Nietzsche, "On Truth and Lies in a Nonmoral Sense," pp. 79–91 in *Philosophy and Truth: Selections from Nietzsche's Notebooks of the Early 1870s*, ed. and trans. Daniel Breazeale (Atlantic Highlands, NJ: Humanities Press, 1979). © by Daniel Breazeale. Reprinted with permission.

Friedrich Nietzsche, *The Will to Power*, trans. Walter Kaufmann and R. J. Hollingdale (New York: Vintage Books, 1968), pp. 289, 292. Reprinted by permission of the publisher.

Friedrich Nietzsche, *Beyond Good and Evil*, trans. Helen Zimmern (Edinburgh and London: T. N. Foulis, 1909), pp. 5–6.

Friedrich Nietzsche, *Twilight of the Idols*, trans. R. J. Hollingdale (London: Penguin, 1968), p. 41. Reprinted by permission of Penguin Books Ltd.

It is remarkable that this was brought about by the intellect, which was certainly allotted to these most unfortunate, delicate, and ephemeral beings merely as a device for detaining them a minute within existence. For without this addition they would have every reason to flee this existence as quickly as Lessing's son.[3] The pride connected with knowing and sensing lies like a blinding fog over the eyes and senses of men, thus deceiving them concerning the value of existence. For this pride contains within itself the most flattering estimation of the value of knowing. Deception is the most general effect of such pride, but even its most particular effects contain within themselves something of the same deceitful character.

As a means for the preserving of the individual, the intellect unfolds its principle powers in dissimulation, which is the means by which weaker, less robust individuals preserve themselves – since they have been denied the chance to wage the battle for existence with horns or with the sharp teeth of beasts of prey. This art of dissimulation reaches its peak in man. Deception, flattering, lying, deluding, talking behind the back, putting up a false front, living in borrowed splendor, wearing a mask, hiding behind convention, playing a role for others and for oneself – in short, a continuous fluttering around the *solitary* flame of vanity – is so much the rule and the law among men that there is almost nothing which is less comprehensible than how an honest and pure drive for truth could have arisen among them. They are deeply immersed in illusions and in dream images; their eyes merely glide over the surface of things and see "forms." Their senses nowhere lead to truth; on the contrary, they are content to receive stimuli and, as it were, to engage in a groping game on the backs of things. Moreover, man permits himself to be deceived in his dreams every night of his life. His moral sentiment does not even make an attempt to prevent this, whereas there are supposed to be men who have stopped snoring through sheer will power. What does man actually know about himself? Is he, indeed, ever able to perceive himself completely, as if laid out in a lighted display case? Does nature not conceal most things from him – even concerning his own body – in order to confine and lock him within a proud, deceptive consciousness, aloof from the coils of the bowels, the rapid flow of the blood stream, and the intricate quivering of the fibers! She threw away the key. And woe to that fatal curiosity which might one day have the power to peer out and down through a crack in the chamber of consciousness and then suspect that man is sustained in the indifference of his ignorance by that which is pitiless, greedy, insatiable, and murderous – as if hanging in dreams on the back of a tiger. Given this situation, where in the world could the drive for truth have come from?

Insofar as the individual wants to maintain himself against other individuals, he will under natural circumstances employ the intellect mainly for dissimulation. But at the same time, from boredom and necessity, man wishes to exist socially and with the herd; therefore, he needs to make peace and strives accordingly to banish from his world at least the most flagrant *bellum omni contra omnes.*[4] This peace treaty brings in its wake something which appears to be the first step toward acquiring that puzzling truth drive: to wit, *that* which shall count as "truth" from now on is established. That is to say, a uniformly valid and binding designation is invented for things, and this legislation of language likewise establishes the first laws of truth. For the contrast between truth and lie arises here for the first time. The liar is a person who uses the valid designations, the words, in order to make something which is unreal appear to be real. He says, for example, "I am rich," when the proper designation for his condition would be "poor." He misuses fixed conventions by means of arbitrary substitutions or even reversals of names. If he does this in a selfish and moreover harmful manner, society will cease to trust him and will thereby exclude him. What men avoid by excluding the liar is not so much being defrauded as it is being harmed by means of fraud. Thus, even at this stage, what they hate is basically not deception itself, but rather the unpleasant, hated consequences of certain sorts of deception. It is in a similarly restricted sense that man now wants nothing but truth: he desires the pleasant, life-preserving consequences of truth. He is indifferent toward pure knowledge which has no consequences; toward those truths which are possibly harmful and destructive he is even hostilely inclined. And besides, what about these linguistic conventions themselves? Are they perhaps products of knowledge, that is, of the sense of truth? Are designations congruent with things? Is language the adequate expression of all realities?

It is only by means of forgetfulness that man can ever reach the point of fancying himself to possess a "truth" of the grade just indicated. If he will not be satisfied with truth in the form of tautology, that is to say, if he will not be content with empty husks, then he will always exchange truths for illusions. What is a word? It is the copy in sound of a nerve stimulus. But the further inference from the nerve stimulus to a cause outside of us is already the result of a false and unjustifiable application of the principle of sufficient reason.[5] If truth alone had been the deciding factor in the genesis of language, and if the standpoint of certainty had been decisive for designations, then how could we still dare to say "the stone is hard," as if "hard" were something otherwise familiar to us, and not merely a totally subjective stimulation! We separate things according to gender, designating the tree as masculine and the plant as feminine. What arbitrary assignments![6] How far this oversteps the canons of certainty! We speak of a "snake": this designation touches only upon its ability to twist itself and could therefore also fit a worm.[7] What arbitrary differentiations! What one-sided preferences, first for this, then for that property of a thing! The various languages placed side by side show that with words it is never a question of truth, never a question of adequate expression; otherwise, there would not be so many languages.[8] The "thing in itself" (which is precisely what the pure truth, apart from any of its consequences, would be) is likewise something quite incomprehensible to the creator of language and something not in the least worth striving for. This creator only designates the relations of things to men, and for expressing these relations he lays hold of the boldest metaphors. To begin with, a nerve stimulus is transferred into an image:[9] first metaphor. The image, in turn, is imitated in a sound: second metaphor. And each time there is a complete overleaping of one sphere, right into the middle of an entirely new and different one. One can imagine a man who is totally deaf and has never had a sensation of sound and music. Perhaps such a person will gaze with astonishment at Chladni's sound figures; perhaps he will discover their causes in the vibrations of the string and will now swear that he must know what men mean by "sound." It is this way with all of us concerning language: we believe that we know something about the things themselves when we speak of trees, colors, snow, and flowers; and yet we possess nothing but metaphors for things – metaphors which correspond in no way to the original entities.[10] In the same way that the sound appears as a sand figure, so the mysterious X of the thing in itself first appears as a nerve stimulus, then as an image, and finally as a sound. Thus the genesis of language does not proceed logically in any case, and all the material within and with which the man of truth, the scientist, and the philosopher later work and build, if not derived from never-never land,[11] is at least not derived from the essence of things.

In particular, let us further consider the formation of concepts. Every word instantly becomes a concept precisely insofar as it is not supposed to serve as a reminder of the unique and entirely individual original experience to which it owes its origin; but rather, a word becomes a concept insofar as it simultaneously has to fit countless more or less similar cases — which means, purely and simply, cases which are never equal and thus altogether unequal. Every concept arises from the equation of unequal things. Just as it is certain that one leaf is never totally the same as another, so it is certain that the concept "leaf" is formed by arbitrarily discarding these individual differences and by forgetting the distinguishing aspects. This awakens the idea that, in addition to the leaves, there exists in nature the "leaf": the original model according to which all the leaves were perhaps woven, sketched, measured, colored, curled, and painted — but by incompetent hands, so that no specimen has turned out to be a correct, trustworthy, and faithful likeness of the original model. We call a person "honest," and then we ask "why has he behaved so honestly today?" Our usual answer is, "on account of his honesty." Honesty! This in turn means that the leaf is the cause of the leaves. We know nothing whatsoever about an essential quality called "honesty"; but we do know of countless individualized and consequently unequal actions which we equate by omitting the aspects in which they are unequal and which we now designate as "honest" actions. Finally we formulate from them a *qualitas occulta*[12] which has the name "honesty." We obtain the concept, as we do the form, by overlooking what is individual and actual; whereas nature is acquainted with no forms and no concepts, and likewise with no species, but only with an X which remains inaccessible and undefinable for us. For even our contrast between individual and species is something anthropomorphic and does not originate in the essence of things; although we should not presume to claim that this contrast does not correspond to the essence of things: that would of course be a dogmatic assertion and, as such, would be just as indemonstrable as its opposite.

What then is truth? A movable host of metaphors, metonymies, and anthropomorphisms: in short, a sum of human relations which have been poetically and rhetorically intensified, transferred, and embellished, and which, after long usage, seem to a people to be fixed, canonical, and binding. Truths are illusions which we have forgotten are illusions; they are metaphors that have become worn out and have been drained of sensuous force, coins which have lost their embossing and are now considered as metal and no longer as coins.

We still do not yet know where the drive for truth comes from. For so far we have heard only of the duty which society imposes in order to exist: to be truthful means to employ the usual metaphors. Thus, to express it morally, this is the duty to lie according to a fixed convention, to lie with the herd and in a manner binding upon everyone. Now man of course forgets that this is the way things stand for him. Thus he lies in the manner indicated, unconsciously and in accordance with habits which are centuries old; and precisely *by means of this unconsciousness* and forgetfulness he arrives at his sense of truth. From the sense that one is obliged to designate one thing as "red," another as "cold," and a third as "mute," there arises a moral impulse in regard to truth. The venerability, reliability, and utility of truth is something which a person demonstrates for himself from the contrast with the liar, whom no one trusts and everyone excludes. As a *"rational"* being, he now places his behavior under the control of abstractions. He will no longer tolerate being carried away by sudden impressions, by intuitions. First he universalizes all these impressions into less color-ful, cooler concepts, so that he can entrust the guidance of his life and conduct to them. Everything which distinguishes man from the animals depends upon this ability to volatilize perceptual metaphors[13] in a schema, and thus to dissolve an image into a concept. For something is possible in the realm of these schemata which could never be achieved with the vivid first impressions: the construction of a pyramidal order according to castes and degrees, the creation of a new world of laws, privileges, sub-ordinations, and clearly marked boundaries – a new world, one which now confronts that other vivid world of first impressions as more solid, more universal, better known, and more human than the immediately perceived world, and thus as the regulative and imperative world. Whereas each perceptual metaphor is individual and without equals and is therefore able to elude all classification, the great edifice of concepts displays the rigid regularity of a Roman columbarium[14] and exhales in logic that strength and coolness which is characteristic of mathematics. Anyone who has felt this cool breath [of logic] will hardly believe that even the concept – which is as bony, foursquare, and transposable as a die – is nevertheless merely the *residue of a metaphor*, and that the illusion which is involved in the artistic transference of a nerve stimu-lus into images is, if not the mother, then the grandmother of every single concept.[15] But in this conceptual crap game "truth" means using every die in the designated manner, counting its spots accurately, fashioning the right categories, and never vio-lating the order of caste and class rank. Just as the Romans and Etruscans cut up the heavens with rigid mathematical lines and confined a god within each of the spaces thereby delimited, as within a *templum*,[16] so every people has a similarly mathemati-cally divided conceptual heaven above themselves and henceforth thinks that truth demands that each conceptual god be sought only within *his own* sphere. Here one may certainly admire man as a mighty genius of construction, who succeeds in piling up an infinitely complicated dome of concepts upon an unstable foundation, and, as it were, on running water. Of course, in order to be supported by such a foundation, his construction must be like one constructed of spiders' webs: delicate enough to be carried along by the waves, strong enough not to be blown apart by every wind. As a genius of construction man raises himself far above the bee in the following way: whereas the bee builds with wax that he gathers from nature, man builds with the far more delicate conceptual material which he first has to manufacture from himself. In this he is greatly to be admired, but not on account of his drive for truth or for pure knowledge of things. When someone hides something behind a bush and looks for it again in the same place and finds it there as well, there is not much to praise in such seeking and finding. Yet this is how matters stand regarding seeking and finding "truth" within the realm of reason. If I make up the definition of a mammal, and then, after inspecting a camel, declare "look, a mammal," I have indeed brought a truth to light in this way, but it is a truth of limited value. That is to say, it is a thoroughly anthropomorphic truth which contains not a single point which would be "true in itself" or really and universally valid apart from man. At bottom, what the investigator of such truths is seeking is only the metamorphosis of the world into man. He strives to understand the world as something analogous to man, and at best he achieves by his struggles the feeling of assimilation. Similar to the way in which astrologers considered the stars to be in man's service and connected with his happiness and sorrow, such an investigator considers the entire universe in connection with man: the entire universe as the infinitely fractured echo of one original sound – man; the entire universe as the infinitely multiplied copy of one original picture – man. His method is to treat man as the measure of all things, but in doing so he again proceeds from the error of believing that he has these things [which he intends to measure] immediately before him as mere objects. He forgets that the original perceptual metaphors are metaphors and takes them to be the things themselves.

Only by forgetting this primitive world of metaphor can one live with any repose, security, and consistency: only by means of the petrification and coagulation of a mass of images which originally streamed from the primal faculty of human imagination like a fiery liquid, only in the invincible faith that *this* sun, *this* window, *this* table is a truth in itself, in short, only by forgetting that he himself is an *artistically creating* subject, does man live with any repose, security, and consistency. If but for an instant he could escape from the prison walls of this faith, his "self consciousness" would be immediately destroyed. It is even a difficult thing for him to admit to himself that the insect or the bird perceives an entirely different world from the one that man does, and that the question of which of these perceptions of the world is the more correct one is quite meaningless, for this would have to have been decided previously in accordance with the criterion of the *correct perception*, which means, in accordance with a criterion which is *not available*. But in any case it seems to me that "the correct perception" – which would mean "the adequate expression of an object in the subject" – is a contradictory impossibility.[17] For between two absolutely different spheres, as between subject and object, there is no causality, no correctness, and no expression; there is, at most, an *aesthetic* relation:[18] I mean, a suggestive transference, a stammering translation into a completely foreign tongue – for which there is required, in any case, a freely inventive intermediate sphere and mediating force. "Appearance" is a word that contains many temptations, which is why I avoid it as much as possible. For it is not true that the essence of things "appears" in the empirical world. A painter without hands who wished to express in song the picture before his mind would, by means of this substitution of spheres, still reveal more about the essence of things than does the empirical world. Even the relationship of a nerve stimulus to the generated image is not a necessary one. But when the same image has been generated millions of times and has been handed down for many generations and finally appears on the same occasion every time for all mankind, then it acquires at last the same meaning for men it would have if it were the sole necessary image and if the relationship of the original nerve stimulus to the generated image were a strictly causal one. In the same manner, an eternally repeated dream would certainly be felt and judged to be reality. But the hardening and congealing of a metaphor guarantees absolutely nothing concerning its necessity and exclusive justification.

Every person who is familiar with such considerations has no doubt felt a deep mistrust of all idealism of this sort: just as often as he has quite clearly convinced himself of the eternal consistency, omnipresence, and infallibility of the laws of nature. He has concluded that so far as we can penetrate here – from the telescopic heights to the microscopic depths – everything is secure, complete, infinite, regular, and without any gaps. Science will be able to dig successfully in this shaft forever, and all the things that are discovered will harmonize with and not contradict each other. How little does this resemble a product of the imagination, for if it were such, there should be some place where the illusion and unreality can be divined. Against this, the following must be said: if each of us had a different kind of sense perception – if we could only perceive things now as a bird, now as a worm, now as a plant, or if one of us saw a stimulus as red, another as blue, while a third even heard the same stimulus as a sound – then no one would speak of such a regularity of nature, rather, nature would be grasped only as a creation which is subjective in the highest degree. After all, what is a law of nature as such for us? We are not acquainted with it in itself, but only with its effects, which means in its relation to other laws of nature – which, in turn, are known to us only as sums of relations. Therefore all these relations always refer again to others and are thoroughly incomprehensible to us in their essence. All that we actually know about these laws of nature is what we ourselves bring to them – time and space, and therefore relationships of succession and number. But everything marvelous about the laws of nature, everything that quite astonishes us therein and seems to demand our explanation, everything that might lead us to distrust idealism: all this is completely and solely contained within the mathematical strictness and inviolability of our representations of time and space. But we produce these representations in and from ourselves with the same necessity with which the spider spins. If we are forced to comprehend all things only under these forms, then it ceases to be amazing that in all things we actually comprehend nothing but these forms. For they must all bear within themselves the laws of number, and it is precisely number which is most astonishing in things. All that conformity to law, which impresses us so much in the movement of the stars and in chemical processes, coincides at bottom with those properties which we bring to things. Thus it is we who impress ourselves in this way. In conjunction with this it of course follows that the artistic process of metaphor formation with which every sensation begins in us already presupposes these forms and thus occurs within them. The only way in which the possibility of subsequently constructing a new conceptual edifice from metaphors themselves can be explained is by the firm persistence of these original forms. That is to say, this conceptual edifice is an imitation of temporal, spatial, and numerical relationships in the domain of metaphor.[19]

2

We have seen how it is originally *language* which works on the construction of concepts, a labor taken over in later ages by *science*.[20] Just as the bee simultaneously constructs cells and fills them with honey, so science works unceasingly on this great columbarium of concepts, the graveyard of perceptions. It is always building new, higher stories and shoring up, cleaning, and renovating the old cells; above all, it takes pains to fill up this monstrously towering framework and to arrange therein the entire empirical world, which is to say, the anthropomorphic world. Whereas the man of action binds his life to reason and its concepts so that he will not be swept away and lost, the scientific investigator builds his hut right next to the tower of science so that he will be able to work on it and to find shelter for himself beneath those bulwarks which presently exist. And he requires shelter, for there are frightful powers which continuously break in upon him, powers which oppose scientific "truth" with completely different kinds of "truths" which bear on their shields the most varied sorts of emblems.

The drive toward the formation of metaphors is the fundamental human drive, which one cannot for a single instant dispense with in thought, for one would thereby dispense with man himself. This drive is not truly vanquished and scarcely subdued by the fact that a regular and rigid new world is constructed as its prison from its own ephemeral products, the concepts. It seeks a new realm and another channel for its activity, and it finds this in *myth* and in *art* generally. This drive continually confuses the conceptual categories and cells by bringing forward new transferences, metaphors, and metonymies. It continually manifests an ardent desire to refashion the world which presents itself to waking man, so that it will be as colorful, irregular, lacking in results and coherence, charming, and eternally new as the world of dreams. Indeed, it is only by means of the rigid and regular web of concepts that the waking man clearly sees that he is awake; and it is precisely because of this that he sometimes thinks that he must be dreaming when this web of concepts is torn by art. Pascal is right in maintaining that if the same dream came to us every night we would be just as occupied with it as we are with the things that we see every day. "If a workman were sure to dream for twelve straight hours every night that he was king," said Pascal, "I believe that he would be just as happy as a king who dreamt for twelve hours every night that he was a workman."[21] In fact, because of the way that myth takes it for granted that miracles are always happening, the waking life of a mythically inspired people – the ancient Greeks, for instance – more closely resembles a dream than it does the waking world of a scientifically disenchanted thinker. When every tree can suddenly speak as a nymph, when a god in the shape of a bull can drag away maidens, when even the goddess Athena herself is suddenly seen in the company of Peisastratus driving through the market place of Athens with a beautiful team of horses[22] – and this is what the honest Athenian believed – then, as in a dream, anything is possible at each moment, and all of nature swarms around man as if it were nothing but a masquerade of the gods, who were merely amusing themselves by deceiving men in all these shapes.

But man has an invincible inclination to allow himself to be deceived and is, as it were, enchanted with happiness when the rhapsodist tells him epic fables as if they were true, or when the actor in the theater acts more royally than any real king. So long as it is able to deceive without *injuring*, that master of deception, the intellect, is free; it is released from its former slavery and celebrates its Saturnalia. It is never more luxuriant, richer, prouder, more clever and more daring. With creative pleasure it throws metaphors into confusion and displaces the boundary stones of abstractions, so that, for example, it designates the stream as "the moving path which carries man where he would otherwise walk." The intellect has now thrown the token of bondage from itself. At other times it endeavors, with gloomy officiousness, to show the way and to demonstrate the tools to a poor individual who covets existence; it is like a servant who goes in search of booty and prey for his master. But now it has become the master and it dares to wipe from its face the expression of indigence. In comparison with its previous conduct, everything that it now does bears the mark of dissimulation,[23] just as that previous conduct did of distortion.[24] The free intellect copies human life, but it considers this life to be something good and seems to be quite satisfied with it. That immense framework and planking of concepts to which the needy man clings his whole life long in order to preserve himself is nothing but a scaffolding and toy for the most audacious feats of the liberated intellect. And when it smashes this framework to pieces, throws it into confusion, and puts it back together in an ironic fashion, pairing the most alien things and separating the closest, it is demonstrating that it has no need of these makeshifts of indigence and that it will now be guided by intuitions rather than by concepts. There is no regular path which leads from these intuitions into the land of ghostly schemata, the land of abstractions. There exists no word for these intuitions; when man sees them he grows dumb, or else he speaks only in forbidden metaphors and in unheard-of combinations of concepts. He does this so that by shattering and mocking the old conceptual barriers he may at least correspond creatively to the impression of the powerful present intuition.

There are ages in which the rational man and the intuitive man stand side by side, the one in fear of intuition, the other with scorn for abstraction. The latter is just as irrational as the former is inartistic. They both desire to rule over life: the former, by knowing how to meet his principle needs by means of foresight, prudence, and regularity; the latter, by disregarding these needs and, as an "overjoyed hero," counting as real only that life which has been disguised as illusion and beauty. Whenever, as was perhaps the case in ancient Greece, the intuitive man handles his weapons more authoritatively and victoriously than his opponent, then, under favorable circumstances, a culture can take shape and art's mastery over life can be established. All the manifestations of such a life will be accompanied by this dissimulation, this disavowal of indigence, this glitter of metaphorical intuitions, and, in general, this immediacy of deception: neither the house, nor the gait, nor the clothes, nor the clay jugs give evidence of having been invented because of a pressing need. It seems as if they were all intended to express an exalted happiness, an Olympian cloudlessness, and, as it were, a playing with seriousness. The man who is guided by concepts and abstractions only succeeds by such means in warding off misfortune, without ever gaining any happiness for himself from these abstractions. And while he aims for the greatest possible freedom from pain, the intuitive man, standing in the midst of a culture, already reaps from his intuition a harvest of continually inflowing illumination, cheer, and redemption – in addition to obtaining a defense against misfortune. To be sure, he suffers more intensely, *when* he suffers; he even suffers more frequently, since he does not understand how to learn from experience and keeps falling over and over again into the same ditch. He is then just as irrational in sorrow as he is in happiness: he cries aloud and will not be consoled. How differently the stoical man who learns from experience and governs himself by concepts is affected by the same misfortunes! This man, who at other times seeks nothing but sincerity, truth, freedom from deception, and protection against ensnaring surprise attacks, now executes a masterpiece of deception: he executes his masterpiece of deception in misfortune, as the other type of man executes his in times of happiness. He wears no quivering and changeable human face, but, as it were, a mask with dignified, symmetrical features. He does not cry; he does not even alter his voice. When a real storm cloud thunders above him, he wraps himself in his cloak, and with slow steps he walks from beneath it.

Notes

1   A more literal, though less English, translation of *Über Wahrheit und Lüge im ausser-moralischem Sinne* might be "On Truth and Lie in the Extramoral Sense."

2   *Pathos.*

3   A reference to the offspring of Lessing and Eva König, who died on the day of his birth.

4   "War of each against all."

5   Note that Nietzsche is here engaged in an implicit critique of Schopenhauer, who had been guilty of precisely this misapplication of the principle of sufficient reason in his first book, *The Fourfold Root of the Principle of Sufficient Reason.* It is quite wrong to think that Nietzsche was ever wholly uncritical of Schopenhauer's philosophy (see, for example, the little essay, *Kritik der Schopenhauerischen Philosophie* from 1867, in *MA*, I, pp. 392–401).

6   *welche willkürlichen Übertragungen.* The specific sense of this passage depends upon the fact that all ordinary nouns in the German language are assigned a gender: the tree is *der Baum;* the plant is *die Pflanze.* This assignment of an original sexual property to all things is the "transference" in question.

7   This passage depends upon the etymological relation between the German words *Schlange* (snake) and *schlingen* (to wind or twist), both of which are related to the old High German *slango.*

8   What Nietzsche is rejecting here is the theory that there is a sort of "naturally appropriate" connection between certain words (or sounds) and things. Such a theory is defended by Socrates in Plato's *Cratylus.*

9   *Ein Nervenreiz, zuerst übertragen in ein Bild.* The "image" in this case is the visual image, what we "see."

10 *Wesenheiten.*

11 *Wolkenkukuksheim:* literally, "cloud–cuckoo–land."

12 "Occult quality."

13 *die anschaulichen Metaphern.* The adjective *anschaulich* has the additional sense of "vivid" – as in the next sentence ("vivid first impressions").

14 A columbarium is a vault with niches for funeral urns containing the ashes of cremated bodies.

15 I.e. concepts are derived from images, which are, in turn, derived from nerve stimuli.

16 A delimited space restricted to a particular purpose, especially a religiously sanctified area.

17 *ein widerspruchsvolles Unding.*

18 *ein ästhetisches Verhalten.* A more literal translation of *Verhalten* is "behavior," "attitude," or perhaps "disposition."

19 This is where section 2 of the fair copy made by von Cersdorff ends. But according to Schlechta (in Schlechta/Anders, pp. 14–15) Nietzsche's preliminary version continued as follows:

"Empty space and empty time are ideas which are possible at any time. Every concept, thus an empty metaphor, is only an imitation of these first ideas: space, time, and causality. Afterwards, the original imaginative act of transference into images: the first provides the matter, the second the qualities which we believe in. Comparison to music. How can one speak of it?"

20 *Wissenschaft.*

21 *Pensées,* number 386. Actually, Pascal says that the workman would be "almost as happy" as the king in this case!

22 According to the story told by Herodotus (*Histories* I, 60) the tyrant Peisistratus adopted the following ruse to secure his popular acceptance upon his return from exile: he entered Athens in a chariot accompanied by a woman named Phye who was dressed in the costume of Athena. Thus the people were supposed to have been convinced that it was the goddess herself who was conducting the tyrant back to the Acropolis.

23 *Verstellung.*

24 *Verzerrung.*

From *The Will to Power*

"No matter how strongly a thing may be believed, strength of belief is no criterion of truth." But what is truth? Perhaps a kind of belief that has become a condition of life? In that case . . . strength could be a criterion.

[. . .]

If the character of existence should be false – which would be possible – what would truth, all our truth, be then? – An unconscionable falsification of the false? The false raised to a higher power.

In a world that is essentially false, truthfulness would be an antinatural tendency: such a tendency could have meaning only as a means to a higher power of falsehood. In order for a world of the true, of being, to be invented, the truthful man would first have to be created (including the fact that such a man believes himself "truthful").

Simple, transparent, not in contradiction with himself, durable, remaining always the same, without wrinkle, volt, concealment, form: a man of this kind conceives a world of being as "God" in his own image.

For truthfulness to be possible, the whole sphere of man must be very clean, small and, respectable; advantage in every sense must be with the truthful man. – Lies, deception, dissimulation must arouse astonishment –

From *Beyond Good and Evil*

What really is this "Will to Truth" in us? In fact we made a long halt at the question as to the origin of this Will – until at last we came to an absolute standstill before a yet more fundamental question. We inquired about the *value* of this Will. Granted that we want the truth: *why not rather* untruth? And uncertainty? Even ignorance? The problem of the value of truth presented itself before us — or was it we who presented ourselves before the problem? Which of us is the Œdipus here? Which the Sphinx?

"*How could* anything originate out of its opposite? For example, truth out of error? or the Will to Truth out of the will to deception? or the generous deed out of self-ishness? or the pure sun-bright vision of the wise man out of covetousness? Such genesis is impossible; whoever dreams of it is ... worse than a fool; things of the highest value must have a different origin, an origin of *their own* — in this transitory, seductive, illusory, paltry world, in this turmoil of delusion and cupidity, they cannot have their source." [...] [T]hrough this "belief" of theirs, they exert themselves for their "knowledge," for something that is in the end solemnly christened "the Truth."

From *Twilight of the Idols*

How the 'Real World' at last Became a Myth ("History of an Error")

6. We have abolished the real world: what world is left? the apparent world perhaps? ... But no! *with the real world we have also abolished the apparent world!* (Mid-day; moment of the shortest shadow; end of the longest error; zenith of mankind; INCIPIT ZARATHUSTRA).

2

PRAGMATISM'S CONCEPTION OF TRUTH

William James

When Clerk–Maxwell was a child it is written that he had a mania for having every-thing explained to him, and that when people put him off with vague verbal accounts of any phenomenon he would interrupt them impatiently by saying, 'Yes; but I want you to tell me the *particular go* of it!' Had his question been about truth, only a prag-matist could have told him the particular go of it. I believe that our contemporary pragmatists, especially Messrs. Schiller and Dewey, have given the only tenable account of this subject. It is a very ticklish subject, sending subtle rootlets into all kinds of crannies, and hard to treat in the sketchy way that alone befits a public lecture. But the Schiller–Dewey view of truth has been so ferociously attacked by rationalistic philosophers, and so abominably misunderstood, that here, if anywhere, is the point where a clear and simple statement should be made.

I fully expect to see the pragmatist view of truth run through the classic stages of a theory's career. First, you know, a new theory is attacked as absurd; then it is admit-ted to be true, but obvious and insignificant; finally it is seen to be so important that its adversaries claim that they themselves discovered it. Our doctrine of truth is at present in the first of these three stages, with symptoms of the second stage having begun in certain quarters. I wish that this lecture might help it beyond the first stage in the eyes of many of you.

Truth, as any dictionary will tell you, is a property of certain of our ideas. It means their 'agreement', as falsity means their disagreement, with 'reality'. Pragmatists and intellectualists both accept this definition as a matter of course, They begin to quarrel only after the question is raised as to what may precisely be meant by the term 'agree-ment', and what by the term 'reality', when reality is taken as something for our ideas to agree with.

In answering these questions the pragmatists are more analytic and painstaking, the intellectualists more offhand and irreflective. The popular notion is that a true idea

William James, "Pragmatism's Conception of Truth," in *Pragmatism: A New Name for Some Old Ways of Thinking* (London: Longman, 1907), pp. 197–236.

must copy its reality. Like other popular views, this one follows the analogy of the most usual experience. Our true ideas of sensible things do indeed copy them. Shut your eyes and think of yonder clock on the wall, and you get just such a true picture or copy of its dial. But your idea of its 'works' (unless you are a clockmaker) is much less of a copy, yet it passes muster, for it in no way clashes with the reality. Even though it should shrink to the mere word 'works', that word still serves you truly; and when you speak of the 'time-keeping function' of the clock, or of its spring's 'elasticity', it is hard to see exactly what your ideas call copy.

You perceive that there is a problem here. Where our ideas cannot copy definitely their object, what does agreement with that object mean? Some idealists seem to say that they are true whenever they are what God means that we ought to think about that object. Others hold the copy-view all through, and speak as if our ideas possessed truth just in proportion as they approach to being copies of the Absolute's eternal way of thinking.

These views, you see, invite pragmatistic discussion. But, the great assumption of the intellectualists is that truth means essentially an inert static relation, When you've got your true idea of anything, there's an end of the matter. You're in possession; you *know*; you have fulfilled your thinking destiny. You are where you ought to be mentally; you have obeyed your categorical imperative; and nothing more need follow on that climax of your rational destiny. Epistemologically you are in stable equilibrium.

Pragmatism, on the other hand, asks its usual question, 'Grant an idea or belief to be true,' it says, 'what concrete difference will its being true make in any one's actual life? How will the truth be realized? What experiences will be different from those which would obtain if the belief were false? What, in short, is the truth's cash-value in experiential terms?'

The moment pragmatism asks this question, it sees the answer: *True ideas are those that we can assimilate, validate, corroborate and verify. False ideas are those that we can not.* That is the practical difference it makes to us to have true ideas; that, therefore, is the meaning of truth, for it is all that truth is known-as.

This thesis is what I have to defend. The truth of an idea is not a stagnant property inherent in it. Truth *happens* to an idea. It *becomes* true, is *made* true by events. Its verity *is* in fact an event, a process: the process namely of its verifying itself, its veri-*fication*, Its validity is the process of its valid-*ation*.

But what do the words verification and validation themselves pragmatically mean? They again signify certain practical consequences of the verified and validated idea. It is hard to find any one phrase that characterizes these consequences better than the ordinary agreement-formula – just such consequences being what we have in mind whenever we say that our ideas 'agree' with reality. They lead us, namely, through the acts and other ideas which they instigate, into or up to, or towards, other parts of experience with which we feel all the while – such feeling being among our potentialities – that the original ideas remain in agreement. The connexions and transitions come to us from point to point as being progressive, harmonious, satisfactory. This function of agreeable leading is what we mean by an idea's verification. Such an account is vague and it sounds at first quite trivial, but it has results which it will take the rest of my hour to explain.

Let me begin by reminding you of the fact that the possession of true thoughts means everywhere the possession of invaluable instruments of action; and that our duty to gain truth, so far from being a blank command from out of the blue, or a 'stunt' self-imposed by our intellect, can account for itself by excellent practical reasons.

The importance to human life of having true beliefs about matters of fact is a thing too notorious. We live in a world of realities that can be infinitely useful or infinitely harmful. Ideas that tell us which of them to expect count as the true ideas in all this primary sphere of verification, and the pursuit of such ideas is a primary human duty. The possession of truth, so far from being here an end in itself, is only a preliminary means towards other vital satisfactions. If I am lost in the woods and starved, and find what looks like a cow-path, it is of the utmost importance that I should think of a human habitation at the end of it, for if I do so and follow it, I save myself. The true thought is useful here because the house which is its object is useful. The practical value of true ideas is thus primarily derived from the practical importance of their objects to us. Their objects are, indeed, not important at all times. I may on another occasion have no use for the house; and then my idea of it, however verifiable, will be practically irrelevant, and had better remain latent. Yet since almost any object may some day become temporarily important, the advantage of having a general stock of *extra* truths, of ideas that shall be true of merely possible situations, is obvious. We store such extra truths away in our memories, and with the overflow we fill our books of reference. Whenever such an extra truth becomes practically relevant to one of our emergencies, it passes from cold-storage to do work in the world and our belief in it grows active. You can say of it then either that 'it is useful because it is true' or that 'it is true because it is useful'. Both these phrases mean exactly the same thing, namely that here is an idea that gets fulfilled and can be verified. True is the name for whatever idea starts the· verification-process, useful is the name for its completed function in experience. True ideas would never have been singled out as such, would never have acquired a class-name, least of all a name suggesting value, unless they had been useful from the outset in this way.

From this simple cue pragmatism gets her general notion of truth as something essentially bound up with the way in which one moment in our experience may lead us towards other moments which it will be worth while to have been led to. Primarily, and on the common-sense level, the truth of a state of mind means this function of a *leading that is worth while*. When a moment in our experience, of any kind whatever, inspires us with a thought that is true, that means that sooner or later we dip by that thought's guidance into the particulars of experience again and make advantageous connexion with them. This is a vague enough statement, but I beg you to retain it, for it is essential.

Our experience meanwhile is all shot through with regularities. One bit of it can warn us to get ready for another bit, can 'intend' or be 'significant of' that remoter object. The object's advent is the significance's verification. Truth, in these cases, meaning nothing but eventual verification, is manifestly incompatible with waywardness on our part. Woe to him whose beliefs play fast and loose with the order which realities follow in his experience; they will lead him nowhere or else make false connexions.

By 'realities' or 'objects' here, we mean either things of common sense, sensibly present, or else common-sense relations, such as dates, places, distances, kinds, activities. Following our mental image of a house along the cow-path, we actually come to see the house; we get the image's full verification. *Such simply and fully verified leadings are certainly the originals and prototypes of the truth-process.* Experience offers indeed other forms of truth-process, but they are all conceivable as being primary verifications arrested, multiplied or substituted one for another.

Take, for instance, yonder object on the wall. You and I consider it to be a 'clock', although no one of us has seen the hidden works that make it one. We let our notion pass for true without attempting to verify. If truths mean verification-processes essentially, ought we then to call such unverified truths as this abortive? No, for they form the overwhelmingly large number of the truths we live by. Indirect as well as direct verifications pass muster. Where circumstantial evidence is sufficient, we can go without eyewitnessing. Just as we here assume Japan to exist without ever having been there, because it *works* to do so, everything we know conspiring with the belief, and nothing interfering, so we assume that thing to be a clock. We *use* it as a clock, regulating the length of our lecture by it. The verification of the assumption here means its leading to no frustration or contradiction. Verifi*ability* of wheels and weights and pendulum is as good as verification, For one truth-process completed there are a million in our lives that function in this state of nascency. They turn us *towards* direct verification; lead us into the *surroundings* of the objects they envisage; and then, if everything runs on harmoniously, we are so sure that verification is possible that we omit it, and are usually justified by all that happens.

Truth lives, in fact, for the most part on a credit system. Our thoughts and beliefs 'pass', so long as nothing challenges them, just as banknotes pass so long as nobody refuses them. But this all points to direct face-to-face verifications somewhere, without which the fabric of truth collapses like a financial system with no cash-basis whatever. You accept my verification of one thing, I yours of another. We trade on each other's truth. But beliefs verified concretely by *somebody* are the posts of the whole superstructure.

Another great reason – beside economy of time – for waiving complete verification in the usual business of life is that all things exist in kinds and not singly. Our world is found once for all to have that peculiarity. So that when we have once directly verified our ideas about one specimen of a kind, we consider ourselves free to apply them to other specimens without verification. A mind that habitually discerns the kind of thing before it, and acts by the law of the kind immediately, without pausing to verify, will be a 'true' mind in ninety-nine out of a hundred emergencies, proved so by its conduct fitting everything it meets, and getting no refutation.

Indirectly or only potentially verifying processes may thus be true as well as full verification-processes. They work as true processes would work, give us the same advantages, and claim our recognition for the same reasons. All this on the common-sense level of matters of fact, which we are alone considering.

But matters of fact are not our only stock in trade. *Relations among purely mental ideas* form another sphere where true and false beliefs obtain, and here the beliefs are absolute, or unconditional. When they are true they bear the name either of definitions or of principles. It is either a principle or a definition that 1 and 1 make 2, that 2 and 1 make 3, and so on; that white differs less from grey than it does from black; that when the cause begins to act the effect also commences. Such propositions hold of all possible 'ones', of all conceivable 'whites' and 'greys' and 'causes'. The objects here are mental objects. Their relations are perceptually obvious at a glance, and no sense-verification is necessary. Moreover, once true, always true, of those same mental objects. Truth here has an 'eternal' character. If you can find a concrete thing anywhere that is 'one' or 'white' or 'grey' or an 'effect,' then your principles will everlastingly apply to it. It is but a case of ascertaining the kind, and then applying the law of its kind to the particular object. You are sure to get truth if you can but name the kind rightly, for your mental relations hold good of everything of that kind without exception. If you then, nevertheless, failed to get truth concretely, you would say that you had classed your real objects wrongly.

In this realm of mental relations, truth again is an affair of leading. We relate one abstract idea with another, framing in the end great systems of logical and mathematical truth, under the respective terms of which the sensible facts of experience eventually arrange themselves, so that our eternal truths hold good of realities also. This marriage of fact and theory is endlessly fertile. What we say is here already true in advance of special verification, *if we have subsumed our objects rightly.* Our ready-made ideal framework for all sorts of possible objects follows from the very structure of our thinking. We can no more play fast and loose with these abstract relations than we can do so with our sense-experiences. They coerce us; we must treat them consistently, whether or not we like the results. The rules of addition apply to our debts as rigorously as to our assets. The hundredth decimal of π, the ratio of the circumference to its diameter, is predetermined ideally now, though no one may have computed it. If we should ever need the figure in our dealings with an actual circle we should need to have it given rightly, calculated by the usual rules; for it is the same kind of truth that those rules elsewhere calculate.

Between the coercions of the sensible order and those of the ideal order, our mind is thus wedged tightly. Our ideas must agree with realities, be such realities concrete or abstract, be they facts or be they principles, under penalty of endless inconsistency and frustration.

So far, intellectualists can raise no protest. They can only say that we have barely touched the skin of the matter.

Realities mean, then, either concrete facts, or abstract kinds of thing and relations perceived intuitively between them. They furthermore and thirdly mean, as things that new ideas of ours must no less take account of, the whole body of other truths already in our possession. But what now does 'agreement' with such threefold realities mean? – to use again the definition that is current.

Here it is that pragmatism and intellectualism begin to part company. Primarily, no doubt, to agree means to copy, but we saw that the mere word 'clock' would do instead of a mental picture of its works, and that of many realities our ideas can only be symbols and not copies. 'Past time', 'power', 'spontaneity' – how can our mind copy such realities?

To 'agree' in the widest sense with a reality *can only mean to be guided either straight up to it or into its surroundings, or to be put into such working touch with it as to handle either it or something connected with it better than if we disagreed.* Better either intellectually or practically! And often agreement will only mean the negative fact that nothing contradictory from the quarter of that reality comes to interfere with the way in which our ideas guide us elsewhere. To copy a reality is, indeed, one very important way of agreeing with it, but it is far from being essential. The essential thing is the process of being guided. Any idea that helps us to *deal*, whether practically or intellectually, with either the reality or its belongings, that doesn't entangle our progress in frustrations, that *fits*, in fact, and adapts our life to the reality's whole setting, will agree sufficiently to meet the requirement. It will hold true of that reality.

Thus, *names* are just as 'true' or 'false' as definite mental pictures are. They set up similar verification-processes, and lead to fully equivalent practical results.

All human thinking gets discursified; we exchange ideas; we lend and borrow verifications, get them from one another by means of social intercourse. All truth thus gets verbally built out, stored up, and made available for every one. Hence, we must *talk* consistently just as we must *think* consistently: for both in talk and thought we deal with kinds. Names are arbitrary, but once understood they must be kept to. We mustn't now call Abel 'Cain' or Cain 'Abel'. If we do, we ungear ourselves from the whole book of Genesis, and from all its connexions with the universe of speech and fact down to the present time. We throw ourselves out of whatever truth that entire system of speech and fact may embody.

The overwhelming majority of our true ideas admit of no direct or face-to-face verification – those of past history, for example, as of Cain and Abel. The stream of time can he recounted only verbally, or verified indirectly by the present prolongations or effects of what the past harbored. Yet if they agree with these verbalities and effects, we can know that our ideas of the past are true. *As true as past time itself was,* so true was Julius Cæsar, so true were antediluvian monsters, all in their proper dates and settings. That past time itself was, is guaranteed by its coherence with everything that's present. True as the present *is*, the past *was* also.

Agreement thus turns out to be essentially an affair of leading – leading that is useful because it is into quarters that contain objects that are important. True ideas lead us into useful verbal and conceptual quarters as well as directly up to useful sensible termini. They lead to consistency, stability and flowing human intercourse. They lead away from eccentricity and isolation, from foiled and barren thinking. The untrammelled flowing of the leading-process, its general freedom from clash and contradiction, passes for its indirect verification; but all roads lead to Rome, and in the end and eventually, all true processes must lead to the face of directly verifying sensible experiences *somewhere*, which somebody's ideas have copied.

Such is the large loose way in which the pragmatist interprets the word agreement. He treats it altogether practically. He lets it cover any process of conduction from a present idea to a future terminus, provided only it run prosperously. It is only thus that 'scientific' ideas, flying as they do beyond common sense, can be said to agree with their realities. It is, as I have already said, *as if* reality were made of ether, atoms or electrons, but we mustn't think so literally. The term 'energy' doesn't even pretend to stand for anything 'objective'. It is only a way of measuring the surface of phenomena so as to string their changes on a simple formula.

Yet in the choice of these man-made formulas we can not be capricious with impunity any more than we can be capricious on the common-sense practical level. We must find a theory that will *work*; and that means something extremely difficult; for our theory must mediate between all previous truths and certain new experiences. It must derange common sense and previous belief as little as possible, and it must lead to some sensible terminus or other that can be verified exactly. To 'work' means both these things; and the squeeze is so tight that there is little loose play for any hypothesis. Our theories are wedged and controlled as nothing else is. Yet sometimes alternative theoretic formulas are equally compatible with all the truths we know, and then we choose between them for subjective reasons. We choose the kind of theory to which we are already partial; we follow 'elegance' or 'economy'. Clerk-Maxwell somewhere says it would be 'poor scientific taste' to choose the more complicated of two equally well-evidenced conceptions; and you will all agree with him. Truth in science is what gives us the maximum possible sum of satisfactions, taste included, but consistency both with previous truth and with novel fact is always the most imperious claimant.

I have led you through a very sandy desert. But now, if I may be allowed so vulgar an expression, we begin to taste the milk in the coconut. Our rationalist critics here discharge their batteries upon us, and to reply to them will take us out from all this dryness into full sight of a momentous philosophical alternative.

Our account of truth is an account of truths in the plural, of processes of leading, realized *in rebus*, and having only this quality in common, that they *pay*. They pay by guiding us into or towards some part of a system that dips at numerous points into sense-percepts, which we may copy mentally or not, but with which at any rate we are now in the kind of commerce vaguely designated as verification. Truth for us is simply a collective name for verification-processes, just as health, wealth, strength, etc., are names for other processes connected with life, and also pursued because it pays to pursue them. Truth is *made*, just as health, wealth, and strength are made, in the course of experience.

Here rationalism is instantaneously up in arms against us. I can imagine a rationalist to talk as follows:

'Truth is not made,' he will say; 'it absolutely obtains, being a unique relation that does not wait upon any process, but shoots straight over the head of experience, and hits its reality every time. Our belief that yon thing on the wall is a clock is true already, although no one in the whole history of the world should verify it. The bare quality of standing in that transcendent relation is what makes any thought true that possesses it, whether or not there be verification. You pragmatists put the cart before the horse in making truth's being reside in verification-processes. These are merely signs of its being, merely our lame ways of ascertaining after the fact, which of our ideas already has possessed the wondrous quality. The quality itself is timeless, like all essences and natures. Thoughts partake of it directly, as they partake of falsity or of irrelevancy. It can't be analysed away into pragmatic consequences.'

The whole plausibility of this rationalist tirade is due to the fact to which we have already paid so much attention. In our world, namely, abounding as it does in things of similar kinds and similarly associated, one verification serves for others of its kind, and one great use of knowing things is to be led not so much to them as to their associates, especially to human talk about them. The quality of truth, obtaining *ante rem*, pragmatically means, then, the fact that in such a world innumerable ideas work better by their indirect or possible than by their direct and actual verification. Truth *ante rem* means only verifiability, then; or else it is a case of the stock rationalist trick of treating the *name* of a concrete phenomenal reality as an independent prior entity, and placing it behind the reality as its explanation. Professor Mach quotes somewhere an epigram of Lessing's:

> Sagt Hänschen Schlau zu Vetter Fritz,
> 'Wie kommt es, Wetter Fritzen,
> Dass grad' die Reichsten in der Welt,
> Das meiste Geld besitzen?'

Hänschen Schlau here treats the principle 'wealth' as something distinct from the facts denoted by the man's being rich. It antedates them; the facts become only a sort of secondary coincidence with the rich man's essential nature.

In the case of 'wealth' we all see the fallacy. We know that wealth is but a name for concrete processes that certain men's lives play a part in, and not a natural excellence found in Messrs. Rockefeller and Carnegie, but not in the rest of us.

Like wealth, health also lives *in rebus*. It is a name for processes, as digestion, circulation, sleep, etc., that go on happily, though in this instance we are more inclined to think of it as a principle and to say the man digests and sleeps so well *because* he is so healthy.

With 'strength' we are, I think, more rationalistic still, and decidedly inclined to treat it as an excellence pre-existing in the man and explanatory of the herculean performances of his muscles.

With 'truth' most people go over the border entirely, and treat the rationalistic account as self-evident. But really all these words in *th* are exactly similar. Truth exists *ante rem* just as much and as little as the other things do.

The scholastics, following Aristotle, made much of the distinction between habit and act. Health *in actu* means, among other things, good sleeping and digesting. But a healthy man need not always be sleeping, or always digesting, any more than a wealthy man need be always handling money, or a strong man always lifting weights. All such qualities sink to the status of 'habits' between their times of exercise; and similarly truth becomes a habit of certain of our ideas and beliefs in their intervals of rest from their verifying activities. But those activities are the root of the whole matter, and the condition of there being any habit to exist in the intervals.

'The true', to put it very briefly, is only the expedient in the way of our thinking, just as 'the right' is only the expedient in the way of our behaving. Expedient in almost any fashion; and expedient in the long run and on the whole of course; for what meets expediently all the experience in sight won't necessarily meet all farther experiences equally satisfactorily. Experience, as we know, has ways of *boiling over*, and making us correct our present formulas.

The 'absolutely' true, meaning what no further experience will ever alter, is that ideal vanishing-paint towards which we imagine that all our temporary truths will some day converge. It runs on all fours with the perfectly wise man, and with the absolutely complete experience; and, if these ideals are ever realized, they will all be realized together. Meanwhile we have to live today by what truth we can get today, and be ready tomorrow to call it falsehood. Ptolemaic astronomy, Euclidean space, Aristotelian logic, scholastic metaphysics, were expedient for centuries, but human experience has boiled over those limits, and we now call these things only relatively true, or true within those borders of experience. 'Absolutely' they are false; for we know that those limits were casual, and might have been transcended by past theorists just as they are by present thinkers,

When new experiences lead to retrospective judgements, using the past tense, what these judgements utter *was* true, even though no past thinker had been led there. We live forwards, a Danish thinker has said, but we understand backwards. The present sheds a backward light on the world's previous processes. They may have been truth-processes for the actors in them. They are not so for one who knows the later revelations of the story.

This regulative notion of a potential better truth to be established later, possibly to be established some day absolutely, and having powers of retroactive legislation, turns its face, like all pragmatist notions, towards concreteness of fact, and towards the future. Like the half-truths, the absolute truth will have to be *made*, made as a relation incidental to the growth of a mass of verification-experience, to which the half-true ideas are all along contributing their quota.

I have already insisted on the fact that truth is made largely out of previous truths. Men's beliefs at any time are so much experience *funded*. But the beliefs are themselves parts of the sum total of the world's experience, and become matter, therefore, for the next day's funding operations. So far as reality means experienceable reality, both it and the truths men gain about it are everlastingly in process of mutation – mutation towards a definite goal, it may be – but still mutation.

Mathematicians can solve problems with two variables. On the Newtonian theory, for instance, acceleration varies with distance, but distance also varies with acceleration. In the realm of truth-processes facts come independently and determine our beliefs provisionally. But these beliefs make us act, and as fast as they do so, they bring into sight or into existence new facts which redetermine the beliefs accordingly. So the whole coil and ball of truth, as it rolls up, is the product of a double influence. Truths emerge from facts; but they dip forward into facts again and add to them; which facts again create or reveal new truth (the word is indifferent) and so on indefinitely. The 'facts' themselves meanwhile are not *true*. They simply *are*. Truth is the function of the beliefs that start and terminate among them.

The case is like a snowball's growth, due as it is to the distribution of the snow on the one hand, and to the successive pushes of the boys on the other, with these factors co-determining each other incessantly.

The most fateful point of difference between being a rationalist and being a pragmatist is now fully in sight. Experience is in mutation, and our psychological ascertainments of truth are in mutation – so much rationalism will allow; but never that either reality itself or truth itself is mutable. Reality stands complete and ready-made from all eternity, rationalism insists, and the agreement of our ideas with it is that unique unanalysable virtue in them of which she has already told us. As that intrinsic excellence, their truth has nothing to do with our experiences. It adds nothing to the content of experience. It makes no difference to reality itself; it is supervenient, inert, static, a reflexion merely. It doesn't *exist*, it *holds* or *obtains*, it belongs to another dimension from that of either facts or fact-relations, belongs, in short, to the epistemological dimension – and with that big word rationalism closes the discussion.

Thus, just as pragmatism faces forward to the future, so does rationalism here again face backward to a past eternity. True to her inveterate habit, rationalism reverts to 'principles', and thinks that when an abstraction once is named, we own an oracular solution.

The tremendous pregnancy in the way of consequences for life of this radical difference of outlook will only become apparent in my later lectures. I wish meanwhile to close this lecture by showing that rationalism's sublimity does not save it from inanity.

When, namely, you ask rationalists, instead of accusing pragmatism of desecrating the notion of truth, to define it themselves by saying exactly what *they* understand by it, the only positive attempts I can think of are these two:

1 'Truth is the system of propositions which have an unconditional claim to be recognized as valid.'[1]
2 Truth is a name for all those judgements which we find ourselves under obligation to make by a kind of imperative duty.[2]

The first thing that strikes one in such definitions is their unutterable triviality. They are absolutely true, of course, but absolutely insignificant until you handle them pragmatically. What do you mean by 'claim' here, and what do you mean by 'duty'? As summary names for the concrete reasons why thinking in true ways is overwhelmingly expedient and good for mortal men, it is all right to talk of claims on reality's part to be agreed with, and of obligations on our part to agree. We feel both the claims and the obligations, and we feel them for just those reasons.

But the rationalists who talk of claim and obligation *expressly say that they have nothing to do with our practical interests or personal reasons.* Our reasons for agreeing are psychological facts, they say, relative to each thinker, and to the accidents of his life. They are his evidence merely, they are no part of the life of truth itself. That life transacts itself in a purely logical or epistemological, as distinguished from a psychological, dimension, and its claims antedate and exceed all personal motivations whatsoever. Though neither man nor God should ever ascertain truth, the word would still have to be defined as that which *ought* to he ascertained and recognized.

There never was a more exquisite example of an idea abstracted from the concretes of experience and then used to oppose and negate what it was abstracted from.

Philosophy and common life abound in similar instances. The 'sentimentalist fallacy' is to shed tears over abstract justice and generosity, beauty, etc., and never to know these qualities when you meet them in the street, because the circumstances make them vulgar. Thus I read in the privately printed biography of an eminently rationalistic mind: 'It was strange that with such admiration for beauty in the abstract, my brother had no enthusiasm for fine architecture, for beautiful painting, or for flowers.' And in almost the last philosophic work I have read, I find such passages as the following: 'Justice is ideal, solely ideal. Reason conceives that it ought to exist, but experience shows that it can not. . . . Truth, which ought to be, can not be. . . . Reason is deformed by experience. As soon as reason enters experience it becomes contrary to reason.'

The rationalist's fallacy here is exactly like the sentimentalist's. Both extract a quality from the muddy particulars of experience, and find it so pure when extracted that they contrast it with each and all its muddy instances as an opposite and higher nature. All the while it is *their* nature. It is the nature of truths to be validated, verified. It pays for our ideas to be validated. Our obligation to seek truth is part of our general obligation to do what pays. The payments true ideas bring are the sole why of our duty to follow them. Identical whys exist in the case of wealth and health.

Truth makes no other kind of claim and imposes no other kind of ought than health and wealth do. All these claims are conditional; the concrete benefits we gain are what we mean by calling the pursuit a duty. In the case of truth, untrue beliefs work as perniciously in the long run as true beliefs work beneficially. Talking abstractly, the quality 'true' may thus be said to grow absolutely precious and the quality 'untrue' absolutely damnable: the one may be called good, the other bad, unconditionally. We ought to think the true, we ought to shun the false, imperatively.

But if we treat all this abstraction literally and oppose it to its mother soil in experience, see what a preposterous position we work ourselves into.

We cannot then take a step forward in our actual thinking. When shall I acknowledge this truth and when that? Shall the acknowledgement be loud? – or silent? If sometimes loud, sometimes silent, which *now*? When may a truth go into cold-storage in the encyclopedia? and when shall it come out for battle? Must I constantly be repeating the truth 'twice two are four' because of its eternal claim on recognition? or is it sometimes irrelevant? Must my thoughts dwell night and day on my personal sins and blemishes, because I truly have them? – or may I sink and ignore them in order to be a decent social unit, and not a mass of morbid melancholy and apology?

It is quite evident that our obligation to acknowledge truth, so far from being unconditional, is tremendously conditioned. Truth with a big T, and in the singular, claims abstractly to be recognized, of course; but concrete truths in the plural need be recognized only when their recognition is expedient. A truth must always be preferred to a falsehood when both relate to the situation; but when neither does, truth is as little of a duty as falsehood. If you ask me what o'clock it is and I tell you that I live at 95 Irving Street, my answer may indeed be true, but you don't see why it is my duty to give it. A false address would be as much to the purpose.

With this admission that there are conditions that limit the application of the abstract imperative, *the pragmatistic treatment of truth sweeps back upon us in its fulness.* Our duty to agree with reality is seen to be grounded in a perfect jungle of concrete expediencies.

When Berkeley had explained what people meant by matter, people thought that he denied matter's existence. When Messrs. Schiller and Dewey now explain what people mean by truth, they are accused of denying *its* existence. These pragmatists destroy all objective standards, critics say, and put foolishness and wisdom on one level. A favourite formula for describing Mr Schiller's doctrines and mine is that we are persons who think that by saying whatever you find it pleasant to say and calling it truth you fulfil every pragmatistic requirement.

I leave it to you to judge whether this be not an impudent slander. Pent in, as the pragmatist more than anyone else sees himself to be, between the whole body of funded truths squeezed from the past and the coercions of the world of sense about him, who so well as he feels the immense pressure of objective control under which our minds perform their operations? If anyone imagines that this law is lax, let him keep its commandment one day, says Emerson. We have heard much of late of the uses of the imagination in science. It is high time to urge the use of a little imagination in philosophy. The unwillingness of some of our critics to read any but the silliest of possible meanings into our statements is as discreditable to their imaginations as anything I know in recent philosophic history. Schiller says the true is that which 'works'. Thereupon he is treated as one who limits verification to the lowest material utilities. Dewey says truth is what gives 'satisfaction'. He is treated as one who believes in calling everything true which, if it were true, would be pleasant.

Our critics certainly need more imagination of realities. I have honestly tried to stretch my own imagination and to read the best possible meaning into the rationalist conception, but I have to confess that it still completely baffles me. The notion of a reality calling on us to 'agree' with it, and that for no reasons, but simply because its claim is 'unconditional' or 'transcendent', is one that I can make neither head nor tail of. I try to imagine myself as the sole reality in the world, and then to imagine what more I would 'claim' if I were allowed to. If you suggest the possibility of my claiming that a mind should come into being from out of the void inane and stand and *copy* me, I can indeed imagine what the copying might mean, but I can conjure up no motive. What good it would do me to be copied, or what good it would do that mind to copy me, if further consequences are expressly and in principle ruled out as motives for the claim (as they are by our rationalist authorities) I can not fathom. When the Irishman's admirers ran him along to the place of banquet in a sedan chair with no bottom, he said, 'Faith, if it wasn't for the honour of the thing, I might as well have come on foot.' So here: but for the honour of the thing, I might as well have remained uncopied. Copying is one genuine mode of knowing (which for some strange reason our contemporary transcendentalists seem to be tumbling over each other to repudiate); but when we get beyond copying, and fall back on unnamed forms of agreeing that are expressly denied to be either copyings or leadings or fittings, or any other processes pragmatically definable, the *what* of the 'agreement' claimed becomes as unintelligible as the why of it. Neither content nor motive can be imagined for it. It is an absolutely meaningless abstraction.[3]

Surely in this field of truth it is the pragmatists and not the rationalists who are the more genuine defenders of the universe's rationality.

Notes

1   A. E. Taylor, *Philosophical Review*, 14: 288.
2   H. Rickert, *Der Gegenstand der Erkenntniss; Einführung in die tranzendentale philosophie* (Tübingen, 1904), ch. on 'Die Urtheilsnothwendigkeit'.

3   I am not forgetting that Professor Rickert long ago gave up the whole notion of truth
    being founded on agreement with reality. Reality according to him, is whatever agrees
    with truth, and truth is founded solely on our primal duty. This fantastic flight, together
    with Mr Joachim's candid confession of failure in his book *The Nature of Truth* (Oxford,
    1906), seems to me to mark the bankruptcy of rationalism when dealing with this subject.
    Rickert deals with part of the pragmatistic position under the head of what he calls
    'Relativismus'. I cannot discuss his text here. Suffice it to say that his argumentation in
    that chapter is so feeble as to seem almost incredible in so generally able a writer.

SUGGESTED READING

Allen, Barry, *Truth in Philosophy* (Cambridge, MA: Harvard University Press, 1993).

Dewey, John, "Propositions, Warranted Assertibility, and Truth," *Journal of Philosophy*, 38 (1941), pp. 169–85.

Dewey, John, *John Dewey. The Middle Works, 1899–1924* (Carbondale, IL: Southern Illinois University Press, 1976).

Field, Hartry, "Disquotational Truth and Factually Defective Discourse," *Philosophical Review*, 103/3 (1994), pp. 405–52.

Freud, Sigmund, *Resistances to Psychoanalysis* (Harmondsworth: Pelican Freud Library, 1986).

Freud, Sigmund, *The Freud Reader*, ed. P. Gay (London: W.W. Norton & Company, 1995).

Husserl, Edmund, *The Crisis of European Sciences and Transcendental Phenomenology* (Evanston, IL: Northwestern University Press, 1970).

James, William, *The Meaning of Truth* (Cambridge, MA: Harvard University Press, 1975.

James, William, *Pragmatism* (Cambridge, MA: Harvard University Press, 1975).

Kolakowski, Leszek, "Marx and the Classical Definition of Truth," in *Toward a Marxist Humanism* (New York: Grove Press, 1969).

Marx, Karl, *Selected Writings* (Indianapolis: Hackett, 1994).

Nietzsche, Friedrich, *The Will to Power*, trans. Walter Kaufmann and R. J. Hollingdale (New York: Random House, 1968).

Nietzsche, Friedrich, *Beyond Good and Evil*, trans. Walter Kaufmann (New York: Vintage, 1989).

Russell, Bertrand, "William James's Conception of Truth," in *Philosophical Essays* (London: George Allen & Unwin, 1996).

Schiller, F. C. S. *Studies in Humanism* (London: Macmillan and Co., 1907).

PART II

REPRESENTATION, SUBJECTIVITY, AND INTERSUBJECTIVITY

INTRODUCTION

The central point of convergence among the different selections we have put in dialogue in this section is the discussion of *objectivism* or *metaphysical realism*, i.e. the philosophical perspective that explains truth in terms of an adequacy relation to a language- and mind-independent world.[1] The extracts in this section argue that objectivism rests on the untenable assumption that the truth is "out there," as if the world itself spoke the truth, as if the truth could be revealed independently of the agency of truth-tellers. This objectivist perspective disregards the subjective and intersubjective conditions of truth claims. As Wittgenstein puts it, it ignores the role that truths and falsehoods play "in our lives" (*On Certainty* (*OC*), §138; p. 64 below). Both Wittgenstein and Kierkegaard emphasize that there is a fundamental existential dimension to truth. Their existential approaches call attention to three central features that have become the focus of contemporary discussions of truth: the *pluralism*, the *contextuality*, and the *performativity* of truth.

In the first place, Kierkegaard and Wittgenstein both reject any view that depicts truth as a unique and fixed relation or property. Arguing against the philosophical conception of truth as a homogeneous normative space, they develop different kinds of *pluralism*. Kierkegaard emphasizes the irreducible plurality of subjective experiences of truth-seekers, while Wittgenstein calls our attention to the enormous diversity of truth-seeking activities. Both Kierkegaard and Wittgenstein emphasize that truth is not something that can just happen as an isolated incident. Truth is temporally extended and involves a dialectical process. According to Kierkegaard, truth is inscribed in a complex "dialectic of communication" ("Concluding Unscientific Postscript" (*CUP*), p. 72; p. 48 below) and in the indefinite totality of human existence. Wittgenstein, on the other hand, emphasizes that truth claims come in clusters, that they form "systems" (cf. esp. *OC* §§140–2; p. 64 below). We cannot make sense of a truth claim in isolation and independently of entire systems of truths. But what do these systems of truths consist of? According to Wittgenstein, they include not only sentences, utterances, or beliefs, but also actions and *forms of life*.[2]

In the second place, both Kierkegaard and Wittgenstein argue that truth has to be *situated* in existential contexts. However, although they both agree that these contexts must be communicative contexts, Kierkegaard emphasizes their subjective and private character,[3] whereas Wittgenstein argues for the intersubjective and public nature of these contexts. The contextualization of truth has been developed in many different ways, as the selections in this section and the next indicate. But all contextualist views agree that truth is context-dependent at least in this sense: it involves a relation to particular speakers, times, and places (and perhaps also to communities of speakers and social practices). Does this mean that truth is "relative"? Do truth claims have to be "relativized" to particular contexts and speakers? Does the contextuality of truth leave room for any kind of transcendence? This will be the topic of the next part of the book.

Finally, in the third place, both Kierkegaard and Wittgenstein suggest that truth has an essential *performative* dimension. Truth is entangled in and produced by the chain of performances that constitute our life-world. This is intimated by Kierkegaard's account of the *expressive* dimension of truth. Ironically adapting Hegel's dialectic[4] (see *Suggested Reading*), Kierkegaard contends that "truth is only in the becoming" (*CUP*

p. 78; p. 50 below). On his view, truth is not a given, but something that has to be *made* — in fact something that is *always in the making* and is never finished or completed. In his account of our "existence-relation" to truth as a continuous "striving," Kierkegaard depicts truth as something that cannot be fixed in representations, but can only be *performed* in an open-ended process of communication. On the other hand, Wittgenstein emphasizes that truth is grounded in "our acting" (*OC* §204; p. 68 below). In line with speech act theory, Wittgenstein conceives of truth claims as performative utterances: to speak the truth is to do something (and not just to represent something); it is a human deed (and not just a picture or mirror that passively reflects what is there). Although Austin initially aligned truth with the representational rather than with the performative aspects of language, he also emphasized that assertions have illocutionary force, and that their descriptive content is a vehicle or instrument for doing things with language (see also Strawson in *Suggested Readings*). The performativity of truth will be further discussed in the next part of the book in connection with the dependence of truth on action-contexts.

There is a very interesting general *convergence* in the *existential* accounts of truth developed by Kierkegaard and Wittgenstein: they both suggest that truth is to be looked at from the standpoint of *existing* subjects; and they both treat existence as the point of departure from the representational and objectivist paradigm. But there seems to be also a crucial *divergence* between their views: while Kierkegaard emphasizes the importance of interiority, inwardness, and secrecy, Wittgenstein attacks privacy and calls attention to what is public and intersubjectively shared. So their existential perspectives take different directions: one *subjective*, the other *social*. Are these paths hopelessly opposed? Can they be reconciled? We can articulate an intersubjective reading of Kierkegaard's view of truth. Indeed, his emphasis on "the double-reflection of communication" (CUP pp. 74ff; p. 49 below) speaks against a monological approach; and his thesis of the "paradoxical" nature of truth rests on a relation between a Self and an Other, since it is based on a dialectic of communication that involves intersubjective mediation and criticizes the illusion of immediacy in "direct communication." Arguably, the relation to God or to the infinite implicit in our orientation toward truth should be understood in communicative terms as a relation to the Other. So, on this reading, what is at the core of Kierkegaard's view of truth is the *openness to the Other*. It is precisely this openness that requires that our "striving for truth" be a never-ending striving (a "striving infinitely," not towards a goal; CUP p. 91; p. 53 below). On the other hand, Wittgenstein's intersubjective perspective does not deny the subjective dimension of truth, and he does talk about the subjective conditions both for being "at home" in the truth and for being able to express it: "No one *can* speak the truth if he has still not mastered himself" (*Culture and Value* (*CV*), p. 35).

Drawing on the analytic and pragmatist approaches of Tarski and Quine, rather than on existentialist views, Davidson offers an original account of the holistic, contextual, and performative character of truth. On Davidson's view, truth provides the link between subjectivity and intersubjectivity and constitutes the key concept in a theory of interpretation, for it allows for the translation of the speech of others into my speech or idiolect. Davidson argues that there is an internal relation between truth and meaning and that, therefore, the meaning of a sentence can be captured by specifying the conditions under which the sentence would be true. On this view, in order to interpret the speech of others, what we have to do is: first, find out the sentences she holds true in her language; and second, specify their truth conditions in our language. Davidson's theory of interpretation does not rest on a general account of truth, but rather, on a situated account of truth as disclosed in our communicative practices – that is, truth within a particular language L spoken by particular people at a particular time. For this purpose, Davidson resorts to Tarski's recursive definition of truth-in-L through the mechanism of disquotation as specified in his famous Convention T: "'p' is true if and only if p." So, on this view, the theories of interpretation on which communication relies consist in one-to-one mappings (logical equivalences, really) between sentences in the language to be interpreted (the *object language*) and sentences in the language of the interpreter (the *metalanguage*): e.g. "'Es regnet' is true iff it rains." When a linguist develops a theory of interpretation for the speech of "an alien," what she does is to construct "a characterization of truth-for-the-alien" which yields "a mapping of sentences held true (or false) by the alien on to sentences held true (or false) by the linguist" ("Truth and Meaning", p. 33; p. 72 below). This account has far-reaching implications.

Following Quine's theory of radical translation and his critique of analyticity (cf. *Suggested Reading*), Davidson's truth-conditional semantics shows the impossibility of sharply distinguishing between what we mean and what we believe in, and therefore it blurs the traditional distinction between truths about meaning and truths about the world (so-called analytic and synthetic truths). This semantic theory proceeds holistically by identifying the location of each sentence in the language as a whole. Davidson argues that this holistic enterprise of interpretation is subject to substantive constraints on our communicative practices of interpretation. In particular, successful communication is guided by what he calls *the principle of charity*, according to which a theory of interpretation has to be constructed so as to maximize agreement between speaker and interpreter.[5] The principle of charity is for Davidson a transcendental principle, an inescapable hermeneutic constraint on communication (i.e. on the construction of mappings between idiolects). It follows from this principle that meaningful disagreement can take place only against the background of a massive agreement and that, therefore, the occurrence of a false belief presupposes the presence of mostly true beliefs. On the basis of the interdependence between meaning and belief and the principle of charity, Davidson develops a transcendental argument against skepticism intended to show that, by and large, speakers are always in touch with the truth. Davidson's principle of charity establishes a tight connection between two different kinds of agreement: the *agreement between speakers* and the *agreement between language and the world*. On Davidson's view, these two forms of agreement are inseparable for participants in communication, for communication involves simultaneously interpreting others and interpreting the world they share. As we shall see, some people, such as Rorty, interpret this Davidsonian account of truth as explaining agreement with the world in terms of agreement with each other, thus reducing objectivity to solidarity. Others, however, interpret Davidson's theory as showing that these two forms of agreement are inextricably interwoven and yet irreducible to one another. The relationship between truth and intersubjective agreement will be the topic of the next part of the book.

As a critique of deflationary views of truth inspired by Ramsey, Tarski, and Davidson, and as a defense of *commonsense realism*, the selection from Putnam's Dewey Lectures closing this part provides the perfect link to the next part's debate between contextualism and realism concerning the immanent and transcendent aspects of truth. Putnam argues that we need to dissolve the false dilemma between metaphysical realism and antirealism or deflationism about truth. He proposes to transcend this dilemma by showing the flaws of both of its horns and sketching a viable alternative. For Putnam, such an alternative should preserve the realist intuitions that deflationists deny without endorsing the philosophical illusions of metaphysical realists. What is wrong with metaphysical realism, according to Putnam, is the conception of truth as a freestanding, language- and mind-independent property, which makes truth inaccessible and skepticism inescapable. But, he argues, in distancing themselves from this metaphysical picture, antirealists and deflationists go too far, and they mistakenly deny the claim that truth can be recognition-transcendent in any sense. Putnam contends that being true cannot be identified with being verified (as Dummett's antirealism suggests), or with being assertible (as deflationism, arguably, suggests). And he sets out to articulate, through his interpretation of Wittgenstein, an alternative view of truth that supports a commonsense realism ("a second naiveté") which avoids the metaphysical and epistemic idealizations of his earlier realist views.[6]

This view preserves the core semantic insights of deflationary views: namely, that truth is internal to language and that the face of our cognitive relation to the world is the face of meaning. However, *pace* deflationists and antirealists, Putnam argues that the *new face of cognition* must make room for the concepts of representation and correspondence with reality. According to Putnam, we should reject the idea of representation as an "interface" between two independent relata, language and the world, but we should not give up on "the whole idea of representation." Putnam's suggestion is that the notions of representation and correspondence should be internalized: that is, they should be understood in terms of the representational activities that take place in everyday linguistic practices. This picture depicts the recognition-transcendence of truth as well entrenched in the normative presuppositions of ordinary practices. What this shows, according to Putnam, is the gap between conception and knowledge – that is, between our human capacities to conceive or symbolically represent and our capacities to corroborate and know. What is thus emphasized is that we have a symbolic access to the world, a linguistic contact with reality, which goes beyond our powers of recognition. It is in this "unproblematic," "commonsensical" sense that truth is said to be recognition-transcendent. Thus, through this Wittgensteinian and neopragmatist account of truth, Putnam claims to have rescued realist intuitions without metaphysical or epistemic idealizations.

Our selection starts with Kierkegaard's forceful defense of subjectivism and his critique of the objective perspective on communication and truth, using a classical essay from the nineteenth century to set the stage for the debate of the twentieth century. While acknowledging a crucial connection between truth and our mental life, Russell views subjectivism as a threat to objective correctness which ultimately undermines the normativity of truth. His realism and his correspondence theory of truth are in radical opposition to any subjective account of truth. Wittgenstein, on the other hand, creates problems for the realist or objectivist view by situating truth in our discursive practices or "language games" and emphasizing the dependence of truth-seeking activities on our background agreement in "forms of life." Davidson develops a very different immanent perspective on truth by linking it to the theories of interpretation that speakers use in their communicative practices. The Davidsonian account of meaning, truth, and interpretation has been linked to deflationary views of truth (see Rorty's paper in part III). Arguing against deflationism and verificationism as well as against metaphysical realism, Putnam closes this dialogue with a defense of a commonsense view of truth that tries to preserve basic realist intuitions.

Notes

1   Russell (1959) provides a forceful (and now classic) defense of this perspective through an account of truth as correspondence. According to Russell's correspondence theory, truth consists in an objective relation between mind and world: namely, an isomorphism between beliefs and facts, between a representational "complex" and an "associated complex." For a belief to be true, Russell contends, the objects represented in it and their relation must be properly mapped onto mind-independent correlates – that is, onto corresponding objects in the world standing in the same relation to one another. Russell's realist view emphasizes that although beliefs have a mental existence, their correctness is not determined by our minds, but by the facts themselves: "minds do not *create* truth or falsehood" (p. 129).

2   The holistic nature of truth has been developed in different ways by contemporary philosophers. We can group these different accounts into two broad categories: a *semiotic holism* that views language as a system or network and thematizes the interrelations among linguistic items, and a *pragmatic or existential holism* that is concerned with the interconnectedness of different aspects of human life and practice (whether linguistic or not). Wittgenstein provides the foundations for the latter kind of holism. See José Medina, *The Unity of Wittgenstein's Philosophy* (Albany, NY: SUNY Press, 2002), ch. 6; and *idem*, "Wittgenstein and Nonsense: Psychologism, Kantianism, and the *Habitus*," *International Journal of Philosophical Studies*, 11/3 (2003), pp. 293–318.

3   It is important to note that the subjective dimension that Kierkegaard calls our attention to includes the subjectivity of the other. He links the truth dimension of indirect communication to its emancipatory goal, which is to spark subjectivity – a kind of existential self-consciousness – in the other. This communicative aspect of subjectivity entails that any subjective experience always implicates the subjectivity of a *second person*. In this respect Kierkegaard's view is surprisingly close to Davidson's "second person" approach (see "The Second Person," in his *Subjective, Intersubjective, Objective* (Oxford: Clarendon Press, 2001), pp. 107–22).

4   Of course Kierkegaard entirely repudiates Hegel's understanding of "truth as system," which was the end served by the dialectic for Hegel.

5   There are also important logical desiderata that go along with the maximization of agreement, such as the maximization of self-consistency.

6   While in the 1960s and 1970s Putnam endorsed metaphysical realism and the correspondence theory of truth, in the 1980s he defended an epistemic account of truth based on his *internal realism* (cf. *Suggested Reading*). Trying to overcome the omniscient perspective or God's-eye view presupposed by his former metaphysical realist view, what Putnam's internal realism did was to internalize this ideal observer within our practices so that, instead of being judged according to an external perspective, truth was to be determined according to ideal standards of justification that can be derived from our practices (although our actual practices never reach ideal epistemic conditions). This internal realist view identifies truth with idealized consensus and is in line with Peirce's and (the early) Habermas's epistemic view of truth.

3

TRUTH, SUBJECTIVITY AND COMMUNICATION

Søren Kierkegaard

1.   *The subjective existing thinker is aware of the dialectic of communication.* Whereas objective thinking is indifferent to the thinking subject and his existence, the subjective thinker as existing is essentially interested in his own thinking, is existing in it. Therefore, his thinking has another kind of reflection, specifically, that of inwardness, of possession, whereby it belongs to the subject and to no one else. Whereas objective thinking invests everything in the result and assists all humankind to cheat by copying and reeling off the results and answers, subjective thinking invests everything in the process of becoming and omits the result, partly because this belongs to him, since he possesses the way, partly because he as existing is continually in the process of becoming, as is every human being who has not permitted himself to be tricked into becoming objective, into inhumanly becoming speculative thought.

The reflection of inwardness is the subjective thinker's double-reflection. In thinking, he thanks the universal, but, as existing in this thinking, as acquiring this in his inwardness, he becomes more and more subjectively isolated.

The difference between subjective and objective thinking must also manifest itself in the form of communication.[1] This means that the subjective thinker must promptly become aware that the form of communication must artistically possess just as much reflection as he himself, existing in his thinking, possesses. Artistically, please note, for the secret does not consist in his enunciating the double-reflection directly, since such an enunciation is a direct contradiction.

Ordinary communication between one human being and another is entirely immediate, because people ordinarily exist in immediacy. When one person states something and another acknowledges the same thing verbatim, they are assumed to be in agreement and to have understood each other. Yet because the one making the statement is unaware of the duplexity [*Dobbelthed*] of thought-existence, he is also unable

Søren Kierkegaard, excerpts from *Concluding Unscientific Postscript to* Philosophical Fragments, Vol. 1: Text, ed. and trans. Howard V. Hong and Edna. H. Hong (Princeton: Princeton University Press, 1992), pp. 72–82, 85–6, 91–2, 106–8, 189–94, 198–200, 202–5. © 1992 by Princeton University Press. Reprinted by permission of Princeton University Press.

to be aware of the double-reflection of communication. Therefore, he has no inti-mation that this kind of agreement can be the greatest misunderstanding and natu-rally has no intimation that, just as the subjective existing thinker has set himself free by the duplexity, so the secret of communication specifically hinges on setting the other free, and for that very reason he must not communicate himself directly; indeed, it is even irreligious to do so. This latter applies in proportion to the essentiality of the subjective and consequently applies first and foremost within the religious domain, that is, if the communicator is not God himself or does not presume to appeal to the miraculous authority of an apostle but is just a human being and also cares to have meaning in what he says and what he does.

Therefore, the subjective religious thinker, who has comprehended the duplexity of existence in order to be such a thinker, readily perceives that direct communication is a fraud toward God (which possibly defrauds him of the worship of another person in truth), a fraud toward himself (as if he had ceased to be an existing person), a fraud toward another human being (who possibly attains only a relative God-relationship), a fraud that brings him into contradiction with his entire thought. In turn, to enun-ciate this directly would again be a contradiction, because the form would then become direct despite the entire double-reflection of what is said. To require of a thinker that he contradict his entire thought and his world-view by the form he gives his com-munication, to console him by saying that in this way he will be beneficial, to let him remain convinced that nobody cares about it, indeed, that nobody notices it in these objective times, since such extreme conclusions are merely tomfoolery, which every systematic day laborer regards as nothing – well, that is good advice, and also quite cheap. Suppose it was the life-view of a religiously existing subject that one may not have followers, that this would be treason to both God and men; suppose he were a bit obtuse (for if it takes a bit more than honesty to do well in this world, obtuseness is always required in order to be truly successful and to be truly understood by many) and announced this directly with unction and pathos – what then? Well, then he would be understood and soon ten would apply who, just for a free shave each week, would offer their services in proclaiming this doctrine; that is, in further substantiation of the truth of his doctrine, he would have been so very fortunate as to gain followers who accepted and spread this doctrine about having no follower.

Objective thinking is completely indifferent to subjectivity and thereby to inward-ness and appropriation; its communication is therefore direct. It is obvious that it does not therefore have to be easy. But it is direct, it does not have the illusiveness and the art of double-reflection. It does not have that God-fearing and humane solic-itude of subjective thinking in communicating itself; it can be understood directly; it can be reeled off. Objective thinking is therefore aware only of itself and is therefore no communication,[2] at least no artistic communication, inasmuch as it would always be required to think of the receiver and to pay attention to the form of the com-munication in relation to the receiver's misunderstanding. Objective thinking[3] is, like most people, so fervently kind and communicative; it communicates right away and at most resorts to assurances about its truth, to recommendations and promises about how all people someday will accept this truth – so sure is it. Or perhaps rather so unsure, because the assurances and the recommendations and the promises, which are indeed for the sake of those others who are supposed to accept this truth, might also

be for the sake of the teacher, who needs the security and dependability of a majority vote. If his contemporaries deny him this, he will draw on posterity – so sure is
he. This security has something in common with the independence that, independent
of the world, needs the world as witness to one's independence so as to be certain
of being independent.

The form of a communication is something different from the 'expression of a
communication. When a thought has gained its proper expression in the word, which
is attained through the first reflection, there comes the second reflection, which bears
upon the intrinsic relation of the communication to the communicator and renders
the existing communicator's own relation to the idea. Let us once again cite a few
examples. We do have plenty of time, because what I write is not the awaited final
paragraph that will complete the system. Suppose,[4] then, that someone wanted to
communicate the following conviction: truth is inwardness; objectively there is no
truth, but the appropriation is the truth. Suppose he had enough zeal and enthusiasm to get it said, because when people heard it they would be saved. Suppose he
said it on every occasion and moved not only those who sweat easily but also the
tough people – what then? Then there would certainly be some laborers who had
been standing idle in the marketplace and only upon hearing this call would go forth
to work in the vineyard – to proclaim this teaching to all people. And what then?
Then he would have contradicted himself even more, just as he had from the beginning, because the zeal and enthusiasm for getting it said and getting it heard were
already a misunderstanding. The main point was indeed to become understood, and
the inwardness of the understanding would indeed be that the single individual would
understand this by himself. Now he had even gone so far as to obtain barkers, and a
barker of inwardness is a creature worth seeing.

Actually to communicate such a conviction would require art and self-control:
enough self-control to comprehend inwardly that the God-relationship of the individual human being is the main point, that the meddling busyness of a third person
is a lack of inwardness and a superfluity of amiable obtuseness, and enough art to
vary inexhaustibly, just as inwardness is inexhaustible, the doubly reflected form of the
communication. The more art, the more inwardness – yes, if he had considerable art,
it would even be quite possible for him to say that he was using it with the assurance of being able the next moment to ensure the inwardness of the communication, because he was infinitely concerned to preserve his own inwardness, a concern
that saves the concerned person from all positive chattiness.

Suppose someone wanted to communicate that the truth is not the truth but that
the way is the truth, that is, that the truth is only in the becoming, in the process of
appropriation, that consequently there is no result. Suppose he were a humanitarian
who necessarily had to publicize this to all people. Suppose he took the splendid
shortcut of communicating this in direct form in *Adresseavisen*, by which means he
gained masses of supporters, whereas the artistic way, despite his utmost efforts, would
leave undecided whether or not he had helped anyone – what then? Well, then his
assertion would indeed turn out to be a result.

Suppose someone wanted to communicate that all receiving is a producing.
Suppose he repeated it so frequently that this thesis even came to be used as copy in
teaching penmanship – then he would certainly have gotten his thesis confirmed.

Suppose someone wanted to communicate the conviction that a person's God-relationship is a secret. Suppose he was a very congenial kind of man who was so fond of other people that he simply had to come out with it. Suppose he nevertheless still had enough understanding to sense a bit of the contradiction in communicating this directly and consequently he communicated it under a pledge of secrecy – what then? Then either he must assume that the pupil was wiser than the teacher, that the pupil was actually able to keep silent, something the teacher was unable to do (a superb satire on being a teacher!), or he must become so blissful in gibberish that he completely failed to discover the contradiction. It is a curious thing about these congenial people; it is so touching that they have to come out with it – and it is so vain of them to believe that some other human being needs one's assistance in his God-relationship, as if God were not able to help himself and the person involved. But it is a bit strenuous: in existing to hold on to the thought that one is nothing before God, that all personal effort is only a jest. It is a bit chastening to respect every human being so that one does not dare to meddle directly in his God-relationship, partly because one ought to have enough in dealing with one's own, partly because God is no friend of impertinence.

Wherever the subjective is of importance in knowledge and appropriation is therefore the main point, communication is a work of art; it is doubly reflected, and its first form is the subtlety that the subjective individuals must be held devoutly apart from one another and must not run coagulatingly together in objectivity. This is objectivity's word of farewell to subjectivity.

Ordinary communication, objective thinking, has no secrets; only doubly reflected subjective thinking has secrets; that is, all its essential content is essentially a secret, because it cannot be communicated directly. This is the significance of the secrecy. That this knowledge cannot be stated directly, because the essential in this knowledge is the appropriation itself, means that it remains a secret for everyone who is not through himself doubly reflected in the same way, but that this is the essential form of truth means that this cannot be said in any other way.[5] Therefore, when someone is set on communicating this directly, he is obtuse; and when someone else is set on demanding this of him, he also is obtuse. Faced with such an illusive, artistic communication, ordinary human obtuseness will cry: It is egotism. So, when obtuseness prevails and communication becomes direct, obtuseness will have won so much that the communicator will have become just as obtuse.

It is possible to distinguish between an essential secret and an accidental one. For example, what has been said in a privy council is an accidental secret as long as it is not publicly known, because the statement itself can be understood directly as soon as it is made public. That no one knows what will happen in a year is an accidental secret, because when it has happened it can be understood directly. On the other hand, when Socrates, on account of his daimon, isolated himself from any and every relation and, for instance, *posito* [as a supposition] presumed that everyone had to do it in that way, such a life-view would essentially become a secret or an essential secret, because it could not be communicated directly; at most he was capable of artistically, maieutically helping another person negatively to the same view. Everything subjective, which on account of its dialectical inwardness evades the direct form of expression, is an essential secret.

In its inexhaustible artistry, such a form of communication corresponds to and renders the existing subject's own relation to the idea. In order to make this clear in the form of an imaginary construction, without determining whether someone actually existing has himself been conscious of this or not, i.e., has existed in this way or not, I will characterize the existence-relation.

2. *In his existence-relation to the truth, the existing subjective thinker is just as negative as positive, has just as much of the comic as he essentially has of pathos, and is continually in a process of becoming, that is, striving.* Since the existing subject is existing (and that is the lot of every human being, except the objective ones, who have pure being to be in), he is indeed in the process of becoming. Just as his communication must in form essentially conform to his own existence, so his thought must correspond to the form of existence. Through Hegel, everyone is now familiar with the dialectic of becoming. That which in the process of becoming is the alternation between being and non-being (a category that is nevertheless somewhat unclear, inasmuch as being is itself also the continuity in the alternation) is later the negative and the positive.

In our time, we often enough hear talk about the negative and about negative thinkers, and in that connection often enough hear the preaching of the positive ones and their prayers offering thanks to God and Hegel that they are not like those negative ones but have become positive. In the domain of thinking, the positive can be classed in the following categories: sensate certainty, historical knowledge, speculative result. But this positive is precisely the untrue. Sensate certainty is a delusion (see Greek skepticism and the entire presentation in modern philosophy, from which a great deal can be learned); historical knowledge is an illusion (since it is approximation-knowledge); and the speculative result is a phantom. That is, all of this positive fails to express the state of the knowing subject in existence; hence it pertains to a fictive objective subject, and to mistake oneself for such a subject is to be fooled and to remain fooled. Every subject is an existing subject, and therefore this must be essentially expressed in all of his knowing and must be expressed by keeping his knowing from an illusory termination in sensate certainty, in historical knowledge, in illusory results. In historical knowledge, he comes to know much about the world, nothing about himself; he is continually moving in the sphere of approximation-knowledge, while with his presumed positivity he fancies himself to have a certainty that can be had only in infinitude, in which, however, he cannot be as an existing person but at which he is continually arriving. Nothing historical can become infinitely certain to me except this: that I exist (which in turn cannot become infinitely certain to any other individual, who in turn is only in the same way infinitely cognizant of his own existence), which is not something historical. The speculative result is an illusion insofar as the existing subject, thinking, wants to abstract from his existing and wants to be *sub specie aeterni* [under the aspect of eternity].

The negative thinkers therefore always have the advantage that they have something positive, namely this, that they are aware of the negative; the positive thinkers have nothing whatever, for they are deluded. Precisely because the negative is present in existence [*Tilværelse*] and present everywhere (because being there, existence [*Existents*], is continually in the process of becoming), the only deliverance from it is to become continually aware of it. By being positively secured, the subject is indeed fooled.

The negativity that is in existence, or rather the negativity of the existing subject (which his thinking must render essentially in an adequate form), is grounded in the subject's synthesis, in his being an existing infinite spirit. The infinite and the eternal are the only certainty, but since it is in the subject, it is in existence [*Tilværelse*], and the first expression for it is its illusiveness and the prodigious contradiction that the eternal becomes, that it comes into existence [*blive til*].

It is therefore important for the thinking of the existing subject to have a form in which he is able to render this. If he says this in direct utterance, he says something untrue, because in direct utterance the illusiveness is left out, and consequently the form of the communication interferes, just as when the tongue of an epileptic utters the wrong word, although the speaker may not notice it as clearly as the epileptic.

[. . .]

But the genuine subjective existing thinker [. . .] is never a teacher, but a learner, and if he is continually just as negative as positive, he is continually striving. [. . .]

One who is existing is continually in the process of becoming; the actually existing subjective thinker, thinking, continually reproduces this in his existence and invests all his thinking in becoming. This is similar to having style. Only he really has style who is never finished with something but "stirs the waters of language" whenever he begins, so that to him the most ordinary expression comes into existence with newborn originality.

To be continually in the process of becoming in this way is the illusiveness of the infinite in existence. It could bring a sensate person to despair, for one continually feels an urge to have something finished, but this urge is of evil and must be renounced. The perpetual process of becoming is the uncertainty of earthly life, in which everything is uncertain. Every human being knows this and says so once in a while, especially on a solemn occasion and not without sweat and tears, says it directly and moves himself and others – and shows in action what he has already shown in the form of his utterance, that he does not understand what he himself is saying!

[. . .]

That the existing subjective thinker is continually striving does not mean, however, that in a finite sense he has a goal toward which he is striving, where he would be finished when he reached it. No, he is striving infinitely, is continually in the process of becoming, something that is safeguarded by his being just as negative as positive and by his having just as much of the essentially comic as of the essentially pathos-filled, and that has its basis in the circumstance that he is existing and renders this in his thinking. The process of becoming is the thinker's very existence, from which he can indeed thoughtlessly abstract and become objective. How far the subjective thinker might be along that road, whether a long way or a short, makes no essential difference (it is, after all, just a finitely relative comparison); as long as he is existing, he is in the process of becoming.

Existence itself, existing, is a striving and is just as pathos-filled as it is comic: pathos-filled because the striving is infinite, that is, directed toward the infinite, is a process of infinitizing, which is the highest pathos; comic because the striving is a self-contradiction. From a pathos-filled perspective, one second has infinite value; from a comic perspective, ten thousand years are but a prank, like a yesterday, and yet the time the existing individual is in does consist of such parts. When ten thousand years are simply and directly declared to be a prank, many a fool will go along and find it to be wisdom but forget the other, that a second has infinite value. When a second is said to have infinite value, someone or other will be startled and better understand that ten thousand years have infinite value. And yet the one is just as difficult to understand as the other if only one takes time to understand what is to be understood, or if in another way one is seized so infinitely by the thought of having no time to waste, not one second, that a second acquires infinite value.

[. . .]

Lessing has said: *If God held all truth enclosed in his right hand, and in his left hand the one and only ever-striving drive for truth, even with the corollary of erring forever and ever, and if he were to say to me: Choose! – I would humbly fall down to him at his left hand and say: Father, give! Pure truth is indeed only for you alone!* (See Lessing's *S. W.*, V, p. 100.) [. . .]

But first an assurance here regarding my own lowly person. I am as willing as anyone to fall down in worship before the system if I could only catch a glimpse of it. So far I have not succeeded, and although I do have young legs, I am almost worn out by running from Herod to Pilate. [. . .]

System and conclusiveness are just about one and the same, so that if the system is not finished, there is not any system. Elsewhere I have already pointed out that a system that is not entirely finished is a hypothesis, whereas a half-finished system is nonsense. [. . .]

On the other hand, a continued striving for a system is indeed a striving, and a striving, yes, a continued striving, is indeed what Lessing is talking about. But certainly not a striving for nothing! On the contrary, Lessing speaks of a striving for truth; and he uses a peculiar phrase regarding this urge for truth: *den einzigen immer regen Trieb* [the one and only ever-striving drive]. This word *einzig* [one and only] can scarcely be understood as meaning anything other than the infinite in the same sense as it is higher to have one thought, one only, than to have many thoughts. So these two, Lessing and the systematician, both speak of a continued striving – the only difference is that Lessing is obtuse or truthful enough to call it a continued striving, the systematician sagacious or untruthful enough to call it the system.

[. . .]

Whether truth is defined more empirically as the agreement of thinking with being or more idealistically as the agreement of being with thinking, the point in each case is to pay scrupulous attention to what is understood by being and also to pay attention to whether the knowing human spirit might not be lured out into the indefinite and fantastically become something such as no *existing* human being has ever been or can be, a phantom with which the individual busies himself on occasion. [. . .]

The term "being" in those definitions must, then, be understood much more abstractly as the abstract rendition or the abstract prototype of what being *in concreto* is as empirical being. If it is understood in this way, nothing stands in the way of abstractly defining truth as something finished, because, viewed abstractly, the agreement between thinking and being is always finished, inasmuch as the beginning of the process of becoming lies precisely in the concretion that abstraction abstractly disregards.

But if being is understood in this way, the formula is a tautology; that is, thinking and being signify one and the same, and the agreement spoken of is only an abstract identity with itself. Therefore, none of the formulas says more than that truth is, if this is understood in such a way that the copula is accentuated – truth *is* – that is, truth is a redoubling [*Fordoblelse*]. Truth is the first, but truth's other, that it *is*, is the same as the first; this, its being, is the abstract form of truth. In this way it is expressed that truth is not something simple but in an entirely abstract sense a redoubling, which is nevertheless canceled at the very same moment. [. . .]

For the existing spirit *qua* existing spirit, the question about truth persists, because the abstract answer is only for that *abstractum* which an existing spirit becomes by abstracting from himself *qua* existing, which he can do only momentarily, although at such moments he still pays his debt to existence by existing nevertheless. Consequently, it is an existing spirit who asks about truth, presumably because he wants to exist in it, but in any case the questioner is conscious of being an existing individual human being. [. . .]

When for the existing spirit *qua* existing there is a question about truth, that abstract reduplication [*Reduplikation*] of truth recurs; but existence itself, existence itself in the questioner, who does indeed exist, holds the two factors apart, one from the other, and reflection shows two relations. To objective reflection, truth becomes something objective, an object, and the point is to disregard the subject. To subjective reflection, truth becomes appropriation, inwardness, subjectivity, and the point is to immerse oneself, existing, in subjectivity.

[. . .]

We return, then, to the two ways of reflection and have not forgotten that it is an existing spirit who is asking, simply an individual human being, and are not able to forget, either, that his existing is precisely what will prevent him from going both ways at once, and his concerned questions will prevent him from light-mindedly and fantastically becoming a subject-object. Now, then, which of the ways is the way of truth for the existing spirit? Only the fantastical *I-I* is simultaneously finished with both ways or advances methodically along both ways simultaneously, which for an existing human being is such an inhuman way of walking that I dare not recommend it. [. . .]

The way of objective reflection turns the subjective individual into something accidental and thereby turns existence into an indifferent, vanishing something. The way to the objective truth goes away from the subject, and while the subject and subjectivity become indifferent [*ligegyldig*], the truth also becomes indifferent, and that is precisely its objective validity [*Gyldighed*], because the interest, just like the decision, is subjectivity. The way of objective reflection now leads to abstract thinking, to mathematics, to historical knowledge of various kinds, and always leads away from the subjective individual, whose existence or nonexistence becomes, from an objective point of view, altogether properly, infinitely indifferent, altogether properly, because, as Hamlet says, existence and nonexistence have only subjective significance.

At its maximum, this way will lead to a contradiction, and to the extent that the subject does not become totally indifferent to himself, this is merely an indication that his objective striving is not objective enough. At its maximum, it will lead to the contradiction that only objectivity has come about, whereas subjectivity has gone out, that is, the existing subjectivity that has made an attempt to become what in the abstract sense is called subjectivity, the abstract form of an abstract objectivity. And yet, viewed subjectively, the objectivity that has come about is at its maximum either a hypothesis or an approximation, because all eternal decision is rooted specifically in subjectivity.

But the objective way is of the opinion that it has a security that the subjective way does not have (of course, existence, what it means to exist, and objective security cannot be thought together). It is of the opinion that it avoids a danger that lies in wait for the subjective way, and at its maximum this danger is madness. In a solely subjective definition of truth, lunacy and truth are ultimately indistinguishable, because they may both have inwardness.[6] But one does not become lunatic by becoming objective. At this point I might perhaps add a little comment that does not seem superfluous in an objective age. Is the absence of inwardness also lunacy? The objective truth as such does not at all decide that the one stating it is sensible; on the contrary, it can even betray that the man is lunatic, although what he says is entirely true and especially objectively true.

[. . .]

In order to clarify the divergence of objective and subjective reflection, I shall now describe subjective reflection in its search back and inward into inwardness. At its highest, inwardness in an existing subject is passion; truth as a paradox corresponds to passion, and that truth becomes a paradox is grounded precisely in its relation to an existing subject. In this way the one corresponds to the other. In forgetting that one is an existing subject, one loses passion, and in return, truth does not become a paradox; but the knowing subject shifts from being human to being a fantastical something, and truth becomes a fantastical object for its knowing.

When the question about truth is asked objectively, truth is reflected upon objectively as an object to which the knower relates himself. What is reflected upon is not the relation but that what he relates himself is the truth, the true. If only that to which he relates himself is the truth, the true, then the subject is in the truth. When the question about truth is asked subjectively, the individual's relation is reflected upon subjectively. If only the how of this relation is in truth, the individual is in truth, even if he in this way were to relate himself to untruth.[7]

Let us take the knowledge of God as an example. Objectively, what is reflected upon is that this is the true God; subjectively, that the individual relates himself to a something *in such a way* that his relation is in truth a God-relation. Now, on which side is the truth? Alas, must we not at this point resort to mediation and say: It is on neither side; it is in the mediation? Superbly stated, if only someone could say how an existing person goes about being in mediation, because to be in mediation is to be finished; to exist is to become. An existing person cannot be in two places at the same time, cannot be subject-object. When he is closest to being in two places at the same time, he is in passion; but passion is only momentary, and passion is the highest pitch of subjectivity.

The existing person who chooses the objective way now enters upon all approximating deliberation intended to bring forth God objectively, which is not achieved in all eternity, because God is a subject and hence only for subjectivity in inwardness. The existing person who chooses the subjective way instantly comprehends the whole dialectical difficulty because he must use some time, perhaps a long time, to find God objectively. He comprehends this dialectical difficulty in all its pain, because he must resort to God at that very moment, because every moment in which he does not have God is wasted.[8] At that very moment he has God, not by virtue of any objective deliberation but by virtue of the infinite passion of inwardness. The objective person is not bothered by dialectical difficulties such as what it means to put a whole research period into finding God, since it is indeed possible that the researcher would die tomorrow, and if he goes on living, he cannot very well regard God as something to be taken along at his convenience, since God is something one takes along *à tout prix* [at any price], which, in passion's understanding, is the true relationship of inwardness with God.

[...]

The Socratic ignorance was thus the expression, firmly maintained with all the passion of inwardness, of the relation of the eternal truth to an existing person, and therefore it must remain for him a paradox as long as he exists. Yet it is possible that in the Socratic ignorance there was more truth in Socrates than in the objective truth of the entire system that flirts with the demands of the times and adapts itself to assistant professors.

Objectively the emphasis is on **what** *is said; subjectively the emphasis is on* **how** *it is said.* This distinction applies even esthetically and is specifically expressed when we say that in the mouth of this or that person something that is truth can become untruth. Particular attention should be paid to this distinction in our day, for if one were to express in a single sentence the difference between ancient times and our time, one would no doubt have to say: In ancient times there were only a few individuals who knew the truth; now everyone knows it, but inwardness has an inverse relation to it.[9] Viewed esthetically, the contradiction that emerges when truth becomes untruth in this and that person's mouth is best interpreted comically. Ethically-religiously, the emphasis is again on: *how.* But this is not to be understood as manner, modulation of voice, oral delivery, etc., but it is to be understood as the relation of the existing person, in his very existence, to what is said. Objectively, the question is only about categories of thought; subjectively, about inwardness. At its maximum, this "how" is the passion of the infinite, and the passion of the infinite is the very truth. But the passion of the infinite is precisely subjectivity, and thus subjectivity is truth. From the objective point of view, there is no infinite decision, and thus it is objectively correct that the distinction between good and evil is canceled, along with the principle of contradiction, and thereby also the infinite distinction between truth and falsehood. Only in subjectivity is there decision, whereas wanting to become objective is untruth. The passion of the infinite, not its content, is the deciding factor, for its content is precisely itself. In this way the subjective "how" and subjectivity are the truth.

But precisely because the subject is existing, the "how" that is subjectively emphasized is dialectical also with regard to time. In the moment of the decision of passion,

where the road swings off from objective knowledge, it looks as if the infinite decision were thereby finished. But at the same moment, the existing person is in the
temporal realm, and the subjective "how" is transformed into a striving that is motivated and repeatedly refreshed by the decisive passion of the infinite, but it is nevertheless a striving.

When subjectivity is truth, the definition of truth must also contain in itself an
expression of the antithesis to objectivity, a memento of that fork in the road, and
this expression will at the same time indicate the resilience of the inwardness. Here
is such a definition of truth: *An objective uncertainty, held fast through appropriation with
the most passionate inwardness, is the truth*, the highest truth there is for an *existing* person.
At the point where the road swings off (and where that is cannot be stated objectively, since it is precisely subjectivity), objective knowledge is suspended. Objectively
he then has only uncertainty, but this is precisely what intensifies the infinite passion
of inwardness, and truth is precisely the daring venture of choosing the objective
uncertainty with the passion of the infinite. I observe nature in order to find God,
and I do indeed see omnipotence and wisdom, but I also see much that troubles and
disturbs. The *summa summarum* [sum total] of this is an objective uncertainly, but the
inwardness is so very great, precisely because it grasps this objective uncertainty with
all the passion of the infinite. In a mathematical proposition, for example, the objectivity is given, but therefore its truth is also an indifferent truth.

But the definition of truth stated above is a paraphrasing of faith. Without risk, no
faith. Faith is the contradiction between the infinite passion of inwardness and the
objective uncertainty. If I am able to apprehend God objectively, I do not have faith;
but because I cannot do this, I must have faith. If I want to keep myself in faith, I
must continually see to it that I hold fast the objective uncertainty, see to it that in
the objective uncertainty I am "out on 70,000 fathoms of water" and still have faith.

The thesis that subjectivity, inwardness, is truth contains the Socratic wisdom, the
undying merit of which is to have paid attention to the essential meaning of existing, of the knower's being an existing person. That is why, in his ignorance, Socrates
was in the truth in the highest sense within paganism. [. . .]

When subjectivity, inwardness, is truth, then truth, objectively defined, is a paradox;
and that truth is objectively a paradox shows precisely that subjectivity is truth, since
the objectivity does indeed thrust away, and the objectivity's repulsion, or the expression for the objectivity's repulsion, is the resilience and dynamometer of inwardness.
The paradox is the objective uncertainty that is the expression for the passion of
inwardness that is truth. So much for the Socratic. [. . .]

Viewed Socratically, the eternal essential truth is not at all paradoxical in itself, but
only by being related to an existing person.

Notes

1   Double-reflection is already implicit in the idea of communication itself: that the subjec-
    tive individual (who by inwardness wants to express the life of the eternal, in which all
    sociality and all companionship are inconceivable because the existence-category, move-
    ment, is inconceivable here, and hence essential communication is also inconceivable

because everyone must be assumed to possess everything essentially), existing in the isolation of inwardness, wants to communicate himself, consequently that he simultaneously wants to keep his thinking in the inwardness of his subjective existence and yet wants to communicate himself. It is not possible (except for thoughtlessness, for which all things are indeed possible) for this contradiction to become manifest in a direct form. – It is not so difficult, however, to understand that a subject existing in this way may want to communicate himself. A person in love, for instance, to whom his erotic love is his very inwardness, may well want to communicate himself, but not directly, just because the inwardness of erotic love is the main thing for him. Essentially occupied with continually acquiring the inwardness of erotic love, he has no result and is never finished, but he may nevertheless want to communicate; yet for that very reason he can never use a direct form, since that presupposes results and completion. So it is also in a God-relationship. Just because he himself is continually in the process of becoming in an inward direction, that is, in inwardness, he can never communicate himself directly, since the movement is here the very opposite. Direct communication requires certainty, but certainty is impossible for a person in the process of becoming, and it is indeed a deception. Thus, to employ an erotic relationship, if a maiden in love yearns for the wedding day because this would give her assured certainty, if she wanted to make herself comfortable in legal security as a spouse, if she preferred marital yawning to maidenly yearning, then the man would rightfully deplore her unfaithfulness, although she indeed did not love anyone else, because she would have lost the idea and actually did not love him. And this, after all, is the essential unfaithfulness in an erotic relationship; the incidental unfaithfulness is to love someone else.

2   That is how it always goes with the negative; wherever it is unconsciously present, it transmutes the positive into the negative. In this case, it transmutes communication into an illusion, because no thought is given to the negative in the communication, but the communication is thought of purely and simply as positive. In the deception of double-reflection, consideration is given to the negativity of the communication, and therefore this communication, which seems to be nothing compared with that other mode of communication, is indeed communication.

3   It is always no be borne in mind that I am speaking of the religious, in which objective thinking, if it is supposed to be supreme, is downright irreligiousness. But wherever objective thinking is within its rights, its direct communication is also in order, precisely because it is not supposed to deal with subjectivity.

4   I say only "suppose," and in this form I have permission to present what is most certain and most unreasonable, for even the most certain is not posited as the most certain but is posited as what is assumed for the purpose of shedding light on the matter; and even the most unreasonable is not posited essentially but only provisionally, for the purpose of illustrating the relation of ground and consequent.

5   If in our age there lived a person who, subjectively developed, was aware of the art of communication, he would experience the most glorious buffoonery and farce. He would be turned out of doors as one who is incapable of being objective, until at long last a good-natured objective chap, a systematic devil of a fellow, would most likely have mercy upon him and help him halfway into the paragraphs. What was once regarded as an impossibility – namely, to paint a picture of Mars in the armor that makes him invisible – would now succeed extremely well; in fact, what is even more curious, it would now succeed halfway.

6   Even this is not true, however, because madness never has the inwardness of infinity. Its fixed idea is a kind of objective something, and the contradiction of madness lies in wanting to embrace it with passion. The decisive factor in madness is thus not the subjective, but the little finitude that becomes fixed, something the infinite can never become.

7	The reader will note that what is being discussed here is essential truth, or the truth that is related essentially to existence, and that it is specifically in order to clarify it as inwardness or as subjectivity that the contrast is pointed out.

8	In this way God is indeed a postulate, but not in the loose sense in which it is ordinarily taken. Instead, it becomes clear that this is the only way an existing person enters into a relationship with God: when the dialectical contradiction brings passion to despair and assists him in grasping God with "the category of despair" (faith), so that the postulate, far from being the arbitrary, is in fact *necessary* defense [*Nød værge*], self-defense; in this way God is not a postulate, but the existing person's postulating of God is – a necessity [*Nødvendighed*].

9	See *Stages on Life's Way*, ed. and trans. H. V. Hong and E. H. Hong (Princeton: Princeton University Press, 1988), p. 366 n.

4

REMARKS ON TRUTH
from *On Certainty* and *Culture and Value*

Ludwig Wittgenstein

From *On Certainty*

94.   But I did not get my picture of the world by satisfying myself of its correctness; nor do I have it because I am satisfied of its correctness. No: it is the inherited background against which I distinguish between true and false.

95.   The propositions describing this world-picture might be part of a kind of mythology. And their role is like that of rules of a game; and the game can be learned purely practically, without learning any explicit rules.

96.   It might be imagined that some propositions, of the form of empirical propositions, were hardened and functioned as channels for such empirical propositions as were not hardened but fluid; and that this relation altered with time, in that fluid propositions hardened, and hard ones became fluid.

97.   The mythology may change back into a state of flux, the river-bed of thoughts may shift. But I distinguish between the movement of the waters on the river-bed and the shift of the bed itself; though there is not a sharp division of the one from the other.

98.   But if someone were to say "So logic too is an empirical science" he would be wrong. Yet this is right: the same proposition may get treated at one time as something to test by experience, at another as a rule of testing.

Ludwig Wittgenstein, *On Certainty*, ed. G. E. M. Anscombe and G. H. von Wright, trans. Denis Paul and G. E. M. Anscombe (Oxford: Basil Blackwell, 1969), pp. 15–18, 20–3, 27–8 (§ 94–117, 137–62, 191–206). Reprinted by permission of Blackwell Publishing.

Ludwig Wittgenstein, *Culture and Value: A Selection from the Posthumous Remains*, edited by G. H von Wright in collaboration with Heikki Nyman (second edition of the text by Alois Pichler, translated by Peter Winch) (Oxford: Blackwell, 1998), pp. 41, 64. This book was originally published as *Vermischte Bemerkungen* in 1977 (revised second edition 1994). Reprinted by permission of Blackwell Publishing.

99.   And the bank of that river consists partly of hard rock, subject to no alteration or only to an imperceptible one, partly of sand, which now in one place now in another gets washed away, or deposited.

100.   The truths which Moore says he knows, are such as, roughly speaking, all of us know, if he knows them.

101.   Such a proposition might be e.g. "My body has never disappeared and reappeared again after an interval."

102.   Might I not believe that once, without knowing it, perhaps in a state of unconsciousness, I was taken far away from the earth – that other people even know this, but do not mention it to me? But this would not fit into the rest of my convictions at all. Not that I could describe the system of these convictions. Yet my convictions do form a system, a structure.

103.   And now if I were to say "It is my unshakeable conviction that etc.", this means in the present case too that I have not consciously arrived at the conviction by following a particular line of thought, but that it is anchored in all my *questions and answers*, so anchored that I cannot touch it.

104.   I am for example also convinced that the sun is not a hole in the vault of heaven.

105.   All testing, all confirmation and disconfirmation of a hypothesis takes place already within a system. And this system is not a more or less arbitrary and doubtful point of departure for all out arguments: no, it belongs to the essence of what we call an argument. The system is not so much the point of departure, as the element in which arguments have their life.

106.   Suppose some adult had told a child that he had been on the moon. The child tells me the story, and I say it was only a joke, the man hadn't been on the moon; no one has ever been on the moon; the moon is a long way off and it is impossible to climb up there or fly there. – If now the child insists, saying perhaps there is a way of getting there which I don't know, etc. what reply could I make to him? What reply could I make to the adults of a tribe who believe that people sometimes go to the moon (perhaps that is how they interpret their dreams), and who indeed grant that there are no ordinary means of climbing up to it or flying there? – But a child will not ordinarily stick to such a belief and will soon be convinced by what we tell him seriously.

107.   Isn't this altogether like the way one can instruct a child to believe in a God, or that none exists, and it will accordingly be able to produce apparently telling grounds for the one or the other?

108.   "But is there then no objective truth? Isn't it true, or false, that someone has been on the moon?" If we are thinking within our system, then it is certain that no

one has ever been on the moon. Not merely is nothing of the sort ever seriously reported to us by reasonable people, but our whole system of physics forbids us to believe it. For this demands answers to the questions "How did he overcome the force of gravity?" "How could he live without an atmosphere?" and a thousand others which could not be answered. But suppose that instead of all these answers we met the reply: "We don't know *how* one gets to the moon, but those who get there know at once that they are there; and even you can't explain everything." We should feel ourselves intellectually very distant from someone who said this.

109.   "An empirical proposition can be *tested*" (we say). But how? and through what?

110.   What *counts* as its test? – "But is this an adequate test? And, if so, must it not be recognizable as such in logic?" – As if giving grounds did not come to an end sometime. But the end is not an ungrounded presupposition: it is an ungrounded way of acting.

111.   "I *know* that I have never been on the moon." That sounds quite different in the circumstances which actually hold, to the way it would sound if a good many men had been on the moon, and some perhaps without knowing it. In *this* case one could give grounds for this knowledge. Is there not a relationship here similar to that between the general rule of multiplying and particular multiplications that have been carried out?

I want to say: my not having been on the moon is as sure a thing for me as any grounds I could give for it.

112.   And isn't that what Moore wants to say, when he says he *knows* all these things? — But is his knowing it really what is in question, and not rather that some of these propositions must be solid for us?

113.   When someone is trying to teach us mathematics, he will not begin by assuring us that he *knows* that a + b = b + a.

114.   If you are not certain of any fact, you cannot be certain of the meaning of your words either.

115.   If you tried to doubt everything you would not get as far as doubting anything. The game of doubting itself presupposes certainty.

116.   Instead of "I know . . .", couldn't Moore have said: "It stands fast for me that . . ."? And further: "It stands fast for me and many others. . . ."

117.   Why is it not possible for me to doubt that I have never been on the moon? And how could I try to doubt it?

First and foremost, the supposition that perhaps I have been there would strike me as *idle*. Nothing would follow from it, nothing be explained by it. It would not tie in with anything in my life.

When I say "Nothing speaks for, everything against it," this presupposes a principle of speaking for and against. That is, I must be able to say what *would* speak for
it.

[. . .]

137.   Even if the most trustworthy of men assures me that he *knows* things are thus
and so, this by itself cannot satisfy me that he does know. Only that he believes he
knows. That is why Moore's assurance that he knows . . . does not interest us. The
propositions, however, which Moore retails as examples of such known truths are
indeed interesting. Not because anyone knows their truth, or believes he knows them,
but because they all have a *similar* role in the system of our empirical judgments.

138.   We don't, for example, arrive at any of them as a result of investigation.
     There are e.g. historical investigations and investigations into the shape and also
the age of the earth, but not into whether the earth has existed during the last
hundred years. Of course many of us have information about this period from our
parents and grandparents; but mayn't they be wrong? – "Nonsense!" one will say.
"How should all these people be wrong?" – But is that an argument? Is it not simply
the rejection of an idea? And perhaps the determination of a concept? For if I speak
of a possible mistake here, this changes the role of "mistake" and "truth" in our lives.

139.   Not only rules, but also examples are needed for establishing a practice. Our
rules leave loop-holes open, and the practice has to speak for itself.

140.   We do not learn the practice of making empirical judgments by learning rules:
we are taught *judgments* and their connexion with other judgments. *A totality* of judgments is made plausible to us.

141.   When we first begin to *believe* anything, what we believe is not a single
proposition, it is a whole system of propositions. (Light dawns gradually over the
whole.)

142.   It is not single axioms that strike me as obvious, it is a system in which consequences and premises give one another *mutual* support.

143.   I am told, for example, that someone climbed this mountain many years ago.
Do I always enquire into the reliability of the teller of this story, and whether the
mountain did exist years ago? A child learns there are reliable and unreliable inform-
ants much later than it learns facts which are told it. It doesn't learn *at all* that that
mountain has existed for a long time: that is, the question whether it is so doesn't
arise at all. It swallows this consequence down, so to speak, together with *what* it
learns.

144.   The child learns to believe a host of things. I.e. it learns to act according to
these beliefs. Bit by bit there forms a system of what is believed, and in that system

some things stand unshakeably fast and some are more or less liable to shift. What stands fast does so, not because it is intrinsically obvious or convincing; it is rather held fast by what lies around it.

145.   One wants to say "*All* my experiences shew that it is so". But how do they do that? For that proposition to which they point itself belongs to a particular interpretation of them.

"That I regard this proposition as certainly true also characterizes my interpretation of experience."

146.   We form *the picture* of the earth as a ball floating free in space and not altering essentially in a hundred years. I said "We form the *picture* etc." and this picture now helps us in the judgment of various situations.

I may indeed calculate the dimensions of a bridge, sometimes calculate that here things are more in favour of a bridge than a ferry, etc. etc., – but somewhere I must begin with an assumption or a decision.

147.   The picture of the earth as a ball is a *good* picture, it proves itself everywhere, it is also a simple picture – in short, we work with it without doubting it.

148.   Why do I not satisfy myself that I have two feet when I want to get up from a chair? There is no why. I simply don't. This is how I act.

149.   My judgments themselves characterize the way I judge, characterize the nature of judgment.

150.   How does someone judge which is his right and which his left hand? How do I know that my judgment will agree with someone else's? How do I know that this colour is blue? If I don't trust *myself* here, why should I trust anyone else's judgment? Is there a why? Must I not begin to trust somewhere? That is to say: somewhere I must begin with not-doubting; and that is not, so to speak, hasty but excusable: it is part of judging.

151.   I should like to say: Moore does not *know* what he asserts he knows, but it stands fast far him, as also for me; regarding it as absolutely solid is part of our *method* of doubt and enquiry.

152.   I do not explicitly learn the propositions that stand fast for me. I can *discover* them subsequently like the axis around which a body rotates. This axis is not fixed in the sense that anything holds it fast, but the movement around it determines its immobility.

153.   No one ever taught me that my hands don't disappear when I am not paying attention to them. Nor can I be said to presuppose the truth of this proposition in my assertions etc., (as if they rested on it) while it only gets sense from the rest of our procedure of asserting.

154.   There are cases such that, if someone gives signs of doubt where we do not doubt, we cannot confidently understand his signs as signs of doubt.

   I.e.: if we are to understand his signs of doubt as such, he may give them only in particular cases and may not give them in others.

155. In certain circumstances a man cannot make a *mistake*. ("Can" is here used logically, and the proposition does not mean that a man cannot say anything false in those circumstances.) If Moore were to pronounce the opposite of those propositions which he declares certain, we should not just not share his opinion: we should regard him as demented.

156.   In order to make a mistake, a man must already judge in conformity with mankind.

157.   Suppose a man could not remember whether he had always had five fingers or two hands? Should we understand him? Could we be sure of understanding him?

158.   Can I be making a mistake, for example, in thinking that the words of which this sentence is composed are English words whose meaning I know?

159.   As children we learn facts; e.g., that every human being has a brain, and we take them on trust. I believe that there is an island, Australia, of such-and-such a shape, and so on and so on; I believe that I had great-grandparents, that the people who gave themselves out as my parents really were my parents, etc. This belief may never have been expressed; even the thought that it was so, never thought.

160.   The child learns by believing the adult. Doubt comes *after* belief.

161.   I learned an enormous amount and accepted it on human authority, and then I found some things confirmed or disconfirmed by my own experience.

162.   In general I take as true what is found in text-books, of geography for example. Why? I say: All these facts have been confirmed a hundred times over. But how do I know that? What is my evidence for it? I have a world-picture. Is it true or false? Above all it is the substratum of all my enquiring and asserting.

[. . .]

191. Well, if everything speaks for an hypothesis and nothing against it − is it then certainly true? One may designate it as such. − But does it certainly agree with reality, with the facts? − With this question you are already going round in a circle.

192. To be sure there is justification; but justification comes to an end.

---

193.   What does this mean: the truth of a proposition is *certain*?

194.   With the ward "certain" we express complete conviction, the total absence of doubt, and thereby we seek to convince other people. That is *subjective* certainty.

But when is something objectively certain? When a mistake is not possible. But what kind of possibility is that? Mustn't mistake be *logically* excluded?

195.   If I believe that I am sitting in my room when I am not, then I shall not be said to have *made a mistake*. But what is the essential difference between this case and a mistake?

196.   Sure evidence is what we *accept* as sure, it is evidence that we go by in *acting* surely, acting without any doubt.

What we call "a mistake" plays a quite special part in our language games, and so too does what we regard as certain evidence.

197.   It would be nonsense to say that we regard something as sure evidence because it is certainly true.

198.   Rather, we must first determine the role of deciding for or against a proposition.

199.   The reason why the use of the expression "true or false" has something misleading about it is that it is like saying "it tallies with the facts or it doesn't", and the very thing that is in question is what "tallying" is here.

200.   Really "The proposition is either true or false" only means that it must be possible to decide for or against it. But this does not say what the ground for such a decision is like.

201.   Suppose someone were to ask: "Is it really right for us to rely on the evidence of our memory (or our senses) as we do?"

202.   Moore's certain propositions almost declare that we have a right to rely upon this evidence.

203.   [Everything that we regard as evidence indicates that the earth already existed long before my birth. The contrary hypothesis has *nothing* to confirm it at all.

If everything speaks *for* an hypothesis and nothing against it, is it objectively *certain*? One can *call* it that. But does it *necessarily* agree with the world of facts? At the very best it shows us what "agreement" means. We find it difficult to imagine it to be false, but also difficult to make use of it.]

What does this agreement consist in, if not in the fact that what is evidence in these language games speaks for our proposition? (*Tractatus Logico-Philosophicus*)

204.   Giving grounds, however, justifying the evidence, comes to an end; – but the end is not certain propositions' striking us immediately as true, i.e. it is not a

kind of *seeing* on our part; it is our *acting*, which lies at the bottom of the language-game.

205.   If the true is what is grounded, then the ground is not *true*, nor yet false.

206.   If someone asked us "but is that *true*?" we might say "yes" to him; and if he demanded grounds we might say "I can't give you any grounds, but if you learn more you too will think the same".

    If this didn't come about, that would mean that he couldn't for example learn history.

From *Culture and Value*

One *cannot* speak the truth; – if one has not yet conquered oneself. One *cannot* speak it – but not, because one is still not clever enough.

    The truth can be spoken only by someone who is already *at home* in it; not by someone who still lives in untruthfulness, and does no more than reach out towards it from within untruthfulness.

[. . .]

The truly apocalyptic view of the world is that things do *not* repeat themselves. It is not e.g. absurd to believe that the scientific & technological age is the beginning of the end for humanity, that the idea of Great Progress is a bedazzlement, along with the idea that the truth will ultimately be known; that there is nothing good or desirable about scientific knowledge and that humanity, in seeking it, is falling into a trap. It is by no means clear that this is not how things are.

5

TRUTH AND MEANING

Donald Davidson

We decided a while back not to assume that parts of sentences have meanings except in the ontologically neutral sense of making a systematic contribution to the meaning of the sentences in which they occur. Since postulating meanings has netted nothing, let us return to that insight. One direction in which it points is a certain holistic view of meaning. If sentences depend for their meaning on their structure, and we understand the meaning of each item in the structure only as an abstraction from the totality of sentences in which it features, then we can give the meaning of any sentence (or word) only by giving the meaning of every sentence (and word) in the language. Frege said that only in the context of a sentence does a word have meaning; in the same vein he might have added that only in the context of the language does a sentence (and therefore a word) have meaning.

This degree of holism was already implicit in the suggestion that an adequate theory of meaning must entail *all* sentences of the form '*s* means *m*'. But now, having found no more help in meanings of sentences than in meanings of words, let us ask whether we can get rid of the troublesome singular terms supposed to replace '*m*' and to refer to meanings. In a way, nothing could be easier: just write '*s* means that *p*', and imagine '*p*' replaced by a sentence. Sentences, as we have seen, cannot name meanings, and sentences with 'that' prefixed are not names at all, unless we decide so. It looks as though we are in trouble on another count, however, for it is reasonable to expect that in wrestling with the logic of the apparently non–extensional 'means that' we will encounter problems as hard as, or perhaps identical with, the problems our theory is out to solve.

The only way I know to deal with this difficulty is simple, and radical. Anxiety that we are enmeshed in the intensional springs from using the words 'means that' as filling between description of sentence and sentence, but it may be that the success of our venture depends not on the filling but on what it fills. The theory will have done its work if it provides, for every sentence *s* in the language under study, a matching

Donald Davidson, *Inquiries Into Truth and Interpretation* (Oxford: Clarendon Press: 1984), pp. 22–36. Reprinted by permission of Oxford University Press.

sentence (to replace '*p*') that, in some way yet to be made clear, 'gives the meaning' of *s*. One obvious candidate for matching sentence is just *s* itself, if the object language is contained in the metalanguage; otherwise a translation of *s* in the metalanguage. As a final bold step, let us try treating the position occupied by '*p*' extensionally: to implement this, sweep away the obscure 'means that', provide the sentence that replaces '*p*' with a proper sentential connective, and supply the description that replaces '*s*' with its own predicate. The plausible result is

(*T*)   *s* is *T* if and only if *p*.

What we require of a theory of meaning for a language *L* is that without appeal to any (further) semantical notions it place enough restrictions on the predicate 'is *T*' to entail all sentences got from schema *T* when '*s*' is replaced by a structural description of a sentence of *L* and '*p*' by that sentence.

Any two predicates satisfying this condition have the same extension,[1] so if the metalanguage is rich enough, nothing stands in the way of putting what I am calling a theory of meaning into the form of an explicit definition of a predicate 'is *T*'. But whether explicitly defined or recursively characterized, it is clear that the sentences to which the predicate 'is *T*' applies will be just the true sentences of *L*, for the condition we have placed on satisfactory theories of meaning is in essence Tarski's Convention *T* that tests the adequacy of a formal semantical definition of truth.[2]

The path to this point has been tortuous, but the conclusion may be stated simply: a theory of meaning for a language *L* shows 'how the meanings of sentences depend upon the meanings of words' if it contains a (recursive) definition of truth-in-*L*. And, so far at least, we have no other idea how to turn the trick. It is worth emphasizing that the concept of truth played no ostensible role in stating our original problem. That problem, upon refinement, led to the view that an adequate theory of meaning must characterize a predicate meeting certain conditions. It was in the nature of a discovery that such a predicate would apply exactly to the true sentences. I hope that what I am saying may be described in part as defending the philosophical importance of Tarski's semantical concept of truth. But my defence is only distantly related, if at all, to the question whether the concept Tarski has shown how to define is the (or a) philosophically interesting conception of truth, or the question whether Tarski has cast any light on the ordinary use of such words as 'true' and 'truth'. It is a misfortune that dust from futile and confused battles over these questions has prevented those with a theoretical interest in language – philosophers, logicians, psychologists, and linguists alike – from seeing in the semantical concept of truth (under whatever name) the sophisticated and powerful foundation of a competent theory of meaning.

There is no need to suppress, of course, the obvious connection between a definition of truth of the kind Tarski has shown how to construct, and the concept of meaning. It is this: the definition works by giving necessary and sufficient conditions for the truth of every sentence, and to give truth conditions is a way of giving the meaning of a sentence. To know the semantic concept of truth for a language is to know what it is for a sentence – any sentence – to be true, and this amounts, in one good sense we can give to the phrase, to understanding the language. This at any rate is my excuse for a feature of the present discussion that is apt to shock old hands;

my freewheeling use of the word 'meaning', for what I call a theory of meaning has after all turned out to make no use of meanings, whether of sentences or of words. Indeed, since a Tarski-type truth definition supplies all we have asked so far of a theory of meaning, it is clear that such a theory falls comfortably within what Quine terms the 'theory of reference' as distinguished from what he terms the 'theory of meaning'. So much to the good for what I call a theory of meaning, and so much, perhaps, against my so calling it.[3]

A theory of meaning (in my mildly perverse sense) is an empirical theory, and its ambition is to account for the workings of a natural language. Like any theory, it may be tested by comparing some of its consequences with the facts. In the present case this is easy, for the theory has been characterized as issuing in an infinite flood of sentences each giving the truth conditions of a sentence; we only need to ask, in sample cases, whether what the theory avers to be the truth conditions for a sentence really are. A typical test case might involve deciding whether the sentence 'Snow is white' *is* true if and only if snow is white. Not all cases will be so simple (for reasons to be sketched), but it is evident that this sort of test does not invite counting noses. A sharp conception of what constitutes a theory in this domain furnishes an exciting context for raising deep questions about when a theory of language is correct and how it is to be tried. But the difficulties are theoretical, not practical. In application, the trouble is to get a theory that comes close to working; anyone can tell whether it is right.[4] One can see why this is so. The theory reveals nothing new about the conditions under which an individual sentence is true; it does not make those conditions any clearer than the sentence itself does. The work of the theory is in relating the known truth conditions of each sentence to those aspects ('words') of the sentence that recur in other sentences, and can be assigned identical roles in other sentences. Empirical power in such a theory depends on success in recovering the structure of a very complicated ability – the ability to speak and understand a language. We can tell easily enough when particular pronouncements of the theory comport with our understanding of the language; this is consistent with a feeble insight into the design of the machinery of our linguistic accomplishments.

The remarks of the last paragraph apply directly only to the special case where it is assumed that the language for which truth is being characterized is part of the language used and understood by the characterizer. Under these circumstances, the framer of a theory will as a matter of course avail himself when he can of the built-in convenience of a metalanguage with a sentence guaranteed equivalent to each sentence in the object language. Still, this fact ought not to con us into thinking a theory any more correct that entails ' "Snow is white" is true if and only if snow is white' than one that entails instead:

(S)   'Snow is white' is true if and only if grass is green, provided, of course, we are as sure of the truth of (S) as we are of that of its more celebrated predecessor. Yet (S) may not encourage the same confidence that a theory that entails it deserves to be called a theory of meaning.

The threatened failure of nerve may be counteracted as follows. The grotesqueness of (S) is in itself nothing against a theory of which it is a consequence, provided the theory gives the correct results for every sentence (on the basis of its structure, there being no other way). It is not easy to see how (S) could be party to such an enterprise, but if it were — if, that is, (S) followed from a characterization of the predicate 'is true' that led to the invariable pairing of truths with truths and falsehoods with falsehoods — then there would not, I think, be anything essential to the idea of meaning that remained to be captured.[5]

What appears to the right of the biconditional in sentences of the form '*s* is true if and only if *p*' when such sentences are consequences of a theory of truth plays its role in determining the meaning of *s* not by pretending synonymy but by adding one more brush-stroke to the picture which, taken as a whole, tells what there is to know of the meaning of *s*; this stroke is added by virtue of the fact that the sentence that replaces '*p*' is true if and only if *s* is.

It may help to reflect that (S) is acceptable, if it is, because we are independently sure of the truth of 'Snow is white' and 'Grass is green'; but in cases where we are unsure of the truth of a sentence, we can have confidence in a characterization of the truth predicate only if it pairs that sentence with one we have good reason to believe equivalent. It would be ill advised for someone who had any doubts about the colour of snow or grass to accept a theory that yielded (S), even if his doubts were of equal degree, unless he thought the colour of the one was tied to the colour of the other.[6] Omniscience can obviously afford more bizzare theories of meaning than ignorance; but then, omniscience has less need of communication.

It must be possible, of course, for the speaker of one language to construct a theory of meaning for the speaker of another, though in this case the empirical test of the correctness of the theory will no longer be trivial. As before, the aim of theory will be an infinite correlation of sentences alike in truth. But this time the theory-builder must not be assumed to have direct insight into likely equivalences between his own tongue and the alien. What he must do is find out, however he can, what sentences the alien holds true in his own tongue (or better, to what degree he holds them true). The linguist then will attempt to construct a characterization of truth-for-the-alien which yields, so far as possible, a mapping of sentences held true (or false) by the alien on to sentences held true (or false) by the linguist. Supposing no perfect fit is found, the residue of sentences held true translated by sentences held false (and vice versa) is the margin for error (foreign or domestic). Charity in interpreting the words and thoughts of others is unavoidable in another direction as well: just as we must maximize agreement, or risk not making sense of what the alien is talking about, so we must maximize the self-consistency we attribute to him, on pain of not understanding *him*. No single principle of optimum charity emerges; the constraints therefore determine no single theory. In a theory of radical translation (as Quine calls it) there is no completely disentangling questions of what the alien means from questions of what he believes. We do not know what someone means unless we know what he believes; we do not know what someone believes unless we know what he means. In radical interpretation we are able to break into this circle, if only incompletely, because we can sometimes tell that a person accedes to a sentence we do not understand.[7]

In the past few pages I have been asking how a theory of meaning that takes the form of a truth definition can be empirically tested, and have blithely ignored the

prior question whether there is any serious chance such a theory can be given for a
natural language. What are the prospects for a formal semantical theory of a natural
language? Very poor, according to Tarski; and I believe most logicians, philosophers
of language, and linguists agree.[8] Let me do what I can to dispel the pessimism. What
I can in a general and programmatic way, of course, for here the proof of the pudding
will certainly be in the proof of the right theorems.

Tarski concludes the first section of his classic essay on the concept of truth in
formalized languages with the following remarks, which he italicizes:

> ... *The very possibility of a consistent use of the expression 'true sentence' which is in harmony
> with the laws of logic and the spirit of everyday language seems to be very questionable, and
> consequently the same doubt attaches to the possibility of constructing a correct definition of this
> expression.* (165)

Late in the same essay, he returns to the subject:

> ... the concept of truth (as well as other semantical concepts) when applied to collo-
> quial language in conjunction with the normal laws of logic leads inevitably to confu-
> sions and contradictions. Whoever wishes, in spite of all difficulties, to pursue the
> semantics of colloquial language with the help of exact methods will be driven first to
> undertake the thankless task of a reform of this language. He will find it necessary to
> define its structure, to overcome the ambiguity of the terms which occur in it, and
> finally to split the language into a series of languages of greater and greater extent, each
> of which stands in the same relation to the next in which a formalized language stands
> to its metalanguage. It may, however be doubted whether the language of everyday life,
> after being 'rationalized' in this way, would still preserve its naturalness and whether it
> would not rather take on the characteristic features of the formalized languages. (267)

Two themes emerge: that the universal character of natural languages leads to contradiction (the semantic paradoxes), and that natural languages are too confused and
amorphous to permit the direct application of formal methods. The first point deserves
a serious answer, and I wish I had one. As it is, I will say only why I think we are
justified in carrying on without having disinfected this particular source of conceptual anxiety. The semantic paradoxes arise when the range of the quantifiers in the
object language is too generous in certain ways. But it is not really clear how unfair
to Urdu or to Wendish it would be to view the range of their quantifiers as insufficient to yield an explicit definition of 'true-in-Urdu' or 'true-in-Wendish'. Or, to put
the matter in another, if not more serious way, there may in the nature of the case
always be something we grasp in understanding the language of another (the concept
of truth) that we cannot communicate to him. In any case, most of the problems of
general philosophical interest arise within a fragment of the relevant natural language
that may be conceived as containing very little set theory. Of course these comments
do not meet the claim that natural languages are universal. But it seems to me that
this claim, now that we know such universality leads to paradox, is suspect.

Tarski's second point is that we would have to reform a natural language out of
all recognition before we could apply formal semantical methods. If this is true, it is
fatal to my project, for the task of a theory of meaning as I conceive it is not to

change, improve, or reform a language, but to describe and understand it. Let us look at the positive side. Tarski has shown the way to giving a theory for interpreted formal languages of various kinds; pick one as much like English as possible. Since this new language has been explained in English and contains much English we not only may, but I think must, view it as part of English for those who understand it. For this fragment of English we have, *ex hypothesi*, a theory of the required sort. Not only that, but in interpreting this adjunct of English in old English we necessarily gave hints connecting old and new. Wherever there are sentences of old English with the same truth conditions as sentences in the adjunct we may extend the theory to cover them. Much of what is called for is to mechanize as far as possible what we now do by art when we put ordinary English into one or another canonical notation. The point is not that canonical notation is better than the rough original idiom, but rather that if we know what idiom the canonical notation is canonical *for*, we have as good a theory for the idiom as for its kept companion.

Philosophers have long been at the hard work of applying theory to ordinary language by the device of matching sentences in the vernacular with sentences for which they have a theory. Frege's massive contribution was to show how 'all', 'some', 'every', 'each', 'none', and associated pronouns, in some of their uses, could be tamed; for the first time, it was possible to dream of a formal semantics for a significant part of a natural language. This dream came true in a sharp way with the work of Tarski. It would be a shame to miss the fact that as a result of these two magnificent achievements, Frege's and Tarski's, we have gained a deep insight into the structure of our mother tongues. Philosophers of a logical bent have tended to start where the theory was and work out towards the complications of natural language. Contemporary linguists, with an aim that cannot easily be seen to be different, start with the ordinary and work toward a general theory. If either party is successful, there must be a meeting. Recent work by Chomsky and others is doing much to bring the complexities of natural languages within the scope of serious theory. To give an example: suppose success in giving the truth conditions for some significant range of sentences in the active voice. Then with a formal procedure for transforming each such sentence into a corresponding sentence in the passive voice, the theory of truth could be extended in an obvious way to this new set of sentences.[9]

One problem touched on in passing by Tarski does not, at least in all its manifestations, have to be solved to get ahead with theory: the existence in natural languages of 'ambiguous terms'. As long as ambiguity does not affect grammatical form, and can be translated, ambiguity for ambiguity, into the metalanguage, a truth definition will not tell us any lies. The chief trouble, for systematic semantics, with the phrase 'believes that' in English lies not in its vagueness, ambiguity, or unsuitability for incorporation in a serious science: let our metalanguage be English, and all *these* problems will be carried without loss or gain into the metalanguage. But the central problem of the logical grammar of 'believes that' will remain to haunt us.

The example is suited to illustrating another, and related, point, for the discussion of belief sentences has been plagued by failure to observe a fundamental distinction between tasks: uncovering the logical grammar or form of sentences (which is in the province of a theory of meaning as I construe it), and the analysis of individual words or expressions (which are treated as primitive by the theory). Thus Carnap, in the first edition of *Meaning and Necessity*, suggested we render 'John believes that the earth is round' as 'John responds affirmatively to "the earth is round" as an English sentence'. He gave this up when Mates pointed out that John might respond affirmatively to one sentence and not to another no matter how close in meaning.[10] But there is a confusion here from the start. The semantic structure of a belief sentence, according to this idea of Carnap's, is given by a three-place predicate with places reserved for expressions referring to a person, a sentence, and a language. It is a different sort of problem entirely to attempt an analysis of this predicate, perhaps along behaviouristic lines. Not least among the merits of Tarski's conception of a theory of truth is that the purity of method it demands of us follows from the formulation of the problem itself, not from the self-imposed restraint of some adventitious philosophical puritanism.

I think it is hard to exaggerate the advantages to philosophy of language of bearing in mind this distinction between questions of logical form or grammar, and the analysis of individual concepts. Another example may help advertise the point.

If we suppose questions of logical grammar settled, sentences like 'Bardot is good' raise no special problems for a truth definition. The deep differences between descriptive and evaluative (emotive, expressive, etc.) terms do not show here. Even if we hold there is some important sense in which moral or evaluative sentences do not have a truth value (for example, because they cannot be verified), we ought not to boggle at ' "Bardot is good" is true if and only if Bardot is good'; in a theory of truth, this consequence should follow with the rest, keeping track, as must be done, of the semantic location of such sentences in the language as a whole – of their relation to generalizations, their role in such compound sentences as 'Bardot is good and Bardot is foolish', and so on. What is special to evaluative words is simply not touched: the mystery is transferred from the word 'good' in the object language to its translation in the metalanguage.

But 'good' as it features in 'Bardot is a good actress' is another matter. The problem is not that the translation of this sentence is not in the metalanguage – let us suppose it is. The problem is to frame a truth definition such that ' "Bardot is a good actress" is true if and only if Bardot is a good actress' – and all other sentences like it – are consequences. Obviously 'good actress' does not mean 'good and an actress'. We might think of taking 'is a good actress' as an unanalysed predicate. This would obliterate all connection between 'is a good actress' and 'is a good mother', and it would give us no excuse to think of 'good', in these uses, as a word or semantic element. But worse, it would bar us from framing a truth definition at all, for there is no end to the predicates we would have to treat as logically simple (and hence accommodate in separate clauses in the definition of satisfaction): 'is a good companion to dogs', 'is a good 28-years old conversationalist', and so forth. The problem is not peculiar to the case: it is the problem of attributive adjectives generally.

It is consistent with the attitude taken here to deem it usually a strategic error to undertake philosophical analysis of words or expressions which is not preceded by or at any rate accompanied by the attempt to get the logical grammar straight. For how can we have any confidence in our analyses of words like 'right', 'ought', 'can', and 'obliged', or the phrases we use to talk of actions, events, and causes, when we do not know what (logical, semantical) parts of speech we have to deal with? I would say much the same about studies of the 'logic' of these and other words, and the sentences containing them. Whether the effort and ingenuity that have gone into the study of deontic logics, modal logics, imperative and erotetic logics have been largely futile or not cannot be known until we have acceptable semantic analyses of the sentences such systems purport to treat. Philosophers and logicians sometimes talk or work as if they were free to choose between, say, the truth-functional conditional and others, or free to introduce non-truth-functional sentential operators like 'Let it be the case that' or 'It ought to be the case that'. But in fact the decision is crucial. When we depart from idioms we can accommodate in a truth definition, we lapse into (or create) language for which we have no coherent semantical account – that is, no account at all of how such talk can be integrated into the language as a whole.

To return to our main theme: we have recognized that a theory of the kind proposed leaves the whole matter of what individual words mean exactly where it was. Even when the metalanguage is different from the object language, the theory exerts no pressure for improvement, clarification, or analysis of individual words, except when, by accident of vocabulary, straightforward translation fails. Just as synonymy, as between expressions, goes generally untreated, so also synonymy of sentences, and analyticity. Even such sentences as 'A vixen is a female fox' bear no special tag unless it is our pleasure to provide it. A truth definition does not distinguish between analytic sentences and others, except for sentences that owe their truth to the presence alone of the constants that give the theory its grip on structure: the theory entails not only that these sentences are true but that they will remain true under all significant rewritings of their non-logical parts. A notion of logical truth thus given limited application, related notions of logical equivalence and entailment will tag along. It is hard to imagine how a theory of meaning could fail to read a logic into its object language to this degree; and to the extent that it does, our intuitions of logical truth, equivalence, and entailment may be called upon in constructing and testing the theory.

I turn now to one more, and very large, fly in the ointment: the fact that the same sentence may at one time or in one mouth be true and at another time or in another mouth be false. Both logicians and those critical of formal methods here seem largely (though by no means universally) agreed that formal semantics and logic are incompetent to deal with the disturbances caused by demonstratives. Logicians have often reacted by downgrading natural language and trying to show how to get along without demonstratives; their critics react by downgrading logic and formal semantics. None of this can make me happy: clearly demonstratives cannot be eliminated from a natural language without loss or radical change, so there is no choice but to accommodate theory to them.

No logical errors result if we simply treat demonstratives as constants;[11] neither do any problems arise for giving a semantic truth definition. '"I am wise" is true if and only if I am wise', with its bland ignoring of the demonstrative element in 'I' comes off the assembly line along with '"Socrates is wise" is true if and only if Socrates is wise' with *its* bland indifference to the demonstrative element in 'is wise' (the tense).

What suffers in this treatment of demonstratives is not the definition of a truth predicate, but the plausibility of the claim that what has been defined is truth. For this claim is acceptable only if the speaker and circumstances of utterance of each sentence mentioned in the definition is matched by the speaker and circumstances of utterance of the truth definition itself. It could also be fairly pointed out that part of understanding demonstratives is knowing the rules by which they adjust their refer-ence to circumstance; assimilating demonstratives to constant terms obliterates this feature. These complaints can be met, I think, though only by a fairly far-reaching revision in the theory of truth. I shall barely suggest how this could be done, but bare suggestion is all that is needed: the idea is technically trivial, and in line with work being done on the logic of the tenses.[12]

We could take truth to be a property, not of sentences, but of utterances, or speech acts, or ordered triples of sentences, times, and persons; but it is simplest just to view truth as a relation between a sentence, a person, and a time. Under such treatment, ordinary logic as now read applies as usual, but only to sets of sentences relativized to the same speaker and time; further logical relations between sentences spoken at different times and by different speakers may he articulated by new axioms. Such is not my concern. The theory of meaning undergoes a systematic but not puzzling change; corresponding to each expression with a demonstrative element there must in the theory be a phrase that relates the truth conditions of sentences in which the expression occurs to changing times and speakers. Thus the theory will entail sen-tences like the following:

'I am tired' is true as (potentially) spoken by p at t if and only if p is tired at t.

'That book was stolen' is true as (potentially) spoken by p at t if and only if the book demonstrated by p at t is stolen prior to t.[13]

Plainly, this course does not show how to eliminate demonstratives; for example, there is no suggestion that 'the book demonstrated by the speaker' can be substituted ubiquitously for 'that book' *salva veritate.* The fact that demonstratives are amenable to formal treatment ought greatly to improve hopes for a serious semantics of natural language, for it is likely that many outstanding puzzles, such as the analysis of quota-tions or sentences about propositional attitudes, can be solved if we recognize a con-cealed demonstrative construction.

Now that we have relativized truth to times and speakers, it is appropriate to glance back at the problem of empirically testing a theory of meaning for an alien tongue. The essence of the method was, it will be remembered, to correlate held-true sen-tences with held-true sentences by way of a truth definition, and within the bounds of intelligible error. Now the picture must be elaborated to allow for the fact that sentences are true, and held true, only relative to a speaker and a time. Sentences with demonstratives obviously yield a very sensitive test of the correctness of a theory of meaning, and constitute the most direct link between language and the recurrent macroscopic objects of human interest and attention.[14]

In this paper I have assumed that the speakers of a language can effectively deter-mine the meaning or meanings of an arbitrary expression (if it has a meaning), and that it is the central task of a theory of meaning to show how this is possible. I have argued that a characterization of a truth predicate describes the required kind of struc-ture, and provides a clear and testable criterion of an adequate semantics for a natural language. No doubt there are other reasonable demands that may be put on a theory of meaning. But a theory that does no more than define truth for a language comes far closer to constituting a complete theory of meaning than superficial analysis might suggest; so, at least, I have urged.

Since I think there is no alternative, I have taken an optimistic and programmatic view of the possibilities for a formal characterization of a truth predicate for a natural language. But it must be allowed that a staggering list of difficulties and conundrums remains. To name a few: we do not know the logical form of counterfactual or sub-junctive sentences; nor of sentences about probabilities and about causal relations; we have no good idea what the logical role of adverbs is, nor the role of attributive adjec-tives; we have no theory for mass terms like 'fire', 'water', and 'snow', nor for sen-tences about belief, perception, and intention, nor for verbs of action that imply purpose. And finally, there are all the sentences that seem not to have truth values at all: the imperatives, optatives, interrogatives, and a host more. A comprehensive theory of meaning for a natural language must cope successfully with each of these problems.

Notes

1   Assuming, of course, that the extension of these predicates is limited to the sentences of L.

2   A. Tarski, 'The Concept of Truth in Formalized Languages', in *Logic, Semantics, Metamath-ematics* (Oxford: Oxford University Press, 1965).

3   But Quine may be quoted in support or my usage: '. . . in point of *meaning* . . . a word may be said to be determined to whatever extent the truth or falsehood of its contexts is determined.' ('Truth by Convention', in *The Ways of Paradox and Other Essays* (New York: Random House, 1966), 82.) Since a truth definition determines the truth value of every sentence in the object language (relative to a sentence in the metalanguage), it deter-mines the meaning of every word and sentence. This would seem to justify the title Theory of Meaning.

4   To give a single example: it is clearly a count in favour of a theory that it entails ' "Snow is white" is true if and only if snow is white'. But to contrive a theory that entails this (and works for all related sentences) is not trivial. I do not know a wholly satisfactory theory that succeeds with this very case (the problem of 'mass terms').

5   Critics have often failed to notice the essential proviso mentioned in this paragraph. The point is that (S) could not belong to any reasonably simple theory that also gave the right truth conditions for 'That is snow' and 'This is white'[. . .]

6   This paragraph is confused. What it should say is that sentences of the theory are empiri-cal generalizations about speakers, and so must not only be true but also lawlike. (S) pre-sumably is not a law, since it does not support appropriate counter-factuals. It's also important that the evidence for accepting the (time and speaker relativized) truth condi-tions for 'That is snow' is based on the causal connection between a speaker's assent to the sentence and the demonstrative presentation of snow. [. . .]

7   This sketch of how a theory of meaning for an alien tongue can be tested obviously owes it inspiration to Quine's account of radical translation in Chapter II of *Word and Object*. In suggesting that an acceptable theory of radical translation take the form of a recursive characterization of truth, I go beyond Quine. Toward the end of this paper, in the dis-cussion of demonstratives, another strong point of agreement will turn up.

8   So far as I am aware, there has been very little discussion of whether a formal truth defi-
    nition can be given for a natural language. But in a more general vein, several people
    have urged that the concepts of formal semantics be applied to natural language. See, for
    example, the contributions of Yehoshua Bar-Hillel and Evert Beth to *The Philosophy of
    Rudolph Carnap*, ed. Paul Schilpp (Pub Group West, 1984), and Bar-Hillel's 'Logical Syntax
    and Semantics'. *Language*, 30/2 (1954), pp. 230–7.

9   The *rapprochement* I prospectively imagine between transformational grammar and a sound
    theory of meaning has been much advanced by a recent change in the conception of
    transformational grammar described by Chomsky [. . .] The structures generated by the
    phrase-structure part of the grammar, it has been realized for some time, are those suited
    to semantic interpretation; but this view is inconsistent with the idea, held by Chomsky
    until recently, that recursive operations are introduced only by the transformation rules,
    Chomsky now believes the phrase-structure rules are recursive. Since languages to which
    formal semantic methods directly and naturally apply are ones for which a (recursive)
    phrase-structure grammar is appropriate, it is clear that Chomsky's present picture of the
    relation between the structures generated by the phrase-structure part of the grammar,
    and the sentences of the language, is very much like the picture many logicians and
    philosophers have had of the relation between the richer formalized languages and ordi-
    nary language. (In these remarks I am indebted to Bruce Vermazen.)

10 B. Mates, 'Synonymity', *University of California Publications in Philosophy*, 25 (1950).

11 See W. V. Quine, *Methods of Logic* (Cambridge, MA: Harvard University Press, 1982), p. 8.

12 This claim has turned out to be naïvely optimistic. For some serious work on the subject,
    see S. Weinstein, 'Truth and Demonstratives', *Nous*, 8 (1982), pp. 179–84.

13 There is more than an intimation of this approach to demonstratives and truth in J. L.
    Austin, 'Truth', *Proceedings of the Aristotelian Society*, suppl. vol., 1950, pp. 111–29.

14 These remarks derive from Quine's idea that 'occasion sentences' (those with a demon-
    strative element) must play a central role in constructing a translation manual.

6

THE FACE OF COGNITION

Hilary Putnam

Dummettian Antirealism

[. . .] Michael Dummett sees the problem of realism as having to do with the "recognition transcendence" of truth. Either truth is simply the state of being verified or it transcends what the speaker can verify, he argues, and if it transcends what the speaker can verify, it is not a property whose presence the speaker can "recognize." And if truth is a property whose presence (in some cases, at least) the speaker cannot recognize, then the speaker's alleged "grasp" of the notion of truth becomes a mystery. In effect, Dummett is telling us, if truth is not verifiable, then, short of postulating magical powers of mind, we will not be able to explain how we understand the notion. The rejection of magical powers of mind requires the acceptance of a very radical form of verificationism, according to Dummett's line of thinking – one so radical that it requires us to revise a number of the laws of classical logic, beginning with the Principle of Bivalence.

There is a rajoinder to Dummett's argument that Dummett himself anticipated from the beginning, one that he discusses at length in *The Logical Basis of Metaphysics*. That rejoinder, which in essence goes back to Tarski's celebrated essay on the concept of truth runs as follows: "What is your problem? Take any sentence you like – take a sentence whose truth value we may not be able to find out, if you please. For example, take the sentence:

(1) Lizzie Borden killed her parents with an axe.

Even if the truth of this sentence is 'recognition transcendent', surely you understand what it *means* to say that (1) is true. For you understand (1) itself, and the chief logical principle governing the use of the word 'true' is:

Hilary Putnam, excerpts from "The Face of Cognition," in *The Threefold Cord: Mind, Body, and World* (New York: Columbia University Press, 1999), pp. 49–59, 64–70. Reprinted by permission of Columbia University Press.

[Tarski's Convention T:] *If* S *is the* name of *any sentence, and we write that sentence in the blank in:*

(2)   S *is true if and only if* . . . .
then the resulting sentence will be true.

[Less formally: a sentence that says of another sentence S that S is true is equivalent to S itself. Tarski's famous example was:

(3)   'Snow is white' is true if and only if snow is white.]

In short, you understand 'Lizzie Borden killed her parents with an axe' and you know that

'Lizzie Borden killed her patents with an axe' is true if and only if Lizzie Borden killed her parents with an axe.

So you do understand what it means to say that (1) is true; *it means that Lizzie Borden killed her parents with an axe.*

I want also to note the fact that some philosophers who offer this account of how we understand sentences of the form "S is true" – but not Tarski himself – add the claim that truth is not a "substantive property." These philosophers – I shall refer to them as "deflationists,' in order to distinguish their position from Tarski's own (unmodified) position – claim that the predicate "is true" is just "a logical device." I shall say something about this "deflationist" position shortly.

However, Dummett's reply to the (unmodified) "Tarskian" argument takes us to the heart of his philosophical concerns. "Granted that I understand sentence (1), and other sentences with an unknown truth value, e.g., undecided conjectures in mathematics," he answers (in effect – I am formulating his reply in my own words), "the philosophical problem is *to give an account of what that understanding consists in.*" In short, if you appeal to an *unexplicated* notion of "understanding a sentence," then you are simply ducking all the philosophical problems.

According to Dummett, my understanding of the sentence (1) (i.e., of any sentence) consists in my ability to *recognize if (1) is verified.* In other words, *if (1) should be verified* (by data that I myself perceive), then I *would* be able to tell that it was, and the ability or system of abilities that enables me to do this *constitutes* my understanding of (1). Similarly, I possess the ability to recognize proofs in mathematics, and this allows me to say that if I were given a proof of the conjecture that there are infinitely many twin primes (primes such that one is obtained by adding or subtracting two to a prime), I could recognize that it *was* a proof. And that is how I can say that I *understand* the Twin Prime Conjecture.

Dummett, of course, would concede the "Tarskian" points that he also understands the statement that (1) is true and the statement that the Twin Prime Conjecture is true, and that he knows that the statement that (1) is true is equivalent to (1) itself, etc. "But notice," he will point out (my words again!), "If my account is right, a speaker's understanding of the statement that (1) is true involves the speaker's understanding what it is for (1) to be verified – and this property, being verified, is a property that (1) and its negation may *both* lack; it does not require the speaker to know anything about a property – call it 'classical truth' – that must be possessed either by (1) or else by (1)'s negation, independently of whether anyone can tell which one possesses it, as it postulated by classical logic." In short, if Dummett's verificationist account of *what constitutes understanding* is right, then either truth is a useless metaphysical abstraction or else there is nothing to the claim that *truth* is *a bivalent property*, the claim that characterizes "two-valued" logic. (It is thus that Dummett is led to the radical claim that a sound philosophy of language requires the revision of classical logic itself.)

I want now to consider the response of the "deflationist philosophers" I mentioned a few moments ago. These philosophers agree with Dummett in thinking of our understanding of our sentences as *consisting in* our knowledge of the conditions under which they are verified, although they reject Dummett's notion of "conclusive verification," replacing that notion with a notion of degrees of verification. They also reject Dummett's claim that we must not think of truth as a bivalent property, although they do agree that it is not a "substantive property" about which some metaphysical story needs to be told; rather they claim that rejecting that metaphysical picture of what truth is does not require us to give up the Law of the Excluded Middle, "p v $-p$." As just mentioned, the deflationists even allow us to assert Bivalence:

(3) "Either p is true or the negation of p is true,"

where p is any declarative sentence, but they interpret the assertion of (3) as a mere linguistic practice, free of commitment to the existence of a property "truth" that is determinately possessed either by the sentence or else by the negation of the sentence. That is, if we put sentence (1) for p, what (3) means, they say, is

(4) Either Lizzie Borden killed her parents with an axe or Lizzie Borden did not kill her parents with an axe.

– and (4), it will be noted, does not contain the word *true*.

But why should we accept (4)? Deflationists give different answers. Carnap and Ayer said that the acceptance of sentences of the form "p or not-p" is a linguistic convention; Quine, rejecting that answer, says simply that such sentences are "obvious" (sometimes he says "central" to our reasoning). But does not the "obviousness" of (4) depend on our belief that there is a fact of the matter as to whether Lizzie Borden did or did not administer the famous "forty whacks"? And if uttering a sentence (whether or not I also employ the "logical device" of saying that the sentence "is true") is just following a communitywide practice of assigning it a degree of assertability "as a function of observable circumstances," how do we so much as make sense of the idea of a fact of the matter as to the rightness of statements that are *neither* confirmed nor disconfirmed by those observable circumstances?

If we structure the debate in the way in which both Dummett and the deflationists do, then we are left with a forced choice between (a) either Dummettian antirealism or deflationism about truth, or (b) a retreat to metaphysical realism. Both

Dummett's "global antirealist" and the deflationist advertise their accounts as rescuing us from metaphysical realism. But surely one of the sources of the continuing appeal of metaphysical realism in contemporary philosophy is a dissatisfaction with the only apparent alternatives. The metaphysical realist will want to reply to the deflationist (and the antirealist) as follows:

"Realism requires us to say that either (1) or the negation of (1) is true. If a philosopher advises us to retain 'Either (1) is true or the negation of (1) is true' as something we are permitted to say while reinterpreting *what we are doing when we say it* in such a way as to deprive us of what we ordinarily mean (when we say of a sentence that it is true), then he is disguising the radically revisionary character of his theory through a terminological sleight of hand. That is what the deflationist, in effect, does. He allows us to hold on to the thought that 'Either (1) is true or the negation of (1) is true' only in the attenuated sense that he advises us to follow a policy of assigning all grammatical sentences of the syntactic *shape* 'p v $-p$' the degree of assertability (the "level of confidence," in Horwich's phrase) one. This attenuated sense in which the deflationist continues to permit us to speak of a sentence's being true fails to capture what is significant about true sentences (as opposed to false ones): true sentences possess a substantive property that false sentences lack – namely, the property of corresponding to a reality. Deflationism is thus unable, for example, to acknowledge the reality of past events (as things that truly happened), even though it retains the old form of words ('It happened or it didn't happen') as a *mere* form of words. Deflationism, in effect, follows the lead of logical positivism in refusing to think of our sentences as subject to serious terms of normative appraisal, of appraisal in terms of the possession or absence of a substantive property of rightness that is different from verifiability. On the deflationist account, when one asserts the whole sentence '(1) is true or the negation of (1) is true' one is not saying that one of the *disjuncts* possess the relevant sort of substantive rightness. The deflationist is unable to do justice to the sense in which one of the disjuncts of this sentence possesses the same sort of substantive rightness as does (if you are presently reading this essay) the sentence 'You are right now reading these words in front of you.' The deflationist (by regarding degree of assertability, but not truth, as a property that is more than just a logical device) is therefore unable to capture the sense in which certain statements about the past (namely, the true ones) are fully as *right* as statements about the present. Dummett perceives the situation more clearly than the deflationists in that he at least recognizes – indeed emphasizes – that his account of understanding commits him to antirealism about the past (and not only about the past). Neither Dummett nor the deflationist, however, can accommodate the ordinary sense in which certain statements about the past are substantively true."

What is the difference between the realism of the metaphysical realist (whose response to deflationism I just sketched) and the commonsense realism that I wish to attribute to Wittgenstein? In a different context (in response to a Platonist about rule following) Wittgenstein writes,

> Really the only thing wrong with what you say is the expression "in a queer way." The rest is all right; and the sentence only seems queer when one imagines a different language-game for it from the one in which we actually use it.

Wittgenstein would, I believe, reply to the metaphysical realist's response to the deflationist (which I have sketched above) by saying, "Really the only thing wrong with what you say is the expression 'substantive property' (and related uses of 'substantive', as in 'substantive sort of rightness' and 'substantively true')." Thus, from Wittgenstein's point of view, most of the words that the metaphysical realist finds himself moved to say (in response to the deflationist) are perfectly all right. But the metaphysical realist makes these words seem fated to say something *queer* by calling upon them to bear an explanatory burden – to bear metaphysical weight – in accounting for the relation between Thought and Reality. The metaphysical realist feels that the deflationist has drained our ordinary ways of speaking and acting of their substance, and so he seeks to reinfuse them somehow with substance. It is to this end that he ineffectually invokes the notion of a "substantive property." The metaphysical realist (in trying to do justice, for example, to our ordinary realism about the past) feels compelled to appeal to something that *underlies* our language games: a mysterious property that stands behind – both in the sense of remaining invisibly in the background and in the sense of guaranteeing – our ordinary ways of speaking and acting. The metaphysical realist and the deflationist share a common picture in that it seems to both a queer thing that certain statements (for example, about the past) can be said to be true.

The Error (and the Insight) in Verificationism

Part of what is right in the metaphysical realist's response to the deflationist is the realization that that view does not (as advertised) successfully undercut Dummettian antirealism. On the contrary, deflationism about truth – as long as it involves (as it has since Ramsey introduced the position in the 1920s) a verificationist account of understanding – adopts the most disastrous feature of the antirealist view, the very feature that brings about the loss of the world (and the past). It differs from antirealism in this regard only in that it attempts to disguise that feature by means of a superficial terminological conservatism. The metaphysical realist is thus to this extent right: to undercut Dummett's antirealism requires challenging his account of understanding, not adopting it. But what makes the metaphysical realist's response *metaphysical* is its acceptance of the idea (which it shares with the Dummettian antirealist) that our ordinary realism – for example, about the past – presupposes a view of truth as a "substantive property." The metaphysical realist, in wanting a property that he can ascribe to all and only true sentences, wants a property that corresponds to the assertoric force of a sentence. But this is a very funny property. To avoid identifying this property of "truth" with that of assertability, the metaphysical realist needs to argue that there is something we are saying when we say of a particular claim that it is true over and above what we are saying when we simply assert the claim. He wants Truth to be something that *goes beyond* the content of the claim and to be that in virtue of which the claim is true. This forces the metaphysical realist to postulate that there is some single thing we are saying (over and above what we are claiming) whenever we make a truth claim, no matter what sort of statement we are discussing, no matter what the circumstances under which the statement is said to be true, and no matter what the pragmatic point of calling it true is said to be.

The right alternative to thinking of truth as a "substantive property" à la the meta-physical realist is *not* to think of our statements as mere marks and noises that our community has taught us to associate with conditions for being conclusively verified (as in the account of Dummett's "global antirealist") or to associate with "betting behavior" in a way that is "a function of observable circumstances" (as in Horwich's account). The right alternative is to recognize that empirical statements already make claims about the world − many different sorts of claims about the world − whether or not they contain the words *is true*. What is wrong in deflationism is that it cannot properly accommodate the truism that certain claims about the world are (not merely assertable or verifiable but) *true*. What is right in deflationism is that if I assert that "it is true that *p*," then I assert the same thing as if I simply assert *p*. Our confidence, when we make statements about the past, that we are saying something whose right-ness or wrongness depends on *how things were back then* (when we claim, for example, that "It is true that Lizzie Borden killed her parents with an axe") is not something that requires the metaphysical idea that there is a "substantive property" whose exis-tence underwrites the very possibility of using the word *true*.

In order to see more clearly the difference between the commonsense realism I am defending and the kind of metaphysical realism we are right to recoil from, let us shift our attention for a moment from discourse about observable things, such as deer grazing on the meadow, to discourse about unobservables, e.g., microbes. [Earlier] I remarked that the use of instruments should be viewed as a way of extending our natural powers of observation. But the use of language is also a way of extending our natural powers of observation. If I could not understand talk about "things too small to see with the naked eye," the microscope would be at best a toy (like the kaleido-scope); what I saw when I looked through the eyepiece would mean nothing to me. However, it would be a mistake to conclude that the dependence goes both ways. The phrase "too small to see with the naked eye" does not depend for its intelligi-bility on the invention of an instrument that allows us to see things smaller than the things the naked eye can see (nor did we regard it as changing its sense when the microscope was invented). What is mistaken about verificationism is the claim that the meaning of an expression like "things too small to see with the naked eye" depends on there being methods of verifying the existence of such things, and the related claim that the meaning of such an expression changes as these methods of verification change (e.g., with the invention of the microscope). However there is a philosophical danger of rejecting what is right in verificationism in the course of rejecting what is wrong with it. What is right in verificationism is that a great deal of scientific talk does depend for its full intelligibility on the provision of the kind of thick explanatory detail that is impossible if one has no familiarity with the use of scientific instruments. For example, in Democritus's writings, as we know of them, the notion of an atom was a metaphysical one, but one to which *we* can give a sense, even if Democritus himself could not. Thus scientific instruments and scientific ways of talking are both ways of extending our perceptual and conceptual powers, and those ways are highly interdependent; indeed, they can fuse into a single complex practice.

The ways in which language extends the mental abilities that we share with other animals are almost endless; our ability to construct sophisticated scientific theories is only one example. A very different sort of example is provided by the role of logical constants, for example, the words *all* and *no*. An animal or a child that has not yet learned to use these words may have expectations that we who have acquired them can and do describe with the aid of these words. For example, imagine that someone with modest skills at sleight of hand causes a handkerchief to "vanish" in front of a child's very eyes, and the child displays astonishment. We might say that the child believes (believed) that "handkerchiefs do not vanish into thin air just like that" – i.e., that *no* handkerchiefs vanish into thin air just like that. Of course, that generalization does not have any consequences that the child can understand not possessed by the generalization: "*Observed* handkerchiefs do not vanish into thin air just like that." Yet we would not dream of using the latter words to described the child's attitude to the event. We would not know how to make sense of the suggestion that a child is only concerned to make a judgment about the behavior of *observed* hankerchiefs. This is the case *not* because we take the child to be concerned with making judgments about both observed *and* unobserved hankerchiefs; the distinction between the two generalizations is not one that belongs to the child's intellectual repertoire. It is a part of *our* repertoire (and which description we use may make a difference to *us* under certain circumstances: "Fine shades of behavior. Why are they *important?* They have important consequences." *Philosophical Investigations*, p. 204). We describe even primitive preverbal attitudes as attitudes toward objects of which people may or may not be aware, and not just toward the part of the world that the child (or we) can "verify." Our sophisticated adult talk about certain features of the world (such as "those that are observable to us") rests upon – is parasitic upon – just such a primitive preverbal attitude toward the world.

A quite different aspect of the extension of our conceptual abilities brought about by the possession of words for generality is the possibility of formulating conjectures that transcend even "ideal verifiability," such as "There are no intelligent extraterrestrials." The fact that this conjecture may not be verifiable even "in principle" does not mean that it does not correspond to a reality; but one can only say what reality corresponds to it, if it is true, by using the words themselves. And this is not deflationism; on the contrary, deflationism, by identifying understanding with possession of verification abilities, makes it mysterious that we should find these words intelligible. Once again, the difficulty here lies in keeping what is right in verificationism (or in this case in deflationism) while throwing out what is wrong.

Nothing in what I just said requires us to think of our ability to conceive of such things as microbes (or of our ability to think that there are no intelligent extraterrestrials) as a freestanding ability, independent of a great many other abilities and independent of scientific and other institutions and practices. But, conversely, nothing in Wittgenstein's insistence on the ways in which conception and practical interaction with the world depend upon one another, and on the plurality of kinds of conception and practice involved, requires us to think of conception as the mere manipulation of syntactic objects in response to perceptual "inputs" (as "cognitive scientists" tend to do. I do not wish to accuse Michael Dummett of consciously holding that picture of conception, but his emphasis on *formal proof* as a model of verification, and his insistence that the goal of philosophy of language should be to *specify recursively* how the sentences of the language can be verified, suggest to me that his picture of language use is closer to the "cognitive scientific" version of the Cartesian cum materialist picture than he himself may realize. Dummett has been primarily concerned to combat "holistic" versions of that picture – versions in which the unit of significance is the whole network of sentences rather than the single sentence – in favor of a "molecular" version – a version in which each sentence has its own isolated method of verification; but this is a debate about the *details* of the picture. Dummett sees no alternative to the picture as a whole except to postulate mysterious mental acts; and that is because he has from the beginning felt obliged to regard his own thoughts as if they were syntactic objects that require rules of manipulation. But there is an alternative, as more than one philosopher has recently pointed out – namely, to distinguish carefully between the activity of "representation" (as something in which we engage) and the idea of a "representation" as an *interface* between ourselves and what we think about, and to understand that giving up the idea of representations as interfaces requiring a "semantics" is not the same thing as giving up on the whole idea of representation.

[. . .]

Wittgenstein on Truth

How, then, do we understand "recognition transcendent" uses of the word *true*, as, for example, when we say that the sentence "Lizzie Borden killed her parents with an axe" may well be true even though we may never be able to establish for certain that it is? Tarski (who was not a deflationist in my sense, because he did not subscribe to the verificationist account of understanding in any of its versions) expressed a genuine insight in pointing out (as Frege had before him) that there is an intimate connection between understanding a sentence and understanding the claim that that sentence is true. If we accept it that understanding the sentence "Lizzie Borden killed her parents with an axe" is not simply a matter of being able to recognize a verification in our own experience – accept it, that is, that we are able to conceive of how things that we cannot verify *were* – then it will not appear as "magical" or "mysterious" that we can understand the claim that that sentence is *true*. What makes it true, if it is, is simply that Lizzie Borden killed her parents with an axe. The recognition transcendence of truth comes, in this case, to no more than the "recognition transcendence" of some killings. And did we ever think that all killers can be recognized as such? Or that the belief that there are certain determinate individuals who are or were killers and who cannot be detected as such by us is a belief in magical powers of the mind?

There is, however, something that Tarski ignores, and that is the fact that there are perfectly well-formed declarative sentences that are *neither* true nor false; indeed, in Tarski's theory, it was supposed to be a theorem of logic (given what Tarski calls an "adequate definition" of the truth predicate) that each sentence is either true or false (has a true negation). But there are many reasons why a sentence may fail to have a truth value: for example, the vagueness of some of its terms ("The number of trees in Canada is even") or the failure of the world to behave the way it should if the terms it employs are to work (e.g., many sentences about the simultaneity of events were *discovered* to lack a truth value when relativity theory appeared on the scene;

this is quite different from ordinary vagueness, of the kind that it requires only "linguistic intuition" to perceive). The use of true and false in "Such and such a sentence is *neither true nor false*" is inadmissible in Tarskian semantics. Those who regard "true" as a mere "device for disquotation" (e.g., asserting sentences without actually using them) also ignore or deny this clearly predicative use of *true* and *false*.

One thinker who did *not* ignore or deny this was Wittgenstein. In an important (but frequently misunderstood) section of *Philosophical Investigations* (§136), he writes:

> At bottom, giving "This is how things are" as the general form of propositions is the same as giving the definition: a proposition is whatever can be true or false. For instead of "This is how things are" I could have said "This is true". (Or again "This is false".) But we have
>
> 'p' is true = p
> 'p' is false = not-p
>
> And to say that a proposition is whatever can be true or false amounts to saying: we call something a proposition when *in our language* we apply the calculus of truth functions to it.
>
> Now it looks as if the definition – a proposition is whatever can be true or false – determined what a proposition was, by saying: what fits the concept 'true,' or whatever the concept 'true' fits, is a proposition. So it is as if we had a concept of true and false which we could use to determine what is and what is not a proposition. What *engages* with the concept of truth (as with a cogwheel) is a proposition.
>
> But this is a bad picture. It is as if one were to say "The king in chess is *the* piece that one can check." But this can mean no more than that in our game of chess we only check the king. Just as the proposition that only a *proposition* can be true or false can say no more than that we only predicate "true" and "false" of what we call a proposition. And what a proposition is in one sense determined by the rules of sentence formation (in English, for example), and in another sense by the use of the sign in the language-game. And the use of the words "true" and "false" may be among the constituent parts of the game; and if so it *belongs* to our concept 'proposition' but does not '*fit*' it. As we might also say, check *belongs* to our concept of the king in chess (as so to speak a constituent part of it). To say that check did not *fit* our concept of the pawns, would mean that a game in which pawns were checked, in which, say, the players who lost their pawns lost, would be uninteresting or stupid or too complicated or something of the kind.

Kripke, who quotes only "But we have

'p is true = p'"

– sees *PI* §136 as a clear expression of deflationism. But I do not believe this can be what Wittgenstein intended for the following reasons:

(1)   We know that Wittgenstein does not oppose the idea that empirical propositions "correspond to realities"; indeed, he elsewhere discusses the sense of this correspondence and distinguishes it from the very different sense in which mathematical

propositions correspond to reality; rather the thrust of the whole passage is clearly directed against the metaphysical realist's understanding of such platitudinous thoughts as the though that "This chair is blue" can correspond to the fact that a particular chair is blue. The essential point Wittgenstein makes in *PI* §136 is that we do not recognize that something is a proposition by seeing that it "fits" the concept "truth," where truth is conceived of as a freestanding property. But it would be just as much of a mistake to think that we can explain what truth is by saying that for any *proposition* p, p is true = p, as it is to think that we can explain what a proposition is by saying that a proposition is what is true or false. In both cases we are simply making grammatical observations; we must not confuse what are virtually tautologies for metaphysical discoveries. The notion of truth and the notion of a proposition mesh together like a pair of gears in a machine; neither is a foundation on which the other rests. Our understanding of what truth comes to, in any particular case (and it can come to very different things), is given by our understanding of the proposition, and that is dependent on our mastery of "the language-game," by which Wittgenstein means here "the whole, consisting of language and the actions into which it is woven." There is a certain "holism" here; knowing what truth is in a particular case depends on knowing the *use* of signs in the language game just as knowing what checking is depends on knowing the use of the various pieces in chess.

(2)   When we *ourselves* are willing to apply truth functions to a sentence – note how Wittgenstein emphasizes *in our language* – we regard the sentence as true or false, as a genuine *Satz*.

(3)   A grammatical string of sounds or marks that is *neither* true nor false is simply not a sentence (*Satz*) in Wittgenstein's sense. This is what Wittgenstein means by speaking of "*the definition* – a proposition is whatever can be true or false" (my emphasis). There is no suggestion in this that adding the words "is true" is a "logical device" that we can apply to "declarative sentences" ad libitum.

The possibility that I see in Wittgenstein's writings, of doing full justice to the principle that to call a proposition true is equivalent to asserting the proposition (doing full justice to what I called "Tarski's insight") without committing the errors of the deflationists, is a condition of preserving our commonsense realism while appreciating the enormous *difference* between that commonsense realism and the elaborate metaphysical fantasy that is traditional realism – the fantasy of imagining that the form of all knowledge claims is fixed once and for all in advance. That fantasy goes with the equally fantastic idea that there must be just one *way* in which a knowledge claim can be responsible to reality – by "corresponding" to it, where "correspondence" is thought to be a mysterious relation that somehow underwrites the very possibility of there being knowledge claims. Indeed, a rejection of the idea that we can speak once and for all of "all propositions" as if these constituted a determinate and surveyable totality, and of one single "truth predicate," whose meaning is fixed once and for all, is also one that the later Wittgenstein shared with Tarski.

Instead of looking for a freestanding property of "truth," in the hope that when we find what that property is we will know what the *nature* of propositions is and what the *nature* of their correspondence to reality is, Wittgenstein wants us to *look* at ethical language (and not the kind of ethical language that only occurs in philosophy), to look at religious language, to look at mathematical language, which is itself, he says, a "motley," to look at imprecise language that manages to be perfectly "clear" in context ("Stand roughly here"), to look at talk that is sometimes nonsensical and to look at the very same sentences when they function perfectly well (talk of "what is going on in so-and-so's head" is an example of this), to look and *see* the differences in the way these sorts of discourse function, all the very different ways in which they relate to reality.

If Wittgenstein was right, how should his reflections affect our view of the concept of truth? On the one hand, to regard an assertion or a belief or a thought as true or false *is* to regard it as being right or wrong; on the other hand, just what sort of rightness or wrongness is in question varies enormously with the *sort* of discourse. *Statement, true, refers*, indeed, *belief, assertion, thought, language* – all the terms we use when we think about logic (or "grammar") in the wide sense in which Wittgenstein understands that notion – have a plurality of uses, and new uses are constantly added as new forms of discourse come into existence. On the other hand, that does not mean that any practices at all of employing "marks and noises" can be recognized by us as adding up to a form of discourse – for not every way of producing marks and noises is "one in which there is the face of meaning at all." Part of what I have been trying to show in these lectures is that what we recognize as the face of meaning is, in a number of fundamentally important cases, also the face of our natural cognitive relations to the world – the face of perceiving, of imagining, of expecting, of remembering, and so on – even though it is also the case that as language extends those natural cognitive relations to the world, it also transforms them. Our journey has brought us back to the familiar: truth is sometimes recognition transcendent because what goes on in the world is sometimes beyond our power to recognize, even when it is not beyond our power to conceive.

[. . .] I have had occasion to discuss not only perception and understanding but a number of topics that are usually thought to be far removed from the philosophy of mind: such topics as truth (and deflationism about truth), necessity, and the realism/antirealism debate. But it should be clear by now that a nice allocation of philosophical problems to different philosophical "fields" makes no real sense. To suppose that philosophy divides into separate compartments labeled "philosophy of mind," "philosophy of language," "epistemology," "value theory," and "metaphysics," is a sure way to lose all sense of how the problems are connected, and that means to lose all understanding of the sources of our puzzlement. Indeed, we have seen how the arguments in the realism/antirealism debate over the very possibility of representing a reality "external" to our minds (or to our brains) constantly appeal to assumptions about perception and to assumptions about understanding – in particular, the assumption that we face a forced choice between explaining the very possibility of understanding by appeal to one or another metaphysical mystery, on the one hand, and accepting a verificationist account of understanding, on the other – and how that assumption in turn supports deflationist and antirealist accounts of truth. [Earlier] I spoke of the need to get a deeper understanding of the causes of our tendency to "recoil" from one horrendous position to another in philosophy. [Here] I have focused on what seem to me to be the two principle causes of this tendency.

The first of those causes is a certain kind of reductionism, the kind of reductionism that makes it impossible to see that when concepts are interlinked, as *perception, understanding, representation, verification, truth* are interlinked, the philosophical task must be to explore the circle rather than to reduce all the points on the circle to just one point. The second of these causes is the prevalence of the sort of assumption just mentioned – the all too seductive assumption that we know what the philosophical options are, and that they amount in each case to a forced choice between a funny metaphysical something standing behind our talk (whether it be talk of "truth" or "reference" or "necessity" or "understanding") and "tough-minded" reductionism (verificationism, or deflationism, or antirealism, or whatever). No matter which of these causes is responsible for any given case of the tendency – and usually they operate in tandem – the surest symptom of their presence is an inability to see that giving up on the funny metaphysical somethings does not require us to give up on concepts that, whatever our philosophical convictions, we employ and must employ when we live our lives. Until now I have not mentioned the word *pragmatism* [. . .]. But if there was one great insight in pragmatism, it was the insistence that what has weight in our lives should also have weight in philosophy.

SUGGESTED READING

Austin, J. L., "Truth," *Proceedings of the Aristotelian Society*, 24 (1950), pp. 111–29.

Austin, J. L., "Unfair to Facts," in *Philosophical Papers* (Oxford: Clarendon Press, 1961), pp. 102–22.

Davidson, Donald, *Inquiries into Truth and Interpretation* (New York: Oxford University Press, 1984).

Davidson, Donald, "The Folly of Trying to Define Truth," *Journal of Philosophy*, 93/6 (1996), pp. 263–78.

Dummett, Michael, *Truth and Other Enigmas* (London: Duckworth, 1978).

Hegel, G. W. F., *Phenomenology of Spirit*, trans. A. V. Miller (Oxford: Oxford University Press, 1977), esp. pp. 3–4, 22–3, and "The Truth of Self-Certainty," pp. 104–38.

Lynch, Michael, *Truth in Context: An Essay on Pluralism and Objectivity* (Cambridge, MA: MIT Press, 1998).

Putnam, Hilary, *Meaning and the Moral Sciences* (London: Routledge & Kegan Paul, 1978); see esp. Lecture II, pp. 18–33.

Putnam, Hilary, *Reason, Truth, and History* (Cambridge: Cambridge University Press, 1981).

Quine, W. V., "Two Dogmas of Empiricism," *Philosophical Review*, 60 (1951), pp. 20–43.

Quine, W. V., *The Pursuit of Truth* (Cambridge, MA: Harvard University Press, 1990).

Ramsey, F. P., "Facts and Propositions," *Proceedings of the Aristotelian Society*, 7 (1927), pp. 153–70.

Russell, Bertrand, "Truth and Falsehood," in *The Problems of Philosophy* (New York: Oxford University Press, 1959), pp. 119–30.

Sartre, Jean-Paul, *Truth and Existence*, trans. Adrian Van Den Hoven (Chicago: University of Chicago Press, 1995).

Sellars, Wilfrid, "Truth and 'Correspondence'," *Journal of Philosophy*, 59 (1962), pp. 29–55.

Strawson, P. F., "Truth," *Proceedings of the Aristotelian Society*, 24 (1950), pp. 129–56.

Tarski, Alfred, "The Semantic Conception of Truth and the Foundations of Semantics," *Philosophy and Phenomenological Research*, 4 (1944), pp. 341–75.

PART III

TRUTH, CONSENSUS, AND TRANSCENDENCE

INTRODUCTION

The central topic that unifies the debates on truth of this section is how best to understand the *social* nature of truth and the relation between truth and *consensus*. The papers collected in this section reflect different positions on whether a social account of truth developed from the standpoint of our claim-making and justificatory practices leaves room for any kind of *transcendence*, i.e. context- and practice-independence. On this issue there is a split among philosophers who can be called, in a broad sense, *pragmatists*. On the one hand, some pragmatists (such as Habermas, Putnam, Brandom, and McDowell) defend a *minimal or commonsensical realism*, arguing that an immanent perspective can and must accommodate the context-transcendent aspects of truth. On the other hand, there are pragmatist philosophers (most notably Rorty) who contend that a thoroughgoing immanent perspective must unmask transcendence as an illusion and lead to *deflationism* and/or *antirealism* with respect to truth (cf. Horwich and Wright, among others). The first three papers of this section constitute a dialogue between Rorty and two of his critics, Habermas and McDowell. This debate between different pragmatist perspectives is expanded and supplemented with a selection from Feyerabend which represents a social perspective on truth in the philosophy of science. This last selection echoes deflationary points about truth elaborated by other philosophers of science such as Kuhn and Fine, but it can also be read as a response to some of the critical arguments developed by Habermas and McDowell.

The relevant background to the debate between Rorty and his critics is provided by a *social-practice approach* to truth that cuts across philosophical traditions. The basic strategy of this approach consists in elucidating truth by appealing to what we actually *do*: that is, to the communicative practices in which truth claims are raised, critically examined, and settled. This approach has been developed in different traditions by philosophers as different as Dewey, Heidegger, Wittgenstein, and Sellars. It constitutes a reaction to *representationalism*, which views truth as correspondence and rests on strong metaphysical commitments concerning the representational relations between language and the world. This view is ascribed to many figures in the history of philosophy (starting with Plato) and to many early analytic philosophers such as Frege, Russell, Tarski, and Carnap (cf. *Suggested Readings*; and see also Part II). Rorty argues that within the social-practice camp there is the danger of falling into the representationalist paradigm when we are tempted to think of truth as going beyond the limits of our practices and the consensus of their participants. We are so tempted when we are led to believe that correctness has an external or transcendent dimension as well as an internal or immanent one. Viewed immanently, the correctness of our claims is determined by their internal relations within the conceptual frameworks or schemas of our practices. But our practices change, and so do their conceptual schemas, which can be more or less adequate, correct or incorrect. This may suggest that we need an extra dimension of validity that relates our practices to something beyond themselves. This is what Rorty characterizes as "an unfortunate slide back into representationalism and metaphysics." According to Rorty, both Heidegger and Sellars are "backsliding" social-practice theorists because the external or transcendent dimension of correctness is retained in the former's notion of "disclosedness" and in the latter's notion of "picturing."

So Rorty proposes a "non-backsliding" social-practice account of truth, a thorough-going internalism and deflationism that eradicates the illusion of transcendence once and for all. Following Davidson, he argues that our communicative practices do not contain fixed criteria of assertibility or conceptual schemes. On Rorty's and Davidson's view, communication consists in a seamless process of weaving and re-weaving webs of belief. But how do ascriptions of truth figure in this process? According to Davidson and Rorty, they should not be understood as ascriptions of a property that ties statements to a conceptual scheme or a set of assertibility criteria or seman-tic rules. Instead, they insist, truth ascriptions are expressions of assent and agreement, for they express harmony between our assertoric attitude and that of others with respect to particular claims. This can be explained through an elucidation of the *dis-quotational* use of the truth predicate. As suggested by Tarski's Convention T, in dis-quotational contexts what the use of the truth predicate does is to express commitment to the assertion quoted and, therefore, it is equivalent to its repetition (hence the redun-dancy property of truth): " 'p' is true = p." This exemplifies the Sellarsian and David-sonian strategy of explaining truth in terms of one's own language ("idiolect" for Davidson) or web of belief. But Rorty insists that this strategy does not identify ascrip-tions of truth with ascriptions of justified assertibility. Against the charge of a naïve and parochial identification between truth and assertibility, Rorty emphasizes the importance of the *cautionary* use of the truth predicate in statements such as "it may be justified and assertible but not true." For Rorty, the gap between truth and justifi-cation does not take truth outside our justificatory practices or make it independent of agreement. It simply reflects the fallibilist attitude in our orientation toward truth; that is, it is indicative of our openness to be proven wrong about the truth claims we endorse (no matter how well justified they happen to be). Far from being incompatible with the social-practice strategy of explaining objectivity in terms of *solidarity*, the cau-tionary use of the truth predicate falls squarely within it, for it expresses our willing-ness to widen agreement and extend it beyond our community: it is a call for more solidarity, not for transcending agreement. On this view, validity is always intersubjec-tive validity; and, Rorty insists, appealing to a stronger notion of correctness – an agree-ment-independent notion – involves sliding back into an illusory metaphysical picture of truth. Against this regressive "backsliding" Rorty defends a daring philosophical *rad-icalism* as the direction that social-practice accounts of truth should take. He finds the principal proponents of this radicalism in Davidson and Derrida. In his controversial interpretations of their views, Rorty sees a strong convergence between Derrida and Davidson as "non-backsliding" social-practice theorists who have radicalized the anti-representational strategy inaugurated by their predecessors, Heidegger and Sellars.

Rorty's *radical philosopher* is not afraid of accepting that truth is always context-dependent, that there is an inescapable connection between truth and the fallible agreements reached in our justificatory practices. Rorty's contextualism and his con-sensus theory of truth have been criticized by many and in many different ways. But most of the objections that have been raised complain about a lack of *normativity* and a lack of *realism*. In the papers we have selected, both Habermas and McDowell argue that Rorty's view fails to accommodate the normative attitudes and the realist intu-itions of participants in communicative practices.[1] But while Habermas's argument focuses on the *unconditionality* of truth, McDowell develops his objection through an argument about the *objectivity* of truth.

Habermas argues that Rorty's radical "epistemization" of truth reduces validity to coherence with current standards and therefore neglects what was right about the correspondence theory of truth: namely, the notion of *unconditional* validity. Without this notion, Habermas argues, we can't account for the distinction between believing and knowing unreservedly which is implicit in our truth claims. According to Habermas, in order to explain the unconditional character of our truth claims, we need to explain the *internal connection* between truth and justification – that is, we have to explain "the fact that a justification successful in our justificatory context points in favor of the context-independence truth of the justified proposition." Habermas proposes a formal-pragmatic account of this internal relation and, therefore, of unconditionality. This account is an elucidation of the formal presuppositions that link the action-contexts of the lifeworld and the discursive contexts of our justificatory practices. According to this account, validity first takes the form of behavioral certainty in the "language games" and practices that constitute the lifeworld; but the behavioral certainties of the lifeworld can be problematized, and we then need to resort to discourses that can settle our disputes. These discourses proceed through the rational attitude of submitting to nothing other than the force of the best reason. And since the order of reasons goes beyond any particular action-context, Habermas contends, the discursive vindication or "redemption" of validity claims can establish a renewed certainty that is context-transcendent. Thus the rational adjudication of validity claims rests on and at the same time extends the realist attitude of agents whose practices of cooperation and communication cannot function without the supposition of an independent reality. So, for Habermas, unconditionality is rooted in the *everyday realism* of our communicative practices (it is a formal presupposition of the participants in communication in the lifeworld which extends itself into the discourses in which their problematized claims are vindicated or "redeemed"). Habermas maintains that what a philosophical radicalism à la Rorty misses is precisely this everyday realism that provides the "normative reference point" for our truth claims and their discursive "redemption."

McDowell, on the other hand, argues that what Rorty's pragmatism misses is the *objectivity* of truth: that is, the *answerability to the world* of our truth-seeking practices of inquiry. McDowell warns that Rorty and other relativists try to impose a false dichotomy on us: inquiry is either thought to be answerable to a language- and mind-independent reality, or, alternatively, to be answerable to nothing but the norms of current practice. McDowell agrees with Rorty that we should reject the illusory transcendence of a language- and mind-independent reality, but he insists that we should understand the *internality* of truth differently. On his view, that truth is internal to our practices of inquiry does not mean that it is reducible to agreement within those practices, but rather that it involves an orientation to the world that is embedded in the normative standpoint of our practices. McDowell contends that the norms of inquiry transcend consensus: they demand of truth-seekers that they have *the world in view*. Having *the world in view*, he argues, constitutes an "innocuous transcendence" – a harmless appearance/reality distinction – which does not require any metaphysical picture, for it is fully explicable in terms of the norms of objectivity immanent in our practices. According to these norms, inquiry is normatively beholden both to our practices and to its subject matter.

In contrast with Habermas's and McDowell's calls for universality and objectivity, the last selection of this section presents a pluralist perspective on truth applied to what is taken to be the most universal and objective domain of all: the domain of science. The radical pluralism of Feyerabend calls into question the role of universality and objectivity in the scientific search for truth, raising warnings and challenges for realist claims such as Habermas's and McDowell's. Whereas McDowell was concerned with the rehabilitation of objectivity, Feyerabend is concerned with the rehabilitation of relativism. Against the alethic monism of intellectualist views, he argues that truths should remain concrete and relative to the plural and heterogeneous experiences of ordinary people, rather than being unified by abstract theories.

Following Protagoras, Feyerabend calls for "a return to common sense in matters of truth." Against the elitism of intellectualist views that put the power of adjudicating truth claims in the hands of a few, he argues for a *democratic relativism* according to which disputes concerning truth should be settled through debates in which no one in particular is given a special weight, not by experts with special rights to lay claim to truth. One of the most original insights of Feyerabend's democratic relativism is that it calls into question the direction of fit assumed by traditional theories of truth: he argues that what is most important to our truth claims is the direction of fit from world to language, not from language to world. So we could say that Feyerabend's view puts the emphasis on *Making Truth*, rather than on *Being Truth* as most philosophical theories have done and continue to do. In this sense he argues that what is in question in the dispute between Platonic intellectualism and Protagorean relativism is who should hold the power to reshape the world in one's image, the experts or the people (see also Lyotard in *Suggested Reading*). Feyerabend insists that, ultimately, this power should reside in the common men and women. He warns us against the false pretensions of scientism, which presents science as the sole possessor of truth and as providing a unified picture of the world for the rest of society. Feyerabend argues that, despite grandiloquent promises of unification, our most advanced versions of scientific research fail to give us the *unity* of universal and objective truths: science is divided into multifarious regions of knowledge in which truths take very different shapes. This thoroughgoing pluralism (or "regionalism") is reminiscent of the deflationary approaches to truth developed, among others, by Arthur Fine and Michael Williams in philosophy of science and epistemology (see *Suggested Reading*). According to these approaches, "truth" is not the name of a property or a content that remains the same across contexts and can be thematized by a philosophical theory, be it a metaphysical, epistemic, or semantic theory. According to deflationism, no philosophical theory can give a unified meaning to "truth." On this *no-theory* approach to truth, there is room only for piecemeal elucidations of the use of the truth predicate in different practices.

Note

1   Rorty has written brief responses to Habermas and McDowell (see *Suggested Reading*). In these responses Rorty argues that Habermas's appeal to unconditional validity and McDowell's appeal to objectivity are ways of sliding back into a metaphysical picture that can have no place in a social-practice account of truth. He insists that a Davidsonian deflationary account of truth offers a robust enough notion of validity and objectivity in terms of solidarity.

7

REPRESENTATION, SOCIAL PRACTICE, AND TRUTH

Richard Rorty

Some years ago, Robert Brandom suggested that recent philosophy of language divides up into two schools. For the first, or representationalist, school (typified by Frege, Russell, Tarski and Carnap), Brandom says, "the essential feature of language is its capacity to represent the way things are."[1] Representationalists, he continues, "take truth to be the basic concept in terms of which a theory of meaning, and hence a theory of language, is to be developed." The second school (typified by Dewey and Wittgenstein) starts off from a conception of language as a set of social practises. Members of this school start off from assertibility, and then squeeze the notion of truth in as best they can.

As Brandom says, both the early Heidegger and Sellars are members of the latter school. There is, I think, a useful comparison to be made between the way in which those two social-practise theorists handle the distinction between assertibility and truth. The Heidegger of *Being and Time*, as Brandom says in a later article,[2] defends "the ontological primacy of the social" on the basis of "pragmatism concerning authority." For the Heidegger of this period, truth as accuracy of representation, as mere correctness [*Richtigkeit, adaequatio*], is identified with warranted assertibility, treated as a matter of conformity to current practise. He takes the traditional pseudo-problems of the relation of language to *beings*, problems engendered by representationalism, to be solved by the discovery of the primacy of the social. But he thinks that "truth" still names a central philosophical topic – viz., the relation between *Being* and changing "understandings of Being" [*Seinsverstaendnisse*]. So Heidegger distinguishes between correctness and disclosedness, between *Richtigkeit* and *Erschlossenheit* or *aletheia*. Disclosedness is a relation between vocabularies, conceptual systems, and Being – as opposed to the correctness relation which holds between sentences and beings.

Sellars makes the same sort of move. He takes the traditional representationalist problematic of the relation of language and thought to the world to be resolved by

Richard Rorty, "Representation, Social Practice, and Truth," from *Philosophical Studies* 54 (1988), pp. 215–28. Reprinted with kind permission of Kluwer Academic Publishers and the author.

recognizing that, as he says in *Science and Metaphysics*, "semantical statements of the Tarski–Carnap variety do not assert relations between linguistic and extra-linguistic items."[3] Sellars spells out his social-practise construal of the notion of truth as follows: "for a proposition to be true is for it to be assertible . . . correctly assertible, that is, in accordance with the relevant semantical rules and on the basis of such additional, though unspecified, information as these rules may require. . . ."[4] His substitution of inference-tickets for assertions of word–world correspondence is illustrated by his claim that a Tarskian T-sentence is "a consequence of the above *intensional* definition of 'true' [as S-assertibility], in the sense that the assertion of the right-hand side of the implication statement is a *performance* of the kind authorized by the truth statement on the left."[5]

Like Heidegger, however, Sellars is not content to leave the matter at that. After analyzing truth as S-assertibility, he goes on to discuss the question of what happens when the semantical rules themselves change, when we have a change of "framework." This is the point at which he introduces his notion of "adequacy of picturing." Picturing is for Sellars what disclosedness is for Heidegger. It is the extra dimension which relates social practises to something beyond themselves, and thus recaptures the Greek problematic of humanity's relation to the non-human (of *nomos* vs. *physis*). In Sellars' case this non-human something is "the world." In Heidegger's case it is "Being."

Many of those who owe their philosophical formation to Heidegger, notably Derrida, see his desire to save this traditional problematic, and thus his talk of Being and of disclosedness, as pious nostalgia, further evidence of the dominion of Greece over Germany. They view that desire, and that kind of talk, as a slide back into metaphysics. Many of us whose minds were formed by reading Sellars think of Sellars' doctrine of picturing as an unfortunate slide back into representationalism – a last-minute recrudescence of the pious hope that the great problems formulated by the philosophical tradition (and, more particularly, by Kant) were not *altogether* illusory.

Are Heidegger or Sellars in fact backsliding? Or has one or the other, or both, found a happy *via media* between the uncritical representationalism of the philosophical tradition and an overenthusiastic pragmatism which throws Being and the World overboard? One way to get this question into better focus is to take a look at Davidson. Davidson's disdain for the idea of "conceptual frameworks," as relic of the analytic–synthetic distinction, is well known. His refusal to admit questions about a relation between scheme and content – for example, about the adequacy of some historically-given language-game to "the world" – is part of this disdain. So Davidson seems a good candidate for the position of *non*-backsliding "social practises" theorist.

Davidson, however, may seem to resist Brandom's classification. For, as I said earlier, Brandom makes it a mark of representationalism to "take truth to be the basic concept in terms of which a theory of meaning, and hence a theory of language, is to be developed." On a first reading of his "Truth and Meaning" (1967), Davidson seems an arch-representationalist. But, as I have argued elsewhere,[6] by the time Davidson has finished (in some twenty years' worth of subsequent articles) with the notion of truth, it is as little suited for representationalist purposes as it is when Sellars has finished with it. For what Davidson now calls his "coherence theory" of truth says that only evidence – that is, other beliefs, as opposed to experience, sensory stimulation, or the world – can make beliefs true. Since "making true" is the inverse of "representing," this doctrine makes it impossible for Davidson to talk about language representing the world – standing to it as scheme to content.

This contrast between "evidence" and "world" may seem to repeat Sellars' point that "true" does not name a word–world relation, but instead is to be analyzed as "S-assertible." But such an assimilation is blocked by Davidson's urging us to leave "true" *unanalyzed*, to take it as primitive.[7] Davidson would resist Sellars' analysis because he wants to de-epistemologize the notion of truth – to keep it as separate from questions of justification as Sellars keeps the notion of picturing. He thinks that although truth is, indeed, "the basic concept in terms of which a theory of meaning is to be developed," only a de-epistemologized conception of truth will get that job done.

To clarify what such a concept of truth is like, consider the difference between the ways in which Sellars and Davidson handle the familiar anti-pragmatist point that a sentence can be assertible without being true. Sellars distinguishes two senses in which this point is sound. One is that there is a distinction between assertibility from the point of view of a finite individual user of a conceptual system and assertibility from the point of view of an omniscient user. Omniscient Jones makes only *correct* assertions, because he has all the additional information which the rules require him to have before opening his mouth. Finite Smith, by contrast, is justified in making incorrect assertions by his lack of world enough and time. So truth has to be defined as S-assertibility, assertibility by Jones, rather than ordinary assertibility by you, me, or Smith, The *second* sense in which this anti-pragmatist point is sound is that Jones, despite his omniscience, may be using a second-rate set of semantical rules. He may, for example, be a Neanderthal or an Aristotelian. So his assertions, though correct by his lights, are still, we moderns are inclined to say, false. That is why Sellars wants to bring in picturing as distinct from truth, to allow for ever better S-assertibilities.

By contrast, Davidson wants to describe the distinction between assertibility and truth without reference to semantical rules or conceptual systems. He regards these latter notions as arbitrary divisions of a seamless and endless process of reweaving webs of belief, a seamless process of altering criteria of assertibility. So for him there is no way to construct a notion of "ideal" assertibility with which to identify truth, nor is there any need to worry about the difference between us and the Neanderthals, or us and the Galactics. On his view, truth and assertibility have *nothing* to do with one another. Truth is not the name of a property, and in particular not the name of a relational property which ties a statement to the world or to a set of semantical rules as followed by an omniscient being. Ascriptions of truth are to be treated disquotationally, or, more generally, anaphorically. As Brandom says in the article I cited at the beginning, you need a notion of truth as distinct from assertibility to do semantics – and in particular to handle inferences involving compound sentences – but you may not need it for anything else. Assertibility, for Davidson, *is* the name of a property, but it is always assertibility by some finite Smith (or group of Smiths) in some situation at some time – assertibility relative to some *given*, actual, finite web of beliefs.

This contrast between Sellars' and Davidson's strategy stands out in the following passage from Davidson:

[the principle that] whatever there is to meaning must he traced back to experience, the given, or patterns of sensory stimulation, something intermediate between belief and the usual objects our beliefs are about . . . open[s] the door to skepticism. Trying to make meaning accessible has made truth inaccessible. When meaning goes epistemological in this way, truth and meaning are necessarily divorced. One can, of course, arrange a shotgun wedding by redefining truth as what we are justified in asserting. But this does not marry the original mates.[8]

Davidson's point is that one can epistemologize meaning by tying it to the given, or one can epistemologize truth by tying it to justification, but *either* tie-up will lead either to skepticism or to extravagantly complicated, ultimately unsuccessful, efforts to evade skepticism. Either will lead us back into the maze of blind alleys which is the representationalist tradition. So the thing to do is to marry truth and meaning to nothing and nobody but each other. The resulting marriage will be so intimate a relationship that a theory of truth will *be* a theory of meaning, and conversely. But that theory will be of no use to a representationalist epistemology, not to any other sort of epistemology. It will be an explanation of what people *do*, rather than of a non-causal, representing, relation in which they stand to non-human entities. I suspect that Davidson would say that Sellars is still held captive by a representationalist picture. In this picture, Neanderthal or Aristotelian sentences have meaning – that is, are translatable by us – by virtue of their referring, albeit unperspicuously, to what really exists – viz., the objects referred to in the ideal, Peircian, conceptual system. For if Sellars were free of this picture, it would not seem of importance to him to set up the baroque Tractarian apparatus with the aid of which he tries to explicate "the concept of a domain of objects which are pictured in one way (less adequate) by one linguistic system, and in another way (more adequate) by another."[9] As with all other accounts of meaning which insist on a tie with the world as a condition of meaningfulness, Sellars opens the gates to skepticism. For now he has to give an account of the notion of "more adequate picturing" which will serve as what he calls "an Archimedean point outside the series of actual and possible beliefs."[10] But any such account will lead back to skepticism. For Sellars' very description of the picturing relation raises doubts of the sort associated with what Putnam has called "metaphysical realism." We begin to wonder how we could ever know whether our increasing success at predicting and controlling our environment as we moved from Neanderthal through Aristotelian to Newtonian was an index of a non-intentional "matter-of-factual" relation called "adequate picturing." Perhaps the gods see things otherwise. Perhaps they are amused by seeing us predicting better and better while picturing worse and worse.

This sort of skeptical doubt, Davidson will urge, can never be resolved. For Sellars himself has to admit that there is no super-language, neutral between the three conceptual schemes just mentioned, in which we can formulate a criterion of adequacy. His own principles force him to agree with the point which Putnam makes against Kripke: that you cannot *specify* a non-intentional Archimedean tie with the world, a point outside a series of beliefs. For the non-intentional relations you specify will be as theory-relative, as belief-relative, as everything else. So either "CS_j pictures more adequately than CS_i" just *means* "CS_j is better suited to our needs than CS_i," or it does not. If it does, then we can dispense with the Tractarian apparatus which is sup-

posed to unite all such conceptual systems. If it does not, and if we cannot say anything more about what it *does* mean, then surely we can forgo talk of picturing altogether. As Rosenberg puts it, talk of correct picturing is "in a sense idle" because "the
sense of such claims of ontological adequacy or absolute correctness is given only in
terms of the notion of conceptual schemes and retrospective collective justifiabilities
constitutive of the very diachronic process we have been describing."[11]

The difference between Sellars and Davidson here is the difference between somebody who takes seriously the question "Does what we are talking about really exist?"
and somebody who does not. This difference in attitude toward the reality–appearance distinction accounts for two more differences between the two philosophers.
The first is that Davidson, unlike both Quine and Sellars, has no special interest in
physical science. He cares nothing for the relation of intentional or moral locutions
to the disposition of elementary particles. He has no reductionist impulses, no preferred vocabulary in which to describe the world, no particular regard for the vocabulary of unified natural science. His attitude toward Eddington's two tables is the
Deweyan one which Sellars thinks childish: he says "both." This is also his attitude
toward the difference between the manifest and the scientific image: use whatever
image is handy for the purpose at hand, without worrying about which is closer to
reality.

This absence of reductionist impulses leads to an insouciance about the analytic
–synthetic distinction. It leads, in particular, to the view that philosophers' "conceptual analyses" are usually just remnants of what Davidson calls an "adventitious puritanism" (of, e.g., empiricism) or of the morbid scientistic fear (common in Vienna
and Berlin during the 1920s) that one may be using seemingly referring expressions
which in fact do not refer. It also leads to the view that, as I said earlier, nothing is
gained by talking about "conceptual systems" that could not be had more easily by
just talking about change in linguistic behavior – change which can be described
either as change of meaning or as change of belief, depending upon whether (as
Harman puts it) it seems more convenient to revise our encyclopedias or our
dictionaries.

So much for the differences between Davidson and Sellars. The similarities are, I
think, more important. For, at bottom, their anti–representationalist strategy is the same.
This strategy consists in appealing to *what we do* as a resolution of familiar representationalist problems. More specifically, it consists in letting self-referential indexicals
play a role in philosophical explanation. Sellars, to my mind, is the great pioneer in
this area. He was the first analytic philosopher to break with the idea that philosophy
must be done from what Putnam calls a "God's eye view." This traditional representationalist conception of objectivity was shattered when Sellars (in his early article "A
Semantical Solution of the Mind–Body Problem") suggested that the reason why
intentional discourse was irreducible to non-intentional discourse was simply that
intentional discourse was token-reflexive discourse and non-intentional discourse was
not. More specifically, Sellars suggested that we explain what it is to be a language by
reference to what *we* do – not "we" in some vague generic sense in which it is equivalent to "humanity" but in the sense of what you and I are currently doing. As he said
in "Being and Being Known," "the basic role of signification statements is to say that
two expressions, at least one of which is in *our own* vocabulary, have the same use."[12]

This seems to me an epoch-making step, for it is the beginning of the end of what Rosenberg has called the Myth of Mind Apart. It opens the way for Sellars' habitual appeals to inference-tickets and patterns of practical reasoning – his appeals to what *we* do – to explicate the concept of truth, to vindicate induction, and to expound the moral point of view. For such appeals presuppose that a philosophical account of our practises need *not* take the form of descriptions of our relation to something not ourselves, but need *merely* describe our practises. The desired "relation to the world" which representationalists fear may be lacking is, Sellars was implying, *built into* the fact that these are *our* practises – the practises of real live human beings engaged in causal interaction with the rest of nature.

The claim that reference to the practises of real live people is all the philosophical justification anybody could want for anything, and the only defense against the skeptic anybody needs, is central to Davidson's philosophical strategy as well. To bring this out, let me take the slightly circuitous route of citing some exasperated criticisms made of Davidson by one of his most acute representationalist critics. Jonathan Bennett has said that Davidson is unable or unwilling to carry out what Bennett sees as "the philosopher's task" – viz., "to take warm, familiar aspects of the human condition and look at them coldly and with the eye of a stranger."[13]

What annoys Bennett most is Davidson's habit of acting as if Grice had lived in vain, as if there were no need to ask what makes a language a language, as if "he could just rely on the premise that *he speaks a language*," without subjecting that premise "to any kind of explanation or analytical scrutiny." Bennett goes on to say that "With one strange exception . . . he [Davidson] tells us nothing about what it is for a behavioral system to be a language, or for a sound or movement to be (a token of) a sentence." He continues: "Davidson seems willing to take that concept on trust, as something whose instances are dropped into our laps without the need for philosophical work."[14]

The "strange exception" which Bennett mentions is Davidson's claim that Convention T "makes essential use of the notion of translation into a language we know."[15] As Bennett goes on to say, Davidson holds that "each person's concept of truth brings in a particular language – or a particular small set of languages – because *each person's concept of truth is partly self-referential.*" Here, I think, Bennett gets to the core of Davidson's position. But it is also, as I have been saying, the core of Sellars' position. These two social-practise theorists share a willingness to do what Bennett thinks fantastic: to "explain *true* in terms of *language I know.*"[16]

Representationalists like Bennett construe as mysterious relations between the human and the non-human what social-practise theorists like Sellars and Davidson construe as elliptical descriptions of practises – practises which we humans have developed in the course of interacting with non-human things. So when Davidson says that most of our beliefs, most of Aristotle's beliefs, and most of your average Neanderthal's beliefs, were true, Bennett diagnoses what he calls "incurious parochialism." He would say the same of Sellars' account of intentional discourse as explicated by self-referential indexicals. For if this account is sufficient there will be no way of explicating the notion of "intending" without reference to *our* own vocabulary. So there will be no way for Gricean speech-act theory to carry out its program.

If Sellars and Davidson are right in suggesting that philosophical explication is always going to lead back to self-referential indexicals, then there is something seriously wrong with Bennett's idea that philosophers can step back from warm, familiar aspects of the human condition and look at them with the eye of a stranger. Bennett's phrasing gets to the heart of the representationalist philosopher's motives. It also gets to the heart of the initial Greek attempt to distinguish *nomos* from *physis* – an attempt which Heidegger links to the beginnings of *Seinsvergessenheit*. Hegel, Sellars' early hero, was properly suspicious of the idea that philosophers can take this step back. He thought that the great mistake of the Kantians was to try to view knowledge as a medium, or as an instrument.[17] He insisted that the proper starting-point for philosophy was not an aloof transcendental standpoint but rather the particular point in world-history at which we find ourselves. It may be the great mistake of the kind of neo-Kantian philosophy of language which Bennett represents to think that we can treat language as a medium or an instrument – that we can *avoid* doing what Bennett rightly says Davidson does: "explaining *true* in terms of *language I know*."[18]

The question of whether there is anything for philosophers to appeal to save the way *we* live now, what *we* do now, how *we* talk now – anything beyond *our* own little moment of world-history – is the decisive issue between representationalist and social-practise philosophers of language. More generally, it is the decisive issue between an approach to philosophy which takes for granted what Rosenberg calls "the Myth of Mind Apart" and one which assumes that something is, indeed, dropped into the philosopher's lap – namely, her own linguistic know-how, or more generally, her own patterns of practical reasoning the ways in which her community copes with the world. The alternative to this assumption would seem to be that what was dropped into her lap was a gift from heaven called "clarity of thought" or "powerful analytic techniques" or "critical distance" – a heaven-sent ability to wrench one's mind free from one's community's practises, to turn away from *nomos* toward *physis*.

So much for what seems to me the common core of Davidson and Sellars, and the source of the bafflement with which both men's views are greeted by representationalists. Now let me turn back to the differences between their respective treatments of the notion of truth. I said earlier that Sellars tried to take the curse off his Deweyan identification of truth with assertibility by distinguishing, first, Omniscient Jones' use of our conceptual system (CSO) from finite Smith's use, and second, CSO from a sequence of CS_is which lead up to the limit CS. This limit conceptual system, CSP, is the conceptual scheme used by speakers of Peircish at the ideal end of inquiry. By these distinctions, he hopes to grant the skeptic his point that we may be getting everything wrong while still maintaining that "true" does not name a word–world relation. By contrast, Davidson's way with the skeptic is much quicker and dirtier. It is summed up in the following passage:

> In order to doubt or wonder about the provenance of his beliefs an agent must know what belief is. This brings with it the concept of objective truth, for the notion of a belief is the notion of a state that may or may not jibe with reality. But beliefs are also identified, directly and indirectly, by their causes. What an omniscient interpreter knows a fallible interpreter gets right enough if he understands a speaker, and this is just the complicated causal truth that makes us the believers we are, and fixes the contents of our beliefs. The agent has only to reflect on what a belief is to appreciate that most of his basic beliefs are true, and among his beliefs, those most securely held and that cohere with the main body of his beliefs are the most apt to be true.[19]

Notice, in this passage, the claim that all that omniscience could know about our relation to the world is "the complicated causal truth that makes us the believers we are." Davidson's point is that knowing *that* truth would automatically enable omniscience to translate our utterances and to recognize most of them as truths. If we bear Sellars' distinctions in mind, we may be tempted to ask whether the Omniscience in question is merely Omniscient Jones using CSO, or rather Omniscient Jones in glory, using CSP. Davidson will reply that it simply doesn't matter. The difference between CSO and CSP is, for him, philosophically insignificant. Davidson and Sellars agree that what shows us that life is not just a dream, that our beliefs are in touch with reality, is the *causal* non-intentional, non-representational, links between us and the rest of the universe. But Sellars thinks that it takes a long time (all the way to the end of inquiry) for these causal links to whip us into properly correspondent shape, and that in the meantime we may be talking about what does not exist. In contrast, Davidson thinks that they had already whipped us into the relevant shape as soon as they made us language-users.

For Sellars, the primitive animists and the Aristotelians employed referring expressions most of which did not pick out entities in the world, and the same may be true of *us*, who have not yet reached CSP. For Davidson, everybody has always talked about mostly real things, and has made mostly true statements. The only difference between primitive animists and us, or us and the Galactics, is that the latecomers can make a few extra true statements which their ancestors did not know how to make (and avoid a few falsehoods). But these little extras – the difference between wood-nymphs and microbiology, or between our microbiology and its successor in Galactic unified science – are just icing on the cake. A massive amount of true belief and successful picking-out was already in place when the first Neanderthal went metalinguistic and found words in which to explain to her mate that one of his beliefs was false. For the Neanderthal lived in the same world that the omniscient user of CSP lives in, and the same causal forces which led most of her and her mate's linguistic behavior to consist of true assertions will lead an omniscient user to say mostly what she said. The complicated causal story about how this happened goes much the same, whether told in Neanderthal, Newtonian or Peircish; the details just get a bit more complicated at each successive stage.

The difference between Sellars and Davidson parallels a difference between Sellars and Rosenberg, or, more exactly, between Sellars and early Rosenberg on the one hand and slightly later Rosenberg on the other. In the first book, *Linguistic Representation*, Rosenberg took chapter 5 of *Science and Metaphysics* at face value and developed an account of proto-correlational isomorphisms, Jumblese et al. He wanted, at that time, to preserve Sellars' notion of "one truth about the world" – the one told according to the semantic rules of CSP. But in his second book, *One World and our Knowledge of It*, from which I earlier quoted the passage about the "idleness" of the notion of "correct picturing," he drops the idea of "one truth" and settles for that of "one world." Now he says that the fact that a successor conceptual scheme is more nearly (absolutely) correct than its predecessor *consists* in its adoption or espousal as a successor being warranted or justified."[20] That sentence closes off the skeptical "metaphysical realist" possibility which was left open in both *Science and Metaphysics* and *Linguistic Representation*. These books made picturing a matter-of-factual relation causally independent of social practises; so they left open the possibility that successive schemes might predict better and better by picturing worse and worse. The later Rosenberg precludes this possibility. For he has made "pictures more correctly than" mean something like "accepted (for good reasons, in a relatively domination-free communication situation) later than."

The only important difference between this latter Rosenbergian account and Davidson's is the residual scientism which Rosenberg shares with Sellars, and from which Davidson is free. This scientism makes Sellars and Rosenberg take the notion of "conceptual scheme" seriously, and its absence lets Davidson shrug it off. Scientism, in this sense, is the assumption that every time science lurches forward philosophy must redescribe the face of the whole universe. Scienticists think that every new discovery of micro-structure casts doubt on the "reality" of manifest macro-structure and of any intervening middle structures. If one takes this claim seriously, one may well feel torn between van Fraassen's instrumentalism and Sellars' realism. If one does not, as Davidson does not, then one will simply not ask which of Eddington's two tables is real, and one will be baffled about the difference between van Fraassen's ready belief in tables and his more tentative attitude toward electrons.[21] One will (with Bain and Peirce) take beliefs as rules for actions rather than elements in a representational system, and say that it is well to have lots of different sets of rules for dealing with tables – in order to be prepared for the various different contexts in which one may encounter them (in the dining room, under the electron microscope, etc.). One will be as obstinately Oxonian about the word "real" as Austin was, able to wield it when distinguishing real diamonds from paste and real cream from non-dairy whitener, but not when distinguishing primary from secondary qualities.

One can think of scientism in the relevant sense as going back to the latter distinction. Philosophers like Locke thought that they heard from Newton and Boyle the language which Plato and St. Paul had hoped to hear beyond the grave: the language which specified clearly and distinctly what we had previously spoken of obliquely and confusedly. In our own century, enthusiastic readers of *The Encyclopedia of Unified Science* hoped that that language was now actually in sight. So they retained the representationalist problematic of modern philosophy which Locke had initiated by distinguishing between ideas which did and did not resemble their objects.[22] Sellars thinks that we must take this problematic seriously, and that we can use the results of social-practise philosophy of language to answer questions posed by representationalist philosophy of language. Like the early Heidegger, he thinks that we can pour new wine into old bottles, and write in a way which is continuous with the philosophical tradition – that we can combine what Brandom calls "pragmatism about authority" with something like traditional ontology. More radical social-practise theorists such as Derrida and Davidson think that one cannot, and that attempts to do so amount to backsliding.[23] Though my own leanings are obviously toward radicalism, I have not attempted to adjudicate the issue between Davidson's quick and dirty dissolution of the traditional problematic and Sellars' attempt at a happy *via media*. I have merely tried to get that issue into sharper focus.

Notes

1   'Truth and Assertibility', *Journal of Philosophy*, 73 (1976), p. 137.
2   'Heidegger's Categories in *Being and Time*', *The Monist*, 66 (1983), pp. 387–409.
3   *Science and Metaphysics* (New York: Humanities Press, 1968), p. 82.
4   Ibid., p. 101.
5   Ibid., italics added.
6   'Pragmatism, Davidson and Truth', in *Objectivity, Relativism and Truth* (New York: Cambridge University Press, 1991).
7   Davidson, 'A Coherence Theory of Truth and Knowledge', in E. LePore (ed.), *Truth and Interpretation* (Oxford: Blackwell, 1986), p. 308.
8   Ibid., p. 313.
9   *Science and Metaphysics*, p. 140.
10 Ibid., p. 142.
11 Jay Rosenberg, *One World and Our Knowledge of It* (Dordrecht: Reidel, 1980), p. 186.
12 *Science, Perception and Reality* (London: Routledge and Keagan Paul, 1963), p. 56; italics added.
13 'Critical Notice' of *Inquires into Truth and Interpretation, Mind*, (1985), p. 619.
14 Ibid.
15 Ibid., p. 626, citing *Inquiries*, p. 194f.
16 Ibid.
17 Hegel, 'Introduction' to *The Phenomenology of Spirit*, trans. A. V. Miller (Oxford: Oxford University Press, 1977), p. 47. 'Should we not be concerned as to whether this fear of error is not just the error itself? Indeed, this fear takes something – a great deal, in fact – for granted as truth, supporting its scruples and inferences on what is itself in need of prior scrutiny to see if it is true. To be specific, it takes for granted certain ideas about cognition as an *instrument* and *a medium*, and assumes that there is a *difference between ourselves and this cognition*'.
18 Bennett, 'Critical Notice', p. 626.
19 Davidson, 'A Coherence Theory', pp. 318–19.
20 *One World and Our Knowledge of It*, p. 117.
21 On dissolving the issue between Stellars and van Fraassen, see Gary Gutting, 'Scientific Realism vs. Constructive Empiricism: A Dialogue', in *Images of Science: Essays on Realism and Empiricism*, ed. Paul M. Churchland and Clifford A. Hooker (Chicago: Univ. of Chicago Press, 1985).
22 Note that recent defenders of the primary–secondary quality distinction such as Thomas Nagel and Bernard Williams join Bennett in thinking that it is possible, and for some purposes useful, to step back from warm, familiar aspects of the human condition and view them with the eye of a stranger. That is why Nagel says that a full-fledged Wittgensteinian social-practise view of language is incompatible with realism. (See Nagel, *The View From Nowhere* (Oxford: Oxford University Press, 1986), p. 106.
23 For the convergence of Davidson and Derrida, see Samuel Wheeler, 'Indeterminacy of French Interpretation: Derrida and Davison', in *Truth and Interpretation: Perspectives on the Philosophy of Donald Davidson*, ed. Ernest LePore (Oxford and New York: Basil Blackwell, 1986), pp. 477–94.

8

RICHARD RORTY'S
PRAGMATIC TURN

Jürgen Habermas

From the pragmatic radicalization of the linguistic turn Rorty obtains a nonrealist understanding of knowledge. In order to test whether he radicalizes the linguistic turn in the right way, I will then compare the contextualist approach with the epistemological doubt of the modern skeptic. In doing so I will recall a problem that was always connected with coherence conceptions of truth: the problem of how truth is to be distinguished from rational acceptability. In responding to this question, there is a parting of philosophical ways. Whereas Rorty assimilates truth to justification at the expense of everyday realist intuitions, others attempt to take account of intuitions even within the linguistic paradigm, whether with the help of a deflationary strategy as regards the problem of truth or through an idealization of the process of justification itself. On the one hand, I will take issue with the deflationary strategy that relies on a semantic conception of truth, emphasizing instead the advantages of a pragmatic viewpoint. On the other hand, again from a pragmatic perspective, I will criticize a kind of epistemization of the idea of truth that I myself once proposed. In doing so I will develop an alternative to the liquidation of unconditional claims to truth. It is this liquidation that has ultimately compelled Rorty to effect a problematic naturalization of linguistified reason – or, at any rate, one that leads to further problems.

[...]

Contextualism and Skepticism as Problems Specific
to Particular Paradigms

When Rorty regards contextualism as the necessary consequence of a fully executed linguistic turn, he is right in one respect: contextualism designates a problem that can occur only when we reckon on a reason embodied in linguistic practices. But

Jürgen Habermas, "Richard Rorty's Pragmatic Turn," in *Rorty and His Critics*, ed. Robert Brandom (Oxford: Blackwell, 2000), p. 32 (excerpt), 37–55. Reprinted by permission of Blackwell Publishing.

he is wrong to see contextualism at the same time as the solution to the problem. This view has its roots, if I am correct, in a problematic understanding of philosophical paradigms.

Like, for example, Apel and Tugendhat, Rorty regards the history of philosophy as a succession of three paradigms. He speaks of metaphysics, epistemology, and the philosophy of language.[1] Of course, the philosophy of language has detached itself only halfheartedly from mentalism. Rorty believes that the linguistic turn can be carried through consistently to its conclusion only in the form of a critique of reason that takes its leave of philosophy as such. It is not just the problems but the way of posing problems that changes with the leap from one paradigm to the next:

> This picture of ancient and medieval philosophy as concerned with *things*, the philosophy of the seventeenth through the nineteenth centuries with *ideas*, and the enlightened contemporary philosophical scene with *words* has considerable plausibility. But this sequence should not be thought of as offering three contrasting views about what is primary, or what is foundational. It is not that Aristotle thought that one could best explain ideas and words in terms of things, whereas Descartes and Russell rearranged the order of explanation. It would be more correct to say that Aristotle did not have – did not feel the need of – a theory of knowledge, and that Descartes and Locke did not have a theory of meaning. Aristotle's remarks about knowing do not offer answers, good or bad, to Locke's questions, any more than Locke's remarks about language offer answers to Frege's.[2]

This *discontinuity* means that philosophical questions are not settled through finding the right answers; rather, they fall into disuse once they have lost their market value. This also holds for the question of the objectivity of knowledge.

On the mentalist view, objectivity is ensured when the representing subject refers to his objects in the right way. He checks the subjectivity of his representations against the objective world: "'subjective' contrasts with 'corresponding to what is out there,' and thus means something like 'a product only of what is in here.'"[3] On the linguistic view, the subjectivity of beliefs is no longer checked directly through confrontation with the world but rather through public agreement achieved in the communication community: "a 'subjective' consideration is one which has been, or would be, or should be, set aside by rational discussants."[4] With this, the intersubjectivity of reaching understanding replaces the objectivity of experience. The language–world relation becomes dependent on communication between speakers and hearers. The vertical world-relation of representations of something, or of propositions about something, is bent back, as it were, into the horizontal line of the cooperation of participants in communication. The intersubjectivity of the lifeworld, which subjects inhabit in common, *displaces* the objectivity of a world that a solitary subject confronts: "For pragmatists, the desire for objectivity is not the desire to escape the limitations of one's community, but simply the desire for as much intersubjective agreement as possible."[5] Rorty wants to say: the paradigm shift transforms perspectives in such a way that epistemological questions as such are passé.

The contextualist understanding of the linguistic turn from which this anti-realism emerges goes back to a conception of the rise and fall of paradigms that excludes continuity of theme between paradigms as well as learning processes that extend across paradigms. In fact, the terms in which we undertake a comparison of paradigms reflect our hermeneutic starting point – and, thus, our own paradigm. That Rorty selects for his comparison the frame of reference of objectivity, subjectivity, and intersubjectivity results from the basic conceptual perspective from which we now describe the linguistic turn of mentalism. On the other hand the picture of a contingent succession of incommensurable paradigms does not in any way fit with this description. Rather, from the perspective of that frame of reference, a subsequent paradigm appears as an answer to a problem bequeathed to us by the devaluation of a preceding paradigm. Contrary to what Rorty supposes, paradigms do not form an arbitrary sequence but a dialectical relationship.

Nominalism robbed things of their inner nature or essence and declared general concepts to be constructions of a finite mind. Since then, comprehending that which is (das Seiende) in thought has lacked a foundation in the conceptual constitution of beings themselves. The correspondence of mind with nature could no longer be conceived as an ontological relation, the rules of logic no longer reflected the laws of reality. Pace Rorty, mentalism responded to this challenge by reversing the order of explanation. If the knowing subject can no longer derive the standards for knowledge from a disqualified nature, it has to supply these standards from a reflexively disclosed subjectivity itself. Reason, once embodied objectively in the order of nature, retreats to subjective spirit. With this, the being-in-itself (das Ansich) of the world is transformed into the objectivity of a world that is given for us, the subjects – a world of represented objects or phenomena. Whereas up to then, the constitution of the world of being-in-itself had enabled a correspondence of thought with reality – true judgments – the truth of judgments is now supposed to be measured against the certainty of evident subjective experiences (Erlebnisse). Representational thought leads to objective knowledge insofar as it comprehends the phenomenal world.

The concept of subjectivity introduced a dualism between inner and outer that seemed to confront the human mind with the precarious task of bridging a chasm. With this, the way was cleared for skepticism in its modern form. The private character of my particular subjective experiences, on which my absolute certainty is based, simultaneously provides reason to doubt whether the world as it appears to us is not in fact an illusion. This skepticism is anchored in the constitutive concepts of the mentalist paradigm. At the same time it conjures up memories of the comforting intuition that sustained the ontological paradigm: the idea that the truth of judgments is guaranteed by a correspondence with reality that is grounded in reality itself. This "residual" intuition, as it were, which had lost none of its suggestive power with the switch of paradigm, joined forces with the new skeptical question of whether – and if so, how – the agreement between representation and represented object is to be grounded on the basis of the evidence of our subjective experiences. It is this question that first provokes the epistemological quarrel between Idealism and Empiricism.[6] However, in light of this genealogy it becomes apparent – and this is my main point here – that contextualism is built into the basic concepts of the linguistic paradigm just as skepticism is built into mentalism. And once again, the intuitions regarding truth that carry over or stick with us from the preceding paradigms lead to an intensification of these problems.

Just as the dispute about universals at the end of the Middle Ages contributed to the devaluation of objective reason, the critique of introspection and psychologism at the end of the nineteenth century contributed to the shaking up of subjective reason.

With the displacement of reason from the consciousness of the knowing subject to language as the medium by means of which acting subjects communicate with one another, the order of explanation changes once more. Epistemic authority passes over from the knowing subject, which supplies from within herself the standards for the objectivity of experience, to the justificatory practices of a linguistic community. Up to then the intersubjective validity of beliefs had resulted from the subsequent convergence of thoughts or representations. Interpersonal agreement had been explained by the ontological anchoring of true judgments or by the shared psychological or transcendental endowments of knowing subjects. Following the linguistic turn, however, all explanations take the primacy of a common language as their starting point. Description of states and events in the objective world, like the self-representation of experiences to which the subject has privileged access, is dependent on the interpreting use of a common language. For this reason, the term 'intersubjective' no longer refers to the result of an *observed* convergence of the thoughts or representations of various persons, but to the prior commonality of a linguistic pre-understanding or horizon of the lifeworld – which, from the perspective of the participants themselves, is presupposed – within which the members of a communication community find themselves before they reach understanding with one another about something in the world. Finally, the contextualist question, which should not be confused with the epistemological doubt of skepticism, results from this primacy of the intersubjectivity of shared beliefs over confrontation with reality (a reality that is always already interpreted).

The pragmatic turn leaves no room for doubt as to the existence of a world independent of our descriptions. Rather, from Peirce to Wittgenstein, the idle Cartesian doubt has been rejected as a performative contradiction – "if you tried to doubt everything you would not get as far as doubting anything. The game of doubting itself presupposes certainty."[7] On the other hand, all knowledge is fallible and, when it is problematized, dependent on justification. As soon as the standard for the objectivity of knowledge passes from private certainty to public practices of justification, "truth" becomes a three-place concept of validity. The validity of propositions that are fallible in principle is shown to be validity that is justified *for* a public.[8] Moreover, because in the linguistic paradigm truths are accessible only in the form of rational acceptability, the question now arises of how in that case the truth of a proposition can still be isolated from the context in which it is justified. Unease with regard to this problem brings older intuitions about truth onto the scene. It awakens memory of a correspondence between thought and reality or of a contact with reality that is sensorially certain. These images, which are still suggestive despite having lost their bearings, are behind the question of how the fact that we cannot transcend the linguistic horizon of justified beliefs is compatible with the intuition that true propositions fit the facts. It is no accident that the contemporary rationality debates circle around the concepts of truth and reference.[9] Just as skepticism does not simply assimilate being to appearance but rather gives expression to the uneasy feeling that we *might* be unable to separate the one from the other convincingly, neither does contextualism, properly understood, equate truth with justified assertibility. Contextualism is rather an expression of the embarrassment that would ensue if we did have to assimilate the one to the other. It makes us aware of a problem to which cultural relativism presents a solution that is false because it contains a performative self-contradiction.

Truth and Justification

Even in the comprehension of elementary propositions about states or events in the world, language and reality interpenetrate in a manner that for us is *indissoluble*. There is no natural possibility of isolating the constraints of reality that make a statement true from the semantic rules that lay down these truth conditions. We can explain what a fact is only with the help of the truth of a statement of fact, and we can explain what is real only in terms of what is true. Being, as Tugendhat says, is veritative being.[10] Since the truth of beliefs or sentences can in turn be justified only with the help of other beliefs and sentences, we cannot break free from the magic circle of our language. This fact suggests an anti-foundationalist conception of knowledge and a holistic conception of justification. Because we cannot confront our sentences with anything that is not itself already saturated linguistically, no basic propositions can be distinguished that would be privileged in being able to legitimate themselves, thereby serving as the basis for a linear chain of justification. Rorty rightly emphasizes "that nothing counts as justification unless by reference to what we already accept," concluding from this "that there is no way to get outside our beliefs and our language so as to find some test other than coherence."[11]

This does not mean, of course, that the coherence of our beliefs is sufficient to clarify the meaning of the concept of truth – which has now become central. Certainly, within the linguistic paradigm, the truth of a proposition can no longer be conceived as correspondence with something in the world, for otherwise we would have to be able to "get outside of language" while using language. Obviously, we cannot compare linguistic expressions with a piece of uninterpreted or "naked" reality – that is, with a reference that eludes our linguistically bound inspection.[12] None the less, the correspondence idea of truth was able to take account of a fundamental aspect of the meaning of the truth predicate. This aspect – the notion of unconditional validity – is swept under the carpet if the truth of a proposition is conceived as coherence with other propositions or as justified assertibility within an interconnected system of assertions. Whereas well-justified assertions can turn out to be false, we understand truth as a property of propositions "that cannot be lost." Coherence depends on practices of justification that let themselves be guided by standards that change from time to time. This accounts for the question: "Why does the fact that our beliefs hang together, supposing they do, give the least indication that they are true?"[13]

The "cautionary" use of the truth predicates[14] shows that, with the truth of propositions, we connect an unconditional claim that points beyond all the evidence available to us; on the other hand, the evidence that we bring to bear in our contexts of justification has to be sufficient to entitle us to raise truth claims. Although truth cannot be reduced to coherence and justified assertibility, there has to be an internal relation between truth and justification. How, otherwise, would it be possible to explain that a justification of "*p*," successful according to our standards, points in favor of the truth of "*p*," although truth is not an achievement term and does not depend on how well a proposition can be justified. Michael Williams describes the problem as a dispute between two equally reasonable ideas: "First, that if we are to have knowledge of an objective world, the truth of what we believe about the world must be independent of our believing it; and second, that justification is inevitably a matter of supporting beliefs by other beliefs, hence in this minimal sense a matter of coherence."[15] This leads to the contextualist question: "Given only knowledge of what we believe about the world, and how our beliefs fit together, how can we show that these beliefs are likely to be true?"[16]

This question should not, however, be understood in a skeptical sense, for the conception according to which we, as socialized individuals, always already find ourselves within the linguistically disclosed horizon of our lifeworld implies an unquestioned background of intersubjectively shared convictions, proven true in practice, which makes nonsense of total doubt as to the accessibility of the world. Language, which we cannot "get outside of" should not be understood in analogy to the inwardness of a representing subject who is as if cut off from the external world of representable objects. The relationship between justifiability and truth, although in need of clarification, signals no gulf between inner and outer, no dualism that would have to be *bridged* and that could give rise to the skeptical doubt as to whether our world *as a whole* is an illusion. The pragmatic turn pulls the rug from under this skepticism. There is a simple reason for this. In everyday practices, we cannot use language without *acting*. Speech itself is effected in the mode of speech acts that for their part are embedded in contexts of interaction and entwined with instrumental actions. As actors, that is, as interacting and intervening subjects, we are always already in contact with things about which we can make statements. Language games and practices are *interwoven*, "At some point . . . we have to leave the realm of sentences (and texts) and draw open agreement in action and experience (for instance, in using a predicate)."[17] From the point of view of the philosophy of language, Husserl's phenomenological conclusion that we "are always already in contact with things" is confirmed.

For this reason, the question as to the internal connection between justification and truth – a connection that explains why we may, in light of the evidence available to us, raise an unconditional truth claim that aims beyond what is justified – is not an epistemological question. It is not a matter of being or appearance. What is at stake is not the correct representation of reality but everyday practices that must not fall apart. The contextualist unease betrays a worry about the smooth functioning of language games and practices. Reaching understanding cannot function unless the participants refer to a single objective world, thereby stabilizing the intersubjectively shared public space with which everything that is merely subjective can be contrasted.[18] This supposition of an objective world that is independent of our descriptions fulfills a functional requirement of our processes of cooperation and communication. Without this supposition, everyday practices, which rest on the (in a certain sense) Platonic distinction between believing and knowing unreservedly, would come apart at the seams.[19] If it were to turn out that we cannot in any way make *this* distinction, the result would he more of a pathological self-misunderstanding than an illusionary understanding of the world. Whereas skepticism suspects an epistemological mistake, contextualism supposes a faulty construction in the way we live.

Contextualism thus raises the question of whether and, as the case may be, how the intuition that we can in principle distinguish between what-is-true and what-is-held-to-be-true can be brought into the linguistic paradigm. This intuition is not "realist" in an epistemological sense. Even within pragmatism there is a parting of ways with regard to this question. Some are pragmatist enough to take seriously realist everyday intuitions and the internal relation between coherence and truth to which they attest. Others regard the attempt to clarify this internal relation as hopeless, treating everyday realism as an illusion. Rorty wants to combat this illusion by rhetorical means and pleads for *reeducation*. We ought to get used to replacing the desire for objectivity with the desire for solidarity and, with William James, to understanding "truth" as no more than that in which it is good for "us" — the liberal members of Western culture or Western societies — to believe.

> [Pragmatists) should see themselves as working at the interface between the common sense of their community, a common sense much influenced by Greek metaphysics and by patriarchal monotheism . . . They should see themselves as involved in a long-term attempt to change the rhetoric, the common sense, and self-image of their community.[20]

Before I deal with this proposal, I would like to examine whether the alternatives are as hopeless as Rorty assumes. Are there not plausible explanations for the fact that a justification successful in our justificatory context points in favor of the context-independent truth of the justified proposition? I am interested above all in two attempts at explanation: a deflationary one, which disputes that "truth" has any nature at all that could be explicated; and epistemic one, which inflates the idea of a justified assertion to such an extent that truth becomes the limit concept of the justificatory process. Of course, deflationism is permitted to de-thematize the concept of truth only to the extent that this concept can continue to sustain realist intuitions, while the epistemic conception is allowed to idealize the justificatory conditions only to the extent that its idea of argumentation removed from everyday practices remains within the reach of "our" practices.[21]

The Semantic Conception of Truth and the Pragmatic Perspective

Tarski's Convention T — "'*p*' is true if and only if *p*" — relies on a disquotational use of the truth-predicate that can be illustrated, for instance, by the example of confirming another person's statements: "Everything that the witness said yesterday is true." With this, the speaker makes his own "everything that was said," in such a way that he could repeat the corresponding assertions in the stance of the first person. This use of the truth-predicate is noteworthy in two respects. For one thing, it permits a generalizing reference to subject matter that is mentioned but not explicitly reproduced. Tarski uses this property in order to construct a theory of truth that generalizes about all instances of "T." For another, the truth-predicate when used in this way establishes a relation of equivalence between two linguistic expressions — the whole point of the Tarskian strategy of explanation depends on this. For, through exploiting the disquotational function, the inaccessible "relation of correspondence" between language and world or sentence and fact can, it appears, be reflected onto the tangible semantic relation between the expressions of an object language and those of a metalanguage. No matter how one conceives of the representational function of statements, whether as "satisfaction" of truth conditions or as "fitting" the facts to the sentences, what is envisaged in every case are pictures of relations that extend beyond language. It now seems possible to clarify these pictures with the help of interrelations that are *internal to language*. This initial idea allows us to understand why weak realist connotations are connected with the semantic conception of truth even if it is clear that this conception cannot sustain a strong epistemological realism in the manner of Popper.[22]

Now, it was already noticed at an early stage that the semantic conception of truth cannot vindicate its claim to be an explication of the full meaning of the truth-predicate.[23] The reason for this is that the disquotational function is not sufficiently informative because it already presupposes the representational function. One understands the meaning of Convention T when one knows what is *meant* (*gemeint*) with the right-hand side of the biconditional. The meaning of the truth-predicate in the sentence "Everything that the witness said yesterday is true" is parasitic on the assertoric mode of the witness's assertions. Before an assertion can be quoted it must be "put forward." This presupposed assertoric meaning can he analyzed in an exemplary way by looking at the "yes" and "no" positions of participants in argumentation who raise or refute objections; it can also be seen in the "cautionary" use of the truth-predicate, which recalls the experience of participants in argumentation that even propositions that have been justified convincingly can turn out to be false.

The truth-predicate belongs – though not exclusively – to the language game of argumentation. For this reason its meaning can be elucidated (at least partly) according to its functions in this language game, that is, in the *pragmatic dimension* of a particular employment of the predicate. Whoever confines herself to the semantic dimension of sentences and of metalinguistic commentaries on sentences comprehends only the reflection of a prior linguistic practice that, as remains to be shown, extends even into everyday practices. However, the deflationary treatment of the concept of truth, through its semantic dimming of the pragmatic meaning of truth, has the advantage of avoiding discussions about the "nature" of truth without having to forfeit a minimal orientation toward the distinction between knowing and believing, between being-true and being-held-to-be-true. This strategy aims at uncoupling these elementary distinctions from the dispute about substantial epistemological views. If it can be shown that the semantic conception of truth is sufficient to explain the usual methods of inquiry and theory selection – that is, sufficient also to explain what counts as "success" or "growth in knowledge" in the scientific enterprise – we can rescue the weak realist supposition of a world independent of our descriptions without boosting up the concept of truth in an epistemological–realist way.[24]

On the other hand, science is not the only sphere – and not even the primary one – in which the truth-predicate has a use. Even if a deflationary concept of truth were sufficient for elucidating the fact of science, for rendering the functioning of our practices of inquiry transparent, this would still not dissipate the contextualist doubt. For this doubt extends not only to the construction and selection of theories, indeed, not only to practices of argumentation in general: with respect to the pretheoretical orientation toward truth inherent in everyday practices, a semantic conception of truth simply does not help us at all.

What is at issue in the lifeworld is the pragmatic role of a Janus-faced notion of truth that mediates between behavioral certainty and discursively justified assertibility. In the network of established practices, implicitly raised validity claims that have been accepted against a broad background of intersubjectively shared convictions constitute the rails along which behavioral certainties run. However, as soon as these certainties lose their hold in the corset of self-evident beliefs, they are jolted out of tranquility and transformed into a corresponding number of questionable topics that thereby become subject to debate. In moving from action to rational discourse,[25] what is initially naively held-to-be-true is released from the mode of behavioral certainty and assumes the form a hypothetical proposition whose validity is left open for the duration of the discourse. The argumentation takes the form of a competition for the better arguments in favor of, or against, controversial validity claims, and serves the cooperative search for truth.[26]

With this description of justificatory practices guided by the idea of truth, however, the problem is posed anew of how the systematic mobilization of good reasons, which at best lead to justified beliefs, is supposed nonetheless to be adequate for the purpose of discriminating between justified and unjustified truth claims. To begin with, I simply want to keep hold of the picture of a circular process that presents itself to us from a perspective expanded by means of the theory of action: shaken-up behavioral certainties are transformed on the level of argumentation into controversial validity claims raised for hypothetical propositions; these claims are tested discursively – and, as the case may be, vindicated – with the result that the discursively accepted truths can return to the realm of action; with this, behavioral certainties (as the case may be, new ones), which rely on beliefs unproblematically held to be true, are produced once more. What still remains to be explained is the mysterious power of the discursively achieved agreement that *authorizes* the participants in argumentation, in the role of actors, to accept unreservedly justified assertions as truths. For it is clear from the description from the point of view of action theory that argumentation can fulfill the role of *troubleshooter* with regard to behavioral certainties that have become problematic only if it is guided by truth in a context-independent – that is, unconditional – sense.

Although when we adopt a reflexive attitude we know that all knowledge is fallible, in everyday life we cannot survive with hypotheses alone, that is, in a persistently fallibilist way. The organized fallibilism of scientific inquiry can deal hypothetically with controversial validity claims indefinitely because it serves to bring about agreements that are *uncoupled* from action. This model is not suitable for the lifeworld. Certainly, we have to make decisions in the lifeworld on the basis of incomplete information; moreover, existential risks such as the loss of those closest to us, sickness, old age, and death are the mark of human life. However, notwithstanding these uncertainties, everyday routines rest on an unqualified trust in the *knowledge* of lay people as much as experts. We would step on no bridge, use no car, undergo no operation, not even eat an exquisitely prepared meal if we did not consider the knowledge used to be safeguarded, if we did not hold the assumptions employed in the production and execution of our actions to be true. At any rate, the performative need for behavioral certainty rules out a reservation in principle with regard to truth, even though we know, as soon as the naive performance of actions is interrupted, that truth claims can be vindicated only discursively – that is, only within the relevant context of justification. Truth may be assimilated neither to behavioral certainty nor to justified assertibility. Evidently, only strong conceptions of knowledge and truth – open to the accusation of Platonism – can do justice to the unity of the illocutionary meaning of assertions, which take on different roles in the realms of action and discourse respectively. Whereas in everyday practices "truths" prop up behavioral certainties, in discourses they provide the reference point for truth claims that are in principle fallible.

The Epistemic Conception of Truth in a Pragmatic Perspective

The stubborn problem of the relation between truth and justification makes understandable the attempt to distinguish "truth" from "rational acceptability" through an idealization of the conditions of justification. This attempt proposes that a proposition justified according to "our" standards is distinguished from a true proposition in the same way that a proposition justified in a given context is distinguished from a proposition that could be justified in any context. A proposition is "true" if it could be justified under ideal epistemic conditions (Putnam)[27] or could win argumentatively reached agreement in an ideal speech situation (Habermas)[28] or in an ideal communication community (Apel).[29] What is true is what may be accepted as rational under ideal conditions. Convincing objections have been raised to this proposal, which dates back to Peirce. The objections are directed in part against conceptual difficulties with the ideal state adopted; in part they show that an idealization of justificatory conditions cannot achieve its goal because it either distances truth too far from justified assertibility or not far enough.

The first kind of objection draws attention to the paradoxical nature of the notion of "complete" or "conclusive" knowledge fixed as a limit concept – that, when its incompleteness and fallibility is taken away from it, would no longer be (human) knowledge.[30] Paradoxical, too, is the idea of a final consensus or definitive language that would bring to a standstill all further communication or all further interpretation, "with the result that what is *meant* as a situation of ideal mutual understanding stands revealed as a situation beyond the necessity for (and the problems connected with) linguistic processes of reaching understanding."[31] This objection is directed not just against an idealization that hypostatizes final states *as attainable* states in the world. Even if the ideal reference points are understood as aims that are not attainable in principle, or attainable only approximately, it remains "paradoxical that we would be obliged to strive for the realization of an ideal whose realization would be the end of human history."[32] As a regulative idea, the critical point of the orientation toward truth becomes clear only when the formal or processual properties of argumentation, and *not its aims*, are idealized.

The second kind of objection leads to the same conclusion. These objections are directed not against the incoherent results of the idealization of the targeted states but against the operation of idealization itself. No matter how the value of the epistemic conditions is enhanced through idealizations, either they satisfy the unconditional character of truth claims by means of requirements that cut off all connection with the practices of justification familiar to us, or else they retain the connection to practices familiar to us by paying the price that rational acceptability does not exclude the possibility of error even under these ideal conditions, that is, does not simulate a property "that cannot be lost": "It would he apparent either that those conditions allow the possibility of error or that they are so ideal as to make no use of the intended connection with human abilities."[33]

In his debates with Putnam, Apel, and me, Rorty makes use of these objections not in order to discredit the epistemization of truth but in order to radicalize it. With his opponents he shares the view that the standards for the rational acceptability of propositions, although they change historically, do not always do so arbitrarily. At least from the perspective of the participants, rationality standards are open to critique and can be "reformed," that is, improved on the basis of good reasons. Unlike Putnam, however, Rorty does not want to take account of the fact of learning processes by conceding that justificatory practices are guided by an idea of truth that transcends the justificatory context in question. He completely rejects idealizing limit concepts and interprets the difference between justification and truth in such a way that a proponent is prepared in principle to defend her views not only here and now but even in front of another audience. Whoever is oriented toward truth in this sense is willing "to justify his convictions in front of a competent audience" or "to increase the size or diversity of the conversational community."[34] On Rorty's view, every idealization that goes beyond this will founder on the problem that in idealizing we must always take something familiar as our point of departure; usually it is "us," that is, the communication community as we are familiar with it: "I cannot see what 'idealized rational acceptability' can mean except 'acceptability to an ideal community.' Nor can I see, given that no such community is going to have a God's eye view, that this ideal community can be anything more than us as we should like to be. Nor can I see what 'us' can mean here except: us educated, sophisticated, tolerant, wet liberals, the people who are always willing to hear the other side, to think out all their implications, etc."[35]

Of course, it can be objected to this that an idealization of the justificatory conditions does not in any way have to take the "thick" characteristics of one's own culture as its point of departure; rather, it can start with the formal and processual characteristics of justificatory practices in general that, after all, are to be found in all cultures – even if not by any means always in institutionalized form. The fact that the practice of argumentation compels the participants themselves to make pragmatic assumptions with a counterfactual fits in well with this. Whoever enters into discussion with the serious intention of becoming convinced of something through dialogue with others has to presume performatively that the participants allow their "yes" or "no" to be determined solely by the force of the better argument. However, with this they assume – normally in a counterfactual way – a speech situation that satisfies improbable conditions: openness to the public, inclusiveness, equal rights to participation, immunization against external or inherent compulsion, as well as the participants' orientation toward reaching understanding (that is, the sincere expression of utterances).[36] In these unavoidable presuppositions of argumentation, the intuition is expressed that true propositions are resistant to spatially, socially, and temporally unconstrained attempts to refute them. What we hold to be true has to be defendable on the basis of good reasons, not merely in a different context but in all possible contexts, that is, at any time and against anybody. This provides the inspiration for the discourse theory of truth: a proposition is true if it withstands all attempts to refute it under the demanding conditions of rational discourse.[37]

However, this does not mean that it is also true *for this reason*. A truth claim raised for "p" says that the truth conditions for "p" are satisfied. We have no other way of ascertaining whether or not this is the case expect by way of argumentation, for direct access to uninterpreted truth conditions is denied to us. But the fact that the truth conditions are satisfied does not itself become an epistemic fact just because we can only *establish* whether these conditions are satisfied by way of discursive vindication of truth claim – whereby we have already had to interpret the truth conditions in light of the relevant sorts of reasons for the claim in question.

A consistently epistemic reading of the discourse-theoretical explanation of truth already founders on the problem that not all of the processual properties mentioned retain a "connection with human abilities." Nonetheless, with regard to the argumentative presuppositions of general inclusiveness, equal rights to participation, freedom from repression, and orientation toward reaching understanding, we can imagine in *the present* what an approximately ideal satisfaction would look like. This does not hold for anticipation of the future, of future corroboration (*Bewährung*). To be sure, the orientation toward the future, too, *essentially* has the critical point of reminding us of the ethnocentric limitation and the fallibility of every actually achieved agreement, no matter how rationally motivated; that is, it serves as a reminder to us of the possible further decentering of the perspective of our justification community. Time, however, is a constraint of an ontological kind. Because all real discourses, conducted in actual time, are limited with regard to the future, we cannot know whether propositions that are rationally acceptable today will, even under approximately ideal conditions, assert themselves against attempts to refute them in the future as well. On the other hand, this very limitedness condemns our finite minds to be content with rational acceptability as *sufficient proof* of truth: "Whenever we raise truth claims on the basis of good arguments and convincing evidence we *presume* . . . that no new arguments or evidence will crop up in the future that would call our truth claim into question."[38]

It is not so difficult to understand why participants in argumentation, as subjects capable of speech and action, have to behave in this way if we look at a pragmatic description of their discourses, which are embedded in the lifeworld. In everyday practices, as we have seen, socialized individuals are dependent on behavioral certainties, which remain certainties only so long as they are sustained by a knowledge that is accepted unreservedly. Corresponding to this is the grammatical fact that, when we put forward the assertion "p" in a performative attitude, we have to believe that "p" is true unconditionally even though, when we adopt a reflexive attitude, we cannot rule out that tomorrow, or somewhere else, reasons and evidence could emerge that could invalidate "p." However, this does not yet explain why we are *permitted* to regard a truth claim explicitly raised for "p" as vindicated as soon as the proposition is rationally accepted under conditions of rational discourse. What does it mean to say that truth claims can be "vindicated" discursively?

The Pragmatic Conception of Truth

It is still unclear what it is that *authorizes* us to regard as true a proposition that is presumed to be justified ideally – within the limits of finite minds. Wellmer speaks in this regard of a "surplus" residing in the "anticipation of future corroboration." Perhaps it would be better to say that participants in argumentation who convince themselves of the justification of a controversial validity claim have reached a point where they have been brought by the unconstrained force of the better argument to a certain *shift in perspective*. When, in the course of a process of argumentation, participants attain the conviction that, having taken on board all relevant information and having weighed up all the relevant reasons, they have exhausted the reservoir of potential possible objections to "*p*," then all motives for continuing argumentation have been, as it were, used up. At any rate there is no longer any rational motivation for retaining a hypothetical attitude toward the truth claim raised for "*p*" but temporarily left open. From the perspective of actors who have temporarily adopted a reflexive attitude in order to restore a partially disturbed background understanding, the de-problematization of the disputed truth claim means that a license is issued for return to the attitude of actors who are involved in dealing with the world more naively. As soon as the differences in opinion are resolved between "us" and "others" with regard to what is the case, "our" world can merge once more with "the" world.

When this shift takes place we, who as participants in argumentation accept the truth claim for "*p*" as justified, reappoint the state of affairs "that *p*" – problematized up to now – with its rights as an assertion M*p* that can be raised from the perspective of the first person. An assertion that has been *disposed of* argumentatively in this way and returned to the realm of action takes its place in an intersubjectively shared lifeworld from within whose horizon we, the actors, refer to something in a single objective world. It is a matter here of a *formal* supposition, not one that prejudges specific content nor one that suggests the goal of the "correct picture of the nature of things" that Rorty always connects with a realist intuition. Because acting subjects have to cope with "the" world, they cannot avoid being realists in the context of their lifeworld. Moreover, they are allowed to be realists because their language games and practices, so long as they function in a way that is proof against disappointment, "prove their truth" (*sich bewähren*) in being carried on.

This pragmatic authority responsible for certainty – interpreted in a realist way with the help of the supposition of an objective world – is suspended on the reflexive level of discourses, which are relieved of the burdens of action and where only arguments count. Here, our gaze turns away from the objective world, and the disappointments we experience in our direct dealings with it, to focus exclusively on our conflicting interpretations of the world. In this intersubjective dimension of contested interpretations, an assertion "proves its truth" solely on the basis of reasons, that is, with reference to the authority responsible for possible refutation, not for practically experienced disappointment. Here, however, the fallibilist consciousness that we can err even in the case of well-justified beliefs depends on an orientation toward truth whose roots extend into the realism of everyday practices – a realism no longer in force within discourse. The orientation toward unconditional truth, which compels participants in argumentation to presuppose ideal justificatory conditions and requires of them an ever-increasing decentering of the justification community, is a reflex of that other difference – required in the lifeworld – between believing and knowing; this distinction relies on the supposition, anchored in the communicative use of language, of a single objective world.[39] In this way, the lifeworld with its strong, action-related conceptions of truth and knowledge projects into discourse and provides the reference point – transcending justification – that keeps alive among participants in argumentation a consciousness of the fallibility of their interpretations. Conversely, this fallibilist consciousness also reacts back upon everyday practices without thereby destroying the dogmatism of the lifeworld. For actors, who as participants in argumentation have learned that no conviction is proof against criticism, develop in the lifeworld, too, rather less dogmatic attitudes toward their problematized convictions.

This stereoscopic perception of processes of cooperation and communication, layered according to action-contexts and discourses, allows us recognize the *embeddedness* of discourses it the lifeworld. Convictions play a different role in action than in discourse and "prove their truth" in a different way in the former than in the latter. In everyday practices, a prereflexive "coping with the world" decides whether convictions "function" or are drawn into the maelstrom of problematization, whereas in argumentation it depends solely on reasons whether controversial validity claims deserve rationally motivated recognition. It is true that the question of the internal relation between justification and truth poses itself only on the reflexive level; however, only the interaction between actions and discourses permits an answer to this question. The contextualist doubt cannot be dissipated so long as we persist in remaining on the level of argumentation and neglect the transformation – secured by personal union, as it were – of the knowledge of those who act into the knowledge of those who argue, while equally neglecting the transfer of knowledge in the opposite direction. Only the entwining of the two different pragmatic roles played by the Janus-faced concept of truth in action-contexts and in rational discourses respectively can explain why a justification successful in a local context points in favor of the context-independent truth of the justified belief. Just as, on the one hand, the concept of truth allows translation of shaken-up behavioral certainties into problematized propositions, so too, on the other hand, does the firmly retained orientation toward truth permit the *translation back* of discursively justified assertions into reestablished behavioral certainties.

To explain this we have only to bring together in the right way the partial statements assembled here up to now. In the lifeworld actors depend on behavioral certainties. They have to cope with a world presumed to be objective and, for this reason, operate with the distinction between believing and knowing.[40] There is a *practical* necessity to rely intuitively on what is unconditionally held-to-be-true. This mode of unconditionally holding-to-be-true is reflected on the discursive level in the connotations of truth claims that point beyond the given context of justification and require the supposition of ideal justificatory conditions – with a resulting decentering of the justification community. For this reason, the process of justification can be guided by a notion of truth that *transcends justification* although it is *always already operatively effect-*

ive in the realm of action. The function of the validity of statements in everyday practices explains why the discursive vindication of validity claims may at the same time be interpreted as the satisfaction of a pragmatic need for justification. This need for justification, which sets in train the transformation of shaken-up behavioral certainties into problematized validity claims, can be satisfied only by a translation of discursively justified beliefs back into behavioral truths.

Because it is, in the end, this interaction that dissipates the contextualist doubt about everyday realist intuitions, an objection seems likely that the whole dispute is prejudiced by my tendentious description of the embedding of discourses in the lifeworld. Rorty would certainly not deny the connection between rational discourse and action. He would also agree with our establishing a connection between the two perspectives: between the perspective of the participants in argumentation who seek to convince each other of the correctness of their interpretations, and the perspective of acting subjects involved in their language games and practices. However, Rorty would not distinguish these perspectives from each other in such a way that the one is relativized against the other. For the purpose of his description, he borrows from the perspective of participants in argumentation the imprisonment in dialogue that prevents us from breaking free from contexts of justification; at the same time, he borrows from the perspective of actors the mode of coping with the world. It is through the *blending into one another* of these opposing perspectives that the ethnocentric certainty is formed – a certainty that prompts Rorty to ask the question of why we should in the first place attempt to bring the contextualist knowledge obtained through reflexive experiences in argumentation into harmony with the everyday realism ascribed to the lifeworld. If the actors in the lifeworld – temporarily – cannot avoid being "realists," so much the worse for them. In that ease it is up to the philosophers to reform the misleading commonsense conception of truth.

To be sure, deflationism, operating along the lines of Michael Williams with a semantic conception of truth, is still too strong for this purpose. Instead, Rorty rigorously carries through to its conclusion an epistemization of the concept of truth. Because there is nothing apart from justification, and because nothing follows for the truth of a proposition from its justified assertibility, the concept of truth is superfluous. "The difference between justification and truth is one which makes no difference except for the reminder that justification to one audience is not justification to another."[41] Even the only nonredundant use of the truth-predicate – the "cautionary" one – requires reinterpretation. It is a matter of inventing and implementing a new vocabulary that does without a concept of truth and eliminates realist intuitions (such as the supposition of an objective world, talk of representing facts, and so forth): "We simply refuse to talk in a certain way, the Platonic way . . . Our efforts at persuasion must take the form of gradual inculcation of new ways of speaking, rather than of straightforward argumentation with old ways of speaking."[42]

The Naturalization of Linguistified Reason

Rorty's program of reeducation has provoked questions and objections.[43] In the first instance, Rorty himself must shoulder the burden of proof for his unwillingness to leave the language of common sense as it is. As a rule, pragmatists make substantial allowances for themselves on the basis that their views are at one with common sense. Strangely enough, neopragmatists boast of their role as "atheists in an overwhelmingly religious culture." Their therapy is supposed to reach through the pathological language games of philosophers to the distortions for which Platonism is responsible in daily life itself. In order to make plausible Platonism's idealist violence, Rorty has to let himself in for a diagnosis of the history of Western metaphysics as a history of decline. However, what Heidegger or Derrida, for example, have to say in their own fairly metaphysical ways about the critique of metaphysics is, on Rorty's estimation, more part of the "edifying" literature that is supposed to be reserved for private perfection of the self and cannot, at any rate, serve the public critique of alienated living conditions.[44]

Of course, more important than the motivation for this enterprise is the question of its viability. I would like to conclude with just two questions in this regard:

(a)　Is the envisaged revision of our self-understanding compatible with the fact of an ability to learn that is not already constricted *a priori*?

(b)　What is to happen to the normative character of reason, and how counterintuitive is the proposed neo-Darwinist self-description of rational beings?

(a)　The program of a rational revision of deeply rooted Platonic prejudices presumes we are capable of a learning process that not only can take place within a given vocabulary and according to the standards prevailing in a given context but that seizes hold of the vocabulary and standards themselves. This reason alone requires Rorty to provide a suitable equivalent for an orientation toward truth that aims beyond the prevailing context of justification. If, however, the distinction between "true" and "justified" shrinks to the fact that the proponent is prepared to defend "*p*" even in front of a *different* audience, the reference point for such an anticipation [of truth] is missing. Rorty counters this objection by conceding a cautious idealization of justificatory conditions. He allows that what traditionally was called the "pursuit of truth" might just as well be described as the "pursuit of intersubjective, unforced agreement among larger and larger groups of interlocutors": "We hope to justify our belief to as many and as large audiences as possible."[45] Rorty, it is true, does not want this to be understood as an orientation toward an "ever-retreating goal," that is, as a regulative idea. Even the larger audience and the overarching context are supposed to be no more than a different audience and a different context. Nonetheless, Rorty adds to this description the qualifications mentioned: ever-expanding size and ever-increasing diversity – that is, conditions that hamper the possible success of argumentation in certain, not completely arbitrary, ways.

Rorty cannot explain this impediment to the success of argumentation that is unnecessary from a functional point of view. With the orientation toward "more and more," "larger and larger," and "increasingly diverse" audiences, Rorty brings a weak idealization into play that, on his premise, is far from self-evident. As soon as the concept of truth is eliminated in favor of a context-dependent epistemic validity-for-us, the normative reference point necessary to explain why a proponent should endeavor to seek agreement for "*p*" *beyond the boundaries of her own group* is missing. The information that the agreement of an increasingly large audience gives us increasingly less reason to fear that we will be refuted presupposes the very interest that has to be explained: the desire for "as much intersubjective agreement as possible." If something is "true" if and only if it is recognized as justified "by us" because it is good "for us," there is no rational motive for expanding the circle of members. No reason exists for the decentering expansion of the justification community especially since Rorty defines "my own ethnos" as the group in front of which I feel obliged to give an account of myself. There is, however, no normative justification for any further orientation toward the agreement of "strangers," merely an explanatory pointer toward the arbitrary features of a "liberal Western culture" in which "we intellectuals" adopt a more or less undogmatic attitude. But even we are assured by Rorty that, "we must, in practice, privilege our own group, even though there can be no noncircular justification for doing so."[46]

(b)   In losing the regulative idea of truth, the practice of justification loses that point of orientation by means of which standards of justification are distinguished from "customary" norms. The sociologizing of the practice of justification means a naturalization of reason. As a rule, social norms can be described not merely from the point of view of a sociological observer but also from the perspective of participants in light of the standards they hold to be true. Without a reference to truth or reason, however, the standards themselves would no longer have any possibility of self-correction and would thus for their part forfeit the status of norms capable of being justified. In this respect, they would no longer even be customary norms. They would be *nothing more than* social facts, although they would continue to claim validity "for us," the relevant justification community. If, despite this, the practice of justification is not to collapse, and if the predicate "rational" is not to lose its normative character — that is, if both are to continue to be able to function — the rationality standards valid for us have to be, if not justified, then at least explained.

For this Rorty falls back on a naturalist description of human beings as organisms that develop tools in order to adapt themselves optimally to their environment with the aim of satisfying their needs. Language, too, is such a tool — and not, for instance, a medium for representing reality: "No matter whether the tool is a hammer or a gun or a belief or a statement, tool-using is part of the interaction of the organism with its environment."[47] What appears to us as the normative dimension of the linguistically constituted human mind merely gives expression to the fact that intelligent operations are functional for the preservation of a species that, through acting, must "cope" with reality. This neo-Darwinist self-description demands an ironic price. For Rorty, in replacing the "correct description of facts" with "successful adaptation to the environment," merely exchanges one kind of objectivism for another: the objectivism of "represented" reality for the objectivism of instrumentally "mastered" reality. Although admittedly, with this, the direction of fit for interaction between human beings and world is changed, what remains the same is the reference point of an objective world as the totality of everything that we can, in the one case, "represent," in the other, "deal with."

The pragmatic turn was supposed to replace the representationalist model of knowledge with a communication model that sets successful intersubjective mutual understanding (*Verständigung*) in the place of a chimerical objectivity of experience. It is, however, precisely this intersubjective dimension that is in turn closed off in an objectivating description of processes of cooperation and communication that can be grasped as such only from the perspective of participants. Rorty uses a jargon that no longer permits any differentiation between the perspectives of the participant and the observer. Interpersonal relationships, which are owed to the intersubjective possession of a shared language, are assimilated to the pattern of adaptive behavior (or instrumental action). A corresponding de-differentiation between the strategic and the non-strategic use of language, between action oriented toward success and action oriented toward reaching understanding, robs Rorty of the conceptual means for doing justice to the intuitive distinctions between convincing and persuading, between motivation through reasons and causal exertion of influence, between learning and indoctrination. The counterintuitive mingling of the one with the other has the unpleasant consequence that we lose the critical standards operating in everyday life. Rorty's naturalist strategy leads to a categorial leveling of distinctions of such a kind that our descriptions lose their sensitivity for differences that do make a difference in everyday practices.[48]

Notes

1   Cf. H. Schnädelbach, "Philosophie," in E. Martens and H. Schnädelbach, eds. *Grundkurs Philosophie* (Hamburg, 1985), pp. 37–76.
2   R. Rorty, *Philosophy and the Mirror of Nature* (Princeton, NJ, 1979), p. 263.
3   Ibid., p. 339.
4   Ibid., p. 338.
5   R. Rorty, *Philosophical Papers I: Objectivity, Relativism, and Truth* (Cambridge, 1991), p. 23.
6   Only the empiricists were prepared to call "objective" the experience (*Erfahrung*) that "corresponds to what is there outside" (Rorty). The transcendental idealists, by contrast, reduce even the objectivity of experience to necessary subjective conditions of possible experience.
7   L. Wittgenstein, *On Certainty*, trans. D. Paul and G. E. M. Anscombe (Oxford, 1969), §115, p. 125.
8   H. Schnädelbach, "Thesen über Geltung und Wahrheit," in *Zur Rehabilitierung des animal rationale* (Frankfurt, 1992), pp. 104–15.
9   With respect to a critique of Rorty's approach, I will confine myself in the following to the problem of truth. However, I would like to indicate, at least, that we would not be able to explain the possibility of learning processes without reference to the capacity for recognizing the same entities under different descriptions.
10 E. Tugendhat, *Traditional and Analytical Philosophy*, trans. P. A. Gorner (Cambridge, 1982), pp. 50ff.
11 R. Rorty, *Philosophy and the Mirror of Nature*, p. 178.

12   Cf. M. Williams, *Unnatural Doubts* (Princeton, NJ, 1966), p. 232: "We need only ask whether or not the 'direct' grasping of facts on which such comparison depends is supposed to be a cognitive state with propositional content. If it isn't, it can have no impact on verification. But if it is, what we have been given is another kind of belief."

13   Ibid., p. 267.

14   R. Rorty, "Pragmatism, Davidson, and Truth," in E. Lepore, ed., *Truth and Interpretation* (Oxford, 1986), p. 343.

15   Williams, *Unnatural Doubts*, p. 266.

16   Ibid., p. 249.

17   F. Kambartel, "Universalität richtig verstanden," *Deutsche Zeitschrift für Philosophie* 44 (1996): 249.

18   It is no accident that I introduced the formal-pragmatic concept of the grammatical supposition of an objective world in the context of the theory of action. Cf. J. Habermas, *The Theory of Communicative Action*, trans. T. McCarthy, vol. 1 (Boston, 1984), pp. 75–101; vol. 2 (Boston, 1987), pp. 119ff.

19   Cf. Williams, *Unnatural Doubts*, p. 238: "All that is involved in the idea of an objective world as 'what is there anyway' is that an objective proposition's being true is one thing and our believing it to be true, or being justified in believing it to be true, something else again."

20   R. Rorty, "Is Truth a Goal of Inquiry? Davidson vs. Wright," *Philosophical Quarterly* 45 (1995): 281–300 (here, p. 300).

21   D. Davidson pursues a third strategy that could be called "theoreticist" or, as he himself proposes, "methodological"; cf. D. Davidson, "The Folly of Trying to Define Truth," *Journal of Philosophy* 93 (1996): 263–78. Davidson uses the semantic conception of truth, understood in a nondeflationary way, as the undefined basic concept for an empirical theory of language. Both the concept of truth, which is used as a theoretical term in his theory of language, and the theory itself, which is supposed to explain the comprehension of linguistic expressions, can prove their truth (*sich bewähren*) at one and the same time. For this reason, Davidson's implicit "theory of truth" can be discussed only in connection with his theory as a whole. In general, I see the following difficulty: on the one hand, Davidson disputes that the concept of truth has a content capable of being explicated, to this extent allying himself with the deflationist polemic against attempts to explain the meaning of truth; on the other hand, he has to secure for the truth-predicate, over and above its disquotational function, a certain content as far as the theory of rationality is concerned in order to explain the veridical nature of beliefs. To this extent he joins forces with Putnam and Dummett, who insist that Tarski's Convention T says nothing about the actual meaning of truth. Standing between these two positions, Davidson, instead of merely using the concept, sees himself compelled to write learned treatises on a concept he declares to be "indefinable" – treatises in which he does, at least, in a metacritical way, isolate the realist intuitions bound up with truth. Cf. D. Davidson, "The Structure and Content of Truth," *Journal of Philosophy* 87 (1990): 279–328. Davidson holds onto the idea that we can know something of an objective world "which is not of our own making." This view separates him from Rorty who attempts in vain to pull Davidson over to his own side of an abolitionist understanding of truth. Cf. D. Davidson, "A Coherence Theory of Truth and Knowledge," in A. Malachowski, ed., *Reading Rorty* (Oxford, 1990), pp. 120–39; cf. also Rorty, "Pragmatism, Davidson, and Truth." For a comparison of Davidson's and my own approaches to the theory of language, see B. Fultner, *Radical Interpretation or Communicative Action* (PhD dissertation, Northwestern University, 1995).

22   K. R. Popper, "Truth, Rationality and the Growth of Scientific Knowledge," in *Conjectures and Refutations* (London, 1963), pp. 215–50.

23 E. Tugendhat, "Tarskis semantische Definition der Wahrheit," *Philosophische Rundschau* 8 (1960): 131–59, reprinted in his *Philosophische Aufsätze* (Frankfurt, 1992), pp. 179–213.

24 I refer here to positions held by P. Horwich and A. Fine; cf. M. Williams, "Do We (Epistemologists) Need to Theory of Truth?," *Philosophical Topics* 14 (1986): 223–42.

25 I introduced this distinction in the Christian Gauss Lectures on founding sociology in the theory of language (1971); cf. J. Habermas, *Vorstudien und Ergänzungen zur Theorie des kommunikativen Handelns* (Frankfurt, 1984), pp. 1–126, especially pp. 104ff.

26 Habermas, *Theory of Communicative Action*, vol. 1, pp. 22–42.

27 H. Putnam, "Introduction," in *Realism and Reason* (Cambridge, 1983).

28 J. Habermas, "Wahrheitstheorie," in Habermas, *Vorstudien und Ergänzungen zur Theorie des kommunikativen Handelns*.

29 K. O. Apel, "Fallibilismus, Konsenstheorie der Wahrheit und Letzbegründung," in Forum für Philosophie, ed., *Philosophie und Begründung* (Frankfurt, 1987), pp. 116–211.

30 C. Lafont, "Spannungen im Wahrheitsbegriff," *Deutsche Zeitschrift für Philosophie* 42 (1994): 1007–23; Williams, *Unnatural Doubts*, pp. 233ff.

31 A. Wellmer, "Ethics and Dialogue," in *The Persistence of Modernity*, trans. D. Midgley (Cambridge, MA, 1991), p. 175 (amended translation).

32 A. Wellmer, "Wahrheit, Kontingenz, Moderne," in *Endspiele* (Frankfurt, 1993), p. 162. English translation as *Endgames: Essays and Lectures on the Irreconcilable, Nature of Modernity* (Cambridge, MA, 1998).

33 Davidson, "The Structure and Content of Truth," p. 307.

34 R. Rorty, "Sind Aussagen universelle Geltungsansprüche?," *Deutsche Zeitschrift für Philosophie* 6 (1994): 982f.

35 R. Rorty, "Putnam and the Relativist Menace," *Journal of Philosophy* 90 (1993): 451f.

36 J. Habermas, "Remarks on Discourse Ethics," in *Justification and Application*, trans. C. Cronin (Cambridge, MA, 1993), pp. 30ff., pp. 58f.

37 L. Wingert, *Gemeinsinn und Moral* (Frankfurt, 1993), p. 277.

38 A. Wellmer, "Wahrheit," p. 163; cf. the corresponding reflections on "superassertibility" in C. Wright, *Truth and Objectivity* (Cambridge, MA, 1992).

39 Cf. Lafont, "Spannungen im Wahrheitsbegriff," p. 1021: "Only the presupposition of a single objective world . . . permits [us] to make the unconditional validity of truth compatible with a fallible understanding of knowledge."

40 I cannot in the present context deal with moral and other normative validity claims that have a built-in orientation toward discursive vindication. They lack the property of "transcending justification" that accrues to truth claims through the supposition of a single objective world built into the communicative use of language. Normative validity claims are raised for interpersonal relationships within a social world that is not independent of "our making" in the same way as is the objective world. The discursive treatment of normative claims is, however, "analogous to truth" insofar as the participants in practical discourse are guided by the goal of a commanded, permitted, or forbidden "single right answer." The social world is intrinsically historical, that is, ontologically constituted in a different way than the objective world. For this reason, in the case of the social world, the idealization of the justificatory conditions cannot include an "anticipation of future corroboration (*Bewährung*)," in the sense of an anticipated refutation of future objections (Wingert), but only in the critical sense of a proviso concerning approximation, that is, a proviso concerning the justification community's actually achieved state of decentering. The discursive indication of a truth claim says that the truth conditions, interpreted as assertibility conditions, are satisfied. In the case of a normative validity claim, the discursively achieved agreement grounds the corresponding norm's worthiness to be recognized;

to this extent the agreement itself contributes to the satisfaction of the norm's conditions of validity. Whereas rational acceptability merely indicates the truth of a proposition, it provides a constructive contribution to the validity of norms.

41   R. Rorty, "Is Truth a Goal of Inquiry?," p. 300.

42   R. Rorty, "Relativism: Finding and Making," MS (1995), p. 5.

43   T. McCarthy, "Philosophy and Social Practice: Richard Rorty's 'New Pragmatism,'" in *Ideals and Illusions* (Cambridge, MA, 1991), pp. 11–34.

44   R. Rorty, "Habermas, Derrida, and the Functions of Philosophy," *Revue Inernationale de Philosophie* 49 (1995), 437–60; cf. my reply in ibid., pp. 553–6.

45   R. Rorty, "Is truth a Goal of Inquiry?," p. 298.

46   R. Rorty, *Philosophical Papers* I, p. 29.

47   R. Rorty, "Relativism: Finding and Making," pp. 11f.

48   The same objectivism and the same kind of insensitivity could be shown through reference to Rorty's egocentric or ethnocentric description of processes of interpretation, for example, of hard cases of intercultural understanding (*Verständigung*). Unlike Gadamer, Rorty does not have recourse to the symmetrical conditions for an adoption of perspectives learned by speakers and hearers in learning the system of personal pronouns and making possible a reciprocal convergence of interpretive horizons that, initially, are far apart. Instead, he takes as his starting point an asymmetrical relationship between "us" and "them," so that we have to judge their utterances according to our standards and assimilate their standards to ours; cf. J. Habermas, *Postmetaphysical Thinking*, trans. W. M. Hohengarten (Cambridge, MA, 1992), pp. 135ff. This assimilatory model of understanding (*Verstehen*) partially coincides with Davidson's model of interpretation. However, what for Davidson is the result of a methodological decision to view the interpretation of linguistic expression as the application of the hypotheses of an empirically turned theory of truth, results for Rorty from the decision (of strategic significance for his theory) in favor of a naturalist descriptive vocabulary.

9

TOWARDS REHABILITATING
OBJECTIVITY

John McDowell

1.   Richard Rorty is notorious among philosophers for his campaign against epistemology practiced in the manner of the Cartesian and British-empiricist tradition. But
putting it like that underplays how drastic Rorty's thinking about epistemology is.
For Rorty, an activity in that vein is simply what the label "epistemology" means. He
has no time for a different, and perhaps useful, kind of reflection that might still
deserve to count as epistemological. My main aim in this paper is to urge that what
I take to be Rorty's basic convictions, with which I sympathize, do not require so
completely dismissive a stance towards the very idea of epistemology. Indeed, I want
to urge that Rorty's basic project positively requires a more hospitable attitude to
something that may as well be counted as epistemological reflection.

   An illuminating context for Rorty's campaign against epistemology is a Deweyan
narrative of Western culture's coming to maturity.[1] For Dewey's own growing-up, it
was important to disburden himself of the oppressive sense of sin inculcated into him
by his mother, and this feature of his own life shaped his picture of what it would
be for humanity at large to come of age.

   In simple outline, the story goes like this. The sense of sin from which Dewey
freed himself was a reflection of a religious outlook according to which human beings
were called on to humble themselves before a non-human authority. Such a posture
is infantile in its submissiveness to something other than ourselves.[2] If human beings
are to achieve maturity, they need to follow Dewey in liberating themselves from this
sort of religion, a religion of abasement before the divine Other.[3] But a humanism
that goes no further than that is still incomplete. We need a counterpart secular emancipation as well. In the period in the development of Western culture during which
the God who figures in that sort of religion was stricken, so to speak, with his mortal
illness, the illness that was going to lead to the demise famously announced by Nietzsche, some European intellectuals found themselves conceiving the secular world, the
putative object of everyday and scientific knowledge, in ways that paralleled that

John McDowell, "Towards Rehabilitating Objectivity," in *Rorty and His Critics*, ed. Robert Brandom
(Oxford: Blackwell, 2000), pp. 109–23. Reprinted by permission of Blackwell Publishing.

humanly immature conception of the divine. This is a secular analog to a religion of abasement, and human maturity requires that we liberate ourselves from it as well as from its religious counterpart.

What Rorty takes to parallel authoritarian religion is the very idea that in everyday and scientific investigation we submit to standards constituted by the things themselves, the reality that is supposed to be the topic of the investigation. Accepting that idea, Rorty suggests, is casting the world in the role of the non-human Other before which we are to humble ourselves. Full human maturity would require us to acknowledge authority only if the acknowledgment does not involve abasing ourselves before something non-human. The only authority that meets this requirement is that of human consensus. If we conceive inquiry and judgment in terms of making ourselves answerable to the world, as opposed to being answerable to our fellows, we are merely postponing the completion of the humanism whose achievement begins with discarding authoritarian religion.

The idea of answerability to the world is central to the discourse of objectivity. So Rorty's call is to abandon the discourse, the vocabulary, of objectivity, and work instead towards expanding human solidarity. Viewed in the context I have just sketched, this invitation has a world-historical character. As Rorty sees things, participating in the discourse of objectivity merely prolongs a cultural and intellectual infantilism, and persuading people to renounce the vocabulary of objectivity should facilitate the achievement of full human maturity. This would be a contribution to world history that is, perhaps surprisingly, within the power of mere intellectuals.

2.   I share Rorty's conviction that we ought to try to get out from under the seeming problems of epistemology in the Cartesian and British-empiricist vein, rather than taking then at face value and attempting to solve them. (It was largely from him that I learned to think like that.) I think, too, that there may be illumination to be had from a parallel between the conception of the world that figures in epistemology in that vein, on the one hand, and a certain conception of the divine, on the other. But it is possible to go that far with Rorty and still dissent from his suggestion that, in order to avoid entanglement in that familiar unprofitable epistemological activity, we need to discard the very idea of being answerable to something other than ourselves.

What gives the seeming problems of mainstream modern epistemology their seeming urgency is not the sheer idea that inquiry is answerable to the world. The culprit, rather, is a frame of mind in which the world to which we want to conceive our thinking as answerable threatens to withdraw out of reach of anything we can think of as our means of access to it. A gap threatens to open between us and what we should like to conceive ourselves as knowing about, and it then seems to be a task for philosophy to show us ways to bridge the gulf. It is this threat of inaccessibility on the part of the world that we need to dislodge, in order to unmask as illusory the seeming compulsoriness of mainstream epistemology. And the threat of inaccessibility is not part of the very idea of the world as something other than ourselves to which our investigative activities are answerable.

This allows us to make the parallel between epistemology and religion more pointed. The world as it figures in mainstream epistemology is a counterpart, not to just any idea of the divine as non-human and authoritative, but to the conception of *deus absconditus*, God as withdrawn into a mysterious inaccessibility. A telling Deweyan protest against epistemology, as practiced in the Cartesian and British-empiricist style, can be cast as a protest against the idea of philosophy as priestcraft, supposedly needed to mediate between this *mundus absconditus* and ordinary human beings who aspire to knowledge of it.

The idea that inquiry is answerable to the world does not by itself commit us to believing that there is a need for philosophy as priestcraft. We can accept that inquiry is answerable to the things themselves and still suppose, correctly, that the resources of ordinary investigative activity can suffice to put us in touch with the subject matter of investigation, without need of special philosophical mediation. That is: we can follow Dewey in rejecting philosophy as priestcraft, without needing to abandon the very vocabulary of objectivity. What we need to dislodge is the idea of the world as withdrawn into inaccessibility, and that is quite another matter.

3.   If we separate the idea of objectivity from the threat of withdrawal on the part of the world, we can make better sense of the position of Cartesian and British-empiricist epistemology in the history of philosophy.

For one thing, this makes it easier to ensure that a Deweyan protest against an epistemology with priestly pretensions is aimed in an appropriate historical direction. The idea of being answerable to the subject matter of inquiry is surely not new with modern philosophy. Rorty sometimes cites Plato's manipulation of the contrasts between knowledge and opinion, and between reality and appearance, as a paradigm of what goes wrong in the metaphysics of objectivity.[4] But the familiar supposed problems of modern epistemology are not just more of something that we already find in Plato. That would make it a mystery that two more millennia had to pass before philosophy began to be obsessed with the anxieties of Cartesian epistemology. It took something further and more specific to make what people wanted to think of as the target of their investigations threaten to withdraw out of reach of what they wanted to think of as their means of access to it.

What figures in Plato as a distance between mere appearance and reality is not the distance that generates the characteristic anxiety of modern epistemology. Perhaps both the Platonic and the Cartesian conceptions can be captured in terms of an image of penetrating a veil of appearance and putting ourselves in touch with reality, but the image works differently in the two contexts. In the Platonic context, appearance does not figure as something that after all constitutes access to knowable reality, although it takes philosophy to show us how it can do so. Philosophy in Plato does not show how to bridge a gulf between appearance and an empirically knowable reality; it does not picture appearance as an avenue to knowledge at all. Correspondingly, the acknowledged and embraced remoteness of the knowable in Plato is quite unlike the threatened, but to be overcome, remoteness of the knowable in modern philosophy. Plato is nothing like a Cartesian skeptic or a British empiricist.

Attacking the vocabulary of objectivity as such, as Rorty does, rather than the conception of the world as withdrawn, distracts attention from a necessary task. If we are to achieve a satisfactory exorcism of the problematic of mainstream modern epistemology, we need to uncover and understand the specific historical influences – which, as I have been insisting, are much more recent than the vocabulary of objectivity itself

– that led to a seeming withdrawal on the part of what we wanted to see as the empirically knowable world, and thus to philosophy's coming to center on epistemology in the sense of the attempt to bridge the supposed gulf.[5] Freeing the vocabulary of objectivity from contamination by the threat of withdrawal can be the project of epistemology in a different sense. This is an activity whose very point would converge with the point Rorty is making, when he rejects the idea that philosophy holds the secret to the possibility of empirical knowledge.

If we focus on the threat of withdrawal, we not only enable ourselves to raise diagnostic questions at the right point in history, the beginning of modern philosophy; we also make room, perhaps usefully, for a conception of Kant that differs from Rorty's. Rorty finds figures congenial to his world-historical conception of what philosophers ought to be doing only quite recently in the history of philosophy, with the emergence of self-consciously subversive thinkers such as Nietzsche. The only significance Rorty finds in Kant is that Kant's enormous prestige enabled the professionalization of philosophy, in the sense of the activity Rorty deplores as merely prolonging human immaturity.[6] But Kant precisely aims to combat the threat of a withdrawal on the part of the world we aspire to know. Kant undermines the idea that appearance screens us off from knowable reality; he offers instead a way of thinking in which – to put it paradoxically from the point of view of the style of epistemology he aims to supersede – appearance just is the reality we aspire to know (unless things have gone wrong in mundane ways). It is a fundamentally Kantian thought that the truth about the world is within the reach of those who live in the realm of appearance – to use a Platonic turn of phrase that is now rendered safe, deprived of any tendency to encourage the idea that we need philosophical gap-bridging. This is fully in the spirit of a Deweyan protest against the idea that epistemology is needed for a priestly mediation between us and a world that has withdrawn from us.[7] So if we reconceive Rorty's world-historical project, so as to direct it specifically against the epistemological problematic of withdrawal rather than the vocabulary of objectivity, we can see Kant as an ally, not an enemy. For what it is worth, this version of the crusade might do better at engaging professors of philosophy.

4.   One aspect of the immaturity that Rorty finds in putting objectivity rather than solidarity at the focus of philosophical discourse is a wishful denial of a certain sort of argumentative or deliberative predicament. On the face of it, certain substantive questions are such that we can be confident of answers to them, on the basis of thinking the matter through with whatever resources we have for dealing with questions of the relevant kind (for instance, ethical questions); there is no need for a sideways glance at philosophy. But even after we have done our best at marshalling considerations in favor of an answer to such a question, we have no guarantee that just anyone with whom we can communicate will find our answer compelling. That fact – perhaps brought forcibly home by our failing to persuade someone – can then induce the sideways glance, and undermine the initial confidence. Rorty's suggestion is that the vocabulary of objectivity reflects a philosophical attempt to shore up the confidence so threatened, by wishfully denying the predicament. The wishful idea is that in principle reality itself fills this gap in our persuasive resources; any rational subject who does not see things aright must be failing to make proper use of humanly universal

capacities to be in tune with the world. If we fall into this way of thinking, we are trying to exploit the image of an ideal position in which we are in touch with something greater than ourselves – a secular counterpart to the idea of being at one with the divine – in order to avoid acknowledging the ineliminable hardness of hard questions, or in order to avoid facing up to the sheer contingency that attaches to our being in a historically evolved cultural position that enables us to find compelling just the considerations we do find compelling.[8]

Here too we can make a separation. This wishful conception of attunement with how things really are, as a means of avoiding an uncomfortable acknowledgment of the limitations of reason and the contingency of our capacities to think as we believe we should, can be detached from the very idea of making ourselves answerable to how things are. We can join Rorty in deploring the former without needing to join him in abandoning the very idea of aspiring to get things right.

I can bring out how these are two different things by looking at a feature of Rorty's reading of Plato.

Rorty follows Nietzsche in suggesting that Platonic conceptions in ethics reflect an inability to face up to the kind of hard choices that are the stuff of an ethically complex life – as if the idea were that getting in touch with the Forms would carry one through life without need for the effort of deliberation.[9] But I think this reading misses the point of Platonic ethics. Being in touch with the Forms is not meant to be a substitute for hard thinking about what to do. On the contrary, the Forms are an image to enable us to sustain the idea that there is such a thing as getting things right, precisely in the absence of ways to make answers to ethical questions universally compelling. It is not a Platonic thought that putting someone in touch with the Forms is in principle a way to compel assent, on disputed questions about how to live, from anybody at all who is rational enough to engage in discussion of the questions.

I think this is brought out by the treatment of Callicles, in the *Gorgias*, and Thrasymachus, in the *Republic*: places where, on Rorty's reading, one would expect to find Plato wheeling in a reality larger than mere human beings, as if it could fill gaps in the arguments that we can come up with apart from resorting to it. That is not what happens in those dialogues. Each of those opponents of ethical orthodoxy is reduced to a sulk, before anything specifically Platonic even appears on the scene, by arguments whose quality is quite uneven, but which are, at the worst, transparently sophistical (so that one can easily sympathize with the sulking). Thrasymachus introduces the question whether one should live in accord with what Socrates would recognize as virtue, but is himself driven into an angry silence in the first book of the *Republic*. Thereafter Plato turns to something that does not look like even a promissory note for a way of rendering an affirmative answer to the question universally compelling, compelling even to people like Thrasymachus. Instead, with Thrasymachus himself conspicuously taking no part in the conversation, Plato has Socrates characterize the knowledge that matters for knowing how to live as what results from a proper education. And education here is not, as Rorty's reading might lead one to expect, a honing of purely intellectual capacities, to put them in tune with a reality one might conceive as accessible independently of contingencies of cultural position. Plato insists that a proper education is an education of the sentiments no less than the intellect (to put it in eighteenth-century terms). There is a similar structure in the *Gorgias*, with Callicles figuring in the conversation as a patently unconvinced "yea"-sayer – remarkably enough, in view of the fuss Plato has Socrates make, earlier in the dialogue, about how important it is to him to secure the sincere assent of his interlocutors (compare 472b with 501c). I think the moral, in both dialogues, most be meant to be something on these lines: people who raise such questions are dangerous, and should he forced into silence, or acquiescence, by whatever means are available; people whose character is in good order will have confidence in right answers to the questions, a confidence that should not be threatened by the fact that questioners such as Callicles or Thrasymachus cannot be won over by persuasive argument.[10]

It is true, of course, that Plato gives a cognitive slant to his picture of what it is to have one's character in good order; he sees it as a capacity to arrive at the truth about a certain subject matter. But there is no implication that this capacity to arrive at the truth somehow insures one against tragic predicaments, or bypasses the need for hard thinking about difficult questions.

One would not expect Plato to have had the sort of concern Rorty has with contingency. But it is one thing to lack that concern, and quite another to have a metaphysical picture that excludes it. Plato's metaphysical picture can perfectly well accommodate the thought that it is a contingency that certain people can get things right; this formulation smoothly combines an acknowledgment of contingency with an employment of the vocabulary of objectivity, in a way that ought to be incoherent if Rorty were right about the vocabulary of objectivity. There is nothing alien to Plato in supplying, say, Glaucon and Adeimantus in the *Republic* with a thought on these lines: "How fortunate we are to have been born Greeks, not barbarians, and thus to have had an upbringing that made us capable of seeing things aright on these matters."

Of course it would be absurd to suggest that one can set aside Rorty's reading of Plato on the strength of a few quick sentences. But I do not need to carry conviction on the alternative I have sketched; it is enough for my purposes here that it should be so much as intelligible. This shows that the very idea of aspiring to get things right, of making ourselves answerable to how things are, has no necessary connection with what Rorty deplores: an inability to face up to contingency, and the fantasy of transferring the burden of hard thinking to the world itself.[11]

5.   So far I have been taking issue, at a general level, with Rorty's suggestion that the very vocabulary of objectivity commits us to a wishful denial of contingency, and that it saddles us with the idea that philosophy is needed, in order to supply a guarantee for the capacity of inquiry to make contact with its subject matter. I agree with Rorty that we should be open-eyed about contingency, and hostile to philosophy's claim to be a necessary underpinning for other sorts of intellectual activity, but I have urged that this does not warrant his dismissive attitude to the very idea of making ourselves answerable to the world.

I want now to point to a flaw in the way Rorty treats the vocabulary of objectivity when he goes into analytical detail about it.

Hilary Putnam has argued, to put it in Rorty's words, that "notions like 'reference' – semantic notions which relate language to nonlanguage – are internal to our overall view of the world."[12] Rorty cites Putnam's argument with approval. He writes, giving more examples of the notions to which the argument applies: "From the standpoint of the representationalist, the fact that notions like representation, reference, and truth are deployed in ways that are internal to a language or a theory is no reason to drop them."[13] The figure here labeled "the representationalist" is someone who refuses to give up the vocabulary of objectivity in favor of the vocabulary of solidarity. Of course Rorty is not suggesting we should drop the uses of these semantical notions to which Putnam's argument applies, uses that are internal to a world view. But he thinks "the representationalist" tries to use the notions in a way that is not internal to a world view. It is this supposed external use, according to Rorty, that is in question in the discourse of objectivity. So his view is that we need to distinguish the discourse of objectivity from the innocent internal use of the semantical notions that Putnam discusses.

One could define the discourse of objectivity as involving a certain supposed external use of the semantical notions, and in that case I would have no problem with Rorty's attitude to it. But Rorty suggests that rejecting these supposed external uses requires rejecting any form of the idea that inquiry is answerable to the world. I think this deprives us of something that is not inextricably implicated with what Putnam unmasks as illusion, and in depriving us of something we can innocently want, the move is damaging to Rorty's own philosophical project.

Rorty's picture is on these lines. If we use an expression like "accurate representation" in the innocent internal way, it can function only as a means of paying "empty compliments" to claims that pass muster within our current practice of claim-making.[14] Now "the representationalist" finds a restriction to this sort of assessment unacceptably parochial. Recoiling from that, "the representationalist" tries to make expressions like "true" or "accurate representation" signify a mode of normative relatedness – conformity – to something more independent of us than the world as it figures in our world view. This aspiration is well captured by Thomas Nagel's image of "trying to climb outside of our own minds."[15] The image fits a conception, or supposed conception, of reality that threatens to put it outside our reach, since the norms according to which we conduct our investigations cannot of course be anything but our current norms. Recoiling from the idea that we are restricted to paying "empty compliments" to bits of our world view, "the representationalist" tries to conceive the relation between what we want to see as our world view and its subject matter from sideways on, rather than from the vantage point of the world view – now only problematically so called – itself. This way, it comes to seem that referential relations – to focus on the case that originally figured in Putnam's argument – would have to be intelligible in the "Augustinian" way Wittgenstein considers at the beginning of *Pilosophical Investigations*; not, that is, from the midst of an understanding of linguistic practice as a going concern, but as if they could be prior building blocks in an explanation, from first principles, of how language enables us to give expression to thought at all.

This conception is naturally reflected in just the sorts of philosophical wonderment at, for instance, the meaningfulness of language, or the fact that we so much as have an "overall view of the world," that Rorty tellingly deplores. In this conception, being genuinely in touch with reality would in a radical way transcend whatever we can do within our practices of arriving at answers to our questions. Thus a familiar gulf seems to open between us and what we should like to be able to think of ourselves as able to get to know about. And the only alternative, as Rorty sees things, is to take our inquiry not to be subject to anything but the norms of current practice. This picture of the options makes it look as if the very idea of inquiry as normatively beholden not just to current practice but to its subject matter is inextricably connected with the "Augustinian" picture and the impulse to climb outside of our own minds. But a piece of mere sanity goes missing here.

6.   It will help to focus on just one of the notions that figure in this line of thought, the notion of truth.

Rorty thinks there are three potentially relevant "uses" of "true": a commending or normative use, a "disquotational" use, and a "cautionary" use.[16]

The "cautionary" use is employed when we say, of some claim that we have so far not managed to find anything wrong with, that it may, even so, not be true. Rorty thinks such a remark is a reminder that, even though the claim's credentials have passed muster in the eyes of all qualified audiences to whom we have so far exposed it, we may in the future encounter an audience who finds fault with it, in a way that, as we shall acknowledge, reflects the fact that the future audience is better qualified.

So far, Rorty thinks, so good. The trouble comes if we take this "cautionary" use to be expressive of a norm. That way, we persuade ourselves that we understand compellingness to any audience as a norm for our activities of inquiry, and for the claim-making that gives expression to their results. And now we are liable to picture this universal compellingness in terms of a conformity to reality that would need to be contemplated from outside any local practice of investigation.

No doubt it is a good thing to aspire to overcome parochiality in the persuasiveness of the warrants we can offer for what we believe; that is part of the content of Rorty's own praise of solidarity. But this does not make universal compellingness intelligible as a norm. Rorty writes: "to say something like 'we hope to justify our belief to as many and as large audiences as possible' . . . is to offer only an ever-retreating goal, one which fades for ever and for ever when we move. It is not even what common sense would call a goal. For it is not even something to which we might get closer, much less something we might realize we had finally reached."[17] Trying to identify this "ever-retreating goal," only dubiously conceivable as a goal at all, with truth as a norm for inquiry and judgment is a way into a picture of the obligations of inquirers that has nothing to do with devising arguments in order to convince particular groups of human beings – a picture in which aiming at being genuinely in touch with reality seems appropriately captured by the image of trying to climb outside our own minds. The aspiration to overcome parochiality, then, is all very well; but the only norm, at this level of generality, that intelligibly governs inquiry is that of coming up with claims that our peers, competent in the norms of our current practices of claim-making, will let us get away with.[18] If we try to make sense of a further norm, involving responsibility to the subject matter of inquiry, we land ourselves in the "Augustinian" or sideways-on picture of our relation to that subject matter.

Now, to begin with, there is something unsatisfactory about the way Rorty separates the first two of these three uses of "true," the normative use and the "disquotational" use. Rorty claims that the "disquotational" use of "true" is "descriptive," and as such not merely to be distinguished from, but incapable of being combined in a unified discourse with, any use of "true" that treats truth as a norm for inquiry and claim-making.[19] But this makes no room for such truisms as the following: what makes it correct among speakers of English to make a claim with the words "Snow is white" (to stay with a well-worn example) is that snow is (indeed) white.

The idea of disquotation, literally interpreted, fits the "T-sentences" that are to be provable in a Tarskian theory of truth for a language, formulated in a metalanguage that expands the object language only by adding semantic vocabulary. But we can extend the idea of disquotation to fit the case of a Tarskian theory whose object language is not contained in the metalanguage in which the theory is stated – a theory that might be put to the Davidsonian purpose of capturing an interpretation of one language in another.[20] Here what figures, not quoted, on the right-hand side of a T-sentence is no longer the very same sentence that appears between quotation marks, or otherwise designated, before "is true if and only if" on the left-hand side. But it is a sentence that, if the theory is a good one, has the same effect; its use here cancels the semantic ascent effected by the quotation marks or other method of designation, and so disquotes in an extended sense. A sentence that is true, in the sense of "true" whose conditions of application to the sentences of this or that language Tarski showed how to pin down in a theory (provided that we can find a suitable logical form in, or impose a suitable logical form on, the sentences of the language), is – we can naturally say – disquotable. And this idea of disquotability is not separate, as Rorty suggests, from anything normative. For a given sentence to be true – to be disquotable – is for it to be correctly usable to make a claim just because . . . , where in the gap we insert, not quoted but used, the sentence that figures on the right-hand side of the T-sentence provided for the sentence in question by a good Tarskian theory for its language (the sentence itself, in the case in which we can exploit the unextended idea of disquotation). Truth in the sense of disquotability is unproblematically normative for sentences uttered in order to make claims.[21]

Now let us reconsider Rorty's treatment of the "cautionary" use. In a passage in which he is explicitly wondering whether he suffers from a blind spot, Rorty writes that, apparently unlike Davidson, he sees "no significance in the fact that we use the same word to designate what is preserved by valid inference as we use to caution people that beliefs justified to us may not be justified to other, better, audiences."[22] But what is preserved by valid inference, which is presumably truth as expressed by a commending or normative use of "true," is simply disquotability. That disquotability is normative for conclusions of inference, and hence that disquotability must be preserved by good patterns of inference, is just part of what it means for disquotability to be normative, in the unproblematic way it is, for claim-making. Moreover, disquotability yields a straightforward gloss on the cautionary use of "true" as well. One can express the cautionary point not only with an explicit use of "true," but also with a kind of augmented disquotation: that is, by making a claim in which one modifies a non-quoting use of the words that figure in the original claim, or the words that appear on the right-hand side of a non-homophonic T-sentence for the sentence uttered in making it, by adding a modal operator and a negation sign. Rorty's cautionary use is exemplified in a form of words such as " 'All life forms are carbon-based' may not (after all) be true"; but one could achieve exactly the same effect by saying "There may (after all) be life forms that are not carbon-based." What one warns oneself or others that a claim may not have, in spite of its passing muster so far, is just disquotability. I think this shows that the blind spot Rorty wonders about is indeed there. That we use the same word simply reflects the fact that it is the same status, disquotability, that is, on the one hand, preserved by valid inference and, on the other, possibly lacked by beliefs, or claims, on which there is present consensus among qualified judges.

The same blind spot is operative in a thesis Rorty puts by saying "justification is relative to an audience."[23] Taken one way, indeed, the thesis is obviously correct; whenever one carries conviction by giving reasons, it is some particular audience that one persuades. Now Rorty thinks that is the only way to take the thesis; he thinks the only hygienically available conception of what it is for, say, a claim to be justified (or warranted, or rationally acceptable) must be relative to some particular audience, on pain of our purporting to have an idea of justification that is implicated with the sideways-on picture and the aspiration to climb outside our own minds. Failing the sideways-on picture, he suggests, "the terms 'warranted,' 'rationally acceptable,' etc., will always invite the question 'to whom?'."[24] This idea is what underwrites the argument I rehearsed a few paragraphs back, that, although persuasiveness to audiences other than our peers is a worthy aspiration, the only way justification (or warrant, or rational acceptability) can constitute a norm for claim-making is in the guise of ability to pass muster with our peers. But here the norm constituted by disquotability goes missing. An utterance of "Cold fusion has not been achieved, so far, in the laboratory" has (if I am right about the physics) a warrant, a justifiedness, that consists not in one's being able to get away with it among certain conversational partners, but in – now I disquote, and implicitly make a claim – cold fusion's not having been achieved, so far, in the laboratory. Here the terms "warranted," "rationally acceptable," etc., have collected an obvious answer, not to the question "to whom?," but to the question "in the light of what?," and the question "to whom?" need not be in the offing at all.

Notice that in order to insist on these lines that we can make sense of a notion of justification for which the relevant question is "in the light of what?," all I need is my (rather rudimentary) ability to make claims about whether or not cold fusion has occurred. Rorty thinks any purported notion of warrant or justifiedness that is not relative to an audience would have to be implicated with the sort of philosophy that involves trying to climb outside our own minds. But one does not pretend to climb outside one's own mind if one gives expression, as I just did, to the norm constituted by disquotability. One formulates the relevant normative condition on a given assertoric utterance by disquoting (possibly in the extended sense) the words whose assertoric utterance is governed by the norm one is invoking; that is, by using words (for instance, "Cold fusion has not been achieved") that would figure on the right-hand side of the relevant T-sentence, words in whose norm-governed employment one is (more or less) competent.

It is true that we have only whatever lights are at our disposal to go on in bringing such a norm to bear – which involves deciding what to say about, for instance, whether or not cold fusion has occurred. We understand what the norm of disquotability comes to, potential utterance by potential utterance, from the midst of a current practice of claim-making; we understand it by the lights constituted by being a (more or less) competent party to the practice. But it does not follow that nothing can be normative for moves within the practice except ensuring that one's peers will let one get away with them. There is a norm for making claims with the words "Cold fusion has not occurred" that is constituted by whether or not cold fusion has occurred; and whether or not cold fusion has occurred is not the same as whether or not saying it has occurred will pass muster in the current practice. On topics on which there is no dispute, it will always seem from within a practice of investigation that the answers to such pairs of questions coincide, but that should not prevent us from seeing that the questions differ. Moreover, anyone who can be recognized as self-consciously participating in a practice of claim-making must be able to see that the questions differ. Without this difference, there would be no ground for conceiving one's activity as making claims about, say, whether or not cold fusion has occurred, as opposed to achieving unison with one's fellows in some perhaps purely decorative activity on a level with a kind of dancing. The distinguishability of the questions amounts to the availability of the notion of a claim's being justified in the light of how things stand with its subject matter. And the questions are distinguishable from within our practice of claim-making; insisting on the distinction is not an expression of the fantasy that one can conceive the practice's conformity to reality from sideways on.

Seeing how the questions differ, we can see how the thought that some claim is true is not – as in Rorty's "empty compliment" idea – the thought that it would pass muster in the relevant claim-making practice as presently constituted. It is the thought that things really are a certain way: for instance, that cold fusion really has not occurred. To insist on this distinction is not to try to think and speak from outside our practices; it is simply to take it seriously that we can really mean what we think and say from within them. It is not just "the representationalist," someone who thinks we need to climb outside our own minds in order to understand how thought and speech relate to reality, who can be expected to recoil from a denial of this.

There are two different things that might be meant by saying, as Rorty applauds Putnam for saying, that norms expressible with notions like that of truth are internal to our world view. Putnam's insight is that we must not succumb to the illusion that we need to climb outside our own minds, the illusion that though we aim our thought and speech at the world from a standpoint constituted by our present practices and competences, we must be able to conceive the conformity of our thought and speech to the world from outside any such standpoint. But to unmask that as an illusion is not to say, with Rorty, that the norms that govern claim-making can only be norms of consensus, norms that would be fully met by earning the endorsement of our peers for our claims. We must indeed avoid the illusion of transcendence that Putnam's insight rejects, but we do not put our capacity to do so at risk if we insist that in claim-making we make ourselves answerable not just to the verdicts of our fellows but to the facts themselves. That is, if you like, to say that norms of inquiry transcend consensus. But this transcendence is quite distinct from the transcendence Putnam unmasks as an illusory aspiration. These norms are internal to our world view, just as Putnam urged that the relevant norms must be. It is just that the world view to which

they are internal has the world in view otherwise than as constituted by what linguistic performances will pass muster in our present practice. But that is merely a
requirement for us to have the world in view at all – for moves within the relevant
practices to be expressive of a world view, as opposed to merely aspiring to vocalize
in step with one another. Taking this transcendence in stride requires no more than
confidence in our capacity to direct our meaning at, say, whether or not cold fusion
has occurred.[25]

7.   What I have been urging is that truth as disquotability is a mode of justifiedness
that is not relative to some particular audience; the question that this mode of justifiedness raises is not "to whom?" but "in the light of what?". This mode of justifiedness is, innocuously, normative for inquiry and the judgments and claims it aims
at. For all the efforts of philosophers to put it in doubt, something we can conceive
in terms of satisfaction of such a norm is unproblematically achievable from the local
standpoints that are the only standpoints we can occupy in intellectual activity.

Contrast Rorty's picture, in which there is nothing for truth, as a mode of justifiedness that is not relative to a particular audience, to be except the "ever-retreating
goal" of being convincing to ever more and larger audiences. Of course the "ever-
retreating goal" cannot be achieved, and Rorty says as much. But his blind spot about
disquotability leads him to think this correct point can be put by saying something
to this effect: if we conceive truth as a mode of justifiedness that transcends consensus, we are conceiving something that would not be achievable. This rejects the
innocuous transcendence along with the illusory one. And the effect is to make urgent
just the sorts of question that Rorty wants to discourage.

As I said, taking the innocuous transcendence in stride requires no more than confidence in our capacity to direct our meaning at, say, whether or not cold fusion has
occurred. Philosophers have contrived to shake this confidence, to make such a capacity look mysterious, by moves whose effect is to make it seem that comprehension of
how inquiry, judgment, and claim-making are related to reality would require the other
kind of transcendence, the kind that is an illusory aspiration. Rorty's own refusal to
countenance norms for claim-making that go beyond consensus is of course motivated by his well-placed hostility to this idea, the idea that we need to climb outside
our own minds in order to occupy a point of view from which to conceive the relation of thought to reality. But throwing out the innocuous transcendence along with
the illusory aspiration has exactly the effect he deplores; it makes a mystery of how
we manage to direct our thought and speech as it were past the endorsement of our
fellows and to the facts themselves. Rorty is committed to taking imagery on those
lines as irredeemably expressive of the hankering after climbing outside our own
minds. But the imagery comes to nothing more than an insistence that we speak and
think – of course from the midst of our practices – about, say, whether or not cold
fusion has occurred. And Rorty's own move makes a mystery of how we manage to
do that, in just the sort of way in which he rightly wants not to let philosophy make
a mystery of such things.

If one has a steadfast understanding of truth as disquotability, one can be immune
to philosophically induced anxiety about how thought and speech, undertaken from
the midst of our local practices, can make contact with reality. But consider someone

who has a merely inchoate understanding of truth as disquotability, a norm for inquiry concerning which the relevant question is not "to whom?" but "in the light of what?". Suppose such a person is confronted with Rorty's pronouncement that there is no attaining truth except in the guise of convincingness to one's peers. The pronouncement puts in question the achievability of a kind of conformity of thought and speech to the world that – as such a person realizes, though *ex hypothesi* only inchoately – ought to be unproblematic. It would be only natural to recoil into just the kind of gap-bridging philosophical activity that Rorty deplores.

8.   Rorty aims to discourage a certain genre of philosophy, and I have been urging that his treatment of truth is counter-productive by his own lights. It is a connected point that this treatment of truth is, I believe, fundamentally unDeweyan. Philosophers seduce people into the kind of anxiety Rorty follows Dewey in deploring; they induce anxiety by manipulating the thought that we have only our own lights to go on in any inquiry. The thought is actually innocent, but it can be made to seem that having only our own lights to go on is a confinement, something that would threaten to cut us off from reality itself. This makes it seem that we need a special philosophical viewpoint, one that contemplates inquiry's relation to reality from sideways on, so that we can be reassured that ordinary inquiry makes contact with its intended subject matter. On this kind of conception, it is only by the grace of philosophy that truth is attainable in ordinary investigative activity. Rorty follows Dewey in his hostility towards this kind of pretension on the part of philosophy, and as I have indicated, I have no problem with that. But Dewey put the point by saying such things as this: "Truth is a collection of truths; and these constituent truths are in the keeping of the best available methods of inquiry and testing as to matters-of-fact; methods which are, when collected under a single name, science."[26] As Davidson comments: "Dewey's aim was to bring truth, and with it the pretensions of philosophers, down to earth."[27] Dewey insisted that truth is within the reach of ordinary inquiry. Rorty, quite differently, thinks he can achieve the desired effect – cutting down the pretensions of philosophy – by cheerfully affirming that truth in the relevant sense is not within reach at all. That is just the sort of pronouncement that triggers the kind of philosophy Dewey and Rorty deplore, and it is not an effective consolation, or deterrent, to add "not even within the reach of philosophy."[28]

    What about the idea that the vocabulary of objectivity reflects an intellectual and cultural immaturity? I have been urging that disquotability is unproblematically normative, and that a proper understanding of the point yields a good gloss on the idea that inquiry is answerable to the world. It seems to me that it would be absurd to equate accepting this simple thought with abasing ourselves before the world, so as to fail to live up to our capacity for human maturity. Indeed, I am inclined to suggest that the boot is on the other foot. If there is a metaphysical counterpart to infantilism anywhere in this vicinity, it is in Rorty's phobia of objectivity, and the suggestion that we should replace talk of our being answerable to the world with talk of ways of thinking and speaking that are conducive to our purposes.[29] This fits a truly infantile attitude, one for which things other than the subject show up only as they impinge on its will. Acknowledging a non-human external authority over our thinking, so far from being a betrayal of our humanity, is merely a condition of growing up.[30]

I applaud Rorty's hostility to the sort of philosophy that sets itself up as providing necessary foundations for intellectual activity in general. But I think he is wrong in supposing that the way to cure people of the impulse towards that sort of philosophy is to proscribe, or at least try to persuade people to drop, the vocabulary of objectivity, and centrally the image of the world as authoritative over our investigations. I think this policy of Rorty's involves a misconception of an innocuous notion of truth. Once we understand that, we can see why Rorty's attempt to dislodge people from the vocabulary tends to have an effect that is exactly opposite to the one he wants. The way to cure ourselves of unwarranted expectations for philosophy is not to drop the vocabulary of objectivity, but to work at understanding the sources of the deformations to which the vocabulary of objectivity has historically been prone. If we could do that, it would enable us to undo the deformations, and see our way clear of the seemingly compulsory philosophical problematic that Rorty wants us to get out from under. This would be an epistemological achievement, in a perfectly intelligible sense of "epistemological" that does not restrict epistemology to accepting the traditional problematic. It is the deformations, to which Rorty's discussions of truth reveal him to be a party, and not the vocabulary itself, that lead to philosophical trouble.

Notes

1   Elaborating this context was a central theme in the stimulating lectures Rorty delivered, under the overall title "Anti-Authoritarianism in Epistemology and Ethics," in Girona, Catalonia, during his 1996 tenure of the Ferrater Mora Chair in Contemporary Thought. My formulation of the Deweyan narrative is a simplified version of the way Rorty presented it in those lectures. See also, e.g., "Solidarity or Objectivity?," in Rorty's *Objectivity, Relativism, and Truth* (Cambridge University Press, Cambridge, 1991), pp. 21–34.

2   This phase of the story invites a Freudian formulation, which Rorty gave in his Girona lectures. There are also obvious resonances with Nietzsche.

3   Notice that this is not the same as liberating ourselves from religion *tout court*, as Dewey's own example makes clear.

4   See, e.g., "Solidarity or Objectivity?," p. 22.

5   In *Philosophy and the Mirror of Nature* (Princeton University Press, Princeton, 1979) Rorty did concern himself with the historical question I am pointing to here (though I do not think he got the answer right). In respect of responsiveness to this historical question, more recent writings like "Solidarity or Objectivity?" seem to represent a backward step.

6   See chapter III of *Philosophy and the Mirror of Nature*.

7   See, e.g., *Experience and Nature* (Dover, New York, 1958), p. 410: "the profuseness of attestations to supreme devotion to truth on the part of philosophy is matter to arouse suspicion. For it has usually been a preliminary to the claim of being a peculiar organ of access to highest and ultimate truth. Such it is not." See the opening remarks in the written version of Donald Davidson's Dewey lectures, "The Structure and Content of Truth," *Journal of Philosophy* 87 (1990), 279–328, from which I have borrowed this quotation.

8   This theme is central in Rorty's *Contingency, Irony, and Solidarity* (Cambridge University Press, Cambridge, 1989).

9   See "Solidarity or Objectivity?," p. 32.

10 Rorty says of Orwell's O'Brien: "Orwell did not invent O'Brien to serve as a dialectical foil, as a modern counterpart to Thrasymachus. He invented him to warn us against him, as one might warn against a typhoon or a rogue elephant." (*Contingency, Irony, and Solidarity*, p. 176.) I think that makes O'Brien pretty much exactly a modern counterpart to Thrasymachus as Plato actually uses him.

11 "Fantasy" is not the way Rorty would put this; he thinks such terms of criticism concede too much to the metaphysics of objectivity, and he would simply say that such conceptions have not proved useful. This seems to me to be pragmatism gone over the top, depriving itself of a useful critical notion. But this depends on something I am about to argue, that it is only by way of a conflation that Rorty comes to think resisting the kinds of philosophy he rightly sees as unprofitable requires resistance to the very vocabulary of objectivity.

12 *Objectivity, Relativism, and Truth*, p. 6. See, e.g., Putnam's *Meaning and the Moral Sciences* (Routledge and Kegan Paul, London, 1978).

13 Ibid.

14 For the phrase "empty compliment," see *Philosophy and the Mirror of Nature*, p. 10.

15 *The View from Nowhere* (Oxford University Press, New York, 1986), p. 9; see *Objectivity, Relativism, and Truth*, p. 7.

16 See "Pragmatism, Davidson and Truth," in *Objectivity, Relativism, and Truth*, pp. 126–50, at p. 128.

17 "Is Truth a Goal of Enquiry? Davidson vs. Wright," *Philosophical Quarterly* 45(1995), 281–300, at p. 298.

18 Rorty writes: "I view warrant as a sociological matter, to be ascertained by observing the reception of S's statement by her peers." ("Putnam and the Relativist Menace," *Journal of Philosophy* 90 (1993), 443–61, at p. 449.) At a different level, we would have to specify the norms of the current practices themselves.

19 See "Pragmatism, Davidson and Truth."

20 See Davidson's writings on interpretation, collected in his *Inquiries into Truth and Interpretation* (Clarendon Press, Oxford, 1984). For the extended notion of disquotation (cancelation of semantic ascent), see W. V. Quine, *Philosophy of Logic* (Prentice-Hall, Englewood Cliffs, NJ, 1970), pp. 10–13.

21 Rorty thinks he is following Davidson in glossing disquotation in terms of a causal relation between bits of language and things that are not bits of language, and concluding from the gloss that "the disquotational use of 'true'," so far from being normative itself, cannot even be coherently combined with normative talk. I think this pretty much misses the point of Davidson's writings about interpretation. I urged this at pp. 152–3 of my *Mind and World* (Harvard University Press, Cambridge, MA, 1994). I think this feature of Rorty's thinking descends directly from the frequent, and never satisfactory, engagements of Wilfrid Sellars with Tarskian semantics; it would be an interesting exercise to trace the line of descent in detail.

22 "Is Truth a Goal of Enquiry?," p. 286. For the belief that the "cautionary" use of "true" "is captured neither by a common-sensical account of its approbative force nor by a disquotational account," see also "Putnam and the Relativist Menace," p. 460.

23 "Is Truth a Goal of Enquiry?," p. 283. See also the passage quoted in n. 18 above.

24 "Putnam and the Relativist Menace," p. 452.

25 Rorty makes a helpful distinction between relativism and ethnocentrism, and disavows relativism. (See "Solidarity or Objectivity?") Ethnocentrism is the insistence that we speak from the midst of historically and culturally local practices; it amounts to a rejection of the illusory transcendence involved in the image of trying to climb outside of our own minds. But in refusing to allow the in fact perfectly innocent thought that in speaking

from the midst of the practices of our ethnos, we make ourselves answerable to the world itself (for instance, to how things stand with respect to cold fusion), Rorty makes a move whose effect is to collapse his own helpful distinction. The thesis that "justification is relative to an audience" is, as explicitly stated, relativistic, not just ethnocentric. This is at least some excuse for what Rorty complains of (e.g. in "Putnam and the Relativist Menace"), namely Putnam's continuing to count Rorty as a relativist even in the face of Rorty's disclaimer.

26   *Experience and Nature*; quoted by Davidson, "The Structure and Content Truth," p. 279,

27   Ibid.

28   Rorty writes: "To try to make truth approachable and reachable is to do what Davidson deplores, to humanize truth" ("Is Truth a Goal of Enquiry?," p. 298). I think this is a misreading of Davidson's opposition to an "epistemic" conception of truth. Davidson opposes the idea that an account of what it is for a claim to be true needs to incorporate a reference to, for instance, human powers of recognition. That is not at all to say that it is all right to conceive truth as out of reach of human powers of recognition.

29   For a sounding of this note in the context of Rorty's anti-authoritarianism, consider the following passage: "my preferred narrative is a story of human beings as having recently gotten out from under the thought of, and the need for, authority. I see James's suggestion that we carry utilitarianism over from morals into epistemology as crucial to this anti-authoritarianism of the spirit. For James shows us how to see Truth not as something we have to respect, but as a pointless nominalization of the useful adjective we apply to beliefs that are getting us what we want. Ceasing to see Truth as the name of an authority and coming to see the search for stable and useful beliefs as simply one more part of the pursuit of happiness are essential if we are to have the experimental attitude toward social existence that Dewey commended and the experimental attitude toward individual existence that Romanticism commended." ("Response to Bernstein," in Herman J. Saatkamp, Jr., ed., *Rorty and Pragmatism: The Philosopher Responds to His Critics* (Vanderbilt University Press, Nashville and London, 1995), pp. 68–71, at p. 71.)

30   This thought too could be put in Freudian terms.

10

NOTES ON RELATIVISM

Paul Feyerabend

Three Initial Statements of the Relativist Position

R1: Man is the measure of all things; of those that are that they are; and of those that are not, that they are not.

R2: Whatever seems to somebody, is to him to whom it seems.

R3: That the laws, customs, facts that are being put before the citizens ultimately rest on the pronouncements, beliefs and perceptions of human beings and that important matters should therefore be referred to the (perceptions and thoughts of the) people concerned and not to abstract agencies and distant experts.

Truth and Reality in Protagoras

The distinction between being and seeming, truth and falsehood, the facts as they are and the facts as they are said or thought to be, was a familiar (though often only implied) part of common discourse long before Protagoras had formulated R1. 'As in the most contemporary idiom, so in Homer and Sophocles the man who speaks the truth "tells it like it is" and the liar tells it otherwise.'[1]

The presocratic philosophers, especially Parmenides, sharpened the distinction and made the duality (true–false) explicit. In addition they gave unified accounts of everything that could be said to be. These accounts conflicted with the unphilosophical ways of 'telling it like it is'. For the philosophers the conflict showed that common-sense was incapable of reaching truth. Democritus, for example, asserted that 'bitter and sweet are opinions, colour is an opinion – in truth there are atoms and the void',[2] while Parmenides rejected the 'ways of humans' (B1, 27), of 'the many' (B6, 7) who, being guided by 'habits based on much experience' (B7, 3), 'drift along, deaf as well

Paul Feyerabend, "Notes on Relativism," in *Farewell to Reason* (London and New York: Verso, 1987), pp. 49–62. Reprinted by permission of the publisher.

as blind, disturbed and undecided' (B6, 6ff). Thus statements such as 'this is red', or 'that moves' which describe important events in the lives of artists, physicians, generals, navigators as well as ordinary human beings were summarily excluded from the domain of truth.

One of Protagoras' aims seems to have been to restore such statements to their former eminence. 'You and I,' Protagoras seems to say, 'our physicians, artists, artisans know many things and we live as we do because of this knowledge. Now these philosophers call our knowledge opinions based on shiftless experience and contrast "the many", i.e. people like us, with the enlightened few, i.e. themselves and their strange theories. Well, as far as I am concerned truth lies with us, with our "opinions" and "experiences" and we, "the many", not abstract theories, are the measure of things.'[3] Protagoras' reference to sensations (*Theaet.*, 152b1ff) can be seen in this light: 'sensations', for Protagoras, are neither the technical entities Plato constructs to get R1 into trouble (156a2ff) nor Ayerian sense-data; they are what common people rely on when judging their surroundings. Things are hot or cold for a person when the person feels them to be hot or cold, and not when a philosopher, using theory, pronounces the presence of The Hot or The Cold (two of Empedocles's abstract 'elements'). Protagoras's comments on mathematics (a circle cannot touch a ruler at only a single point – Aristotle, *Met.*, 998a) reflect the same attitude: practical concepts overrule concepts that have been separated from human action (modern constructivists proceed in an analogous way).[4] Both the arguments [outlined earlier] ('measuring' depends on circumstances; 'opinions' can be obtained in highly sophisticated ways) and the present considerations show that Protagoras reintroduced commonsense ways of establishing truth and defended them against the abstract claims of some of his predecessors. This, however, is not yet the whole story.

The reason is that Protagoras combined his return to common sense in matters of truth with rather uncommonsensical ideas about falsehood. According to *Euthydemus* 286c and *Theaet.* 167a7ff., he thought it impossible to (try to speak truthfully and yet) make a false assertion. It seems that this doctrine was connected with the idea, found in Parmenides (B 2, 8; B 8, 7) and exploited by Gorgias (*On the Non Existent or on Nature*), that false statements, being about nothing, also say nothing: perception and opinion, the customary measures of truth, are infallible measures and the worlds projected by different individuals, groups, nations are as they perceive and describe them – they are all equally real. However, *they are not equally good or beneficial* (to those who live in them). A sick person lives in a world where everything tastes sour and therefore is sour (166e2ff.) – but he is not happy in it. The members of a racist society live in a world where people fall into sharply defined groups, some creative and benevolent, others parasitical and evil – but their lives are not very comfortable. A desire for change may arise in either case. How can the change be effected?

According to Protagoras changes are caused by wise men (166d1ff.). Wise men cannot change falsehood into truth or appearance into reality – but they can change an uncomfortable, painful and threatening reality into a better world. Just as a physician, using medicine, changes a real but distressful state of an individual into an equally real but agreeable state (of the same individual – or of a changed individual), in the same way a wise man, using words, changes an evil and ruinous state (of an individual or of an entire city) into a beneficial state. Note that according to this account it is the individual or the state, not the wise man, who judges the success of the procedure. Note also that this judgement, acting back on the wise man, may improve his own state of expertise and thus turn him into a better advisor. Note, finally, that in a democracy the 'wise man' is the community of citizens as represented by the general assembly: what the assembly says is both a truth about society and an instrument for changing it, and the reality brought about by its statements is an instrument for changing the procedures and the opinions of the assembly in turn. This is how Protagoras' theory of truth and reality can be used to explain the workings of a direct democracy.

It is interesting to compare Protagoras's views with the more familiar forms of philosophical and scientific objectivism. Objectivism asserts that everybody, no matter what their perceptions and opinions, lives in the same world. Special groups (astronomers, physicists, chemists, biologists) explore this world, other special groups (politicians, industrialists, religious leaders) make sure that people can survive in it. First the manufacturers of an objective reality go on their flights of fancy, then the material and social engineers connect the results with the needs and wishes of the common folk, that is, with reality as defined by Protagoras. Protagoras collapses the two procedures into one: 'reality' (to speak the objectivists' language) is explored by attempting to satisfy human wishes in a more direct way; thought and emotions work together (and are perhaps not even separated). We might say that the approach of Protagoras is an engineering approach, while the objectivists who separate theory and practice, thought and emotion, nature and society, and who carefully distinguish between objective reality on the one side and experience and everyday life on the other, introduce sizeable metaphysical components. Trying to change their surroundings so that they look more and more like this reality (and thus make them feel comfortable), the objectivists act of course like pure Protagoreans, but not like Protagorean wise men. To become wise, they must 'relativize' their approach. There are many indications that this is already part of their practice.

To start with, objectivists have not constructed one world, but many. Of course, some of these worlds are more popular than others, but this is due to a preference for certain values (in addition to the value of objectivity – see section 2), not to intrinsic advantages: results of measurement are preferred to qualities because technological changes are preferred to harmonious adaptations; laws of nature overrule divine principles because they act in a more monotonous way – and so on. The plurality affects the sciences which contain highly valued experimental enterprises such as molecular biology side by side with despised qualitative disciplines such as botany or rheology. The most fundamental science, physics, has so far failed to give us a unified account of space, time and matter. What we have, therefore (apart from grandiloquent promises and superficial popularizations), is a variety of approaches based on a variety of models and successful in restricted domains, i.e. what we have is a Protagorean practice.

Secondly, the transition from a particular model to practical matters often involves such sizeable modifications that we would do better to speak of an entirely new world. Industry in various countries confirms this conjecture by decoupling its research from universities and engineering schools and developing procedures more suited to its own particular needs. Social programmes, ecological studies, impact reports for technological projects often raise problems unanswered by any existing science; those engaged in the studies are forced to extrapolate, redraw boundaries, or develop entirely new ideas to overcome the limits of specialist knowledge. Thirdly, objectivist approaches, especially in health, agriculture and social engineering, may succeed by forcing reality into their patterns; the distorted societies then start showing traces of the patterns imposed. This is again a truly Protagorean procedure except that it inverts the Protagorean chain of command: what counts is the judgement of the interfering scientists and not the judgement of the people interfered with. Fourth, the interference often upsets a delicate equilibrium of aims and means and so does more harm than good – and this is now recognized by the 'developers' themselves. In his study *The Constitution of Liberty*, Chicago 1960, chapter 4, p. 54, F. A. von Hayek distinguishes between what he calls 'two different traditions in the theory of liberty', 'one empirical and unsystematic, the other speculative and rationalistic – the first based on an interpretation of traditions and institutions which had spontaneously grown up and were but imperfectly understood, the second aiming at the construction of a Utopia, which has often been tried, but never successfully', and he explains why the former is to be preferred to the latter. But the former tradition is closely related to the Protagorean point of view whose 'seeming' reflects partly comprehended, partly unnoticed adaptations to what the nature of the moment happens to be. If debates play an important role in the adaptations and if the debates are carried out by an assembly of free citizens so that everybody has the right to act as a 'wise man', then we have what I shall call a *democratic relativism*. In the next section I shall describe this form of society in somewhat greater detail. Before that, however, I wish to make some comments on the notion of a debate.

One of the main objections against Protagoras is that different Protagorean worlds cannot clash and that debates between their inhabitants are therefore impossible. This may be true for an outside observer; it is not true for the participants who, perceiving a conflict, can start a quarrel without asking his permission. The parties to a debate (I shall call them A and B) need not share any elements (meanings, intentions, propositions) that can be detached from their interaction and examined independently of the role they play in it. Even if such elements existed the question would still arise how, being outside human lives, they can enter them and affect them in the specific way in which an assertion, or a thesis, or a belief affects the consciousness and the actions of the participants. What is needed is that A has the impression that B shares something with him, seems to be aware of this, acts accordingly; that a semanticist C, examining A and B, can develop a theory of what is shared and how what is shared affects the conversation; and that A and B, on reading C, have the impression that he has hit the nail on the head. Actually, what is needed is much less: A and B need not accept what they find when reading C – C may still survive and be respected if there exists a profession that values his ideas. Reputations, after all, are made and broken by the impression the actions of some people make on others. Appeals to a higher authority are empty words unless the authority is noticed, i.e. appears in the consciousness of the one or the other individual.

Democratic Relativism

R1, interpreted as R3, is of far greater importance than modern philosophical analyses and 'clarifications' would make us believe. It can guide people in their dealings with nature, social institutions and with each other. To explain I shall first give some historical background.

Most societies that depend on a close collaboration between diverse groups have experts, people with special knowledge and special skills. Hunters and gatherers, it seems, possessed all the knowledge and all the skills necessary for survival. Large-scale hunts and agriculture then led to a division of labour and tighter social controls. Experts arose from this development: the Homeric warriors were experts in the conduct of war; rulers like Agamemnon, in addition, knew how to unite different tribes under a single purpose; physicians healed bodies, mantics interpreted omens and predicted the future. The social position of experts did not always correspond to the importance of their services. Warriors might be servants of society, to be called upon in times of danger, but without special powers in times of peace; on the other hand, they might be its masters, shaping it in accordance with their own warlike ideology. Scientists once had no greater influence than plumbers; today large sections of society reflect their view of things. Experts were a matter of course in Egypt, Sumeria, Babylonia, Assyria, among the Hittites, the Hurrites, the Phoenicians and the many other peoples that populated the ancient Near East. They played an important role in the Stone Age as is shown by the amazing remnants of Stone Age astronomy and Stone Age mathematics that have been discovered over the years. The first recorded discussion of the problems of expert knowledge occurred in Greece, in the fifth and fourth centuries B.C., among the sophists, and then in Plato and Aristotle.

The discussion anticipated most modern problems and positions. The ideas it produced are simple and straightforward and unencumbered by the useless technicalities of modern intellectual debates. We can all learn from these old thinkers, their argument and their views.

The discussion also went beyond the authority of special fields, such as medicine and navigation; it included inquiries concerning the good life and the right form of government: should a city be governed by a traditional authority such as a king, or by a board of political experts, or should government be a matter for all?

Two views emerged from the discussion. According to the *first view* an expert is a person who produces important knowledge and has important skills. His knowledge and his skills must not be questioned or changed by non-experts. They must be taken over by society in precisely the form suggested by the experts. High priests, kings, architects, physicians occasionally saw their function in this way – and so did some of the societies in which they worked. In Greece (Athens, fifth century B.C.) this view was an object of ridicule.[5]

Representatives of the *second view* pointed out that experts in arriving at their results often restrict their vision. They do not study all phenomena but only those in a special field; and they do not examine all aspects of these special phenomena but only those related to their occasionally rather narrow interests. It would therefore be foolish to regard expert ideas as 'true', or as 'real' – period – without further studies that go beyond expert limits. And it would be equally foolish to introduce them into society without having made sure that the professional aims of the experts agree with the aims of society. Even politicians cannot be left unattended, for though they deal with society as a whole they deal with it in a narrow way, being guided by party interests and superstitions and only rarely by what others might regard as 'true knowledge'.

According to Plato, who held the view just described, the further studies are the task of super-experts, namely philosophers. Philosophers define what it means to know and what is good for society. Many intellectuals favour this *authoritarian approach*. They may overflow with concern for their fellow human beings, they may speak of 'truth', 'reason', 'objectivity', even of 'liberty', but what they really want is the power to reshape the world in their own image. There is no reason to assume that this image will be less one-sided than the ideas it wants to control and so it, too, must be examined. But who will carry out *this* examination? And how can we be sure that the authority to which we entrust the matter does not again introduce its own narrow conceptions?

The answer given by the *democratic approach* (in a sense to be clarified as the argument proceeds) arose in particular historical circumstances. 'Natural' societies 'grew' without much conscious planning on the part of those who lived in them. In Greece major changes, in special fields as well as in society at large, gradually became a matter of debate and explicit reconstruction. Athenian democracy at the time of Pericles took care that every free man could have his say in the debate and could temporarily assume any position, however powerful. We do not know the steps that led to this very specific type of adaptation and it is by no means certain that the development was beneficial in all respects. Some of the difficulties that trouble us today suggest that debate and 'rational discourse' in particular are not a universal panacaea, that they may be too crude to capture the more subtle threats to our well being and that there may be better ways of conducting the business of life.[6] But societies that are committed to it and define liberty and a worthwhile life accordingly, cannot exclude a single opinion, however outlandish. For what are political debates about? They are about the needs and the wishes of the citizens. And who are better judges of these needs and wishes than the citizens themselves? It is absurd first to declare that a society serves the needs of 'the people' and then to let autistic experts (liberals, Marxists, Freudians, sociologists of all persuasions) decide what 'the people' 'really' need and want. Of course, popular wishes have to take the world into account and this means: the available resources, the intentions of the neighbours, their weapons, their policies – even the possibility that strong popular desires and aversions are unconscious and accessible to special methods only. According to Plato and his modern successors (scientists, politicians, business leaders), it is here that the need for expert advice arises. But experts are just as confused about fundamental matters as those they are supposed to advise and the variety of their suggestions is at least as large as the variety implicit in public opinion.[7] They often commit grievous mistakes. Besides, they never consider all aspects that affect the rest of the population but only those that happen to correspond to the current state of their speciality. This state is often far removed from the problems faced by the citizens. Citizens, guided but not replaced by experts, can pinpoint such shortcomings and work towards their removal.[8] Every trial by jury provides examples of the limits and contradictions inherent in expert testimony and encourages the jurors to make reasonable guesses in recondite fields. The citizens of a democracy, Protagoras would say, expressing the political ideas of Periclean Athens (which differed from the science-ridden democracies of today and was less inhibited by restrictions), receive this kind of education not merely once or twice in their lifetime, but every single day of their lives. They live in a state – small and manageable Athens – where information freely flows from one citizen to the next. They not only *live* in this state, they also *conduct its business*; they discuss important problems in the general assembly and occasionally lead the discussions, they participate in law courts and artistic competitions, they judge the work of writers who are now regarded as some of the greatest dramatists of 'civilised humanity' (Aeschylus, Sophocles, Euripides, Aristophanes all competed for public prizes), they initiate and terminate wars and auxiliary expeditions, they receive and examine the reports of generals, navigators, architects, food merchants, they arrange foreign aid, welcome foreign dignitaries, listen to and debate with sophists, garrulous Socrates included – and so on. They use experts all the time – but in an advisory capacity, and they make the final decisions themselves. According to Protagoras the knowledge the citizens acquire during this unstructured but rich, complex and active process of learning (learning is not separated from living, it is part of it – the citizens learn while carrying out the duties that need the knowledge acquired) suffices for judging all events in the city, the most complex technical problems included. Examining a particular situation (such as the danger of a meltdown in a nearby nuclear reactor – to use a modern example), the citizens will, of course, have to study new things – but they have acquired a facility of picking up unusual items and, most importantly, they have a sense of perspective that allows them to see the strong points and the limitations of the proposals under review. No doubt the citizens will commit mistakes – everybody commits mistakes – and they will suffer from them. But suffering from their mistakes they will also become wiser while the mistakes of experts, being hidden away, create trouble for everybody but enlighten only a privileged few. We may sum up this point of view by declaring that

R4:   citizens, and not special groups have the last word in deciding what is true or false, useful or useless for their society.

So far, a short and very sketchy account of ideas that are found, in traces, in Protagoras and in Periclean Athens. I shall call the point of view they adumbrate *democratic relativism*.

Democratic relativism is a form of *relativism*; it says that different cities (different societies) may look at the world in different ways and regard different things as acceptable. It is *democratic* because basic assumptions are (in principle) debated and decided upon by all citizens. Democratic relativism has much to recommend it, especially for us in the West, but it is not the one and only possible way of living. Many societies are built up in a different way and yet provide a home and means of survival for their inhabitants [. . .].

Democratic relativism has interesting ancestors, the *Oresteia* of Aeschylus among them: Orestes avenged his father; this satisfies the law of Zeus, represented by Apollo. To avenge his father Orestes has to kill his mother; this mobilises the Eumenides who oppose the murder of blood relatives. Orestes flees and seeks protection at the altar of Athene. To solve the problem created by the conflicting moralities, Athene initiates a 'rational debate' between Apollo and the Eumenides, with Orestes participating. Part of the debate is the question of whether a mother is a blood relative. The Eumenides say she is: Orestes spilt the blood of a blood relative and must be punished. Apollo says she is not: the mother provides warmth, protection and nourishment for the seed, she is a breeding oven, but she does not contribute her blood to the child (this view was held for a long time after). Today the debate would be resolved by experiments and expert judgement: experts would withdraw into their laboratories and Apollo, Orestes and Athene would have to wait for their findings. In Aeschylus the matter is decided by a vote: a court of Athenian citizens is informed about the case and gives its opinion. The votes are equally balanced after Athene adds her own vote in favour of Orestes (she was born without a mother) and so Orestes is released from the revenge of the Eumenides. But Athene also declares that their world view will not be discarded: the city needs *all* the agencies that made it grow, it cannot afford to lose a single one of them. True, there are now new laws and a new morality – the laws of Zeus as represented by Apollo. But these laws are not permitted to sweep aside what came before. They are granted entrance into the city *provided* they share the power with their predecessors. Thus a generation before Herodotus popular laws and customs were declared to be *valid* while their validity was *restricted* to make room for other, but equally important laws and customs. [. . .]

Democratic relativism does not exclude the search for an objective, i.e. a thought-, perception- and society-independent reality. It welcomes research dedicated to finding objective facts but controls it by (subjective) public opinion. It thus denies that showing the objectivity of a result means showing that it is binding for all. Objectivism is treated as one tradition among many, not as a basic structure of society. There is no reason to be troubled by such a procedure and to fear that it will destroy important achievements. For although objectivists have discovered, delineated and presented situations and facts that exist and develop independently of the act of discovery, they cannot guarantee that the situations and facts are also independent of the entire tradition that led to their discovery [. . .]. Besides, even the most determined (and best paid) application of what many Western intellectuals regard as the most advanced versions of objective research have so far failed to give us the unity the idea of a universal and objective truth suggests. There are grandiloquent promises, there are blunt assertions of unifications already achieved but what we have *in fact* are regions of knowledge similar in structure to the regionalism Herodotus described so vividly in his history. Physics, the alleged core of chemistry and, via chemistry, of biology, has at least three principal subdivisions: the domain of the very large ruled by gravitation and tamed by Einstein's theory of general relativity (and various modifications thereof); the domain of the very small, ruled by the strong nuclear forces but not yet tamed by any comprehensive theory (the 'Grand Unified Theories' or 'GUTs' are, according to Gell-Mann, 'neither grand, nor unified; it might even be said that they are not even theories – just glorified models'); and, finally, an intermediate domain where quantum theory reigns supreme. Outside physics we have qualitative knowledge which contains commonsense and parts of biology, chemistry, geology as yet unreduced to the 'basic science' of the moment. The theories or points of view that define the processes in all these domains either clash, or cease to make sense when universalised, i.e. when assumed to be valid under all circumstances. Hence we may either interpret them as instruments of prediction with no relevance for what is true, or real, or we may say that they are 'true for' special areas which are defined by special questions, procedures, principles. Alternatively, we may assert that one theory reflects the basic structure of the world while the others deal with secondary phenomena. In this case speculation rather than empirical research becomes the measure of truth. Pluralism survives, but it is lifted on to the metaphysical plane. Speaking in the manner of Herodotus we can summarise the situation in the following way:

R5:   the world, as described by our scientists and anthropologists, consists of (social and physical) regions with specific laws and conceptions of reality. In the social domain we have relatively stable societies which have demonstrated an ability to survive in their own particular surroundings and possess great adaptive powers. In the physical domain we have different points of view, valid in different areas, but inapplicable outside. Some of these points of view are more detailed – these are our scientific theories; others simpler, but more general – these are the various philosophical or commonsense views that affect the construction of 'reality'. The attempt to enforce a universal truth (a universal way of finding truth) has led to disasters in the social domain and to empty formalisms combined with never-to-be-fulfilled promises in the natural sciences.

Note that *R5 is not meant to be read as a universal truth*. It is a statement made within a particular tradition (Western intellectual debate starting from and leading towards scientific results), explained and defended (more or less competently) according to the rules of this tradition and indicating that the tradition is incoherent. The statement is of no interest to a Pygmy, or to a follower of Lao-Tsu (although the latter may study it for historical reasons). Note also that parts of R5 depend on a special evaluation of knowledge claims: quantum mechanics and relativity are assumed to offer equally important, equally successful, and equally acceptable accounts of the material universe. Some critics (Einstein among them) judge the situation differently. For them relativity physics goes to the bottom of things while the quantum theory is an important but highly unsatisfactory prelude to more substantial views. These physicists reject R5 and assert that universally valid theories already exist. As I said above, this introduces metaphysical conjectures where assertions concerning objectivity depend on a subjective weighing of knowledge claims. There are again many such approaches (the orthodox one among them) which means that plurality is transformed (it is made metaphysical), it is not removed. [. . .]

Democratic relativism is not the philosophy that guides modern 'democracies': power, here, is delegated to distant power centres, and important decisions are made by experts, or the 'representatives of the people', hardly ever by 'the people' themselves. Still, it seems a good starting point for Western intellectuals trying to improve their own life and the lives of their fellow human beings (it seems a good starting point for citizens' initiatives). It encourages debate, argument, and social reconstruction based on both. It is a specific political view, restricted in appeal and not necessarily better than the more intuitive procedures of 'primitive' societies. Yet since it invites the participation of all it may lead to the discovery that there are many ways of being in the world, that people have a right to use the ways that appeal to them and that using these ways they may lead a happy and fulfilling life.[9]

Notes

The statements of the relativist position at the beginning (and elsewhere) have been extracted from a longer, more nuanced discussion in the original paper, and have been renumbered for this occasion – editors.

1   Charles Kahn, *The Verb Be*, Dordrecht 1973, p. 363; cf. pp. 365, 369. For what follows see also Ch. 2 of Felix Heinimann, *Nomos and Physis*, Basel 1945, and Kurt von Fritz, 'Nous, Noein and their Derivatives in Presocratic Philosophy', *Classical Philology*, Vol. 40 (1945), pp. 223ff; Vol. 41 (1946), pp. 12ff.

2   Diels-Kranz, Fragment B9. According to Reinhardt (V. E. Alfieri, *Atomos Idea*, Florence 1953, p. 127), the word *nomo* in the fragment is used in parallel to Parmenides' *nenomistai* (B6, 8) which in turn (Heinimann, *op. cit.*, 74ff) may be rendered as 'being customarily believed by the many' (but not true).

3   On the phrase 'the many' in Greek philosophical discourse from Homer to Aristotle cf. Hans-Dieter Voigtländer, *Der Philosophe und die Vielen*, Wiesbaden 1980. Protagoras is dealt with on pp. 81ff. 'Nobody can pretend', writes Victor Ehrenberg, *From Solon to Socrates*, Methuen, London and New York 1973, p. 340, 'that the sentence (R1) or its translations is clear and meaningful. It needs further explanation and that is by no means obvious . . . It is likely that Protagoras went beyond the meaning of mere sense perception . . . The main point, the one clearly positive and the one which impressed people at once and for all time, is the *metron anthropos*, the central position given to man.' I would add: to man insofar as he is engaged in his ordinary, day-to-day activities, not to man the inventor of abstract theories.

4   This interpretation was suggested by E. Kapp, *Gnomon*, Vol. 12 (1936), pp. 70ff. Kurt von Fritz adopts Kapp's views [. . .]; in his article 'Protagoras' [. . .] he compares Protagoras' statement with the complaints of the author of *Ancient Medicine* that medical theoreticians describe illnesses and cures in terms of abstract entities such as The Hot, The Cold, The Wet, The Dry without saying a word about the particular food (hot milk? lukewarm water?) that is supposed to be taken or the particular ailment (diarrhoea) that affects the patient. Considering such parallels, von Fritz infers (p. 114) that Protagoras' statement 'was not originally designed to formulate a consistent sensualism, relativism or subjectivism but rather wanted to confront the strange philosophy of the Eleatics (according to whom Being had not part and did not change), or Heraclitus [according to whom there was only change] and of others who had left the communis opinio far behind with a commonsense philosophy just as the author of (*Ancient Medicine*) confronted a medical school which derived its science from general philosophical and scientific principles with a purely empirical medicine and added explicitly that a medical theory could be of value only if comprehensible for a layman.' Cf. also F. M. Cornford, *Plato's Theory of Knowledge*, New York 1957, p. 69: 'All that the objections (raised in *Theaet.* 164c–165e) in fact established was that "perception" must be stretched to include awareness of memory images.'

5   Cf. e.g. J. Burkhardt, *Griechische Kulturgeschichte*, Munich 1977, Vol. 4, pp. 118ff.

6   The problem alluded to forms a vast subject which we are only slowly beginning to understand. For example, it is becoming clear that the difficulties of some so-called 'Third World' countries may be results of the manipulative rationality of the West rather than of an

original barrenness of the land, or of the incompetence of those tending it. The expansion of Western civilization robbed many indigenous people of their dignity and their means of survival. Wars, slavery, simple murder was for a long time the right way of dealing with 'primitives'. But the humanitarians have not always fared better than the gangsters. Imposing their own views of what it means to be human and what a good life consists in, they have often added to the destruction wrought by their colonial predecessors. [. . .]

7   As an example consider the many ways in which Freudians, existentialists, geneticists, behaviourists, neurophysiologists, Marxists, theologians (hardcore Catholics; liberation theologists) define human nature and the great variety of suggestions they make on topics such as education, war, crime, etc.

8   Robert Jungk, in an interesting and provocative book about nuclear power (*The New Tyranny*, New York 1979), reports that citizens are often better informed about relevant scientific literature than scientists and that, having different and wider interests (for example, they are interested in the future wellbeing of their children), they may consider effects not yet examined by scientists. A concrete example of the impact of citizens' initiatives is examined in R. Meehan, *The Atom and the Fault*, Cambridge, Mass. 1984.

9   Some modern liberals grant foreign cultures the right to exist provided they participate in international trade, permit Western doctors to heal them and Western missionaries (of science and of other religions) to explain the wonders of science and Christianity to their children. But the idea of a peaceful Commonwealth of Nations whose members learn from each other thus constantly rising to new stages of knowledge and awareness is not shared by the Pygmies (for example) who prefer to be left alone (C. M. Turnbull, 'The Lesson of the Pygmies', *Scientific American* 208 (1), 1963). Rationalists such as Karl Popper (*The Open Society and its Enemies*, Vol. 1, New York 1963, p. 118) have no objection to applying pressure at this point: the entrance into mature humanity may have to be enforced 'by some form of imperialism'. I don't think that the achievements of science and rationalism are sufficiently dazzling to justify such a procedure.

SUGGESTED READING

Brandom, Robert, "Pragmatism, Phenomenalism, and Truth Talk," *Midwest Studies in Philosophy*, 12 (1988), pp. 75–93.

Brandom, Robert, *Making It Explicit* (Cambridge, MA: Harvard University Press, 1994).

Carnap, Rudolf, "Empiricism, Semantics, and Ontology," *Revue Internationale de Philosophie*, 11 (1950), pp. 20–40.

Carnap, Rudolf, "Intellectual Autobiography," in P. A. Schilpp (ed.), *The Philosophy of Rudolf Carnap* (La Salle, IL: Open Court, 1963), pp. 1–84.

Dewey, John, *Experience and Nature*, in *John Dewey: The Later Works, 1925–1953*, vol. 1 (Carbondale, IL: Southern Illinois University Press, 1988).

Dewey, John, *The Quest for Certainty*, in *John Dewey: The Later Works, 1925–1953*, vol. 4 (Carbondale, IL: Southern Illinois University Press, 1988).

Fine, Arthur, "Truthmongering: Less is True," *Canadian Journal of Philosophy*, 19 (1989), pp. 611–16.

Frege, Gottlob, "The Thought: A Logical Inquiry," *Mind*, 65 (1956), pp. 289–311.

Heidegger, Martin, *Being and Time*, trans. J. Stambaugh (Albany, NY: SUNY Press, 1996).

Horwich, Paul, *Truth* (Oxford: Oxford University Press, 1998).

Kuhn, Thomas, *The Structure of Scientific Revolutions* (Chicago: University of Chicago Press, 1962).

Latour, Bruno, "Clothing the Naked Truth," in Hilary Lawson (ed.), *Dismantling Truth: Reality in the Post-Modern World* (New York: St Martin's Press, 1989), pp. 101–26.

Lyotard, Jean-Fraçois, *The Postmodern Condition: A Report on Knowledge* (Minneapolis: University of Minnesota Press, 1979).

Lyotard, Jean-François, *The Differend: Phrases in Dispute*, trans. Georges Van Den Abbeele (Minneapolis: University of Minnesota Press, 1988).

Nancy, Jean-Luc, *The Inoperative Community*, trans. Christopher Fynsk (Minneapolis: University of Minnesota Press, 1991).

Rorty, Richard, "Response to Jürgen Habermas," in Robert Brandom (ed.), *Rorty and his Critics* (Oxford: Blackwell, 2000), pp. 56–64.

Rorty, Richard, "Response to John McDowell," in Robert Brandom (ed.), *Rorty and his Critics* (Oxford: Blackwell, 2000), pp. 124–8.

Sellars, Wilfrid, *Science and Metaphysics: Variations of Kantian Themes* (New York: Humanities Press, 1968).

Williams, Michael, "Do We (Epistemologists) Need a Theory of Truth?," *Philosophical Topics*, 14 (1986), pp. 223–42.

Williams, Michael, "Meaning and Deflationary Truth," *Journal of Philosophy*, 96/11 (1999), pp. 545–64.

Wright, Crispin, "Truth: A Traditional Debate Reviewed," in S. Blackburn and K. Simmons (eds), *Truth* (Oxford: Oxford University Press, 1999), pp. 203–38.

PART IV

NON-PROPOSITIONAL TRUTH: LANGUAGE, ART, AND WORLD

INTRODUCTION

Few doubt that truth is to be understood propositionally. But this idea seems to rest on the twin assumptions that truth begins with language, and that language is essentially propositional. Each of these claims is strongly contested here. Such contestation is provoked by: revisionary thoughts about the nature of language (Derrida), by dwelling as the creative and critical taking up of tradition along with a multiplicity of other voices (Vattimo), by the dependence of reflective truth on a more fundamental perceptual engagement in the world (Merleau-Ponty), and by the essential creativity of our deployment of language in novel circumstances (Margolis).

These various thinkers have no single view on how truth is tied up with the non- or pre-propositional, but they share the sense that truth is not simply a technical expression that can be given an isolated theoretical treatment. The very idea of a theory of truth would seem to privilege theoretical reflection on the nature of truth, just when that is in question. In part, this accounts for the fact that the term 'truth' here often seems to be used in a rather broad-brush kind of way. But it would be more to the point to say that 'truth' is understood not just as a particular philosophical problem, but as a fundamental philosophical and cultural value, and we cannot adequately recognize that value even theoretically without bringing it into play with other major philosophical categories – history, perception, world, body, language, social practices, etc.

All of these contributors have, in one way or another, been touched by phenomenology, by the sense that philosophy has to do with a response to the complexity of human experience. This is clear enough in the case of Merleau-Ponty, whose name for that experience is "perception" – understood not just as being struck by stimuli, nor as imposing categories on things, but rather as an active engagement in the world. It is clear for Vattimo, as he draws on Heidegger and Gadamer in developing a critical account of the dwelling presupposed by any sense of truth as propositional. Derrida and Margolis are more complex cases. One of Derrida's most scholarly works (*Speech and Phenomena*[1]) is a careful "deconstruction" of the phenomenological privilege of the voice as a primary source and carrier of meaning. In our selection here, Derrida expands his target to include the whole theory of the sign as a derivative phenomenon representing some deeper level of meaning. Instead Derrida will emphasize the disseminating power of language as "writing."[2] On this account, the creativity of language begins when it is acknowledged that it is not tied down to a pre-given layer of meaning that would escape its play. The direct focus of Margolis's concerns is the repudiation of the prejudice of bivalence in truth – the assumption that our only options are true and false. But he achieves this by appealing to the intentional features of cultural phenomena, features which require interpretation, and for which a certain relativism is quite compatible with objectivity. As we have seen, for Margolis, both on the side of the object, and on "our" side, we can find sites of resistance to bivalent apriorism. Works of art (and literature, and even theories of science) elicit multiple "incongruent" but singly plausible readings. And more basically, the historically sedimented social practices that give rise to these various senses of the objective have to respond creatively to novel situations in which the right way to apply a certain concept will not always have been charted.

Margolis's position is unlike all the others in the way in which he harnesses logical and formal considerations in the service of his defense of relativism. This is a particularly intriguing move, opening the way to interpretive pluralism by courteously spelling out just what the "rules" of operating with multivalent truth-assignations would look like. This raises the fascinating question as to whether phenomenology is not too precipitate in opposing itself to science, reflection, nature, etc. If it had been aware of the full range of logics, would it have been so eager to postulate pre-propositional levels of truth? We return to this issue below.

Throughout this book, we stress the idea of truth as a basic philosophical and cultural value. Each of these contributors is identifying a "strong" version of this value as something we need to set aside. And it is revealing that for many of the Europeans here, this strong version is identified directly or indirectly with *theology*, which often takes the shape of the absolutism targeted by both Nietzsche and James (see Part I above).[3] We can capture what is implied here as a certain shape of thought – the idea of "truth" as a point of legitimating reference that would be outside or beyond the mundane operation of human decision, judgment, choice – a fixed point by which one could move the world. We may suppose we had long since abandoned such an idea, or that it is a confusion even to connect it with the contemporary question of truth. But when it is targeted by Derrida, for example, it is clear that he sees this "theology" as inhabiting many contemporary accounts of language, especially those based on the idea of the "sign." If we understand the sign as a signifier linked to a signified[4] and then suppose that the layer of the signified is one of meaning no longer subjected to the play of difference, to history, to changes in our practices – *that* is theology. And when Margolis identifies Platonism, or the idea that what is objective has to have a fixed essence, as the indefensible presupposition of the usual understanding of truth (bivalence), he is making a similar point. We may find it strange to see the word 'theology' used in this way. Such a use combines the formal sense (positing something outside the system that nevertheless controls the system)[5] and the historical sense that philosophy and theology have long been deeply intertwined.[6] To the extent that the value of truth is caught up in such a structure or logic, we will not be surprised to learn that the struggle against the operation of such regimes of truth is long and difficult and often takes a political form. (See Part VI below.) And Derrida confirms this when he writes here that "one does not leave the epoch whose closure one can outline." Margolis, for example, successfully resists the idea that the link between essentialism and bivalence requires that we ditch bivalence entirely. Rather, we limit its scope, and deny its universality.

The challenge that Derrida sets to those who draw sustenance from phenomenology, albeit hermeneutically enhanced with a richer account of language and history, is to show that phenomenology does not just reinscribe this "theological" structure. In a remark he perhaps directed at both Husserl and Merleau-Ponty, Derrida once claimed that "There never has been any perception."[7] The implication is that what Merleau-Ponty claims to find in perception (perceptual "faith," as he sometimes puts it) is a version of the same theological structure: positing grounds immune from the vagaries of the world they support. And Merleau-Ponty, as we know, describes this perceptual engagement as the space of truth. It is clear that there are, for Merleau-Ponty, substantive dimensions to this engagement, not least the spatial, temporal, and significative dimensions sustained by our mobile embodiment. But Merleau-Ponty might well respond that perception is not the site of some pristine essentialism, but precisely one of "difference" – of action, change, ambiguity, relationality, etc. – one in which meaning is not fixed but is constantly being created, with others, by engagement with what is given. We can treat this claim as an epistemological one, but, as Merleau-Ponty says in his concluding sentence, it is no less "an ethics." To call it an ethics, is, I suggest, to say that we cannot understand "science," "reflection," "language," without the capacity for return – a turning back to "the naive evidence of things." This is undertaken not to verify this or that propositional claim, but rather to recall thoughtfully the background against which critical, theoretical claims alone make sense.

A similar move can be found in Paul Ricoeur's hermeneutics, when he insists on the "circle" in which science arises.[8] It may redescribe the real, but science is a social practice that begins in, and never leaves, the pre-scientific human world. For Ricoeur, this is the first step in a complex account differentiating various orders of truth dialectically in play. But whether it is science, or religious insight, or politics, he does not mystify the pre-reflective; rather, he sets it up as a pole in a dialectic of totalization and problematization. In the case of Vattimo (and Ricoeur), we may wonder just how far they really are from Derrida. In a later essay,[9] Derrida speaks of the need to "go through the undecidable," as an ethical imperative, where the "undecidable" can be glossed as the desperate but unavoidable inadequacy of bivalent conceptualization. Vattimo suggests that he differs from Derrida in understanding the multiplicity of voices that surround us as various responses to the call of transforming tradition, not as "mere confusion or arbitrariness."[10]

In some ways, Merleau-Ponty's hyper-reflection,[11] Margolis's restrictive deployment of bivalence, and Vattimo's creative dwelling could be treated as transformations of the same idea, albeit expressed in different terms. In the light of Vattimo's attempts to emphasize the creative and transformative relation to tradition, over against the somewhat more conservative tendencies of Gadamer, Gadamer might respond that when, for example, he understands poetry as a self-standing entity, impervious to translation,[12] he is explaining how it is that the multiplicity of voices does not just include living humans, but also their cultural products, that acquire a certain autonomy. While Derrida associates the metaphysical sense of truth with what we have called the "theological" structure of control from beyond the fray, and treats the phonocentric privilege of the voice in Husserl's phenomenology as an exemplary instance, Gadamer's account of the special status of the poem is precisely one in which any connection to what the poet meant is severed. So in this respect, poetry's contribution to the search for truth takes us away from the subjective, just as it does with Derrida and Margolis. And it shows us how tradition can still speak to us.[13]

These papers represent a range of different traditions: phenomenology (Merleau-Ponty), hermeneutics (Vattimo), neo-pragmatism (Margolis), and deconstruction (Derrida). The challenge of drawing them into conversation begins with the challenge of translating from one idiom to another. So far, we have arraigned these various authors around the question of the "theological" structure of truth, and found various complementarities lurking in the shadows of surface incongruency. But it is worth taking up further a question we raised earlier – whether Margolis's creative attention to the alethic dimension of interpretation – that of the formal and logical rules we operate with – does not open up ways forward that would weaken the justification for phenomenological moves. No longer would we see "representation" as such in need of re-connection to the truth. We would first have to consider the poverty of our particular ways of representing things. For example, we should not attack "logic" for excluding ambiguity until we have sampled a few fuzzy logics. There is a lesson to be learned here, but it is not precisely this one. Margolis does not merely introduce liberal alethic options – this is a facilitating move that opens onto taking seriously the ontological requirements of a world that is dynamic and often complexly intentional. What we can fruitfully keep in mind is the way in which what we call "truth" is not indeed some simple relation of agreement, adequation, or conformity, let alone some achievable ground of "presence," but is inseparable from what are often quite counter-intuitive structures.

We conclude by considering two such structures, exemplified by Derrida's logic of the supplement[14] and Nietzsche's association of truth and woman.[15]

Derrida describes the logic of the supplement as exhibited by a term which, by supplementing a system deemed to be already complete, actually completes it. For example, a supposedly pure and complete "spoken word" is "completed" by "writing" – that is, by being articulated and preserved within a system of public, external signs. The recognition of the "incompleteness" of the spoken word (or a "private language") displaces what we take to be the privileged site of truth from the private to the public. Analogously, his substitution of the word "trace" for the normal "sign" is accompanied by the insistence that the trace is not a trace of anything. There are just more traces, and no privileged meanings. This structure is further elaborated by Baudrillard's account of the simulacrum, an appearance without an original, which is his verdict on the contemporary world.[16] But we typically do not see things like this: "The simulacrum is never that which conceals the truth – it is the truth which conceals that there is none."[17] Derrida and Baudrillard both build on Nietzsche's account (at the end of his "How the Real World at last became a Myth"[18]) of the fate of appearances after the reality to which they have been opposed has evaporated. This makes the ideal of truth into a species of illusion. And again it is Nietzsche who reminds us that while science and art are both illusions, art is to be preferred because it, at least, knows that this is so.

The second and not unrelated paradoxical structure from which truth can no longer be separated, is that of desire. This, surely, is the point of Nietzsche's question: "Suppose truth were a woman, what then?"[19] It reappears in Kierkegaard's reference to Lessing's supposition that God might offer us a choice between the truth and the perpetual striving after truth. The point is that while there is an intimate connection between truth and desire, it may also be that the paradox of desire infects the ideal of truth – that it is destroyed by its fulfillment.[20] This seems paradoxical. When Husserl talks about truth and self-evidence, it is precisely the prospect of fulfillment that is held out. Vattimo's insistence on the need to accommodate the desire for the *patency* of truth points in the same direction. And yet the main drift of the French readings of Hegel in the twentieth century has been to try to dissociate the dialectic from its *telos* – the achievement of Absolute Knowledge.

Our response may be that there is nothing wrong with achieving our goals, fulfilling our desires. Clearly this is often true. But to the extent that desires motivate us, give us direction, even give shape and meaning to our lives, it is often important that they not be fulfilled. The donkey will stop moving if it catches up with the carrot dangled in front of its nose. But the more thoughtful point is that there are many things we misunderstand if we think they can be achieved at some point in time. And this misunderstanding can be dangerous. It is for this reason that some would promote eschatology, in the face of the temptations of clerical authority.[21] Eschatology projects a unity "manifested at the last day," allowing the Christian to "live among the extremest multiplicity of the orders of truth with the hope of 'one day' comprehending unity."

If indeed the significance and value of what philosophers call "truth" cannot be disentangled from these paradoxes – it does not necessarily invalidate the focus on works of art as intentional unities by Merleau-Ponty or Margolis (or Heidegger or Gadamer),[22] as exemplary occasions for truth claims, but it does give us pause. It may be that the attempt to connect back representational truth to pre-representational dimensions of language, art, and perception opens up not so much primitive grounds of reassurance as labyrinths of complexity, and paradox – Vattimo's word for this is "unfounding" – and the ethical requirement is that we do not forget this when we speak of truth.

If we ask ourselves why or how such paradoxes arise, it is tempting to suppose that they are the product of over-confidence in our capacity to represent the real. If we draw a complete picture of the world that leaves out the drawing of the picture, something like Derrida's logic of the supplement should not come as a surprise. Nor should the fact that guiding ideals lose their force once realized. Perhaps the lesson to be learned here is that we let the fly out of the fly-bottle either by understanding truth as a complex practice, not as a representation, or by understanding representation itself as an embedded practice.

But are we sure we know what a *practice* is? In Part V ("Disclosure and Testimony") we discuss the inaugurating and sustaining dimensions of disclosure, and the challenges and demands of testimony and witnessing. Are these practices of interruption, or the interruptions of practice?

Notes

1   *Speech and Phenomena*, trans. David B. Allison (Evanston, IL: Northwestern University Press, 1973).
2   He means by "writing" any significant activity in any medium, including the voice, gesture, etc., where the traditional judgment on writing that, compared to speech, it is merely secondary, cut off from the source, is embraced as a virtue.
3   It is, however, important to acknowledge that theology does not always operate in this way. In the hands of a Kierkegaard, a Benjamin, or a Levinas, it serves to *interrupt* any sense of truth as objective and complete.
4   This is the language of Saussure and structuralism, but any theory of language that posits meanings as well as words has the same shape to it.
5   Nietzsche once made a similar point by saying that we have not got rid of God if we still believe in grammar.

6   See Heidegger, "The Onto-theo-logical Constitution of Metaphysics", in *Identity and Difference*, trans. Joan Stambaugh (Chicago: University of Chicago Press, 2002).

7   *Speech and Phenomena*, p. 97.

8   See e.g. Paul Ricoeur, "Truth and Falsehood," in *History and Truth*, trans. Charles A. Kelbley (Evanston, IL: Northwestern University Press, 1965). This is a paper we would happily have included in a longer version of this collection.

9   See "Force of Law", in *Deconstruction and the Possibility of Justice*, ed. Drucilla Cornell et al. (New York and London: Routledge, 1992), p. 24. Derrida writes: "A decision that did not go through the ordeal of the undecidable would not be a free decision, it would only be the programmable application or unfolding of a calculable process."

10   In fact, this would be a misleading caricature of Derrida's position. Derrida often speaks of the need to respond to the weight or pressure of the times. And Vattimo's sense of a ground which is "unfounding," i.e. which does not supply any determinate foundation, is one to which Derrida would be sympathetic.

11   Merleau-Ponty uses the words "hyper-dialectic" and "hyper-reflection" pretty much interchangeably in *The Visible and the Invisible*. "What we call hyper-dialectic is a thought that, on the contrary, is capable of reaching truth because it envisages without restriction the plurality of the relationships and what has been called ambiguity. The bad dialectic is that which thinks it recomposes being by a thetic thought, by an assemblage of statements, by thesis, antithesis, and synthesis; the good dialectic is that which is conscious of the fact that every thesis is an idealization, that Being is not made up of idealizations or of things said, as the old logic believed, but of bound wholes": *The Visible and the Invisible* (Evanston, IL: Northwestern University Press, 1968), p. 94.

12   See e.g., Gadamer's important essay, "On the Contribution of Poetry to the Search for Truth," in *The Relevance of the Beautiful and other Essays*, trans. Nicholas Walker, ed. Robert Bernesconi (Cambridge: Cambridge University Press, 1987). Gadamer argues for poetry as offering a distinctive experience of truth, one severed from the original voice of the author. The poem "stands written," much like a legal or religious text, and like a pledge or a proclamation has a performative dimension. On his reading, if poetry has any overriding significance, it is in the way in which it draws our attention to our being at home in the world, to what Vattimo, after Heidegger, calls "dwelling." The question Vattimo pushes in our selection here has to do with our creative relation to that dwelling. We must not forget what Heidegger called the experience of the *unheimlich*, not-quite-being-at-home, that is required for truly being-at-home!

13   What should we make of Gadamer's sense of poetry's autonomous capacity for expressing a self-fulfilling truth? We might fasten on the idea of "self-fulfillment" as a sign of a renewed essentialism. Or we could read Gadamer as describing the way in which works of art embody intentional structures. To say they are "self-fulfilling" is to say that they hold up a mirror to the consensual community (as Margolis would have it), whose language they speak. And that too would explain how a poem (and a legal judgment, and a religious declaration) can highlight, with authority, the world's familiarity. For that familiarity is a reflection of the local ways in which meaning is made and the world experienced. In a word: truth.

14   The logic of the supplement is elaborated in Derrida's ". . . That Dangerous Supplement," Part II.2 of *Of Grammatology* (Baltimore: Johns Hopkins University Press, 1974).

15   "Supposing that Truth is a woman – what then?," the first line of the Preface to *Beyond Good and Evil*, trans. Walter Kaufmann (New York: Vintage, 1989). For a wide range of discussions of this and similar remarks, see Kelly Oliver and Marilyn Pearsall (eds), *Feminist Interpretations of Friedrich Nietzsche* (University Park, PA: Pennsylvania State University Press, 1998).

16 See our selection in Part VII from Baudrillard, *Simulacra and Simulation*, trans. Shiela Faria Glaser (Ann Arbor: University of Michigan Press, 1994).

17 Ibid.

18 In *Twilight of the Idols*, trans. R. J. Hollingdale (New York: Viking, 1990)

19 We discuss this remark again in Part VI. Nietzsche is explicitly working within a hetero-normative culture, the dominant tradition of philosophy (what Derrida calls phallogo-centrism), "deconstructing" it in his particular way.

20 It is worth noting here that Ramsey (forefather of deflationary accounts of truth in ana-lytic philosophy, accounts that tend to treat "is true" as adding little to "p") defined "true" as an "achievement term," as a sign of satisfaction. This has been described as a success semantics.

21 See Ricoeur, "Truth and Falsehood."

22 See Merleau-Ponty's "Cézanne's Doubt" (short extracts included here), Margolis (see ch. 12), Heidegger's "The Origin of the Work of Art" (short extract included in ch. 16), and Gadamer's "The Contribution of Poetry to the Search for Truth".

11

THE TRUTH OF HERMENEUTICS
and "The Decline of the Subject and
the Problem of Testimony"

Gianni Vattimo

How does hermeneutic ontology speak about truth? This question must take into account the widely held suspicion that the philosophical position of hermeneutics is relativist, anti–intellectualist and irrationalist (or, at best, traditionalist). For it lacks that instance of truth which the metaphysical tradition has always thought in terms of patency (the incontrovertible givenness of the thing) and the correspondence of the proposition to the evidence of the thing. The Heideggerian critique of the notion of truth as correspondence seems to deprive hermeneutics of this instance, and even to make it impossible for hermeneutics to "save the phenomena," to acknowledge the experience of truth common to us all. This experience occurs when we openly espouse the validity of an affirmation, put forward a rational critique of the existing order (a mythical tradition, an *idolum fori*, an unjust social structure), or correct a false opinion by passing from appearance to truth. Without these usages of truth, thought seems to abdicate its vocation. Yet can they still be guaranteed without some idea of patency, and thus of correspondence?

One can reply to such a question only by trying to reconstruct, or perhaps construct, the positive terms of a hermeneutic conception of truth. This must be done on the basis of, and beyond, the "destruction" of correspondence-truth as carried out by Heidegger. At the beginning, however, let us recall the essential motives for Heidegger's rejection of the notion of truth as correspondence.

We are concerned to put to rest the misapprehension that in *Being and Time* Heidegger looks for a more adequate description of the meaning of Being and the idea of truth, as if the notions of Being handed down to us by the metaphysical tradition were partial, incomplete, inadequate, and therefore false descriptions of Being

Gianni Vattimo, "The Truth of Hermeneutics," © 1991 from *Questioning Foundations*, ed. Hugh Silverman (London: Routledge, 1991), pp. 11–28, 255–6 (notes). Reprinted by permission of Routledge/Taylor & Francis Books, Inc.

Gianni Vattimo, excerpts from *The Adventure of Difference: Philosophy after Nietzsche and Heidegger*, trans. Cyprian Blamires (Baltimore: Johns Hopkins University Press, 1993), pp. 40, 41, 50, 52, 54, 58. Reprinted by permission of Polity Press.

as it is *really* given, and truth as it *really* occurs. That this might not be Heidegger's intention is, from the very beginning, less than clear. However, it may be appreciated well enough if one reflects that such an intention would inevitably be contradictory, even in light of the features at play within truth as correspondence itself. With the evolution of Heidegger's work after *Being and Time* it becomes clear that his ontology cannot in any way be taken for a kind of existentially phrased neo-Kantianism (the structure of reason and its a priori having fallen into the thrownness and finitude of Dasein's project).

At the same time, it is clear that the objection to the conception of truth as correspondence is not made solely on the basis of its being inadequate to describe the experience of truth faithfully. For with the acknowledgment of inadequacy, one sees that one cannot retain a conception of truth as correspondence, since this implies a conception of Being as *Grund*, as the insuperable first principle which reduces all questioning to silence. Moreover, precisely the meditation on the insufficiency of the idea of truth as the correspondence of judgment to thing has put us on the track of Being as event. Admittedly, to say that "Being is event" (as Heidegger, quite rightly, never actually said)[1] is apparently *also* to give a descriptive proposition that claims to be "adequate." But to remark upon this superficially, as occurs repeatedly in all the "winning" arguments of metaphysics (the argument against skepticism is a typical example), is to placate and satisfy only those who bow before the ontological implications of the principle of noncontradiction. It does not persuade anyone to change their view, however. And above all, it does not allow thought to take a further step. In general, Heidegger has taught us to reject the untroubled identification of the structures of Being with the structures of our historical grammar and language. Thus, he has also taught us to reject the immediate identification of Being with what is sayable without performative contradictions in the context of the language we speak.

To say that Being "is" event means to pronounce in some way, still in the language of metaphysics, consciously accepted and *verwunden*, the ultimate proposition of metaphysics. The logic of foundation is being carried to extremes. It is the same process of unfounding (*sfondamento*), albeit experienced differently, that Nietzsche "described" with the proposition "God is dead."

It would not be rash to reconstruct the middle Heidegger's thought as an elaboration of this contradiction. This would resolve (dissolve) the *Kehre* entirely in *Verwindung*, in the resigned resumption-distortion-acceptance of metaphysics and nihilism. We recall this ensemble of problems only to remind ourselves that, in attempting to construct a hermeneutic conception of the experience of truth in positive terms, beyond the destruction of correspondence-truth, we must let ourselves be guided by the same motives that led Heidegger to that destruction in the first place. Such motives are not reducible to the search for a description that is truer because it is more adequate. They have, instead, to do with the impossibility of still thinking Being as *Grund*, as first principle, given only to the exact contemplation, panoramic but soundless, of *nous*. Recalling the motives for Heidegger's criticism of correspondence-truth is crucial if we are to overcome the aporias that seem to threaten the hermeneutic conception of truth, and not only in the view of its critics. Such a conception must be constructed on the basis of what Heidegger calls "opening." It will avoid the risks to which the critics of hermeneutics have drawn our attention

(irrationalism, relativism, and traditionalism), only to the extent that we remain faithful to the motives of the Heideggerian destruction. This destruction did not set out
to propose a more adequate conception of truth, hut aimed to "respond" to the
meaning of Being as event.

Referring to this guiding thread, we can resolve, or at least articulate in a more
positive manner, a problem that post-Heideggerian hermeneutics does not seem to
have posed in the right terms: the question of the relation between truth as opening
and truth as correspondence (or, what is in many ways the same thing, between truth
in philosophy and the human sciences and truth in the positive sciences). Every reader
of *Truth and Method* will appreciate that it is not clear whether Gadamer intends to
suggest that the human sciences have a truth of their own, founded upon interpretation, or whether he wishes to affirm this "model" of truth as valid for every experience of truth in general (and thus for the experimental sciences too). Either way,
this "obscurity" in Gadamer may be easily explained by noting that in *Truth and
Method* the Heidegger to which he makes most constant and wide-ranging reference
is the Heidegger of *Being and Time*.[2]

Now, on the basis of *Being and Time*, we can say that the simple presence to which
both banal everydayness and scientific objectivism are reduced arises from a partial
attitude that cannot serve as the only model for thinking Being. Inauthentic thought,
which is the ontology that needs to be destroyed, and will later become the metaphysics that forgets Being in favor of beings, takes simple presence and the objectivity of objects as models for thinking not only entities within the world, but also Being
itself. To escape inauthenticity or the "lethean" distortions of metaphysics, we must
avoid this undue extension of the simple presence of entity-objects to Being.

Gadamer does not seem to venture further than this in his criticism of modern
scientism in *Truth and Method*. For him, such scientism is not the fatal outcome of
metaphysics. Still less is it a fact bound up with the destiny and history of metaphysics, as it clearly is for Heidegger after *Being and Time*. Even Rorty's thesis in *Philosophy and the Mirror of Nature*, in which he distinguishes between "epistemology"
and "hermeneutics" in terms that may well be drawn back to correspondence and
opening, seems to be a reformulation ("urbanized" like Gadamer's) of a position whose
basis may be found in *Being and Time*.[3] Epistemology is the construction of a body
of rigorous knowledge and the solution of problems in light of paradigms that lay
down rules for the verification of propositions. To be sure, these rules do not necessarily imply that whoever follows them gives a truthful account of the state of things,
but at least they do not exclude it. Moreover, they allow a conception of science and
scientific practice to survive which are for the most part in harmony with the traditional metaphysical vision of the proposition–thing correspondence.

Hermeneutics, by contrast, unfolds in the encounter with different paradigmatic
horizons. Resisting evaluation on the basis of any correspondence (to rules or to the
thing), such horizons manifest themselves as "poetic" proposals of other worlds, of the
institution of different rules (within which a different "epistemology" is in force).

We will not pursue the suggestions or problems that arise from Rorty's hypothesis, which seems common to a Gadamerian perspective, although Gadamer has always
been very reticent on the subject of the relation between knowledge in the interpretive sciences and knowledge in the strict, or natural sciences. One relevant differ-

ence between his position and Rorty's consists in the fact that, on the moral plane at least, Gadamer grants a kind of supremacy to knowledge in the human sciences (especially in *Reason in the Age of Science*). The natural sciences, inevitably linked to technology and with a tendency toward specialization (not only in knowledge, but also in pursuing ever more specific ends, possibly in conflict with the general interests of society), must be "legitimized" by a thought which relates them back to the *logos*, to the common consciousness expressed in the natural-historical language of a society and its shared culture. The continuity of this consciousness, even in the sense of a *critical* reconstruction, is assured precisely by the human sciences, and by philosophy above all. In the terminology of *Being and Time* (and later, *Vom Wesen der Wahrheit*), the opening, which occurs in language and its founding events (like the work of art), is truth in its most original sense. It serves, too, as a point of reference for the legitimation of correspondence-truth in the sciences.

The sciences, however, insofar as they specialize via the construction of artificial languages, "do not think," as Heidegger and Gadamer have said. As for Rorty, his Position seems to be more radical than Gadamer's. There is no residue of the distinction between the natural sciences and the human sciences. Each form of knowledge may be in either a hermeneutic "phase" or in an epistemological one, according to whether it is living through a "normal" or "revolutionary" period. However, this excludes any possible hierarchy between types of knowledge. It also excludes any privileged place for human rationality in general, such as Gadamer's logos-language (and common sense, dense with history).

Yet just how radical is this difference between Gadamer and Rorty? Both relate truth as correspondence back to truth as opening. This is understood either (in Gadamer) as an historico-cultural horizon shared by a community that speaks the same language, or (in Rorty) as a paradigm that, without necessarily being identified with a linguistic community or cultural universe, nonetheless contains the rules for the solutions of its own problems and shows itself to be a foundation that is not founded, not even by that historical continuity still active in Gadamer. However, the problem ultimately remains the same for both thinkers. For Gadamer too the historical continuity which legitimizes the opening, and prevents its reduction to an arbitrary and casual paradigm, is nonetheless a limited community. It cannot be extended to a limit such as would link it with humanity in general, at least not explicitly. There holds for Rorty, but probably for Gadamer as well, a certain "Weberian" relativism. One can speak of truth in the sense of conformity with rules, given with the opening itself, only within an historical-cultural opening or paradigm. At the same time, the opening as such cannot be said to be "true" on the basis of criteria of conformity, but is (at least for Gadamer) original truth. For it institutes the horizons within which all verification and falsification are possible. The "hermeneutic" experience of the opening is more or less explicitly "aesthetic." This is clear in Rorty, who thinks the encounter with other paradigms as an encounter with a new system of metaphors.[4] Not by chance does Gadamer himself begin *Truth and Method* by affirming the significance of truth in art. But in Gadamer the encounter with other openings of the world, which is interpretation, is an aesthetic experience only to the extent that the latter is thought in historical terms, as an integration, or better, as a present "application" of a call whose origin lies in the past.

In effect, we should turn more to Gadamer than to Rorty for an articulation of the hermeneutic doctrine of truth as opening. This is so even if in Gadamer the problems entailed by this conception are brought into relief, forcing us to return to Heidegger, to his thought after *Being and Time*, and to what have seemed to be the fundamental demands motivating the critique of correspondence-truth found in that work.

If truth as opening is not thought as the incontrovertible givenness of an object possessed by a clear and distinct idea and adequately described in a proposition that faithfully reflects the idea, then the truth of the opening can, it seems, only be thought on the basis of the metaphor of dwelling. At bottom, this holds not only for Gadamer, but for Rorty as well. I can do epistemology, I can formulate propositions that are valid according to certain rules, only on the condition that I dwell in a determinate linguistic universe or paradigm. Dwelling is the first condition of my saying the truth. But I cannot describe it as a universal, structural, and stable condition. There are two reasons for this: because historical experience (and that of the history of science as well) displays the irreducibility of heterogenous paradigms and cultural universes, and because in order to describe the opening as a stable structure, I would need a criterion of conformity which would then be the more original opening.

I shall speak, then, of truth as opening in terms of dwelling. I call it truth because, like rules with respect to individual propositions, it is the first condition of every single truth.

Dwelling in the truth is, to be sure, very different from showing and rendering explicit what already is. In this respect Gadamer is right when he observes that belonging to a tradition, or even in Wittgensteinian terms, to a form of life, does not mean passively undergoing the imposition of a system of prejudices. In certain contemporary readings of Nietzsche, this would be equivalent to the total reduction of truth to a play of forces.[5] Dwelling implies, rather, an interpretive belonging that involves both consensus and the possibility of critical activity. Not for nothing, one could add, do modern dictatorships give an ever greater place to the techniques of organizing consensus. Dominion through consensus is more secure and more stable. There is a certain difference from pure constriction established here, which perhaps humanizes the exercise of even the most despotic power. It certainly recognizes, albeit paradoxically, the decisive significance of a conscious adhesion to a tradition, and the always active interpretive character of staying in a tradition. As a metaphor for speaking of hermeneutic truth, dwelling would need to be understood as though one were dwelling in a library. Whereas the idea of truth as correspondence represents knowledge as the possession of an "object" by way of an adequate representation, the truth of dwelling is, by contrast, the competence of the librarian who does not possess entirely, in a point-like act of transparent comprehension, all of the contents of all the books among which he lives, nor even the first principles upon which the contents depend. One cannot compare knowledge as possession by command of first principles to the competence of the librarian. The librarian knows where to look because he knows how the volumes are classified and has a certain idea of the "subject catalogue."

It is therefore senseless and misleading to accuse hermeneutics of being reduced to relativism or irrationalism, whereby each articulation within the opening, each epistemology, would be merely the revelation of what always already is. The conflict of interpretations would then be nothing but a conflict of forces that have no "argument" whatsoever to offer, other than the violence by which their predomination is secured. But thrownness into a historical opening is always inseparable from an active participation in its constitution, its creative interpretation and transformation.

However, these suspicions about hermeneutics are always renewed by the fact that it seems incapable of describing "original" truth as dwelling without recourse to a metaphor rooted deeply in the metaphysical tradition: that of "community," or in Hegelian terms, of "beautiful, ethical life." The persistent force of this reference may be seen, most recently, in Habermas's *Theory of Communicative Action* where the *Lebenswelt* is thought in reference to the ideal of an organic community characterized in terms of ethical life, and has both a normative and a foundational role. If there is to be a moment of "patency" included in hermeneutic dwelling without recourse to the model of correspondence, then "ethical life" seems to be indispensable. In other words, truth as opening also seems to involve a moment of "recognition," a "sensation" of incontrovertibility, of full patency. In accordance with the characteristic aesthetic quality of the hermeneutic experience of truth, but also with its links to pragmatism (those promoted by Rorty are legitimized by the pragmatist approach of the existential analytic of *Being and Time*), this comes to be understood as the recognition of a harmonious integration rather than the appropriation of a content via an adequate representation. Classical doctrines of patency as characteristic not only of certainty but also of truth (until phenomenology) have always forced themselves to accept this sensation of integration and harmony as a sign and symptom to which the truth of the content of experience could not be reduced. Yet they have done so without ever producing convincing proof that this difference really existed.

Nietzsche acknowledges this, too, when he invites us to doubt precisely what appears to be most evident, certain, indisputable. In the hermeneutic conception of truth as opening, this transition is comprehensively eliminated. The truth of opening is not an object whose cognitive possession may be attested to by the sensation of patency, completeness, and integration that we may feel in any given moment. This integration is the original truth itself, the condition of our Being in the true, upon which depends the possibility of making true judgments, verified in the light of rules of correspondence.

Can these complications and problems connected with them be avoided by reducing truth to merely "secondary" truth, to correspondence-truth, as metaphysics has always done (with the exception of Kant)? Yes, but only by "reducing Being to beings," or at the price of remaining prisoners of ideology by identifying the paradigm or cultural universe into which we are thrown with the real world *tout court*. This, it is understood, *we cannot do*. We cannot knowingly reconstruct myth, we cannot artificially assume a natural attitude – so the problem of truth as opening poses itself in such a way that it cannot be ignored. And it does so in the form of the problem of opening as truth. Not to consider the historical-cultural condition into which we are thrown to be a problem of truth means to take it, more or less consciously, as a brute fact, whose fatal reduction to an effect of force is only a sign of its remaining within the sphere of a metaphysics of foundations – a prisoner once more of *Grund* as the ultimate point of reference beyond which we do not pass and which silences all questioning. Thus we cannot help but pose the problem of opening. Why should we consider the world to be identical to our historical description of it, which in the meantime, as a result of the revolution of metaphysics into nihilism, has appeared to us as *such*? We cannot help but pose the problem of opening in terms of truth, for otherwise we shall end up by taking it to be a brute fact, a *Grund*.

Yet this seems to be "prohibited" for two reasons: first, by the need to distinguish the opening from its articulation (the hermeneutical from the epistemological), which can no longer be ignored after Marx, Nietzsche, and Heidegger; second, because what becomes unthinkable with the experience of the distinction between the opening and single truths (with the ontological difference), is precisely something like *Grund*. The impossibility of continuing to think Being in terms of *Grund* inspired Heidegger to his critique of correspondence, which simply could not have been motivated by the desire to find a more adequate description than that founded upon adequation.

Yet, does the difficulty posed by this impossibility find a repose in the reduction of the givenness of an object to an aesthetic experience of *fulfilment*, of the harmonious integration into a community, of the with–itself of Hegelian spirit? It is not simply a matter of regarding with suspicion the aestheticism which this hermeneutic conception of truth seems necessarily to involve. For in the end, such is the referal of the sensation of objective patency back to a recognition of integration within the world in which one "dwells" and in which one feels at home, as though in beautiful ethical life. This aestheticism is suspect only insofar as it does not take its leave of the true as the *Grund*, but seems instead to be a still more monumental and peremptory version of it.

The solution of the problems and discomforts created by life in a "society" held together only by contractual, mechanical, and conventional links is not the reconstruction of an organic community. Just as the recovery of a notion of virtue within a concrete historical horizon of shared values (through belonging to a common tradition) is not the solution to the subjectivist aporias in which modern rationalist ethics has issued. As in MacIntyre, the criticisms of modern ethical rationalism conclude – perhaps not by chance – with the proposal of a return to a premodern morality. This outcome illustrates a risk run to an equal degree by the hermeneutic conception of truth.

On certain pages of Gadamer, it seems to be something more than a risk. Yet, in Gadamer, as in Rorty, there are the instruments needed to prevent the "aesthetic" model from leading to "aesthetical" results. Recognizing these elements maintains the proposal that guided the Heideggerian critique of truth as correspondence. In this way, one would also be more faithful to an "aesthetic" model no longer thought in anachronistic classical terms.

Hermeneutics replaces truth, as the appropriation of a thing via its adequate representation, with thought as dwelling and as aesthetic experience. But this aesthetic experience is in its turn thought on the basis of its actual configuration in the epoch of the end of metaphysics, to which hermeneutic ontology also belongs. For this experience, the false work of art, *kitsch*, is presented today with the characteristics of completeness, roundness, and the harmonious reconciliation and perfect compenetration of content and form that were thought to be characteristics of art in the classical sense. The connection between hermeneutics and aesthetics in the epoch of the end of metaphysics could also be formulated in this way: to assert the importance of aesthetic experience with respect to truth, and to propose it as a "model" for a conception of truth free from scientism (from the idea of truth as correspondence and the patency of the object) only becomes possible when aesthetic experience is modified to such a degree that it loses its "classical" characteristics. Corresponding to this transformation of the aesthetic, which, with Heidegger, must be considered as a feature of the destiny of Being, there is also a radical transformation of cognitive experience in the sciences. Indeed, this occurs to such an extent that the function of a "model of truth" put forward for aesthetic experience might no longer appear foreign or opposed to the very self-knowledge concurrently matured in the sciences.

The critique of the idea of truth as correspondence leads hermeneutics to conceive of truth on the model of dwelling and aesthetic experience. But this experience still tends to be presented according to classicist images of integration, harmony, and roundness which correspond to art in the epoch of metaphysics. If hermeneutics gives in to this tendency, it will end up opposing correspondence-truth with nothing more than an idealization of the beautiful ethical life. Instead of escaping the peremptoriness of *Grund* (and its forgetful identification of Being and beings), it would merely reassert an even more monumental foundationalism, expressing itself in the pure and simple identification of the opening with the brute factuality of a certain form of life not open to discussion.

A more accurate recognition of the aesthetic experience serving as a model here leads instead to a different outcome.[6] It leads away from the emphasis that metaphysical thought has always placed upon the subjective sensation of certainty as a sign of truth. Regardless of every effort to the contrary, it seems impossible, after Nietzsche, to still think of clear and distinct ideas as the model for truth, or of the experience of the true as the incontrovertible certainty of consciousness before a given content. The Nietzschean "school of suspicion" cannot but lead to a demystification so radical as to demystify the suspicion itself. Such a result, however, is not equivalent to a recuperation, pure and simple, of the experience of patency. If it wishes to be faithful to the intentions (and the good reasons) that motivated the Heideggerian critique of truth as correspondence, hermeneutics cannot simply offer another explanation of the experience of patency, referring the sensation of fullness back to a cause distinct from the manifestation of the thing in its simple presence (for example, the sense of integration in a community thought as the Hegelian beautiful ethical life).

For hermeneutics it is a matter, rather, of recognizing completely the link between that very patency of consciousness and metaphysics. Indeed, the manner of truth's being given as a clear and distinct idea and as incontrovertible evidence belongs to the very history of metaphysics. Here too, as with all elements of the history of metaphysics, thought cannot remain under the illusion that it can perform a true and proper overcoming. Instead it must work at a *Verwindung*, a resumption and distortion, which will maintain the model of correspondence as a secondary moment of the experience of truth.[7]

After Nietzsche, but in the end simply after Kant (whose transcendental foundation already places single truths and corresponding propositions on a secondary level), we no longer think of truth as the correspondence of a proposition to the state of things. Truth as correspondence, even as incontrovertible patency experienced in the certainty of consciousness, is only a secondary moment within the experience of truth, and reveals itself as such when metaphysics matures toward its completion. This can be seen, for example, in the advent of modern experimental science. Its technological consequences and its transformation of the scientific undertaking into a social project of gigantic proportions have rendered irrelevant the mythical moment of discovery and certainty of consciousness, upon which metaphysics constructed its idea of truth. Just as conceiving the encounter with the work of art in classical terms is anachronistic, illusory, and decidedly *kitsch* (nowadays only merchandise promoted in advertising is presented in this way), so too conceiving the "eureka" of the scientist in his laboratory as the supreme moment, as the very model for the significance of the experience of truth, is ideological and mystifying. Perhaps the experience of truth *begins* from there, as one then sets out toward certainty on a voyage to discover the conditions which render it possible (or perhaps belie it), where these are never given once and for all in sheer patency.

In opposition to *Erklärung*, to positive-scientific "explanation" which subsumes a single case under a general law (which is itself given as evident), hermeneutics does not propose a *Verstehen* which, as a lived experience of sympathy and common belonging, reproduces the same "silencing" peremptoriness of objective evidence, only at the level of vitalistic immediacy. Instead, it sets in opposition what one might call, with Heidegger, an *Erörterung*. This is an unfounding (*sfondante*) "collocation" which indeed has many traits of aesthetic experience, but as it is given at the end of metaphysics (and as a moment of its "overcoming" in the form of a *Verwindung*). Perhaps the research opened up by Kant on the conditions of possibility for physics as a science reaches its culmination here. Physics as a science, or modern technical science as it is set out in the world of *Gestell*, is possible only on the condition of no longer thinking truth according to the model of patency given to consciousness. The modern scientific project itself heralds the consummation of that model and the relegation of correspondence-truth to a second level. Ultimately, this is the ever more accentuated divarication between the real, as that which is given in the immediacy of a cogent intuition, and the true, as that which is established only by virtue of its being situated within an unfounding horizon (*un orizzonte sfondante*).

All of which, naturally, one would have to argue in greater detail via reconstruction of the rise of self-consciousness in the sciences between the nineteenth and twentieth centuries. This would also have to include a consideration of the debates over realism and conventionalism, and a discussion of such examples as the methodological anarchism of Feyerabend, as well as the reproposal of "realism" and its various significations.

From the point of view of hermeneutics, the features of *Erörterung* as an alternative to the metaphysical "model of truth" (and to its variations in the sense of the organic community) are brought out more clearly if we reflect further upon the metaphor of dwelling. To offer a declension of this metaphor with the example of dwelling in a library merely serves to underline a feature which is, however, common to all dwelling: being introduced not into a "natural" space thought as an abstract, geometrical space, but into a landscape marked by a tradition. The library in which late-modern man lives, and in which his experience of truth is set, is a "library of Babel," to use Borges's expression. The elements for this specification of the concept of *Erörterung* can already be traced in the distinction marked out in *Being and Time* between tradition as *Tradition* and tradition as *Überlieferung* (the latter understood as the active inheritance of the past as an open possibility, not as a rigidly determined and determining schema). What constitutes the truth of single truths given in propositions (that "correspond") is their referral back to conditions of possibility which cannot be articulated in propositions (which themselves correspond).

Such conditions are given as an unending network of references, a network constituted by the multiple voices of the *Überlieferung*, of the handing down (not necessarily from the past), which resound in the language in which those propositions are formulated. These voices speak as an irreducible multiplicity resisting every attempt to draw them back to a unity. This is an especially modern experience, making inevitable the link between the happening of truth as *Erörterung* and the ending of metaphysics.

Does the closed and definitive system of Kantian categories not also crumble because of the discovery of the multiplicity of cultural universes, and thus of the irreducible plurality of a priori conditions of knowledge? This multiplicity, however, would remain only a factual given, lacking any philosophical significance, if philosophy, for its part, did not link it to the discovery of temporality as constitutive of Being. The irreducible multiplicity of cultural universes becomes philosophically relevant only in light of the mortality constitutive of *Dasein*. This mortality does not confer upon the *Überlieferung* the character of a confused superposition of perspectives, but rather the dignity of the *Geschick*, the giving of Being as the sending of openings which vary from time to time, as do the generations of man. This must be kept in mind in order to understand how the tradition, within which propositions (that correspond) acquire their most authentic truth, is not only a Babel, but is also "impoverished." This marks it as an unfounding provenance compared to a giving of Being as simple presence.

This aspect of the *Überlieferung*, in which the sense of transmission and the more specific sense of sending and source are brought together, is recognized explicitly here in order to avoid yet another metaphysical equivocation. This equivocation can be seen in all versions of hermeneutics as a philosophy of the irreducible multiplicity of perspectives. In Heideggerian hermeneutics this multiplicity is opened by the mortality constitutive of *Dasein*, which finds itself always already thrown into a project, into a language, a culture, which it *inherits*. The awareness of the multiplicity of perspectives is *also inherited*. The conception of truth as dwelling in the library of Babel is not a true description of the experience of truth that would ultimately replace the false one given by metaphysics. It is, rather, the outcome of the articulation of metaphysics as the reduction of Being to presence. This includes its culmination in technoscience and the consequent dissolution of the very idea of reality in the multiplicity of interpretations. Situating truths, propositions that "correspond," within truth as opening does not mean suspending their ultimate cogency within a multiplicity of perspectives. (This might stand as a description of the deconstructionist version of hermeneutics proposed by Jacques Derrida). By contrast, the hermeneutic *Erörterung* places truths against the background (*sfondo*) of the irreducible multiplicity of voices which make them possible. It experiences this collocation as a response to a call that comes from the *Überlieferung*, and which keeps this groundlessness (*sfondamento*) from being mere confusion or arbitrariness.[8]

This seems to be the only way to pose not only the problem of truth as opening, but also the problem of opening as truth. The horizon cannot be reduced to a brute fact, insuperable and equipped with the same peremptory authority as a metaphysical *Grund*. The multiplicity of voices against which single truths acquire authenticity is not an ultimate structure given as true in place of Being as unity, *archē*, foundation. It is, rather, provenance. Being, given in metaphysics as simple presence, is itself always on the point of turning into an object (of measurement, of manipulation, etc.). It is given today as multiplicity, temporality, mortality. To recognize this giving as an event, not as an already-*given*, peremptory structure, means to find in the multiplicity of voices not merely an anarchic confusion, but the call of a *Geschick*. This is a destiny that no longer has the characteristics of a metaphysical ground. The *Geschick* retains something of the metaphysical *Grund* and of its capacity for legitimation, but only in the paradoxical, nihilistic form of a propensity for dissipation that cannot present itself with a metaphysical cogency. It represents, nonetheless, a possible rationality for thought, a possible "truth of the opening." Thus, in the sphere of this dissolute destiny of Being, the succession of scientific paradigms and science's growing awareness of its own historically situated character are not to be resolved by substituting a relativistic metaphysics for the realist metaphysics of the tradition.

The divarication of the *true* and the *real*, one of the most striking implications of the development of modern science, would become an aspect of the completion and dissolution of metaphysics. In this history, Being is given, at the end, as that which *is not*, at least in the sense of an object. It occurs as the opening which, while making possible single truths as propositions corresponding to the given, withdraws itself explicitly from any kind of appropriative stating. The conquest of the true would thus follow a path leading away from the real as the immediate pressure of the given and the incontrovertible imposition of the *in itself*. To use an example from psychoanalysis, this is similar to the fascination of the imaginary and its games of identification, as in Lacan, from which we can only withdraw via a passage at the level of the symbolic.[9]

The unfounding (*sfondante*) horizon within which the single truths (even as "corresponding" statements of the sciences) acquire their authentic truth, i.e., come to be "founded" [*fondati*], would not be the historically determined paradigm containing the rules of their formulation, which cannot be interrogated further (like a form of life which legitimizes itself by the very fact of its existing). Nor would it be the disordered multiplicity of the paradigms that would effectively suspend any pretensions to the definitive status of single truths. To stand in the opening is not to achieve a harmonious (traditionalist, conservative) integration in a received canon shared by an organic community, but neither is it the pure relativist-historicist separation of the blasé. For the Mannheim of *Ideology and Utopia*, this constitutes the only possible point of view not limited by ideology, and which is taken up not by the Marxian proletariat, but by the European intellectual formed in and by the knowledge of many cultural universes.[10]

By contrast, we get back to truth as opening by taking the unfounding (*sfondamento*) as destiny. If the developments of science demonstrate a growing divarication of the true from the real, then this destiny means that the divarication attests not only to the insuperable historical relativity of the paradigms, with all the consequences this involves (first among which is the temptation to skepticism), but it also attests to Being's propensity for reduction, for the dissolution of strong characteristics. This presents itself as a possible guiding thread for interpretations, choices, and even moral options, well beyond the simple affirmation of a plurality of paradigms.[11]

What remains in this perspective of the "traditional" notion of truth as correspondence and the patency of the object? Paradoxically, the *critical* function of truth is enhanced here, in the form of a leap into the *logoi*, an ever renewed passage "from here to there," to use the Platonic expression. This is so inasmuch as even the consciousness of patency is forever reinterrogated regarding its conditions, forever drawn back into the horizon of the opening that constitutes its permanent unfounding (*sfondamento*). In scientific research today the "discovery" itself is increasingly entrusted to measurements, instrumental verifications, and the establishment of continuity and "tests" between objects. Consequently, the sensation of success and the feeling of fullness that accompany "discovery" are relegated to the range of secondary effects of truth. Or they serve as points of departure too heavily compromised by the pressure of the "real," from which one must therefore separate oneself – a separation that began with the distinction between primary and secondary qualities, and in general with the ideal of disinterestedness and scientific objectivity.

The growing historical-political self-awareness of science can probably be counted as one of the aspects of this transformation of the notion of truth. The ideal of correspondence is not thereby explicitly denied, but situated on a second and lower level with respect to truth as opening.

Despite appearances, this does not amount to a reaffirmation of the supremacy of philosophy and the human sciences over the physical sciences. Even Rorty's distinction between "epistemology" and "hermeneutics" is probably too schematic: it draws too rigid a distinction between a work of articulation within a paradigm, i.e., the solution of puzzles, and the revolutionary transformation of the paradigm itself. But scientific work, from the viewpoint of Popperian falsificationism, is not readily described as a simple articulation of rules given when checking the correspondence between propositions and states of things. On the other hand, the institution of historical openings, of new horizons of truth, is perhaps a less aesthetically emphatic event than Rorty seems to think.

Nor is the other metaphysical usage of truth (guaranteeing the universal validity of true statements on the basis of the thing being given "in person") entirely lost in the hermeneutic reformulation of truth as opening. Here, the merely postulated universality of true propositions – always linked to the surreptitious identification of the "we" of a determinate scientific community or specific cultural universe with humanity in general – is replaced by an assemblage of single truths with the multiplicity of perspectives constituting the network that supports them and makes them possible. Once again, the hermeneutic conception of truth is not an affirmation of the "local" over the "global," or any other "parochial" reduction of the true. To articulate the connections and the stratifications that echo in every true statement means to activate the memory of an indefinite network of relations. (I am thinking of Wittgenstein's family resemblances.) This network constitutes the very basis of a possible universality, namely, the persuasiveness of that statement, ideally, for everyone.

It is a case of universality and criticality *verwunden*. They are taken up again in their earlier metaphysical determinations, pursued and distorted accordingly, that is, in hearing a call of Being which resounds in the epoch of the completion of metaphysics. These, too, are the transformations on account of which Heidegger believed it necessary to refer the more original essence of truth to "freedom."[12] Hermeneutics must always reflect upon this turn.

Notes

1   On the decisive sense of this term in Heidegger, and the continuation of his thought in the direction of a way out of metaphysics, cf. the final chapter of my *The End of Modernity: Nihilism and Hermeneutics*, trans. and intro. Jon R. Snyder (Baltimore: Johns Hopkins University Press, 1988) and my contributions to *Filosofia* 86 and *Filosofia* 87, ed. Gianni Vattimo (Torino, 1986 and 1987).

2   Apart from the pages dedicated to Heidegger in Hans-Georg Gadamer's *Truth and Method* (New York: Seabury Press, 1976), an important document in this respect is Gadamer's meeting with Adriano Fabris published in *Teoria* (fasc. 1, 1982) in which Gadamer insists on his closeness to the "second Heidegger," but also that the second Heidegger must be related back to the first, since it is ultimately a matter of retranslating into the language of *Being and Time* what the later works presented under the form of "visions."

3   See Richard Rorty, *Philosophy and the Mirror of Nature* (Ithaca: Cornell University Press, 1979).

4   See ibid.

5   For example, this is Foucault's position, at least according to Paul Veyne's radical interpretation, of which one should see above all "E possible una morale per Foucault?," in *Effeto Foucault*, ed. P. A. Rovatti (Milan: Feltrinelli, 1986), pp. 30–8.

6   For a wider illustration of this point, see my contribution to the Royaumont Colloquium in 1987, "L'impossible outbli," in *Usages de l'oubli*, ed. Yosef H. Yerushalmi et al. (Paris: Seuil, 1988).

7   Cf. Vattimo, *Filosofia* 86 and 87.

8   Speaking of "arbitrary" strategies of the thought of difference, Derrida explicitly evokes Mallarmé's *coup de dès*, and this reference has more than a casual significance: see Jacques Derrida's "Différance," in *Margins of Philosophy*, trans. Alan Bass (Chicago; University of Chicago Press, 1982).

9   I am using the Lacanian terminology here without any pretense to fidelity to his text; all the more since alongside the imaginary and the symbolic, he proposes also the "real," which in my schema only seems to have a place on the side of the imaginary.

10 Cf. Karl Mannheim, *Ideology and Utopia* (San Diego: Harcourt Brace Jovanovich, 1985), in which historical relativism is limited by the view that ideological points of view can be integrated into a "comprehensive totality" that serves as the basis for a scientific politics.

11 A fuller discussion of this can be found in my essay "Ethics of Communication or Ethics of Interpretation?," in *The Transparent Society* (Cambridge: Polity, 1992), pp. 105–20.

12 This is the theme of Martin Heidegger's "On the Essence of Truth," in *Martin Heidegger: Basic Writings,* ed. David Farrell Krell, trans. John Sallis (New York; Harper and Row, 1977).

From "The Decline of the Subject and the Problem of Testimony"

Any appeal to the idea of testimony nowadays can justifiably be labelled anachronistic. At least for anyone who was educated during the early postwar period in Europe, the word 'testimony' seems inextricably linked to [. . .] the era of existentialism. Testimony [. . .] is a reminder of the profound intensity with which from the time of Kierkegaard existentialism has always viewed the unrepeatable existence of the individual and his particular and highly personal relationship with truth, a relationship to which a person commits himself wholly, exclusively and in isolation [. . .] Today's philosophical climate shows little interest in this kind of subject. (p. 40)

[. . .] Of late there has in fact been a wave of 'impersonalism' both at the level of the most penetrating philosophical research and at the level of more fleeting cultural trends. [. . .] I [. . .] do not believe that it has only a negative influence and ought to be resisted, rather, it is a symptom of a real turn in our way of thinking and a transformation in the fundamental conditions of existence. Any discourse on testimony must begin [. . .] with the crisis of the notion of the subject itself. (p. 41)

In *Being and Time* the inauthenticity in which Dasein always, already and primordially exists is tied to the fact that Dasein exists with others, in society, and consequently always tends to take common opinion as the basis for its projects. But once metaphysics has been recognized as destiny, the individual's belonging to a historical world becomes a possibility that is constitutive. One does not become authentic by leaving the world of the *they* in a personal assumption of responsibility; entry into the sphere of authentic existence [. . .] can only occur (if it actually can) through the modification of this world, through the transformation of one epoch of Being into another. (p. 50)

That is, the real meaning of the ontological turn in Heidegger's philosophy after *Being and Time* lies in the recognition that the bourgeois/Christian idea of the subject is an inadequate one in which to interpret the historical experience of modern man. (p. 52)

To pose the problem of testimony – however approximate the meaning of this term in the person–truth nexus – means [. . .] restating the problem of the meaning of action and historical choice. We have discovered that history *does not* play itself out on the level of our conscious individual decisions, whether because such decisions only mask and conceal decisions and choices already taken, of which we are unaware, though they guide us, or because what is at stake in those very decisions that we take to be our own is our belonging to a historical world, to a class, a language that conditions and *defines* us. (p. 54)

Whether or not we accept Marxian terminology, the points made by Marx need to be borne in mind. After the decline of the subject, the only way to restore meaning to the notion of testimony, as well as to that historical action on the part of human beings to which the notion of testimony is tied, is to rid ourselves of all residual objectivism in our conception of Being. At the same time we must stop thinking of the bourgeois/Christian individual as the only possible subject of history and the only centre of initiative. And these requirements must both be satisfied at the same time (pp. 5–8).

12

RELATIVISM AND CULTURAL RELATIVITY

Joseph Margolis

It is a truism at once baffling and reassuring that there are apt bilinguals for every known natural language. It is the corollary, of course, of an equally baffling and equally reassuring truism, namely, that a newborn child can have learned any language as its first language if it can have learned the language it eventually acquires. And yet, at the point of mature competence, everyone is aware of the deep uncertainty of understanding the speech and behavior of others belonging to the same culture as well as to another culture. In fact, we may as well admit that we are not always clear whether we understand ourselves at certain critical moments or, indeed, are clear about what we may have done or said or made at some moment in our past. Plato broadly suggests in the *Ion* that the gods make captive the minds of poets in order to express through them their own thoughts. But the gods are notoriously difficult to understand. Furthermore, we are hardly confident about what it is we do when we understand ourselves, one another, those of our own culture, and those of another culture. No one, I think, has satisfactorily answered the question.

When we ponder these familiar puzzles, we begin to suspect that often – possibly always – what we call understanding and knowledge may not be capable of being as crisp or as univocal or as confirmable as we should like. If, to take a compelling example, I stand before a number of Paul Klee's enigmatic drawings, I am aware that part of their great charm rests with the fact that I can place them with assurance in an art tradition I am well acquainted with, though I am unable to state their meaning and what their purposive structure is with a precision and assurance matching their obvious mastery. I fall back to weaker claims, and I take the Klees to convey not so much a dearth of evidence I might otherwise have collected as a sign I am at the limit of what could possibly be added in the way of evidence that could ever bring my interpretive conjectures to any single, final, exclusive truth about these pieces.

Joseph Margolis, excerpts from "Relativism and Cultural Relativity," in *What, After All, Is a Work of Art?: Lectures in the Philosophy of Art* (University Park, PA: Pennsylvania State University Press, 1999), pp. 41–65. © 1999 by The Pennsylvania State University. Reprinted by permission of the publisher.

I am myself impressed with the uncertainty (that is, the certainty) that what Klee produced might not be able to support any uniquely valid description or interpretation or explanation of their "meaning," and that what holds for the Klees holds everywhere, or for the most part, or often enough that we must make conceptual room for such occasions. Others may not believe as I do, may not be struck in the same way I am. It is for that reason I confess I am a relativist, though I am aware that others are not.

Of course, in mentioning the Klees, I am not insisting so much on the possibility of alternative interpretations of any particular piece as I am on the initially problematic nature of first confronting a Klee. Anyone familiar with the usual Klee prints and paintings knows how difficult it is to determine what to regard as the right way to "read" them. No telltale clues reassure us, confirming that we're simply right, after all. We are obliged to construct (within our sense of the tradition of receiving art) what we judge to be a fair way of entering the (Intentional) "world" of any particular Klee. (I am convinced that the same is true as well in getting our bearings on, say, a more "legible" Vermeer.) But the deeper point is that *how* we enter Klee's "world" is a function of how we ourselves have been formed and altered by the ongoing history of painting we suppose we are able to master, well after the original Klees were produced.

In the West, the history of relativism is a conceptual disaster: not, as one might imagine, because of the futile efforts in its defense but rather because of the remarkable constancy of philosophy's adverse judgment that relativism cannot possibly be made coherent. It is an extraordinary fact that, from ancient times to the very end of [the twentieth] century, there have been no more than one or two principal objections against the coherence of relativism – already formulated by Plato and Aristotle – that have been thought so decisive that we still invoke the ancient arguments almost without modification.

As far as I know, there is no other doctrine of comparable importance – skepticism (which is altogether different) springs to mind – that shows the same degree of philosophical inertia. The ancients thought of the matter primarily in logical or formal terms (even if ontologically or epistemologically), and in the modern world, the ancient puzzles have been additionally complicated by the general admission of historical and cultural diversity (the consequence, I should say, of philosophy's reflections on the meaning of the French Revolution). You see the difference at once when comparing Plato's *Theaetetus* and Aristotle's *Metaphysics* Gamma (both addressed to Protagoras) to the more diffuse accounts of Thomas Kuhn's *The Structure of Scientific Revolutions* and Michel Foucault's "Nietzsche, Genealogy, and History."[1] Of course, the modern exemplars are hardly canonical in the same sense the ancient texts are thought to be. But the plain fact is, the ancient arguments are remarkably easy to defeat (though they have hardly been strengthened over the centuries) and the modern discussions are not so much arguments one way or another as unavoidable confirmations of the kind of cultural site at which the threat of relativism must be met. Any proper defense of relativism must address both themes.

I am convinced that the ancient and modern ways of rejecting relativism depend on the same unearned conviction, namely, that whatever is truly real possesses some unchangeable structure, that whatever changes occur in the real world may be explained only in terms of what is changeless, and that whatever we come to know of reality involves a grasp (however approximate) of that underlying structure.

The opponents of relativism are aware that its deepest defense relies on its *not* being demonstrable that this executive conviction can ever be shown to be necessary or inviolable in reality or in thought – that is, to avoid paradox or self-contradiction. Aristotle is entirely explicit on the matter. In fact, what I have just offered is a summary of his argument in *Metaphysics* Gamma, and Plato's sketch of Protagoras's thesis on the meaning of truth shows how opposing the canonical view of fixity (in at least one way, certainly not in every eligible way) instantly produces a self-defeating paradox.

Protagoras seems to have been aware of the underlying confrontation between necessary invariance and flux; very possibly, he meant his famous doctrine, "Man is the measure," to accord with the rejection of Parmenides' dictum, which (we may suppose) Plato and Aristotle wished to reconcile with the reality (or the appearance of reality) of the changing everyday world. But I must warn you in the bargain that part of the argument that is needed cannot altogether escape certain formal considerations. (I intend to press these to advantage.)

You see how complicated the underlying quarrel is. I have no wish to pursue it here, though its relevance can never be rightly ignored. In the modern world, the ancient doctrine of invariance is most compellingly championed in the familiar dictum that nature is governed by universal, changeless, and exceptionless laws, and that the work of the sciences is directed toward their discovery or approximation.[2] The fact is, now, at the end of the twentieth century, even that notion is no longer thought unassailable: the laws of nature, we suppose, may (without contradiction) be artifacts or idealizations of some sort from the informal and imperfect regularities of the observed world.[3] Furthermore, the world of human culture – of language, languaged thought, history, technology, art, and, most provocatively, whatever we suppose are the competence of science and the conditions of the world's intelligibility – is clearly contingently formed, impressively variable in structure, eminently alterable by human intervention, problematically intelligible under conditions that change with changing history, and endlessly novel and creative.

In that sense, the prospects of defending relativism are paradigmatically focused in the puzzles of interpreting the art world. For, it may be argued, if relativism can be defended in the world of the arts, then, assuming that modal invariance cannot be secured philosophically and that it cannot be unreasonable to regard our conceptual resources as common coin for theorizing about nature and culture alike, what is gained in one corner of inquiry may be pressed into service in another. Seen that way, you realize that the contest regarding the defense of relativism harbors rather grand pretensions – for instance, about essentialism and the fixed conditions of intelligibility. I set these aside here, but only as an economy. The fact remains that the classic defeat of relativism is given in ontological terms or in logical terms brought into accord with an unquestioned ontology.

Now, the defense of relativism joins two lines of reasoning: one is more or less confined to formal, uninterpreted, or logical considerations bearing on the treatment of truth or what we should take our truth-values to be, as far as admissible inferences go; the other addresses what, regarding one or another local sector of reality and knowledge, favors or disfavors the relativistic preferences arrived at in the first. The division is obviously artificial, since the intended benefits of the first are offered in the service of the second, and the possibilities the second suggests must be shown not to produce difficulties for the first.

For convenience, I tag inquiries of the first sort "alethic," and inquiries of the second, "ontic" and "epistemic"; also, I urge they be viewed as no more than distinct aspects of a single indivisible inquiry. You see, therefore, that a responsible relativism must provide an alternative "logic" on which its larger rationale depends, but it cannot pursue the large claim if it does not exceed the alethic issue. By the same token, attacks on relativism that are purely formal but are thought to bear on epistemic or ontic issues (once the coherence or nonparadoxicality of relativism is admitted) are, to put it mildly, philosophically irresponsible.

The alethic question is entitled to a certain priority, however, because if it may be shown that relativism's logic cannot but be self-defeating, there would be little point to going on to the ontic and epistemic questions art-works and other cultural artifacts oblige us to consider (that is, in defense of relativism). But, of course, if you take seriously the inseparability of the two sorts of question, you see at once that its priority is no more than a convenience. For what the appropriate logic should be, in servicing, say, the interpretation of the arts, will be a function of what we take the objective features of the arts to be. Alethic, ontic, and epistemic questions are inseparable from one another relative to truth-claims because they are inseparable within objective inquiries. To deny that would be no more than to favor another version of the invariantist thesis: for instance, to claim that, regarding reality, only some form of bivalence (taking True and False as disjunctive and exhaustive truth-values) could possibly serve coherently and adequately. That is exactly Aristotle's claim in the *Metaphysics.*

No evidence shows one cannot depart, coherently, from an all-encompassing bivalence, and there is no reason to object to the compatibility of employing both a bivalent and a relativistic logic – wherever wanted – provided only that such policies be properly segregated, on grounds of relevance, so as to avoid avoidable difficulties. It is also excessive to insist that no such division of labor may be conducted in as informal a way as we please, for all that is needed is that we fit the picture of our practice to what is reasonably close to the actual practice. [. . .]

I have introduced three important caveats in approaching the alethic question. I find them reasonable and compelling. More than that, they are not noticeably skewed in relativism's favor. Before going on and in order to avoid misunderstanding, I restate them here: (1) alethic, ontic, and epistemic questions are inseparable in analyzing would-be truth-claims; (2) the proper "logic" of any set of truth-claims is a function of what we take to be the domain of inquiry and the conditions of knowledge; and (3) no formal reason precludes us from mingling the "logics" of different sorts of truth-claims, provided only they are rightly segregated on grounds of relevance.

[. . .]

[. . .] The opponents of relativism usually ignore the inseparability of alethic and both ontic and epistemic matters. They claim we must adhere in an invariant way to bivalence wherever truth-claims are at stake, but they neglect to explain why our local "logic" should not be tailored to what we believe a given sector of reality can rightly support in the way of truth-claims, and they cannot satisfactorily explain why a restriction in the scope of bivalence should be thought to produce an insuperable paradox. For instance, they surely cannot show that a three-valued logic is inherently self-defeating, or that a would-be bivalent logic cannot accommodate truth-value gaps.[4] Here, of course, I am approaching the logical needs of an interpretive practice addressed to the Intentional complexities of artworks. I therefore invite your patience.

I can now provide an answer to the alethic question. The following are the essential elements of a relativistic logic – where, by a "logic," I mean nothing more than a policy regarding the formal conditions for the choice and assignment of truth-values affecting admissible inferences in the space in which they are applied, without (yet) specifying the evidentiary grounds on which they are empirically assigned: (1) the concept and practice of a bivalent logic are assumed to be in general play in all our inquiries, but the bivalent values themselves (True/False) are restricted in scope or denied application among the truth-claims admitted to the domain in question; (2) within relativism's scope, the values True and False are treated asymmetrically: False is retained, but True is denied application, and a many-valued set of truth-values (not a three-valued set – one that merely adds Indeterminate to the usual bivalent pair) replaces True, so that "not false" is no longer equivalent, as in a standard bivalent logic, to "true," but is equivalent instead to values drawn from the replacing many-valued values; (3) within the scope of (1)–(2), truth-claims that, on a bivalent logic but not now, would be formally contradictory or incompatible may be logically compatible when assigned one or another of the replacing many-valued values; these may be termed "incongruent" values, meaning, by that term of art, that what they permit would be incompatible on a bivalent logic but are (now) formally consistent within the alethic scope intended; also, that further constraints of inconsistency and contradiction may be admitted (on substantive grounds) involving opposing the value False and one or another of the replacing values; (4) bivalent and relativistic logics remain compatible and may be jointly used, provided only the scope and relevance constraints binding different sets of truth-values and their applications are segregated – in as ad hoc a way as we please; (5) the resultant logic may, when rightly joined to ontic and epistemic considerations, be as *realist* in import as the applications of any standard bivalent logic; and (6) the values invoked remain entirely formal – lack all epistemic and ontic import – until the domain in which they are applied is pertinently interpreted.

[. . .]

A few explanatory remarks may be helpful here. For one thing, I treat cultural entities in a "realist" way – in other words, no more than that they are real and that their properties may be fairly said to be discerned. In this minimal sense, *realism* is neutral as between bivalence and a relativistic logic (though, of course, many would not be willing to admit as much). Second, on my view, a relativism regarding interpretation is not precluded from treating certain "descriptive" (even certain "interpretive") attributions bivalently; that is just what I had in mind in admitting an informal and relatively ad hoc mix of bivalent and relativistic values in interpreting familiar artworks (for instance, speaking of Hamlet's procrastination). But admitting this much goes no distance toward admitting *any* antecedently fixed general range of application of bivalent values in interpretive contexts, and what we should understand as the right relationship between description and interpretation depends on our theory of what an artwork is. It certainly cannot be decided by appeal to how things may go (analogously) in speaking, say, of physical objects. This is often overlooked.[5] Third, in defending relativism, it is irrelevant that interpreters often believe their own accounts preclude other "incongruent" interpretations, if a disciplined practice (as among professional critics and scholars) – that is, a collective practice, as opposed to an individual idiosyncrasy – finds it worth conceding that such interpretations may be jointly valid. And fourth, the entire issue is worth very little if the alethic questions are disjoined from a reasonably ramified account of the ontology of art and the epistemology of interpretation. It is extraordinary how many discussants disregard these very modest constraints.

[. . .]

I should perhaps add that I am entirely willing to label my many-valued values in any way that suits the occasion in hand ("apt," "reasonable," "plausible," or the like). All I insist on is that, thus far at least, they are merely "alethic" – that is, *not yet* interpreted epistemically or ontically. It is of course entirely possible that such values as "apt" or "plausible" should also be construed in evidentiary ways. However, if you allow them here in the alethic sense, they are not yet epistemically informed. I should say that something similar obtains in a many-valued logic that admits "probable" or "probably true," although it is characteristically linked to a bivalent logic and likely to be intended in nonrelativistic ways. There may be many such loosely similar distinctions to consider. (Relativist values, however, are not probabilistic values of any kind.)

We have reached a stalemate, then, on the alethic issue. Whatever advantages accrue to bivalence or relativism depend entirely on our picture of the world in which they apply. Even that is a stunning gain. For, if you review the history of relativism, you will not fail to see that it has never been conceded that a relativism close to Protagoras's conception could possibly escape one or another lethal paradox. That now turns out to have been a mistake.

I trust you approve my initial constraints on the airing of relativism's prospects. I have, in the foregoing, confined my analysis to the alethic in order to demonstrate, within the usual terms the canonical opponents of relativism insist on, that relativism remains as coherent as bivalence – and need not even refuse to be linked to the use of bivalence. In arguing thus, I may have prompted objections of two related sorts that I should like to offset. For, many will say, if you treat relativism in the alethic way, you have yourself fallen in with relativism's opponents; you must believe that a relativistic logic is, on objectivist grounds, the right logic to prefer everywhere. By "objectivism," I mean no more than there is an "independent" order of reality – including artworks and other cultural entities – and we are fortunately endowed with the cognitive capacity to discern its determinate structure as it exists "independently."[6]

No. What I have offered in the foregoing is an attempt to vindicate relativism within the terms of reference the opponents of relativism insist on: my limited claim here is that they fail under that constraint. But I also want to insist, first of all, that the entire alethic policy I am advocating is *not* detachable from the encompassing ontic and epistemic considerations relative to which a relativistic logic (or a bivalent logic, for that matter) works at all; and second, that here the invariances and modal necessities of the "objectivist" orientation are to be rejected.

You will notice that I have avoided introducing flux or historicity or incommensurability in speaking of the mere alethic structure of relativism. That was meant to preclude certain irrelevant objections. Nevertheless, *once*, on independent grounds, you acknowledge historicity, the range of application for a relativistic logic is bound to be much larger than might otherwise be supposed. Relativism is hardly interesting, presented as a mere abstract possibility. It gains standing only by being put to use in one important sector of inquiry or another. Here, of course, I am attempting to show its advantage in the criticism of the arts, but I set no antecedent limitations on its use. On the contrary, you see that vindicating relativism in the formal sense is only a small part of recovering the puzzle that the modernist/postmodernist dispute obscures.

I

Matters change abruptly once we turn from formal to substantive considerations, for relativism has its best inning in judgments about cultural phenomena. Even if admitting that were tantamount to admitting a restriction on relativism's range of application, nothing would be lost: as I have said, relativism need not be an all-or-nothing affair. The opponents of relativism forever point to inquiries that (as they believe) could not possibly recommend a relativistic logic. Perhaps. But if relativism may be defended piece-meal, for different sectors of inquiry, the objection would be irrelevant. [. . .]

[. . .] Wherever we want to admit "incongruent" truth-claims, we need only fall back to a relativistic logic. The question remains whether there are any such sectors of inquiry — whether it would be no more than stonewalling to deny they exist. Of course they do! I shall come to the argument in a moment. But, more to the point, you must realize that what remains to be supplied is not so much a further formal defense of relativism as an ontic and epistemic characterization of the phenomena of certain exemplary inquiries and of what it is possible to claim and confirm about them. These, it may be hoped, can be shown to fit especially well the peculiar resources of a relativistic logic. What this shows is the misplaced zeal with which relativism is usually condemned and the profound mistake of conflating relativism with skepticism — or worse. For to justify relativism is to qualify the logical variety of admissibly objective truth-claims and to explain why relativism should be favored in certain domains at least. That runs absolutely contrary to skepticism's objective — as well as anarchism's and nihilism's, for that matter. [. . .]

By "cultural relativity," then, I mean no more than the pedestrian fact that different societies have different histories, languages, customs, values, theories, and the like. I do *not* mean, in that sense, that what is true is also different among different peoples,

or that knowledge differs among different peoples because knowledge must be relativized to what is already relativized in the way of truth. Such a position would be
a conceptual blunder as well as a complete *non sequitur*. What, substantively, is claimed
to be true will doubtless differ from one cultural orientation to another, but truth
and knowledge, as such, cannot be construed, on pain of contradiction, as culturally
variable. For that would mean what is (rightly) true might also be (rightly) false. This
is the reason for distinguishing between truth and truth-claims.

Simply put, the theme of cultural relativity is a matter of first-order fact, whereas
the relativist's thesis is a matter of second-order legitimation. That languages and
customs differ is no more than a tiresome first-order fact; but that a relativistic logic
should fit certain inquiries better than a bivalent logic, *without yet implicating any vari-
ability in truth or knowledge as such*, is a question open to serious second-order philosophical dispute. I see no quarrel here. By themselves, the bare facts regarding cultural
relativity have no philosophical importance at all. They acquire importance only when
they are pressed in the direction of the blundering thesis I have just flagged or of
whatever, more defensibly, may accord with relativism proper. This matter is almost
universally overlooked.

What is potentially interesting about cultural relativity is that the differences noted
between cultures may also obtain within them – that intersocietal differences are no
different in any principled way from intrasocietal differences; therefore, it is just as
philosophically difficult to fix objective truth and knowledge within any one society
or culture as it is between very different societies or cultures. That, I should say, was
the absolutely splendid thesis of W. V. Quine's enormously influential book *Word and
Object*, though that connection is never pointedly addressed in *Word and Object* (in
the sense relevant to relativism) or anywhere else in Quine's publications.[7] For, of
course, it is also the central thesis of Kuhn's *Structure of Scientific Revolutions* and Foucault's "Nietzsche, Genealogy, and History," which, by and large, are inchoate rela-
tivisms addressed to the possible philosophical importance of cultural relativity and
historical change. For what Kuhn and Foucault were willing to concede – which
Quine was not – was that what we count as truth and knowledge (that is, the legit-
imated concepts, not the bare, first-order facts accumulated by different societies) are
artifacts of history in the very same way first-order facts are. Yet that is no longer mere
cultural relativity but relativity housing relativism, the conjunction of alethic and
ontic/epistemic issues.

We don't actually know what Kuhn's and Foucault's theories of relativism were.
They were never explicit enough. Kuhn was content to deny that we could ever
directly discern any principle of "neutrality" regarding objective truth (objectivism),
and Foucault had no patience with the question. The usual philosophical error spun
from the facts of cultural relativity is, in effect, the same error Socrates attributes to
Protagoras in the well-known exchange with Protagoras's student, in the *Theaetetus*.
"True" for Protagoras, Socrates affirms, means "true-for-*x*." Truth is an inherently
relational notion, relativized to whatever, contingently, merely "appears" – or is
"believed" – true by this person or that, or by the same person at different times.
This has become the standard reading of Protagoras's doctrine over twenty-five
hundred years.[8] Of course, if that is what relativism comes to, then certainly relativism
is absurd – because it is self-defeating in an insuperable way.

One could never, for instance, say what anyone took to be true by his or her own or anyone else's lights; every effort to do so would be caught in the "relationalism" of the original definition of "true." I trust it is clear that I have, by what has already been offered in the way of analyzing relativism's logic, completely obviated the need to fall back to this preposterous reading of either cultural relativity or Protagoras's doctrine. We must go further. I do acknowledge that a bewildering number of commentators suppose either that cultural relativity *is* what relativism comes to or that, in virtue of cultural relativity, adopting relativism is tantamount to admitting Socrates' formula.[9] But that is surely a *non sequitur.* I am unconditionally opposed to both readings.

All this is by way of clearing the air. The primary point about cultural relativity is not mere first-order variety but rather that, within such variety, we must single out the possible import of its being the case that expressive, representational, stylistic, rhetorical, symbolic, semiotic, linguistic, traditional, institutional, and otherwise significative features of artworks and other cultural phenomena fall within the scope of the culturally variable. For, if such properties are subject to cultural relativity, then it must dawn on us that we may not be able to defend the objectivity of truth-claims about them in the usual bivalent way. We may have to fall back to the relativist's option. Such is the full connection between the two questions I originally distinguished.

I call all such properties (the expressive and the representational, for instance) "Intentional" properties, which means they designate meanings assignable to certain structures or meaningful structures as a result of the various forms of culturally informed activity (speech, deeds, manufacture, artistic creation), such that suitably informed persons may claim to discern these properties and interpret them objectively. "Intentionality" is a term of art here, which I designate by capitalizing the initial "I." (I have introduced the notion before, informally.) I use the term predicatively, to mark a family of *sui generis* properties confined to the cultural world – that is, to designate the collective, intrinsically interpretable features of societal life. I do *not* equate the term to the essentially solipsistic, ahistorical, and acultural forms of intentionality featured in the theories of Brentano and Husserl, yet I apply "Intentionality" in a way that still provides for something like the use they intended, but only under enculturing conditions (the conditions of acquiring, in infancy, a natural language and a grasp of the practices of one's surrounding society).[10]

That is a large story of its own, which I cannot properly relate here.[11] I merely co-opt the benefit of admitting its relevance. The most strategic theorem it offers – not the most important for our question – rests with the fact (congenial to cultural relativity) that Intentional properties are quite real. For convenience, I recommend the following postulate: the Intentional is equal to the cultural. For what is normally contested (remember Danto) in admitting the world of human culture is whether it is real at all – as real (say) as physical nature – and, *qua* real, marked by the *sui generis* properties I've just collected (the Intentional). That, of course, lays a proper ground for the objectivity of interpretive truth-claims that is conveniently indifferent to the alethic quarrel between bivalent and relativistic logics.

There's much more to the story than that. I'm being more than cautious in drawing your attention to the unfinished tale on which the completion of the argument favoring relativism depends. It's not needed in any narrow sense here, but it would help to reassure you that, both prephilosophically and philosophically, questioning the reality of the cultural world would produce instant and insuperable paradox. On my own argument, it would involve questioning our own existence. As I see matters, we ourselves (or "selves") are also artifacts of cultural life formed by transforming the members of *Homo sapiens* into linguistically and culturally apt subjects, marked (by that process) for discerning the Intentional features of whatever, as selves, we make and do. To put the point in its most provocative form, one could assert that no principled ground exists on which to disjoin the realist reading of human selves and the realist reading of the artifacts of their world; both are culturally constituted in similar ways and subject to similar interpretive interests. I would not press the point, except for the fact that the most fashionable analytic theories in the West (particularly in the philosophy of mind) completely discount the reality of the cultural (and the intentional in general) or make it entirely derivative, logically, from whatever may be specified in purely biological or computational terms.[12]

Even that might not be troubling, since these theorists often have little interest in the philosophical problems of the cultural world. But what should we say when leading theorists of the arts – Arthur Danto, most notably – commit themselves to the *denial* of the reality of the cultural (or the Intentional).[13] I must alert you to the fact that even a bivalent account of the objectivity of literary and art criticism would utterly founder on anything like Danto's thesis; so that admitting the reality – *a fortiori*, the discernibility – of the Intentional structure of artworks and human careers lays a needed ontic and epistemic ground for the would-be objectivity of critical interpretations and histories, *whether construed bivalently or relativistically, objectivistically or constructivistically*. Allow the gain, if you will, however provisionally: it does not quite reach to what is decisive for or against relativism, but it makes the debate worth the bother.

Let me summarize what I have already established in this chapter, with an eye to securing a further goal. Thus far we have (1) distinguished a relativistic logic from a bivalent logic and shown its formal coherence; (2) discovered that the defense of relativism, as in a relativistic theory of interpretation or history, is largely occupied with demonstrating, ontically and epistemically, a certain suitable fit between manageable inquiries in one or another sector of the world and the resources and advantages of a relativistic logic; (3) acknowledged that no insurmountable paradox results from using a bivalent and a relativistic logic together, even in a lax and ad hoc way; and (4) determined that relativism and cultural relativity are entirely different doctrines, since the first is a second-order thesis and the second is a first-order thesis. We want, of course, to know how relativism and cultural relativity may be fruitfully linked so that an obviously robust practice – such as the ongoing work of a professional cohort of historians or art critics, or lawyers or moralists, for that matter – could be sustained or would strike us as worthwhile (not prone to any serious loss of investigative rigor) and would actually be less arbitrary and more rewarding than champions of the bivalent canon suppose.

The general answer is plain enough: on the one hand, the defenders of the bivalent canon cannot make their own case everywhere and, indeed, inevitably betray their awareness that they cannot; on the other hand, we already have the favorable evidence of the exemplary practices of interpretive critics and historians. The essential clue is this: the switch from bivalence to relativistic values is not a change in rigor at all but a change in what we understand to be the nature of the *objects* on which the relevant rigor is to be practiced. In claiming that the Intentional structure of art-works definitely favors relativism over bivalence, I take the general failure on the part of most critics of relativism to analyze Intentionality to be knockdown evidence of their failure to address the full question of relativism itself. For Intentional attributes are not determinate – though, under interpretive conditions, they are determinable – when compared with what is usually taken to be the determinate nature of physical or non-Intentional attributes. It's this issue that needs to be pursued – along with, of course, its bearing on the question of objectivity. [. . .]

It may also be that a potential social benefit results from calling *all* pretensions of objectivity into question at the present time. I am willing to concede the possibility, but it is not my principal concern here. Nevertheless, I'll add in all frankness that to reject "objectivity" because one rejects "objectivism" is excessive – and more than misleading. Because, we obviously need *some* normative sense of the rigor of inquiry and the attribution of truth-values. Whatever is best in that sense is what we must recover as objectivity. (There's a danger here of being misunderstood.) But strict post-modernism is conceptual anarchy: whatever first-order recovery may be defended implicates some form of second-order legitimation.[14]

For present purposes, I bridge the difference between the two issues by admitting straight out that what counts as objectivity is – ineluctably – a reasoned artifact of how we choose to discipline our truth-claims in any sector of inquiry. The assumption is that there is simply no way to *discover* the true norms of objectivity in any domain at all. Acceptable norms will have to be constructed as one or another disputed second-order proposal fitted to what we claim are our best first-order interests in this domain or that. What's important is that such a construction is not tantamount to relativism – in the straightforward sense that even our adherence to a bivalent logic (in physics, say) may have to take a constructivist turn. Constructivism is not, as such, equivalent to relativism.

Kuhn may well be right to say that it is "hopeless" to pretend to discover the changeless marks of objectivity.[15] Some claim to see in this a return to Socrates' interpretation of Protagoras. But that would be a mistake, a complete *non sequitur*. For, as already remarked, "true" is laid down in the *Theaetetus* as meaning "true-for-x" and is thereafter rigorously applied (if possible), whereas, here, it is not a question of the meaning or criteria of "true" at all but of how, socially, the practices of what we call objective inquiry are first formed. There is no ulterior judgment to the effect that what is posited as a defensible practice in this regard is tantamount to, or entails, the finding that that (also) *is true-for-x* (where "*x*" is now the society that supports the practice).

II

[. . .]

[. . .] Relativism is not inherently a subversive doctrine, a way of destroying the fabric of decent society. It is, rather, the upshot of a quite sober reckoning of the false pretensions of a canon that might well wreck us with its own misguided zeal.

Imagine that the champions of some political *status quo* insisted they had found the true norms of invariant human nature and therefore were obliged to treat moral, legal, political, and religious questions in accord with a strict bivalence *informed by those ulterior truths*: that would be the analogue of Beardsley's and Hirsch's doctrines. They can't possibly work: the Intentionality of the human world is far too complex, far too equivocal, far too mongrelized, far too transient, and far too easily altered by our own efforts to determine its meaning. Here, you begin to see the advantage of conceding no more than the Intentionality of artworks and the formal resources of relativism.

Please explain yourself, you're bound to say. Don't just rail against the honest labor of more conventional theorists. Tell us how you would reconcile relativism and objectivity – in criticism, for example. Tell us that, or go away! Fair enough. I accept the complaint, but my answer stares you in the face. A proper elucidation would doubtless be interminable, but the essential clue is clear enough: Intentional properties – expressive, semiotic, representational, and all the other significative properties I've gathered under the umbrella term "Intentional" – cannot be determined criterially, algorithmically, evidentially, except in ways that are already subaltern to the consensual (not criterial) tolerance of the apt agents of the collective practices of a particular society. That is the reason all analogies drawn from physical nature won't do, for cultural phenomena exhibit, and physical phenomena lack, Intentional properties. Hence, what we mean by description and interpretation is not quite the same in the two domains (though they are not disjoint either).

In our own time, the thesis may be drawn, in different ways, from Wittgenstein's notions of a *Lebensform* and a "language game" and from Kuhn and Foucault as well.[16] Historically, I am convinced it captures the leanest way to read Hegel's notion of *sittlich* as well as *Geist*.[17] It appears as a recognizable stream of thought running from Hegel through Marx, Nietzsche, Dilthey, Heidegger, Horkheimer, and Gadamer, down to Foucault. If you grasp the point, you see at once it is not possible to segregate the theory of interpreting artworks from a general theory of cultural reality. Professional work will have its local policy, to be sure, but its logic and its sense of a viable practice will be governed by our general conception of the *sui generis* features of the culture we share – any culture, as we now understand matters.

The important point to bear in mind is that a proper analysis of Intentionality is in no way hostage to a favorable policy on relativism. It's the other way around: Intentional properties, which distinguish the world of human culture – *a fortiori*, literary and art criticism and, on a plausible argument, even explanatory theories in the physical sciences – will ultimately signal what our alethic, ontic, and epistemic policies should be.

The entire contest can be decided by reviewing two corollaries of my characterization of Intentionality – applied, if adopted, to the special concerns of professional critics, historians, or the like. First of all, predication in general cannot be epistemically managed on criterial or algorithmic grounds unless, *per impossibile*, Platonism is proved viable. I claim that general predicates, Intentional predicates in particular, cannot be extended to new instances, except informally, in terms of what, consensually, may be tolerated as effective or incremental extensions from acknowledged exemplars. Any difficulties incurred – for example, in the sciences, with respect to would-be laws, prediction, explanation, or technological control – can be readily resolved along alternative lines that will have to proceed as before.[18]

But the hopelessness of all theories of universals – realist, nominalist, conceptualist – remains confirmed quite independently of all that. If so, then bivalence will *always* be subject to a policy of accommodating predicative similarities that cannot itself be strictly applied (algorithmically, for instance) in bivalent terms. This concession is generally ignored by the opponents of relativism, even though the tolerance that must be admitted is not inherently relativistic in its own right. Bivalence itself must be applied in a constructivist way to predicables. Even a bivalent treatment of predicative truth must acknowledge that informality.

If you add to this (the first corollary) the obvious adjustment – that the particular exemplars on which extended predicative tolerance depends will always be subject to replacement, on the strength of changing convictions of what to look for in the way of observable similarities – then *whatever* we judge to be objective in the predicative way will elude the impossible strictures of any (bivalent) policy informed by one or another form of invariance. What I say here is that objectivity must be a constructed artifact of our consensual practice – whether construed bivalently or relativistically. Furthermore, what holds for predication holds for reference and denotation and for all linguistic powers that bear on servicing truth-claims. I challenge the opponents of relativism to explain how, if Platonism cannot be invoked, the objective practice of making and confirming truth-claims can possibly be restricted in the bivalent way. I think there cannot be an answer.

The second corollary concerns Intentional predicates and the nature of artworks in particular. Imagine someone asks you for the meaning of Anselm Kiefer's use of Nazi symbolism in his enormously intriguing paintings – which may be judged (by opposed lines of reasoning) to be celebrating or exorcising the world's unresolved memory of that terrible past. How should we decide such a dispute? I suggest you take stock of the following notions. First of all, any predicative attribution will be *sittlich* – in the minimal (perhaps pirated) sense I have already sketched but not previously named. (I now borrow the term in the slimmest possible way from Hegel.) The perception of predicative similarity lacks, in the last instance, adequate criteria or algorithms of application, because, as I say, to presume otherwise would be to favor a form of Platonism. Thus, if the scope of a general predicate – any predicate – is extended in real-world terms, it escapes utter arbitrariness only by appealing to the *sittlich*, the actual practices of a society of apt speakers. Questions of the fit between such extensions and the theoretical and practical interests of those speakers affect only the choice among various lines of extension amid an indefinite run of such possibilities. Such a choice never affords more powerful epistemic resources. Hence, the fortunes of bivalence cannot fail to be subordinated to deeper epistemic and ontic considerations.

By parity of reasoning, our aptitude for discerning relevant similarities in a run of would-be cases – any cases – signifies our mastery of the same *sittlich* practices within whose bounds such similarities obtain or are reasonably extended. In the art world, Intentional properties bring into play meanings and other significative structures (Kiefer's images, for instance). So – I mention as a second consideration – Intentional properties complicate the initial question of perceptual similarity (in any generous sense of "similarity" by drawing in (within the bounds of the first) specifically interpretive attributions of semiotic similarities. Is Prokofiev's *Classical Symphony* Mozartean, for instance? Is *Miss Lonelyhearts* a fair analogue of Milton's *Paradise Regained*?

To admit these questions is to admit the unlikelihood of adhering to a strict bivalence – yet without refusing the advantage of a laxer use of bivalence under consensual conditions. If you bear in mind that ordinary discourse is the usual exemplar of our treatment of truth-claims – both in the sense that any would-be greater precision of reference and predication is tethered to the possibilities of conversational precision and in the sense that, at the conversational level, consensual solidarity (again, *not* in the criterial way) cannot fail to be in play – you must grasp as well that the precision of critical discourse (like the precision of science) cannot exceed the precision with which we understand ourselves and one another. In this sense, relativism is a reminder of our epistemic frailties. How could it be otherwise?

[. . .] In cultural matters, some form of constructivism seems inevitable; and if in pursuing the import of the analysis of predication, reference, and discursive contexts, we find we cannot segregate our discourse about the natural world and the world of human culture, then some sort of constructivism will be implicated once again. As I have said, however, constructivism is *not* tantamount to relativism. Neither is cultural relativity, nor the relativity of truth-value assignments on evidentiary grounds formed in accord with the first-order patterns of cultural relativity. All that is often overlooked – or misconstrued. Certainly, saying the ascription of "true" to a given statement is relative to a society's evidentiary practice is not equivalent to agreeing that "true" means "true-for-*x*" in anything like the relational sense Socrates cleverly imposes on Theaetetus. Beyond that, if human thought is, as I suggest, historicized as well, and if objectivity must (as in the predicative case) be artifactually constructed in accord with our consensual practices, then (I suggest) it is well-nigh impossible that relativism will not have a very strong inning in interpretive and other cultural contexts (and elsewhere as well). Nevertheless, I insist I have built the argument up from the least contestable considerations.

Notes

1   Thomas S. Kuhn, *The Structure of Scientific Revolutions*, 2d ed., enl. (Chicago: University of Chicago Press, 1970); Michel Foucault, "Nietzsche, Genealogy, and History," in *Language, Countermemory, Practice: Selected Essays and Interviews*, trans. Donald F. Bouchard and Sherry Simon, ed. Donald F. Bouchard (Ithaca: Cornell University Press, 1977).

2   See, for instance, Carl G. Hempel, "The Function of General Laws in History," *in Aspects of Scientific Explanation and Other Essays in the Philosophy of Science* (New York: Free Press, 1965); and Wesley C. Salmon, *Scientific Explanation and Causal Structure of the World* (Princeton: Princeton University Press, 1984).

3   See, for instance, Nancy Cartwright, *How the Laws of Physics Lie* (Oxford: Clarendon Press, 1983); and Bas C. van Fraassen, *Laws and Symmetry* (Oxford: Clarendon Press, 1989).

4   See, in this connection, W. V. Quine, *Word and Object* (Cambridge: Harvard University Press, 1960), sections 15–16; and P. F. Strawson, "On Referring," *Mind* 14 (1950).

5   The complication regarding description and interpretation is overlooked in Richard
    Shusterman, "Beneath Interpretation: Against Hermeneutic Holism," *The Monist* 73 (1990).

6   See, further, Richard J. Bernstein, *Beyond Objectivism and Relativism: Science, Hermeneutics,
    and Praxis* (Philadelphia: University of Pennsylvania Press, 1983); and Joseph Margolis, *The
    Truth About Relativism* (Oxford: Basil Blackwell, 1991).

7   See Quine, *Word and Object,* chaps. 1–2.

8   It is repeated, for instance, by Myles Burnyeat, a specialist on Plato, in "Protagoras and
    Self-Refutation in Plato's *Theaetetus,*" *Philosophical Review* 85 (1976).

9   See, for instance, Hilary Putnam, "Why Reason Can't Be Naturalized," *Philosophical Papers,*
    vol. 1 (Cambridge: Cambridge University Press, 1983), 235–37.

10 For a convenient summary, see Jitendra Nath Mohanty, *The Concept of Intentionality* (St.
    Louis: Warren H. Green, 1972).

11 For a sense of its bearing on the defense of relativism, see, further, Joseph Margolis,
    Historied Thought, Constructed World: A Conceptual Primer for the Turn of the Millennium
    (Berkeley and Los Angeles: University of California Press, 1995).

12 See, for instance, Paul M. Churchland, *A Neurocomputational Perspective: The Nature of Mind
    and the Structure of Science* (Cambridge: MIT Press, 1989); and John R. Searle, *The Con-
    struction of Social Reality* (New York: Free Press, 1995).

13 See Arthur C. Danto, "The Artworld," *Journal of Philosophy* 61 (1964); and the meaning
    of "transfiguration" in Danto's *The Transfiguration of the Commonplace: A Philosophy of Art*
    (Cambridge: Harvard University Press, 1981).

14 Since giving these lectures, I have read Barbara Herrnstein Smith, *Belief and Resistance:
    Dynamics of Contemporary Intellectual Controversy* (Cambridge: Harvard University Press,
    1997). There is much that Smith and I share (and have shared in earlier publications).
    But, with due appreciation of her rhetorical intent, I find she slights the recuperative side
    of the epistemological and methodological issues. This gives her account a cast that is
    more sympathetic with Rorty's postmodernism, Feyerabend's anarchism, or the claims of
    the Scottish sociologists of knowledge than I would favor. I condede that all of these
    options make their contribution, but I also find them all (finally) inadequate.

15 Compare Kuhn, *The Structure of Scientific Revolutions,* section 10.

16 See Ludwig Wittgenstein, *Philosophical Investigations,* trans. G. E. M. Anscombe (New York:
    Macmillan, 1953).

17 See G. W. E. Hegel, *Phenomenology of Spirit,* trans. A. V. Miller (Oxford: Oxford University
    Press, 1977). The sense of the *"sittlich"* extends, I believe, beyond the "ethical."

18 See Joseph Margolis, "The Politics of Predication," *Philosophical Forum* 27 (1996).

13

PERCEPTION AND TRUTH
from "An Unpublished Text," "Cézanne's Doubt," and "Reflection and Interrogation"

Maurice Merleau-Ponty

From "An Unpublished Text"

We never cease living in the world of perception, but we go beyond it in critical thought – almost to the point of forgetting the contribution of perception to our idea of truth.[1] For critical thought encounters only *bare propositions* which it discusses, accepts or rejects. Critical thought has broken with the naive evidence of *things*, and when it affirms, it is because it no longer finds any means of denial. However necessary this activity of verification may be, specifying criteria and demanding from our experience its credentials of validity, it is not aware of our contact with the perceived world which is simply there before us, beneath the level of the verified true and the false. Nor does critical thought even define the positive steps of thinking or its most valid accomplishments.

My first two works sought to restore the world of perception. My works in preparation aim to show how communication with others, and thought, take up and go beyond the realm of perception which initiated us to the truth.

The perceiving mind is an incarnated mind. I have tried, first of all, to reestablish the roots of the mind in its body and in its world, going against doctrines which treat perception as a simple result of the action of external things on our body as well as against those which insist on the autonomy of consciousness. These philoso-

Maurice Merleau-Ponty, "An Unpublished Text by Maurice Merleau-Ponty: A Prospectus of His Work," trans. Arleen B. Dallery, in *Primacy of Perception*, ed. James M. Edie (Evanston, IL: Northwestern University Press, 1964), pp. 3–11. Reprinted by permission of Éditions Gallimard and Northwestern University Press.

Maurice Merleau-Ponty, excerpts from "Cézanne's Doubt," in *Sense and Non-Sense*, trans. Hubert L. Dreyfus and Patricia Allen Dreyfus (Evanston, IL: Northwestern University Press, 1964), pp. 13–16. Reprinted by permission of Éditions Gallimard and Northwestern University Press.

Maurice Merleau-Ponty, excerpts from "Reflection and Interrogation," in *The Visible and the Invisible*, ed. Claude Lefort, trans. Alphonso Lingis (Evanston, IL: Northwestern University Press, 1968), pp. 41–3, 49. Reprinted by permission of Éditions Gallimard and Northwestern University Press.

phies commonly forget – in favor of a pure exteriority or of a pure interiority – the insertion of the mind in corporeality, the ambiguous relation which we entertain with our body and, correlatively, with perceived things. When one attempts, as I have in *The Structure of Behavior*, to trace out, on the basis of modern psychology and physiology, the relationships which obtain between the perceiving organism and its milieu one clearly finds that they are not those of an automatic machine which needs an outside agent to set off its pre-established mechanisms. And it is equally clear that one does not account for the facts by superimposing a pure, contemplative consciousness on a thinglike body. In the conditions of life – if not in the laboratory – the organism is less sensitive to certain isolated physical and chemical agents than to the constellation which they form and to the whole situation which they define. Behaviors reveal a sort of prospective activity in the organism, as if it were oriented toward the meaning of certain elementary situations, as if it entertained familiar relations with them, as if there were an "*a priori* of the organism," privileged conducts and laws of internal equilibrium which predisposed the organism to certain relations with its milieu. At this level there is no question yet of a real self-awareness or of intentional activity. Moreover, the organism's prospective capability is exercised only within defined limits and depends on precise, local conditions.

The functioning of the central nervous system presents us with similar paradoxes. In its modern forms, the theory of cerebral localizations has profoundly changed the relation of function to substrate. It no longer assigns, for instance, a pre-established mechanism to each perceptual behavior. "Coordinating centers" are no longer considered as storehouses of "cerebral traces," and their functioning is qualitatively different from one case to another, depending on the chromatic nuance to be evoked and the perceptual structure to be realized. Finally, this functioning reflects all the subtlety and all the variety of perceptual relationships.

The perceiving organism seems to show us a Cartesian mixture of the soul with the body. Higher-order behaviors give a new meaning to the life of the organism, but the mind here disposes of only a limited freedom; it needs simpler activities in order to stabilize itself in durable institutions and to realize itself truly as mind. Perceptual behavior emerges from these relations to a situation and to an environment which are not the workings of a pure, knowing subject.

In my work on the *Phenomenology of Perception* we are no longer present at the emergence of perceptual behaviors; rather we install ourselves in them in order to pursue the analysis of this exceptional relation between the subject and its body and its world. For contemporary psychology and psychopathology the body is no longer merely *an object in the world*, under the purview of a separated spirit. It is on the side of the subject; it is our *point of view on the world*, the place where the spirit takes on a certain physical and historical situation. As Descartes once said profoundly, the soul is not merely in the body like a pilot in his ship; it is wholly intermingled with the body. The body, in turn, is wholly animated, and all its functions contribute to the perception of objects – an activity long considered by philosophy to be pure knowledge.

We grasp external space through our bodily situation. A "corporeal or postural schema" gives us at every moment a global, practical, and implicit notion of the relation between our body and things, of our hold on them. A system of possible movements, or "motor projects," radiates from us to our environment. Our body is not in space like things; it inhabits or haunts space. It applies itself to space like a hand to an instrument, and when we wish to move about we do not move the body as we move an object. We transport it without instruments as if by magic, since it is ours and because through it we have direct access to space. For us the body is much more than an instrument or a means; it is our expression in the world, the visible form of our intentions. Even our most secret affective movements, those most deeply tied to the humoral infrastructure, help to shape our perception of things.

Now if perception is thus the common act of all our motor and affective functions, no less than the sensory, we must rediscover the structure of the perceived world through a process similar to that of an archaeologist. For the structure of the perceived world is buried under the sedimentations of later knowledge. Digging down to the perceived world, we see that sensory qualities are not opaque, indivisible "givens," which are simply exhibited to a remote consciousness – a favorite idea of classical philosophy. We see too that colors (each surrounded by an affective atmosphere which psychologists have been able to study and define) are themselves different modalities of our co-existence with the world. We also find that spatial forms or distances are not so much relations between different points in objective space as they are relations between these points and a central perspective – our body. In short, these relations are different ways for external stimuli to test, to solicit, and to vary our grasp on the world, our horizontal and vertical anchorage in a place and in a here-and-now. We find that perceived things, unlike geometrical objects, are not bounded entities whose laws of construction we possess a priori, but that they are open, inexhaustible systems which we recognize through a certain style of development, although we are never able, in principle, to explore them entirely, and even though they never give us more than profiles and perspectival views of themselves. Finally, we find that the perceived world, in its turn, is not a pure object of thought without fissures or lacunae; it is, rather, like a universal style shared in by all perceptual beings. While the world no doubt co-ordinates these perceptual beings, we can never presume that its work is finished. Our world, as Malebranche said, is an "unfinished task."

If we now wish to characterize a subject capable of this perceptual experience, it obviously will not be a self-transparent thought, absolutely present to itself without the interference of its body and its history. The perceiving subject is not this absolute thinker; rather, it functions according to a natal pact between our body and the world, between ourselves and our body. Given a perpetually new natural and historical situation to control, the perceiving subject undergoes a continued birth; at each instant it is something new. Every incarnate subject is like an open notebook in which we do not yet know what will be written. Or it is like a new language; we do not know what works it will accomplish but only that, once it has appeared, it cannot fail to say little or much, to have a history and a meaning. The very productivity or freedom of human life, far from denying our situation, utilizes it and turns it into a means of expression.

This remark brings us to a series of further studies which I have undertaken since 1945 and which will definitively fix the philosophical significance of my earlier works while they, in turn, determine the route and the method of these later studies.

I found in the experience of the perceived world a new type of relation between the mind and truth. The evidence of the perceived thing lies in its concrete aspect, in the very texture of its qualities, and in the equivalence among all its sensible properties — which caused Cézanne to say that one should be able to paint even odors. Before our undivided existence the world is true; it exists. The unity, the articulations of both are intermingled. We experience in it a truth which shows through and envelops us rather than being held and circumscribed by our mind.

Now if we consider, above the perceived world, the field of knowledge properly so called — i.e., the field in which the mind seeks to possess the truth, to define its objects itself, and thus to attain to a universal wisdom, not tied to the particularities of our situation — we must ask: Does not the realm of the perceived world take on the form of a simple appearance? Is not pure understanding a new source of knowledge, in comparison with which our perceptual familiarity with the world is only a rough, unformed sketch? We are obliged to answer these questions first with a theory of truth and then with a theory of intersubjectivity, both of which I have already touched upon in essays such as "Le doute de Cézanne," "Le Roman et la métaphysique,"[2] and, on the philosophy of history, in *Humanisme et terreur* [1947]. But the philosophical foundations of these essays are still to be rigorously elaborated. I am now working on two books dealing with a theory of truth.

It seems to me that knowledge and the communication with others which it presupposes not only are original formations with respect to the perceptual life but also they preserve and continue our perceptual life even while transforming it. Knowledge and communication sublimate rather than suppress our incarnation, and the characteristic operation of the mind is in the movement by which we recapture our corporeal existence and use it to symbolize instead of merely to coexist. This metamorphosis lies in the double function of our body. Through its "sensory fields" and its whole organization the body is, so to speak, predestined to model itself on the natural aspects of the world. But as an active body capable of gestures, of expression, and finally of language, it turns back on the world to signify it. As the observation of apraxics shows, there is in man, superimposed upon actual space with its self-identical points, a "virtual space" in which the spatial values that a point *would receive* (for any other position of our corporal co-ordinates) are also recognized. A system of correspondence is established between our spatial situation and that of others, and each one comes to symbolize all the others. This insertion of our factual situation as a particular case within the system of other possible situations begins as soon as we *designate* a point in space with our finger. For this pointing gesture, which animals do not understand, supposes that we are already installed in virtual space — at the end of the line prolonging our finger in a centrifugal and cultural space. This mimic usage of our body is not yet a conception, since it does not cut us off from our corporeal situation; on the contrary, it assumes all its meaning. It leads us to a concrete theory of the mind which will show the mind in a relationship of reciprocal exchange with the instruments which it uses, but uses only while rendering to them what it has received from them, and more.

In a general way expressive gestures (in which the science of physiognomy sought in vain for the sufficient signs of emotional states) have a univocal meaning only with respect to the situation which they underline and punctuate. But like phonemes, which have no meaning by themselves, expressive gestures have a diacritical value:

they announce the constitution of a symbolical system capable of redesigning an infinite number of situations. They are a first language. And reciprocally language can be
treated as a gesticulation so varied, so precise, so systematic, and capable of so many
convergent expressions [*recoupements*] that the internal structure of an utterance can
ultimately agree only with the mental situation to which it responds and of which
it becomes an unequivocal sign. The meaning of language, like that of gestures, thus
does not lie in the elements composing it. The meaning is their common intention,
and the spoken phrase is understood only if the hearer, following the "verbal chain,"
goes beyond each of its links in the direction that they all designate together.

It follows that even solitary thought does not cease using the language which supports it, rescues it from the transitory, and throws it back again. Cassirer said that
thought was the "shuttlecock" of language. It also follows that perhaps, taken piece
by piece, language does not yet contain its meaning, that all communication supposes
in the listener a creative re-enactment of what is heard. Language leads us to a thought
which is no longer ours alone, to a thought which is presumptively universal, though
this is never the universality of a pure concept which would be identical for every
mind. It is rather the call which a situated thought addresses to other thoughts, equally
situated, and each one responds to the call with its own resources. An examination
of the domain of algorithm would show there too, I believe, the same strange
function which is at work in the so-called inexact forms of language. Especially when
it is a question of conquering a new domain for exact thought, the most formal
thought is always referred to some qualitatively defined mental situation from which
it extracts a meaning only by applying itself to the configuration of the problem. The
transformation is never a simple analysis, and thought is never more than relatively
formal.

Since I intend to treat this problem more fully in my work *L'Origine de la vérité*,
I have approached it less directly in a partially written book dealing with literary language. In this area it is easier to show that language is never the mere clothing of a
thought which otherwise possesses itself in full clarity. The meaning of a book is
given, in the first instance, not so much by its ideas as by a systematic and unex-
pected variation of the modes of language, of narrative, or of existing literary forms.
This accent, this particular modulation of speech – if the expression is successful – is
assimilated little by little by the reader, and it gives him access to a thought to which
he was until then indifferent or even opposed. Communication in literature is not
the simple appeal on the part of the writer to meanings which would be part of an
a priori of the mind; rather, communication arouses these meanings in the mind
through enticement and a kind of oblique action. The writer's thought does not
control his language from without; the writer is himself a kind of new idiom, constructing itself, inventing ways of expression, and diversifying itself according to its
own meaning. Perhaps poetry is only that part of literature where this autonomy is
ostentatiously displayed. All great prose is also a re-creation of the signifying instrument, henceforth manipulated according to a new syntax. Prosaic writing, on the
other hand, limits itself to using, through accepted signs, the meanings already accepted
in a given culture. Great prose is the art of capturing a meaning which until then
had never been objectified and of rendering it accessible to everyone who speaks the
same language. When a writer is no longer capable of thus founding a new universality and of taking the risk of communicating, he has outlived his time. It seems to

me that we can also say of other institutions that they have ceased to live when they show themselves incapable of carrying on a poetry of human relations – that is, the call of each individual freedom to all the others.

Hegel said that the Roman state was the prose of the world. I shall entitle my book *Introduction à la prose du monde*.[3] In this work I shall elaborate the category of prose beyond the confines of literature to give it a sociological meaning.

For these studies on expression and truth approach, from the epistemological side, the general problem of human interrelations – which will be the major topic of my later studies. The linguistic relations among men should help us understand the more general order of symbolic relations and of institutions, which assure the exchange not only of thoughts but of all types of values, the co-existence of men within a culture and, beyond it, within a single history. Interpreted in terms of symbolism, the concept of history seems to escape the disputes always directed to it because one ordinarily means by this word – whether to accept it or to reject it – an external Power in the name of which men would be dispossessed of consciousness. History is no more external to us than language. There *is* a history of thought: the succession of the works of the spirit (no matter how many detours we see in it) is really a single experience which develops of itself and in whose development, so to speak, truth capitalizes itself.[4] In an analogous sense we can say that there is a history of humanity or, more simply, *a* humanity. In other words, granting all the periods of stagnation and retreat, human relations are able to grow, to change their avatars into lessons, to pick out the truth of their past in the present, to eliminate certain mysteries which render them opaque and thereby make themselves more translucent.

The idea of a single history or of a logic of history is, in a sense, implied in the least human exchange, in the least social perception. For example, anthropology supposes that civilizations very different from ours are comprehensible to us, that they can be situated in relation to ours and vice-versa, that all civilizations belong to the same universe of thought, since the least use of language implies an idea of truth. Also we can never pretend to dismiss the adventures of history as something foreign to our present action, since even the most independent search for the most abstract truth has been and is a factor of history (the only one, perhaps, that we are sure is not disappointing). All human acts and all human creations constitute a single drama, and in this sense we are all saved or lost together. Our life is essentially universal.

But this methodological rationalism is not to be confused with a dogmatic rationalism which eliminates historical contingency in advance by supposing a "World Spirit" (Hegel) behind the course of events. If it is necessary to say that there is a total history, a single tissue tying together all the enterprises of simultaneous and successive civilizations, all the results of thought and all the facts of economics, it must not be in the guise of a historical idealism or materialism – one handing over the government of history to thought; the other, to matter. Because cultures are just so many coherent systems of symbols and because in each culture the modes of work, of human relations, of language and thought, even if not parallel at every moment, do not long remain separated, cultures can be compared and placed under a common denominator. What makes this connection of meaning between each aspect of a culture and all the rest, as between all the episodes of history, is the permanent, harmonious thought of this plurality of beings who recognize one another as "*semblables*," even when some seek to enslave others, and who are so commonly situated that adversaries are often in a kind of complicity.

Our inquiries should lead us finally to a reflection on this *transcendental man*, or this "natural light" common to all, which appears through the movement of history – to a reflection on this Logos which gives us the task of vocalizing a hitherto mute world. Finally, they should lead us to a study of the Logos of the perceived world which we encountered in our earliest studies in the evidence of things. Here we rejoin the classical questions of metaphysics, but by following a route which removes from them their character as *problems* – that is to say, as difficulties which could be solved cheaply through the use of a few metaphysical entities constructed for this purpose. The notions of Nature and Reason, for instance, far from explaining the metamorphoses which we have observed from perception up to the more complex modes of human exchange, make them incomprehensible. For by relating them to separated principles, these notions mask a constantly experienced moment, the moment when an existence becomes aware of itself, grasps itself, and expresses its own meaning.

The study of perception could only teach us a "bad ambiguity," a mixture of finitude and universality, of interiority and exteriority. But there is a "good ambiguity" in the phenomenon of expression, a spontaneity which accomplishes what appeared to be impossible when we observed only the separate elements, a spontaneity which gathers together the plurality of monads, the past and the present, nature and culture into a single whole. To establish this wonder would be metaphysics itself and would at the same time give us the principle of an ethics.

Notes

1   This text was preceded by the following "Introductory Note" signed by Martial Gueroult: "The text given below was sent to me by Merleau-Ponty at the time of his candidacy to the Collège de France, when I was putting together a report of his qualifications for presentation to the assembly of professors. In this report Merleau-Ponty traces his past and future as a philosopher in a continuous line, and outlines the perspectives of his future studies from *L'Origine de la vérité* to *L'Homme transcendental*. In reading these unpublished and highly interesting pages, one keenly regrets the death which brutally interrupted the élan of a profound thought in full possession of itself and about to fulfill itself in a series of original works which would have been landmarks in contemporary French philosophy."
2   These are the first two essays in *Sens et non-sens* (Paris, 1948). – *Trans.*
3   This work was never published as such, though some of the studies it occasioned are the basis of the early chapters of *Signes* (Paris, 1960). – *Trans.*
4   That is, truth becomes Truth by "building up its capital." – *Trans.*

From "Cézanne's Doubt"

Cézanne could not convince by his arguments and preferred to paint instead. Rather than apply to his work dichotomies more appropriate to those who sustain traditions than to those men, philosophers or painters, who initiate these traditions, he preferred to search for the true meaning of painting, which is continually to question tradition. Cézanne did not think he had to choose between feeling and thought, between order and chaos. He did not want to separate the stable things which we see and the shifting way in which they appear; he wanted to depict matter as it takes on form, the birth of order through spontaneous organization. He makes a basic distinction not between "the senses" and "the understanding" but rather between the spontaneous organization of the things we perceive and the human organization of ideas and sciences. We see things; we agree about them; we are anchored in them; and it is with "nature" as our base that we construct our sciences. Cézanne wanted to paint this primordial world, and his pictures therefore seem to show nature pure, while photographs of the same landscapes suggest man's works, conveniences, and imminent presence. Cézanne never wished to "paint like a savage." He wanted to put intelligence, ideas, sciences, perspective, and tradition back in touch with the world of nature which they must comprehend. He wished, as he said, to confront the sciences with the nature "from which they came."

By remaining faithful to the phenomena in his investigations of perspective, Cézanne discovered what recent psychologists have come to formulate: the lived perspective, that which we actually perceive, is not a geometric or photographic one.

[. . .]

Cézanne does not try to use color to *suggest* the tactile sensations which would give shape and depth. These distinctions between touch and sight are unknown in primordial perception. It is only as a result of a science of the human body that we finally learn to distinguish between our senses. The lived object is not rediscovered or constructed on the basis of the contributions of the senses; rather, it presents itself to us from the start as the center from which these contributions radiate. We *see* the depth, the smoothness, the softness, the hardness of objects; Cézanne even claimed that we see their odor. If the painter is to express the world, the arrangement of his colors must carry with it this indivisible whole, or else his picture will only hint at things and will not give them in the imperious unity, the presence, the insurpassable plenitude which is for us the definition of the real. That is why each brushstroke must satisfy an infinite number of conditions. Cézanne sometimes pondered hours at a time before putting down a certain stroke, for, as Bernard said, each stroke must "contain the air, the light, the object, the composition, the character, the outline, and the style." Expressing what *exists* is an endless task.[1]

[. . .] The painter who conceptualizes and seeks the expression first misses the mystery − renewed every time we look at someone − of a person's appearing in nature. In *La Peau de chagrin* Balzac describes a "tablecloth white as a layer of newly fallen snow, upon which the place-settings rise symmetrically, crowned with blond rolls." "All through youth," said Cézanne, "I wanted to paint that, that tablecloth of new snow. . . . Now I know that one must will only to paint the place-settings rising symmetrically and the blond rolls. If I paint 'crowned' I've had it, you understand? But if I really balance and shade my place-settings and rolls as they are in nature, then you can be sure that the crowns, the snow, and all the excitement will be there too."

From "Reflection and Interrogation"

[. . .] Each perception is mutable and only probable − it is, if one likes, only an *opinion*; but what is not opinion, what each perception, even if false, verifies, is the belong-ingness of each experience to the same world, their equal power to manifest it, as *possibilities of the same world*. If the one takes the place of the other so well − to the point that one no longer finds any trace of it a moment after the illusion − it is pre-cisely because they are not successive hypotheses about an unknowable Being, but perspectives upon the same familiar Being, which we know cannot exclude the one without including the other and which we know in any case to be itself beyond con-testation. And this is why the very fragility of a perception, attested by its breakup and by the substitution of another perception, far from authorizing us to efface the index of "reality" from them all, obliges us to concede it to all of them, to recognize all of them to be variants of the same world, and finally to consider them not as all false but as "all true," not as repeated failures in the determination of the world but as progressive approximations. Each perception envelops the possibility of its own replacement by another, and thus of a sort of disavowal from the things. But this also means that each perception is the term of an approach, of a series of "illusions" that were not merely simple "thoughts" in the restrictive sense of Being-for-itself and the "merely thought of," but possibilities that could have been, radiations of this unique world that "there is" . . . − and which, as such, never revert to nothingness or to sub-jectivity as if they had never appeared, but are rather, as Husserl puts it well, "crossed out" or "cancelled" by the "new" reality. The philosophy of reflection is not wrong in considering the false as a mutilated or partial truth: its error is rather to act as if the partial were only a *de facto* absence of the totality, which does not need to be accounted for. This finally destroys any consistency proper to the appearance, inte-grates it in advance into Being, deprives it of its tenor of truth because it is partial, makes it disappear into an internal adequation where Being and the reasons for being are one. The movement toward adequation, to which the facts of dis-illusion bear witness, is not the returning to itself of an adequate Thought that would have inex-plicably lost sight of itself − nor is it a blind progress of probability, founded on the number of signs and concordances. It is the prepossession of a totality which is there before one knows how and why, whose realizations are never what we would have imagined them to be, and which nonetheless fulfills a secret expectation within us, since we believe in it tirelessly.

   [. . .] It is a question of reconsidering the interdependent notions of the active and the passive in such a way that they no longer place us before the antinomy of a phi-losophy that accounts for being and the truth, but does not take the world into account, and a philosophy that takes the world into account, but uproots us from being and the truth.

[. . .]

My access to a universal mind via reflection, far from finally discovering what I always was, is motivated by the intertwining of my life with the other lives, of my body with the visible things, by the intersection of my perceptual field with that of the others, by the blending in of my duration with the other durations. If I pretend to find, through reflection, in the universal mind the premise that had always backed up my experience, I can do so only by forgetting this non-knowing of the beginning which is not nothing, and which is not the reflective truth either, and which also must be accounted for.

14

THE END OF THE BOOK AND THE BEGINNING OF WRITING

Jacques Derrida

Socrates, he who does not write — Nietzsche[1]

However the topic is considered, the *problem of language* has never been simply one problem among others. But never as much as at present has it invaded, *as such*, the global horizon of the most diverse researches and the most heterogeneous discourses, diverse and heterogeneous in their intention, method, and ideology. The devaluation of the word "language" itself, and how, in the very hold it has upon us, it betrays a loose vocabulary, the temptation of a cheap seduction, the passive yielding to fashion, the consciousness of the avant-garde, in other words — ignorance — are evidences of this effect. This inflation of the sign "language" is the inflation of the sign itself, absolute inflation, inflation itself. Yet, by one of its aspects or shadows, it is itself still a sign: this crisis is also a symptom. It indicates, as if in spite of itself, that a historico-metaphysical epoch *must* finally determine as language the totality of its problematic horizon. It must do so not only because all that desire had wished to wrest from the play of language finds itself recaptured within that play but also because, for the same reason, language itself is menaced in its very life, helpless, adrift in the threat of limitlessness, brought back to its own finitude at the very moment when its limits seem to disappear, when it ceases to be self-assured, contained, and *guaranteed* by the infinite signified which seemed to exceed it.

The Program

By a slow movement whose necessity is hardly perceptible, everything that for at least some twenty centuries tended toward and finally succeeded in being gathered under the name of language is beginning to let itself be transferred to, or at least summa-

Jacques Derrida, *Of Grammatology*, trans. Gayatri Chakravorty Spivak (Baltimore and London: The Johns Hopkins University Press, 1976), pp. 6–26, 323–5 (notes). © 1997 by The Johns Hopkins University Press. Reprinted with the permission of The Johns Hopkins University Press.

rized under, the name of writing. By a hardly perceptible necessity, it seems as though the concept of writing – no longer indicating a particular, derivative, auxiliary form of language in general (whether understood as communication, relation, expression, signification, constitution of meaning or thought, etc.), no longer designating the exterior surface, the insubstantial double of a major signifier, *the signifier of the signifier* – is beginning to go beyond the extension of language. In all senses of the word, writing thus *comprehends* language. Not that the word "writing" has ceased to designate the signifier of the signifier, but it appears, strange as it may seem, that "signifier of the signifier" no longer defines accidental doubling and fallen secondary. "Signifier of the signifier" describes on the contrary the movement of language: in its origin, to be sure, but one can already suspect that an origin whose structure can be expressed as "signifier of the signifier" conceals and erases itself in its own production. There the signified always already functions as a signifier. The secondarity that it seemed possible to ascribe to writing alone affects all signifieds in general, affects them always already, the moment they *enter the game*. There is not a single signified that escapes, even if recaptured, the play of signifying references that constitute language. The advent of writing is the advent of this play; today such a play is coming into its own, effacing the limit starting from which one had thought to regulate the circulation of signs, drawing along with it all the reassuring signifieds, reducing all the strongholds, all the out-of-bounds shelters that watched over the field of language. This, strictly speaking, amounts to destroying the concept of "sign" and its entire logic. Undoubtedly it is not by chance that this *overwhelming* supervenes at the moment when the extension of the concept of language effaces all its limits. We shall see that this overwhelming and this effacement have the same meaning, are one and the same phenomenon. It is as if the Western concept of language (in terms of what, beyond its plurivocity and beyond the strict and problematic opposition of speech (*parole*) and language (*langue*), attaches it *in general* to phonematic or glossematic production, to language, to voice, to hearing, to sound and breadth, to speech) were revealed today as the guise or disguise of a primary writing:[2] more fundamental than that which, before this conversion, passed for the simple "supplement to the spoken word" (Rousseau). Either writing was never a simple "supplement," or it is urgently necessary to construct a new logic of the "supplement." It is this urgency which will guide us further in reading Rousseau.

These disguises are not historical contingencies that one might admire or regret. Their movement was absolutely necessary, with a necessity which cannot be judged by any other tribunal. The privilege of the *phonē* does not depend upon a choice that could have been avoided. It responds to a moment of *economy* (let us say of the "life" of "history" or of "being as self-relationship"). The system of "hearing (understanding) oneself-speak" through the phonic substance – which *presents itself* as the nonexterior, nonmundane, therefore nonempirical or noncontingent signifier – has necessarily dominated the history of the world during an entire epoch, and has even produced the idea of the world, the idea of world-origin, that arises from the difference between the worldly and the non-worldly, the outside and the inside, ideality and nonideality, universal and nonuniversal, transcendental and empirical, etc.[3]

With an irregular and essentially precarious success, this movement would apparently have tended, as toward its *telos*, to confine writing to a secondary and instrumental function: translator of a full speech that was fully *present* (present to itself, to its signified, to the other, the very condition of the theme of presence in general), technics in the service of language, *spokesman*, interpreter of an originary speech itself shielded from interpretation.

Technics in the service of language: I am not invoking a general essence of technics which would be already familiar to us and would help us in *understanding* the narrow and historically determined concept of writing as an example. I believe on the contrary that a certain sort of question about the meaning and origin of writing precedes, or at least merges with, a certain type of question about the meaning and origin of technics. That is why the notion of technique can never simply clarify the notion of writing.

It is therefore as if what we call language could have been in its origin and in its end only a moment, an essential but determined mode, a phenomenon, an aspect, a species of writing. And as if it had succeeded in making us forget this, and in *wilfully misleading us*, only in the course of an adventure: as that adventure itself. All in all a short enough adventure. It merges with the history that has associated technics and logocentric metaphysics for nearly three millennia. And it now seems to be approaching what is really its own *exhaustion*; under the circumstances – and this is no more than one example among others – of this death of the civilization of the book, of which so much is said and which manifests itself particularly through a convulsive proliferation of libraries. All appearances to the contrary, this death of the book undoubtedly announces (and in a certain sense always has announced) nothing but a death of speech (of a *so-called* full speech) and a new mutation in the history of writing, in history as writing. Announces it at a distance of a few centuries. It is on that scale that we must reckon it here, being careful not to neglect the quality of a very heterogeneous historical duration: the acceleration is such, and such its qualitative meaning, that one would be equally wrong in making a careful evaluation according to past rhythms. "Death of speech" is of course a metaphor here: before we speak of disappearance, we must think of a new situation for speech, of its subordination within a structure of which it will no longer be the archon.

To affirm in this way that the concept of writing exceeds and comprehends that of language, presupposes of course a certain definition of language and of writing. If we do not attempt to justify it, we shall be giving in to the movement of inflation that we have just mentioned, which has also taken over the word "writing," and that not fortuitously. For some time now, as a matter of face, here and there, by a gesture and for motives that are profoundly necessary, whose degradation is easier to denounce than it is to disclose their origin, one says "language" for action, movement, thought, reflection, consciousness, unconsciousness, experience, affectivity, etc. Now we tend to say "writing" for all that and more: to designate not only the physical gestures of literal pictographic or ideographic inscription, but also the totality of what makes it possible; and also, beyond the signifying face, the signified face itself. And thus we say "writing" for all that gives rise to an inscription in general, whether it is literal or not and even if what it distributes in space is alien to the order of the voice: cinematography, choreography, of course, but also pictorial, musical, sculptural "writing." One might also speak of athletic writing, and with even greater certainty of military or political writing in view of the techniques that govern those domains today. All this to describe not only the system of notation secondarily connected with these activities but the essence and the content of these activities themselves. It is also in this sense that the contemporary biologist speaks of writing and *program* in relation to the most elementary processes of information within the living cell. And, finally, whether it has essential limits or not, the entire field covered by the cybernetic *program* will be the field of writing. If the theory of cybernetics is by itself to oust all metaphysical concepts — including the concepts of soul, of life, of value, of choice, of memory — which until recently served to separate the machine from man,[4] it must conserve the notion of writing, trace, *grammē* [written mark], or grapheme, until its own historico-metaphysical character is also exposed. Even before being determined as human (with all the distinctive characteristics that have always been attributed to man and the entire system of significations that they imply) or nonhuman, the *grammē* — or the *grapheme* — would thus name the element. An element without simplicity. An element, whether it is understood as the medium or as the irreducible atom, of the arche-synthesis in general, of what one must forbid oneself to define within the system of oppositions of metaphysics, of what consequently one should not even call *experience* in general, that is to say the origin of *meaning* in general.

This situation has always already been announced. Why is it today in the process of making itself known *as such* and *after the fact*? This question would call forth an interminable analysis. Let us simply choose some points of departure in order to introduce the limited remarks to which I shall confine myself. I have already alluded to *theoretical* mathematics; its writing — whether understood as a sensible *graphie* (manner of writing) (and that already presupposes an identity, therefore an ideality, of its form, which in principle renders absurd the so easily admitted notion of the "sensible signifier"), or understood as the ideal synthesis of signifieds or a trace operative on another level, or whether it is understood, more profoundly, as the *passage* of the one to the other — has never been absolutely linked with a phonetic production. Within cultures practicing so-called phonetic writing, mathematics is not just an enclave. That is mentioned by all historians of writing; they recall at the same time the imperfections of alphabetic writing, which passed for so long as the most convenient and "the most intelligent"[5] writing. This enclave is also the place where the practice of scientific language challenges intrinsically and with increasing profundity the ideal of phonetic writing and all its implicit metaphysics (metaphysics *itself*), particularly, that is, the philosophical idea of the *epistēmē*; also of *istoria*, a concept profoundly related to it in spite of the dissociation or opposition which has distinguished one from the other during one phase of their common progress. History and knowledge, *istoria* and *epistēmē* have always been determined (and not only etymologically or philosophically) as detours *for the purpose of* the reappropriaton of presence.

But beyond theoretical mathematics, the development of the *practical methods* of information retrieval extends the possibilities of the "message" vastly, to the point where it is no longer the "written" translation of a language, the transporting of a signified which could remain spoken in its integrity. It goes hand in hand with an extension of phonography and of all the means of conserving the spoken language, of making it function without the presence of the speaking subject. This development, coupled with that of anthropology and of the history of writing, teaches us that phonetic writing, the medium of the great metaphysical, scientific, technical, and economic adventure of the West, is limited in space and time and limits itself even as it is in the process of imposing its laws upon the cultural areas that had escaped it. But this nonfortuitous conjunction of cybernetics and the "human sciences" of writing leads to a more profound reversal.

The Signifier and Truth

The "rationality" – but perhaps that word should be abandoned for reasons that will appear at the end of this sentence – which governs a writing thus enlarged and radicalized, no longer issues from a logos. Further, it inaugurates the destruction, not the demolition but the de-sedimentation, the de-construction, of all the significations that have their source in that of the logos. Particularly the signification of *truth*. All the metaphysical determinations of truth, and even the one beyond metaphysical ontotheology that Heidegger reminds us of, are more or less immediately inseparable from the instance of the logos, or of a reason thought within the lineage of the logos, in whatever sense it is understood: in the pre-Socratic or the philosophical sense, in the sense of God's infinite understanding or in the anthropological sense, in the pre-Hegelian or the post-Hegelian sense. Within this logos, the original and essential link to the *phonē* has never been broken. It would be easy to demonstrate this and I shall attempt such a demonstration later. As has been more or less implicitly determined, the essence of the *phonē* would be immediately proximate to that which within "thought" as logos relates to "meaning," produces it, receives it, speaks it, "composes" it. If, for Aristotle, for example, "spoken words (ta en tē phonē) are the symbols of mental experience (pathēmata tes psychēs) and written words are the symbols of spoken words" (*De interpretatione*, 1, 16a 3) it is because the voice, producer of *the first symbols*, has a relationship of essential and immediate proximity with the mind. Producer of the first signifier, it is not just a simple signifier among others. It signifies "mental experiences" which themselves reflect or mirror things by natural resemblance. Between being and mind, things and feelings, there would be a relationship of translation or natural signification; between mind and logos, a relationship of conventional symbolization. And the *first* convention, which would relate immediately to the order of natural and universal signification, would be produced as spoken language. Written language would establish the conventions, interlinking other conventions with them

> Just as all men have not the same writing so all men have not the same speech sounds, but mental experiences, of which these are the *primary symbols* (*semeīa prótos*), are the same for all, as also are those things of which our experiences are the images. (*De interpretatione*, 1, 16a; italics added)

The feelings of the mind, expressing things naturally, constitute a sort of universal language which can then efface itself. It is the stage of transparence. Aristotle can sometimes omit it without risk.[6] In every case, the voice is closest to the signified, whether it is determined strictly as sense (thought or lived) or more loosely as thing. All signifiers, and first and foremost the written signifier, are derivative with regard to what would wed the voice indissolubly to the mind or to the thought of the signified sense, indeed to the thing itself (whether it is done in the Aristotelian manner that we have just indicated or in the manner of medieval theology, determining the *res* as a thing created from its *eidos*, from its sense thought in the logos or in the infinite understanding of God). The written signifier is always technical and representative. It has no constitutive meaning. This derivation is the very origin of the notion of the "signifier." The notion of the sign always implies within itself the distinction between signifier and signified, even if, as Saussure argues, they are distinguished simply as the two faces of one and the same leaf. This notion remains therefore within the heritage of that logocentrism which is also a phonocentrism: absolute proximity of voice and being, of voice and the meaning of being, of voice and the ideality of meaning. Hegel demonstrates very clearly the strange privilege of sound in idealization, the production of the concept and the self-presence of the subject.

> This ideal motion, in which through the sound what is as it were the simple subjectivity (*Subjektivität*), the soul of the material thing expresses itself, the ear receives also in a theoretical (*theoretisch*) way, just as the eye shape and colour, thus allowing the interiority of the object to become interiority itself (*läßt dadurch das Innere der Gegenstände für das Innere selbst werden*) (*Esthétique*, III. I tr. fr. p. 16).[7] ... The ear, on the contrary, perceives [*vernimmt*] the result of that interior vibration of material substance without placing itself in a practical relation toward the objects, a result by means of which it is no longer the material form [*Gestalt*] in its repose, but the first, more ideal activity of the soul itself which is manifested [*zum Vorschein kommt*]. (p. 296)[8]

What is said of sound in general is a fortiori valid for the *phonē* by which, by virtue of hearing (understanding)-oneself-speak – an indissociable system – the subject affects itself and is related to itself in the element of ideality.

We already have a foreboding that phonocentrism merges with the historical determination of the meaning of being in general as *presence*, with all the subdeterminations which depend on this general form and which organize within it their system and their historical sequence (presence of the thing to the sight as *eidos*, presence as substance/essence/existence [*ousia*], temporal presence as point [*stigmē*] of the now or of the moment [*nun*], the self-presence of the cogito, consciousness, subjectivity, the co-presence of the other and of the self, intersubjectivity as the intentional phenomenon of the ego, and so forth). Logocentrism would thus support the determination of the being of the entity as presence. To the extent that such a logocentrism is not totally absent from Heidegger's thought, perhaps it still holds that thought within the epoch of onto-theology, within the philosophy of presence, that is to say within philosophy *itself*. This would perhaps mean that one does not leave the epoch whose closure one can outline. The movements of belonging or not belonging to the epoch are too subtle, the illusions in that regard are too easy, for us to make a definite judgment.

The epoch of the logos thus debases writing considered as mediation of mediation and as a fall into the exteriority of meaning. To this epoch belongs the difference between signified and signifier, or at least the strange separation of their "parallelism," and the exteriority, however extenuated, of the one to the other. This appurtenance is organized and hierarchized in a history. The difference between signified and signifier belongs in a profound and implicit way to the totality of the great epoch covered by the history of metaphysics, and in a more explicit and more systematically articulated way to the narrower epoch of Christian creationism and infinitism when these appropriate the resources of Greek conceptuality. This appurtenance is essential and irreducible; one cannot retain the convenience or the "scientific truth" of the Stoic and later medieval opposition between *signans* and *signatum* without also bringing with it all its metaphysico-theological roots. To these roots adheres not only the distinction between the sensible and the intelligible – already a great deal – with all that it controls, namely, metaphysics in its totality. And this distinction is generally accepted as self-evident by the most careful linguists and semiologists, even by those who believe that the scientificity of their work begins where metaphysics ends. Thus, for example:

> As modern structural thought has clearly realized, language is a system of signs and linguistics is part and parcel of the science of signs, or *semiotics* (Saussure's *sémiologie*). The mediaeval definition of sign – "*aliquid stat pro aliquo*" – has been resurrected and put forward as still valid and productive. Thus the constitutive mark of any sign in general and of any linguistic sign in particular is its twofold character: every linguistic unit is bipartite and involves both aspects – one sensible and the other intelligible, or in other words, both the *signans* "signifier" (Saussure's *signifiant*) and the *signatum* "signified" (*signifié*). These two constituents of a linguistic sign (and of sign in general) necessarily suppose and require each other.[9]

But to these metaphysico-theological roots many other hidden sediments cling. The semiological or, more specifically, linguistic "science" cannot therefore hold on to the difference between signifier and signified – the very idea of the sign – without the difference between sensible and intelligible, certainly, but also not without retaining, more profoundly and more implicitly, and by the same token the reference to a signified able to "take place" in its intelligibility, before its "fall," before any expulsion into the exteriority of the sensible here below. As the face of pure intelligibility, it refers to an absolute logos to which it is immediately united. This absolute logos was an infinite creative subjectivity in medieval theology: the intelligible face of the sign remains turned toward the word and the face of God.

Of course, it is not a question of "rejecting" these notions; they are necessary and, at least at present, nothing is conceivable for us without them. It is a question at first of demonstrating the systematic and historical solidarity of the concepts and gestures of thought that one often believes can be innocently separated. The sign and divinity have the same place and time of birth. The age of the sign is essentially theological. Perhaps it will never *end*. Its historical *closure* is, however, outlined.

Since these concepts are indispensable for unsettling the heritage to which they belong, we should be even less prone to renounce them. Within the closure, by an oblique and always perilous movement, constantly risking falling back within what is being deconstructed, it is necessary to surround the critical concepts with a careful and thorough discourse – to mark the conditions, the medium, and the limits of their effectiveness and to designate rigorously their intimate relationship to the machine whose deconstruction they permit; and, in the same process, designate the crevice through which the yet unnameable glimmer beyond the closure can be glimpsed. The concept of the sign is here exemplary. We have just marked its metaphysical appurtenance. We know, however, that the thematics of the sign have been for about a century the agonized labor of a tradition that professed to withdraw meaning, truth, presence, being, etc., from the movement of signification. Treating as suspect, as I just have, the difference between signified and signifier, or the idea of the sign in general, I must state explicitly that it is not a question of doing so in terms of the instance of the present truth, anterior, exterior or superior to the sign, or in terms of the place of the effaced difference. Quite the contrary. We are disturbed by that which, in the concept of the sign – which has never existed or functioned outside the history of (the) philosophy (of presence) – remains systematically and genealogically determined by that history. It is there that the concept and above all the work of deconstruction, its "style," remain by nature exposed to misunderstanding and nonrecognition.

The exteriority of the signifier is the exteriority of writing in general, and I shall try to show later that there is no linguistic sign before writing. Without that exteriority, the very idea of the sign falls into decay. Since our entire world and language would collapse with it, and since its evidence and its value keep, to a certain point of derivation, an indestructible solidity, it would be silly to conclude from its placement within an epoch that it is necessary to "move on to something else," to dispose of the sign, of the term and the notion. For a proper understanding of the gesture that we are sketching here, one must understand the expressions "epoch," "closure of an epoch," "historical genealogy" in a new way; and must first remove them from all relativism.

Thus, within this epoch, reading and writing, the production or interpretation of signs, the text in general as fabric of signs, allow themselves to be confined within secondariness. They are preceded by a truth, or a meaning already constituted by and within the element of the logos. Even when the thing, the "referent," is not immediately related to the logos of a creator God where it began by being the spoken/thought sense, the signified has at any rate an immediate relationship with the logos in general (finite or infinite), and a mediated one with the signifier, that is to say with the exteriority of writing. When it seems to go otherwise, it is because a metaphoric mediation has insinuated itself into the relationship and has simulated immediacy; the writing of truth in the soul, opposed by *Phaedrus* (278a) to bad writing (writing in the "literal" [*propre*] and ordinary sense, "sensible" writing, "in space"), the book of Nature and God's writing, especially in the Middle Ages; all that functions as *metaphor* in these discourses confirms the privilege of the logos and founds the "literal" meaning then given to writing: a sign signifying a signifier itself signifying an eternal verity, eternally thought and spoken in the proximity of a present logos. The paradox to which attention must be paid is this: natural and universal writing, intelligible and nontemporal writing, is thus named by metaphor. A writing that is sensible, finite, and so on, is designated as writing in the literal sense; it is thus thought on the side of culture, technique, and artifice; a human procedure, the ruse of a being accidentally incarnated or of a finite creature. Of course, this metaphor remains enigmatic and refers to a "literal" meaning of writing as the first metaphor. This "literal" meaning is yet unthought by the adherents of this discourse. It is not, therefore, a matter of inverting the literal meaning and the figurative meaning but of determining the "literal" meaning of writing as metaphoricity itself.

In "The Symbolism of the Book," that excellent chapter of *European Literature and the Latin Middle Ages*, E. R. Curtius describes with great wealth of examples the evolution that led from the *Phaedrus* to Calderon, until it seemed to be "precisely the reverse" (tr. fr. p. 372)[10] by the "newly attained position of the book" (p. 374) [p. 306]. But it seems that this modification, however important in fact it might be, conceals a fundamental continuity. As was the case with the Platonic writing of the truth in the soul, in the Middle Ages too it is a writing understood in the metaphoric sense, that is to say a *natural*, eternal, and universal writing, the system of signified truth, which is recognized in its dignity. As in the *Phaedrus*, a certain fallen writing continues to be opposed to it. There remains to be written a history of this metaphor, a metaphor that systematically contrasts divine or natural writing and the human and laborious, finite and artificial inscription. It remains to articulate rigorously the stages of that history, as marked by the quotations below, and to follow the theme of God's book (nature or law, indeed natural law) through all its modifications.

Rabbi Eliezer said: "If all the seas were of ink, and all ponds planted with reeds, if the sky and the earth were parchments and if all human beings practised the art of writing – they would not exhaust the Torah I have learned, just as the Torah itself would not be diminished any more than is the sea by the water removed by a paint brush dipped in it."[11]

Galileo: "It [the book of Nature] is written in a mathematical language."[12]

Descartes: ". . . to read in the great book of Nature . . ."[13]

Demea, in the name of natural religion, in the *Dialogues*, . . . of Hume: "And this volume of nature contains a great and inexplicable riddle, more than any intelligible discourse or reasoning."[14]

Bonnet: "It would seem more philosophical to me to presume that our earth is a book that God has given to intelligences far superior to ours to read, and where they study in depth the infinitely multiplied and varied characters of His adorable wisdom."
G. H. von Schubert: "This language made of images and hieroglyphs, which supreme Wisdom uses in all its revelations to humanity – which is found in the inferior [*nieder*] language of poetry – and which, in the most inferior and imperfect way [*auf der allerniedrigsten und unvollkommensten*], is more like the metaphorical expression of the dream than the prose of wakefulness, . . . we may wonder if this language is not the true and wakeful language of the superior regions. If, when we consider ourselves awakened, we are not plunged in a millennial slumber, or at least in the echo of its dreams, where we only perceive a few isolated and obscure words of God's language, as a sleeper perceives the conversation of the people around him."[15]

Jaspers: "The world is the manuscript of an other, inaccessible to a universal reading, which only existence deciphers."[16]

Above all, the profound differences distinguishing all these treatments of the same metaphor must not be ignored. In the history of this treatment, the most decisive separation appears at the moment when, at the same time as the science of nature, the determination of absolute presence is constituted as self-presence, as subjectivity. It is the moment of the great rationalisms of the seventeenth century. From then on, the condemnation of fallen and finite writing will take another form, within which we still live: it is non-self-presence that will be denounced. Thus the exemplariness of the "Rousseauist" moment, which we shall deal with later, begins to be explained. Rousseau repeats the Platonic gesture by referring to another model of presence: self-presence in the senses, in the sensible cogito, which simultaneously carries in itself the inscription of divine law. On the one hand, *representative*, fallen, secondary, instituted writing, writing in the literal and strict sense, is condemned in *The Essay on the Origin of Languages* (it "enervates" speech; to "judge genius" from books is like "painting a man's portrait from his corpse," etc.). Writing in the common sense is the dead letter, it is the carrier of death. It exhausts life. On the other hand, on the other face of the same proposition, writing in the metaphoric sense, natural, divine, and living writing, is venerated; it is equal in dignity to the origin of value, to the voice of conscience as divine law, to the heart, to sentiment, and so forth.

> The Bible is the most sublime of all books, . . . but it is after all a book. . . . It is not at all in a few sparse pages that one should look for God's law, but in the human heart where His hand deigned to write. (*Lettre à Vernes*)[17]

> If the natural law had been written only in the human reason, it would be little capable of directing most of our actions. But it is also engraved in the heart of man in ineffacable characters. . . . There it cries to him. (*L'état de guerre*)[18]

Natural writing is immediately united to the voice and to breath. Its nature is not grammatological but pneumatological. It is hieratic, very close to the interior holy voice of the *Profession of Faith*, to the voice one hears upon retreating into oneself: full and truthful presence of the divine voice to our inner sense: "The more I retreat into myself, the more I consult myself, the more plainly do I read these words written in my soul: be just and you will be happy. . . . I do not derive these rules from the principles of the higher philosophy, I find them in the depths of my heart written by nature in characters which nothing can efface."[19]

There is much to say about the fact that the native unity of the voice and writing is *prescriptive*. Arche-speech is writing because it is a law. A natural law. The beginning word is understood, in the intimacy of self-presence, as the voice of the other and as commandment.

There is therefore a good and a bad writing: the good and natural is the divine inscription in the heart and the soul; the perverse and artful is technique, exiled in the exteriority of the body. A modification well within the Platonic diagram: writing of the soul and of the body, writing of the interior and of the exterior, writing of conscience and of the passions, as there is a voice of the soul and a voice of the body. "Conscience is the voice of the soul, the passions are the voice of the body" (p. 249). One must constantly go back toward the "voice of nature," the "holy voice of nature," that merges with the divine inscription and prescription; one must encounter oneself within it, enter into a dialogue within its signs, speak and respond to oneself in its pages.

It was as if nature had spread out all her magnificence in front of our eyes to offer its
text for our consideration. . . . I have therefore closed all the books. Only one is open
to all eyes. It is the book of Nature. In this great and sublime book I learn to serve and
adore its author.

The good writing has therefore always been *comprehended*. Comprehended as that
which had to be comprehended: within a nature or a natural law, created or not, but
first thought within an eternal presence. Comprehended, therefore, within a totality,
and enveloped in a volume or a book. The idea of the book is the idea of a totality, finite or infinite, of the signifier; this totality of the signifier cannot be a totality,
unless a totality constituted by the signified preexists it, supervises its inscriptions and
its signs, and is independent of it in its ideality. The idea of the book, which always
refers to a natural totality, is profoundly alien to the sense of writing. It is the ency-
clopedic protection of theology and of logocentrism against the disruption of writing,
against its aphoristic energy, and, as I shall specify later, against difference in general.
If I distinguish the text from the book, I shall say that the destruction of the book,
as it is now under way in all domains, denudes the surface of the text. That necessary violence responds to a violence that was no less necessary.

The Written Being/The Being Written

The reassuring evidence within which Western tradition had to organize itself and
must continue to live would therefore be as follows: the order of the signified is
never contemporary, is at best the subtly discrepant inverse or parallel – discrepant by
the time of a breath – from the order of the signifier. And the sign must be the unity
of a heterogeneity, since the signified (sense or thing, noeme or reality) is not in itself
a signifier, a *trace*: in any case is not constituted in its sense by its relationship with a
possible trace. The formal essence of the signified is *presence*, and the privilege of its
proximity to the logos as *phonē* is the privilege of presence. This is the inevitable
response as soon as one asks: "what is the sign?," that is to say, when one submits the
sign to the question of essence, to the "ti esti." The "formal essence" of the sign can
only be determined in terms of presence. One cannot get around that response, except
by challenging the very form of the question and beginning to think that the sign
is that ill-named thing, the only one, that escapes the instituting question of philosophy: "what is . . .?"[20]
    Radicalizing the concepts of *interpretation, perspective, evaluation, difference*, and all the
"empiricist" or nonphilosophical motifs that have constantly tormented philosophy
throughout the history of the West, and besides, have had nothing but the inevitable
weakness of being produced in the field of philosophy, Nietzsche, far from remaining
simply (with Hegel and as Heidegger wished) *within* metaphysics, contributed a great
deal to the liberation of the signifier from its dependence or derivation with respect
to the logos and the related concept of truth or the primary signified, in
whatever sense that is understood. Reading, and therefore writing, the text were for
Nietzsche "originary"[21] operations (I put that word within quotation marks for reasons to appear later) with regard to a sense that they do not first have to transcribe

or discover, which would not therefore be a truth signified in the original element and presence of the logos, as *topos noetos*, divine understanding, or the structure of a priori necessity. To save Nietzsche from a reading of the Heideggerian type, it seems that we must above all not attempt to restore or make explicit a less naive "ontology," composed of profound ontological intuitions acceding to some originary truth, an entire fundamentality hidden under the appearance of an empiricist or metaphysical text. The virulence of Nietzschean thought could not be more competely misunderstood. On the contrary, one must *accentuate* the "naiveté" of a breakthrough which cannot attempt a step outside of metaphysics, which cannot *criticize* metaphysics radically without still utilizing in a certain way, in a certain type or a certain style of *text*, propositions that, read within the philosophic corpus, that is to say according to Nietzsche ill-read or unread, have always been and will always be "naivetés," incoherent signs of an absolute appurtenance. Therefore, rather than protect Nietzsche from the Heideggerian reading, we should perhaps offer him up to it completely, underwriting that interpretation without reserve; in a *certain way* and up to the point where, the content of the Nietzschean discourse being almost lost for the question of being, its form regains its absolute strangeness, where his text finally invokes a different type of reading, more faithful to his type of writing: Nietzsche has *written what* he has written. He has written that writing − and first of all his own − is not originarily subordinate to the logos and to truth. And that this subordination has *come into being* during an epoch whose meaning we must deconstruct. Now in this direction (but only in this direction, for read otherwise, the Nietzschean demolition remains dogmatic and, like all reversals, a captive of that metaphysical edifice which it professes to overthrow. On that point and in that *order of reading*, the conclusions of Heidegger and Fink are irrefutable), Heideggerian thought would reinstate rather than destroy the instance of the logos and of the truth of being as "primum signatum:" the "transcendental" signified ("transcendental" in a certain sense, as in the Middle Ages the transcendental − *ens, unum, verum, bonum* − was said to be the "primum cognitum") implied by all categories or all determined significations, by all lexicons and all syntax, and therefore by all linguistic signifiers, though not to be identified simply with any one of those signifiers, allowing itself to be precomprehended through each of them, remaining irreducible to all the epochal determinations that it nonetheless makes possible, thus opening the history of the logos, yet itself being only through the logos; that is, *being nothing* before the logos and outside of it. The logos *of* being, "Thought obeying the Voice of Being,"[22] is the first and the last resource of the sign, of the difference between *signans* and *signatum*. There has to be a transcendental signified for the difference between signifier and signified to be somewhere absolute and irreducible. It is not by chance that the thought of being, as the thought of this transcendental signified, is manifested above all in the voice: in a language of words (*mots*). The voice *is heard* (understood) − that undoubtedly is what is called conscience − closest to the self as the absolute effacement of the signifier: pure auto-affection that necessarily has the form of time and which does not borrow from outside of itself, in the world or in "reality," any accessory signifier, any substance of expression foreign to its own spontaneity. It is the unique experience of the signified producing itself spontaneously, from within the self, and nevertheless, as signified concept, in the element of ideality or universality. The unworldly character of this substance of expression is constitutive of this ideality. This experience of the effacement of the signifier in the voice is not merely one illusion among many – since it is the condition of the very idea of truth – but I shall elsewhere show in what it does delude itself. This illusion is the history of truth and it cannot be dissipated so quickly. Within the closure of this experience, the word (*mot*) is lived as the elementary and undecomposable unity of the signified and the voice, of the concept and a transparent substance of expression. This experience is considered in its greatest purity – and at the same time in the condition of its possibility – as the experience of "being." The word "being," or at any rate the words designating the sense of being in different languages, is, with some others, an "originary word" ("*Urwort*"),[23] the transcendental word assuring the possibility of being-word to all other words. As such, it is precomprehended in all language and – this is the opening of *Being and Time* – only this precomprehension would permit the opening of the question of the sense of being in general, beyond all regional ontologies and all metaphysics: a question that broaches philosophy (for example, in the *Sophist*) and lets itself be taken over by philosophy, a question that Heidegger repeats by submitting the history of metaphysics to it. Heidegger reminds us constantly that the sense of being is neither the word "being" nor the concept of being. But as that sense is nothing outside of language and the language of words, it is tied, if not to a particular word or to a particular system of language (concesso non dato), at least to the possibility of the word in general. And to the possibility of its irreducible simplicity. One could thus think that it remains only to choose between two possibilities. (1) Does a modern linguistics, a science of signification breaking the unity of the word and breaking with its alleged irreducibility, still have anything to do with "language?" Heidegger would probably doubt it. (2) Conversely, is not all that is profoundly meditated as the thought or the question of being enclosed within an old linguistics of the word which one practices here unknowingly? Unknowingly because such a linguistics, whether spontaneous or systematic, has always had to share the presuppositions of metaphysics. The two operate on the same grounds.

It goes without saying that the alternatives cannot be so simple.

On the one hand, if modern linguistics remains completely enclosed within a classical conceptuality, if especially it naively uses the word *being* and all that it presupposes, that which, within this linguistics, deconstructs the unity of the word in general can no longer, according to the model of the Heideggerian question, as it functions powerfully from the very opening of *Being and Time*, be circumscribed as ontic science or regional ontology. In as much as the question of being unites indissolubly with the precomprehension of the *word being*, without being reduced to it, the linguistics that works for the deconstruction of the constituted unity of that word has only, in fact or in principle, to have the question of being posed in order to define its field and the order of its dependence.

Not only is its field no longer simply ontic, but the limits of ontology that correspond to it no longer have anything regional about them. And can what I say here of linguistics, or at least of a certain work that may be undertaken within it and thanks to it, not be said of all research *in as much as and to the strict extent that* it would finally deconstitute the founding concept-words of ontology, of being in its privilege? Outside of linguistics, it is in psychoanalytic research that this breakthrough seems at present to have the greatest likelihood of being expanded.

Within the strictly limited space of this breakthrough, these "sciences" are no longer *dominated* by the questions of a transcendental phenomenology or a fundamental ontology. One may perhaps say, following the order of questions inaugurated by *Being and Time* and radicalizing the questions of Husserlian phenomenology, that this breakthrough does not belong to science itself, that what thus seems to be produced within an ontic field or within a regional ontology, does not belong to them by rights and leads back to the question of being itself.

Because it is indeed the *question* of being that Heidegger asks metaphysics. And with it the question of truth, of sense, of the logos. The incessant meditation upon that question does not restore confidence. On the contrary, it dislodges the confidence at its own depth, which, being a matter of the meaning of being, is more difficult than is often believed. In examining the state just before all determinations of being, destroying the securities of onto-theology, such a meditation contributes, quite as much as the most contemporary linguistics, to the dislocation of the unity of the sense of being, that is, in the last instance, the unity of the word.

It is thus that, after evoking the "voice of being," Heidegger recalls that it is silent, mute, insonorous, wordless, originarily *a-phonic* (*die Gewähr der lautlosen Stimme verborgener Quellen . . .*). The voice of the sources is not heard. A rupture between the originary meaning of being and the word, between meaning and the voice, between "the voice of being" and the "*phonē*," between "the call of being," and articulated sound; such a rupture, which at once confirms a fundamental metaphor, and renders it suspect by accentuating its metaphoric discrepancy, translates the ambiguity of the Heideggerian situation with respect to the metaphysics of presence and logocentrism. It is at once contained within it and transgresses it. But it is impossible to separate the two. The very movement of transgression sometimes holds it back short of the limit. In opposition to what we suggested above, it must be remembered that, for Heidegger, the sense of being is never simply and rigorously a "signified." It is not by chance that that word is not used; that means that being escapes the movement of the sign, a proposition that can equally well be understood as a repetition of the classical tradition and as a caution with respect to a technical or metaphysical theory of signification. On the other hand, the sense of being is literally neither "primary," nor "fundamental," nor "transcendental," whether understood in the scholastic, Kantian, or Husserlian sense. The restoration of being as "transcending" the categories of the entity, the opening of the fundamental ontology, are nothing but necessary yet provisional moments. From *The Introduction to Metaphysics* onward, Heidegger renounces the project of and the word ontology.[24] The necessary, originary, and irreducible dissimulation of the meaning of being, its occultation within the very blossoming forth of presence, that retreat without which there would be no history of being which was completely *history* and history of *being*, Heidegger's insistence on noting that being is produced as history only through the logos, and is nothing outside of it, the difference between being and the entity — all this clearly indicates that fundamentally nothing escapes the movement of the signifier and that, in the last instance, the difference between signified and signifier *is nothing*. This proposition of transgression, not yet integrated into a careful discourse, runs the risk of formulating regression itself. One must therefore *go by way of* the question of being as it is directed by Heidegger and by him alone, at and beyond onto-theology, in order to reach the rigorous thought of that strange nondifference and in order to determine it correctly. Heidegger occasionally reminds us that "being," as it is fixed in its general syntactic and lexicological forms within linguistics and Western philosophy, is not a primary and absolutely irreducible signified, that it is still rooted in a system of languages and an historically determined "significance," although strangely privileged as the virtue of disclosure and dissimulation; particularly when he invites us to meditate on the "privilege" of the "third person singular of the present indicative" and the "infinitive." Western metaphysics, as the limitation of the sense of being within the field of presence, is produced as the domination of a linguistic form.[25] To question the origin of that domination does not amount to hypostatizing a transcendental signified, but to a questioning of what constitutes our history and what produced transcendentality itself. Heidegger brings it up also when in *Zur Seinsfrage*, for the same reason, he lets the word "being" be read only if it is crossed out (*kreuzweise Durchstreichung*). That mark of deletion is not, however, a "merely negative symbol" (p. 31) (p. 83). That deletion is the final writing of an epoch. Under its strokes the presence of a transcendental signified is effaced while still remaining legible. Is effaced while still remaining legible, is destroyed while making visible the very idea of the sign. In as much as it de-limits onto-theology, the metaphysics of presence and logocentrism, this last writing is also the first writing.

To come to recognize, not within but on the horizon of the Heideggerian paths, and yet in them, that the sense of being is not a transcendental or trans-epochal signified (even if it was always dissimulated within the epoch) but already, in a truly *unheard of* sense, a determined signifying trace, is to affirm that within the decisive concept of ontico-ontological difference, *all is not to be thought at one go*; entity and being, ontic and ontological, "ontico-ontological," are, in an original style, *derivative* with regard to difference; and with respect to what I shall later call *différance*, an economic concept designating the production of differing/deferring. The ontico-ontological difference and its ground (*Grund*) in the "transcendence of Dasein" (*Vom Wesen des Grundes* (Frankfurt am Main, 1955), p. 16 (p. 29)) are not absolutely originary. Différance by itself would be more "originary," but one would no longer be able to call it "origin" or "ground," those notions belonging essentially to the history of ontotheology, to the system functioning as the effacing of difference. It can, however, be thought of in the closest proximity to itself only on one condition: that one begins by determining it as the ontico-ontological difference before erasing that determination. The necessity of passing through that erased determination, the necessity of that *trick of writing* is irreducible. An unemphatic and difficult thought that, through much unperceived mediation, must carry the entire burden of our question, a question that I shall provisionally call *historial* (*historiale*). It is with its help that I shall later be able to attempt to relate différance and writing.

The hestitation of these thoughts (here Nietzsche's and Heidegger's) is not an "incoherence": it is a trembling proper to all post-Hegelian attempts and to this passage between two epochs. The movements of deconstruction do not destroy structures from the outside. They are not possible and effective, nor can they take accurate aim, except by inhabiting those structures. Inhabiting them *in a certain way*, because one always inhabits, and all the more when one does not suspect it. Operating necessarily from the inside, borrowing all the strategic and economic resources of subversion from the old structure, borrowing them structurally, that is to say without being able to isolate their elements and atoms, the enterprise of deconstruction always in a certain way falls prey to its own work. This is what the person who has begun the same work in another area of the same habitation does not fail to point out with zeal. No exercise is more widespread today and one should be able to formalize its rules.

Hegel was already caught up in this game. *On the one hand*, he undoubtedly *summed up* the entire philosophy of the logos. He determined ontology as absolute logic; he assembled all the delimitations of philosophy as presence; he assigned to presence the eschatology of parousia, of the self-proximity of infinite subjectivity. And for the same reason he had to debase or subordinate writing. When he criticizes the Leibnizian characteristic, the formalism of the understanding, and mathematical symbolism, he makes the same gesture: denouncing the being-outside-of-itself of the logos in the sensible or the intellectual abstraction. Writing is that forgetting of the self, that exteriorization, the contrary of the interiorizing memory, of the *Erinnerung* that opens the history of the spirit. It is this that the *Phaedrus* said: writing is at once mnemotechnique and the power of forgetting. Naturally, the Hegelian critique of writing stops at the alphabet. As phonetic writing, the alphabet is at the same time more servile, more contemptible, more secondary ("alphabetic writing expresses *sounds* which are themselves signs. It consists therefore of the signs of signs ('*aus Zeichen der Zeichen*'," *Enzyklopädie*, §459))[26] but it is also the best writing, the mind's writing; its effacement before the voice, that in it which respects the ideal interiority of phonic signifiers, all that by which is sublimates space and sight, all that makes of it the writing of history, the writing, that is, of the infinite spirit relating to itself in its discourse and its culture:

> It follows that to learn to read and write an alphabetic writing should be regarded as a means to infinite culture (*unendliches Bildungsmittel*) that is not enough appreciated; because thus the mind, distancing itself from the concrete sense-perceptible, directs its attention on the more formal moment, the sonorous word and its abstract elements, and contributes essentially to the founding and purifying of the ground of interiority within the subject.

In that sense it is the *Aufhebung* of other writings, particularly of hieroglyphic script and of the Leibnizian characteristic that had been criticized previously through one and the same gesture. (*Aufhebung* is, more or less implicitly, the dominant concept of nearly all histories of writing, even today. It is *the* concept of history and of teleology.) In fact, Hegel continues: "Acquired habit later also suppresses the specificity of alphabetic writing, which consists in seeming to be, in the interest of sight, a detour (*Umweg*) through hearing to arrive at representations, and makes it into a hieroglyphic script for us, such that in using it, we do not need to have present to our consciousness the mediation of sounds."

It is on this condition that Hegel subscribes to the Leibnizian praise of nonphonetic writing. It can be produced by deaf mutes, Leibniz had said. Hegel:

> Beside the fact that, by the practice which transforms this alphabetic script into hieroglyphics, the aptitude for abstraction acquired through such an exercise *is conserved* [italics

added], the reading of hieroglyphs is for itself a deaf reading and a mute writing (*ein taubes Lesen und ein stummes Schreiben*). What is audible or temporal, visible or spatial, has each its proper basis and in the first place they are of equal value; but in alphabetic script there is only *one* basis and that following a specific relation, namely, that the visible language is related only as a sign to the audible language; intelligence expresses itself immediately and unconditionally through speech. (ibid.)

What writing itself, in its nonphonetic moment, betrays, is life. It menaces at once the breath, the spirit, and history as the spirit's relationship with itself. It is their end, their finitude, their paralysis. Cutting breath short, sterilizing or immobilizing spiritual creation in the repetition of the letter, in the commentary or the *exegesis*, confined in a narrow space, reserved for a minority, it is the principle of death and of difference in the becoming of being. It is to speech what China is to Europe: "It is only to the exegeticism[27] of Chinese spiritual culture that their hieroglyphic writing is suited. This type of writing is, besides, the part reserved for a very small section of a people, the section that possesses the exclusive domain of spiritual culture. . . . A hieroglyphic script would require a philosophy as exegetical as Chinese culture generally is" (ibid.).

If the nonphonetic moment menaces the history and the life of the spirit as self-presence in the breath, it is because it menaces substantiality, that other metaphysical name of presence and of *ousia*. First in the form of the substantive. Nonphonetic writing breaks the noun apart. It describes relations and not apellations. The noun and the word, those unities of breath and concept, are effaced within pure writing. In that regard, Leibniz is as disturbing as the Chinese in Europe: "This situation, the analytic notation of representations in hieroglyphic script, which seduced Leibniz to the point of wrongly preferring this script to the alphabetic, rather contradicts the fundamental exigency of language in general, namely the noun. . . . All difference [*Abweichung*] in analysis would produce another formation of the written substantive."

The horizon of absolute knowledge is the effacement of writing in the logos, the retrieval of the trace in parousia, the reappropriation of difference, the accomplishment of what I have elsewhere called[28] the *metaphysics of the proper* (*le propre* – self-possession, propriety, property, cleanliness).

Yet, all that Hegel thought within this horizon, all, that is, except eschatology, may be reread as a meditation on writing. Hegel is *also* the thinker of irreducible difference. He rehabilitated thought as the *memory productive* of signs. And he reintroduced, as I shall try to show elsewhere, the essential necessity of the written trace in a philosophical – that is to say Socratic – discourse that had always believed it possible to do without it; the last philosopher of the book and the first thinker of writing.

Notes

1   "Aus dem Gedankenkreise der Geburt der Tragödie," I. 3. *Nietzsche Werke* (Leipzig, 1903), vol. 9, part 2, i, p. 66.

2   To speak of a primary writing here does not amount to affirming a chronological priority of fact. That debate is well-known; is writing, as affirmed, for example, by Metchaninov

and Marr, then Loukotka, "anterior to phonetic language?" (A conclusion assumed by the first edition of the Great Soviet Encyclopedia, later contradicted by Stalin. On this debate, cf. V. Istrine, "Langue et écriture," *Linguistique*, op. cit., pp. 35, 60. This debate also forms around the theses advanced by P. van Ginneken. On the discussion of these propositions, cf. James Février, *Histoire de l'écriture* (Payot, 1948–59), pp. 5 f.). I shall try to show below why the terms and premises of such a debate are suspicious.

3 I shall deal with this problem more directly in *La voix et le phénomène* (Paris, 1967) (*Speech and Phenomenon*, op. cit.).

4 Wiener, for example, while abandoning "semantics," and the opposition, judged by him as too crude and too general, between animate and inanimate etc., nevertheless continues to use expressions like "organs of sense," "motor organs," etc. to qualify the parts of the machine.

5 Cf., e.g., *L'écriture et la psychologic des peuples* (proceedings of a Colloquium 1963), pp. 126, 148, 355, etc. From another point of view, cf. Roman Jakobson, *Essais de linguistique générale* (tr. fr. (Nicolas Ruwet, Paris, 1963), p. 116). (Jakobson and Morris Halle, *Fundamentals of Language* (The Hague, 1956), p. 16).

6 This is shown by Pierre Aubenque (*Le problème de l'être chez Aristotle* (Paris, 1966), pp. 106 f.). In the course of a provocative analysis, to which I am here indebted, Aubenque remarks: "In other texts, to be sure, Aristotle designates as symbol the relationship between language and things: 'It is not possible to bring the things themselves to the discussion, but, instead of things, we can use their names as symbols.' The intermediary constituted by the mental experience is here suppressed or at least neglected, but this suppression is legitimate, since, mental experiences behaving like things, things can be substituted for them immediately. On the other hand, one cannot by any means substitute names for things" (pp. 107–8).

7 Georg Wilhelm Friedrich Hegel, *Werke*, Suhrkamp edition (Frankfurt am Main, 1970), vol. 14, p. 256; translated as *The Philosophy of Fine Art* by F. P. Osmaston (London, 1920), vol. 3, pp. 15–16.

8 Hegel, p. 134; Osmaston, p. 341.

9 Roman Jakobson, *Essais de linguistique générale*, tr. fr., p. 162 ("The Phonemic and Grammatical Aspects of Language in their Interrelations," *Proceedings of the Sixth International Congress of Linguistics* (Paris, 1949), p. 6). On this problem, on the tradition of the concept of the sign, and on the originality of Saussure's contribution within this continuity, cf. Edmond Ortigues, *Le discoure et le symbole* (Aubier, 1962), pp. 54 f.

10 Ernst Robert Curtius, "Das Buch als Symbol," *Europäische Literatur und lateinisches Mittelalter* (Bern, 1948), p. 307. French translation by Jean Bréjoux (Paris, 1956): translated as *European Literature and the Latin Middle Ages*, by Willard R. Trask, Harper Torchbooks edition (New York, 1963), pp. 305, 306.

11 Cited by Emmanuel Levinas, in *Difficile liberté* (Paris, 1963), p. 44.

12 Quoted in Curtius, op. cit. (German), p. 326, (English), p. 324; Galileo's word is "philosophy" rather than "nature."

13 Ibid. (German) p. 324, (English) p. 322.

14 David Hume, *Dialogues Concerning Natural Religion*, ed. Norman Kemp Smith (Oxford, 1935), p. 193.

15 Gotthilf Heinrich von Schubert, *Die Symbolik des Traumes* (Leipzig, 1862), pp. 23–4.

16 Quoted in Paul Ricoeur, *Gabriel Marcel et Karl Jaspers* (Paris, 1947), p. 45.

17 *Correspondance complète de Jean Jacques Rousseau*, ed. R. A. Leigh (Geneva, 1967), vol. V. pp. 65–6. The original reads "l'évangile" rather than "la Bible."

18 Rousseau, *Oeuvres complètes*, Pléiade edition, vol. III, p. 602.

19 Derrida's reference is *Emile*, Pléiade edition, vol. 4, pp. 589, 594. My reference is *Emile*,

tr. Barbara Foxley (London, 1911), pp. 245, 249. Subsequent references to this translation
are placed within brackets.

20 I attempt to develop this theme elsewhere (*Speech and Phenomena*).

21 This does not, by simple inversion, mean that the signifier is fundamental or primary. The
"primacy" or "priority" of the signifier would be an expression untenable and absurd to
formulate illogically within the very logic that it would legitimately destroy. The signifier
will never by rights precede the signified, in which case it would no longer be a signifier and the "signifying" signifier would no longer have a possible signified. The thought
that is announced in this impossible formula without being successfully contained therein
should therefore be stated in another way; it will clearly be impossible to do so without
putting the very idea of the sign into suspicion, the "sign-of" which will always remain
attached to what is here put in question. At the limit therefore, that thought would destroy
the entire conceptuality organized around the concept of the sign (signifier and signified,
expression and content, and so on).

22 Postface to *Was ist Metaphysik?* (Frankfurt am Main, 1960), p. 46. The insistence of the
voice also dominates the analysis of *Gewissen* (conscience) in *Sein und Zeit* (pp. 267 f.)
(pp. 312 f.).

23 Cf. *Das Wesen der Sprache* ("The Nature of Language"), and *Das Wort* ("Words"), in *Unter-
wegs zur Sprache* (Pfüllingen), 1959 (*On the Way to Language*, tr. Peter D. Hertz (New York,
1971)).

24 (Martin Heidegger, *Einführung in die Metaphysik* (Tübingen, 1953) translated as *An Introduction to Metaphysics* by Ralph Mannheim (New Haven, 1959)). Tr. French Gilbert Kahn
(Paris, 1967), p. 50.

25 *Introduction à la métaphysique*, tr. fr. p. 103 (*Einführung* p. 70; *Introduction*, p. 92). "All this
points in the direction of what we encountered when we characterized the Greek experience and interpretation of being. If we retain the usual interpretation of being, the word
'being' takes its meaning from the unity and determinateness of the horizon which guided
our understanding. In short: we understand the verbal substantive 'Sein' through the infinitive, which in turn is related to the 'is' and its diversity that we have described. The definite and particular verb form 'is,' the *third person singular of the present indicative*, has here
a pre-eminent rank. We understand 'being' not in regard to the 'thou art,' 'you are,' 'I am,'
or 'they would be,' though all of these, just as much as 'is,' represent verbal inflections of
'to be.' . . . And involuntarily, almost as though nothing else were possible, we explain the
infinitive 'to be' to ourselves through the 'is.'

"Accordingly, 'being' has the meaning indicated above, recalling the Greek view of the
essence of being, hence a determinateness which has not just dropped on us accidentally
from somewhere but has dominated our historical being-there since antiquity. At one
stroke our search for the definition of the meaning of the word 'being' becomes explicitly what it is, namely a reflection on the source of our hidden history." I should, of
course, cite the entire analysis that concludes with these words.

26 *Enzyklopädie der philosophischen Wissenschaften in Grundrisse*, Suhrkamp edition (Frankfurt
am Main, 1970), pp. 273–6).

27 *dem Statarischen*, an old German word that one has hitherto been tempted to translate as
"immobile" or "static" (see (Jean) Gibelin, (tr. *Leçons sur la philosophie de la religion* (Paris,
1959)), pp. 255–7.

28 "La parole soufflée," in *L'écriture et la différence* (Paris: Seuil, 1967).

SUGGESTED READING

Baudrillard, Jean, *Simulacra and Simulation*, trans. Shiela Faria Glaser (Ann Arbor: University of Michigan Press, 1994).

Derrida, Jacques, *Speech and Phenomena*, trans. David B. Allison (Evanston, IL: Northwestern University Press, 1973).

Derrida, Jacques, ". . . That Dangerous Supplement," Part II.2 of *Of Grammatology* (Baltimore: Johns Hopkins University Press, 1974).

Derrida, Jacques, "Passe-Partout," Introduction to *The Truth in Painting*, trans. Ian McLeod and Geoff Bennington (Chicago: University of Chicago Press, 1987).

Derrida, Jacques, "Force of Law," in *Deconstruction and the Possibility of Justice*, ed. Drucilla Cornell et al. (New York and London: Routledge, 1992).

Gadamer, Hans-Georg, *Truth and Method* (New York: Seabury Press, 1975).

Gadamer, Hans-Georg, *Philosophical Hermeneutics*, trans. David E. Linge (Berkeley: University of California Press, 1976).

Gadamer, Hans-Georg, "On the Contribution of Poetry to the Search for Truth," in *The Relevance of the Beautiful and Other Essays*, trans. Nicholas Walker, ed. Robert Bernasconi (Cambridge: Cambridge University Press, 1987).

Heidegger, Martin, "The Origin of the Work of Art," in *Poetry, Language, Thought*, trans. and ed. Albert Hofstadter (New York: Harper & Row, 1971)

Heidegger, Martin, "The Onto-theo-logical Constitution of Metaphysics," in *Identity and Difference*, trans. Joan Stambaugh (Chicago: University of Chicago Press, 2002).

Margolis, Joseph, *Historied Thought, Constructed World: A Conceptual Primer for the Turn of the Millennium* (Berkeley: University of California Press, 1995).

Margolis, Joseph, *Interpretation Radical but Not Unruly: The New Puzzle of the Arts and History* (Berkeley and Los Angeles: University of California Press, 1995).

Margolis, Joseph, *Selves and Other Texts: The Case for Cultural Realism* (University Park, PA: Pennsylvania State University Press, 2001).

Margolis, Joseph, *Reinventing Pragmatism: American Philosophy at the End of the Twentieth Century* (Ithaca, NY: Cornell University Press, 2002).

Merleau-Ponty, Maurice, "Cézanne's Doubt," in *Sense and Non-Sense* (Evanston, IL: Northwestern University Press, 1964).

Merleau-Ponty, Maurice, *The Primacy of Perception*, trans. William Cobb (Evanston, IL: Northwestern University Press, 1964).

Merleau-Ponty, Maurice, *The Visible and the Invisible* (Evanston, IL: Northwestern University Press, 1968).

Oliver, Kelly, and Marilyn Pearsall (eds), *Feminist Interpretations of Friedrich Nietzsche* (University Park, PA: Pennsylvania State University Press, 1998).

Ricoeur, Paul, *History and Truth*, trans. Charles A. Kelbley (Evanston, IL: Northwestern University Press, 1965).

Ricoeur, Paul, *Hermeneutics and the Human Sciences* (Cambridge: Cambridge University Press, 1981).

Ricoeur, Paul, *Oneself as Another*, trans. Kathleen Blamey (Chicago: University of Chicago Press, 1994).

PART V

DISCLOSURE AND TESTIMONY

INTRODUCTION

In an important essay from the 1970s, Vattimo wrote: "Any appeal to the idea of testimony nowadays can justifiably be labeled anachronistic."[1] The very idea of testimony seemed to him linked to the era of existentialism, and to the kind of individual "subject" for whom freedom, choice, responsibility, and death would be fundamental issues. At the time Vattimo was writing, the "death of the subject" was in full swing, and the whole question of testimony seemed *passé*. But since then, remarkably, the climate has changed. On the continent, Levinas, Derrida, and Nancy have made these kinds of question respectable again, even if freedom and responsibility have been recast to accommodate a deconstructed subject.[2] And in analytical philosophy there has been a resurgence of interest in a related cluster of themes in moral psychology: notably trust, belief, lying, promising, etc. The conversation Vattimo wanted to kick-start is now in full swing.

It remains the case, however, that some need persuading that the question of *truth* is importantly tied up with disclosure and testimony at all, however urgent these issues might be. And yet once we move away from the assumption that language is essentially propositional (or perhaps *essentially* anything), and concern ourselves with its practical and performative dimensions, the connections with disclosure, testimony, and witnessing seem more compelling. Disclosure here alludes to the most basic ways in which the world is available or open to us, a usage commonly associated with Heidegger's account of truth as disclosedness of being. Whether this *ontological* understanding of disclosure displaces or actually contributes to understanding truth as a social practice is a matter of some dispute. According to Levinas at least, he and Heidegger occupy polar positions, with disclosure tied to anonymous Being by Heidegger, while Levinas ties testimony to the other person's self-exposure. The performative dimension of language is much clearer.[3] It is first important to distinguish instrumental from constitutive dimensions. Instrumentally, we say things to bring about certain effects (perlocutions), but we also do some things *just by* uttering certain words under the right conditions (illocutions). Saying "Aye" under the right conditions *is* voting. Both disclosure and testimony are constitutive in this sense.

Husserl, Heidegger, and Levinas, phenomenologists of different stripes, share the sense that truth begins with what we might call a self-manifesting moment. One of the ways in which they differ is in their understanding of how this bears on the normativity of truth. Phenomenology is the philosophical product of a sensibility nurtured on the intuitable clarity of logic and mathematics demanding that standard for knowledge in general. Husserl's fundamental normative commitment is to be found in his view that phenomenology was the only way in which philosophy could preserve humanity against a nihilistic divorce from the roots of significance. It was only by a scrupulous return to something like "intuitive fulfillment," each of us being able to "see" that something is so, that culture in general could escape the fate of moving around the board empty, meaningless expressions, the reign of the *flatus voci*. Husserl will link these concerns to that of responsibility – literally being able to validate for oneself, and make available to others, the grounds of one's truth claims. So the connection between adequation, self-evidence, and truth is both an epistemological one and also an ethical one.[4] The difference between Husserl and the positivism of Carnap and Ayer some years later is that Husserl was not reductively empirical about the question of testing and validation. Indeed, he identified truth and validation with the elaboration of the intentional structure of knowing, thinking, judging, etc. What we might think of as concepts are for Husserl primarily and originally varieties of intentional "act."

Although there are indeed sophisticated phenomenalists in the positivist movement, the realists and naive verificationists among the logical positivists reduced the problem of intentionality to a correspondence theory of truth (what James would call "the copy theory"). While Husserl thinks that there is more to intentionality than mere correspondence or passive mirroring, that human meaning draws on the spontaneous representational and formative activities of the mind. James's version of this claim (see Part I) is that ideas are not mere *copies* of things, but symbols (compare Rorty's critique of the realist conception of the mind as a mirror of nature). James would go on to account for these symbols as tools in human praxis, in our dealings with the world and with each other. This dimension is less apparent in the selection we include here from Husserl than it is in his later concept of the *lifeworld* as the requisite background and constitutive framework of the activity of symbolization.[5]

The problem of "truth" might be said to begin with the fact that in perception, imagination, and language we find ourselves with productive capacities that do not have built-in quality control. We produce thoughts, images, and sentences that, as interesting as they might be, are vague, misleading, or just plain false. On Husserl's view, the defect they share is that while they are candidates for truth by virtue of their form, they lack, in various ways, full "adequation," "self-evidence," or what Vattimo (in Part IV) called "patency." For Husserl, it is important to stress, phenomenology concerns itself with neither a psychological study of the facts of the mind nor any "objective" study of the world. It concerns itself, rather, with the ideal structures of consciousness, hence with the links between truth and adequation. Husserl is not a Platonist, but he is an essentialist, and this selection from his *Logical Investigations* offers a powerful statement of how the conceptual matrix of the language of truth is grounded in consciousness. If for Nietzsche and James, however (see Part I), Husserl's position seems like a desperate but doomed attempt to defend an absolutist conception of truth, other parts of his *Logical Investigations* provide a series of pointed arguments against any kind of relativism or pragmatism about truth.[6]

We have said that Heidegger and Levinas share with Husserl the sense that truth begins with what we might call a self-manifesting moment. Where they differ, indeed split, is over the significance of the social, and this is where Elgin's paper begins to bite. For Husserl, truth's "adequacy" is a condition for my being able to make a responsible claim to others. For Heidegger, the level at which I respond to the disclosure of being impacts on the authenticity of my being-with-others. For Levinas, the other person's testimony is the primary ethical moment, and it is only through this that I have access to the other in any real sense. Elgin's concerns are in some ways closer to Husserl's, bringing out the complexity of the social dimension in a way that Husserl never does, and bringing out the normativity of testimony at the opposite end of the spectrum from Levinas. For Elgin, testimony is like promising, in that it licenses the other to believe me, and in so doing shows more broadly how epistemological and ethical considerations overlay one another. Levinas focuses not on the license to believe that testimony issues to the witness, but rather on why testimony has that power. We might say that Levinas focuses not on the other's right to believe me, but on my obligation to believe the other. This does not mean that the other cannot be lying, that testimony cannot be false. Rather, it is saying that the kind of testimony we call witnessing is best thought of not as a claim that happens to be true, but as a "speaking of the truth" in a context in which what is being said, and who is saying it, is a matter of some significance. To be clear, it may be that witnessing in this sense is a special case that does not generalize to all testimony. But what is at stake finds a parallel in disputes about perception between phenomenalism and realism – whether the ways we can be mistaken should properly be allowed to change our understanding of the normal case, or be treated as exceptions. The phenomenalist claims that if we stick to the phenomena, we can pick up the error in the interpretive phase at which we talk about things and the world. The realist insists that what we hear is the motorbike, not motorbike sounds. If someone sets us up with a recording, then we are deceived, but we should not conclude anything more general as a consequence.[7] Similarly, we may say that the false witness is *not* bearing witness at all, because bearing witness means "telling it as it was." Someone who "gets it wrong" (suffering a memory lapse, etc.) is trying to bear witness, but unknown to everyone, failing. What Levinas and the realist about perception share is the presumption of veracity, and a sense of why that presumption is justified. There is little epistemological reflexivity in Levinas's account. Elgin, on the other hand, is more willing to dissect the performance of testimony to draw out the aspect of warranting belief from the broader act of testimony. In Elgin's case, truth seems to be restricted to the propositional content of testimony, while for Levinas truth appears in its fundamental form *as* testimony. How do we understand truth in this second sense?

The central split between Heidegger and Levinas, between truth as disclosure and truth as testimony, between (crudely) the ontological and the ethical, is one that Levinas has had the advantage of being able to frame publicly in the essay reprinted here. On his view, there is a broader battle within philosophy between that influenced by the Greek tradition, in which a kind of ethical neutrality prevails, and that which takes seriously ethics "as first philosophy." The Greek tradition concerns itself with metaphysics, ontology, and epistemology, and it takes for granted the substitutability of subject-positions. With the opening of ethics, as Levinas presents it, we have instead a fundamental asymmetry, in which I am responsible for the other, but he or she is not responsible for me. For Levinas, what this asymmetry is opposed to is the neutrality of ontology, the "view from nowhere," or what we might call the detached viewpoint. The position taken up by Hegel or Heidegger is the obvious counterpoint here. In some ways, Levinas's response to Heidegger parallels Kierkegaard's response to Hegel. While for Hegel, the truth lies in the correction and overcoming of every partial perspective – he famously said that truth took the form of a system – for Kierkegaard, this position throws the baby out with the bathwater. Without a position, a perspective, knowing cannot take place, let alone the kinds of affirmations of self that we think of as promising, testimony, or witnessing. Levinas's position is somewhat the reverse of Kierkegaard's in the sense that for him it is not my subjectivity that a neutral ontological standpoint eliminates, it is the claim the other makes upon me, the fundamental ethical moment. The conflict with

Heidegger over truth is particularly revealing, because Heidegger could also be said to be contesting a certain limitation of ontology. In *Being and Time* (1926), Heidegger had argued for the destruction of the history of ontology, what we might call a critical rereading of the history of philosophy, in order to make its basis "decisions" come alive again. Heidegger claims that Being is not just there, but is rather intimately connected with its appearing, not in the sense of appearance that leads to skepticism, but rather in the sense of self-manifesting, or – self-disclosing. Walking like a duck, looking like a duck, talking like a duck, are *what-it-is to be a duck*. And it is in this grasp of the disclosedness of being that Heidegger first locates truth. We might say that in understanding being this way, particularly understanding our own (human) being as uniquely tied up with *possibility*, we choose (or fail to choose) to live *in the truth*, or authentically. So for Heidegger, truth is tied to the disclosedness of being, which has a subsequent impact on my authentic self-understanding and my relations with others, while for Levinas it is tied from the beginning to a capacity, indeed obligation, to respond to the testimony of others. And it is this disagreement about *priority* that makes it more than just a disagreement about the meaning of the word *truth*.

We have mobilized *existential* disclosedness – associated with Heidegger's account of authenticity – to question the rigidity of Levinas's opposition between ontological disclosedness and ethical testimony. But a fuller account would also develop the way in which, for Heidegger, disclosedness is not just an individual phenomenon, but reflects the historical and cultural possibilities open to a community. This is made clear in his accounts (in "The Origin of the Work of Art") of how a work of art "opens a world," and how the Greek temple provides the space for a community to come together. To speak of the gods of the temple is to speak of how it is that truth discloses itself to a people - how they come to understand themselves, their destiny, their possibilities. Clearly this is not unproblematic. What brings people together will also exclude others or mobilize "a people" for war against the "enemy." It is at just such a point that Nancy, Lyotard, and Derrida attempt to rework Heidegger in less conservative directions.[8] And it is worth noting that in *The Differend*, Lyotard sets the problem of the witness in a legal and political context that explodes the ontological versus ethical frame we have worked with here. Lyotard focuses on the defendant in a court of law who "cannot be heard" for reasons of discursive incommensurability (including race/ethnicity, gender/sexuality, nationality, language, class). For Levinas the political realm is already one that excludes the singular ethics of the face-to-face relation. But in recognizing that "the third" is always present, even Levinas cannot maintain the purity of that version of the ethical.

Elgin and Heidegger allow us to imagine different responses to Levinas's position here. Heidegger's focus on the ontological might draw our attention to the Hobbesian assumptions about human nature that Levinas seems to be making, such that the ethical imperative becomes a necessary corrective.[9] And Elgin offers us a less rigid assessment of the place of the ethical – as tied up with epistemological and ontological questions in a messier way that Levinas is proposing. She also offers us a sense of the reciprocity of the ethical rather than what is for Levinas its essential asymmetry – that I am responsible for you, but not vice versa.[10]

While it is difficult to know quite how to weigh these considerations, especially in the light of contemporary skepticism about any form of self-authorization in a world of floating signifiers (see our final *Supplement* in Part VII), it would be remiss of us not to mention if only in a gestural way two powerful background historical considerations that seem to be driving the interest in truth as disclosure and as testimony, as well as the broader resurgence in moral and political philosophy. The first we could call the growth of technology and commodification, social and industrial development. These have brought with them immense gains, but for many people this has been at the price of a sense of loss, that our contact with the "real" is being prepackaged, mediated, commodified, subjected to rules, concepts, and algorithms. These allow for greater complexity and organization, but the savor of the singular contact with the real can seem threatened. The emphasis on truth as disclosure, indeed the broader phenomenological thrust, can be seen as an attempt to counteract this tendency. At the same time, testimony, bearing witness, have been thrust into the limelight first by the reports of survivors of the Holocaust, by the testimony of countless people who have suffered at the hands of regimes which, for periods of time, exercised closed tyrannical control over their populations, and by veterans returning from war having seen things they wish they had not seen. Testimony has meant being able to tell a free world what happened. And in the case of South Africa's Truth and Reconciliation Commission, it meant confession as well as testimony, all with a view to being able to move forward to create a more peaceful and just society. These two factors – combating commodification and breaking deadly silences – have given the question of truth a renewed political dimension. And the essay by Vattimo to which we first alluded stresses ways of understanding testimony in a less individualistic sense. These more political issues we take up in Part VI.

Notes

1   We append an excerpt from this essay to Vattimo's paper "The Truth of Hermeneutics" in Part IV.

2   Speaking of a "deconstructed" subject is shorthand for a range of transformations. A well-known collection brought many of these strands together: *Who Comes After the Subject?*, ed. E. Cadava, P. Connor, and J.-L. Nancy (London: Routledge, 1991). The central theme was precisely new forms of responsibility, and an awareness of the importance of a certain passivity that lies beyond the usual distinction between agency and passivity.

3   See J. L. Austin, *How to Do Things with Words* (Oxford: Oxford University Press, 1962), and John Searle, *Speech Acts* (Cambridge: Cambridge University Press, 1969).

4   This insistence on the reliability of what others say is fundamental to science. Reports of experiments are presented as replicable by anyone with the appropriate skills.

5   See Edmund Husserl, *Crisis of European Sciences and Transcendental Phenomenology*, trans. David Carr (Evanston, IL: Northwestern University Press, 1970).

6   Edmund Husserl, *Logical Investigations*, trans. J. N. Findlay (London: Routledge, 2001). It is important to add here that quite what relativism about truth *means*, and whether James or even Nietzsche are strict relativists, are both open to discussion. Barry Allen for instance (in his excellent *Truth in Philosophy* (Cambridge, MA: Harvard University Press, 1993)), denies this, emphasizing James's naturalism and neo-Darwinianism. Husserl, however, argues that any naturalistic view of *truth* is self-contradictory.

7   Putnam's rejection of the interface model of cognition may involve just such a move; see Putnam in Part II, and also Alcoff in Part VI.

8   See J.-L. Nancy, *Being Singular Plural* (Stanford, CA: Stanford University Press, 2000); J. F.
    Lyotard *The Differend* (Minneapolis: University of Minnesota Press, 1988); J. Derrida, *The
    Other Heading: Reflections on Today's Europe* (Bloomington: Indiana University Press, 1992).
9   See David Wood, "Where Levinas Went Wrong", in *The Step Back: Ethics and Politics after
    Deconstruction* (Albany: SUNY Press, 2005), ch. 3.
10 Elgin's work is connected to an important resurgence of work in moral psychology con-
    nected with issues of personal and interpersonal truth – trust, honesty, sincerity, lying, self-
    deception. See writings on trust and moral psychology more broadly by Trudy Govier,
    Cheshire Calhoun, Karen Jones, Nomy Arpaly, Naomi Scheman, Sue Campbell, Victoria
    McGeer, et al. See *Suggested Reading* for other examples.

15

SELF-EVIDENCE AND TRUTH
and "Relativism in an Extended Sense"

Edmund Husserl

§36 Introduction

In our discussions up to this point we have said nothing of the *qualities* of acts, nor presumed anything in regard to them. Possibility and impossibility have indeed no special relation to these qualities. It makes no difference, e.g., to the possibility of a proposition, whether we realize the propositional matter as matter for an act of *assertion* (not of an act that assents to something in the accepting or recognizing manner of approval, but in the manner of a simple act of belief or taking for true), or whether we use it, in qualitatively modified fashion, as the matter of a pure presentation. A proposition is always 'possible', when the concrete act of propositional meaning permits of a fulfilling identification with an objectively complete intuition of matching material. It is likewise irrelevant if this fulfilling intuition is a percept, or a pure construction of fantasy, etc. Since the summoning up of imaginative pictures is more subject, in varying degrees, to our will, than that of percepts and assertions, we incline to relate possibility specially to the picture-life of fantasy. A thing counts as possible, if it allows itself, objectively speaking, to be realized in the form of an adequate imaginative picture, whether we ourselves, as particular empirical individuals, succeed in thus realizing it or not. But through the ideal linkage between perception and imagination, which assures us *a priori* that to each percept a possible image corresponds, this proposition is equivalent to our own, and the limitation of the concept to imagination not essential.

What we have now to do, quite briefly, is to discuss the effect of these just indicated differences upon relationships of fulfilment, so that our treatments may at least reach a provisional term, as well as a view over further researches.

Edmund Husserl, *Logical Investigations*, Vol. I, trans. J. N. Findlay (London: Routledge & Kegan Paul, 1970), pp. 760–70. Reprinted by permission of Taylor & Francis Books Ltd.

Edmund Husserl, excerpt from *Logical Investigations*, trans. J. N. Findlay (London: Routledge & Kegan Paul, 1970), pp. 144–5. Reprinted by permission of Taylor & Francis Books Ltd.

§37 The Fulfilling Function of Perception:
The Ideal of Ultimate Fulfilment

We have seen that differences in the completeness of 'fulness' have an important bearing on the manner in which objects are made present in presentations. Signitive acts constitute the lowest step: they possess no fulness whatever. Intuitive acts have fulness, in graded differences of more and less, and this is already the case within the sphere of imagination. The perfection of an imagination, however great, still leaves it different from a perception: it does not present the object itself, not even in part, it offers only its image, which, as long as it is an image at all, never is the thing itself. The latter we owe to perception. Even this, however, 'gives' us the object in varied gradations of perfection, in differing degrees of 'projection'. The intentional charac-ter of perception, as opposed to the mere representation of imagination, is that of direct presentation. This is, as we know, an *internal* difference of acts, more precisely of their interpretative form. But 'direct' presentation does not in general amount to a true being-present, but only to an appearance of presence, in which objective pres-ence, and with it the perfection of veridicity (*Wahr-nehmung*, perception) exhibits degrees. This is shown by a glance at the corresponding scale of fulfilment, to which all exemplification of perfection in presentation is here, as elsewhere, referred. We thereby become clear that a difference extends over the fulness of perception that we sought to cover by our talk of perceptual *projection*, a difference that does not concern fulness in respect of its sensuous stuff, its internal character, but means a graded exten-sion of its character *as* fulness, i.e. of the interpretative character of the act. From this point of view many elements of fulness count for us − quite apart from anything genetic, for we know full well that these, like all similar differences, have an associa-tive origin − as *final presentations* of the corresponding objective elements. They offer themselves as identical with these last, not as their mere representatives: they are *the thing itself* in an absolute sense. Other cases again count as mere adumbrations of colour, perspectival foreshortenings etc., in which case it is clear that to such locu-tions something corresponds in the phenomenological content of the act prior to all reflection. We have already dealt with these 'projective' differences, and found them, pictorially transferred, in the case of imagination. Every projection is representative in character, and represents by way of similarity, but the manner of this representation by similarity differs according as the representation takes the projected content as picture or self-presentation (self-projection) of the object. The ideal limit, which an increase of fulness of projection permits, is, in the case of perception, the absolute self of the thing (as in imagination it is its absolutely resembling image), and that for every side and for every presented element of the object.

The discussion of possible relationships of fulfilment therefore points to *a goal in which increase of fulfilment terminates, in which the complete and entire intention has reached its fulfilment,* and that not intermediately and partially, but ultimately and finally. The intuitive substance of this last fulfilment is the absolute sum of possible fulness; the intuitive representative is the object itself, as it is in itself. Where a presentative inten-tion has achieved its last fulfilment, the genuine *adaequatio rei et intellectus* has been brought about. *The object is actually 'present' or 'given', and present as just what we have intended it*; no partial intention remains implicit and still lacking fulfilment.

And so also, *eo ipso*, the ideal of every fulfilment, and therefore of a *significative* fulfilment, is sketched for us; the *intellectus* is in this case the thought-intention, the intention of meaning. And the *adaequatio* is realized when the object meant is in the strict sense *given* in our intuition, and given as just what we think and call it. No thought-intention could fail of its fulfilment, of its last fulfilment, in fact, in so far as the fulfilling medium of intuition has itself lost all implication of unsatisfied intentions.

One sees that the perfection of the adequation of thought to thing is twofold: on the one hand there is a perfect adaptation to intuition, since the thought means nothing that the fulfilling intuition does not completely present as belonging to the thought. In this the two previously distinguished 'perfections' are plainly compre-hended: they yield what we called the 'objective completeness' of the fulfilment. On the other hand the complete intuition itself involves a perfection. The intuition fulfils the intention which terminates in it as not itself again being an intention which has need of further fulfilment, but as offering us the *last* fulfilment of our intention. We must therefore draw a distinction between the perfection of the *adaptation to intuition*, which is 'adequation' in the natural, wider sense, and the perfection of final fulfilment which presupposes this fulfilment, and which is an adequation with the 'thing itself'. Each faithful, unalloyed description of an intuitive object or event provides an example of the former perfection. If the object is something in interior experience, and is grasped as it is in reflex perception, then the second perfection may be added, as when, for instance, looking back on a categorical judgement just made, we speak of the subject-presentation in this judgement. The first perfection is, however, lacking, when we call the tree standing before us a 'cultivated' variety of apple-tree, or when we speak of the 'vibratory frequency' of the note just dying away, or, in general, when we speak of such properties of perceptual objects as, however much they may be mar-ginally meant in our perceiving intention, are not even more or less projectively present in what actually appears.

The following observation is also in place. Since an ultimate fulfilment may contain absolutely no unfulfilled intentions, it must issue out of a *pure* percept. An objectively complete percept, but one achieved by the continuous synthesis of impure percepts, will not fill the bill.

Against our mode of treatment, which places the final fulfilment of all intentions in perception, it may be objected that the realized consciousness of the universal, the consciousness which gives fulness to conceptually general presentations, and which sets the 'universal object itself' before our eyes, rests on a ground of mere imagina-tion, or is at least indifferent to the difference between perception and imagination. The same is obviously true, as a consequence of what has just been said, of all self-evident general assertions, which make themselves plain to us, in axiomatic fashion, 'from our very notions alone'.

This objection points to a gap in our investigation that has already been touched on from time to time. We first took perception, with immediate obviousness, as being the same as *sense*-perception, intuition as being the same as sensuous intuition. Tacitly, without any clear consciousness, we have frequently gone beyond the bounds of these notions, e.g. in connection with our discussions of compatibility. We regularly did this, when, e.g., we spoke of intuiting a conflict or a union, or some other synthesis as such. In our next chapter, which deals generally with categorial forms we shall show the need to widen the concepts of perception and other sorts of intuition. To remove our objection, we shall now only say that the imagination, which serves as basis for generalizing abstraction, does not therefore exercise an actual, authentic function of fulfilment, and so does not play the part of a 'corresponding' intuition. What is individually singular in phenomena, is not itself, as we have several times stressed, the universal, nor does it contain the universal as a real (*reell*) 'piece' of itself.

§38 Assertive Acts in the Function of Fulfilment: Self-Evidence in the Loose and Strict Sense

Under the rubric of 'intentions', assertive and non-assertive acts have so far been indiscriminately ranged. Nonetheless, though the general character of fulfilment essentially depends on the 'matter' of acts, which alone is relevant to an array of most important relationships, the quality of acts shares in the determination of others, and to such a degree that talk of intention, of directed aiming, really only seems to suit assertive acts. Our *thought* (*Meinung*) aims at a thing, and it hits its mark, or does not hit it, according as it agrees or does not agree in a certain way with perception (which is here an assertive act). Assertion then agrees with assertion: the intending and fulfilling act are alike in this quality. Mere presentation, however, is passive: it leaves matters 'in suspense'. Where by chance an adequate percept accompanies a mere presentation, a fulfilling coincidence certainly issues from the mutually fitting 'matters' of the acts: in the transition, however, the presentation acquires an assertive note, and the unity of coincidence itself certainly has this note quite homogeneously. *Each actual identification or differentiation is an assertive act*, whether itself founded on assertions or not. This last briefly-worded proposition adds an all-important characterization to the results of our last chapter, a characterization determining all relationships of compatibility: the theory of identifications and differentiations thereby reveals itself, with more clearness than before, as a chapter in the theory of judgement. For according as assertive or non-assertive acts function in our intentions or their fulfilments, they illuminate distinctions like that between *illustration*, perhaps *exemplification*, on the one hand, and *verification or confirmation* and its opposite *refutation*, on the other. The concept of verification relates exclusively to *assertive acts in relation to their assertive fulfilment*, and ultimately to their *fulfilment through percepts*.

To this last pre-eminent case we now give closer consideration. It is a case in which the ideal of adequation yields us *self-evidence* (*Evidenz*). We speak somewhat loosely of self-evidence wherever an assertive intention (a statement in particular) finds verification in a corresponding, fully accommodated percept, even if this be no more than a well-fitting synthesis of coherent single percepts. To speak of *degrees and levels of self-evidence* then has a good sense. Here are relevant all approximations of percepts to the objective completeness of their presentation of their object, all further steps towards the final ideal of perfection, the ideal of adequate perception, of the complete self-manifestation of the object, however it was referred to in the intention to be fulfilled. But the *epistemologically pregnant sense* of self-evidence is exclusively concerned with this last unsurpassable goal, *the act of this most perfect synthesis of fulfilment*, which gives to an intention, e.g. the intention of judgement, the absolute fulness of content, the fulness of the object itself. The object is not merely meant, but in the strictest sense *given*, and given as it is meant, and made one with our meaning-reference. It does not matter, for the rest, whether one is dealing with an individual or a universal object, with an object in the narrower sense or with a state of affairs, the correlate of an identifying or distinguishing synthesis.

Self-evidence itself, we said, is the act of this most perfect synthesis of fulfilment. Like every identification, it is an objectifying act, its objective correlate being called *being in the sense of truth*, or simply *truth* – if one does not prefer to award this term to another concept of the many that are rooted in the said phenomenological situation. Here, however, a closer discussion is needed.

§39 Self-Evidence and Truth

1.   If we at first keep to the notion of truth just suggested, *truth* as the correlate of an identifying act is a *state of affairs* (*Sachverhalt*), as the correlate of a coincident identity it is an *identity*: *the full agreement* of what is meant with what is *given as such*. This agreement we *experience* in self-evidence, in so far as self-evidence means the actual carrying out of an adequate identification. The proposition that self-evidence is the 'experience' of truth cannot, however, be simply interpreted as telling us that the self-evidence is the perception (in a sufficiently wide sense) of truth, and, in the case of strict self-evidence, the *adequate perception of truth*. For [. . .] we must allow that the carrying out of an identifying coincidence is not as yet an actual perception of objective agreement, but becomes so only through its own act of objectifying interpretation, its own looking towards present truth. Truth is indeed 'present'. Here we have always the *a priori* possibility of looking towards this agreement, and of laying it before our intentional consciousness in an adequate percept.

2.   A second concept of truth concerns the *ideal relationship* which obtains in the unity of coincidence which we defined as self-evidence, *among the epistemic essences of the coinciding acts*. While truth in sense 1 was the *objective* item corresponding to the act of self-evidence, truth in *this* sense is the Idea which belongs to the act-form: *the epistemic essence interpreted as the ideal essence of the empirically contingent act of self-evidence, the Idea of absolute adequation as such.*

3.   We also experience in self-evidence, from the side of the act which furnishes 'fulness', *the object given in the manner of the object meant*: so given, the object is fulness itself. This object can also be called being, truth, the 'truth' in so far as it is here not experienced as in the merely adequate percept, but as the ideal fulness for an intention, as that which makes an intention true (or as the ideal fulness for the intention's *specific* epistemic essence).

4.   Lastly, considered from the standpoint of the intention, the notion of the relationship of self-evidence yields us truth as the *rightness of our intention* (and especially that of our judgement), its adequacy to its true object, or *the rightness of the intention's epistemic essence in specie*. We have, in the latter regard, the rightness, e.g., of the judgement in the logical sense of the proposition: the proposition 'directs' itself to the thing itself, it says that it is so, and it really is so. In this we have the expression of the ideal, and therefore general, possibility that a proposition of such and such a 'matter' admits of fulfilment in the sense of the most rigorous adequation.

We must further particularly note that the 'being' here in   question in our first objective sense of truth, is not to be confused with the 'being' covered by the *copula* in the affirmative categorical judgement. Self-evidence is a matter of *total coincidence*, whereas the 'being' of the copula corresponds generally, if not invariably to partial identifications (i.e. judgements of quality).

But even where total identification is predicated, the two 'beings' will not coincide. For we must observe that in the case of a self-evident judgement, i.e. of a self-evident predicative assertion, *being in the sense of truth is experienced but not expressed*, and so never coincides with the being meant and experienced in the 'is' of the assertion. This second 'being' is the synthetic moment in what *is* in the sense of *is true* – how could it express the fact that the latter is true? There are in fact *several agreements* which are here brought to synthesis: *one* of these, the partial, predicative one, is meant assertively and perceived adequately, and so self-presented. (What this means will become clearer in the next chapter by way of the more general doctrine of categorial objectification.) This is the *agreement of subject with predicate*, the suiting of predicate to subject. We have, in the second place, *the agreement which constitutes the synthetic form of the act of self-evidence*, and therefore of the total coincidence of the meaning-intention of our assertion with the percept of the state of affairs itself, a coincidence naturally achieved in stages, which do not here concern us further. *This* agreement is plainly not asserted, it is not objective like the first agreement, which belongs to the state of affairs judged. No doubt it *can* always be asserted and asserted with self-evidence. It then becomes the verifying state of affairs for a new self-evidence, of which the like is true, and so on. At each step, however, one must distinguish the verifying state of affairs from the state of affairs constitutive of the self-evidence itself, we must distinguish the objectified from the not-objectified state of affairs.

The distinctions just drawn lead to the following general discussion.

In our exposition of the relationships of the concepts of self-evidence and truth, we have not drawn a distinction which touches the *objective* side of the acts which, whether functioning as intentions or fulfilments, find their absolute adequation in self-evidence: we have not, that is, distinguished between states of affairs, on the one hand, and other objects, on the other. We have paid no heed, correspondingly, to the phenomenological difference between acts which relate, on the one hand – acts of agreement and disagreement, predicative acts – and acts which do not relate, on the other. We have paid no heed, therefore, to the difference between relational and non-relational meanings, or to the relational–non-relational distinction among ideally apprehended essences in general. Strict adequation can bring non-relating as much as relating intentions into union with their complete fulfilments. If we now particularly consider the field of expressions, we need not concern ourselves with judgements as assertive intentions or assertive fulfilments; acts of naming can also achieve their adequation. The concepts of truth, rightness, the true, are generally interpreted more narrowly than we have done: they are connected with judgements and propositions, or with the states of affairs which are their objective correlates. 'Being' is meanwhile mainly spoken of in relation to absolute objects (not states of affairs), though no definite lines are drawn. Our right to our more general interpretation of these concepts is unassailable. The very nature of the case demands that the concepts of truth and falsehood, should, in the first instance at least, be fixed so widely as to span the whole sphere of objectifying acts. It seems therefore most suitable that the concepts of truth and being should be so distinguished, that our concepts of truth – a certain range of equivocation remaining inevitable but hardly dangerous once our concepts are clarified – are applied *from the side of the acts themselves* and their ideally graspable moments, whereas the concepts of *being* (genuine being) are applied to the corresponding *objective correlates*. Truth would then have to be defined in the manner of (2) and (4) as the Idea of adequation, or as the rightness of objectifying assertion and meaning. Being would then have to be pinned down according to (1) and (3) as the identity of the object at once meant and given in adequation, or (in conformity with the natural sense of words) as the adequately perceivable thing as such, in an indefinite relation to an intention that it is to make true or fulfil adequately.

After our concepts have been thus widely fixed and assured phenomenologically, we may pass on, having regard to the distinction between relational and non-relational acts (predications versus absolute assertions) to define *narrower concepts of truth and being*. The narrower concept of truth would be limited to the ideal adequation of a *relational* act to the corresponding adequate percept of a state of affairs: just so the narrower concept of being would concern the being of absolute objects, and would separate this off from the 'subsistence' of the state of affairs.

The following is accordingly clear: if one defines a judgement as an assertive act in general, then the sphere of judgement, subjectively speaking, coincides with the joint spheres of the concepts *true* and *false* in the widest sense of these words. But if one defines it by way of the statement and its possible fulfilment, and ranges under judgements only the sphere of relational assertions, then the same coincidence obtains again, provided that the *narrower* concepts of truth and falsehood are again used as a basis.

In one-sided fashion we have hitherto favoured the case of self-evidence, the act described as one of total coincidence. But, turning to the correlated case of conflict, we encounter *absurdity*, the experience of the total conflict between intention and quasi-fulfilment. To the concepts of truth and being the correlated concepts of *falsehood* and *non-being* then correspond. The phenomenological clarification of these concepts can be carried out without particular difficulty, once all foundations have been prepared. The negative ideal of an *ultimate frustration* would first have to be exactly circumscribed.

When self-evidence is conceived strictly, in the manner made basic here, it is plain that such doubts as have from time to time been expressed in modern times are absurd, doubts as to whether the experience of self-evidence might not be associated with the matter A for one man, while absurdity is associated with it for another. Such doubts are only possible as long as self-evidence and absurdity are interpreted as peculiar (positive or negative) *feelings* which, contingently attaching to the act of judgement, impart to the latter the specific features which we assess logically as truth and falsehood. If someone experiences the self-evidence of A, it is *self-evident* that no second person can experience the absurdity of this same A, for, that A is self-evident, means that A is not merely meant, but also genuinely given, and given as precisely what it is thought to be. In the strict sense it is itself present. But how could a second person refer in thought to this same thing A, while the thought that it is A is genuinely excluded by a genuinely given non-A? One is, it is plain, dealing with a matter of essence, the same matter, in fact, that the law of contradiction (into whose ambiguities the correlations discussed above naturally enter) successfully expresses.

It is reliably clear, as a result of our analyses, that being and non-being are not concepts which in their origin express opposition among the *qualities* of our judgements. Following our interpretation of the phenomenological relationships involved, every judgement is assertive: this assertion does not characterize the 'is' of which the 'is not' is the *qualitative* contrary. The qualitative contrary of a judgement is a mere presentation having the same 'matter'. Differences between 'is' and 'is not' are differences in intentional 'matter'. Just as an 'is' expresses predicative agreement after the manner of a meaning-intention, so an 'is not' expresses a predicative conflict.

Relativism in an Extended Sense

§37 General Observation: The Concept of Relativism in an Extended Sense

Our two forms of relativism are special cases of relativism in the widest sense of the word, as a doctrine which somehow derives the pure principles of logic from facts. Facts are 'contingent': they might very well not have been the case, they might have been different. If the facts then differ, logical principles also will differ; they will also be contingent, with a being relative to the facts on which they are founded. I do not wish to counter this by merely bringing in the apodeictic inner evidence of logical laws, points argued for in former chapters: I wish to bring in another point which is more important in this context [. . .]. Anyone can see from my statements up to this point that for me the pure truths of logic are all the ideal laws which have their whole foundation in the 'sense', the 'essence' or the 'content', of the concepts of Truth, Proposition, Object, Property, Relation, Combination, Law, Fact etc. More generally stated, they have their whole foundation in the sense of the concepts which make up the heritage of *all* science, which represent the categories of constituents out of which science as such is essentially constituted. Laws of this sort should not be violated by any theoretical assertion, proof or theory, not because such a thing would render the latter false – so would conflict with any truth – but because it would render them inherently absurd. An assertion, e.g., whose content quarrels with the principles whose roots lie in the *sense* of truth as such, is self-cancelling. For to assert, is to maintain the truth of this or that content. A proof whose content quarrels with the principles rooted in the *sense* of the relation of ground and consequent, is self-cancelling. For to prove, is to state that there is such and such a relation of ground and consequent etc. That an assertion is 'self-cancelling', is 'logically absurd', means that its particular content (sense, meaning) contradicts the general demands of its own, pertinent meaning-categories, contradicts what has its general root in the general meaning of those categories. It is now clear that, in this pregnant sense, any theory is logically absurd which deduces logical principles from any matters of fact. To do so is at variance with the general sense of the concepts of 'logical principle' and 'fact', or, to speak more precisely and more generally, of the concepts of 'truth based on the mere content of concepts' and 'truth concerning individual existence'. It is easy to see that the objections against the above discussed relativistic theory are, in the main, objections to relativism in the most general sense.

16

ON THE ESSENCE OF TRUTH
and "The Origin of the Work of Art"

Martin Heidegger

Our topic is the *essence* of truth. The question regarding the essence of truth is not concerned with whether truth is a truth of practical experience or of economic calculation, the truth of a technical consideration or of political sagacity, or, in particular, a truth of scientific research or of artistic composition, or even the truth of thoughtful reflection or of cultic belief. The question of essence disregards all this and attends to the one thing that in general distinguishes every "truth" as truth.

Yet with this question concerning essence do we not soar too high into the void of generality which deprives all thinking of breath? Does not the extravagance of such questioning bring to light the groundlessness of all philosophy? A radical thinking that turns to what is actual must surely from the first insist bluntly on establishing the actual truth which today gives us a measure and a stand against the confusion of opinions and reckonings. In the face of this actual need what use is the question concerning the essence of truth, this "abstract" question that disregards everything actual? Is not the question of essence the most inessential and superfluous that could be asked?

No one can evade the evident certainty of these considerations. None can lightly neglect their compelling seriousness. But what is it that speaks in these considerations? "Sound" common sense. It harps on the demand for palpable utility and inveighs against knowledge of the essence of beings, which essential knowledge has long been called "philosophy."[1]

Martin Heidegger, "On the Essence of Truth," trans. John Sallis, in *Basic Writings* (revised and expanded edition) ed. David Farrell Krell (London: Routledge & Kegan Paul, 1993), pp. 117–41. English translation © 1977, 1993 by HarperCollins Publishers, Inc. General introduction and introductions to each selection © 1997, 1993 by David Farrell Krell. Reprinted with permission of HarperCollins Publishers, Inc. and Taylor and Francis Ltd.

The German text is contained in Martin Heidegger, *Wegmarken* (Frankfurt am Main: Vittorio Klostermann Verlag, 1967), pp. 73–97. This translation is based on the fourth edition of the essay, published by Klostermann in 1961.

Martin Heidegger, excerpts from "The Origin of the Work of Art," in *Poetry, Language, Thought*, trans. and ed. Albert Hofstadter (New York: Harper & Row, 1971), pp. 35–6, 38, 41–5, 62, 71. © 1971 by Martin Heidegger. Reprinted by permission of HarperCollins Publishers, Inc.

Common sense has its own necessity; it asserts its rights with the weapon pecu-
liarly suitable to it, namely, appeal to the "obviousness" of its claims and considerations. However, philosophy can never refute common sense, for the latter is deaf to
the language of philosophy. Nor may it even wish to do so, since common sense is
blind to what philosophy sets before its essential vision.

Moreover, we ourselves remain within the sensibleness of common sense to the
extent that we suppose ourselves to be secure in those multiform "truths" of practical
experience and action, of research, composition, and belief. We ourselves intensify that
resistance which the "obvious" has to every demand made by what is questionable.

Therefore even if some questioning concerning truth is necessary, what we then
demand is an answer to the question as to where we stand today. We want to know
what our situation is today. We call for the goal which should be posited for man in
and for his history. We want the actual "truth." Well then − truth!

But in calling for the actual "truth" we must already know what truth as such
means. Or do we know this only by "feeling" and "in a general way"? But is not
such vague "knowing" and our indifference regarding it more desolate than sheer
ignorance of the essence of truth?

1. The Usual Concept of Truth

What do we ordinarily understand by "truth"? This elevated yet at the same time
worn and almost dulled word "truth" means what makes a true thing true. What is
a true thing? We say, for example, "It is a true joy to cooperate in the accomplishment of this task." We mean that it is purely and actually a joy. The true is the actual.
Accordingly, we speak of true gold in distinction from false. False gold is not actually what it appears to be. It is merely a "semblance" and thus is not actual. What is
not actual is taken to be the opposite of the actual. But what merely seems to be
gold is nevertheless something actual. Accordingly, we say more precisely: actual gold
is genuine gold. Yet both are "actual," the circulating counterfeit no less than the
genuine gold. What is true about genuine gold thus cannot be demonstrated merely
by its actuality. The question recurs: what do "genuine" and "true" mean here?
Genuine gold is that actual gold the actuality of which is in accordance (*in der
Übereinstimmung steht*) with what, always and in advance, we "properly" mean by
"gold." Conversely, wherever we suspect false gold, we say: "Here something is not
in accord" (*stimmt nicht*). On the other hand, we say of whatever is "as it should be":
"It is in accord." The *matter* is in accord (*Die Sache stimmt*).

However, we call true not only an actual joy, genuine gold, and all beings of
such kind, but also and above all we call true or false our statements about beings,
which can themselves be genuine or not with regard to their kind, which can be
thus or otherwise in their actuality. A statement is true if what it means and says is
in accordance with the matter about which the statement is made. Here too we say,
"It is in accord." Now, though, it is not the matter that is in accord but rather the
proposition.

The true, whether it be a matter or a proposition, is what accords, the accordant
(*das Stimmende*). Being true and truth here signify accord, and that in a double sense:

on the one hand, the consonance (*Einstimmigkeit*) of a matter with what is supposed in advance regarding it and, on the other hand, the accordance of what is meant in the statement with the matter.

This dual character of the accord is brought to light by the traditional definition of truth: *veritas est adaequatio rei et intellectūs.* This can be taken to mean: truth is the correspondence (*Angleichung*) of the matter to knowledge. But it can also be taken as saying: truth is the correspondence of knowledge to the matter. Admittedly, the above definition is usually stated only in the formula *veritas est adaequatio intellectūs ad rem* (truth is the adequation of intellect to thing). Yet truth so conceived, propositional truth, is possible only on the basis of material truth (*Sachwahrheit*), of *adaequatio rei ad intellectum* (adequation of thing to intellect). Both concepts of the essence of *veritas* have continually in view a conforming to . . . (*Sichrichten nach* . . .), and hence think truth as *correctness* (*Richtigkeit*).

Nonetheless, the one is not the mere inversion of the other. On the contrary, in each case *intellectus* and *res* are thought differently. In order to recognize this we must trace the usual formula for the ordinary concept of truth back to its most recent (i.e., the medieval) origin. *Veritas* as *adaequatio rei ad intellectum* does not imply the later transcendental conception of Kant – possible only on the basis of the subjectivity of man's essence – that "objects conform to our knowledge." Rather, it implies the Christian theological belief that, with respect to what it is and whether it is, a matter, as created (*ens creatum*), *is* only insofar as it corresponds to the idea preconceived in the *intellectus divinus*, i.e., in the mind of God, and thus measures up to the idea (is correct) and in this sense is "true." The *intellectus humanus* too is an *ens creatum*. As a capacity bestowed upon man by God, it must satisfy its *idea*. But the understanding measures up to the idea only by accomplishing in its propositions the correspondence of what is thought to the matter, which in its turn must be in conformity with the *idea*. If all beings are "created," the possibility of the truth of human knowledge is grounded in the fact that matter and proposition measure up to the idea in the same way and therefore are fitted to each other on the basis of the unity of the divine plan of creation. *Veritas* as *adaequatio rei (creandae) ad intellectum (divinum)* guarantees *veritas* as *adaequatio intellectūs (humani) ad rem (creatam)*. Throughout, *veritas* essentially implies *convenientia*, the coming of beings themselves, as created, into agreement with the Creator, an "accord" with regard to the way they are determined in the order of creation.

But this order, detached from the notion of creation, can also be represented in a general and indefinite way as a world-order. The theologically conceived order of creation is replaced by the capacity of all objects to be planned by means of a worldly reason (*Weltvernunft*) which supplies the law for itself and thus also claims that its procedure is immediately intelligible (what is considered "logical"). That the essence of propositional truth consists in the correctness of statements needs no further special proof. Even where an effort is made – with a conspicuous lack of success – to explain how correctness is to occur, it is already presupposed as being the essence of truth. Likewise, material truth always signifies the consonance of something at hand with the "rational" concept of its essence. The impression arises that this definition of the essence of truth is independent of the interpretation of the essence of the Being of all beings, which always includes a corresponding interpretation of the essence of man as the bearer and executor of *intellectus*. Thus the formula for the essence of truth (*veritas est adaequatio intellectūs et rei*) comes to have its general validity as something immediately evident to everyone. Under the domination of the obviousness which this concept of truth seems to have but which is hardly attended to as regards its essential grounds, it is considered equally obvious that truth has an opposite, and that there is untruth. The untruth of the proposition (incorrectness) is the non-accordance of the statement with the matter. The untruth of the matter (non-genuineness) signifies non-agreement of a being with its essence. In each case untruth is conceived as a non-accord. The latter falls outside the essence of truth. Therefore when it is a question of comprehending the pure essence of truth, untruth, as such an opposite of truth, can be put aside.

But then is there any further need at all for a special unveiling of the essence of truth? Is not the pure essence of truth already adequately represented in the generally accepted concept, which is upset by no theory and is secured by its obviousness? Moreover, if we take the tracing back of propositional truth to material truth to be what in the first instance it shows itself to be, namely a theological explanation, and if we then keep the philosophical definition completely pure of all admixture of theology and limit the concept of truth to propositional truth, then we encounter an old – though not the oldest – tradition of thinking, according to which truth is the accordance (*homoiōsis*) of a statement (*logos*) with a matter (*pragma*). What is it about statements that here remains still worthy of question – granted that we know what is meant by accordance of a statement with the matter? Do we know that?

2. The Inner Possibility of Accordance

We speak of accordance in various senses. We say, for example, considering two five-mark coins lying on the table: they are in accordance with one another. They come into accord in the oneness of their outward appearance. Hence they have the latter in common, and thus they are in this regard alike. Furthermore, we speak of accordance whenever, for example, we state regarding one of the five-mark coins: this coin is round. Here the statement is in accordance with the thing. Now the relation obtains, not between thing and thing, but rather between a statement and a thing. But wherein are the thing and the statement supposed to be in accordance, considering that the relata are manifestly different in their outward appearance? The coin is made of metal. The statement is not material at all. The coin is round. The statement has nothing at all spatial about it. With the coin something can be purchased. The statement about it is never a means of payment. But in spite of all their dissimilarity the above statement, as true, is in accordance with the coin. And according to the usual concept of truth this accord is supposed to be a correspondence. How can what is completely dissimilar, the statement, correspond to the coin? It would have to become the coin and in this way relinquish itself entirely. The statement never succeeds in doing that. The moment it did, it would no longer be able as a statement to be in accordance with the thing. In the correspondence the statement must remain – indeed even first become – what it is. In what does its essence, so thoroughly different from every thing, consist? How is the statement able to correspond to something else, the thing, precisely by persisting in its own essence?

Correspondence here cannot signify a thing-like approximation between dissimilar kinds of things. The essence of the correspondence is determined rather by the kind of relation that obtains between the statement and the thing. As long as this "relation" remains undetermined and is not grounded in its essence, all dispute over the possibility and impossibility, over the nature and degree, of the correspondence loses its way in a void. But the statement regarding the coin relates "itself" to this thing in that it presents (*vor-stellt*) it and says of the presented how, according to the particular perspective that guides it, it is disposed. What is stated by the presentative statement is said of the presented thing in just such manner *as* that thing, as presented, is. The "such-as" has to do with the presenting and its presented. Disregarding all "psychological" preconceptions as well as those of any "theory of consciousness," to present here means to let the thing stand opposed as object. As thus placed, what stands opposed must traverse an open field of opposedness (*Entgegen*) and nevertheless must maintain its stand as a thing and show itself as something withstanding (*ein Ständiges*). This appearing of the thing in traversing a field of opposedness takes place within an open region, the openness of which is not first created by the presenting but rather is only entered into and taken over as a domain of relatedness. The relation of the presentative statement to the thing is the accomplishment of that *bearing* (*Verhältnis*) which originally and always comes to prevail as a comportment (*Verhalten*). But all comportment is distinguished by the fact that, standing in the open region, it adheres to something opened up *as such*.[2] What is thus opened up, solely in this strict sense, was experienced early in Western thinking as "what is present" and for a long time has been named "being."

Comportment stands open to beings. Every open relatedness is a comportment. Man's open stance varies depending on the kind of beings and the way of comportment. All working and achieving, all action and calculation, keep within an open region within which beings, with regard to what they are and how they are, can properly take their stand and become capable of being said. This can occur only if beings present themselves along with the presentative statement so that the latter subordinates itself to the directive that it speak of beings *such-as* they are. In following such a directive the statement conforms to beings. Speech that directs itself accordingly is correct (true). What is thus said is the correct (the true).

A statement is invested with its correctness by the openness of comportment; for only through the latter can what is opened up really become the standard for the presentative correspondence. Open comportment must let itself be assigned this standard. This means that it must take over a pregiven standard for all presenting. This belongs to the openness of comportment. But if the correctness (truth) of statements becomes possible only through this openness of comportment, then what first makes correctness possible must with more original right be taken as the essence of truth.

Thus the traditional assignment of truth exclusively to statements as the sole essential locus of truth falls away. Truth does not originally reside in the proposition. But at the same time the question arises of the ground of the inner possibility of the open comportment which pregives a standard, which possibility alone lends to propositional correctness the appearance of fulfilling the essence of truth at all.

3. The Ground of the Possibility of Correctness

Whence does the presentative statement receive the directive to conform to the object and to accord by way of correctness? Why is this accord involved in determining the essence of truth? How can something like the accomplishment of a pregiven direct-edness occur? And how can the initiation into an accord occur? Only if this pregiv-ing has already entered freely into an open region for something opened up which prevails there and which binds every presenting. To free oneself for a binding directedness is possible only by *being free* for what is opened up in an open region. Such being free points to the heretofore uncomprehended essence of freedom. The openness of comportment as the inner condition of the possibility of correctness is grounded in freedom. *The essence of truth is freedom.*

But does not this proposition regarding the essence of correctness substitute one obvious item for another? In order to be able to carry out any act, and therefore one of presentative stating and even of according or not according with a "truth," the actor must of course be free. However, the proposition in question does not really mean that an unconstrained act belongs to the execution of the statement, to its pronouncement and reception; rather, the proposition says that freedom is the *essence* of truth itself. In this connection "essence" is understood as the ground of the inner possibility of what is initially and generally admitted as known. Nevertheless, in the concept of freedom we do not think truth, and certainly not at all its essence. The proposition that the essence of truth (correctness of statements) is freedom must consequently seem strange.

To place the essence of truth in freedom – doesn't this mean to submit truth to human caprice? Can truth be any more radically undermined than by being surren-dered to the arbitrariness of this "wavering reed"? What forced itself upon sound judg-ment again and again in the previous discussion now all the more clearly comes to light: truth is here driven back to the subjectivity of the human subject. Even if an objectivity is also accessible to this subject, still such objectivity remains along with subjectivity something human and at man's disposal.

Certainly deceit and dissimulation, lies and deception, illusion and semblance – in short, all kinds of untruth – are ascribed to man. But of course untruth is also the opposite of truth. For this reason, as the non-essence of truth, it is appropriately excluded from the sphere of the question concerning the pure essence of truth. This human origin of untruth indeed only serves to confirm by contrast the essence of truth "in itself" as holding sway "beyond" man. Metaphysics regards such truth as the imperishable and eternal, which can never be founded on the transitoriness and fragility that belong to man's essence. How then can the essence of truth still have its subsistence and its ground in human freedom?

Resistance to the proposition that the essence of truth is freedom is based on pre-conceptions, the most obstinate of which is that freedom is a property of man. The essence of freedom neither needs nor allows any further questioning. Everyone knows what man is.

4. The Essence of Freedom

However, indication of the essential connection between truth as correctness and freedom uproots those preconceptions – granted of course that we are prepared for a transformation of thinking. Consideration of the essential connection between truth and freedom leads us to pursue the question of the essence of man in a regard which assures us an experience of a concealed essential ground of man (of Dasein), and in such a manner that the experience transposes us in advance into the originally essential domain of truth. But here it becomes evident also that freedom is the ground of the inner possibility of correctness only because it receives its own essence from the more original essence of uniquely essential truth. Freedom was first determined as freedom for what is opened up in an open region. How is this essence of freedom to be thought? That which is opened up, that to which a presentative statement as correct corresponds, are beings opened up in an open comportment. Freedom for what is opened up in an open region lets beings be the beings they are. Freedom now reveals itself as letting beings be.

Ordinarily we speak of letting be whenever, for example, we forgo some enterprise that has been planned. "We let something be" means we do not touch it again, we have nothing more to do with it. To let something be has here the negative sense of letting it alone, of renouncing it, of indifference and even neglect.

However, the phrase required now – to let beings be – does not refer to neglect and indifference but rather the opposite. To let be is to engage oneself with beings. On the other hand, to be sure, this is not to be understood only as the mere management, preservation, tending, and planning of the beings in each case encountered or sought out. To let be – that is, to let beings be as the beings which they are – means to engage oneself with the open region and its openness into which every being comes to stand, bringing that openness, as it were, along with itself. Western thinking in its beginning conceived this open region as *ta alētheia*, time unconcealed. If we translate *alētheia* as "unconcealment" rather than "truth," this translation is not merely more literal; it contains the directive to rethink the ordinary concept of truth in the sense of the correctness of statements and to think it back to that still uncomprehended disclosedness and disclosure of beings. To engage oneself with the disclosedness of beings is not to lose oneself in them; rather, such engagement withdraws in the face of beings in order that they might reveal themselves with respect to what and how they are and in order that presentative correspondence might take its standard from them. As this letting-be it exposes itself to beings as such and transposes all comportment into the open region. Letting-be, i.e., freedom, is intrinsically exposing, ek-sistent.[3] Considered in regard to the essence of truth, the essence of freedom manifests itself as exposure to the disclosedness of beings.

Freedom is not merely what common sense is content to let pass under this name: the caprice, turning up occasionally in our choosing, of inclining in this or that direction. Freedom is not mere absence of constraint with respect to what we can or cannot do. Nor is it on the other hand mere readiness for what is required and necessary (and so somehow a being). Prior to all this ("negative" and "positive" freedom), freedom is engagement in the disclosure of beings as such. Disclosedness itself is conserved in ek-sistent engagement, through which the openness of the open region; i.e., the "there" ("*Da*"), is what it is.

In Da-sein the essential ground, long ungrounded, on the basis of which man is able to ek-sist, is preserved for him. Here "existence" does not mean *existentia* in the sense of occurring or being at hand. Nor on the other hand does it mean, in an "existentiell" fashion, man's moral endeavor in behalf of his "self," based on his psychophysical constitution. Ek-sistence, rooted in truth as freedom, is exposure to the disclosedness of beings as such. Still uncomprehended, indeed, not even in need of an essential grounding, the ek-sistence of historical man begins at that moment when the first thinker takes a questioning stand with regard to the unconcealment of beings by asking: what are beings? In this question unconcealment is experienced for the first time. Being as a whole reveals itself as *physis*, "nature," which here does not yet mean a particular sphere of beings but rather beings as such as a whole, specifically in the sense of emerging presence (*aufgehendes Anwesen*). History begins only when beings themselves are expressly drawn up into their unconcealment and conserved in it, only when this conservation is conceived on the basis of questioning regarding beings as such. The primordial disclosure of being as a whole, the question concerning beings as such, and the beginning of Western history are the same; they occur together in a "time" which, itself unmeasurable, first opens up the open region for every measure.

But if ek-sistent Da-sein, which lets beings be, sets man free for his "freedom" by first offering to his choice something possible (a being) and by imposing on him something necessary (a being), human caprice does not then have freedom at its disposal. Man does not "possess" freedom as a property. At best, the converse holds: freedom, ek-sistent, disclosive Da-sein, possesses man – so originally that only *it* secures for humanity that distinctive relatedness to being as a whole as such which first founds all history. Only ek-sistent man is historical. "Nature" has no history.

Freedom, understood as letting beings be, is the fulfillment and consummation of the essence of truth in the sense of the disclosure of beings. "Truth" is not a feature of correct propositions which are asserted of an "object" by a human "subject" and then "are valid" somewhere, in what sphere we know not; rather, truth is disclosure of beings through which an openness essentially unfolds (*west*). All human comportment and bearing are exposed in its open region. Therefore man *is* in the manner of ek-sistence.

Because every mode of human comportment is in its own way open and plies itself to that toward which it comports itself, the restraint of letting-be, i.e., freedom, must have granted it its endowment of that inner directive for correspondence of presentation to beings. That man ek-sists now means that for historical humanity the history of its essential possibilities is conserved in the disclosure of beings as a whole. The rare and the simple decisions of history arise from the way the original essence of truth essentially unfolds.

However, because truth is in essence freedom, historical man can, in letting beings be, also *not* let beings be the beings which they are and as they are. Then beings are covered up and distorted. Semblance comes to power. In it the non-essence of truth comes to the fore. However, because ek-sistent freedom as the essence of truth is not a property of man; because on the contrary man ek-sists and so becomes capable of history only as the property of this freedom; the non-essence of truth cannot first arise subsequently from mere human incapacity and negligence. Rather, untruth must derive from the essence of truth. Only because truth and untruth are, *in essence, not* irrelevant to one another but rather belong together is it possible for a true proposition to enter into pointed opposition to the corresponding untrue proposition. The question concerning the essence of truth thus first reaches the original domain of what is at issue when, on the basis of a prior glimpse of the full essence of truth, it has included a consideration of untruth in its unveiling of that essence. Discussion of the non-essence of truth is not the subsequent filling of a gap but rather the decisive step toward an adequate posing of the *question* concerning the essence of truth. Yet how are we to comprehend the non-essence in the essence of truth? If the essence of truth is not exhausted by the correctness of statements, then neither can untruth be equated with the incorrectness of judgments.

5. The Essence of Truth

The essence of truth reveals itself as freedom. The latter is ek-sistent, disclosive letting beings be. Every mode of open comportment flourishes in letting beings be and in each case is a comportment to this or that being. As engagement in the disclosure of being as a whole as such, freedom has already attuned all comportment to being as a whole. However, being attuned (attunement)[4] can never be understood as "experience" and "feeling," because it is thereby simply deprived of its essence. For here it is interpreted on the basis of something ("life" and "soul") that can maintain the semblance of the title of essence only as long as it bears in itself the distortion and misinterpretation of being attuned. Being attuned, i.e., ek-sistent exposedness to beings as a whole, can be "experienced" and "felt" only because the "man who experiences," without being aware of the essence of the attunement, is always engaged in being attuned in a way that discloses beings as a whole. Every mode of historical man's comportment – whether accentuated or not, whether understood or not – is attuned and by this attunement is drawn up into beings as a whole. The openedness of being as a whole does not coincide with the sum of all immediately familiar beings. On the contrary: where beings are not very familiar to man and are scarcely and only roughly known by science, the openedness of beings as a whole can prevail more essentially than it can where the familiar and well-known has become boundless, and nothing is any longer able to withstand the business of knowing, since technical mastery over things bears itself without limit. Precisely in the leveling and planing of this omniscience, this mere knowing, the openedness of beings gets flattened out into the apparent nothingness of what is no longer even a matter of indifference but rather is simply forgotten.

Letting beings be, which is an attuning, a bringing into accord, prevails throughout and anticipates all the open comportment that flourishes in it. Man's comportment is brought into definite accord throughout by the openedness of being as a whole. However, from the point of view of everyday calculations and preoccupations this "as a whole" appears to be incalculable and incomprehensible. It cannot be understood on the basis of the beings opened up in any given case, whether they belong to nature or to history. Although it ceaselessly brings everything into definite accord, still it remains indefinite, indeterminable; it then coincides for the most part with what is most fleeting and most unconsidered. However, what brings into accord is not nothing but rather a concealing of beings as a whole. Precisely because letting be always lets beings be in a particular comportment which relates to them and thus discloses them, it conceals beings as a whole. Letting-be is intrinsically at the same time a concealing. In the ek-sistent freedom of Da-sein a concealing of being as a whole comes to pass [*ereignet sich*]. Here there *is* concealment.

6. Untruth as Concealing

Concealment deprives *alētheia* of disclosure yet does not render it *sterēsis* (privation); rather, concealment preserves what is most proper to *alētheia* as its own. Considered with respect to truth as disclosedness, concealment is then undisclosedness and accordingly the untruth that is most proper to the essence of truth. The concealment of beings as a whole does not first show up subsequently as a consequence of the fact that knowledge of beings is always fragmentary. The concealment of beings as a whole, untruth proper, is older than every openedness of this or that being. It is also older than letting-be itself which in disclosing already holds concealed and comports itself toward concealing. What conserves letting-be in this relatedness to concealing? Nothing less than the concealing of what is concealed as a whole, of beings as such, i.e., the mystery; not a particular mystery regarding this or that, but rather the one mystery — that, in general, mystery (the concealing of what is concealed) as such holds sway throughout man's Da-sein.

In letting beings as a whole be, which discloses and at the same time conceals, it happens that concealing appears as what is first of all concealed. Insofar as it ek-sists, Da-sein conserves the first and broadest undisclosedness, untruth proper. The proper non-essence of truth is the mystery. Here non-essence does not yet have the sense of inferiority to essence in the sense of what is general (*koinon, genos*), its *possibilitas* and the ground of its possibility. Non-essence is here what in such a sense would be a pre-essential essence. But "non-essence" means at first and for the most part the deformation of that already inferior essence. Indeed, in each of these significations the non-essence remains always in its own way essential to the essence and never becomes inessential in the sense of irrelevant. But to speak of non-essence and untruth in this manner goes very much against the grain of ordinary opinion and looks like a dragging up of forcibly contrived *paradoxa*. Because it is difficult to eliminate this impression, such a way of speaking, paradoxical only for ordinary *doxa* (opinion), is to be renounced. But surely for those who know about such matters the "non-" of the primordial non-essence of truth, as untruth, points to the still unexperienced domain of the truth of Being (not merely of beings).

As letting beings be, freedom is intrinsically the resolutely open bearing that does not close up in itself.[5] All comportment is grounded in this bearing and receives from it directedness toward beings and disclosure of them. Nevertheless, this bearing toward concealing conceals itself in the process, letting a forgottenness of the mystery take precedence and disappearing in it. Certainly man takes his bearings (*verhält sich*) constantly in his comportment toward beings; but for the most part he acquiesces in this or that being and its particular openedness. Man clings to what is readily available and controllable even where ultimate matters are concerned. And if he sets out to extend, change, newly assimilate, or secure the openedness of the beings pertaining to the most various domains of his activity and interest, then he still takes his directives from the sphere of readily available intentions and needs.

However, to reside in what is readily available is intrinsically not to let the concealing of what is concealed hold sway. Certainly among readily familiar things there are also some that are puzzling, unexplained, undecided, questionable. But these self-certain questions are merely transitional, intermediate points in our movement within the readily familiar and thus not essential. Wherever the concealment of beings as a whole is conceded only as a limit that occasionally announces itself, concealing as a fundamental occurrence has sunk into forgottenness.

But the forgotten mystery of Dasein is not eliminated by the forgottenness; rather, the forgottenness bestows on the apparent disappearance of what is forgotten a peculiar presence (*Gegenwart*). By disavowing itself in and for forgottenness, the mystery leaves historical man in the sphere of what is readily available to him, leaves him to his own resources. Thus left, humanity replenishes its "world" on the basis of the latest needs and aims, and fills out that world by means of proposing and planning. From these man then takes his standards, forgetting being as a whole. He persists in them and continually supplies himself with new standards, yet without considering either the ground for taking up standards or the essence of what gives the standard. In spite of his advance to new standards and goals, man goes wrong as regards the essential genuineness of his standards. He is all the more mistaken the more exclusively he takes himself, as subject, to be the standard for all beings. The inordinate forgetfulness of humanity persists in securing itself by means of what is readily available and always accessible. This persistence has its unwitting support in that *bearing* by which Dasein not only ek-sists but also at the same time *in-sists*, i.e., holds fast to what is offered by beings, as if they were open of and in themselves.

As ek-sistent, Dasein is insistent. Even in insistent existence the mystery holds sway, but as the forgotten and hence "inessential" essence of truth.

7. Untruth as Errancy

As insistent, man is turned toward the most readily available beings. But he insists only by being already ek-sistent, since, after all, he takes beings as his standard. However, in taking its standard, humanity is turned away from the mystery. The insistent turning toward what is readily available and the ek-sistent turning away from the mystery belong together. They are one and the same. Yet turning toward and away from is based on a turning to and fro proper to Dasein. Man's flight from the mystery toward what is readily available, onward from one current thing to the next, passing the mystery by – this is *erring*.[6]

Man errs. Man does not merely stray into errancy. He is always astray in errancy, because as ek-sistent he in-sists and so already is caught in errancy. The errancy through which man strays is not something which, as it were, extends alongside man like a ditch into which he occasionally stumbles; rather errancy belongs to the inner constitution of the Da-sein into which historical man is admitted. Errancy is the free space for that turning in which insistent ek-sistence adroitly forgets and mistakes itself constantly anew. The concealing of the concealed being as a whole holds sway in that disclosure of specific beings, which, as forgottenness of conceal-ment, becomes errancy.

Errancy is the essential counter-essence to the primordial essence of truth. Errancy opens itself up as the open region for every opposite to essential truth. Errancy is the open site for and ground of *error.* Error is not just an isolated mistake but rather the realm (the domain) of the history of those entanglements in which all kinds of erring get interwoven.

In conformity with its openness and its relatedness to beings as a whole, every mode of comportment has its mode of erring. Error extends from the most ordinary wasting of time, making a mistake, and miscalculating, to going astray and venturing too far in one's essential attitudes and decisions. However, what is ordinarily and even according to the teachings of philosophy recognized as error, incorrectness of judg-ments and falsity of knowledge, is only one mode of erring and, moreover, the most superficial one. The errancy in which any given segment of historical humanity must proceed for its course to be errant is essentially connected with the openness of Dasein. By leading him astray, errancy dominates man through and through. But, as leading astray, errancy at the same time contributes to a possibility that man is capable of drawing up from his ek-sistence – the possibility that, by experiencing errancy itself and by not mistaking the mystery of Da-sein, he *not* let himself be led astray.

Because man's in-sistent ek-sistence proceeds in errancy, and because errancy as leading astray always oppresses in some manner or other and is formidable on the basis of this oppression of the mystery, specifically as something forgotten, in the ek-sistence of his Dasein man is *especially* subjected to the rule of the mystery and the oppression of errancy. He is in the *needful condition of being constrained* by the one and the other. The full essence of truth, including its most proper non-essence, keeps Dasein in need by this perpetual turning to and fro. Dasein is a turning into need. From man's Dasein and from it alone arises the disclosure of necessity and, as a result, the possibility of being transposed into what is inevitable.

The disclosure of beings as such is simultaneously and intrinsically the concealing of being as a whole. In the simultaneity of disclosure and concealing errancy holds sway. Errancy and the concealing of what is concealed belong to the primordial essence of truth. Freedom, conceived on the basis of the in-sistent ek-sistence of Dasein, is the essence of truth (in the sense of the correctness of presenting) only because freedom itself originates from the primordial essence of truth, the rule of the mystery in errancy. Letting beings be takes its course in open comportment. However, letting beings as such be as a whole occurs in a way befitting its essence only when from time to time it gets taken up in its primordial essence. Then resolute openness toward the mystery (*Ent-schlossenheit zum Geheimnis*) is under way into errancy as such. Then the question of the essence of truth gets asked more originally. Then the ground of the intertwin-ing of the essence of truth with the truth of essence reveals itself. The glimpse into the mystery out of errancy is a question – in the sense of that unique question of what being as such is as a whole. This questioning thinks the question of the *Being* of beings, a question that is essentially misleading and thus in its manifold meaning is still not mastered. The thinking of Being, from which such questioning primordially originates, has since Plato been understood as "philosophy" and later received the title "metaphysics."

8. Philosophy and the Question of Truth

In the thinking of Being the liberation of man for ek-sistence, the liberation that grounds history, is put into words. These are not just the "expression" of an opinion but are always already the ably conserved articulation of the truth of being as a whole. How many have ears for these words matters not. Who those are that can hear them determines man's standpoint in history. However, in the same period in which the beginning of philosophy takes place, the *marked* domination of common sense (sophistry) also begins.

Sophistry appeals to the unquestionable character of the beings that are opened up and interprets all thoughtful questioning as an attack on, an unfortunate irritation of, common sense.

However, what philosophy is according to the estimation of common sense, which is quite justified in its own domain, does not touch on the essence of philosophy, which can be determined only on the basis of relatedness to the original truth of being as such as a whole. But because the full essence of truth contains the non-essence and above all holds sway as concealing, philosophy as a questioning into this truth is intrinsically discordant. Philosophical thinking is gentle releasement that does not renounce the concealment of being as a whole. Philosophical thinking is especially the stern and resolute openness that does not disrupt the concealing but entreats its unbroken essence into the open region of understanding and thus into its own truth.

In the gentle sternness and stern gentleness with which it lets being as such be as a whole, philosophy becomes a questioning which does not cling solely to beings yet which also can allow no externally imposed decree. Kant presaged this innermost need that thinking has. For he says of philosophy:

> Here philosophy is seen in fact to be placed in a precarious position which is supposed to be stable – although neither in heaven nor on earth is there anything on which it depends or on which it is based. It is here that it has to prove its integrity as the keeper of its laws [*Selbsthalterin ihrer Gesetze*], not as the mouthpiece of laws secretly communicated to it by some implanted sense or by who knows what tutelary nature. (*Grundlegung zur Metaphysik der Sitten, Werke*, Akademieausgabe IV, 425; *Groundworth of the Metaphysics of Morals*, trans. H. J. Paton (New York: Harper & Row, 1964), translation modified)

With this essential interpretation of philosophy, Kant, whose work introduces the final turning of Western metaphysics, envisions a domain which to be sure he could understand only on the basis of his fundamental metaphysical position, founded on subjectivity, and which he had to understand as the keeping of its laws. This essential view of the determination of philosophy nevertheless goes far enough to renounce every subjugation of philosophical thinking, the most destitute kind of which lets philosophy still be of value as an "expression" of "culture" (Spengler) and as an ornament of productive mankind.

However, whether philosophy as "keeper of its laws" fulfills its primordially decisive essence, or whether it is not itself first of all kept and appointed to its task as keeper by the truth of that to which its laws pertain – this depends on the primordiality with which the original essence of truth becomes essential for thoughtful questioning.

The present undertaking takes the question of the essence of truth beyond the confines of the ordinary definition provided in the usual concept of essence and helps us to consider whether the question of the essence of truth must not be, at the same time and even first of all, the question concerning the truth of essence. But in the concept of "essence" philosophy thinks Being. In tracing the inner possibility of the correctness of statements back to the ek-sistent freedom of letting-be as its "ground," likewise in pointing to the essential commencement of this ground in concealing and in errancy, we want to show that the essence of truth is not the empty "generality" of an "abstract" universality but rather that which, self-concealing, is unique in the unremitting history of the disclosure of the "meaning" of what we call Being – what we for a long time have been accustomed to considering only as being as a whole.

9. Note

The question of the essence of truth arises from the question of the truth of essence. In the former question essence is understood initially in the sense of whatness (*quidditas*) or material content (*realitas*), whereas truth is understood as a characteristic of knowledge. In the question of the truth of essence, essence is understood verbally; in this word, remaining still within metaphysical presentation, Being is thought as the difference that holds sway between Being and beings. Truth signifies sheltering that lightens [*lichtendes Bergen*] as the basic characteristic of Being. The question of the essence of truth finds its answer in the proposition *the essence of truth is the truth of essence*. After our explanation it can easily be seen that the proposition does not merely reverse the word order so as to conjure the specter of paradox. The subject of the proposition – if this unfortunate grammatical category may still be used at all – is the truth of essence. Sheltering that lightens is – i.e., lets essentially unfold – accordance between knowledge and beings. The proposition is not dialectical. It is no proposition at all in the sense of a statement. The answer to the question of the essence of truth is the saying of a turning [*die Sage einer Kehre*] within the history of Being. Because sheltering that lightens belongs to it, Being appears primordially in the light of concealing withdrawal. The name of this lighting [*Lichtung*] is *alētheia*.

Already in the original project the lecture "On the Essence of Truth" was to have been completed by a second lecture "On the Truth of Essence." The latter failed for reasons that are now indicated in the "Letter on Humanism" in *Martin Heidegger: Basic Writings*, ed. David F. Krell (New York: Harper & Row, 1993).

The decisive question (in *Being and Time*, 1927) of the meaning, i.e., of the project-domain [. . .], i.e., of the openness, i.e., of the truth of Being and not merely of beings, remains intentionally undeveloped. Our thinking apparently remains on the path of metaphysics. Nevertheless, in its decisive steps, which lead from truth as correctness to ek-sistent freedom, and from the latter to truth as concealing and as errancy, it accomplishes a change in the questioning that belongs to the overcoming of metaphysics. The thinking attempted in the lecture comes to fulfillment in the essential experience that a nearness to the truth of Being is first prepared for historical man on the basis of the Da-sein into which man can enter. Every kind of anthropology and all subjectivity of man as subject is not merely left behind – as it was already in *Being and Time* – and the truth of Being sought as the ground of a transformed historical position; rather, the movement of the lecture is such that it sets out to think from this other ground (Da-sein). The course of the questioning is intrinsically the way of a thinking which, instead of furnishing representations and concepts, experiences and tries itself as a transformation of its relatedness to Being.

Notes

1 Throughout the translation *das Seiende* is rendered as "being" or "beings," *ein Seiendes* as "a being," *Sein* as "Being," *das Seiende im Ganzen* as either "being as a whole" or "beings as a whole" depending on the context. – TR.

2 The text reads, "ein Offenbares *als ein solches.*" In ordinary German *offenbar* means "evident," "manifest." However, the context which it has here through its link with "open region" (*das Offene*), "open stance" (*Offenständigkeit*), and "openness" (*Offenheit*) already suggests the richer sense that the word has for Heidegger: that of something's being so opened up as to reveal itself, to be manifest (as, for example, a flower in bloom), in contrast to something's being so closed or sealed up within itself that it conceals itself. – TR.

3 This variant of the word *Existenz* indicates the ecstatic character of freedom, its standing outside itself. – TR.

4 The text reads, "*Die Gestimmtheit (Stimmung). . . .*" *Stimmung* refers not only to the kind of attunement which a musical instrument receives by being tuned but also to the kind of attunement that constitutes a mood or a disposition of Dasein. The important etymological connection between *Stimmung* and the various formations based on *stimmen* (to accord) is not retained in the translation. – TR.

5 "Resolutely open bearing" seeks to translate *das entschlossene Verhältnis. Entschlossen* is usually rendered as "resolute," but such a translation fails to retain the word's structural relation to *verschlossen*, "closed" or "shut up." Significantly, this connection is what makes it possible for Heidegger to transform the sense of the word: he takes the prefix as a privation rather than as indicating establishment of the condition designated by the word to which it is affixed. Thus, as the text here makes quite clear, *entschlossen* signifies just the opposite of that kind of "resolve" in which one makes up his mind in such fashion as to close off all other possibilities: it is rather a kind of keeping *un-closed*. – TR.

6 "To err" may translate *irren* only if it is understood in its root sense derived from the Latin *errare*, "to wander from the right way," and only secondarily in the sense "to fall into error." – TR.

From "The Origin of the Work of Art"

The equipmental quality of equipment was discovered. But how? Not by a description and explanation of a pair of shoes actually present; not by a report about the process of making shoes; and also not by the observation of the actual use of shoes occurring here and there; but only by bringing ourselves before Van Gogh's painting. This painting spoke. In the vicinity of the work we were suddenly somewhere else than we usually tend to be.

The art work let us know what shoes are in truth. It would be the worst self-deception to think that our description, as a subjective action, had first depicted everything thus and then projected it into the painting. If anything is questionable here, it is rather that we experienced too little in the neighborhood of the work and that we expressed the experience too crudely and too literally. But above all, the work did not, as it might seem at first, serve merely for a better visualizing of what a piece of equipment is. Rather, the equipmentality of equipment first genuinely arrives at its appearance through the work and only in the work.

What happens here? What is at work in the work? Van Gogh's painting is the disclosure of what the equipment, the pair of peasant shoes, *is* in truth. This entity emerges into the unconcealedness of its being. The Greeks called the unconcealedness of beings *alētheia*. We say "truth" and think little enough in using this word. If there occurs in the work a disclosure of a particular being, disclosing what and how it is, then there is here an occurring, a happening of truth at work.

In the work of art the truth of an entity has set itself to work. "To set" means here: to bring to a stand. Some particular entity, a pair of peasant shoes, comes in the work to stand in the light of its being. The being of the being comes into the steadiness of its shining.

[. . .]

Yet truth is put into the work. What truth is happening in the work? Can truth happen at all and thus be historical? Yet truth, people say, is something timeless and supertemporal.

[. . .]

We now ask the question of truth with a view to the work. But in order to become more familiar with what the question involves, it is necessary to make visible once more the happening of truth in the work. For this attempt let us deliberately select a work that cannot be ranked as representational art.

A building, a Greek temple, portrays nothing. It simply stands there in the middle of the rock-cleft valley. The building encloses the figure of the god, and in this concealment lets it stand out into the holy precinct through the open portico. By means of the temple, the god is present in the temple. This presence of the god is in itself the extension and delimitation of the precinct as a holy precinct. The temple and its precinct, however, do not fade away into the indefinite. It is the temple-work that first fits together and at the same time gathers around itself the unity of those paths and relations in which birth and death, disaster and blessing, victory and disgrace, endurance and decline acquire the shape of destiny for human being. The all-governing expanse of this open relational context is the world of this historical people. [. . .]

Standing there, the building rests on the rocky ground. This resting of the work draws up out of the rock the mystery of that rock's clumsy yet spontaneous support. Standing there, the building holds its ground against the storm raging above it and so first makes the storm itself manifest in its violence. [. . .] We call this ground the *earth*. What this word says is not to be associated with the idea of a mass of matter deposited somewhere, or with the merely astronomical idea of a planet. Earth is that whence the arising brings back and shelters everything that arises without violation. In the things that arise, earth is present as the sheltering agent.

The temple-work, standing there, opens up a world and at the same time sets this world back again on earth, which itself only thus emerges as native ground.

[. . .]

To be a work means to set up a world. But what is it to be a world? The answer was hinted at when we referred to the temple. On the path we must follow here, the nature of world can only be indicated. What is more, this indication limits itself to warding off anything that might at first distort our view of the world's nature.

The world is not the mere collection of the countable or uncountable, familiar and unfamiliar things that are just there. But neither is it a merely imagined frame-work added by our representation to the sum of such given things. The *world worlds*, and is more fully in being than the tangible and perceptible realm in which we believe ourselves to be at home. World is never an object that stands before us and can be seen. World is the ever-nonobjective to which we are subject as long as the paths of birth and death, blessing and curse keep us transported into Being. Wherever those decisions of our history that relate to our very being are made, are taken up and abandoned by us, go unrecognized and are rediscovered by new inquiry, there the world worlds. [. . .] By the opening up of a world, all things gain their lingering and hastening, their remoteness and nearness, their scope and limits. In a world's world-ing is gathered that spaciousness out of which the protective grace of the gods is granted or withheld. Even this doom of the god remaining absent is a way in which world worlds.

[. . .]

The establishing of truth in the work is the bringing forth of a being such as never was before and will never come to be again. The bringing forth places this being in the Open in such a way that what is to be brought forth first clears the openness of the Open into which it comes forth. Where this bringing forth expressly brings the openness of beings, or truth, that which is brought forth is a work. Creation is such a bringing forth. As such a bringing, it is rather a receiving and an incorporating of a relation to unconcealedness.

[. . .]

In the work, the happening of truth is at work and, indeed, at work according to the manner of a work. Accordingly the nature of art was defined to begin with as the setting-into-work of truth. Yet this definition is intentionally ambiguous. It says on the one hand: art is the fixing in place of a self-establishing truth in the figure. This happens in creation as the bringing forth of the unconcealedness of what is. Setting-into-work, however, also means: the bringing of work-being into movement and happening. This happens as preservation. Thus art is: the creative preserving of truth in the work. *Art then is the becoming and happening of truth.*

17

TRUTH OF DISCLOSURE AND TRUTH OF TESTIMONY

Emmanuel Levinas

1. Truth and Being

The *true* as a synonym for the *real*, as a presentation *in the original* of disclosed being, assumes the indifference of the presented being with regard to its thematization by consciousness and, in a certain manner, its security with respect to the subjective fantasies that would project themselves onto its discovered aspect, onto its nudity.

The term *objectivity* (which, today, it is perhaps wrong to identify with the result of a process of reification, for it is in its place in every awareness, be it the awareness of becoming, of relation, of a norm, or of life and oneself) expresses this indifference, and thereby the very being of that which is. But this indifference – or this security, this objectivity – does not appear as an attribute that qualifies the disclosed realities, nor as a modality of relations among the terms that constitute the real, nor as the character of the configuration of all these terms in a system. Indifference *signifies* when being is referred to consciousness, the claim of which – to affect in any way whatsoever the order which, through consciousness, shows itself – being would, precisely, impugn.

Yet everything happens as though the signifyingness or the intelligibility of the relations among terms or relations, the arrangement of the structures of being among themselves, the intelligibility of the thematized system, were precisely the very way of impugning the interference of the gaze in being as made manifest to it. The indifference of the disclosed with respect to consciousness is not, indeed, evenly apportioned in the theme, and is dependent upon intelligibility. Signifyingness and the brilliance of appearing go, in a certain manner, together. A shadow is cast over the terms if they are taken outside the relation, over the relations and structures taken outside the system in which they are implicated; it is cast over them when, still

Emmanuel Levinas, "Truth of Disclosure and Truth of Testimony," trans. Iain MacDonald, in *Basic Philosophical Writings*, ed. Adriaan T. Peperzak, Simon Critchley, and Robert Bernasconi (Bloomington and Indianapolis: Indiana University Press, 1996), pp. 98–107, 184–5 (notes). Reprinted by permission of Flammarion.

isolated or already abstract, terms and relations have yet to take their place in conjuncture, when the structures have yet to be secured in a system. An order made manifest, in which the terms of the structures or the elements of a system are held together
as abstractions, despite its thematization, offers some resistance to the light, and is not
made wholly manifest. The structure is, indeed, intelligible or rational or signifying,
whereas the terms on their own have no meaning. It is *in* the relation that the terms
acquire a brilliance that finds itself tarnished as soon as they are separated from it.

A *lag* between the fact of *being thematized* and the fact of *being made manifest in
intelligibility* can thus be adduced, a *passage* from thematization to manifestation within
intelligibility. In the movement from the one to the other, a hesitation, a time, a certain
risk, good or bad fortune, can be made out – the necessity of an effort for the structures to be secured. This event or this becoming within intelligibility itself can be
called subjectivity. But then subjectivity thinks itself fully on the basis of objective
intelligibility, come to celebrate a noon without shadows where, without proper
density, it does not even cast its own shadow. Disappearing into the intelligibility or
the objectivity of structures, the subject becomes aware of itself as called forth by
intelligibility. Rational, theoretical consciousness in all its purity!

The truth correlative to being – in which the subject, a pure welcome reserved
for the nudity of disclosed being, effaces itself *before* that which manifests itself, and
in which effort, inventiveness, and genius are all just the means, ways, and detours by
which being is dis-covered, by which its phases come together and its structures are
secured – remains, within the thought that issued from Greece, the foundation of
every notion of truth.

The truth resulting from the subject's engagement in the world and history through
labor, cultural creation, and political organization, whereby the subjectivity of the
subject shows itself to be humanity, finitude, care for its being thrown in anticipation
of its end – this truth remains the truth of disclosed being.[1] The reflections of being
in the humanity of the subject, its effects on this humanity, let themselves, precisely,
be thematized. The experience of one who has lived, "been around," "got on in years,"
translates into objective propositions of experience as such, already offering itself to
the human sciences. Everything happens as though, behind the human, lies the subject
that effaces itself *before* the being of its humanity, letting it link up, come together,
and disclose itself. Representation governs the notion of truth, and thereby every
meaning is governed by ontology.

Husserl's famous proposition regarding the *Urdoxa*, residing at the basis of all intentionality – even nontheoretical intentionality – and allowing, *before any reflection on the
act of valuation or acting will*, the transformation of the axiological and practical noe-
matic sense into the doxical, into a meaning that is a pure position of being, establishes the priority of truth understood as disclosure and thereby the priority of the
gathering together (of the ensemble) of the *synchrony of being*, in relation to every other
way of signifying.[2] By taking up Brentano's thesis in this form – for Brentano every
psychical act was either a representation or founded upon representation – Husserl
finds himself affirming not so much the privilege contemplation would enjoy with
respect to action (for, as has been rightly noted, within the Husserlian ideal of knowledge, it is easy to discern an ongoing task: the necessity of manual intervention in
the laboratory and in the writing indispensable to the transmission of results obtained

to other researchers in order to further the task − not to mention incidental digressions − the necessity of walking "around the thing," etc.) but rather the priority or ultimacy of *meaning*: being, in all its synchrony, in its nudity without mystery, in its immanence to knowing. In accordance with the tradition running from Aristotle to Heidegger! Every meaning and every psychism, all spirituality, lead back to *dis-covery*, gathering together, synchronous appearing, even if intentional correlation does not remain the ultimate structure. The priority of the doxical thesis in its Husserlian formulation establishes the priority of the truth of being and the universality of immanence.

Every confession of truths comes back to a prior disclosure of being, that is to say, situates within the limits of being every sensible thought, and *subordinates sense to being*. Language either refers to this previous discovery or contributes to it, receiving, in this case, transcendental status; but language in no way would know how to signify beyond being. Testimony − the confession of some knowledge or of an experience by a subject − can be conceived only in relation to the disclosed being which remains the norm; it brings about only indirect truths about being, or about the relations man has with being. These truths are evidently inferior, secondhand, and uncontrollable, distorted by the very fact of their transmission: "self-effacing subjectivity," by circulating information, is capable of bad faith and lying. The critique of testimony − by whatever method (the proliferation and comparison of testimonies, investigation into the credibility of the witness, etc.) − is necessary to draw out the truth (since the *question* is suppressed).[3]

In its most elevated meaning, testimony can doubtless be understood as the schematization of the abstract concept of being in the concreteness of the subject. Art would testify to the truth according to such a schematism. But once again, the structure of discovery reappears in the schema. The disclosure of being governs testimony. The *concreteness of the subject or being*, investigated by the critic or the historian or the philosopher, is schematized and placed on the side of being. *Before* being, the *subject of knowledge* effaces itself.

2. The Meaning of a "Beyond Being"

Does the truth of testimony illuminate only by way of borrowed light? The truth of testimony is certainly irreplaceable everywhere the subject is not just the instance that welcomes the manifestation of being but also the exclusive sphere of "subjective experiences," the enclosed and private domain that opens itself to universality and inspection only through the story that the subject makes of these. But do saying[4] and testimony contribute only a means of communication and intersubjective control to the experience of subjective being?

The conception of the subjectivity of the subject held by the Western tradition assumes that the manifestation of being is the starting point of all sense. In effect, the notion of the soul has been purified over the course of the history of philosophy of any connotation other than that which evokes consciousness or thematizing contemplation. The importance that the concept of intentionality has taken on in recent times marks the culmination of this trend. Is not calling into question such a structure of the psychism to hint at a role for testimony – and for the Saying itself – that would be more directly "veritative" than that which they play when transmitting or communicating ontological experiences? Far from being subordinated to the disclosure of being, are they not the source of a meaning signifying otherwise? Do they not allow a glimpse of a sensible adventure that would not be played out within the limits of being? An intrigue from beyond being? One could doubtless ask whether an intrigue that takes shape beyond being is not a contradiction in terms. But has not the notion of the Good or the One beyond Being already been ventured?[5] And is the concept of transcendence reducible simply to the absurd position of a being behind the scenes in a hinter-world?

At first glance, it would seem so. Do not mind and the manifestation of being go together? Subjectivity, in the form of consciousness and, ultimately, intentionality, is quasi-raised by the event of manifestation. Since being, by its essence, appears, consciousness is consciousness of . . . , whereby all that might escape presentation, all that might signify beyond the synthesis of the present, presents itself, is put together, and synchronized. Nothing changes if the notion of "consciousness of . . ." is expanded to describe it as *access* to being. The exteriority of being presupposed in this manner of speaking is already borrowed from the gathering together of being in a theme that "consciousness of . . ." gives itself. "Access to being" expresses a notion just as tautological as manifestation of being or ontology. The subjective is understood strictly in terms of manifestation.

3. The Psychism as Inspiration

Cannot the psychism be thought of as a relation with the unrepresentable? As a relation with a past on the hither side of every present and every representation, not belonging to the order of presence? I have shown in another study the meaning of the subjectivity included in the everyday and extra-ordinary event of my responsibility toward other humans, that is, of my responsibility for the freedom of others, for a destiny that escapes my will. The freedom of the other (*autrui*) will never have been able to originate in my own, that is to say, will never have been able to fit into the same present, will never have been able to be – or to become again – contemporary with my freedom, or be representable to me. "The unlimited responsibility in which I find myself comes from the hither side of my freedom, from a nonpresent par excellence, from the nonoriginal, from the anarchic, from the hither side of or from beyond essence."[6] Initially approached from responsibility for the other human – beginning from human solidarity or fraternity – the subject *would be alienated in the depths of its identity* – an alienation that would not empty the Same of its identity, but which would constrain it in the unimpugnable summons of me by the other, where no one could stand in for me. *The soul is the other within me*, a sickness of identity, its being out of phase, its diachrony, gasping, shuddering. But *is not the one-for-the-other meaning itself*? A signifyingness of meaning more ancient than manifestation of being, the one-for-the-other, "possession" of the same by the other in responsibility, the other in the same – the soul is already a touch mad, psychism already psychosis. The psychism of the soul is alterity within identity, animation, inspiration. Thought through to the end, the one-for-the-other is no anodyne formal relation, but rather all the gravity of the body, its *conatus* extirpated and capable of giving: *the very possibility of giving*, the for-the-other of subjectivity, nonsubstance, nonquietude. Exposure to the other, but not the exposure of skin to gaze; rather, the vulnerability to which sensibility is reducible before entering, by way of "sensations," in gnoseological play. A sensibility perhaps, coming back to the for-the-other of maternity, on the hither side of being; coming back to the maternity that is the very gestation of the other in the same, of the other in the same that would be the psyche itself.

The union of body and soul, impossible for Descartes without supernatural intervention (because sought by him on the basis of the rationality of representation, of the gathering together, and of the synchrony of terms – the soul being already understood as a thematizing thought), is, as the animation of the same by the other, the one-for-the-other of meaning, the signifyingness of meaning, intelligibility itself. The other within the same, worrying me as responsibility, as the summons of me by the other, does not open the door of non-sense through this exceptional alienation but constrains an irreplaceable subject to substitution. A subjectivity of human flesh and blood more passive in its extradition to the other than the passivity of the effect in a causal chain; as tearing-away-from-oneself-for-the-other in giving-to-the-other-the-bread-from-one's-mouth, identity here indicts itself neither in the confirmation of self by self, nor by self-coincidence, nor by repose in itself, but precisely by the *accusation* that summons me, the unique me, that summons me and not the Ego in me; an accusation that summons me without there being anyone to answer in my stead. As Dostoyevsky writes, "every one of us is guilty before all, for everyone and everything, and I more than others. . . ."[7]

4. Testimony

The one-for-the-other of subjectivity, unlike the generosity of a voluntary act (which would, all things considered, resuscitate intentionality, representational and taking initiatives), but all at once like extradition to the other. Responsibility for the other does not amount to a beginning: my relation with another freedom does not fit into a free decision. The two freedoms cannot be gathered in a presence. Responsibility for the other precedes every decision, it is before the origin. An-archy. Here, the without-beginning is nevertheless not the bad infinity of the extrapolation of the present by pure negation, since responsibility moves positively toward the other. A responsibility in which obligation increases in obedience while culpability augments with saintliness – an infinity which therefore is not simply that of a *Sollen*, which is asymptotic with its Ideal located at infinity, at the infinity of the bad infinite. A glorious Infinite.[8] The infinite would not know how to enter into appearance – to become a phenomenon – to become a theme without letting itself be contained, without accepting limits in immanence. This refusal to appear is thus, positively, the very responsibility for the other, anterior to every memorable present, coming from a past that was never present, that was never the freedom of a subject, ordering me to the other, to the first to come along, to the neighbor, without showing itself to me, but entering me by the simple effect of traumatism, by breaking and entering. My responsibility for the other is precisely this relation with an unthematizable Infinity. It is neither the experience of Infinity nor proof of it: it *testifies* to Infinity.

This *testimony* is not appended to a "subjective experience" in order to proclaim the ontological "conjuncture" disclosed to the subject. This testimony belongs to the very glory of the Infinite. The infinity of responsibility happens precisely as the dissipation of every secret, as the rupture of every interiority, wherein the subject, protected from obsession with the other, might escape. The glory of the Infinite is the egress of the subject from the dark corners of its *reserve*, which might offer an escape route from the summons of the other – like the thickets of Paradise wherein after sinning Adam hid, hearing the voice of God "moving through the garden from the way whence comes the day."[9] Glory is the response to the summons without any possible evasion, a surprise to the respondent himself, but by which, driven out, he develops sincerity or Saying. Indeed, sincerity is not an attribute of the Saying. It is the Saying that, unencumbered by any possessions in being, achieves the extradition of sincerity.[10] No Said recovers sincerity, and none is adequate to it. Saying without said, apparently a talking for nothing, a sign given to the other, "as simple as 'hello,'" and, within the Saying, a sign given of this giving of a sign – the pure transparency of a confession – testimony.

The Saying as testimony precedes all saying. The Saying, before stating a Said – and even the Saying of a Said – is the approach of the other and already testimony. The vocative neither harbors nor expresses its ultimate meaning. In the sign given in every proposition said to the other (for whom I am responsible and before whom I am responsible), I expose myself to the summons of this responsibility as though placed under a blazing sun that eradicates every residue of mystery, every ulterior motive, every loosening of the thread that would allow evasion – already sincere, testifying to the Infinite, not in relating it as a fact, but in unfolding, by the rupture of silence, its very glory, in breaking open the secret of Gyges,[11] the invisible-seeing-subject (*sujet-voyant-invisible*).

The glory of the Infinite does not, therefore, come to affect me as would a representation, nor as would an interlocutor in a "dialogue," before *which* or before *whom* I locate myself. It commands me from my own mouth. Interiority is precisely this reversal: the eminently exterior or the transcendent, by reason of this eminence, disproportionate to the present of the theme, not being able to be "contained," nor being able to appear, nor coming from an interlocutor, concerns me and surrounds me as a commandment speaking from my mouth. A commandment pronounced from the mouth of the one it commands – exceptional structure, and certainly unique. The very exception to the rule of Being. There is no testimony but that of the Infinite.

This is no psychological wonder but the modality according to which the Infinite comes to pass, signifying through the one to whom it signifies, ordering through the one to whom it orders. Not just an incomprehensible inconsistency or ruse of the Infinite resorting to the medium of humans to reveal itself, and to their psalms to glorify itself – but the very way in which the Infinite passes the finite, or the way in which it comes to pass.

That the Infinite comes to pass in the Saying is what lets the Saying be understood as irreducible to one psychological act among others, by which – we know not why – man would double and surpass his thoughts. True, one can show how and why a Saying must be the Saying of a Said, the exchange of information corresponding to "vital necessities." But the Saying without the Said, a sign given to the Other (*Autrui*), is not appended, as information, to a prior "experience" of the Infinite, as though there could be an experience of the Infinite. In the Saying, by which the subject, driven out, leaves its clandestinity, the Infinite comes to pass. Language, a sign given to the other, is sincerity or veracity, according to which glory is glorified. The Infinite thus has glory only through subjectivity, through the human adventure of the approach of the other, through substitution for the other, through the expiation of the other.

That the way in which the Infinite passes the finite should have an ethical sense does not issue from a project of constructing the "transcendental foundation" of ethical experience. The ethical is the field wherein the very paradox of an Infinite in relation to the finite is significant, without faltering in this relation. Testified to – and not thematized – in the sign given to the other, the Infinite signifies on the basis of responsibility for the other (*autrui*), of the one-for-the-other, of a subject supporting everything – subject to everything – that is, suffering for everyone, but bearing the burden of everything without ever having had the chance to decide whether to take on this burden, gloriously amplifying itself to the extent that it is imposed. An obedience that precedes any hearkening unto the commandment. The possibility of finding, anachronously, the order within obedience itself, and of receiving the order from oneself – this reversal of heteronomy into autonomy is the very way in which the Infinite comes to pass – all of which the metaphor of inscribing the law in consciousness expresses in a remarkable manner, reconciling autonomy and heteronomy (in an ambivalence, of which diachrony is the very meaning, and which, in the present, is ambiguity). An inscription of the order in the *for-the-other* of obedience; an anarchic affection that slips into me "like a thief," through the nets extended by consciousness; a traumatism that surprised me absolutely; the order *has never been represented*, for it has never presented itself – not even in the past that comes forth in remembrance – to the point that it is I who says only – and after the fact – this unheard-of obligation. An ambivalence that is the exception and the subjectivity of the subject, its very psychism, the possibility of inspiration: to be the author of what was, *without my knowledge*, inspired in me – to have received, whence we know not, that of which I am the author. In the responsibility for the other, we are at the heart of this ambiguity of inspiration. The unheard-of saying is enigmatic in its an-archic response, in my responsibility for the other. This ambiguity within the subject is the trace of the infinite, alternately beginning and intermediary, the diachronic ambivalence that makes ethics possible.

5. Testimony and Prophecy

One can call prophecy this reversal whereby the perception of the *order* coincides with the meaning of this order, made up by the one who obeys it. Thus prophecy would be the very psychism of the soul: the other within the same; and all of man's spirituality would thereby be prophetic. The infinite does not announce itself in the testimony as a theme. In the sign given to the other whereby I am torn away from the secret of Gyges, in the Saying without the Said of sincerity, in my "here I am"[12] immediately present in the accusative – I testify to the Infinite. The Infinite is not *before* the witness but rather as though it were outside presence or on the "reverse side" of presence, already past, beyond the grasp: an ulterior motive too elevated to thrust itself to the fore. "Here I am in the name of God," without directly referring myself to a presence. The sentence in which God comes forth, for the first time, and mingles with words, cannot be expressed: "I believe in God." Testifying to God does not consist in stating this extra-ordinary word or phrase, as though glory could be located within a theme, could be made into an essence of being. A sign given to the other of this very giving of a sign, "here I am" signifies me in the name of God, in the service of men, without my having anything by which to identify myself, save the sound of my voice or the movement of my gestures – the saying itself. A recurrence that is not a reflection on oneself. It is just the opposite of the return to the self, of self-consciousness. Recurrence is sincerity, effusion of the self, "extradition" of the self to the neighbor. One might, at the limit, pronounce the word *prayer* here – testimony, kerygma, confession, humility; but what is essential therefore lies – what a disappointment for those friends of the truth that thematizes being and for those of the subject that effaces itself before being! – in the fact that the responses are only heard in the demands, that the "provocation" that comes from God is in my invocation, that gratitude is already gratitude for that state of gratitude. The transcendence of revelation lies precisely in the fact that the epiphany comes, in the Saying, from the one who receives the revelation. The order that orders me leaves me no possibility of putting things right side up – of returning to the exteriority of the infinite as one returns to the exteriority of a theme. It is in prophecy that the Infinite eludes objectivation and dialogue and signifies as *illeity* in the third person, but according to a "tertiality" different from that of the third man, from the third that interrupts the face-to-face of the welcome to the other man, and by which justice arises.

The Infinite ordains the "neighbor" for me without exposing itself to me, especially as proximity draws in. An order that was not the *cause* of my response, nor even a question that would have preceded it in a dialogue; an order that I find in my response itself, in the "here I am" that brought me out of the shadows, where my responsibility could have been eluded, which, consequently, belongs to the very glory to which it testifies. *Illeity* is that direction of the "I know not whence," of that which comes without showing itself, of the nonphenomenon and, consequently, of the nonpresent, of a past that was never a present, of an order to which I am subjected before hearing it or that I hear in my own saying. The anachronism of the prophet more paradoxical, according to the retrievable time of recollection, than the prediction of the future. "Before they call, I will answer,"[13] a phrase to be understood literally: in approaching the neighbor, I am always late for the appointed time. But this singular obedience, without agreement or understanding, this allegiance prior to any oath – responsibility prior to engagement – is, precisely, the *other-in-the-same*, inspiration, prophecy – the pneuma of the soul.

I can, certainly, also give myself the God testified to as a Said. An extra-ordinary expression, the only one not to extinguish the Saying in the Said; a Said unique in its genre, fitting neither into grammatical categories as a word (neither a proper nor a common noun), nor into the rules of logic as meaningful (an excluded third of being and nothingness). But a *Said* that receives its meaning from testimony and which thematization betrays in theology by introducing it into a system of language, into the order of the Said, wherein its expression immediately inter-dicts itself (*s'inter-dit*). Thematization, certainly indispensable – for the meaning itself to take shape – a sophism inevitably committed wherever philosophy arises – but a betrayal that philosophy must reduce. A reduction that continually must be attempted because of the trace of sincerity that the words themselves bear. A testimony borne by every saying as sincerity, even when it is a Saying of a Said that the Said dissimulates; but a dissimulation that the saying always seeks to unsay (*dédire*) – which is its ultimate veracity. In the game that activates the cultural keyboard of language, sincerity and testimony signify through the very ambiguity of every said, through the greeting[14] it offers to the other (*autrui*) – the resounding "in the name of God" of all language. But prophecy, through its ambiguities, is not the last resort of a lame revelation. It belongs to the glory of the Infinite. That the prophecy should be able to take on the appearance of a subjective Saying, arising in the subject or in the influences to which the subject is submitted – to begin with, those influences stemming from the subject's physiology – there lies the enigma – the ambiguity – of transcendence. Transcendence would vanish in the very proof we would like to give of it; the Infinite would enter into conjunction with the subject who discloses it. Transcendence is obliged to interrupt the essence of being, to reach the world even while signifying the beyond of being. It needs ambiguity – a frontier at once ineffaceable and finer than the outline (*le tracé*) of an ideal line.

Notes

1   Cf. M. Heidegger, *Being and Time*, § 65 (*Endlichkeit*), §38 (*Geworfenheit*) § 44 (*Wahrheit*), §§46ff. (*Sein zum Tode*).
2   *Ideas* § 104, 113–15, Husserl refers to Brentano in §85. Cf. Brentano's *Psychologie von empirischen Standpunkt* (Hamburg: Meiner, 1874); trans. A. C. Rancurello et at., *Psychology from an Empirical Standpoint* (London: Routledge, 1973). Cf. also Levinas TIP 91–7; TIH 57–61.
3   Levinas probably intends a double entendre in using *la question* for an interrogation under torture. Has the philosophical critique of testimonial truth in its various (for instance, religious) forms not suppressed the most important question (the question of the Good)?
4   With the expression *le dire*, which can be read as a synonym for "to testify" or "to give testimony," Levinas makes a transition to his technical use of the expression *le Dire*, as explained in chap. 1 of *Otherwise than Being*, trans. Alphonso Lingis (Pittsburgh: Duquesne University Press, 1998).
5   See Plato, *Republic* 508e; Plotinus, Enneads VI, 9.
6   Levinas refers here to p. 279 of "Au-delà de l'essence," published in *Revue de Métaphysique et de Morale* 75 (1970), pp. 265–83. The quote does not appear on p. 279, however, but a somewhat different version is found on p. 273. This version, again slightly changed, appears also in chap. 1 of *Otherwise than Being*, AE 12; OB 10.
7   F. Dostoyevsky, *The Brothers Karamazov*, trans. D. Magarshack (Harmondsworth: Penguin, 1984), vol. 1, p. 339. (Translation modified to reflect the French translation given by Levinas. The English translation reads: "every one of us is responsible for everyone else in every way, and I most of all.")

8 The "glory" of Jahweh indicates the epiphany of God's majesty and sanctity. Cf., for example, Exodus 14:18; 16:7–10; 24:15ff.; 33:18; 39:21–9; Isaiah 6:1ff.; 35:1–4; 44:23.

9 Genesis 3:8. The translation reflects that of Levinas in the French. The King James translation reads: "walking in the garden in the cool of the day."

10 Levinas adds here the following note: After or before the lies that the Saying undergoes in the Said – in the words and verbal indifference in which information is exchanged – pious vows issue forth – and responsibilities are avoided.

11 Cf. Plato, *Republic* 359c–360d.

12 *Me voici.*

13 Isaiah 65:24. Levinas's translation insists on "me": "Avant qu'ils appellent, moi, je repondrai."

14 The "salut" in "le salut qu'il rend à autrui" means at the same time "greeting" and "salvation."

18

WORD GIVING, WORD TAKING

Catherine Z. Elgin

We live, sociologists tell us, in an information age. People continually impart information, purporting to speak with authority. "Take my word for it," they urge. "You can rely on me." Nevertheless, it is not altogether clear what it is to take someone's word or when it is reasonable to do so. In investigating such matters, a good place to start is *The Realm of Rights*, where Judith Jarvis Thomson provides an insightful discussion of word giving. She advocates accepting

The Assertion Thesis: *Y* gives *X* his or her word that a proposition is true if and only if *Y* asserts that proposition to *X*, and

(i)   in so doing *Y* is inviting *X* to rely on its truth, and
(ii) *X* receives and accepts the invitation (there is uptake).[1]

If the Assertion Thesis is correct, word giving requires two parties: a word giver and a word taker. The word giver issues an invitation; the word taker accepts it, thereby acquiring a right. In particular, she acquires a claim against the word giver, a claim that is infringed if the proposition in question is not true.

Thomson focuses on promising, where the moral dimension of word giving is particularly salient. But she recognizes that there are other modes of word giving as well. In what follows, I use her account as a springboard for investigating a different species of word giving, the one that epistemologists (perhaps misleadingly) label testimony. I do not want to endorse everything Thomson says about word giving. But appreciating the virtues of theft over honest toil, I propose to steal what I can use from her analysis. With her unwitting help, I hope to shed some light on the epistemology of testimony.

Catherine Z. Elgin, "Word Giving, Word Taking," in *Fact and Value: Essays for Judith Jarvis Thomson*, ed. Alex Byrne, Robert Stalnaker, Ralph Wedgwood (Cambridge, Mass.: MIT Press, 2001), pp. 97–116. © 2001 by MIT Press. Reprinted by permission of MIT Press.

Testimony is a mechanism for information transfer. Here are some examples: The guide says, "The cave paintings at Les Eyzies are 14,000 years old." The reporter announces, "The Dow lost twenty-three points today on heavy trading." The physician warns, "Obesity increases the risk of heart attack." The passerby obliges with directions, "The museum is two blocks down, on the left." In each case, the speaker represents herself as in a position to speak with authority. Although she intimates that her assertion is backed by epistemically adequate reasons, she does not supply them. Testimony, then, conveys information without supplying arguments or evidence to back it up.[2] To be sure, an idle assertive aside could do that. But because testimony is a mode of word giving, it does more. The testifier invites her word receiver to believe on the basis of her say-so. She assures him that her testimony is true. Should her testimony turn out to be false, she will have done him a wrong.

If we understand the nature of that wrong, we get a handle on what the good of testimony is, what benefits it provides. Here the contrast with promising is helpful. Promising provides a framework for voluntarily restricting one's freedom. It facilitates planning and fosters cooperation. Thomson identifies several characteristics of the type of word giving that constitutes promising. (1) Promising is future directed. The propositions whose truth a promisor commits herself to are in the future tense. I can promise that I will eat my spinach. But if I give my word that I am now eating my spinach or that I ate my spinach yesterday, my word giving is not a case of promising. (2) Promising has the promisor as its subject. I can promise that I will eat my spinach. I can promise that I will do my best to get Sam to eat his spinach. But I cannot promise that he will eat his spinach. The reason, evidently, is that no act or omission of mine can ensure his compliance. Promising, then, is essentially first personal. (3) Only a limited range of acts or refrainings or states of affairs fall within the scope of promising. I cannot promise that I will live to be 150, for I lack the capacity to bring that about.[3] Taken together, these features show that promising is restricted to future contingents that are within the agent's power. To the extent that it is indeterminate which states of affairs are contingent in the relevant sense, and which of those are within an agent's power, the scope of promising is indeterminate as well.

Testimony consists of statements of (purportedly) established fact. It has no restrictions as to tense or person. I can testify that Woodrow Wilson was president of Princeton University, that $E = mc^2$, that I am a resident of Massachusetts. I can't testify that I will eat my spinach, though, for despite my best intentions, I might not. Future contingents then lie outside the scope of testimony. But not all statements about the future are excluded. If a prediction is so grounded in established facts and laws that its truth is not up for grabs, it can be the content of testimony. A scientist can testify that a sample of plutonium will continue to emit radiation for hundreds of thousands of years, since established physical facts and laws ensure that the prediction is true. They may, of course, be some question as to what facts and laws are capable of underwriting testimony about the future. So whether a particular prediction qualifies as testimony may be controversial. But a statement's being in the future tense does not automatically rule it out.

Talk of future contingents and freedom to act is apt to induce flutters of metaphysical anxiety. Is the future genuinely open? Is it open in the ways that we think it is? Do we even have a clear conception of what it means to say that it is? Are human beings genuinely free to choose and able to act as they choose? Are we free and able in the ways that we think we are? Do we have a clear conception of what that means? These are legitimate questions whose answers are by no means obvious. If we have to answer them correctly in order to explicate word giving, our prospects are bleak. Luckily, I think we need not do anything so ambitious. Promising, testimony, and other modes of word giving are human practices. They depend for their utility not on what is *really* the case with regard to contingency or human freedom but on shared assumptions about these matters. Even if human beings can, through a sheer act of will, live to be a hundred and fifty years old, no one believes that we can do this. So we are unwilling either to make or to accept a promise to live that long. Even if a psychologist's predictions about infants' eventual career choices have as high an objective probability as physicists' predictions about radioactive decay, we do not believe that psychological predictions are anywhere near that good. So a responsible psychologist would not proffer, nor would we accept, such a prediction as testimony. Promising, testimony, and other modes of word giving are circumscribed by shared, commonsensical assumptions about metaphysical matters. Many of these assumptions are vague and inarticulate. Some, no doubt, are false. But because they are shared, they supply the mutual understanding that we need for the issuing and accepting of invitations to rely on a statement's truth.

To explicate testimony and promising, we need to recognize the shared metaphysical assumptions that underwrite them. We understand a good deal about practices when we see how those assumptions function. If everyone agrees that people have the ability to return books that they borrow, we permit one another to promise to return books and hold them responsible for their failures to do so. If everyone agrees that some people are cognitively competent to calculate the rate of radioactive decay and to report the results of their calculations accurately, we count suitable assertions about such matters as testimony and consider testifiers blameworthy if their reports are wrong. By reference to the presuppositions in effect, then, we can make sense of the actions, motivations, and assessments they give rise to.

"Ought" implies "can." If a person cannot do *p*, he is under no obligation to do *p*, and cannot rightly be faulted for failing to do *p*. Appeal to shared presuppositions explains why we hold people responsible when we do. But if the presuppositions are wildly off the mark, we may be holding people responsible when in fact they are not. Doubtless we sometimes hold people responsible for things they could not avoid. Probably some of our mistakes are due to our faulty views about matters like freedom, agency, and contingency. Still, our word-giving practices are remarkably successful. People frequently behave in the ways they promised they would. Experts often convey information that later events bear out. This suggests that however inaccurate the underlying assumptions are, they are not so far off that they discredit our word-giving practices entirely. I suggest, then, that we bracket concerns about metaphysical underpinnings and proceed on the assumption that our word-giving practices are reasonably well founded and do pretty much what we take them to do.

If I promise you that I will eat my spinach, I give you my word that "I will eat my spinach" is true. I give you a right to expect that I will eat my spinach. Of course, you already had *a* right to expect that. Freedom of thought ensures that you have the right to expect anything you like. You want to expect that I will eat my spinach?

Who's going to stop you? But if an expectation grounded in nothing but freedom of thought is unfulfilled, no one is to blame. When I make a promise, the situation is different. I give you a claim against me. Ceteris paribus, if despite my promise, your expectation is unfulfilled, I am at fault. I gave you a reason to expect that I would eat my spinach, a reason that you otherwise would not have had. In giving you that reason, I increased your warrant for the belief that I will eat my spinach. You have a claim against me, then, because I altered your epistemic circumstances. This epistemic element to promising is, I suggest, what converts the bare right into a claim.

A claim, Thomson argues, is a behavioral constraint. In giving you a claim against me, I agree to keep my behavior within particular bounds.[4] In promising to eat my spinach, I agree to constrain my future behavior so as to include spinach consumption in it. The burden I shoulder is to make "I will eat my spinach" true. Plainly, I am up to the task. But I can testify to all sorts of things that I am utterly powerless to effect. I might, for example, testify that the cave paintings in Les Eyzies are 14,000 years old. Clearly, there is no way that I can make that statement true. The question arises: In so testifying, what claim do I give? How is my behavior constrained? If I don't eat my spinach when I promised that I would, I am subject to censure for failure to eat my spinach. But if the cave paintings are not 14,000 years old, it's hardly my fault. There is no way I can bring it about that the paintings are as old as I say they are. "Ought" implies "can." If I cannot make it the case that the paintings are 14,000 years old, I am under no obligation to do so, and should not be faulted for failing to do so.

Nonetheless, I can be faulted. Why? Perhaps the most obvious answer is causal. My testimony that p caused you to believe that p. So, it might seem that I am to blame for your harboring a false belief. But I can cause you to believe that p in any number of innocent ways. You might, for example, overhear me rehearsing my lines for a play, mistake my utterance for an assertion, and so come to believe what you take me to assert. Although my utterance of p caused your belief, the mistake is surely yours. I am not responsible for your misconstruing my speech act and acquiring a false belief as a result. Maybe a more complicated causal story is needed. Perhaps I am to blame for your falsely believing that p if you come to believe that p because you rightly believe that I believe that p. This is more plausible, but it still won't do. Suppose you overhear me sincerely asserting that p, and rightly conclude that I believe that p. You therefore form the belief that p, on the basis of my assertion. What you don't realize, though, is that I am speaking to my therapist, and that my assertion is (and indeed, I recognize that it is) one of the baseless beliefs that I am in therapy to overcome. Although I have plenty of evidence that $\sim p$, I cannot disabuse myself of the belief that p, having been taught that p at a particularly impressionable age. Again, it seems that I am not at fault for your mistake. It is not enough that I cause you to believe that p or even that I cause you to believe that p by causing you to recognize that I believe that p. I am responsible for your error, not when I cause you to believe that p, but when I entitle you to believe that p. I convey to you not just a belief, but a right to believe. As in promising, you already have a right – a moral right – to believe whatever you like. But neither that right alone nor that right in conjunction with a causal story of how you came to believe gives you a claim against me. You have a claim against me because I invite you to take my word. I volunteer to shoulder the epistemic burden. Testimony, like promising, is a liability-shouldering device.[5]

In testifying that p, I implicate that you can rely on me. For what? Let's look again at promising. When I break my promise, it is not because I failed to eat my spinach simpliciter that I am to blame. People are, in general, under no obligation to eat their spinach. I am to blame because I failed to eat my spinach *having given my word that I would*. Similarly, I am not to blame for the fact that the cave paintings are not 14,000 years old, but for the fact that they are not 14,000 years old *when I gave my word that they are*. In both cases, it seems, what is at issue is a conjunction of the form:

p & Y gives her word to X that p.

The promisor can affect the truth value of each conjunct. She can either bring it about that p or she can refrain from giving her word that p. The testifier can affect only the second. So the locus of blame may be different.[6] The promise breaker is subject to reproach for failing to keep her word. In the case of testimony, there is no question of keeping one's word. Rather, the locus of responsibility lies in the word giving itself. When I promise you that p, the claim I give you constrains my future behavior. I commit myself to behaving in the future so as to ensure the truth of p. When I testify to you that p, the claim I give you manifests a constraint on my current behavior. I present myself as having the resources to underwrite your reliance on p. If p turns out to be false, I am to blame, since I invited you to rely on the truth of p, and I implicated that I was in a position to issue such reliance. The false testifier is blameworthy for having given her word in the first place, for having invited the word taker to rely on it. The proper reproach then is something like: "You shouldn't have said it if you weren't sure." False testimony is morally wrong because it is epistemically wrong.

It is irresponsible to invite someone to rely on your word when your word is not reliable. But when is that? One might think that a person's word is reliable whenever what she says is true, and is unreliable whenever what she says is false. In that case, my promise is reliable whenever I do what I promise to, and unreliable whenever I do not. It is not clear that we should say this, though. Suppose I promised to meet you at the railroad station at 5 P.M., but I had no intention of keeping my promise. Or suppose that although I intended to keep my word, I was obviously unlikely to be able to do so. (In the last five years, the noon train from New York has almost never been on time, as it would have to be for me to arrive in time to keep my promise.) As it turned out, though, my train was early, so I encountered you in the station at five o'clock. Thomson contends that I infringed no claim of yours, since I kept my word. She takes it that the claim my promise gives you lies in the truth of p, and thus is not infringed so long as p turns out to be true.[7] This may be so.[8] But it seems plain that you ought not to have counted on me. It was too nearly a coincidence that we met at the appointed time and place. My word was unreliable. Similarly, if I testified on inadequate grounds that the prehistoric cave paintings served a religious purpose, even if it turns out that my assertion is true, my word was unreliable. You ought not to have relied on it.

Should we say, nevertheless, that my testimony did not infringe your claim? Even if Thomson is right about promising, I do not think that we should. To see why, we need to consider the point of each practice. Promising is future directed and action oriented. Because we in fact met at the station at five o'clock, I did what you were counting on me to do. Hence I did not cause your plans to go awry. Whether or not I ought to have given my word as I did, I arguably infringed no claim, for I (*per accidens*, to be sure) kept my word. Testimony's epistemological function is more central, since testimony serves as a conduit of epistemic entitlement. A speaker cannot convey epistemic entitlement if she has none. And the mere fact that her statement is true is not enough to epistemically entitle her to it. It could just be a lucky guess. If, purely on a hunch, I testify that the cave paintings served a religious purpose, I am not epistemically entitled to say what I do; hence I have no epistemic entitlement to convey to you. This suggests that a testifier infringes a word taker's claim when she testifies to something for which she lacks sufficient grounds.

Let's look at it from the word taker's perspective. If I believe someone's testimony, it is because I believe she speaks with authority, and if it is reasonable for me to believe her testimony, it is reasonable for me to believe that she speaks with authority. In believing she speaks with authority, I don't believe merely that she believes what she says. Nor do I believe merely that she has what she takes to be adequate grounds for her remarks. Rather, to take her word for something involves believing that she has what are in fact adequate grounds. The question then is what constitutes adequate grounds? A seemingly obvious answer is that adequate grounds consist of evidence or reasons that are in fact sufficient to support the assertions that constitute the testimony. But this is not enough. Unless there is good reason to think that the evidence or reasons are adequate, we should not take her word. Suppose a blood test reveals the presence of antibodies that are in fact antibodies to a newly discovered virus. Skeptical worries aside, the antibodies are sufficient evidence of the virus. Dr. No testifies on the basis of the blood test that Zeb has the virus. Unless there is consensus in the medical community that the antibodies in question are the antibodies to that particular virus, Dr. No, although speaking the truth and having what is in fact adequate evidence, does not speak with authority. Until the connection between the antibodies and the virus is established to the satisfaction of the medical community, we ought not take her word.

Should we take someone's word if the evidence she relies on satisfies the standards of the relevant epistemically reputable community, even if the evidence turns out to be misleading? Suppose Professor Cro testifies on the basis of the best available evidence – evidence that satisfies the paleoanthropological community – that the cave paintings are 14,000 years old. The best currently available evidence is circumstantial. There is, to be sure, a margin of error in the dates paleontologists assign. But the experts are confident that 14,000 years old is about the right age, and they have good reason for their confidence. Suppose, though, that they are wrong. If the paintings are in fact 15,000 years old (an age that lies outside the acknowledged margin of error), should we consider Professor Cro epistemically blameworthy for having testified as she did? Does her testimony infringe a claim?

We can and should hold people blameworthy for testifying on the basis of insufficient evidence. If purely on the basis of anecdotal evidence or an experiment run on just twelve subjects, a scientist were to testify that drinking green tea cures poison ivy, we would consider him epistemically remiss. But arguably, the case we are considering is different, for Professor Cro had what everyone concedes was excellent evidence. We might, of course, take a hard-line. You have a right to remain silent, so anything you say can be held against you. Despite the best efforts of the community of paleontologists, which were in fact quite good, Professor Cro testified falsely, and thereby misled scholars who took her word. Hard-liners insist that responsible testimony, like knowledge, requires truth. If so, she should not have testified as she did.

If we take the hard-line, false testimony violates a right, even if at the time of the testimony there was no reason to believe it false and overwhelming reason to believe it true. Perhaps the counterexample to a highly confirmed universal generalization had not yet even arisen. Perhaps the methods required to discredit it had not yet been developed. Nevertheless, if I give you my word that p, and in fact $\sim p$, I infringe your claim. Such a hard-line might seem to violate the maxim "Ought implies can." If I genuinely could not have known that p is false, and/or that the evidence for p is misleading, then I was under no obligation to deny that p. Hence, it may seem, I ought not be faulted for testifying that p. But things are not so simple. For I need not have testified at all. Perhaps I could not have known that p is false. But I surely could have known − indeed, surely did know − that p might be false. I could simply have held my tongue. "Ought implies can" then does not directly discredit the hard-line.

We can avoid imparting falsehoods by exercising our epistemic Miranda rights. In scholarly circles, testimony cannot be compelled. But withholding testimony has a price. In hoarding information, we lose opportunities to advance understanding through education, collaboration, testing and building on other people's findings. It is irresponsible to testify without adequate evidence. It may be equally irresponsible to be excessively demanding in matters of evidence. There is a familiar tension between the desire for well-grounded information and the requirement that the information consist entirely of truths. Reasonable levels of evidence tend to be satisfied by falsehoods as well as truths. If we raise our standards enough to eliminate the falsehoods, cognitively valuable truths are excluded as well. The parallel to arguments that push us toward skepticism is plain. We can avoid judging falsely by refraining from judging at all. We can avoid testifying falsely by refraining from testifying at all. But refusing to believe and refusing to testify are cognitively costly. The risk of error is sometimes worth taking. Nevertheless, if the hard-line is correct, I put myself morally and epistemically at risk every time I testify. That gives me an incentive to increase the level of evidence I demand. To protect myself from inadvertent wrongdoing, I don't just want adequate grounds. I want grounds that I am sure are adequate. That is a more demanding standard. It may be an unsatisfiable one. If Dr. Cro was blameworthy, despite that fact that the test needed to discredit her report had not even been invented at the time she testified, I should hardly be complacent merely because my remarks satisfy contemporary standards. The worry is that the hard-line, by supplying a disincentive to testify, stifles information transfer at the cutting edge of inquiry.

A similar worry can be raised about promising. If my failure to keep my promise, for whatever reason, puts me morally in the wrong, I should be extremely circumspect about making promises. Before I give my word I should be absolutely sure I can deliver. Unfortunately, I cannot be absolutely sure. Neither can anyone else. Should we stop making promises? Given the utility of the practice, that seems a high price to pay. Luckily, we don't have to pay it. Granted, we shouldn't give our word cavalierly, but obsessive caution is not required. When I make you a promise, we both recognize that

I *might* not be able to keep it. Unforeseen circumstances might interfere. Even if I am scrupulous about my moral character, that recognition should not prevent me from giving my word. For part of the institution of promising is that there are forgivable lapses and acceptable excuses. If I failed to keep my promise to meet you to go comparison shopping for grass seed, I infringed the claim I gave you. But if the reason for my absence was that I was negotiating with a deranged student who was holding the dean hostage, my failure to keep my word is excusable. Perhaps I owe you an explanation, but it is not clear that I owe you an apology, since we agree, and know that we agree, that that sort of demand on one's time takes precedence.

We might want to say the same about testimony. Although truth is required and falsehood infringes the word taker's claim, there are forgivable lapses and acceptable excuses. You exonerate me for breaking my promise, saying, "You couldn't have known." My lapse is excusable, for there was no way I could have foreseen the hostage situation that prevented me from keeping my word. The message is this: Had you known that q when you said what you did, you would have been seriously remiss. But since you couldn't have known, you are morally off the hook. We might want to make the same sort of move in the case of false but well-grounded testimony. Had Professor Cro known that the cave paintings were 15,000 years old, or had more accurate dating methods been available, she would have been seriously remiss when she testified that they are 14,000 years old. But since she couldn't have known – since the requisite ferrous oxide dating test will not be developed for another fifty years – her lapse is excusable. We can then retain the hard-line requirement that the content of testimony must be true, while weakening the disincentive to testify by conceding that some false testimony is excusable.

Still, one might wonder whether the truth requirement is an idle wheel. In deciding whether it is reasonable to give or accept testimony that p, we consider whether the assertion that p is well grounded. Even though we recognize that well-groundedness is no assurance of truth, we don't and can't go on to ask the further question: Besides being well grounded, is p also true? For our best hope of discovering whether p is true lies in discovering whether p is well grounded. Current standards of acceptability are the best standards we have for deciding that. It makes no sense, then, to construe the truth requirement as an additional factor that figures in the decision whether to give or to accept testimony that p. Nevertheless, it does not follow that the truth requirement is idle. It may play a different role. Testimony is responsibly proffered and accepted when it satisfies the current standards of the relevant epistemically reputable community of inquiry. Subsequently, new evidence, improved techniques, or refined standards may lead us to conclude that previously accepted testimony is false. If its being false is a sufficient reason to reject it as error, we have the resources to construe revisions in beliefs, methods, and standards as improvements rather than mere changes in our understanding. If the best we can say is that p satisfied the standards accepted at one time but not those accepted at a later time, we do not have such resources. For in that case changes in what it is reasonable to believe or to testify are like changes in fashion. Sometimes one standard or skirt length is in style, sometimes another. A truth requirement is not the only requirement that could play this role, nor is it clearly the best choice.[9] But some such requirement is needed to distinguish advancing understanding from changing intellectual fashions.

Word giving, according to Thomson, requires uptake. The invitee, she says, needs to receive and accept the invitation to rely on the truth of *p*. But, it seems, we are inundated with testimony we have no use for. Textbooks, news reports, lectures, and gossip supply vast amounts of seemingly useless information. Does this discredit Thomson's account? To decide, we need to consider what accepting an invitation involves. To accept my invitation to dinner on Sunday at seven requires appearing for dinner on the appointed day at roughly the appointed time. To accept my invitation to call on me if you need help is different. You accept my invitation if you henceforth consider yourself free to call – if, that is, you adjust your attitudes so that asking me for help is now a live option. You may turn out not to need my help. But even if no call is made, the invitation is accepted. Testifiers issue invitations of both kinds. My testimony may provide you with the specific information you need for a particular purpose. I inform you that in the 1760s Hume was a diplomat in Paris. Relying on my expertise, you incorporate that information into your history of Scottish thought. But not all information transfer is on a need-to-know basis. I make the same remark in an introductory philosophy lecture. I invite my students to rely on its truth, just as I invited you. Most of them will do nothing with it. They have nothing to rely on it for. In my lecture I, as it were, issue an open invitation. I invite my students to rely on the truth of my assertion when and if they need to. If they are prepared to do so, they accept my invitation. Both of these sorts of reliance fit Thomson's model easily. The argument that we receive vast amounts of useless information does not discredit her analysis.

What should we say about proffered testimony that is flatly disbelieved? The invitation to rely is issued, received, and refused. Should we say that such testimony is abortive? If so, there is no word giving without word taking. This seems wrong. The suspect's mother asserts under oath that he was home watching television at the time the crime was committed. No one believes her. Still, it seems, she testifies that he was home. (She couldn't be charged with perjury if she didn't testify.) But simply to jettison the uptake requirement also seems wrong. If my students sleep through the lecture where I assert that Hume was a diplomat, or I make that assertion in a language they don't understand, we would be reluctant to say that I gave them my word that Hume was a diplomat. They can't take my word for it, since they have no idea what my word is. I recommend, then, that the uptake requirement be modified. Testimony is abortive, I suggest, unless the invitation is received. But the invitation need not be accepted. Receiving an invitation to rely on the truth of an assertion is not just having one's sense organs stimulated by the assertion. To receive such an invitation requires understanding the content of the assertion, recognizing it as an assertion, and acknowledging that one has been invited to rely on its truth. This in turn involves recognizing that it has been put forth as having appropriate epistemic backing. I suggest that testimony occurs when a statement of purportedly established fact is offered as someone's word and the offer is understood, recognized, and acknowledged, whether or not it is believed.

When I testify that *p*, what do I invite you to take my word for? The obvious answer is that I invite you to take my word that the sentence I utter – the sentence that replaces the schematic letter *p* – is true. This can't be right, though. For I can give you my word that the cave paintings are 14,000 years old by uttering any of a variety of syntactically and semantically divergent sentences, as well as via contextually appropriate nods, gestures, and inarticulate grunts. I might, for example,

(1) assert, "The cave paintings at Les Eyzies are 14,000 years old."
(2) assert, "At Les Eyzies, the cave paintings are 14,000 years old."
(3) assert, "14K years ago the cave paintings at Les Eyzies were painted."
(4) respond to the question, "How old are they?" by saying, "14,000 years old."
(5) nod when asked, "Are you testifying that they are 14,000 years old?"

As testimony, (1)–(5) amount to the same thing. I issue the same invitation, I shoulder the same epistemic burden, regardless of which of the five I use. The common denominator, Thomson believes, is the proposition they all express. According to Thomson, I invite you to take my word, not for the sentence, if any, that I utter, but for the proposition that I assert.[10] Like Goodman and Quine, I have doubts about the existence of propositions. So I am disinclined to accept this part of Thomson's analysis. But even if we eschew propositions, we are not forced to conclude that every difference between sentences uttered constitutes a difference in the content they convey. Sameness of proposition is not the only criterion of semantic equivalence for sentences. Other, more flexible criteria are available. We might follow Goodman and Scheffler and explicate the equivalence of (1)–(5) in terms of secondary extension.[11] Then (1)–(5) amount to the same thing because they are all that-the-caves-paintings-at-Les-Eyzies-are-14,000-years-old-assertions. Or we might follow Sellars and explicate the equivalence in terms of dot quotes.[12] Other alternatives are also available. We need not decide among them here. Various symbols amount to the same thing in the sense that concerns us just in case a testifier shoulders the same epistemic burden regardless of which of them she uses in giving her word. Let us say that all such symbols *convey the same message*. Doubtless this is imprecise, but further precision is unnecessary for our purposes. Thomson is surely right to recognize that what I invite you to rely on when I give you my word that *p*, is not, or not only, the truth of the particular sentence that I utter. In fact, I would go further and say that it is not, or not only, the truth of the sentence or proposition (if such there be) that I assert.

   If I testify that *p*, I give you my word that *p* is true. But if I testify that the cave paintings are 14,000 years old, I do not commit myself to the truth of the sentence "The cave paintings are 14,000 years old." I would be astounded if they were exactly 14,000 years old. I would consider myself, and be considered by others, to be right, if I was off by no more than a few hundred years. Indeed, in the absence of new evidence, I am apt to utter the very same sentence in my lectures year after year. If I thought the paintings were exactly 14,000 years old this year, I should update my notes and say that they are 14,001 years old next year. Evidently, I use a seemingly precise sentence to convey a considerably vaguer message. It is the truth of the vague message, not the truth of the precise sentence, that my testimony commits me to. There is nothing disingenuous about this. I am not pretending to provide more precision that I do. It is tacitly acknowledged on all sides that the age I ascribe has a fairly generous margin of error. If the actual age of the painting falls within the margin, my testimony counts as true.

Contextual factors also create a discrepancy between medium and message. When in my lecture on prehistoric Europe, I say, "There are no cave paintings of women," my testimony is not falsified by the recent work of a graffiti artist in a cavern in Kentucky, for the scope of my quantifier is tacitly restricted. The message my testimony conveys is that none of the paintings in a contextually circumscribed range (which excludes graffiti in Kentucky) portrays a woman. A testimony's message may diverge considerably from the medium that conveys it — the contents of the conveying sentences, strictly construed.

How then is it that the message conveyed is the message received? What prevents my audience from concluding that my testimony reports the exact date the paintings were produced, or from ascribing to it a significantly different penumbra of vagueness? If all parties to an exchange share the relevant assumptions, there is no mystery. In that case, everyone imposes the same constraints on the interpretation of my words. But why should we think this? If the assumptions have not been expressly agreed to, why should we think that they are shared? Background assumptions plainly vary from one linguistic context to the next. Moreover, they are continually revised and updated as discourse proceeds. But they are neither random nor idiosyncratic. Grice's account explains why. Linguistic communication, he contends, is governed by general principles that focus discussion and coordinate presuppositions. Communication has a variety of functions. Consoling someone may require different principles than informing him does. Grice articulates the maxims that he takes to underlie communication for the purpose of information transfer. I am not confident that the scope of the maxims is as wide as he believes. Producing a sound argument may require stating the obvious, thus violating a maxim of quantity. Nevertheless, I believe that Gricean maxims, or maxims very close to them,[13] apply to testimony, and explain how testimony conveys information when medium and message diverge.

Grice's basic insight is that communication is genuinely interpersonal. Although this does not sound particularly momentous, Grice shows that it is a deep and deeply important point. The informant is not just a spouter of truths; nor is the receiver an empty vessel into which data are poured. Because every interchange involves presuppositions, speaker and hearer must understand each other. This is not just a matter of grasping the words that constitute an utterance or inscription. It involves appreciating why, to what end, and against what background those particular words are uttered or inscribed. To understand an utterance requires understanding its utterer, for communication is a matter of mutual attunement. This is why Grice contends that communication depends on cooperation. Informative exchanges are, he maintains, governed by the Cooperative Principle: "Make your conversational contribution such as is required at the stage at which it occurs, by the accepted purpose or direction of the talk exchange in which you are engaged."[14] To satisfy this principle, he argues, involves satisfying subsidiary maxims. Among these are

(a)   the maxims of quantity:

1.   Make your contribution as informative as is required (for the current purposes of the exchange);

2.   Do not make your contribution more informative than is required.

(b)   a supermaxim of quality:
Try to make your contribution one that is true.

as well as two submaxims:
1.   Do not say what you believe to be false.
2.   Do not say that for which you lack adequate evidence.

and:

(c)   a relevance requirement.[15]

Although the cooperative principle and the maxims are cast as instructions to the speaker, they supply rules for the hearer as well. Ceteris paribus, in order to interpret an informative utterance or inscription correctly, we must construe it as one that satisfies (or at least purports to satisfy) the Gricean rules. In a communicative exchange, not only does each party conform her contributions to the maxims, she also takes it that the other parties are doing so. Interpreting, then, is not a matter of rote application of the homophonic rule or of some regimented principle of inter-linguistic translation. It involves consideration of what interpretation of the speaker's remarks would be one that the speaker could have, or at least believe herself to have, adequate evidence for, what interpretation would yield a statement that the speaker would consider informative, relevant, and so on. You don't take me to have testified that the cave paintings are *exactly* 14,000 years old, because you don't think it remotely likely that I have evidence that could support such a precise statement, nor do you think that such precision is required, or even desirable, in the context in which we are speaking. You take me to have testified that the paintings are in the neighborhood of 14,000 years old, since that is an informative, contextually relevant contention that you think I could have adequate evidence for. You also deploy the maxims in assign-ing the neighborhood a size. What is conceded on all sides goes without saying, for if all parties agree that *p*, "*p*" is uninformative. Therefore, you take me to be saying something more specific than what everyone in the audience already knows anyway. Considerations of relevance provide further constraints. If the discussion requires that the date be specified within 500 years, I am uncooperative if my remark is not that specific. Since you take me to be cooperative, you therefore interpret my remark as saying that the paintings are within 500 years of being 14,000 years old. If we only need a date within 500 years of the right one, it would be uncooperative of me to be much more precise than that. So you have reason to refrain from taking my state-ment to be overly specific.

Gricean considerations show how complex and context-sensitive uptake is. To properly interpret a speaker's testimony involves an awareness of the course and point of the discussion, as well as an appreciation both of what has already been established and of what goes without saying. It also involves epistemic sensitivity. The speaker purports to be satisfying the maxim of quality. So we need to construe her as saying something she has, or takes herself to have, or purports to have adequate evidence for. To do that, we need to be sensitive to the relevant epistemic norms. We need, that is, to understand what sort of and how much evidence is required. To decide among the available interpretations of a speaker's words requires recognizing which of them she can purport to have adequate evidence for, hence what evidence she might have and what evidence would be adequate. Evidential standards vary. A measurement that would be acceptable in the kitchen is apt to be too rough to accept in the lab. Finally, we need interpersonal awareness. It is not enough to know what has actually transpired in the course of the discussion and what is actually required by way of evidence. We also need to understand what each party takes to have transpired and what each takes to be required.

To understand someone's testimony is to construe it as a statement of fact (or a collection of statements of fact) for which the testifier purports to have adequate grounds. People sometimes testify without adequate grounds, being either misleading or misled about the strength of their evidence. In taking someone's word, we assume that she is neither. We take it that she has the adequate grounds that she purports to have. This might be doubted. Suppose Pat says, for no good reason, that p. Although she realizes that Pat has no justification for her remark, Sarah has very good reasons for believing that p, reasons she never brought to bear on the issue prior to hearing Pat's totally unfounded utterance. Sarah is now justified in relying on the truth of p, and came to be justified via Pat's testimony. Still, one wants to say, Sarah does not take Pat's word that p. Pat's statement was a catalyst, but conveyed no epistemic entitlement. Sarah did not accept Pat's invitation to rely on her word, but took the occasion to marshal her own evidence. Sarah did not take Pat's word. There is a harder case, though. Suppose Sasha testifies, on relatively weak grounds, that q. Sasha's grounds are inadequate. But they're not *nothing*. They afford some reason to believe that q. Jenny has additional grounds, which are also insufficient if taken alone. But combined with Sasha's grounds, they yield sufficient evidence for q. Jenny relies partly, but not wholly, on Sasha's testimony. I suggest that the strength of Jenny's reliance on Sasha's testimony is determined by the strength of the backing Jenny takes Sasha's testimony to have. Word taking, then, can be a matter of degree. We may partly rely on the word of someone whose evidence we consider weak.

We are justified in taking someone's word only to the extent that we are justified in thinking her grounds are adequate. But we can take a speaker's word and be justified in doing so without knowing what her grounds are. In some cases, a speaker's behavior might afford ample evidence that she is satisfying the cooperative principle, hence satisfying the second maxim of quality. Sometimes, for example, in reporting one's zip code, that is enough, since this is the sort of thing a normal speaker knows. In cases where evidence of cooperation is not enough, we may know the particular speaker to be morally and epistemically trustworthy. Then even though we lack access to her grounds, we know that she would not be testifying if they were inadequate. In yet other cases, testimony may be given in a context where there are sufficient institutional safeguards to block epistemically irresponsible testimony. The fact that the experts in the field raise no objection indicates that the evidence, whatever it is, satisfies the relevant standards. If the field is epistemically estimable, institutional safeguards are safeguards enough.

Testimony, then, conveys more than the facts that constitute its message. It also conveys that those facts have been established to the satisfaction of the relevant community of inquiry and that the testifier is in a position to epistemically entitle her audience to believe them. That being so, a speaker testifies responsibly only if she is in a position to shoulder the epistemic burden for everything her testimony conveys. It might seem that this does not add to the load. Perhaps a speaker is epistemically entitled to convey anything she is epistemically entitled to believe, and epistemically entitled to believe anything that satisfies the standards of the relevant community of inquiry. If so, the brute fact that she has adequate grounds suffices. She need not be aware that her grounds are adequate. She need not even be aware of what her grounds are.

This is in line with currently popular epistemological theories that hold that a subject can be fully warranted in believing that p, without being aware of what supplies the warrant. Such theories provide an attractive account of perceptual warrant. Seeing a rabbit twenty feet away in the center of his visual field wholly justifies a subject with good eyesight in believing that there is a rabbit in front of him. He need not have the conceptual resources to appreciate that his perception supplies him with grounds, much less know anything about the perceptual mechanisms that make seeing reliable. At least in some cases, then, there is reason to believe that it is the having of grounds, not the awareness that one has grounds, that is required for warrant. But even if this is so, and even if it holds for warranted belief generally, nothing directly follows about what is required to convey warrant.

Being in a position to convey warrant requires more than merely being warranted. A subject who has scattered evidence that warrants her belief that p, but has never put that evidence together, does not realize that she is warranted in believing that p. It does not seem that she can give her word that p, since she is not prepared to shoulder the epistemic burden for the truth of p. A subject whose evidence in fact warrants q might fail to realize that her belief that q is warranted because she thinks that stronger evidence is required. (Perhaps she thinks that Cartesian doubts have to be answered before one is epistemically entitled to believe an empirical theory. Or perhaps, having confused *The Philadelphia Inquirer* with *The National Enquirer*, she considers her source unreliable.) Again, it seems, she is unable to shoulder the epistemic burden, since she considers her grounds inadequate. These examples suggest that in order to testify responsibly, one must not only be justified in believing that p, one must also be justified in believing that one is justified in believing that p.

This sets an additional demand, but not an unsatisfiable one. It does not require ever more evidence for p. Rather, it requires reason to think that one's evidence or grounds for p are adequate. It therefore introduces second-order considerations about the adequacy of grounds. If Jenny is to be justified in believing that she is justified in believing that p, she needs to appreciate her grounds. This requires critical self-awareness. She needs self-awareness because she must be cognizant of the beliefs and perceptual states that supply her grounds. The self-awareness must be critical, for she must recognize that the considerations she adduces qualify as reasons to believe that p. The fox is warranted in believing that there is a rabbit in front of him, but is not justified in believing that his belief is warranted, for he has not idea why he trusts his senses or whether it is reasonable to do so. Jenny also needs some awareness of the relevant epistemic standards. She has to know what sort of evidence and how much evidence is required in a context like this to support a belief like the belief that p. She needs, moreover, to credit those standards. She must consider them reasonable, or at least not unreasonable. If she considered the accepted standards of evidence to be epistemically shoddy, she would have no reason to take their satisfaction to confer epistemic entitlement. Knowing that one's reasons satisfy the standards of the contemporary astrological community does not inspire confidence in the belief they are supposed to support. Finally, she needs to recognize that her grounds satisfy the relevant epistemic standards.

This is fine, one might say, if we are talking about the first link in the chain of epistemic entitlers. If a subject is attuned to the standards of the relevant community of inquiry, recognizes that they are reasonable standards, and realizes that her evidence satisfies those standards, she justifiably believes that she is justified in believing and in testifying that *p*. Often this is not the case. As an intermediate link in the chain, Mike has it on good authority that *p*, and undertakes to pass the information along. He read it in the newspaper, heard it in a lecture, learned it in school. But he is in no position to supply the backing for it. Nor does he have the expertise to recognize or endorse the standards of the community that underwrites his belief. Still, one wants to say that as an informed layman he can testify responsibly that the political situation in Rwanda is unstable, that electrons have negative charge, that Hume was a diplomat. The reason is that an informed layman is not just a gullible stooge. He believes and has good reason to believe that the authorities his judgment rests on are good. The source he relies on to back up his assertion is not only a reliable source; it is also a source he considers reliable and has good reason to consider reliable. Even intermediate links in the chain of epistemic entitlers, then, satisfy the demands of critical self-awareness.

Testimony turns out to be more complex than the idea of information transfer might initially suggest. Testifying that *p* is not just asserting *p*. Nor, of course, is testifying that *p* the same as testifying that one is warranted in testifying that *p*. But it would be unreasonable for you to take my word for it that *p*, if I was not warranted in testifying that *p*. When I testify to you that *p*, then, I do not merely impart the information that *p* is the case. I also give you reason to believe that *p* is warranted and that I am warranted in testifying that *p*. In addition, my testimony gives you moral and epistemic claims against me. If *p* is false (and no exonerating conditions obtain), then in testifying that *p*, I both impart false beliefs and do you a moral wrong. I mislead you about *p*'s epistemic standing by assuring you that it is epistemically safe to rely on the truth of *p*, when in fact it is not. So the ground for the moral wrong is an epistemic wrong. In the realm of rights, epistemology and ethics overlap.

Notes

1   Judith Jarvis Thomson, *The Realm of Rights* (Cambridge, MA: Harvard University Press, 1990), p. 298.
2   There are matters of degree here. Sometimes a speaker supplies some reasons but relies on authority to provide the additional backing that her statements need.
3   Thomson, pp. 299–300.
4   Thomson, p. 64.
5   Thomson, pp. 94–5.
6   It may be, but it need not. We sometimes reproach promise breakers by saying, "You should not have promised what you weren't going to deliver."

7   Thomson, pp. 305–6.

8   I am not sure about this. Thomson may unduly downplay the epistemological factor in promising. My point, though, is that whatever we should say about promising, the epistemological dimension is crucial to the claims given through testimony.

9   See my *Considered Judgment* (Princeton, NJ: Princeton University Press, 1997), chapters 3–4, for an alternative.

10   Thomson, p. 295.

11   Nelson Goodman, *Problems and Projects* (Indianapolis: Hackett Publishing, 1972), pp. 221–38; Israel Scheffler, *Inquiries* (Indianapolis: Hackett Publishing, 1986); see also Catherine Z. Elgin, *Between the Absolute and the Arbitrary* (Ithaca, NY: Cornell University Press, 1997), pp. 110–30.

12   Wilfrid Sellars, *Science and Metaphysics* (London: Routledge and Kegan Paul, 1968), pp. 91–116.

13   I have suggested elsewhere that the first maxim of quality should be revised to "Do not say what you believe to be misleading," rather than "Do not say what you believe to be false."

14   Paul Grice, "Logic and Conversation," in *Studies in the Way of Words* (Cambridge, Mass.: Harvard University Press, 1989), p. 26.

15   Grice, pp. 26–7.

SUGGESTED READING

Allen, Barry, *Truth in Philosophy* (Cambridge, MA: Harvard University Press, 1993).

Austin, J. L., *How to Do Things with Words*, The William James Lectures, 1955 (Oxford: Oxford University Press, 1962).

Ayer, A. J., *Language, Truth, and Logic* (London: Victor Gollancz, 1936).

Baier, Annette, "Trust and Antitrust," *Ethics*, 96 (pp. 231–60). See also her *Postures of the Mind* (1985); *Moral Prejudices: Essays on Ethics* (1996).

Carnap, Rudolf, *Introduction to Semantics* (Cambridge, MA: Harvard University Press, 1942).

Elgin, Catherine Z., *Between the Absolute and the Arbitrary* (Ithaca, NY: Cornell University Press, 1997).

Heidegger, Martin, "The Essence of Truth," in *Basic Writings*, 2nd edn, ed. David Farrell Krell (San Francisco: Harper, 1993).

Heidegger, Martin, "The Origin of the Work of Art," in *Basic Writings*, 2nd edn, ed. David Farrell Krell (San Francisco: Harper, 1993).

Heidegger, Martin, *Being and Time*, trans. Joan Stambaugh (Albany, NY: SUNY Press, 1997).

Husserl, Edmund, *Phenomenology and the Crisis of Philosophy*, trans. Quentin Lauer (New York: Harper, 1965).

Husserl, Edmund, *Crisis of European Sciences and Transcendental Phenomenology*, trans. David Carr (Evanston, IL: Northwestern University Press, 1970).

Husserl, Edmund, *Logical Investigations*, trans. J. N. Findlay (London: Routledge, 2001).

Levinas, Emmanuel, *Totality and Infinity*, trans. Alfonso Lingis (Pittsburgh: Duquesne University Press, 1969).

Levinas, Emmanuel, *Ethics and Infinity*, trans. Richard Cohen (Pittsburgh: Duquesne University Press, 1985).

McGeer, Victoria, "Developing Trust," *Philosophical Explorations*, 5/1 (2002).

Nussbaum, Martha, *Love's Knowledge* (Oxford: Oxford University Press, 1992).

Searle, John, *Speech Acts* (Cambridge: Cambridge University Press, 1969).

PART VI

TRUTH AND POWER

INTRODUCTION

The papers in this part each contribute to a conversation, or perhaps we should say, a struggle, over the relation between truth and power, extending, in particular, the issues of context, consensus, and social practice that are the focus of Part III. In fact there is no single problem or issue about the relation between truth and power, but rather a cluster of interconnected questions that weave their way through this selection.

(1) It is a common unhelpful assumption that we need to choose between a relativistic view of truth and truth as an absolute. Where does this assumption come from? How can it be resisted?

(2) We know that truth can be political in the sense that some "truths" are suppressed for political reasons, and we know that the power to frame the truth – the debates, discussions, and terms of the discourse in which claims to truth are presented – is also a key concern of the powers that be. But does that mean that the value and meaning of "truth" is exhausted by this desire to control the terms of discourse? And what exactly is meant by "power"? Does it coincide with the space of politics, or is it everywhere? And what special problems arise from the specter of totalitarian mass manipulation of opinion?

(3) Does philosophy have some privileged access to or claim to truth (such as metaphysical truth), such that it could plausibly legislate for other people or practices? Or is philosophy at best in a position to analyze and clarify the truth claims of other disciplines? What would philosophical truth look like?

(4) More specifically, if a pragmatist approach broadly speaking connects truth to existing social practices, what opportunities does it offer for any kind of critical perspective? And how does any further critical standpoint avoid being labeled just another narrative, or game, or practice?

(5) What connection is there between truth, interest, and disinterestedness. Obviously, disinterestedness can free itself from the suspicion that its claims are merely the expression of some local commitment. But arguably the interests of those whose voice has been suppressed may be precisely what allows them to correct what would otherwise be a distorted or one-sided picture. Special interests may correct effectively even if they universalize badly.

The papers in this part have deep roots in the history of philosophy. Arendt's discussion of truth in politics draws on the Greek tradition, on Kant and Heidegger, on her experience of German totalitarianism and of the American liberal tradition. Foucault's inaugural lecture at the Collège de France lays out the role of the concept of truth in his work on European practices of prohibition, exclusion, division, and rejection over many centuries, starting out with the distinction between reason and folly, and moving through medical practices, and those connected with defining and regulating sexuality. Finally we include a boundary-crossing paper from Linda Alcoff, at home in both analytic and Continental traditions, and able to thematize the differences, especially over the status of epistemology. She shows we can avoid the extremes of relativism and absolutism without abandoning truth talk.

Early in her paper, Alcoff endorses Elgin's diagnosis of the folly of the philoso-phers' "bipolar disorder" that insists that if answers to philosophical questions are not absolute, they are arbitrary. She will argue that truth is not agent-transcendent, but appropriately, and not arbitrarily, tied up with various social practices. Alcoff is not an official member of the Frankfurt School. A thinker like Horkheimer, for example, would claim that in contemporary thought subjectivism and relativism often live side by side with blind faith, absolutism, and dogmatism, and attempt to explain this pervasive contradiction.[1] What Alcoff shares with Critical Theory is a sense of the need to move beyond this schizophrenic space. She chooses an effective example – conflicting accounts of the formation of the family in seventeenth- and eighteenth-century Britain – to show how a feminist perspective would open up lines of thought otherwise closed off. And a cultural history so informed does not need to choose between the arbitrary and the absolute. Alcoff insists that we need to link truth to social practices to understand how the dilemma can be avoided.

For Critical Theory, broadly speaking, pragmatism forfeits the possibility of deep critique of social practices, while it, not surprisingly, takes such critique seriously. Alcoff formulates her own position somewhat mildly – affirming that "women count . . . and that our optimal life situation is probably not to be found in a condition of life long subordination." Obviously, this claim can be treated as *just another* narrative. Perhaps the answer is that while there may be no privileged *external* position from which to establish or refute that claim, philosophy's emancipatory dimension implies that the demands of social justice are not reducible to formal validation. This is a position close to what was claimed for testimony and witnessing in Part V.

The second set of questions we posed – those to do with power and politics – are more directly addressed by the selections from Arendt and Foucault. Arendt has a more traditional concern with the place that truth, and the commitment to the truth, might have in politics. She takes her cue from Plato's distinction between truth and opinion, his apparent willingness to accept that the political realm is that of opinion, and the implausibility of expecting philosophy to have much of a direct role in public life. Arendt says it matters whether we are talking about factual truth, or rational/philosophical truth. "Facts" are both more manipulable in the short term, and yet have a stubbornness that it is hard to repress forever.[2] Rational or philosophical truth[3] is harder to manipulate, but matters less in politics. Telling the truth is a vocation that really comes into its own only when lying is pervasive. Contemporary political life is threatened by the fact that lying is no longer a way we deceive our enemies: the rulers now first have to deceive themselves, the better to deceive the public. Arendt claims that constitutional states at least place a value on there being institutions – such as universities, the press, courts – that are disinterested and not politicized. Finally, the political is limited by "those things which men cannot change at will," among the most prominent of which is the truth.

Arendt's view of the politics of truth is in sharp contrast to that of Foucault. For while there is no doubt that they would share many of the same social concerns – sympathy with the oppressed – Foucault from the beginning questions the boundary on which Arendt relies between interest and disinterestedness. Following Nietzsche (see Part I), Foucault understands the urgency to distinguish between true and false, reason and folly, to organize fields of knowledge, as driven by a *will to truth*. This is tied intimately to his account of the historical development of the distribution, organization, and legitimation of knowledge and discourse. Foucault is in fact less concerned with truth than with what Kuhn would call paradigms of intelligibility, the space within which various kinds of truth and falsity can arise. The will to truth exerts a particular pressure in such figures as the individual subject, and the author, and the establishing of discrete subject matters for different sciences, where what is always at stake is the reduction of chance, of the unpredictable, and the possibility of a determinable truth. Along with all this, Foucault is accounting for all those forms of social exclusion – from the mad, to the sick, and the criminal – human sacrifices to an ideal of normality maintained by the discourses of the human sciences. When he talks about power, Foucault is not, then, specifically talking about what Arendt calls politics. Rather, as he puts it, "Each society has its régime of truth, its 'general politics' of truth: that is, the types of discourse which it accepts and makes function as true" (p. 333 below). And unlike Arendt, Foucault has no sense of the truth as residing outside power, waiting to correct its excesses. "Truth is a thing of this world: it is produced only by multiple forms of constraint. And it induces regular effects of power" (p. 333 below). There is something of a convergence with Arendt when she describes truth as having a coercive power. But for her this derives from its reference to something outside the political. A conversation with Arendt might perhaps begin by asking Foucault about the status of his own discourse, which certainly sounds like that disinterested discourse that Arendt insists on. Foucault distinguishes the specific from the universal intellectual. The specific intellectual is engaged in local material struggles. The universal intellectual is a Marxist hangover. And yet one has to ask who is the Foucault who distinguishes between the specific and the universal? Is he not above the fray in making that very distinction?

This begins to address the question as to whether philosophers, when they talk about truth, are talking about ordinary, empirical truth – perhaps, as with Foucault, showing it to be discourse-dependent – or whether they do not also have in mind the possibility of truth or truths of a different order. It would be fashionable to dismiss such truths. But many of the essays in this section are struggling with the question of whether philosophy itself is not making truth claims of a different order to those it is analyzing. We might expect this of a Horkheimer, who has a continuing sense of the importance of theoretical coherence, but Alcoff will end her essay with a claim that seems to combine both meta-philosophical and existential elements: "Truth is as dense and multivalent as lived reality, which is, after all, what it is about" (p. 347 below). What Arendt says about the stubbornness of truth are claims of a privileged order, not just statements of fact. And while Foucault's opening remarks express a kind of embarrassment about the need to frame his own discourse in an introduction, he still faces the question about the status of his own discourse. It may be that this formal consequence – that philosophical remarks about truth tend, performatively at least, towards confirming that there are orders of truth – is something that itself needs to be affirmed and explored rather than resisted. If we think we can jettison a distinctively "philosophical" truth, we need to ask whether methodological self-consciousness is really any different.

We have suggested that the voices of the oppressed can function as provocation to a certain narrative or discourse, rather than just another discourse. This might be compared to the *imperative*, the demand the witness makes to be heard. Witnessing, and acknowledging such testimony, would either not be ordinary social practices, or would be privileged practices. One could imagine a strong version of this privilege – that witnessing sets a standard for truth-telling – and should not be subjected to its skeptical validation procedures. Or a weak version – that the voice of the oppressed truly has a privilege – not of supplying the whole truth, but of correcting any vision that would exclude it. Alternatively, it might be argued that philosophizing itself, even articulating the claims of pragmatism, rests if not directly on orders of truth, at least on orders of interest, or of practice. And this would give some confirmation of Arendt's reference to constitutional society's interest in disinterestedness.

The topic "Truth and Power" opens in many directions. These are only some of the ways in which these essays enter into conversation with one another.

Notes

1   See Max Horkheimer, "On the Problem of Truth," trans. Maurice Goldbloom, in *Between Philosophy and Social Science* (Cambridge, MA: MIT Press, 1993); originally published in *The Essential Frankfurt School Reader*, ed. Andrew Arato and Eike Gebhardt (New York: Urizen Books, 1978). Horkheimer (as represented by this paper) is an invisible interlocutor in Part VI. Only considerations of space prevented its inclusion in this collection.
2   Consider claims about weapons of mass destruction used to justify the 2003 US invasion of Iraq.
3   Rational/philosophical truth for Arendt includes "axioms, discoveries, theories" as well as such "philosophical" truths as Socrates' "It is better to suffer wrong than to do wrong."

19

TRUTH AND POLITICS

Hannah Arendt

I

The subject of these reflections is a commonplace. No one has ever doubted that truth and politics are on rather bad terms with each other, and no one, as far as I know, has ever counted truthfulness among the political virtues. Lies have always been regarded as necessary and justifiable tools not only of the politician's or the demagogue's but also of the statesman's trade. Why is that so? And what does it mean for the nature and the dignity of the political realm, on one side, and for the nature and the dignity of truth and truthfulness, on the other? Is it of the very essence of truth to be impotent and of the very essence of power to be deceitful? And what kind of reality does truth possess if it is powerless in the public realm, which more than any other sphere of human life guarantees reality of existence to natal and mortal men – that is, to beings who know they have appeared out of non-being and will, after a short while, again disappear into it? Finally, is not impotent truth just as despicable as power that gives no heed to truth? These are uncomfortable questions, but they arise necessarily out of our current convictions in this matter.

What lends this commonplace its high plausibility can still be summed up in the old Latin adage "*Fiat iustitia, et pereat mundus*" ("Let justice be done though the world may perish") [. . .] and if we put truth in its place – "*Fiat veritas, et pereat mundus*" – the old saying sounds even more plausible. [. . .]

Hannah Arendt, "Truth and Politics," in *The Portable Hannah Arendt* (London: Penguin, 2000), pp. 545–75 (excerpts). Originally published in *Between Past and Future* in *The New Yorker*, February 25, 1967.

This essay was caused by the so-called controversy after the publication of *Eichmann in Jerusalem*. Its aim is to clarify two different, though interconnected, issues of which I had not been aware before and whose importance seemed to transcend the occasion. The first concerns the question of whether it is always legitimate to tell the truth – did I believe without qualification in *"Fiat veritas, et pereat mundus"*? The second arose through the amazing amount of lies used in the "controversy" – lies about what I had written, on one hand, and about the facts I had reported, on the other. The following reflections try to come to grips with both issues. They may also serve as an example of what happens to a highly topical subject when it is drawn into that gap between past and future which is perhaps the proper habitat of all reflections.

[. . .] it will therefore come as something of a surprise that the sacrifice of truth for the survival of the world would be more futile than the sacrifice of any other principle or virtue. For while we may refuse even to ask ourselves whether life would still be worth living in a world deprived of such notions as justice and freedom, the same, curiously, is not possible with respect to the seemingly so much less political idea of truth. What is at stake is survival, the perseverance in existence (*in suo esse perseverare*), and no human world destined to outlast the short life span of mortals within it will ever be able to survive without men willing to do what Herodotus was the first to undertake consciously – namely, λέγειν τα ἐόντα, to say what is. No permanence, no perseverance in existence, can even be conceived of without men willing to testify to what is and appears to them because it is.

The story of the conflict between truth and politics is an old and complicated one, and nothing would be gained by simplification or moral denunciation. Throughout history, the truth-seekers and truthtellers have been aware of the risks of their business; as long as they did not interfere with the course of the world, they were covered with ridicule, but he who forced his fellow-citizens to take him seriously by trying to set them free from falsehood and illusion was in danger of his life: "If they could lay hands on [such a] man . . . they would kill him," Plato says in the last sentence of the cave allegory. The Platonic conflict between truthteller and citizens cannot be explained by the Latin adage, or any of the later theories that, implicitly or explicitly, justify lying, among other transgressions, if the survival of the city is at stake. No enemy is mentioned in Plato's story; the many live peacefully in their cave among themselves, mere spectators of images, involved in no action and hence threatened by nobody. The members of this community have no reason whatever to regard truth and truthtellers as their worst enemies, and Plato offers no explanation of their perverse love of deception and falsehood. If we could confront him with one of his later colleagues in political philosophy – namely, with Hobbes, who held that only "such truth, as opposeth no man's profit, nor pleasure, is to all men welcome" (an obvious statement, which, however, he thought important enough to end his *Leviathan* with) – he might agree about profit and pleasure but not with the assertion that there existed any kind of truth welcome to all men. Hobbes, but not Plato, consoled himself with the existence of indifferent truth, with "subjects" about which "men care not" – e.g., with mathematical truth, "the doctrine of lines and figures" that "crosses no man's ambition, profit or lust." For, Hobbes wrote, "I doubt not, but if it had been a thing contrary to any man's right of dominion, or to the interest of men that have dominion, that the three angles of a triangle should be equal to two angles of a square; the doctrine should have been, if not disputed, yet by the burning of all books of geometry, suppressed, as far as he whom it concerned was able."[1]

No doubt, there is a decisive difference between Hobbes' mathematical axiom and the true standard for human conduct that Plato's philosopher is supposed to bring back from his journey into the sky of ideas, although Plato, who believed that mathematical truth opened the eyes of the mind to all truths, was not aware of it. Hobbes' example strikes us as relatively harmless; we are inclined to assume that the human mind will always be able to reproduce such axiomatic statements as "the three angles of a triangle should be equal to two angles of a square," and we conclude that "the burning of all books of geometry" would not be radically effective. The danger would be considerably greater with respect to scientific statements; had history taken a different turn, the whole modern scientific development from Galileo to Einstein might not have come to pass. And certainly the most vulnerable truth of this kind would be those highly differentiated and always unique thought trains – of which Plato's doctrine of ideas is an eminent example – whereby men, since time immemorial, have tried to think rationally beyond the limits of human knowledge.

The modern age, which believes that truth is neither given to nor disclosed to but produced by the human mind, has assigned, since Leibniz, mathematical, scientific, and philosophical truths to the common species of rational truth as distinguished from factual truth. I shall use this distinction for the sake of convenience without discussing its intrinsic legitimacy. Wanting to find out what injury political power is capable of inflicting upon truth, we look into these matters for political rather than philosophical reasons, and hence can afford to disregard the question of what truth is, and be content to take the word in the sense in which men commonly understand it. And if we now think of factual truths – of such modest verities as the role during the Russian Revolution of a man by the name of Trotsky, who appears in none of the Soviet Russian history books – we at once become aware of how much more vulnerable they are than all the kinds of rational truth taken together. Moreover, since facts and events – the invariable outcome of men living and acting together – constitute the very texture of the political realm, it is, of course, factual truth that we are most concerned with here. Dominion (to speak Hobbes' language) when it attacks rational truth oversteps, as it were, its domain, while it gives battle on its own ground when it falsifies or lies away facts. The chances of factual truth surviving the onslaught of power are very slim indeed; it is always in danger of being maneuvered out of the world not only for a time but, potentially, forever. Facts and events are infinitely more fragile things than axioms, discoveries, theories – even the most wildly speculative ones – produced by the human mind; they occur in the field of the ever-changing affairs of men, in whose flux there is nothing more permanent than the admittedly relative permanence of the human mind's structure. Once they are lost, no rational effort will ever bring them back. Perhaps the chances that Euclidean mathematics or Einstein's theory of relativity – let alone Plato's philosophy – would have been reproduced in time if their authors had been prevented from handing them down to posterity are not very good either, yet they are infinitely better than the chances that a fact of importance, forgotten or, more likely, lied away, will one day be rediscovered.

II

Although the politically most relevant truths are factual, the conflict between truth and politics was first discovered and articulated with respect to rational truth. The opposite of a rationally true statement is either error and ignorance, as in the sciences, or illusion and opinion, as in philosophy. Deliberate falsehood, the plain lie, plays its role only in the domain of factual statements, and it seems significant, and rather odd, that in the long debate about this antagonism of truth and politics, from Plato to Hobbes, no one, apparently, ever believed that organized lying, as we know it today, could be an adequate weapon against truth. In Plato, the truthteller is in

danger of his life, and in Hobbes, where he has become an author, he is threatened
with the burning of his books; mere mendacity is not an issue. It is the sophist and
the ignoramus rather than the liar who occupy Plato's thought, and where he distinguishes between error and lie – that is, between "involuntary and voluntary ψεῦδος"
– he is, characteristically, much harsher on people "wallowing in swinish ignorance"
than on liars.[2] Is this because organized lying, dominating the public realm, as distinguished from the private liar who tries his luck on his own hook, was still
unknown? Or has this something to do with the striking fact that, except for Zoroas-
trianism, none of the major religions included lying as such, as distinguished from
"bearing false witness," in their catalogues of grave sins? Only with the rise of Puritan
morality, coinciding with the rise of organized science, whose progress had to be
assured on the firm ground of the absolute veracity and reliability of every scientist,
were lies considered serious offenses.

However that may be, historically the conflict between truth and politics arose out
of two diametrically opposed ways of life – the life of the philosopher, as interpreted
first by Parmenides and then by Plato, and the way of life of the citizen. To the citizens' ever-changing opinions about human affairs, which themselves were in a state
of constant flux, the philosopher opposed the truth about those things which in their
very nature were everlasting and from which, therefore, principles could be derived
to stabilize human affairs. Hence the opposite to truth was mere opinion, which was
equated with illusion, and it was this degrading of opinion that gave the conflict its
political poignancy; for opinion, and not truth, belongs among the indispensable pre-
requisites of all power. "All governments rest on opinion," James Madison said, and
not even the most autocratic ruler or tyrant could ever rise to power, let alone keep
it, without the support of those who are like-minded. By the same token, every claim
in the sphere of human affairs to an absolute truth, whose validity needs no support
from the side of opinion, strikes at the very roots of all politics and all governments.
This antagonism between truth and opinion was further elaborated by Plato (especially in the *Gorgias*) as the antagonism between communicating in the form of
"dialogue," which is the adequate speech for philosophical truth, and in the form of
"rhetoric," by which the demagogue, as we would say today, persuades the multitude.

Traces of this original conflict can still be found in the earlier stages of the modern
age, though hardly in the world we live in. In Hobbes, for instance, we still read of
an opposition of two "contrary faculties": "solid reasoning" and "powerful eloquence,"
the former being "grounded upon principles of truth, the other upon opinions . . .
and the passions and interests of men, which are different and mutable."[3] More than
a century later, in the Age of Enlightenment, these traces have almost but not quite
disappeared, and where the ancient antagonism still survives, the emphasis has shifted.
In terms of pre-modern philosophy, Lessing's magnificent "*Sage jeder, was ihm Wahrheit
dünkt, und die Wahrheit selbst sei Gott empfohlen*" ("Let each man say what he deems
truth, and let truth itself be commended unto God") would have plainly signified,
Man is not capable of truth, all his truths, alas, are δόξαι, mere opinions, whereas for
Lessing it meant, on the contrary, Let us thank God that we don't know *the* truth.
Even where the note of jubilation – the insight that for men, living in company, the
inexhaustible richness of human discourse is infinitely more significant and meaningful than any One Truth could ever be – is absent, the awareness of the frailty of

human reason has prevailed since the eighteenth century without giving rise to complaint or lamentation. We can find it in Kant's grandiose *Critique of Pure Reason*, in which reason is led to recognize its own limitations, as we hear it in the words of Madison, who more than once stressed that "the reason of man, like man himself, is timid and cautious when left alone, and acquires firmness and confidence in proportion to the number with which it is associated."[4] Considerations of this kind, much more than notions about the individual's right to self-expression, played a decisive part in the finally more or less successful struggle to obtain freedom of thought for the spoken and the printed word.

Thus Spinoza, who still believed in the infallibility of human reason and is often wrongly praised as a champion of free thought and speech, held that "every man is by indefeasible natural right the master of his own thoughts," that "every man's understanding is his own, and that brains are as diverse as palates," from which he concluded that "it is best to grant what cannot be abolished" and that laws prohibiting free thought can only result in "men thinking one thing and saying another," hence in "the corruption of good faith" and "the fostering of . . . perfidy." However, Spinoza nowhere demands freedom of speech, and the argument that human reason needs communication with others and therefore publicity for its own sake is conspicuous by its absence. He even counts man's need for communication, his inability to hide his thoughts and keep silent, among the "common failings" that the philosopher does not share.[5] Kant, on the contrary, stated that "the external power that deprives man of the freedom to communicate his thoughts publicly, *deprives him at the same time of his freedom to think*" (italics added), and that the only guarantee for "the correctness" of our thinking lies in that "we think, as it were, in community with others to whom we communicate our thoughts as they communicate theirs to us." Man's reason, being fallible, can function only if he can make "public use" of it, and this is equally true for those who, still in a state of "tutelage," are unable to use their minds "without the guidance of somebody else" and for the "scholar," who needs "the entire reading public" to examine and control his results.[6]

In this context, the question of numbers, mentioned by Madison, is of special importance. The shift from rational truth to opinion implies a shift from man in the singular to men in the plural, and this means a shift from a domain where, Madison says, nothing counts except the "solid reasoning" of one mind to a realm where "strength of opinion" is determined by the individual's reliance upon "the number which he supposes to have entertained the same opinions" – a number, incidentally, that is not necessarily limited to one's contemporaries. Madison still distinguishes this life in the plural, which is the life of the citizen, from the life of the philosopher, by whom such considerations "ought to be disregarded," but this distinction has no practical consequence, for "a nation of philosophers is as little to be expected as the philosophical race of kings wished for by Plato."[7] We may note in passing that the very notion of "a nation of philosophers" would have been a contradiction in terms for Plato, whose whole political philosophy, including its outspoken tyrannical traits, rests on the conviction that truth can be neither gained nor communicated among the many.

In the world we live in, the last traces of this ancient antagonism between the philosopher's truth and the opinions in the market place have disappeared. Neither the truth of revealed religion, which the political thinkers of the seventeenth century still treated as a major nuisance, nor the truth of the philosopher, disclosed to man in solitude, interferes any longer with the affairs of the world. In respect to the former, the separation of church and state has given us peace, and as to the latter, it ceased long ago to claim dominion – unless one takes the modern ideologies seriously as philosophies, which is difficult indeed since their adherents openly proclaim them to be political weapons and consider the whole question of truth and truthfulness irrelevant. Thinking in terms of the tradition, one may feel entitled to conclude from this state of affairs that the old conflict has finally been settled, and especially that its original cause, the clash of rational truth and opinion has disappeared.

Strangely, however, this is not the case, for the clash of factual truth and politics, which we witness today on such a large scale, has – in some respects, at least – very similar traits. While probably no former time tolerated so many diverse opinions on religious or philosophical matters, factual truth, if it happens to oppose a given group's profit or pleasure, is greeted today with greater hostility than ever before. To be sure, state secrets have always existed; every government must classify certain information, withhold it from public notice, and he who reveals authentic secrets has always been treated as a traitor. With this I am not concerned here. The facts I have in mind are publicly known, and yet the same public that knows them can successfully, and often spontaneously, taboo their public discussion and treat them as though they were what they are not – namely, secrets. That their assertion then should prove as dangerous as, for instance, preaching atheism or some other heresy proved in former times seems a curious phenomenon, and its significance is enhanced when we find it also in countries that are ruled tyrannically by an ideological government. (Even in Hitler's Germany and Stalin's Russia it was more dangerous to talk about concentration and extermination camps, whose existence was no secret, than to hold and to utter "heretical" views on anti-Semitism, racism, and Communism.) What seems even more disturbing is that to the extent to which unwelcome factual truths are tolerated in free countries they are often, consciously or unconsciously, transformed into opinions – as though the fact of Germany's support of Hitler or of France's collapse before the German armies in 1940 or of Vatican policies during the Second World War were not a matter of historical record but a matter of opinion. Since such factual truths concern issues of immediate political relevance, there is more at stake here than the perhaps inevitable tension between two ways of life within the framework of a common and commonly recognized reality. What is at stake here is this common and factual reality itself, and this is indeed a political problem of the first order. And since factual truth, though it is so much less open to argument than philosophical truth, and so obviously within the grasp of everybody, seems often to suffer a similar fate when it is exposed in the market place – namely, to be countered not by lies and deliberate falsehoods but by opinion – it may be worth while to reopen the old and apparently obsolete question of truth versus opinion.

For, seen from the viewpoint of the truthteller, the tendency to transform fact into opinion, to blur the dividing line between them, is no less perplexing than the truthteller's older predicament, so vividly expressed in the cave allegory, in which the philosopher, upon his return from his solitary journey to the sky of everlasting ideas, tries to communicate his truth to the multitude, with the result that it disappears in the diversity of views, which to him are illusions, and is brought down to the uncertain level of opinion, so that now, back in the cave, truth itself appears in the guise of the δοκεῖ μοι ("it seems to me") – the very δόξαι he had hoped to leave behind once and for all. However, the reporter of factual truth is even worse off. He does not return from any journey into regions beyond the realm of human affairs, and he cannot console himself with the thought that he has become a stranger in this world. Similarly, we have no right to console ourselves with the notion that his truth, if truth it should be, is not of this world. If his simple factual statements are not accepted – truths seen and witnessed with the eyes of the body, and not the eyes of the mind – the suspicion arises that it may be in the nature of the political realm to deny or pervert truth of every kind, as though men were unable to come to terms with its unyielding, blatant, unpersuasive stubbornness. If this should be the case, things would look even more desperate than Plato assumed, for Plato's truth, found and actualized in solitude, transcends, by definition, the realm of the many, the world of human affairs. (One can understand that the philosopher, in his isolation, yields to the temptation to use his truth as a standard to be imposed upon human affairs; that is, to equate the transcendence inherent in philosophical truth with the altogether different kind of "transcendence" by which yardsticks and other standards of measurement are separated from the multitude of objects they are to measure, and one can equally well understand that the multitude will resist this standard, since it is actually derived from a sphere that is foreign to the realm of human affairs and whose connection with it can be justified only by a confusion.) Philosophical truth, when it enters the market place, changes its nature and becomes opinion, because a veritable μετάβασις εἰς ἄλλο γένος, a shifting not merely from one kind of reasoning to another but from one way of human existence to another, has taken place.

Factual truth, on the contrary, is always related to other people: it concerns events and circumstances in which many are involved; it is established by witnesses and depends upon testimony; it exists only to the extent that it is spoken about, even if it occurs in the domain of privacy. It is political by nature. Facts and opinions, though they must be kept apart, are not antagonistic to each other; they belong to the same realm. [. . .]

But do facts, independent of opinion and interpretation, exist at all? Have not generations of historians and philosophers of history demonstrated the impossibility of ascertaining facts without interpretation, since they must first be picked out of a chaos of sheer happenings (and the principles of choice are surely not factual data) and then be fitted into a story that can be told only in a certain perspective, which has nothing to do with the original occurrence? No doubt these and a great many more perplexities inherent in the historical sciences are real, but they are no argument against the existence of factual matter, nor can they serve as a justification for blurring the dividing lines between fact, opinion, and interpretation, or as an excuse for the historian to manipulate facts as he pleases. Even if we admit that every generation has the right to write its own history, we admit no more than that it has the right to rearrange the facts in accordance with its own perspective; we don't admit the right to touch the factual matter itself. To illustrate this point, and as an excuse for not pursuing this issue any further: During the twenties, so a story goes, Clemenceau, shortly before his death, found himself engaged in a friendly talk with a representative of the Weimar Republic on the question of guilt for the outbreak of the First World War. "What, in your opinion," Clemenceau was asked, "will future historians think of this troublesome and controversial issue?" He replied "This I don't know. But I know for certain that they will not say Belgium invaded Germany." We are concerned here with brutally elementary data of this kind, whose indestructibility has been taken for granted even by the most extreme and most sophisticated believers in historicism.

It is true, considerably more than the whims of historians would be needed to eliminate from the record the fact that on the night of August 4, 1914, German troops crossed the frontier of Belgium; it would require no less than a power monopoly over the entire civilized world. But such a power monopoly is far from being inconceivable, and it is not difficult to imagine what the fate of factual truth would be if power interests, national or social, had the last say in these matters. Which brings us back to our suspicion that it may be in the nature of the political realm to be at war with truth in all its forms, and hence to the question of why a commitment even to factual truth is felt to be an anti-political attitude.

III

When I said that factual, as opposed to rational, truth is not antagonistic to opinion, I stated a half-truth. All truths – not only the various kinds of rational truth but also factual truth – are opposed to opinion in their *mode of asserting validity*. Truth carries within itself an element of coercion, and the frequently tyrannical tendencies so deplorably obvious among professional truthtellers may be caused less by a failing of character than by the strain of habitually living under a kind of compulsion. Statements such as "The three angles of a triangle are equal to two angles of a square," "The earth moves around the sun," "It is better to suffer wrong than to do wrong," "In August 1914 Germany invaded Belgium" are very different in the way they are arrived at, but, once perceived as true and pronounced to be so, they have in common that they are beyond agreement, dispute, opinion, or consent. For those who accept them, they are not changed by the numbers or lack of numbers who entertain the same proposition; persuasion or dissuasion is useless, for the content of the statement is not of a persuasive nature but of a coercive one. (Thus Plato, in the *Timaeus*, draws a line between men capable of perceiving the truth and those who happen to hold right opinions. In the former, the organ for the perception of truth [νοῦς] is awakened through instruction, which of course implies inequality and can be said to be a mild form of coercion, whereas the latter had merely been persuaded. The views of the former, says Plato, are immovable, while the latter can always be persuaded to change their minds.[8]) What Mercier de la Rivière once remarked about mathematical truth applies to all kinds of truth: "*Euclide est un véritable despote; et les vérités géométriques qu'il nous a transmises, sont des lois véritablement despotiques.*" In much the same vein, Grotius, about a hundred years earlier, had insisted – when he wished to limit the power of the absolute prince – that "even God cannot cause two times two not to make four." He was invoking the compelling force of truth against political power; he was not interested in the implied limitation of divine omnipotence. These two remarks illustrate how truth looks in the purely political perspective, from the viewpoint of power, and the question is whether power could and should be checked not only by a constitution, a bill of rights, and by a multiplicity of powers, as in the system of checks and balances, in which, in Montesquieu's words, "*le pouvoir arrête le pouvoir*" – that is, by factors that arise out of and belong to the political realm proper – but by something that arises from without, has its source outside the political realm, and is as independent of the wishes and desires of the citizens as is the will of the worst tyrant.

Seen from the viewpoint of politics, truth has a despotic character. It is therefore hated by tyrants, who rightly fear the competition of a coercive force they cannot monopolize, and it enjoys a rather precarious status in the eyes of governments that rest on consent and abhor coercion. Facts are beyond agreement and consent, and all talk about them – all exchanges of opinion based on correct information – will contribute nothing to their establishment. Unwelcome opinion can be argued with, rejected, or compromised upon, but unwelcome facts possess an infuriating stubbornness that nothing can move except plain lies. The trouble is that factual truth, like all other truth, peremptorily claims to be acknowledged and precludes debate, and debate constitutes the very essence of political life. The modes of thought and communication that deal with truth, if seen from the political perspective, are necessarily domineering; they don't take into account other people's opinions, and taking these into account is the hallmark of all strictly political thinking.

Political thought is representative. I form an opinion by considering a given issue from different viewpoints, by making present to my mind the standpoints of those who are absent; that is, I represent them. This process of representation does not blindly adopt the actual views of those who stand somewhere else, and hence look upon the world from a different perspective; this is a question neither of empathy, as though I tried to be or to feel like somebody else, nor of counting noses and joining a majority but of being and thinking in my own identity where actually I am not. The more people's standpoints I have present in my mind while I am pondering a given issue, and the better I can imagine how I would feel and think if I were in their place, the stronger will be my capacity for representative thinking and the more valid my final conclusions, my opinion. (It is this capacity for an "enlarged mentality" that enables men to judge; as such, it was discovered by Kant in the first part of his *Critique of Judgment*, though he did not recognize the political and moral implications of his discovery.) The very process of opinion formation is determined by those in whose places somebody thinks and uses his own mind, and the only condition for this exertion of the imagination is disinterestedness, the liberation from one's own private interests. [. . .]

No opinion is self-evident. In matters of opinion, but not in matters of truth, our thinking is truly discursive, running, as it were, from place to place, from one part of the world to another, through all kinds of conflicting views, until it finally ascends from these particularities to some impartial generality. Compared to this process, in which a particular issue is forced into the open that it may show itself from all sides, in every possible perspective, until it is flooded and made transparent by the full light of human comprehension, a statement of truth possesses a peculiar opaqueness. Rational truth enlightens human understanding, and factual truth must inform opinions, but these truths, though they are never obscure, are not transparent either, and it is in their very nature to withstand further elucidation, as it is in the nature of light to withstand enlightenment.

Nowhere, moreover, is this opacity more patent and more irritating than where we are confronted with facts and factual truth, for facts have no conclusive reason whatever for being what they are; they could always have been otherwise, and this annoying contingency is literally unlimited. It is because of the haphazardness of facts that pre-modern philosophy refused to take seriously the realm of human affairs, which is permeated by factuality, or to believe that any meaningful truth could ever be discovered in the "melancholy haphazardness" (Kant) of a sequence of events which constitutes the course of this world. Nor has any modern philosophy of history been able to make its peace with the intractable, unreasonable stubbornness of sheer factuality; modern philosophers have conjured up all kinds of necessity, from the dialectical necessity of a world spirit or of material conditions to the necessities of an allegedly unchangeable and known human nature, in order to cleanse the last vestiges of that apparently arbitrary "it might have been otherwise" (which is the price of freedom) from the only realm where men are truly free. It is true that in retrospect – that is, in historical perspective – every sequence of events looks as though it could not have happened otherwise, but this is an optical, or, rather, an existential, illusion: nothing could ever happen if reality did not kill, by definition, all the other potentialities originally inherent in any given situation.

In other words, factual truth is no more self-evident than opinion, and this may be among the reasons that opinion-holders find it relatively easy to discredit factual truth as just another opinion. Factual evidence, moreover, is established through testimony by eyewitnesses – notoriously unreliable – and by records, documents, and monuments, all of which can be suspected as forgeries. In the event of a dispute, only other witnesses but no third and higher instance can be invoked, and settlement is usually arrived at by way of a majority; that is, in the same way as the settlement of opinion disputes – a wholly unsatisfactory procedure, since there is nothing to prevent a majority of witnesses from being false witnesses. On the contrary, under certain circumstances the feeling of belonging to a majority may even encourage false testimony. In other words, to the extent that factual truth is exposed to the hostility of opinion-holders, it is at least as vulnerable as rational philosophical truth.

I observed before that in some respects the teller of factual truth is worse off than Plato's philosopher – that his truth has no transcendent origin and possesses not even the relatively transcendent qualities of such political principles as freedom, justice, honor, and courage, all of which may inspire, and then become manifest in, human action. We shall now see that this disadvantage has more serious consequences than we had thought; namely, consequences that concern not only the person of the truthteller but – more important – the chances for his truth to survive. Inspiration of and manifestation in human action may not be able to compete with the compelling evidence of truth, but they can compete, as we shall see, with the persuasiveness inherent in opinion. I took the Socratic proposition "It is better to suffer wrong than to do wrong" as an example of a philosophical statement that concerns human conduct, and hence has political implications. My reason was partly that this sentence has become the beginning of Western ethical thought, and partly that, as far as I know, it has remained the only ethical proposition that can be derived directly from the specifically philosophical experience. (Kant's categorical imperative, the only competitor in the field, could be stripped of its Judaeo-Christian ingredients, which account for its formulation as an imperative instead of a simple proposition. Its underlying principle is the axiom of non-contradiction — the thief contradicts himself because he wants to keep the stolen goods as his property — and this axiom owes its validity to the conditions of thought that Socrates was the first to discover.)

The Platonic dialogues tell us time and again how paradoxical the Socratic statement (a proposition, and not an imperative) sounded, how easily it stood refuted in the market place where opinion stands against opinion, and how incapable Socrates was of proving and demonstrating it to the satisfaction not of his adversaries alone but also of his friends and disciples. [. . .]

To the philosopher — or, rather, to man insofar as he is a thinking being — this ethical proposition about doing and suffering wrong is no less compelling than mathematical truth. But to man insofar as he is a citizen, an acting being concerned with the world and the public welfare rather than with his own well-being — including, for instance, his "immortal soul" whose "health" should have precedence over the needs of a perishable body — the Socratic statement is not true at all. The disastrous consequences for any community that began in all earnest to follow ethical precepts derived from man in the singular — be they Socratic or Platonic or Christian — have been frequently pointed out. [. . .]

Since philosophical truth concerns man in his singularity, it is unpolitical by nature. If the philosopher nevertheless wishes his truth to prevail over the opinions of the multitude, he will suffer defeat, and he is likely to conclude from this defeat that truth is impotent — a truism that is just as meaningful as if the mathematician, unable to square the circle, should deplore the fact that a circle is not a square. He may then be tempted, like Plato, to win the ear of some philosophically inclined tyrant, and in the fortunately highly unlikely case of success he might erect one of those tyrannies of "truth" which we know chiefly from the various political utopias, and which, of course, politically speaking, are as tyrannical as other forms of despotism. In the slightly less unlikely event that his truth should prevail without the help of violence, simply because men happen to concur in it, he would have won a Pyrrhic victory. For truth would then owe its prevalence not to its own compelling quality but to the agreement of the many, who might change their minds tomorrow and agree on something else; what had been philosophical truth would have become mere opinion.

Since, however, philosophical truth carries within itself an element of coercion, it may tempt the statesman under certain conditions, no less than the power of opinion may tempt the philosopher. Thus, in the Declaration of Independence, Jefferson declared certain "truths to be self-evident," because he wished to put the basic consent among the men of the Revolution beyond dispute and argument; like mathematical axioms, they should express "beliefs of men" that "depend not on their own will, but follow involuntarily the evidence proposed to their minds."[9] Yet by saying "*We hold these truths to be self-evident*," he conceded, albeit without becoming aware of it, that the statement "All men are created equal" is not self-evident but stands in need of agreement and consent — that equality, if it is to be politically relevant, is a matter of opinion, and not "the truth." [. . .]

The Socratic proposition "It is better to suffer wrong than to do wrong" is not an opinion but claims to be truth, and though one may doubt that it ever had a direct political consequence, its impact upon practical conduct as an ethical precept is undeniable; only religious commandments, which are absolutely binding for the community of believers, can claim greater recognition. Does this fact not stand in clear contradiction to the generally accepted impotence of philosophical truth? And since we know from the Platonic dialogues how unpersuasive Socrates' statement remained for friend and foe alike whenever he tried to prove it, we must ask ourselves how it could ever have obtained its high degree of validity. Obviously, this has been due to a rather unusual kind of persuasion; Socrates decided to stake his life on this truth – to set an example, not when he appeared before the Athenian tribunal but when he refused to escape the death sentence. And this teaching by example is, indeed, the only form of "persuasion" that philosophical truth is capable of without perversion or distortion;[10] by the same token, philosophical truth can become "practical" and inspire action without violating the rules of the political realm only when it manages to become manifest in the guise of an example. [. . .]

This transformation of a theoretical or speculative statement into exemplary truth – a transformation of which only moral philosophy is capable – is a borderline experience for the philosopher: by setting an example and "persuading" the multitude in the only way open to him, he has begun to act. Today, when hardly any philosophical statement, no matter how daring, will be taken seriously enough to endanger the philosopher's life, even this rare chance of having a philosophical truth politically validated has disappeared. In our context, however, it is important to notice that such a possibility does exist for the teller of rational truth; for it does not exist under any circumstances for the teller of factual truth, who in this respect, as in other respects, is worse off. Not only do factual statements contain no principles upon which men might act and which thus could become manifest in the world; their very content defies this kind of verification. A teller of factual truth, in the unlikely event that he wished to stake his life on a particular fact, would achieve a kind of miscarriage. What would become manifest in his act would be his courage or, perhaps, his stubbornness but neither the truth of what he had to say nor even his own truthfulness. For why shouldn't a liar stick to his lies with great courage, especially in politics, where he might be motivated by patriotism or some other kind of legitimate group partiality?

IV

The hallmark of factual truth is that its opposite is neither error nor illusion nor opinion, no one of which reflects upon personal truthfulness, but the deliberate falsehood, or lie. Error, of course, is possible, and even common, with respect to factual truth, in which case this kind of truth is in no way different from scientific or rational truth. But the point is that with respect to facts there exists another alternative, and this alternative, the deliberate falsehood, does not belong to the same species as propositions that, whether right or mistaken, intend no more than to say what is, or how something that is appears to me. A factual statement – Germany invaded Belgium in August 1914 – acquires political implications only by being put in an interpretative context. But the opposite proposition, which Clemenceau, still unacquainted with

the art of rewriting history, thought absurd, needs no context to be of political significance. It is clearly an attempt to change the record, and as such, it is a form of
action. The same is true when the liar, lacking the power to make his falsehood stick,
does not insist on the gospel truth of his statement but pretends that this is his
"opinion," to which he claims his constitutional right. This is frequently done by subversive groups, and in a politically immature public the resulting confusion can be
considerable. The blurring of the dividing line between factual truth and opinion
belongs among the many forms that lying can assume, all of which are forms of
action. [. . .]

To be sure, as far as action is concerned, organized lying is a marginal phenomenon, but the trouble is that its opposite, the mere telling of facts, leads to no action
whatever; it even tends, under normal circumstances, toward the acceptance of things
as they are. (This, of course, is not to deny that the disclosure of facts may be legitimately used by political organizations or that, under certain circumstances, factual
matters brought to public attention will considerably encourage and strengthen the
claims of ethnic and social groups.) Truthfulness has never been counted among the
political virtues, because it has little indeed to contribute to that change of the world
and of circumstances which is among the most legitimate political activities. Only
where a community has embarked upon organized lying on principle, and not only
with respect to particulars, can truthfulness as such, unsupported by the distorting
forces of power and interest, become a political factor of the first order. Where everybody lies about everything of importance, the truthteller, whether he knows it or not,
has begun to act; he, too, has engaged himself in political business, for, in the unlikely
event that he survives, he has made a start toward changing the world.

In this situation, however, he will again soon find himself at an annoying disadvantage. I mentioned earlier the contingent character of facts, which could always
have been otherwise, and which therefore possess by themselves no trace of self-
evidence or plausibility for the human mind. Since the liar is free to fashion his "facts"
to fit the profit and pleasure, or even the mere expectations, of his audience, the
chances are that he will be more persuasive than the truthteller. Indeed, he will usually
have plausibility on his side; his exposition will sound more logical, as it were, since
the element of unexpectedness – one of the outstanding characteristics of all events
– has mercifully disappeared. It is not only rational truth that, in the Hegelian phrase,
stands common sense on its head; reality quite frequently offends the soundness of
common-sense reasoning no less than it offends profit and pleasure.

We must now turn our attention to the relatively recent phenomenon of mass
manipulation of fact and opinion as it has become evident in the rewriting of history,
in image-making, and in actual government policy. The traditional political lie, so
prominent in the history of diplomacy and statecraft, used to concern either true
secrets – data that had never been made public – or intentions, which anyhow do
not possess the same degree of reliability as accomplished facts; like everything that
goes on merely inside ourselves, intentions are only potentialities, and what was
intended to be a lie can always turn out to be true in the end. In contrast, the modern
political lies deal efficiently with things that are not secrets at all but are known to
practically everybody. This is obvious in the case of rewriting contemporary history
under the eyes of those who witnessed it, but it is equally true in image-making of
all sorts, in which, again, every known and established fact can be denied or neglected

if it is likely to hurt the image; for an image, unlike an old-fashioned portrait, is supposed not to flatter reality but to offer a full-fledged substitute for it. And this substitute, because of modern techniques and the mass media, is, of course, much more
in the public eye than the original ever was. [. . .]

Moreover, the traditional lie concerned only particulars and was never meant to
deceive literally everybody; it was directed at the enemy and was meant to deceive
only him. These two limitations restricted the injury inflicted upon truth to such an
extent that to us, in retrospect, it may appear almost harmless. Since facts always occur
in a context, a particular lie — that is, a falsehood that makes no attempt to change
the whole context — tears, as it were, a hole in the fabric of factuality. As every historian knows, one can spot a lie by noticing incongruities, holes, or the junctures of
patched-up places. As long as the texture as a whole is kept intact, the lie will eventually show up as if of its own accord. The second limitation concerns those who are
engaged in the business of deception. They used to belong to the restricted circle of
statesmen and diplomats, who among themselves still knew and could preserve the
truth. They were not likely to fall victims to their own falsehoods; they could deceive
others without deceiving themselves. Both of these mitigating circumstances of the
old art of lying are noticeably absent from the manipulation of facts that confronts
us today.

What, then, is the significance of these limitations, and why are we justified in
calling them mitigating circumstances? Why has self-deception become an indispensable tool in the trade of image-making, and why should it be worse, for the world
as well as for the liar himself, if he is deceived by his own lies than if he merely
deceives others? What better moral excuse could a liar offer than that his aversion to
lying was so great that he had to convince himself before he could lie to others, that,
like Antonio in *The Tempest*, he had to make "a sinner of his memory, To credit his
own lie"? And, finally, and perhaps most disturbingly, if the modern political lies are
so big that they require a complete rearrangement of the whole factual texture — the
making of another reality, as it were, into which they will fit without seam, crack, or
fissure, exactly as the facts fitted into their own original context — what prevents these
new stories, images, and non-facts from becoming an adequate substitute for reality
and factuality?

[. . .]

Such completeness and potential finality, which were unknown to former times,
are the dangers that arise out of the modern manipulation of facts. Even in the free
world, where the government has not monopolized the power to decide and tell what
factually is or is not, gigantic interest organizations have generalized a kind of *raison
d'état* frame of mind such as was formerly restricted to the handling of foreign affairs
and, in its worst excesses, to situations of clear and present danger. And national propaganda on the government level has learned more than a few tricks from business
practices and Madison Avenue methods. Images made for domestic consumption, as
distinguished from lies directed at a foreign adversary, can become a reality for everybody and first of all for the image-makers themselves, who while still in the act of
preparing their "products" are overwhelmed by the mere thought of their victims'

potential numbers. No doubt, the originators of the lying image who "inspire" the hidden persuaders still know that they want to deceive an enemy on the social or the national level, but the result is that a whole group of people, and even whole nations, may take their bearings from a web of deceptions to which their leaders wished to subject their opponents.

What then happens follows almost automatically. The main effort of both the deceived group and the deceivers themselves is likely to be directed toward keeping the propaganda image intact, and this image is threatened less by the enemy and by real hostile interests than by those inside the group itself who have managed to escape its spell and insist on talking about facts or events that do not fit the image. Contemporary history is full of instances in which tellers of factual truth were felt to be more dangerous and even more hostile, than the real opponents. These arguments against self-deception must not be confused with the protests of "idealists," whatever their merit, against lying as bad in principle and against the age-old art of deceiving the enemy. Politically, the point is that the modern art of self-deception is likely to transform an outside matter into an inside issue, so that an international or intergroup conflict boomerangs onto the scene of domestic politics. The self-deceptions practiced on both sides in the period of the Cold War are too many to enumerate, but obviously they are a case in point. Conservative critics of mass democracy have frequently outlined the dangers that this form of government brings to international affairs – without, however, mentioning the dangers peculiar to monarchies or oligarchies. The strength of their argument lies in the undeniable fact that under fully democratic conditions deception without self-deception is well-nigh impossible.

Under our present system of world-wide communication, covering a large number of independent nations, no existing power is anywhere near great enough to make its "image" foolproof. Therefore, images have a relatively short life expectancy; they are likely to explode not only when the chips are down and reality makes its reappearance in public but even before this, for fragments of facts constantly disturb and throw out of gear the propaganda war between conflicting images. However, this is not the only way, or even the most significant way, in which reality takes its revenge on those who dare defy it. The life expectancy of images could hardly be significantly increased even under a world government or some other modern version of the Pax Romana. This is best illustrated by the relatively closed systems of totalitarian governments and one-party dictatorships, which are, of course, by far the most effective agencies in shielding ideologies and images from the impact of reality and truth. [. . .] It has frequently been noticed that the surest long-term result of brainwashing is a peculiar kind of cynicism – an absolute refusal to believe in the truth of anything, no matter how well this truth may be established. In other words, the result of a consistent and total substitution of lies for factual truth is not that the lies will now be accepted as truth, and the truth be defamed as lies, but that the sense by which we take our bearings in the real world – and the category of truth vs. falsehood is among the mental means to this end – is being destroyed.

And for this trouble there is no remedy. It is but the other side of the disturbing contingency of all factual reality. Since everything that has actually happened in the realm of human affairs could just as well have been otherwise, the possibilities for lying are boundless, and this boundlessness makes for self-defeat. Only the occasional

liar will find it possible to stick to a particular falsehood with unwavering consistency; those who adjust images and stories to ever-changing circumstances will find
themselves floating on the wide-open horizon of potentiality, drifting from one possibility to the next, unable to hold on to any one of their own fabrications. Far from
achieving an adequate substitute for reality and factuality they have transformed facts
and events back into the potentiality out of which they originally appeared. And the
surest sign of the factuality of facts and events is precisely this stubborn thereness,
whose inherent contingency ultimately defies all attempts at conclusive explanation.
The images, on the contrary, can always be explained and made plausible – this gives
them their momentary advantage over factual truth – but they can never compete in
stability with that which simply is because it happens to be thus and not otherwise.
This is the reason that consistent lying, metaphorically speaking, pulls the ground from
under our feet and provides no other ground on which to stand. (In the words of
Montaigne, "If falsehood, like truth, had but one face, we should know better where
we are, for we should then take for certain the opposite of what the liar tells us. But
the reverse of truth has a thousand shapes and a boundless field.") The experience of
a trembling wobbling motion of everything we rely on for our sense of direction and
reality is among the most common and most vivid experiences of men under
totalitarian rule. [. . .]

   That facts are not secure in the hands of power is obvious, but the point here is
that power, by its very nature, can never produce a substitute for the secure stability
of factual reality, which, because it is past, has grown into a dimension beyond our
reach. Facts assent themselves by being stubborn, and their fragility is oddly combined
with great resiliency – the same irreversibility that is the hallmark of all human action.
In their stubbornness, facts are superior to power; they are less transitory than power
formations, which arise when men get together for a purpose but disappear as soon
as the purpose is either achieved or lost. This transitory character makes power a
highly unreliable instrument for achieving permanence of any kind, and, therefore,
not only truth and facts are insecure in its hands but untruth and non-facts as well.
The political attitude toward facts must, indeed, tread the very narrow path between
the danger of taking them as the results of some necessary development which men
could not prevent and about which they can therefore do nothing and the danger of
denying them, of trying no manipulate them out of the world.

                                         V

In conclusion, I return to the questions I raised at the beginning of these reflections.
Truth, though powerless and always defeated in a head-on clash with the powers that
be, possesses a strength of its own: whatever those in power may contrive, they are
unable to discover or invent a viable substitute for it. Persuasion and violence can
destroy truth, but they cannot replace it. And this applies to rational or religious truth
just as it applies, more obviously, to factual truth. To look upon politics from the perspective of truth, as I have done here, means to take one's stand outside the political
realm. This standpoint is the standpoint of the truthteller, who forfeits his position –
and, with it, the validity of what he has to say – if he tries to interfere directly

in human affairs and to speak the language of persuasion or of violence. It is to this position and its significance for the political realm that we must now turn our attention.

The standpoint outside the political realm – outside the community to which we belong and the company of our peers – is clearly characterized as one of the various modes of being alone. Outstanding among the existential modes of truthtelling are the solitude of the philosopher, the isolation of the scientist and the artist, the impartiality of the historian and the judge, and the independence of the fact-finder, the witness, and the reporter. (This impartiality differs from that of the qualified, representative opinion, mentioned earlier, in that it is not acquired inside the political realm but is inherent in the position of the outsider required for such occupations.) These modes of being alone differ in many respects, but they have in common that as long as any one of them lasts, no political commitment, no adherence to a cause, is possible. They are, of course, common to all men; they are modes of human existence as such. Only when one of them is adopted as a way of life – and even then life is never lived in complete solitude or isolation or independence – is it likely to conflict with the demands of the political.

It is quite natural that we become aware of the non-political and, potentially, even anti-political nature of truth – *Fiat veritas, et pereat mundus* – only in the event of conflict, and I have stressed up to now this side of the matter. But this cannot possibly tell the whole story. It leaves out of account certain public institutions, established and supported by the powers that be, in which, contrary to all political rules, truth and truthfulness have always constituted the highest criterion of speech and endeavor. Among these we find notably the judiciary, which either as a branch of government or as direct administration of justice is carefully protected against social and political power, as well as all institutions of higher learning, to which the state entrusts the education of its future citizens. To the extent that the Academe remembers its ancient origins, it must know that it was founded by the polis's most determined and most influential opponent. To be sure, Plato's dream did not come true: the Academe never became a counter-society, and nowhere do we hear of any attempt by the universities at seizing power. But what Plato never dreamed of did come true: The political realm recognized that it needed an institution outside the power struggle in addition to the impartiality required in the administration of justice; for whether these places of higher learning are in private or in public hands is of no great importance; not only their integrity but their very existence depends upon the good will of the government anyway. Very unwelcome truths have emerged from the universities, and very unwelcome judgments have been handed down from the bench time and again; and these institutions, like other refuges of truth, have remained exposed to all the dangers arising from social and political power. Yet the chances for truth to prevail in public are, of course, greatly improved by the mere existence of such places and by the organization of independent, supposedly disinterested scholars associated with them. And it can hardly be denied that, at least in constitutionally ruled countries, the political realm has recognized, even in the event of conflict, that it has a stake in the existence of men and institutions over which it has no power.

This authentically political significance of the Academe is today easily overlooked because of the prominence of its professional schools and the evolution of its natural-science divisions, where, unexpectedly, pure research has yielded so many decisive results that have proved vital to the country at large. No one can possibly gainsay the social and technical usefulness of the universities, but this importance is not political. The historical sciences and the humanities, which are supposed to find out, stand guard over, and interpret factual truth and human documents, are politically of greater relevance. The telling of factual truth comprehends much more than the daily information supplied by journalists, though without them we should never find our bearings in an ever-changing world and, in the most literal sense, would never know where we are. This is, of course, of the most immediate political importance; but if the press should ever really becomes the "fourth branch of government," it would have to be protected against government power and social pressure even more carefully than the judiciary is. For this very important political function of supplying information is exercised from outside the political realm, strictly speaking; no action and no decision are, or should be, involved.

Reality is different from, and more than, the totality of facts and events, which, anyhow, is unascertainable. Who says what is – λέγει τὰ ἐόντα – always tells a story, and in this story the particular facts lose their contingency and acquire some humanly comprehensible meaning. It is perfectly true that "all sorrows can be borne if you put them into a story or tell a story about them," in the words of Isak Dinesen, who not only was one of the great storytellers of our time but also – and she was almost unique in this respect – knew what she was doing. She could have added that joy and bliss, too, become bearable and meaningful for men only when they can talk about them and tell them as a story. To the extent that the teller of factual truth is also a storyteller, he brings about that "reconciliation with reality" which Hegel, the philosopher of history *par excellence*, understood as the ultimate goal of all philosophical thought, and which, indeed, has been the secret motor of all historiography that transcends mere learnedness. The transformation of the given raw material of sheer happenings which the historian, like the fiction writer (a good novel is by no means a simple concoction or a figment of pure fantasy), must effect is closely akin to the poet's transfiguration of moods or movements of the heart – the transfiguration of grief into lamentations or of jubilation into praise. We may see, with Aristotle, in the poet's political function the operation of a catharsis, a cleansing or purging of all emotions that could prevent men from acting. The political function of the storyteller – historian or novelist – is to teach acceptance of things as they are. Out of this acceptance, which can also be called truthfulness, arises the faculty of judgment – that, again in Isak Dinesen's words, "at the end we shall be privileged to view, and review, it – and that is what is named the day of judgment."

There is no doubt that all these politically relevant functions are performed from outside the political realm. They require non-commitment and impartiality, freedom from self-interest in thought and judgment. The disinterested pursuit of truth has a long history; its origin, characteristically, precedes all our theoretical and scientific traditions, including our tradition of philosophical and political thought. I think it can be traced to the moment when Homer chose to sing the deeds of the Trojans no less than those of the Achaeans, and to praise the glory of Hector, the foe and the defeated man, no less than the glory of Achilles, the hero of his kinfolk. This had happened nowhere before; no other civilization, however splendid, had been able to look with equal eyes upon friend and foe, upon success and defeat – which since Homer have not been recognized as ultimate standards of men's judgment, even though they are ultimates for the destinies of men's lives. Homeric impartiality echoes throughout Greek history, and it inspired the first great teller of factual truth, who became the father of history: Herodotus tells us in the very first sentences of his stories that he set out to prevent "the great and wondrous deeds of the Greeks *and* the barbarians from losing their due meed of glory." This is the root of all so-called objectivity – this curious passion, unknown outside Western civilization, for intellectual integrity at any price. Without it no science would ever have come into being.

Since I have dealt here with politics from the perspective of truth, and hence from a viewpoint outside the political realm, I have failed to mention even in passing the greatness and the dignity of what goes on inside it. I have spoken as though the political realm were no more than a battlefield of partial, conflicting interests, where nothing counted but pleasure and profit, partisanship, and the lust for dominion. In short, I have dealt with politics as though I, too, believed that all public affairs were ruled by interest and power, that there would be no political realm at all if we were not bound to take care of life's necessities. The reason for this deformation is that factual truth clashes with the political only on this lowest level of human affairs, just as Plato's philosophical truth clashed with the political on the considerably higher level of opinion and agreement. From this perspective, we remain unaware of the actual content of political life – of the joy and the gratification that arise out of being in company with our peers, out of acting together and appearing in public, out of inserting ourselves into the world by word and deed, thus acquiring and sustaining our personal identity and beginning something entirely new. However, what I meant to show here is that this whole sphere, its greatness notwithstanding, is limited – that it does not encompass the whole of man's and the world s existence. It is limited by those things which men cannot change at will. And it is only by respecting its own borders that this realm, where we are free to act and to change, can remain intact, preserving its integrity and keeping its promises. Conceptually, we may call truth what we cannot change; metaphorically, it is the ground on which we stand and the sky that stretches above us.

Notes

1   Ch. 11. Hobbes, *Leviathan*, (eds. R. Tuck, R. Geuss, and Q. Skinner, (Cambridge: Cambridge University Press, 1996).)

2   I hope no one will tell me any more that Plato was the inventor of the "noble lie." This belief rested on a misreading of a crucial passage (414C) in *The Republic*, where Plato speaks of one of his myths – a "Phoenician tale" – as a ψεῦδος. Since the same Greek word signifies "fiction," "error," and "lie" according to context – when Plato wants to distinguish between error and lie, the Greek language forces him to speak of "involuntary" and "voluntary" ψεῦδος – the text can be rendered with Cornford as "bold flight of invention" or be read with Eric Voegelin (*Order and History: Plato and Aristotle*, Louisiana State University, 1957, vol. 3, p. 106) as satirical in intention; under no circumstances can it be understood as a recommendation of lying as we understand it. Plato, of course, was

permissive about occasional lies to deceive the enemy or insane people – *The Republic, 382*; they are "useful . . . in the way of medicine . . . to be handled by no one but a physician," and the physician of the polis is the ruler (388). But, contrary to the cave allegory, no principle is involved in these passages.

3   *Leviathan*, Conclusion.

4   *The Federalist*, no. 49.

5   *Theologico-Political Treatise*, trans. R.H.M. Elwes (New York: Dover, 1951), ch. 20.

6   See "What Is Enlightenment?" and "Was heisst sich im Denken orientieren?"

7   *The Federalist*, no. 49.

8   *Timaeus*, 51D–52.

9   See Jefferson's "Draft Preamble to the Virginia Bill Establishing Religious Freedom."

10 This is the reason for Nietzsche's remark in "Schopenhauer als Erzicher": "Ich mache mir aus einem Philosophen gerade so viel, als er imstande ist, ein Beispiel zu geben."

20

THE DISCOURSE ON LANGUAGE
and "Truth and Power"

Michel Foucault

I would really like to have slipped imperceptibly into this lecture, as into all the others I shall be delivering, perhaps over the years ahead. I would have preferred to be enveloped in words, borne way beyond all possible beginnings. At the moment of speaking, I would like to have perceived a nameless voice, long preceding me, leaving me merely to enmesh myself in it, taking up its cadence, and to lodge myself, when no one was looking, in its interstices as if it had paused an instant, in suspense, to beckon to me. There would have been no beginnings: instead, speech would proceed from me, while I stood in its path – a slender gap – the point of its possible disappearance.

Behind me, I should like to have heard (having been at it long enough already, repeating in advance what I am about to tell you) the voice of Molloy, beginning to speak thus: 'I must go on; I can't go on; I must go on; I must say words as long as there are words, I must say them until they find me, until they say me – heavy burden, heavy sin; I must go on; maybe it's been done already; maybe they've already said me; maybe they've already borne me to the threshold of my story, right to the door opening onto my story; I'd be surprised if it opened.'

A good many people, I imagine, harbour a similar desire to be freed from the obligation to begin, a similar desire to find themselves, right from the outside, on the other side of discourse, without having to stand outside it, pondering its particular, fearsome, and even devilish features. To this all too common feeling, institutions have an ironic reply, for they solemnise beginnings, surrounding them with a circle of silent

Michel Foucault, "The Discourse on Language," trans. Rupert Sawyer in *Social Science Information* (April 1971), pp. 7–30. © 1971 by Sage Publications Ltd and Foundation of the Maison des Science de l'Homme. Reprinted by permission of Sage Publications Ltd.

This lecture was delivered in French at the Collège de France on December 2, 1970. The original French text has been published with the title *L'ordre du discours* (Paris, Gallimard, 1971).

Michel Foucault, "Truth and Power" excerpt from *Power/Knowledge: Selected Interviews and Other Writings 1972–77*, edited by Colin Gordon (Brighton: Harvester Press, 1980), pp. 131–3. Reprinted by permission of Pearson Education Ltd.

Interviewers: Alessandro Fontana, Pasquale Pasquino.

attention; in order that they can be distinguished from far off, they impose ritual forms upon them.

Inclination speaks out: 'I don't want to have to enter this risky world of discourse; I want nothing to do with it insofar as it is decisive and final; I would like to feel it all around me, calm and transparent, profound, infinitely open, with others responding to my expectations, and truth emerging, one by one. All I want is to allow myself to be borne along, within it, and by it, a happy wreck.' Institutions reply: 'But you have nothing to fear from launching out; we're here to show you discourse is within the established order of things, that we've waited a long time for its arrival, that a place has been set aside for it – a place which both honours and disarms it; and if it should happen to have a certain power, then it is we, and we alone, who give it that power.'

Yet, maybe this institution and this inclination are but two converse responses to the same anxiety: anxiety as to just what discourse is, when it is manifested materially, as a written or spoken object; but also, uncertainty faced with a transitory existence, destined for oblivion – at any rate, not belonging to us; uncertainty at the suggestion of barely imaginable powers and dangers behind this activity, however humdrum and grey it may seem; uncertainty when we suspect the conflicts, triumphs, injuries, dominations and enslavements that lie behind these words, even when long use has chipped away their rough edges.

What is so perilous, then, in the fact that people speak, and that their speech proliferates? Where is the danger in that?

Here then is the hypothesis I want to advance, tonight, in order to fix the terrain – or perhaps the very provisional theatre – within which I shall be working. I am supposing that in every society the production of discourse is at once controlled, selected, organised and redistributed according to a certain number of procedures, whose role is to avert its powers and its dangers, to cope with chance events, to evade its ponderous, awesome materiality.

In a society such as our own we all know the rules of *exclusion*. The most obvious and familiar of these concerns what is *prohibited*. We know perfectly well that we are not free to say just anything, that we cannot simply speak of anything, when we like or where we like; not just anyone, finally, may speak of just anything. We have three types of prohibition, covering objects, ritual with its surrounding circumstances, the privileged or exclusive right to speak of a particular subject; these prohibitions interrelate, reinforce and complement each other, forming a complex web, continually subject to modification. I will note simply that the areas where this web is most tightly woven today, where the danger spots are most numerous, are those dealing with politics and sexuality. It is as though discussion, far from being a transparent, neutral element, allowing us to disarm sexuality and to pacify politics, were one of those privileged areas in which they exercised some of their more awesome powers. In appearance, speech may well be of little account, but the prohibitions surrounding it soon reveal its links with desire and power. This should not be very surprising, for psychoanalysis has already shown us that speech is not merely the medium which manifests – or dissembles – desire; it is also the object of desire. Similarly, historians have constantly impressed upon us that speech is no mere verbalisation of conflicts and systems of domination, but that it is the very object of man's conflicts.

But our society possesses yet another principle of exclusion; not another prohibition, but a division and a rejection. I have in mind the opposition: reason and folly. From the depths of the Middle Ages, a man was mad if his speech could not be said to form part of the common discourse of men. His words were considered null and void, without truth or significance, worthless as evidence, inadmissible in the authentification of acts or contracts, incapable even of bringing about transubstantiation – the transformation of bread into flesh – at Mass. And yet, in contrast to all others, his words were credited with strange powers, of revealing some hidden truth, of predicting the future, of revealing, in all their naiveté, what the wise were unable to perceive. It is curious to note that for centuries, in Europe, the words of a madman were either totally ignored or else were taken as words of truth. They either fell into a void – rejected the moment they were proffered – or else men deciphered in them a naive or cunning reason, rationality more rational than that of a rational man. At all events, whether excluded or secretly invested with reason, the madman's speech did not strictly exist. It was through his words that one recognised the madness of the madman; but they were certainly the medium within which this division became active; they were neither heard nor remembered. No doctor before the end of the eighteenth century had ever thought of listening to the content – how it was said and why – of these words; and yet it was these which signalled the difference between reason and madness. Whatever a madman said, it was taken for mere noise; he was credited with words only in a symbolic sense, in the theatre, in which he stepped forward, unarmed and reconciled, playing his role: that of masked truth.

Of course people are going to say all that is over and done with, or that it is in the process of being finished with, today; that the madman's words are no longer on the other side of this division; that they are no longer null and void, that, on the contrary, they alert us to the need to look for a sense behind them, for the attempt at, or the ruins of some 'œuvre'; we have even come to notice these words of madmen in our own speech, in those tiny pauses when we forget what we are talking about. But all this is no proof that the old vision is not just as active as before; we have only to think of the systems by which we decipher this speech; we have only to think of the network of institutions established to permit doctors and psychoanalysts to listen to the mad and, at the same time, enabling the mad to come and speak, or in desperation, to withhold their meagre words; we have only to bear all this in mind to suspect that the old division is just as active as ever, even if it is proceeding along different lines and, via new institutions, producing rather different effects. Even when the role of the doctor consists of lending an ear to this finally liberated speech, this procedure still takes place in the context of a hiatus between listener and speaker. For he is listening to speech invested with desire, crediting itself – for its greater exultation or for its greater anguish – with terrible powers. If we truly require silence to cure monsters, then it must be an attentive silence, and it is in this that the division lingers.

It is perhaps a little risky to speak of the opposition between true and false as a third system of exclusion, along with those I have mentioned already. How could one reasonably compare the constraints of truth with those other divisions, arbitrary in origin if not developing out of historical contingency – not merely modifiable but in a state of continual flux, supported by a system of institutions imposing and manipulating them, acting not without constraint, nor without an element, at least, of violence?

Certainly, as a proposition, the division between true and false is neither arbitrary, nor modifiable, nor institutional, nor violent. Putting the question in different terms, however – asking what has been, what still is, throughout our discourse, this will to truth which has survived throughout so many centuries of our history; or if we ask what is, in its very general form, the kind of division governing our will to know-ledge – then we may well discern something like a system of exclusion (historical, modifiable, institutionally constraining) in the process of development.

It is, undoubtedly, a historically constituted division. For, even with the sixth-century Greek poets, true discourse – in the meaningful sense – inspiring respect and terror, to which all were obliged to submit, because it held sway over all and was pronounced by men who spoke as of right, according to ritual, meted out justice and attributed to each his rightful share; it prophesied the future, not merely announcing what was going to occur, but contributing to its actual event, carrying men along with it and thus weaving itself into the fabric of fate. And yet, a century later, the highest truth no longer resided in what discourse *was*, nor in what it *did*: it lay in what was *said*. The day dawned when truth moved over from the ritualised act – potent and just – of enunciation to settle on what was enunciated itself: its meaning, its form, its object and its relation to what it referred to. A division emerged between Hesiod and Plato, separating true discourse from false; it was a new division for, hence-forth, true discourse was no longer considered precious and desirable, since it had ceased to be discourse linked to the exercise of power. And so the Sophists were routed.

This historical division has doubtless lent its general form to our will to know-ledge. Yet it has never ceased shifting: the great mutations of science may well some-times be seen to flow from some discovery, but they may equally be viewed as the appearance of new forms of the will to truth. In the nineteenth century there was undoubtedly a will to truth having nothing to do, in terms of the forms examined, of the fields to which it addressed itself, nor the techniques upon which it was based, with the will to knowledge which characterised classical culture. Going back a little in time, to the turn of the sixteenth and seventeenth centuries – and particularly in England – a will to knowledge emerged which, anticipating its present content, sketched out a schema of possible, observable, measurable and classifiable objects; a will to knowledge which imposed upon the knowing subject – in some ways taking precedence over all experience – a certain position, a certain viewpoint, and a certain function (look rather than read, verify rather than comment), a will to knowledge which prescribed (and, more generally speaking, all instruments determined) the tech-nological level at which knowledge could be employed in order to be verifiable and useful (navigation, mining, pharmacopoeia). Everything seems to have occurred as though, from the time of the great Platonic division onwards, the will to truth had its own history, which is not at all that of the constraining truths: the history of a range of subjects to be learned, the history of the functions of the knowing subject, the history of material, technical and instrumental investment in knowledge.

But this will to truth, like the other systems of exclusion, relies on institutional support: it is both reinforced and accompanied by whole strata of practices such as pedagogy — naturally — the book-system, publishing, libraries, such as the learned societies in the past, and laboratories today. But it is probably even more profoundly accompanied by the manner in which knowledge is employed in a society, the way in which it is exploited, divided and, in some ways, attributed. It is worth recalling at this point, if only symbolically, the old Greek adage, that arithmetic should be taught in democracies, for it teaches relations of equality, but that geometry alone should be reserved for oligarchies, as it demonstrates the proportions within inequality.

Finally, I believe that this will to knowledge, thus reliant upon institutional support and distribution, tends to exercise a sort of pressure, a power of constraint upon other forms of discourse — I am speaking of our own society. I am thinking of the way Western literature has, for centuries, sought to base itself in nature, in the plausible, upon sincerity and science — in short, upon true discourse. I am thinking, too, of the way economic practices, codified into precepts and recipes — as morality, too — have sought since the eighteenth century, to found themselves, to rationalise and justify their currency, in a theory of wealth and production; I am thinking, again, of the manner in which such prescriptive ensembles as the Penal Code have sought their bases or justifications. For example, the Penal Code started out as a theory of Right; then, from the time of the nineteenth century, people looked for its validation in sociological, psychological, medical and psychiatric knowledge. It is as though the very words of the law had no authority in our society, except insofar as they are derived from true discourse, Of the three great systems of exclusion governing discourse — prohibited words, the division of madness and the will to truth — I have spoken at greatest length concerning the third. With good reason: for centuries, the former have continually tended towards the latter; because this last has, gradually, been attempting to assimilate the others in order both to modify them and to provide them with a firm foundation. Because, if the two former are continually growing more fragile and less certain to the extent that they are now invaded by the will to truth, the latter, in contrast, daily grows in strength, in depth and implacability.

And yet we speak of it least. As though the will to truth and its vicissitudes were masked by truth itself and its necessary unfolding. The reason is perhaps this: if, since the time of the Greeks, true discourse no longer responds to desire or to that which exercises power in the will to truth, in the will to speak out in true discourse, what, then, is at work, if not desire and power? True discourse, liberated by the nature of its form from desire and power, is incapable of recognising the will to truth which pervades it; and the will to truth, having imposed itself upon us for so long, is such that the truth it seeks to reveal cannot fail to mask it.

Thus, only one truth appears before our eyes: wealth, fertility and sweet strength in all its insidious universality. In contrast, we are unaware of the prodigious machinery of the will to truth, with its vocation of exclusion. All those who, at one moment or another in our history, have attempted to remould this will to truth and to turn it against truth at that very point where truth undertakes to justify the taboo, and to define madness; all those, from Nietzsche to Artaud and Tabaille, must now stand as (probably haughty) signposts for all our future work.

There are, of course, many other systems for the control and delimitation of discourse. Those I have spoken of up to now are, to some extent, active on the exterior;

they function as systems of exclusion; they concern that part of discourse which deals with power and desire.

I believe we can isolate another group: internal rules, where discourse exercises its own control; rules concerned with the principles of classification, ordering and distribution. It is as though we were now involved in the mastery of another dimension of discourse: that of events and chance.

In the first place, commentary. I suppose, though I am not altogether sure, there is barely a society without its major narratives, told, retold and varied; formulae, texts, ritualised texts to be spoken in well-defined circumstances; things said once, and conserved because people suspect some hidden secret or wealth lies buried within. In short, I suspect one could find a kind of gradation between different types of discourse within most societies: discourse 'uttered' in the course of the day and in casual meetings, and which disappears with the very act which gave rise to it; and those forms of discourse that lie at the origins of a certain number of new verbal acts, which are reiterated, transformed or discussed; in short, discourse which *is spoken* and remains spoken, indefinitely, beyond its formulation, and which remains to be spoken. We know them in our own cultural system: religious or judicial texts, as well as some curious texts, from the point of view of their status, which we term 'literary'; to a certain extent, scientific texts also.

What is clear is that this gap is neither stable, nor constant, nor absolute. There is no question of there being one category, fixed for all time, reserved for fundamental or creative discourse, and another for those which reiterate, expound and comment. Not a few major texts become blurred and disappear, and commentaries sometimes come to occupy the former position. But while the details of application may well change, the function remains the same, and the principle of hierarchy remains at work. The radical denial of this gradation can never be anything but play, utopia or anguish. Play, as Borges uses the term, in the form of commentary that is nothing more than the reappearance, word for word (though this time it is solemn and anticipated) of the text commented on; or again, the play of a work of criticism talking endlessly about a work that does not exist. It is a lyrical dream of talk reborn, utterly afresh and innocent, at each point; continually reborn in all its vigour, stimulated by things, feelings or thoughts. Anguish, such as that of Janet when sick, for whom the least utterance sounded as the 'word of the Evangelist', concealing an inexhaustible wealth of meaning, worthy to be broadcast, rebegun, commented upon indefinitely: 'When I think', he said on reading or listening; 'When I think of this phrase, continuing its journey through eternity; while I, perhaps, have only incompletely understood it . . .'

But who can fail to see that this would be to annul one of the terms of the relationship each time, and not to suppress the relationship itself? A relationship in continual process of modification; a relationship taking multiple and diverse forms in a given epoch: juridical exegesis is very different – and has been for a long time – from religious commentary; a single work of literature can give rise, simultaneously, to several distinct types of discourse. The *Odyssey*, as a primary text, is repeated in the same epoch, in Berand's translation, in infinite textual explanations and in Joyce's *Ulysses*.

For the time being, I would like to limit myself to pointing out that, in what we generally refer to as commentary, the difference between primary text and secondary text plays two interdependent roles. On the one hand, it permits us to create new discourses ad infinitum: the top-heaviness of the original text, its permanence, its status as discourse ever capable of being brought up to date, the multiple or hidden meanings with which it is credited, the reticence and wealth it is believed to contain, all this creates an open possibility for discussion. On the other hand, whatever the techniques employed, commentary's only role is to say *finally*, what has silently been articulated *deep down*. It must — and the paradox is ever-changing yet inescapable — say, for the first time, what has already been said, and repeat tirelessly what was, nevertheless, never said. The infinite rippling of commentary is agitated from within by the dream of masked repetition: in the distance there is, perhaps, nothing other than what was there at the point of departure: simple recitation. Commentary averts the chance element of discourse by giving it its due: it gives us the opportunity to say something other than the text itself, but on condition that it is the text itself which is uttered and, in some ways, finalised. The open multiplicity, the fortuitousness, is transferred, by the principle of commentary, from what is liable to be said to the number, the form, the masks and the circumstances of repetition. The novelty lies no longer in what is said, but in its reappearance.

I believe there is another principle of rarefaction, complementary to the first: the author. Not, of course, the author in the sense of the individual who delivered the speech or wrote the text in question, but the author as the unifying principle in a particular group of writings or statements, lying at the origins of their significance, as the seat of their coherence. This principle is not constant at all times. All around us, there are sayings and texts whose meaning or effectiveness has nothing to do with any author to whom they might be attributed: mundane remarks, quickly forgotten; orders and contacts that are signed, but have no recognisable author; technical prescriptions anonymously transmitted. But even in those fields where it is normal to attribute a work to an author — literature, philosophy, science — the principle does not always play the same role; in the order of scientific discourse, it was, during the Middle Ages, indispensable that a scientific text be attributed to an author, for the author was the index of the work's truthfulness. A proposition was held to derive its scientific value from its author. But since the seventeenth century this function has been steadily declining; it barely survives now, save to give a name to a theorem, an effect, an example or a syndrome. In literature, however, and from about the same period, the author's function has become steadily more important. Now, we demand of all those narratives, poems, dramas and comedies which circulated relatively anonymously throughout the Middle Ages, whence they come, and we virtually insist they tell us who wrote them. We ask authors to answer for the unity of the works published in their names; we ask that they reveal, or at least display the hidden sense pervading their work; we ask them to reveal their personal lives, to account for their experiences and the real story that gave birth to their writings. The author is he who implants, into the troublesome language of fiction, its unities, its coherence, its links with reality.

I know what people are going to say: 'But there you are speaking of the author in the same way as the critic reinvents him after he is dead and buried, when we are left with no more than a tangled mass of scrawlings. Of course, then you have to put a little order into what is left, you have to imagine a structure, a cohesion, the sort of theme you might expect to arise out of an author's consciousness or his life, even if it is a little fictitious. But all that cannot get away from the fact that the author existed, irrupting into the midst of all the words employed, infusing them with his genius, or his chaos.'

Of course, it would be ridiculous to deny the existence of individuals who write, and invent. But I think that, for some time, at least, the individual who sits down to write a text, at the edge of which lurks a possible *œuvre*, resumes the functions of the author. What he writes and does not write, what he sketches out, even preliminary sketches for the work, and what he drops as simple mundane remarks, all this interplay of differences is prescribed by the author-function. It is from his new position, as an author, that he will fashion – from all he might have said, from all he says daily, at any time – the still shaky profile of his *œuvre*.

Commentary limited the hazards of discourse through the action of an *identity* taking the form of *repetition* and *sameness*. The author principle limits this same chance element through the action of an *identity* whose form is that of *individuality* and the *I*.

But we have to recognise another principle of limitation in what we call, not sciences, but 'disciplines'. Here is yet another relative, mobile principle, one which enables us to construct, but within a narrow framework.

The organisation of disciplines is just as much opposed to the commentary principle as it is to that of the author. Opposed to that of the author, because disciplines are defined by groups of objects, methods, their corpus of propositions considered to be true, the interplay of rules and definitions, of techniques and tools: all these constitute a sort of anonymous system, freely available to whoever wishes, or whoever is able to make use of them, without there being any question of their meaning or their validity being derived from whoever happened to invent them. But the principles involved in the formation of disciplines are equally opposed to that of commentary. In a discipline, unlike in commentary, what is supposed at the point of departure is not some meaning which must be rediscovered, nor an identity to be reiterated; it is that which is required for the construction of new statements. For a discipline to exist there must be the possibility of formulating – and of doing so ad infinitum – fresh propositions.

But there is more, and there is more, probably, in order that there may be less. A discipline is not the sum total of all the truths that may be uttered concerning something; it is not even the total of all that may be accepted, by virtue of some principle of coherence and systematisation, concerning some given fact or proposition. Medicine does not consist of all that may be truly said about disease; botany cannot be defined by the sum total of the truths one could say about plants. There are two reasons for this, the first being that botany and medicine, like other disciplines, consist of errors as well as truths, errors that are in no way residuals, or foreign bodies, but have their own positive functions and their own valid history, such that their roles are often indissociable from that of the truths. The other reason is that, for a proposition to belong to botany or pathology, it must fulfil certain conditions, in a stricter and more complex sense than that of pure and simple truth: at any rate, other conditions. The proposition must refer to a specific range of objects; from the end of the seventeenth century, for example, a proposition, to be 'botanical', had to be concerned with the visible structure of plants, with its system of close and not so close resemblances, or with the behaviour of its fluids; (but it could no longer retain, as had still been the case in the sixteenth century, references to its symbolic value or to the virtues and properties accorded it in antiquity). But without belonging to any discipline, a proposition is obliged to utilise conceptual instruments and techniques of a well-defined type; from the nineteenth century onwards, a proposition was no longer medical – it became 'non-medical', becoming more of an individual fantasy or item of popular imagery – if it employed metaphorical or qualitative terms or notions of essence (congestion, fermented liquids, dessicated solids); in return, it could – it had to – appeal to equally metaphorical notions, though constructed according to a different functional and physiological model (concerning irritation, inflammation or the decay of tissue). But there is more still, for in order to belong to a discipline, a proposition must fit into a certain type of theoretical field. Suffice it to recall that the quest for primitive language, a perfectly acceptable theme up to the eighteenth century, was enough, in the second half of the nineteenth century, to throw any discourse into, I hesitate to say error, but into a world of chimera and reverie – into pure and simple linguistic monstrosity.

Within its own limits, every discipline recognises true and false propositions, but it repulses a whole teratology of learning. The exterior of a science is both more, and less, populated than one might think: certainly, there is immediate experience, imaginary themes bearing on and continually accompanying immemorial beliefs; but perhaps there are no errors in the strict sense of the term, for error can only emerge and be identified within a well-defined process; there are monsters on the prowl, however, whose forms alter with the history of knowledge. In short, a proposition must fulfil some onerous and complex conditions before it can be admitted within a discipline; before it can be pronounced true or false it must be, as Monsieur Canguilhem might say, 'within the true'.

People have often wondered how on earth nineteenth-century botanists and biologists managed not to see the truth of Mendel's statements. But it was precisely because Mendel spoke of objects, employed methods and placed himself within a theoretical perspective totally alien to the biology of his time. But then, Naudin had suggested that hereditary traits constituted a separate element before him; and yet, however novel or unfamiliar the principle may have been, it was nevertheless reconcilable, if only as an enigma, with biological discourse. Mendel, on the other hand, announced that hereditary traits constituted an absolutely new biological object, thanks to a hitherto untried system of filtrage: he detached them from species, from the sex transmitting them, the field in which he observed being that infinitely open series of generations in which hereditary traits appear and disappear with statistical regularity. Here was a new object, calling for new conceptual tools, and for fresh theoretical foundations. Mendel spoke the truth, but he was not *dans le vrai* (within the true) of contemporary biological discourse: it simply was not along such lines that objects and biological concepts were formed. A whole change in scale, the deployment of a totally new range of objects in biology was required before Mendel could enter into the true and his propositions appear, for the most part, exact. Mendel was a true monster, so much so that science could not even properly speak of him. And yet Schleiden, for example, thirty years earlier, denying, at the height of the nineteenth century, vegetable sexuality, was committing no more than a disciplined error.

It is always possible one could speak the truth in a void; one would only be in the true, however, if one obeyed the rules of some discursive 'policy' which would have to be reactivated every time one spoke.

Disciplines constitute a system of control in the production of discourse, fixing its limits through the action of an identity taking the form of a permanent reactivation of the rules.

We tend to see, in an author's fertility, in the multiplicity of commentaries and in the development of a discipline so many infinite resources available for the creation of discourse. Perhaps so, but they are nonetheless principles of constraint, and it is probably impossible to appreciate their positive, multiplicatory role without first taking into consideration their restrictive, constraining role.

There is, I believe, a third group of rules serving to control discourse. Here, we are no longer dealing with the mastery of the powers contained within discourse, nor with averting the hazards of its appearance; it is more a question of determining the conditions under which it may be employed, of imposing a certain number of rules upon those individuals who employ it, thus denying access to everyone else. This amounts to a rarefaction among speaking subjects: none may enter into discourse on a specific subject unless he has satisfied certain conditions or if he is not, from the outset, qualified to do so. More exactly, not all areas of discourse are equally open and penetrable; some are forbidden territory (differentiated and differentiating) while others are virtually open to the winds and stand, without any prior restrictions, open to all.

Here, I would like to recount a little story so beautiful I fear it may well be true. It encompasses all the constraints of discourse: those limiting its powers, those controlling its chance appearances and those which select from among speaking subjects. At the beginning of the seventeenth century, the Shogun heard tell of European superiority in navigation, commerce, politics and the military arts, and that this was due to their knowledge of mathematics. He wanted to obtain this precious knowledge. When someone told him of an English sailor possessed of this marvellous discourse, he summoned him to his palace and kept him there. The Shogun took lessons from the mariner in private and familiarised himself with mathematics after which he retained power and lived to a very old age. It was not until the nineteenth century that there were *Japanese* mathematicians. But that is not the end of the anecdote, for it has its European aspect as well. The story has it that the English sailor, Will Adams, was a carpenter and an autodidact. Having worked in a shipyard he had learnt geometry. Can we see in this narrative the expression of one of the great myths of European culture? To the monopolistic, secret knowledge of oriental tyranny, Europe opposed the universal communication of knowledge and the infinitely free exchange of discourse.

This notion does not, in fact, stand up to close examination. Exchange and communication are positive forces at play within complex but restrictive systems; it is probable that they cannot operate independently of these. The most superficial and obvious of these restrictive systems is constituted by what we collectively refer to as ritual; ritual defines the qualifications required of the speaker (of who in dialogue, interrogation or recitation, should occupy which position and formulate which type of utterance); it lays down gestures to be made, behaviour, circumstances and the whole range of signs that must accompany discourse; finally, it lays down the supposed, or imposed significance of the words used, their effect upon those to whom they are addressed, the limitations of their constraining validity. Religious discourse, juridical and therapeutic as well as, in some ways, political discourse are all barely dissociable from the functioning of a ritual that determines the individual properties and agreed roles of the speakers.

A rather different function is filled by 'fellowships of discourse', whose function is to preserve or to reproduce discourse, but in order that it should circulate within a closed community, according to strict regulations, without those in possession being dispossessed by this very distribution. An archaic model of this would be those groups of Rhapsodists, possessing knowledge of poems to recite or, even, upon which to work variations and transformations. But though the ultimate object of this knowledge was ritual recitation, it was protected and preserved within a determinate group, by the, often extremely complex, exercises of memory implied by such a process. Apprenticeship gained access both to a group and to a secret which recitation made manifest, but did not divulge. The roles of speaking and listening were not interchangeable.

Few such 'fellowships of discourse' remain, with their ambiguous interplay of secrecy and disclosure. But do not be deceived; even in true discourse, even in the order of published discourse, free from all ritual, we still find secret-appropriation and non-interchangeability at work. It could even be that the act of writing, as it is institutionalised today, with its books, its publishing system and the personality of the writer, occurs within a diffuse, yet constraining, 'fellowship of discourse'. The separateness of the writer, continually opposed to the activity of all other writing and speaking subjects, the intransitive character he lends to his discourse, the fundamental singularity he has long accorded to 'writing', the affirmed dissymmetry between 'creation' and any use of linguistic systems – all this manifests in its formulation (and tends moreover to accompany the interplay of these factors in practice) the existence of a certain 'fellowship of discourse'. But there are many others, functioning according to entirely different schemas of exclusivity and disclosure: one has only to think of technical and scientific secrets, of the forms of diffusion and circulation in medical discourse, of those who have appropriated economic or political discourse.

At first sight, 'doctrine' (religious, political, philosophical) would seem to constitute the very reverse of a 'fellowship of discourse'; for among the latter, the number of speakers were, if not fixed, at least limited, and it was among this number that discourse was allowed to circulate and be transmitted. Doctrine, on the other hand, tends to diffusion: in the holding in common of a single ensemble of discourse that individuals, as many as you wish, could define their reciprocal allegiance. In appearance, the sole requisite is the recognition of the same truths and the acceptance of a certain rule – more or less flexible – of conformity with validated discourse. If it were a question of just that, doctrines would barely be any different from scientific disciplines, and discursive control would bear merely on the form or content of what was uttered, and not on the speaker. Doctrinal adherence, however, involves both speaker and the spoken, the one through the other. The speaking subject is involved through, and as a result of, the spoken, as is demonstrated by the rules of exclusion and the rejection mechanism brought into play when a speaker formulates one, or many, inassimilable utterances; questions of heresy and unorthodoxy in no way arise out of fanatical exaggeration of doctrinal mechanisms; they are a fundamental part of them. But conversely, doctrine involves the utterances of speakers in the sense that doctrine is, permanently, the sign, the manifestation and the instrument of a prior adherence – adherence to a class, to a social or racial status, to a nationality or an interest, to a struggle, a revolt, resistance or acceptance. Doctrine links individuals to certain types of utterance while consequently barring them from all others. Doctrine effects a dual subjection, that of speaking subjects to discourse, and that of discourse to the group, at least virtually, of speakers.

Finally, on a much broader scale, we have to recognise the great cleavages in what one might call the social appropriation of discourse. Education may well be, as of right, the instrument whereby every individual, in a society like our own, can gain access to any kind of discourse. But we well know that in its distribution, in what it permits and in what it prevents, it follows the well-trodden battle-lines of social conflict. Every educational system is a political means of maintaining or of modifying the appropriation of discourse, with the knowledge and the powers it carries with it.

I am well aware of the abstraction I am performing when I separate, as I have just done, verbal rituals, 'fellowships of discourse', doctrinal groups and social appropriation. Most of the time they are linked together, constituting great edifices that distribute speakers among the different types of discourse, and which appropriate those types of discourse to certain categories of subject. In a word, let us say that these are the main rules for the subjection of discourse. What is an educational system, after all, if not a ritualisation of the word; if not a qualification of some fixing of roles for speakers; if not the constitution of a (diffuse) doctrinal group; if not a distribution and an appropriation of discourse, with all its learning and its powers? What is 'writing' (that of 'writers') if not a similar form of subjection, perhaps taking rather different forms, but whose main stresses and nonetheless analogous? May we not also say that the judicial system, as well as institutionalised medicine, constitute similar systems for the subjection of discourse?

I wonder whether a certain number of philosophical themes have not come to conform to this activity of limitation and exclusion and perhaps even to reinforce it.

They conform, first of all, by proposing an ideal truth as a law of discourse, and an immanent rationality as the principle of their behaviour. They accompany, too, an ethic of knowledge, promising truth only to the desire for truth itself and the power to think it.

They then go on to reinforce this activity by denying the specific reality of discourse in general.

Ever since the exclusion of the activity and commerce of the Sophists, ever since their paradoxes were muzzled, more or less securely, it would seem that Western thought has seen to it that discourse be permitted as little room as possible between thought and words. It would appear to have ensured that *to discourse* should appear merely as a certain interjection between speaking and thinking; that it should constitute thought, clad in its signs and rendered visible by words or, conversely, that the structures of language themselves should be brought into play, producing a certain effect of meaning.

This very ancient elision of the reality of discourse in philosophical thought has taken many forms in the course of history. We have seen it quite recently in the guise of many themes now familiar to us.

It seems to me that the themes of the founding subject permits us to elide the reality of discourse. The task of the founding subject is to animate the empty forms of language with his objectives; through the thickness and inertia of empty things, he grasps intuitively the meanings lying within them. Beyond time, he indicates the field of meanings – leaving history to make them explicit – in which propositions, sciences, and deductive ensembles ultimately find their foundation. In this relationship with meaning, the founding subject has signs, marks, tracks, letters at his disposal. But he does not need to demonstrate these passing through the singular instance of discourse.

The opposing theme, that of originating experience, plays an analogous role. This asserts, in the case of experience, that even before it could be grasped in the form of a *cogito*, prior significations, in some ways already spoken, were circulating in the world, scattering it all about us, and from the outset made possible a sort of primitive recognition. Thus, a primary complicity with the world founds, for us, a possibility of speaking of experience, in it, to designate and name it, to judge it and, finally, to know it in the form of truth. If there is discourse, what could it legitimately be if not a discrete reading? Things murmur meanings our language has merely to extract; from its most primitive beginnings, this language was already whispering to us of a being of which it forms the skeleton.

The theme of universal mediation is, I believe, yet another manner of eliding the reality of discourse. And this despite appearances. At first sight it would seem that, to discover the movement of a logos everywhere elevating singularities into concepts, finally enabling immediate consciousness to deploy all the rationality in the world, is certainly to place discourse at the centre of speculation. But, in truth, this logos is really only another discourse already in operation, or rather, it is things and events themselves which *insensibly* become discourse in the unfolding of the essential secrets. Discourse is no longer much more than the shimmering of a truth about to be born in its own eyes; and when all things come eventually to take the form of discourse, when everything may be said and when anything becomes an excuse for pronouncing a discourse, it will be because all things having manifested and exchanged meanings, they will then all be able to return to the silent interiority of self-consciousness.

Whether it is the philosophy of a founding subject, a philosophy of originating experience or a philosophy of universal mediation, discourse is really only an activity, of writing in the first case, of reading in the second and exchange in the third. This exchange, this writing, this reading never involve anything but signs. Discourse thus nullifies itself, in reality, in placing itself at the disposal of the signifier.

What civilisation, in appearance, has shown more respect towards discourse than our own? Where has it been more and better honoured? Where have men depended more radically, apparently, upon its constraints and its universal character? But, it seems to me, a certain fear hides behind this apparent supremacy accorded, this apparent logophilia. It is as though these taboos, these barriers, thresholds and limits were deliberately disposed in order, at least partly, to master and control the great proliferation of discourse, in such a way as to relieve its richness of its most dangerous elements; to organise its disorder so as to skate round its most uncontrollable aspects. it is as though people had wanted to efface all trace of its irruption into the activity of our thought and language. There is undoubtedly in our society, and I would not be surprised to see it in others, though taking different forms and modes, a profound logophobia, a sort of dumb fear of these events, of this mass of spoken things, of everything that could possibly be violent, discontinuous, querulous, disordered even and perilous in it, of the incessant, disorderly buzzing of discourse.

If we wish – I will not say to efface this fear – but to analyse it in its conditions, its activity and its effects, I believe we must resolve ourselves to accept three decisions which our current thinking rather tends to resist, and which belong to the three groups of function I have just mentioned: to question our will to truth; to restore to discourse its character as an event; to abolish the sovereignty of the signifier.

These are the tasks, or rather, some of the themes which will govern my work in the years ahead. One can straight away distinguish some of the methodological demands they imply.

A principle of *reversal*, first of all. Where, according to tradition, we think we recognise the source of discourse, the principles behind its flourishing and continuity, in those factors which seem to play a positive role, such as the author discipline, will to truth, we must rather recognise the negative activity of the cutting-out and rarefaction of discourse.

But, once we have distinguished these principles of rarefaction, once we have ceased considering them as a fundamental and creative action, what do we discover behind them? Should we affirm that a world of uninterrupted discourse would be virtually complete? This is where we have to bring other methodological principles into play.

Next, then, the principle of *discontinuity*. The existence of systems of rarefaction does nor imply that, over and beyond them lie great vistas of limitless discourse, continuous and silent, repressed and driven back by them, making it our task to abolish them and at last to restore it to speech. Whether talking in terms of speaking or thinking, we must nor imagine some unsaid thing, or an unthought, floating about the world, interlacing with all its forms and events. Discourse must be treated as a discontinuous activity, its different manifestations sometimes coming together, but just as easily unaware of, or excluding each other.

The principle of *specificity* declares that a particular discourse cannot be resolved by a prior system of significations; that we should not imagine that the world presents us with a legible face, leaving us merely to decipher it; it does not work hand in glove with what we already know; there is no prediscursive fate disposing the word in our favour. We must conceive discourse as a violence that we do to things, or, at all events, as a practice we impose upon them; it is in this practice that the events of discourse find the principle of their regularity.

The fourth principle, that of *exteriority*, holds that we are not to burrow to the hidden core of discourse, to the heart of the thought or meaning manifested in it; instead, taking the discourse itself, its appearance and its regularity, that we should look for its external conditions of existence, for that which gives rise to the chance series of these events and fixes its limits.

As the regulatory principles of analysis, then, we have four notions: event series, regularity and the possible conditions of existence. Term for term we find the notion of event opposed to that of creation, the possible conditions of existence opposing signification. These four notions (signification, originality, unity, creation) have, in a fairly general way, dominated the traditional history of ideas; by general agreement one sought the point of creation, the unity of a work, of a period or a theme, one looked also for the mark of individual originality and the infinite wealth of hidden meanings.

I would like to add just two remarks, the first of which concerns history. We frequently credit contemporary history with having removed the individual event from its privileged position and with having revealed the more enduring structures of history. That is so. I am not sure, however, that historians have been working in this direction alone. Or, rather, I do not think one can oppose the identification of the individual event to the analysis of long term trends quite so neatly. On the contrary, it seems to me that it is in squeezing the individual event, in directing the resolving power of historical analysis onto official price-lists (*mercuriales*), title deeds, parish registers, to harbour archives analysed year by year and week by week, that we gradually perceive – beyond battles, decisions, dynasties and assemblies – the emergence of those massive phenomena of secular or multi-secular importance. History, as it is practised today, does not turn its back on events; on the contrary, it is continually enlarging the field of events, constantly discovering new layers – more superficial as well as more profound – incessantly isolating new ensembles – events, numerous, dense and interchangeable or rare and decisive: from daily price fluctuations to secular inflations. What is significant is that history does not consider an event without defining the series to which it belongs, without specifying the method of analysis used, without seeking out the regularity of phenomena and the probable limits of their occurrence, without enquiring about variations, inflexions and the slope of the curve, without desiring to know the conditions on which these depend. History has long since abandoned its attempts to understand events in terms of cause and effect in the formless unity of some great evolutionary process, whether vaguely homogeneous or rigidly hierarchised. It did not do this in order to seek out structures anterior to, alien or hostile to the event. It was rather in order to establish those diverse converging, and sometimes divergent, but never autonomous series that enable us to circumscribe the 'locus' of an event, the limits to its fluidity and the conditions of its emergence.

The fundamental notions now imposed upon us are no longer those of consciousness and continuity (with their correlative problems of liberty and causality), nor are they those of sign and structure. They are notions, rather, of events and of series, with the groups of notions linked to these; it is around such an ensemble that this analysis of discourse I am thinking of is articulated, certainly not upon those traditional themes which the philosophers of the past took for 'living' history, but on the effective work of historians.

But it is also here that this analysis poses some, probably awesome philosophical or theoretical problems. If discourses are to be treated first as ensembles of discursive events, what status are we to accord this notion of event, so rarely taken into consideration by philosophers? Of course, an event is neither substance, nor accident, nor quality nor process; events are not corporeal. And yet, an event is certainly not immaterial; it takes effect, becomes effect, always on the level of materiality. Events have their place; they consist in relation to, coexistence with, dispersion of, the cross-checking accumulation and the selection of material elements; it occurs as an effect of, and in, material dispersion. Let us say that the philosophy of event should advance in the direction, at first sight paradoxical, of an incorporeal materialism. If, on the other hand, discursive events are to be dealt with as homogeneous, but discontinuous series, what status are we to accord this discontinuity? Here we are not dealing with a succession of instants in time, nor with the plurality of thinking subjects; what is concerned are those caesurae breaking the instant and dispersing the subject in a multiplicity of possible positions and functions. Such a discontinuity strikes and invalidates the smallest units, traditionally recognised and the least readily contested: the instant and the subject. Beyond them, independent of them, we must conceive – between these discontinuous series of relations which are not in any order of succession (or simultaneity) within any (or several) consciousnesses – and we must elaborate – outside of philosophies of time and subject – a theory of discontinuous systematisation. Finally, if it is true that these discursive, discontinuous series have their regularity, within certain limits, it is clearly no longer possible to establish mechanically causal links on an ideal necessity among their constitutive elements. We must accept the introduction of chance as a category in the production of events. There again, we feel the absence of a theory enabling us to conceive the links between chance and thought.

In the sense that this slender wedge I intend to slip into the history of ideas consists in dealing not with meanings possibly lying behind this or that discourse, but with discourse as regular series and distinct events, I fear I recognise in this wedge a tiny (odious, too, perhaps) device permitting the introduction, into the very roots of thought, of notions of *chance*, *discontinuity* and *materiality*. This represents a triple peril which one particular form of history attempts to avert by recounting the continuous unfolding of some ideal necessity. But they are three notions which ought to permit us to link the history of systems of thought to the practical work of historians; three directions to be followed in the work of theoretical elaboration.

Following these principles, and referring to this overall view, the analyses I intend to undertake fall into two groups. On the one hand, the 'critical' group which sets the reversal principle to work. I shall attempt to distinguish the forms of exclusion, limitation and appropriation of which I was speaking earlier; I shall try to show how they are formed, in answer to which needs, how they are modified and displaced, which constraints they have effectively exercised, to what extent they have been worked on. On the other hand, the 'genealogical' group, which brings the three other principles into play: how series of discourse are formed, through, in spite of, or with the aid of these systems of constraint: what were the specific norms for each, and what were their conditions of appearance, growth and variation.

Taking the critical group first, a preliminary group of investigations could bear on what I have designated functions of exclusion. I have already examined one of these for a determinate period: the disjunction of reason and madness in the classical age. Later, we could attempt an investigation of a taboo system in language, that concerning sexuality from the sixteenth to the nineteenth century. In this, we would not be concerned with the manner in which this has progressively – and happily – disappeared, but with the way it has been altered and rearticulated, from the practice of confession, with its forbidden conduct, named, clarified, hierarchised down to the smallest detail, to the belated, timid appearance of the treatment of sexuality in nineteenth-century psychiatry and medicine. Of course, these only amount to somewhat symbolic guidelines, but one can already be pretty sure that the tree will not fall where we expect, and that taboos are not always to be found where we imagine them to be.

For the time being, I would like to address myself to the third system of exclusion. I will envisage it in two ways. Firstly, I would like to try to visualise the manner in which this truth within which we are caught, but which we constantly renew, was selected, but at the same time, was repeated, extended and displaced. I will take first of all the age of the Sophists and its beginning with Socrates, or at least with Platonic philosophy, and I shall try to see how effective, ritual discourse, charged with power and peril, gradually arranged itself into a disjunction between true and false discourse. I shall next take the turn of the sixteenth and seventeenth centuries and the age which, above all in England, saw the emergence of an observational, affirmative science, a certain natural philosophy inseparable, too, from religious ideology – for this certainly constituted a new form of the will to knowledge. In the third place, I shall turn to the beginning of the nineteenth century and the great founding acts of modern science, as well as the formation of industrial society and the accompanying positivist ideology. Three slices out of the morphology of our will to knowledge; three staging posts in our philistinism.

I would also like to consider the same question from quite another angle. I would like to measure the effect of a discourse claiming to be scientific – medical, psychiatric or sociological – on the ensemble of practices and prescriptive discourse of which the penal code consists. The study of psychiatric skills and their role in the penal system will serve as a point of departure and as basic material for this analysis.

It is within this critical perspective, but on a different level, that the analysis of the rules for the limitation of discourse should take place, of those among which I earlier designated the author principle, that of commentary and that of discipline. One can envisage a certain number of studies in this field. I am thinking, for example, of the history of medicine in the sixteenth to nineteenth centuries; not so much an account of discoveries made and concepts developed, but of grasping – from the construction of medical discourse, from all its supporting institutions, from its transmission and its reinforcement – how the principles of author, commentary and discipline worked in practice; of seeking to know how the great author principle, whether Hippocrates, Galen, Paracelsus and Sydenham, or Boerhaave, became a principle of limitation in medical discourse; how, even late into the nineteenth century, the practice of aphorism and commentary retained its currency and how it was gradually replaced by the emphasis on case histories and clinical training on actual cases; according to which model medicine sought to constitute itself as a discipline, basing itself at first on natural history and, later, on anatomy and biology.

One could also envisage the way in which eighteenth- and nineteenth-century literary criticism and history have constituted the character of the author and the form of the work, utilising, modifying and altering the procedures of religious exegesis, biblical criticism, hagiography, the 'lives' of historical or legendary figures, of autobiography and memoirs. One day, too, we must take a look at Freud's role in psychoanalytical knowledge, so different from that of Newton in physics, or from that an author might play in the field of philosophy (Kant, for example, who originated a totally new way of philosophising).

These, then, are some of the projects falling within the critical aspect of the task, for the analysis of instances of discursive control. The genealogical aspect concerns the effective formation of discourse, whether within the limits of control, or outside of them, or as is most frequent, on both sides of delimitation. Criticism analyses the processes of rarefaction, consolidation and unification in discourse; genealogy studies their formation, at once scattered, discontinuous and regulate. To tell the truth, these two tasks are not always exactly complementary. We do not find, on the one hand, forms of rejection, exclusion, consolidation or attribution, and, on a more profound level, the spontaneous pouring forth of discourse, which immediately before or after its manifestation, finds itself submitted to selection and control. The regular forma-tion of discourse may, in certain conditions and up to a certain point, integrate control procedures (this is what happens, for example, when a discipline takes on the form and status of scientific discourse). Conversely, modes of control may take on life within a discursive formation (such as literary criticism as the author's constitutive discourse) even though any critical task calling instances of control into play must, at the same time, analyse the discursive regularities through which these instances are formed. Any genealogical description must take into account the limits at play within real forma-tions. The difference between the critical and genealogical enterprise is not one of object or field, but of point of attack, perspective and delimitation

Earlier on I mentioned one possible study, that of the taboos in discourse on sex-uality. It would be difficult, and in any case abstract, to try to carry out this study, without at the same time analysing literary, religious and ethical, biological and medical, as well as juridical discursive ensembles: wherever sexuality is discussed, wher-ever it is named or described, metaphorised, explained or judged. We are a very long way from having constituted a unitary, regular discourse concerning sexuality; it may be that we never will, and that we are not even travelling in that direction. No matter. Taboos are homogeneous neither in their forms nor their behaviour whether in lit-erary or medical discourse, in that of psychiatry or of the direction of consciousness. Conversely, these different discursive regularities do not divert or alter taboos in the same manner. It will only be possible to undertake this study, therefore, if we take into account the plurality of series within which the taboos, each one to some extent different from all the others, are at work.

We could also consider those series of discourse which, in the sixteenth and sev-enteenth centuries, dealt with wealth and poverty, money, production and trade. Here, we would be dealing with some pretty heterogeneous ensembles of enunciations, for-mulated by rich and poor, the wise and the ignorant, protestants and catholics, royal officials, merchants or moralists. Each one has its forms of regularity and, equally, its systems of constraint. None of them precisely prefigures that other form of regular-ity that was to acquire the momentum of a discipline and which was later to be known, first as 'the study of wealth' and, subsequently, 'political economy'. And yet, it was from the foregoing that a new regularity was formed, retrieving or excluding, justifying or rejecting, this or that utterance from these old forms.

One could also conceive a study of discourse concerning heredity, such as it can be gleaned, dispersed as it was until the beginning of the twentieth century, among a variety of disciplines, observations, techniques and formulae; we would be concerned to show the process whereby these series eventually became subsumed under the single system, now recognised as epistemologically coherent, known as genetics. This is the work François Jacob has just completed, with unequalled brilliance and scholarship

It is thus that critical and genealogical descriptions are to alternate, support and complete each other. The critical side of the analysis deals with the systems enveloping discourse; attempting to mark out and distinguish the principles of ordering, exclusion and rarity in discourse. We might, to play with our words, say it pracrises a kind of studied casualness. The genealogical side of discourse, by way of contrast, deals with series of effective formation of discourse: it attempts to grasp it in its power of affirmation, by which I do not mean a power opposed to that of negation, but the power of constituting domains of objects, in relation to which one can affirm or deny true or false propositions. Let us call these domains of objects positivist and, to play on words yet again, let us say that, if the critical style is one of studied casualness, then the genealogical mood is one of felicitous positivism.

At all events, one thing must be emphasised here: that the analysis of discourse thus understood, does not reveal the universality of a meaning, but brings to light the action of imposed rarity, with a fundamental power of affirmation. Rarity and affirmation; rarity, in the last resort of affirmation — certainly not any continuous outpouring of meaning, and certainly not any monarchy of the signifier.

And now, let those who are weak on vocabulary, let those with little comprehension of theory call all this — if its appeal is stronger than its meaning for them — structuralism. . . .

From "Truth and Power"

[. . .] truth isn't outside power, or lacking in power: contrary to a myth whose history and functions would repay further study, truth isn't the reward of free spirits, the child of protracted solitude, nor the privilege of those who have succeeded in liberating themselves. Truth is a thing of this world: it is produced only by virtue of multiple forms of constraint. And it induces regular effects of power. Each society has its régime of truth, its 'general politics' of truth: that is, the types of discourse which it accepts and makes function as true; the mechanisms and instances which enable one to distinguish true and false statements, the means by which each is sanctioned; the techniques and procedures accorded value in the acquisition of truth; the status of those who are charged with saying what counts as true.

In societies like ours, the 'political economy' of truth is characterised by five important traits. 'Truth' is centred on the form of scientific discourse and the institutions which produce it; it is subject to constant economic and political incitement (the demand for truth, as much for economic production as for political power); it is the object, under diverse forms, of immense diffusion and consumption (circulating through apparatuses of education and information whose extent is relatively broad in the social body, not withstanding certain strict limitations); it is produced and trans-mitted under the control, dominant if not exclusive, of a few great political and eco-nomic apparatuses (university, army, writing, media); lastly, it is the issue of a whole political debate and social confrontation ('ideological' struggles).

It seems to me that what must now be taken into account in the intellectual is not the 'bearer of universal values'. Rather, it's the person occupying a specific posi-tion – but whose specificity is linked, in a society like ours, to the general function-ing of an apparatus of truth. In other words, the intellectual has a three-fold specificity: that of his class position (whether as petty-bourgeois in the service of capitalism or 'organic' intellectual of the proletariat); that of his conditions of life and work, linked to his condition as an intellectual (his field of research, his place in a laboratory, the political and economic demands to which he submits or against which he rebels, in the university, the hospital, etc.); lastly, the specificity of the politics of truth in our societies. And it's with this last factor that his position can take on a general signifi-cance and that his local, specific struggle can have affects and implications which are not simply professional or sectoral. The intellectual can operate and struggle at the general level of that regime of truth which is so essential to the structure and func-tioning of our society. There is a battle 'for truth', or at least 'around truth' – it being understood once again that by truth I do not mean 'the ensemble of truths which are to be discovered and accepted', but rather 'the ensemble of rules according to which the true and the false are separated and specific effects of power attached to the true', it being understood also that it's not a matter of a battle 'on behalf' of the truth but of a battle about the status of truth and the economic and political role it plays. It is necessary to think of the political problems of intellectuals not in terms of 'science' and 'ideology', but in terms of 'truth' and 'power'. And thus the question of the professionalisation of intellectuals and the division between intellectual and manual labour can be envisaged in a new way.

All this must seem very confused and uncertain. Uncertain indeed, and what I am saying here is above all to be taken as a hypothesis. In order for it to be a little less confused, however, I would like to put forward a few 'propositions' – not firm asser-tions, but simply suggestions to be further tested and evaluated.

'Truth' is to be understood as a system of ordered procedures for the production, regulation, distribution, circulation and operation of statements.

'Truth' is linked in a circular relation with systems of power which produce and sustain it, and to effects of power which it induces and which extend it. A 'régime' of truth.

This régime is not merely ideological or superstructural; it was a condition of the formation and development of capitalism. And it's this same régime which, subject to certain modifications, operates in the socialist countries (I leave open here the ques-tion of China, about which I know little).

The essential political problem for the intellectual is not to criticise the ideologi-cal contents supposedly linked to science, or to ensure that his own scientific prac-tice is accompanied by a correct ideology, but that of ascertaining the possibility of constituting a new politics of truth. The problem is not changing people's con-sciousnesses – or what's in their heads – but the political, economic, institutional régime of the production of truth.

It's not a matter of emancipating truth from every system of power (which would be a chimera, for truth is already power) but of detaching the power of truth from the forms of hegemony, social, economic and cultural, within which it operates at the present time.

The political question, to sum up, is not error, illusion, alienated consciousness or ideology; it is truth itself. Hence the importance of Nietzsche.

21

RECLAIMING TRUTH

Linda Martín Alcoff

Epistemology is an especially fruitful and yet relatively neglected arena for dialogue between the Anglo-American, or analytic, and European continental traditions in philosophy. Its neglect can be traced to mistaken views on both sides: many continentalists believe epistemology to be bankrupt as a separate line of normative inquiry given the inadequacy of individual epistemic agency and the politically structured nature of the socially generated procedures of epistemic justification. Meanwhile, many analytics take continental philosophy to have nothing to contribute to epistemology, believing that the analyses of knowledge or of science offered by European philosophers such as Heidegger or Foucault are operating in a different language game from their own.

These views are based on common errors with unfortunate consequences. The refusal to engage with continental treatments of knowledge has kept much of Anglo-American epistemology (with the notable exception of feminist epistemologists) in somewhat of an immature state, particularly in regard to the intersections of epistemology with social and political issues. The refusal to engage with analytic epistemology has sometimes resulted in continental philosophers' accounts of knowledge being under-theorized, with implicit assumptions exempt from inquiry and claims about such important topics as truth undeveloped. Thus, a dialogue on epistemology between these traditions could be fruitful for both.

Of course, there has already been some excellent work done by some continental and analytic philosophers toward just such a dialogue, such as by Merold Westphal, Joseph Rouse, Gary Gutting, Charles Taylor, Ian Hacking, and Richard Rorty among others.[1] Rorty's work is probably the most widely read in this group but, unfortunately, Rorty claims that, after having himself conducted an analysis of both, what is redeemable in continental philosophy "shows" the bankruptcy of the epistemological questions in analytic philosophy. And the work of Westphal, Rouse, Hacking, and

Linda Martín Alcoff, "Reclaiming Truth," a slightly revised version of an article which appeared under this title in *The Hedgehog Review: Critical Reflections on Contemporary Culture*, vol. 3, no. 3 (Fall 2001), pp. 26–41. Reprinted by permission of The Hedgehog Review.

Gutting, despite their model clarity and serious engagement with some of the standard epistemic questions, remains under-read in analytic philosophy, probably because of the figures they are dealing with, e.g. Heidegger, Foucault, and Gadamer.

With the notable exception of Rorty, all of the above listed philosophers believe that both traditions of philosophy can benefit from a serious engagement with the other in the domain of epistemology. It is true that continental work will tend to undercut or at least revise many of the standard analytic epistemic questions, such as those concerning skepticism and the structure of knowledge. But the core aspect of epistemology is its normative concern with knowledge, and the critiques of knowledge given by continental philosophers clearly come out of a normative concern. Analytic philosophers generally eschew the normative motivations of continental critiques of epistemology because of the apparent absence of a concern with truth. Truth talk is all but invisible in much of continental philosophy unless it has figurative, if not literal, quotations marks. Yet without a concern for truth, analytic philosophers have trouble understanding what continental philosophers are doing as philosophy.

However, truth talk has its own controversies in analytic philosophy, some of which are actually identical to the concerns among continental philosophers. In this paper, I try to clarify the points of debate over truth talk and the reasons that both analytic and continental philosophers have for either avoiding it or minimizing its meaningfulness. I will then argue for a reclaiming of truth talk through a demonstration that even a political attentiveness to the way knowledge is produced requires the heuristic guide that only a concern with truth can supply. Next I will compare Rorty and Putnam as two philosophers who are both aiming at a "naive" account of truth in order to avoid its philosophical pitfalls. My ultimate aim will be a conceptualization of truth that can serve as a bridge between analytic and continental philosophical traditions.

I

Catherine Elgin has usefully diagnosed a "bipolar disorder" that continues to incapacitate philosophy and much of contemporary social theory and that inflicts its unwitting sufferers with a perpetual oscillation between equally unhappy alternatives. As she puts it:

> Unless answers to philosophical questions are absolute, they are arbitrary. Unless a position is grounded in agent-neutral, determinate facts, it is right only relative to a perspective that cannot in the end be justified.[2]

Following Elgin, I will define the absolute position as one committed to the belief in determinate truths, as oppose to relative or pluralist ones, and to the possibility of discerning truth in a way that is agent-neutral, or better, agent-transcendent. Both those espousing absolutism as well as those espousing arbitrariness share this conceptualization of truth. The difference is simply in whether or not they are fatalistic in regard to its acquisition.

Many who want to cure philosophy and contemporary social theory of this pathology and transcend the dualism of the absolute and the arbitrary argue that we need to leave behind truth talk altogether. By truth talk I mean here not simply the use of the word "true" but the idea that we can assert more than assertability about our most justified or likely claims, that truth is therefore substantive rather than redundant, that it is not collapsible to or a mere extrapolation from procedures and concepts of justification. In short, truth talk brings in the world. Those who reject truth talk say that it unnecessarily creates absolutist requirements and makes everything non-absolute look like it can have nothing to do with truth and must therefore be arbitrary. Those who argue in this way sometimes say we should aim for edification or for understanding one another or for utility; others say we can retain truth as long as we empty it of content and thus disarm it. Yet the cause of transcending the bipolar disorder of the absolute and the arbitrary is not served well by dispensing with truth talk, since this maintains the assumption that absolute, determinate truth is the only way to cash out the concept.

The repudiation of truth talk can be made for very different reasons. Rorty, having declared the death of metaphysics, wishes to dispense with a metaphysical description of what we know in favor of an aesthetic one. But it makes no sense to call aesthetic judgment "truthful."[3] Elgin argues against the idea that all knowledge is a form of representation, and she takes the association between knowledge and truth to imply that representational models are applicable to every arena of epistemic inquiry. Many philosophers are motivated to move away from truth precisely because of their concern with representation, as if to be true a statement must represent a bit of transcendent reality, where the latter is defined by Dummett as "recognition transcendent," that is, transcendent of any human being's ability to recognize its truth status. The problem for Elgin is with representation's hegemony over conceptions of truth, while for others the problem is with the very notion of representation. How can we recognize that which is recognition-transcendent *as* recognition-transcendent? We obviously cannot, but we *can* recognize meaning, verifiability conditions, instrumental utility, and the normative appropriateness of social practices. So some suggest that we remove the world-condition from truth – since this would seem to require the status of a claim to be recognition-transcendent – and instead define truth in terms of something that we can recognize within a human context.

Some philosophers have also pointed out that to characterize truth as a correct representation of an independent, unmediated world has the nefarious political effect of allowing the one who possesses such a truth to transcend the human world of mediation, and thus the give and take of discussion among fallible inquirers. Simone de Beauvoir was one of the first to describe this problem. In *The Second Sex* she explains that

in *his* hands, as [woman] knows, masculine reasoning becomes an underhand form of force; men's undebatable pronouncements are intended to confuse her. The intention is to put her in a dilemma: either you agree or you do not. . . . in yielding to *him*, he would have her yield to the convincingness of an argument, but she knows that he has himself chosen the premises on which his rigorous deductions depend. As long as she avoids questioning them, he will easily reduce her to silence; nevertheless he will not convince her, for she senses his arbitrariness. And, so annoyed, he will accuse her of being obstinate and illogical; but she refuses to play the game because she knows the dice are loaded.[4]

It might be possible, of course, to open up the game more democratically, and thus to retain a determinate concept of truth without loaded dice, but many have been skeptical at the feasibility of doing this since any characterization of truth that transcends justification would, they think, remove the motivation to listen to alternative or newly developed justificatory considerations.

These various arguments against truth talk can be loosely grouped under four categories: semantic, metaphysical, epistemological, and political. Of course, in many particular critiques, such as Dummett's or Derrida's, more than one rubric is involved. The semantic argument is based on the view that truth talk does no work, or no good work, in the language. It adds nothing substantive to the content of a claim, and any substance it does add is dubious at best. The metaphysical argument characterizes why it is that giving a substantive content to truth is considered dubious: because it offers to characterize a relationship between thought and reality, for example, which cannot be characterized without begging the question. In other words, the metaphysical argument is that truth requires recognition-transcendence. The epistemological argument refers not to what can be stated intelligibly but what can be known, and many agree with Dummett that truth cannot be known because truth, unlike verifiability or assertability, is recognition-transcendent. The concern of the political critique is that, precisely because it postures as recognition-transcendent, truth talk enacts a kind of discursive violence; it is a speech act whose goal is to close down discussion.

The semantic and metaphysical arguments largely motivate, I believe, the epistemological and political arguments. Political concerns, in and of themselves, would not be sufficient to turn away from truth unless one thought that truth was at least suspicious-looking for other reasons as well.[5] The epistemological arguments – that we cannot know the truth – depend heavily on how we understand what the truth is that we are supposed to know, and thus depend upon its semantic and metaphysical characterization. Thus I believe that the main grounds of critique are metaphysical or semantic or, what is often the case, some combination of these two.

Both Rorty and Putnam repudiate absolutism and the possibility of recognition-transcendence, and thus both have adopted some of the main premises on which the repudiation of truth relies, but they have come to different conclusions nonetheless about the viability of truth and representation. To compare their positions, I will take up a specific example of a recent feminist argument in the discipline of history, in order to consider just how plausible, or relevant, any of the arguments pro and con truth talk appear in relation to this example.

Philosophers too often pick relatively easy cases, such as simple perception, or claims in the natural sciences that have a lot of empirical evidence and appear neutral, such as the existence of atoms or electrons. (Philosophers also take pride in turning relatively easy cases into unsolvable conundrums, but even when turned into conundrums these kinds of cases are still of a different order than the case I will be discussing, a case in which there is, as Peirce would say, genuine doubt.) The question of truth is much more difficult, and arises more ordinarily of its own accord without the meddling of philosophers, in more complex, multi-variable explanatory accounts or theories in the social sciences. In cases where empirical evidence is at least a part of the argument, but the grounds for justification are highly interpretive, can we ever claim truth? Even if we think not, it is not so easy simply to dispense with this arena of inquiry as inappropriate to truth talk, since it spans received knowledge from evolutionary biology to the causes of global poverty. There is much *at stake* in these debates in the social sciences, much more than in the question of how to characterize electrons ontologically.

I chose the particular example I will discuss for two main reasons. First, because it is explicitly feminist, and thus useful because some will be suspicious about its truth status just on those grounds: how can a claim be both agent-transcendent and politically motivated? Yet every large claim in the social sciences necessarily begins with some assumptions, and the choice of assumptions almost always reflect some broad political values. It has become especially clear in the domain of historical narrative – the revisions of which continue to elicit debate even in legislative chambers – that political values inform the choice of narrative, as between, for example, a story of "discovery," an "encounter," or an "invasion." Nor can we simply add such various accounts together to achieve the truth; they often directly conflict. Thus, arguably, feminist arguments simply make explicit what is there all the time.

My second reason for choosing this particular example is that the feminist historians I will discuss are on the side of dispensing with truth. Inspired by deconstruction, they refuse to describe their claims as more truthful or likely to be true than those of the historians they criticize, and prefer to speak of their own claims as narratives to be judged by their social effects. Such a rendering of their argument is unnecessarily belittling of it; they are in fact arguing over the truth.

II

Let me turn now to what will have to be a brief and truncated rendition of the example. In a series of powerful critiques, Nancy Armstrong and Leonard Tennenhouse have analyzed two apparently contradictory historical accounts of the formation of the family in seventeenth- and eighteenth-century Britain.[6] Though both of the accounts that Armstrong and Tennenhouse critique argue for different accounts of the history of the family, they both privilege a normative rendition of the nuclear family with a fairly traditional gendered division of labor, one in which children "need their mothers and obey their fathers," and they assume that such families are both natural kinds and natural goods because "a small number of individuals who are together for a long time without outside interference tend to care for one another as for themselves."[7] In other words, these accounts both take the affective ties that emerge from that sort of family as "exempt from history."[8]

The first account that Armstrong and Tennenhouse critique is Peter Laslett's highly influential history of the British family in his *The World We Have Lost*.[9] According to Laslett, "Time was when the whole of life went forward in the family, in a circle of loved, familiar faces, known and fondled objects, all to human size. That time has gone forever."[10] Laslett's thesis is that in the pre-industrial family of early modern England, in which work and family were combined in one unit and one location, family members "enjoyed a closer emotional bonding than was the case during the modern period."[11] Moreover, "Englishmen . . . felt they were parts integrated into an organic whole"[12] with the result that neither modern alienation nor class antagonism existed. Armstrong and Tennenhouse explain that

> By an almost invisible logic of internalization, [Laslett] reasons that even 'the head of the poorest family was at least the head of something.' That each of them was on top of some little heap of humanity apparently made it possible for heads of households to identify with people higher up on the social scale in a way that became impossible once the workplace was detached from the home.[13]

Laslett goes so far as to characterize pre-modern England as a "one-class society,"[14] and he concludes that the eventual destruction of this type of family because of industrialization negatively affected people's emotional and personal lives.

Armstrong and Tennenhouse also look at Lawrence Stone's equally influential history of personal life in his book *The Family, Sex and Marriage, 1500–1800*, which argues, against Laslett, that family ties that were volitional rather than founded as economic units made for a much happier life. Stone also argues that privacy and size made an enormous difference in the capacity to develop happy relationships, and it was only after what he names the "open lineage family" – Laslett's ideal type – becomes replaced by the "closed domesticated nuclear family" – Stone's ideal type – that the household became the site of personal happiness. In regard to the open lineage family, prevalent in the sixteenth century, Stone bemoans the fact that "relations within the nuclear family, between husband and wife and parents and children, were not much closer than those with neighbors, with relatives, or with friends."[15] The closed domesticated nuclear family, by contrast, was the product of what he calls "affective individualism," in which the privacy surrounding the family somehow constituted privacy for individuals within the family, wherein each could develop personal autonomy.

Stone also takes issue with Laslett's preferred family because of its treatment of children. In the early modern period, the use of wet nurses and the widespread tendency to hire children out from just before puberty until their marriage made it virtually impossible to have a "single mothering and nurturing figure."[16] Stone sees this as the "denial" of maternal affection and he uses this fact to explain both the passionate religious enthusiasms of the period as well as its high degree of casual violence and antagonism, on the grounds that the natural emotion rightfully found in mother–child relations had to be deflected into other channels.[17]

Where Laslett paints a regressivist story in which we have lost a world of happiness and equality, Stone offers a progressivist history in which the chances for personal happiness have been enhanced. They differ in the value they confer on privacy, and on the optimism or suspicion by which they regard families based on economic relationships. But Armstrong and Tennenhouse argue that, despite these important differences, both Laslett and Stone make naturalistic assumptions about the impact of family structure on affective life, and they both privilege traditional gender roles within the family, including especially the role of the mother as almost the exclusive nurturing figure.[18] Thus, Armstrong and Tennenhouse charge both Laslett and Stone with romanticizing and revering the traditional male-headed family and neglecting to historicize their own beliefs and preferences about personal life. This cultural terrain is, as Armstrong and Tennenhouse point out, "as close as one comes to sacred ground in a modern secular culture."[19]

Armstrong and Tennenhouse's critiques are first and foremost based on their claim that there is, to put it mildly, questionable evidence for Laslett's and Stone's various claims about the affective history of the family. They make some of the very traditional empirical charges that historians use to challenge each other's accounts, that claims are based on generalizations from evidence that is insufficient, too limited in its scope, and too amenable to contrary interpretations. But the most interesting aspect of their critique for our purposes is that they charge Laslett and Stone with using history to offer support for contemporary ideological convictions espoused in present day pop psychology as well as embedded deeply into our collective common sense. Thus, they argue that historians cannot use their own emotional proclivities or current beliefs and practices in regard to personal life as any kind of ground to theorize the affective lives of people long since dead. They argue, in other words, that interior life itself needs to be historicized and we need to recognize the possibility that our needs and wants, the conditions necessary for our personal happiness, and the texture of our emotional bonds, can change.

Of course, even while they critique the assumptions of Laslett and Stone, it is clear that Armstrong and Tennenhouse are also working with certain assumptions, assumptions that play a critical role in their ability to perceive the weaknesses in Laslett's and Stone's accounts. Some of their assumptions they make explicit, others they don't (and I think their argument would be more persuasive if they did). But it raises the obvious question of whether their arguments are any more legitimate than those they critique. If all historians must work with some assumptions when they try to make sense out of the din of history, and if at least some of these assumptions cannot be proven by uncontroversial empirical methods, then perhaps the deconstructionists are right and we need to treat history as a form of literature.

What are the assumptions made by Armstrong and Tennenhouse themselves? I think there are at least three we can gather just from their critique of Laslett and Stone. The first is that the traditional gendered division of labor in the family is not a manifestation of human nature. This is suggested in part by their demand that interior life be historicized, which of course assumes that interior life *can* be historicized. This is a metaphysical claim about the flexibility of the human self. Even if it is entered here just as a hypothesis that warrants investigation, it is a truth claim.

This assumption is explicit in their overall argument; other assumptions have weaker relations to their argument, but still seem to play a guiding role in the path they take through this material. For example, one might reasonably suppose that Armstrong and Tennenhouse are assuming that women can have the same general wants and needs as men. It is this assumption that would cast doubt on the claim that a patriarchal form of the family, in which the roles and power of father and mother are neither equal nor reciprocal, would be an optimal form of the family from the point of view of the personal happiness of all involved. Laslett relates without comment that in the days of yore, England was an association between the male heads of wealthy families, and that the father ruled the family in more than name only. He does not consider this prima facie evidence for the possibility that the women in these families will experience unhappiness; Armstrong and Tennenhouse clearly do.

A third assumption that Armstrong and Tennenhouse make is that the closed domesticated biologically related form of the family that Stone prefers is not necessarily the best form of family in terms of its effects on society. Stone argues that there are a number of social and political advantages to small families with high levels of privacy in creating the possibility of individual autonomy that will then find its way into anti-authoritarian political movements, for example. Armstrong and Tennenhouse remark that, in criticizing what he balefully calls the exchange of children, Stone "apparently cannot imagine . . . that the presence of other children in the family might have extended the sense of closeness to a community beyond the biological family."[20] This is a possibility Armstrong and Tennenhouse clearly see as a potential social good. This is a truth claim.

Some of these assumptions even look dangerously close to being generalizations, such as the assumption that women have the same basic wants and needs as men. Given their demand for the historicizing of everything, surely Armstrong and Tennenhouse cannot countenance a cross-historical generalization of this sort. But here it should be noted that the demand that we historicize everything does not entail that we will then find that absolutely everything changes; it is simply a demand that we not assume simply on the basis of current sentiment what can and cannot change. We should, in other words, hold nothing back from the cultural historians' examination.[21]

All of these historians, Armstrong and Tennenhouse no less than Laslett and Stone, are working with assumptions and even a political orientation. But not all assumptions have the same kind of epistemic impact. Thus, we can agree, along with Putnam, with William James's claim that all knowledge is mediated without having to then agree that any given mediating influence is equal in its epistemic content to any other. One of the ways assumptions can operate in the production of historical narrative is to make some things appear and others disappear. Because Laslett privileges patriarchy, the particular point of view women may have had on the families he idealizes does not come into view, at least not fully or with prominence. In fact, he doesn't even mention them, nor is gender thematized in *The World We Have Lost*. Stone takes as a given that a central, nurturing maternal figure – not paternal – is necessary for children's well-being. This assumption operated to preempt asking certain kinds of questions, from which other possibilities might have come into view. Armstrong and Tennenhouse, on the other hand, clearly have women in mind when they offer some of their critical analysis about the way in which Laslett and Stone have naturalized a traditional gendered division of labor in the family.

I am not championing feminist assumptions of all sorts as epistemically advantageous in all cases. But at the very least, the assumption that women count, that we may have an independent point of view on things, that we may have the same wants and needs as men, and that our optimal life situation is probably not to be found in a condition of life long subordination, are assumptions proven useful in illuminating new aspects of the historical record unseen before the recent period. To argue for an

epistemic equality between these assumptions and blatantly patriarchal ones — such
that we can forego listening to what women say because they don't know their own
needs, for example — is surely ludicrous. In this light, I find Putnam's project very
interesting, which he has recently (re-)stated as the project to show how a realist commitment, a commitment which he takes to put him in opposition to James, can be
squared with his acceptance of James's claim that perception is never unmediated,
without the two beliefs together leading to skepticism. It seems to me that there are
many "real world examples" such as the one I just discussed which manifest the possibility of squaring these two claims.

III

If the example of feminist historiography suggests that truth claims are operative even
in politically interested historical argument, what kind of truth can we claim here?

As I said, I picked the Armstrong and Tennenhouse example because they retreat
from truth. Although they make what certainly appear to be truth claims throughout
the book, when asked to give a kind of meta-characterization of the epistemic status
of their arguments, Armstrong vigorously denies the referential character of her claims.
She is just offering us a narrative, to be judged by its effects in the present on discourses and practices. She might be able to agree with the claim that her arguments
have assertability, but she will not claim anything approaching truth about the past.
She is, in effect, a Rortyan.

But a narrative can be true or false: narratives tell a story about the world. Even
fictional narratives offer accounts about true things indirectly: true ways in which
human beings can respond to each other, can be affected by a given experience, can
fall into trouble, or pull themselves out of trouble. Although we may compare narratives by what they each allow us to see or appreciate anew, and we may grant that
multiple and even conflicting narratives can be informative about a given event, the
value of a narrative generally rests on the quality and depth of its relation to the
world. In this sense, a narrative is very different from a conversation, which does not
require a relation to the world for it to be good or meaningful; conversations can
resemble lovemaking, play, or chess matches (and philosophy conversations often
resemble the latter), with or without a relation to the world.

Famously for Rorty, however, the ultimate bedrock of comparative judgment is
aesthetic and not epistemic. Rorty's repudiation of truth is based on concerns he has
with all four of the kinds of arguments I listed above: semantic, metaphysical,
epistemological, and political. In general, Rorty has argued that truth talk merely gets
in the way of conversation, posing a requirement that is as unnecessary to conversation as it is likely to lead the conversation off to a dead end. And Rorty of course
portrays himself as carrying on the pragmatist tradition by this argument. To be accurate, Rorty does not argue against *any* use of the word "true" but against a specifically *philosophical* concern with the word or the concept. Thus he holds that the
elimination of a metaphysical project to understand the meaning of truth does not
preclude us from calling some historical accounts true, depending, of course, on how
one construes that metaphysical project. But the question does arise when Rorty

eliminates talk of representation because then the world-content of a historical narrative would be dropped out. By his account, we can call Armstrong and Tennenhouse's account true but we cannot really claim that it represents any truths about the way things really were in pre-modern Britain, in so far as we understand ourselves not to be merely participating in the contestations among historians over how to construct historical narratives but in so far as we are seeking to know as best we can the real nature of people's lives in the past.

Now it may seem as if this is pushing Rorty's anti-metaphysicalism too far. We can make ordinary claims, after all, and claims about the past are ordinary claims. To say that truth is a primitive is not to deny its existence. But for Rorty, unlike for Donald Davidson, for example, to say that truth is a primitive preempts even the possibility of claiming an extra-epistemic meaning to truth, or its relation to an objective world not of our making.[22] Truth is "what is good for *us* to believe," full stop, and the gap between justification and truth, or justified belief and true belief, is simply the gap between the "actual good and the possible better."[23] By contrast, one could bring use in at critical points along the way of inquiry, as Elgin does for example, without it preempting the possibility of giving a world-content to truth. Use here plays the role of mediator, which can reveal or direct us toward certain aspects of reality. It does not serve the cause of transcending the absolute and the arbitrary to present use and objectivity as mutually exclusive choices.

In contrast to Putnam, Davidson, Elgin and others of the pragmatist tradition, Rorty seems to retain rather than argue against the binaries that have structured both foundationalist and postmodern treatments of knowledge. Most important here is the binary between representation and construction. Analytic and continental philosophers are often believed to part company along this divide. Rorty's acceptance of this binary is most apparent in his interpretation of Davidson's epistemology. Rorty argues that Davidson's coherence theory of truth amounts to a kind of constructivism – a belief in the making rather than the discovering of truth. And then he argues that "since 'making true' is the inverse of 'representing,' this doctrine makes it impossible for Davidson to talk about language representing the world – standing to it as scheme to content."[24] He argues further that Davidson "marries" truth and meaning to each other in such a way that the theory of truth (or truth/meaning) that results "will be of no use to a representationalist epistemology, nor to any other sort of epistemology [because it is] an explanation of what people *do*, rather than of a non-causal, representing relation in which they stand to non-human entities."[25] I will set aside the question of whether this is a persuasive reading of Davidson for the moment, to simply note Rorty's contrast between these two types of explanations of truth in so far as it is a conceptualization of the human–world relation: we have the choice of either a non-causal, that is, uninterpreted, relation, or a making relation. I am not inclined to defend the non-causal account, but to explore the possibilities of a third way to describe the relation, a way which in fact shows that "making" and "representing" are not mutually exclusive truth operations.

This is Putnam's latest project, or latest formulation of what his project has been all along. In contrast to Rorty, Putnam does not dispense with truth talk in the sense of a relation with the world, nor even of realism. Though he shares with Rorty the view that a metaphysical project of elucidating the interface between thought and reality is nonsense, he does not go as far as Rorty in dispensing with all forms of metaphysical talk. The differences between Rorty and Putnam are especially interesting to look at because both are more Jamesian than Peircean, especially in their critique of scientism in philosophy and their tendency to psychologize philosophical quandaries.

In his latest book, *The Threefold Cord*, Putnam takes us once again beyond his previous views, or rather, takes his earlier self to be his greatest foil. He argues now against metaphysical realism, internal realism, and pragmatic realism (all positions that he once held) and argues for a form of natural or direct realism. Direct realism is naive realism (what we believe to be true by our best lights is true about the world) but it has a second-order naiveté, having rejected initial naiveté and then moving back to the substance of the naive position after having tried, I suppose, sophistication. It's similar to Nietzsche's notion of the adult playing at playing like a child, thus retaining both the status of sophistication with the benefits of frivolous innocence. The difference between the adult playing like a child and the child playing (like a child) is that the adult knows that s/he is playing like a child, knows the alternatives, and has made a choice.

As this indicates, Putnam's second-order naiveté is not naive. One cannot, after all, return to a carefree bliss in the Garden of Eden once one has seen what lies just beyond the gates. Putnam's realism, thus, and his notion of truth retains some level of its previous sophistication, and thus has a content. Let me explain what I mean.

Putnam argues that direct or naive realism correctly holds that "the world is as it is independently of describers."[26] As I mentioned earlier, one of his aims in this new book is to show how that realist commitment can be squared with the fact that perception is always mediated. Thus, he wants to counter the skeptical conclusions argued for by those who, like Dummett, have realist commitments in their account of what is required for truth but acknowledge that neither human inquiry nor language can transcend its clay feet and thus meet the requirements. As I read it, Putnam's strategy has two stages: (1) to argue against, once again, one of the primary ways these clay feet have been conceptualized – in terms of the "interface" idea in which sense-impressions, qualia, mental representations, or some such are put between human beings and the external world; and (2) after having vanquished this idea, to retrieve the meaningfulness of the concept of representation without it being entangled in the assumption of an interface.[27] Putnam argues, persuasively in my view, that the concept of representation must be retrieved if we are to retain the possibility of veridical discourse, which is precisely discourse that goes beyond conversation to make claims about the world that are in fact true.

Putnam thinks that it is the "interface" idea that keeps mediated inquiry from plausibly achieving relations with the world; without the interface, representation is free to refer to the world rather than to our image of the world. And thus we can return to a naive realism. But it is not really a naive realism that he returns to for, according to Putnam, representations are not thing-like entities at the interface of human beings and the world but practices. And it is because they are practices that we can understand the mediated nature of perception without becoming anti-realists. He uses Wittgenstein's duck–rabbit and Cora Diamond's discussion of two picture faces that have the same expression as examples of the way in which representations can be both real, or accurate as representations, and mediated. In Wittgenstein's example, a single picture can be seen equally well as a duck or a rabbit. In Diamond's example, two pictures of faces represent the same expression despite the fact that it is impossible to point to features of the faces that they have in common and that engender the expression. In each of these examples, one cannot point to anything different about the drawings themselves, anything materially different about them, to explain either the distinction we make on the one hand or the similarity we find on the other.

> Seeing an expression in the picture face is not just a matter of seeing the lines and the dots; rather, it is a matter of seeing something in the lines and the dots – but this is not to say that it is seeing something *besides* the lines and the dots.[28]

By this analogy, Putnam suggests, we can conceptualize the relation of human inquiry to the world. The world "by itself" does not cause us to see a duck or a rabbit, and yet the shapes are there in the world and not merely in our minds. We can affirm simultaneously the fact that the world does not force us to choose duck or rabbit and that our claim to see a duck represents a truth about the world, and not *just* about human perception or human practices, though it may also be about those things.

This, however, is hardly a naive realism. In its substance, it is still the internal realism that Putnam developed in his middle period and has been denying ever since, in that it produces a combination between the aboutness claim of realism and the ontological relativity thesis of pragmatism. It works this out by making a claim about the world that can explain, not how it is possible to have truth at all (which is the metaphysical project Putnam rejects along with Rorty), but how it is possible to have many truths. It is, then, a realism in its claim about the content of truth claims but an internal realism since it holds that human practices must be taken into account to understand which truths will be accepted, or how the world will be seen, at any given moment.

The swing between the absolute and the arbitrary is caused by a conception of truth as determinate and agent-transcendent. But truth is neither of these things. Even in regard to historical argument about the past, where extrapolations are large, complex, and always positional, we aim at the truth, and we can be more or less successful. The mistake is to think that in aiming at the truth we can hit it or miss it, as if truth is an "it." Thinking of truth as an "it" is what makes us think we cannot claim truth. But truth is as dense and multivalent as lived reality, which is, after all, what it is about.

Notes

I am indebted to Marianne Janack for very helpful discussions about the arguments of this paper. I am also grateful to Nancy Armstrong for her feedback on an earlier version.

1 See Joseph Rouse, "Foucault and the Natural Sciences," in *Foucault and the Critique of Institutions*, ed. John Caputo and Mark Yount (University Park, PA: Pennsylvania State

University Press, 1993), pp. 137–62; and *Knowledge and Power: Toward a Political Philosophy of Science* (Ithaca, NY: Cornell University Press, 1987). See Merold Westphal, "Hermeneutics as Epistemology," in *The Blackwell Guide to Epistemology*, ed. John Greco and Ernest Sosa (Oxford: Blackwell, 1999); and *History and Truth in Hegel's* Phenomenology (Atlantic Heights, NJ: Humanities Press International, 1979). See Richard Rorty, *Philosophy and the Mirror of Nature* (Princeton: Princeton University Press, 1979). See Gary Gutting, *Michel Foucault's Archaeology of Scientific Reason* (Cambridge: Cambridge University Press, 1989). See Ian Hacking, *The Social Construction of What?* (Cambridge, MA: Harvard University Press, 1999); and "Language, Truth and Reason," in *Rationality and Relativism*, ed. Martin Hollis and Steven Lukes (Cambridge, MA: MIT Press, 1987). See Charles Taylor, *Philosophical Arguments* (Cambridge, MA: Harvard University Press, 1995).

2 Catherine Elgin, *Between the Absolute and the Arbitrary* (Ithaca, NY: Cornell University Press, 1997), p. 1.

3 Whether his criterion is ultimately aesthetic or political in the end does not matter, since Rorty is among those who equate the two, thus arguing, for example, that a criterion of openness serves poetic vision and political judgment in equal measure, and that, in fact, the two are co-constitutive.

4 Simone de Beauvoir, *The Second Sex*, trans. H. M. Parshley (New York: Random House, 1989), p. 612, my emphasis.

5 Alternatively, one could hold that the political arguments against truth show that there are extra-epistemic reasons for some to hold onto truth, and this provides a prima facie case that we should take a careful look at the metaphysical basis for truth talk. One could read Lyotard and Derrida in this way.

6 Nancy Armstrong and Leonard Tennenhouse, *The Imaginary Puritan: Literature, Intellectual Labor, and the Origins of Personal Life* (Berkeley: University of California Press, 1992).

7 Ibid., p. 84.

8 Ibid., p. 71.

9 Ibid., p. 71.

10 Ibid., p. 72.

11 Ibid., p. 75.

12 Ibid., p. 73.

13 Ibid., p. 72.

14 Ibid., p. 73.

15 Ibid., p. 76.

16 Ibid., p. 81.

17 Ibid., pp. 81–2.

18 Ibid., p. 84.

19 Ibid., p. 85.

20 Ibid., p. 81.

21 This is not to say that all of their feminist assumptions must be put to the test of history, since I am denying that this is possible. Some feminist claims, such as that women have the same wants and needs as men, can be challenged and debated through historical records, but others, such as that women's own views should always be consulted in assessing the past, cannot be coherently challenged. That is, one can accept it or reject it, and give reasons, but it is doubtful that the reasons given on one side will be intelligible to the other – such as that women simply don't know their own interests or cannot interpret the world around them. And it is the latter sort of feminist assumption – that women's own views should always be consulted in assessing the past – that I observe working in Armstrong and Tennenhouse's arguments.

22 See e.g. Richard Rorty, "Solidarity or Objectivity," in *Objectivity, Relativism, and Truth:*

Philosophical Papers, Volume 1 (Cambridge: Cambridge University Press, 1991) p. 22; and Donald Davidson, "A Coherence Theory of Truth and Knowledge," in *Truth and Interpretation: Perspectives on the Philosophy of Donald Davidson*, ed. Ernest LePore (Oxford: Basil Blackwell, 1986).

23 Rorty, "Solidarity or Objectivity," p. 124.

24 Rorty, "Representation, Social Practice, and Truth," in *Objectivity, Relativism, and Truth: Philosophical Papers*, Volume 1 (Cambridge: Cambridge University Press, 1991), p. 153. See also his "Pragmatism, Davidson, and Truth," same volume.

25 Rorty, "Representation, Social Practice, and Truth," p. 154.

26 Hilary Putnam, *The Threefold Cord: Mind, Body, and World* (New York: Columbia University Press, 1999), p. 6.

27 Ibid., p. 59.

28 Ibid., p. 63.

SUGGESTED READING

Alcoff, Linda, *Real Knowing: New Versions of the Coherence Theory* (Ithaca, NY: Cornell University Press, 1996).

Arendt, Hannah, *The Origins of Totalitarianism* (New York: Harvest, 1973).

Arendt, Hannah, *The Human Condition* (Chicago: Chicago University Press, 1998).

Brandom, Robert, *Articulating Reasons* (Cambridge, MA: Harvard University Press, 2000).

Foucault, Michel, *Power/Knowledge*, ed. Colin Gordon (New York: Pantheon, 1980).

Foucault, Michel, *Madness and Civilization*, trans. Alan Sheridan (New York: Vintage, 1988).

Foucault, Michel, *Discipline and Punish*, trans. Alan Sheridan (New York: Vintage, 1995).

Habermas, Jürgen, *Theory of Communicative Action*, trans. Thomas McCarthy (Boston: Beacon Press, 1985).

Habermas, Jürgen, *Philosophical Discourse of Modernity*, trans. Frederick G. Lawrence (Cambridge, MA: MIT Press, 1990).

Honneth, Axel, *The Critique of Power: Reflective Stages in a Critical Social Theory* (Cambridge, MA: MIT Press, 1991).

Horkheimer, Max, *Critical Theory*, trans. Matthew O'Connell (New York: Continuum, 1975).

Horkheimer, Max (and Theodor Adorno), *Dialectic of Enlightenment*, trans. John Cumming (New York: Continuum, 1976).

Kelly, Michael (ed.), *Critique and Power: Recasting the Foucault/Habermas Debate* (Cambridge, MA: MIT Press, 1994).

Lyotard, Jean-François, "Answering the Question: What is Postmodernism?," in Thomas Docherty (ed.), *Postmodernism: A Reader* (New York: Harvester Wheatsheaf, 1993).

Putnam, Hilary, *The Threefold Cord: Mind, Body and World* (New York: Columbia University Press, 1999).

Rorty, Richard, *Objectivity, Relativism and Truth* (Cambridge: Cambridge University Press, 1991).

Rorty, Richard, *Truth and Progress* (Cambridge: Cambridge University Press, 1998).

Sheridan, Alan, *Michael Foucault: The Will to Truth* (London and New York: Tavistock, 1980).

PART VII

A SUPPLEMENT:
RADICALIZATIONS OF TRUTH

INTRODUCTION

Herding cats is a walk in the park compared to trying to do justice to the many ways in which the value of truth is appropriated and deployed by contemporary thinkers. And in this collection we have had to engage in that very mix of selection, ordering, and exclusion that for some, like Foucault and Nietzsche, is the very activity of truth production. It is neither innocent nor "fair." Having completed such a task, it is to be expected that some of the excluded will bang on the gates demanding to be let in, producing the effect of the supplement.[1] Undoubtedly this structure is infinitely replicable, and unless there is a final encore, the musicians will never get home to bed. But we have been moved by the claim for more adequate representation of a number of contemporary thinkers for whom we have not found a place in this volume. If a common thread binds them together, it is perhaps that of the contemporary breakdown of the subordination of the image to the real. The significance of this crisis is of course that philosophers from Plato to Nietzsche (and beyond) have understood clearly that controlling the operation of this relation (between appearance and reality, image and original) is central to the way truth functions in a society. The traditional Marxist version of this claim would be that the dominant ideology is the ideology of the dominant class. But this formulation takes for granted, at least on one level, the continuing operation of the scheme of dominance, by which appearances are subordinated to the real. A more radical move occurs when the assurance of this very structure of domination is shaken, and we are no longer sure that images can be subordinated to the real. We can find traces of this idea in Greek skepticism (Pyrrho, Sextus Empiricus), and these thinkers do not just affirm the immediate epistemological or metaphysical aspects of their position, they lay out its ethical and practical implications. For example, Sextus's attack on the reality of the opposition between Good and Evil moves quickly into a plea for tolerance of cultural diversity.

These issues have been made publicly visible (indeed audible) in debates over the politics of postmodernism, notably between Habermas, Lyotard, and Rorty (see Part III above), but it is worth moving away from the noise of the circus to look more carefully at some of the different ways in which this crisis over the image/reality relationship plays itself out. As we suggested, we can understand this question in an unreconstructedly political way, in which the struggle for power focuses on the struggle to determine the terms in which truth is presented, or as we would now often put it, to discursively "frame" the truth.[2] But the further question arises – what happens if the very idea of the real loses its grip on us? What happens when we hear every appeal to the real as a transparent move in a power game? The response from the left[3] has often been to talk about postmodern irresponsibility; to insist that the critique of oppressive power has to be able to rely on the reality of poverty, discrimination – indeed oppression, or there is no point of leverage, no object of critique, nothing substantial to complain about. There must be a world turning behind the spin.

Engels seems quite clear: "all moral theories [are] . . . the product, in the last analysis of the economic conditions of society obtaining at the time . . . morality has always been class morality."[4] The obvious response to this is to poke away a little at this "last analysis." Does the last analysis subsume all other analyses (cultural, symbolic, psychological)? Well, yes and no: "The economic situation is the basis, but the various elements of the superstructure . . . also exercise their influence upon the course of the historical struggle and in many cases preponderate in determining their *form*."[5] It looks as if the distinction between form and content is coming to the rescue in the face of a threat to the opposition between reality and appearance. Truth is a web of inter-connected forking paths!

Those who do not buy a reductive monism may embrace a pluralistic material-ism, believing that there are many economies (of the body, desire, the other, the image) with their own relative autonomy.[6] But many who take this route have concluded that even in these regional economies, the structure of hierarchical dependence on the bedrock of the real has to be abandoned.

The *locus classicus* of this move is Nietzsche's *How the Real World at Last Became a Myth* ("History of an Error": section 6):

> We have abolished the real world: What world is left? the apparent world perhaps? . . . But no! with the real world we have also abolished the apparent world. . . . Incipit Zarathustra.[7]

What this last phrase indicates is that this metaphysical charge calls for a social trans-formation. And indeed it is with just such a challenge and promise that we began in Part I with Nietzsche and James. If the "last analysis" never comes, or if, in the meantime, we find ourselves caught up in local "economies" that create and distri-bute truth and significance, there are perhaps five domains of contemporary theoreti-cal reflection that bear directly on contemporary struggles over the normativity of truth – feminism, film theory, media studies, psychoanalysis, and queer theory. A con-versation between Butler, Žižek, Deleuze, Irigaray, and Baudrillard would at least begin to show how what looks like an irresponsible sustaining of the autonomy of the image, or at least a radical disturbance of its merely derivative status, actually gener-ates a range of ethical truth practices that would not be intelligible without this theoretical elaboration.

The move to such truth practices is not only possible; in some sense it is neces-sary. Why? Because although we might be tempted to claim *truth* for what Baudrillard (for example) says about the simulacrum (that it hides the absence of the real), or for what Irigaray says about woman (her first strategic option is mimicry), or for what Deleuze says about the false (that the power of the false is creative becoming), there is at least a surface paradox built into these remarks, when seen as *truth* claims. We may suppose that a paradox should be resolved at the level at which it is presented, so that a formal paradox would need a formal solution. From a contra-diction, logicians assure us, anything follows. This is meant to be an argument for steering clear of them. What possible use could we have for something that has so little logical or worldly purchase that "anything follows" from it? But what is re-sidually interesting in this objection is that it is couched in terms of what follows from it, what its implications are, where it leads us. And in such a formulation we find a bridge to the practical. A contradiction is useless, it makes no claim because it is compatible with everything. And if paradoxes are not just empty contradictions, one clue might lie in their distinct practical significance. Indeed it may be that the point of a paradox is to encode a complex recommendation for practice, rather than to defy reason. Suppose it were the case that our thinking cannot but operate with concepts, and that the most powerful ones are ordered in binary pairs (good/ evil, true/false, appearance/reality, image/object, man/woman, self/other, straight/ queer). We may yet conclude that these oppositions are both "necessary" in some sense and yet potentially dangerous, if not fatal to the lucid operation of our intel-ligence, or the productive orientation of our lives. We know that Newtonian mechanics works at the human scale, and believing the earth is flat works in my local neighborhood.

But we deploy these models only with a certain tacit regulative care: "don't take them too literally," or "don't generalize too much." We can continue to use these oppositions, much as one can keep driving a car with bald tires – with extra caution in the rain. This is one way in which the paradoxes and entanglements of truth can be converted into discursive (and other) practices. If truth is caught up in one or more of these oppositions, and if the effective deployment of these oppositions requires these cautions, we can see these paradoxes as yielding recommendations for second-order regulative deployment of *cautionary* principles. This idea can be found in Kierkegaard, Nietzsche, and Wittgenstein. (See our selections above.)

But Nietzsche also advances a stronger principle – not merely that the unthink-ing deployment of these oppositions leads us astray, not merely that what is good enough for everyday use may not work *in extremis*, but that these oppositions even in their standard use serve to maintain an essentially distorted or oppressive reality. Consider Irigaray's claim about the way man/woman operates.[8] This opposition is mapped onto another binary, that of real/imaginary, and positions "woman" in a semiotically subsidiary position. When Nietzsche asks "What if truth were a woman?," he is not asking whether "woman" might be "truth," but whether truth might be an illusion, as much a product of fantasy and distance as woman [for men]. Irigaray pro-poses various strategies of *resistance* to such positioning – from mimicry to the recog-nition of a relation to self (lips that touch) that provides an alternative to entanglement with the male imaginary.

In addition to *caution* and *resistance*, Deleuze proposes *affirmation*. For Deleuze, this practice arises from the need to go beyond simply recognizing the metaphysical inter-dependence of truth and falsity, or original and forgery. For such a recognition arguably remains within the broader horizon of truth. Nietzsche's critique of the will-to-truth opens onto a critical valuation and revaluation of different modes of life – culminating in the character of the artist – "creator of the true" and source of "goodness" and "generosity."[9] Such affirmative practices arise from the overcoming of truth as a play of representations, which would merely negotiate between truth and illusion, appearance and reality.

Another illustration of how working through paradox engenders practical conse-quences can be found in one of Žižek's many brilliant analyses. In *For They Know Not What They Do*, Žižek radicalizes Hegel's understanding of the dialectics of know-ledge. The naive view of knowledge is one in which one "discovers, or discloses some reality that already existed." But "this 'naive' theory overlooks the constitutive char-acter of the process of knowledge with respect to its object: the very knowledge itself modifies its object, confers upon it the form it has as an 'object of knowledge'."[10]

Hegel's account, however, introduces an essential performativity into the equation: "our act of knowledge is included in advance in its substantial content – the path towards truth partakes in truth itself," "the proletariat becomes an actual revolutionary subject by way of integrating the knowledge of its historical role." This performative and processual account is made both possible and necessary when we let go of a static, metaphysical picture of time, truth, and the subject/object relationship. Even more radically, Žižek explains, Hegel also shows us that we must jettison the idea of knowledge as a reflective recovery of an origin we have lost. Rather the very idea of a lost origin is the product of reflection, one we need to let go. (Žižek calls this *retroactive* performativity.) Žižek is not slow to point out the political implications: If we have never had what we thought we had lost (such as "community"), political engagement might better be thought of as permanent struggle (what is original is strife), rather than the restoration of social harmony. And it is revealing that Žižek explicitly repudiates what he takes to be the anti-realism of postmodernism, insisting on the need "for a 'good terror' as the key ingredient of any radical politics"[11] and the ineliminability of the Real.

These contradictions and paradoxes find especially fertile soil in the discourses and practices surrounding sexuality. Foucault wrote: "it is in the area of sex that we must search for the most secret and profound truths about the individual."[12] The idea that there are profound connections between sex and truth has been taken up by gay, lesbian, and gender theorists. Following Foucault and psychoanalysis, queer theory critically studies the normative spaces for the expression of sexual behavior, their presuppositions, and their implications for the lives of sexual beings. The discourses of sexuality and their criteria of truth have thus come under critical scrutiny. Within queer theory, some have argued that the truth about our sexual identities can be liberating when accepted and expressed freely; while others have argued that it is the very assumption that there are truths about sexuality that is oppressive. Sedgwick has argued that modernity has created a normative system of sexual exclusion that oppresses "deviant" sexualities and forces them into closeted lives, while producing obsessive and pathological attitudes toward sexual behavior. She shows that in the discourse of sexuality created by modern culture there are truths that cannot be talked about and yet are obsessively intimated and discussed in indirect ways.[13] The pathology of this discourse involves an obsessive suspicion that calls for an obsessive denial of deviancy (a series of tacit assertions through which one tries to assure oneself and/or others of one's conformity with heteronormativity). In her studies of the normative assumptions and the logic of the "epistemology of the closet," Sedgwick warns about the many twists and turns and often contradictory presuppositions of heteronormative discourse. It is important to keep in mind that these complications, tensions, and contradictions impregnate not only the heteronormative system of exclusion, but also the dialectical moves of their critics. While many queer theorists argue for the subversion of heterosexist norms, others object that the alleged subversion is a dangerous (and infantile) illusion, for any act of subversion is *contained* and taken up by a system of exclusion, so that apparent insurrections always lead to new forms of oppression.[14] Can we really escape the gender and sexual binarism of heterosexist normativity? And how is it related to the binaries of the true and the false, the real and the imaginary?

These issues have been addressed by Judith Butler in conversation with psychoana-lytic and neo-Marxist approaches.[15] She argues that neither the oppositional binaries of the philosophical tradition (real/unreal, true/false) nor those of our heterosexist culture (man/woman, hetero/homo) can be simply erased, but they can be *destabi-lized*. In particular, she calls attention to the destabilizing power of parodic perform-ance (see our Irigaray excerpt too). Butler's performative account of subversive mechanisms rests on an account of *citationality* according to which every utterance or performance cites previous ones and at the same time takes up their meaning in a new direction, so that citation is always *resignification*. She has yet to thematize the normative role of truth in the performative chains of resignification that sustain and transform sexual meanings. Are there "sexual truths"? And whether real or illusory, are "sexual truths" always intimidating and oppressive? Or can they be liberating and transforming? Whatever the answer to these questions, it may be helpful to distin-guish between what Paul Ricoeur would call "different orders of truth," which may be at the service of different systems of sexual exclusion or of different agendas of sexual liberation.[16]

We cite these instances of paradoxical transformation not to endorse their specifics, but rather to point to ways in which a number of highly visible contemporary thinkers have unlocked the social practice implications latent not simply in different accounts of truth, but in the paradoxical entanglements to which the value of truth is so sus-ceptible. These reflections arise less from attempts to define truth (as adequation, as correspondence, as coherence, etc.) than from a recognition that as a normative concept it is inseparable from the oppositions in which it is located and with which it is aligned. And that the way one operates with these oppositions will determine whether "truth" turns into an illusory and schlerotic schematization or an affirmative possibility.

Notes

1   See Derrida's ". . . That Dangerous Supplement . . . ," in *Of Grammatology*, trans. Gayatri
    Spivak (Baltimore: Johns Hopkins University Press, 1976).
2   Another word for this framing is "spin." It is of some interest that framing has both a
    neutral or constitutive sense (in which, in principle, framing supplies a useful orientation),
    and a normatively burdened sense in which a defendant claims that he has been framed,
    set up. The operation of the frame at all has a disturbing effect on a naive understanding
    of truth. Blurring the distinction between a benign and a perverse framing would only
    add to the tribulation.
3   For example, Terry Eagleton and Christopher Norris.
4   Marx and Engels, *Selected Works* (Moscow: Foreign Languages Publishing House, 1962),
    vol. 2, p. 488.
5   Ibid.
6   Such a pluralistic monism is defended by Pierre Bourdieu. His neo-Marxist theory of
    practice treats the social world as a multidimensional space differentiated into relatively
    autonomous fields; and it distinguishes between different kinds of "economy," including
    an "economy" of "symbolic" and "cultural capital." See esp. Pierre Bourdieu, *Language and
    Symbolic Power* (Cambridge, MA: Harvard University Press, 1991).

7   This comes from Nietzsche's *Twilight of the Idols*, trans. R. J. Hollingdale (Harmondsworth: Penguin, 1968), p. 41.

8   Consider more generally Derrida's account of the general strategy of deconstruction as a creative displacement of the rank ordering of such oppositions, in *Positions*, trans. Alan Bass (Chicago: University of Chicago Press, 1981).

9   See our selection from Deleuze.

10 See Slavoj Žižek, *For They Know Not What They Do* (London: Verso, 1991), p. 165.

11 *The Žižek Reader*, ed. Elizabeth Wright and Edmond Wright (Oxford: Blackwell, 1999), p. ix. He continues: "There is no effective freedom without 'terror' – that is, without some form of the unconditional pressure that threatens the very core of our being."

12 *Herculine Barbine* (Brighton: Harvester, 1980), pp. x–xi.

13 Eva K. Sedgwick, *Epistemology of the Closet* (Berkeley and Los Angeles: University of California Press, 1990).

14 For a brilliant discussion of the subversion *versus* containment debate, see Jonathan Dollimore, *Sexual Dissidence* (Oxford: Oxford University Press, 1991).

15 Judith Butler, *Gender Trouble* (New York: Routledge, 1990); idem, *Bodies that Matter* (New York and London: Routledge, 1993); idem, *Excitable Speech* (New York and London: Routledge, 1997).

16 See Paul Ricoeur's "Truth and Falsehood," in *History and Truth* (Evanston, IL: Northwestern University Press, 1965), pp. 165–91, an essay we would like to have included in this volume.

From Slavoj Žižek, *For They Know Not What They Do*

In psychoanalysis [. . .] *truth* belongs to the order of contingency: we vegetate in our everyday life, deep into the universal Lie that structures it, when, all of a sudden, some totally contingent encounter – a casual remark by a friend, an incident we witness – evokes the memory of an old repressed trauma and shatters our self-delusion. Psychoanalysis is here radically anti-Platonic: the Universal is the domain of Falsity *par excellence*, whereas truth emerges as a particular contingent encounter which renders visible its "repressed". The dimension lost in "possibility" is precisely this traumatic, unwarranted character of the emergence of truth: when a truth becomes "possible", it loses the character of an "event", it changes into a mere factual accuracy and thereby becomes part of the ruling universal Lie.

We can see, now, how far Lacanian psychoanalysis is from the pluralist-pragmatic "liberalism" of the Rortyan kind: Lacan's final lesson is not relativity and plurality of truths but the hard, traumatic fact that in every concrete constellation *truth is bound to emerge* in some contingent detail. In other words, although truth is context-dependent – although there is no truth in general, but always the truth *of* some situation – there is none the less in every plural field a particular point which articulates its truth and as such *cannot* be relativized; in this precise sense, truth is always One.

From Judith Butler, *Bodies that Matter*

If, as Žižek argues, "the real itself offers no support for a direct symbolization of it", then what is the rhetorical status of the metatheoretical claim which symbolizes the real for us? Because the real can never be symbolized, this impossibility constitutes the permanent pathos of symbolization. [. . .]

As resistance to symbolization, the "real" functions in an exterior relation to language, as the inverse of mimetic representationalism, that is, as the site where all efforts

Slavoj Žižek, excerpt from *For They Know Not What They Do: Enjoyment as a Political Factor* (London and New York: Verso, 1991), p. 196. Reprinted by permission of the publisher.

Judith Butler, excerpt (© 1993) from *Bodies That Matter: On the Discursive Limits of "Sex,"* (New York and London: Routledge, 1993), p. 207. Reprinted by permission of Routledge/Taylor & Francis Books, Inc. and the author.

Luce Irigaray, "The Power of Discourse and the Subordination of the Feminine," from *This Sex Which Is Not One*, trans. Catherine Porter with Carolyn Burke (New York: Cornell University Press, 1985), selections from pp. 68, 69, 74, 75, 76, 79, 80, 85. Reprinted by permission of the publisher.

Luce Irigaray, "Veiled Lips," in *Marine Lover of Friedrich Nietzsche*, trans. Gillian C. Gill (New York: Columbia University Press, 1991), p. 86. Reprinted by permission of Columbia University Press.

Jean Baudrillard, *Simulacra and Simulacrum*, trans. Shiela Faria Glaser (Ann Arbor: University of Michigan, 1984), selections from pp. 1–7, 12, 27. Reprinted by permission of the University of Michigan Press.

Gilles Deleuze, *Cinema 2. The Time-Image*, trans. H. Tomlinson and R. Galeta (Minneapolis: University of Minneapolis Press, 1989), selections from pp. 129–47. Reprinted by permission of the University of Minnesota Press and Athlone Press.

to represent must founder. The problem here is that there is no way within this frame-work to politicize the relation between language and the real. What counts as the "real," in the sense of the unsymbolizable, is always relative to a linguistic domain that authorizes and produces that foreclosure, and achieves that effect through producing and policing a set of constitutive exclusions. Even if every discursive formation is pro-duced through exclusion, that is not to claim that all exclusions are equivalent: what is needed is a way to assess politically how the production of cultural unintelligibil-ity is mobilized variably to regulate the political field, i.e., who will count as a "subject," who will be required not to count. To freeze the real as the impossible "outside" to discourse is to institute a permanently unsatisfiable desire for an ever elusive referent: the sublime object of ideology. The fixity and universality of this rela-tion between language and the real produces, however, a prepolitical pathos that pre-cludes the kind of analysis that would take the real/reality distinction as the instrument and effect of contingent relations of power.

From Luce Irigaray, "The Power of Discourse and the Subordination of the Feminine"

[W]hat is important is to disconcert the staging of representation according to *exclu-sively* 'masculine' parameters, that is, according to a phallocratic order. It is not a matter of toppling that order so as to replace it – that amounts to the same thing in the end – but of disrupting and modifying it, starting from an 'outside' that is exempt, in part, from phallocratic law.

[. . .] *Why this critique of Freud?*

Because in the process of elaborating a theory of sexuality, Freud brought to light something that had been operative all along though it remained implicit, hidden, unknown: *the sexual indifference that underlies the truth of any science, the logic of every dis-course.* [. . .] Freud does not see *two sexes* whose differences are articulated in the act of intercourse, and [. . .] in the imaginary and symbolic processes [. . .] The 'feminine' is always described in terms of deficiency or atrophy, as the other side of the sex that alone holds a monopoly on value: the male sex. Hence the all to well-known 'penis envy'. [. . .] All Freud's statements describing feminine sexuality overlook the fact that the female sex might possibly have its own 'specificity'.

[. . .]

[I]t is indeed precisely philosophical discourse that we have to challenge, and *disrupt*, inasmuch as this discourse sets forth the law for all others, inasmuch as it constitutes the discourse on discourse. [. . .]

Now, this domination of the philosophical logos stems in large part from its power to *reduce all others to the economy of the Same* [. . .], and [. . .] from its power to *eradicate the difference between the sexes* in systems that are self-representative of a 'masculine subject'.

[. . .]

What is called for instead is an examination of the *operation of 'grammar'* of each figure of discourse. [. . .]

There is, in an initial phase, perhaps only one 'path', the one historically assigned to the feminine: that of *mimicry*. One must assume the feminine role deliberately. Which means already to convert a form of subordination into an affirmation, and thus to begin to thwart it. [. . .]

To play with mimesis is thus, for a woman, to try to recover the place of her exploitation by discourse, without allowing herself to be simply reduced to it.

[. . .]

How, then, are we to try to redefine this language work that would leave space for the feminine? Let us say that every dichotomizing [. . .] break [. . .] has to be disrupted. Nothing is ever to be *posited* that is not also reversed and caught up again in the *supplementarity of this reversal.*

[. . .]

The 'feminine' is never to be identified except by and for the masculine, the reciprocal proposition not being 'true'.

From Luce Irigaray, "Veiled Lips"

She does not set herself up as *one*, as a (single) female unit. She is not closed up or around one single truth or essence. The essence of a truth remains foreign to her. She neither has nor is a being. And she does not oppose a feminine truth to the masculine truth. Because this would once again amount to playing the – man's – game of castration. If the female sex takes place by embracing itself, by endlessly sharing and exchanging its lips, its edges, its borders, and their "content," as it ceaselessly becomes other, no stability of essence is proper to her.

From Jean Baudrillard, "The Precession of the Simulacra"

Today abstraction is no longer that of the map, the double, the mirror or the concept. Simulation is no longer that of a territory, a referential being, or a substance. It is the generation by models of a real without origin or reality: a hyperreal. The territory no longer precedes the map, nor does it survive it. It is nevertheless the map that precedes the territory – *precession of simulacra* – that engenders the territory and if one must return to the fable, today it is the territory whose shreds slowly rot across the extent of the map. It is the real, and not the map, whose vestiges persist here and there in the deserts that are no longer those of the Empire, but ours. *The desert of the real itself.*

[. . .]

Never again will the real have the chance to produce itself – such is the vital function of the model in a system of death, or rather of anticipated resurrection that no longer even gives the event of death a chance. A hyperreal henceforth sheltered from the imaginary, and from any distinction between the real and the imaginary, leaving room only for the orbital recurrence of models and the simulated generation of differences.

[. . .]

Therefore, pretending or dissimulating, leaves the reality principle intact: the difference is always clear, it is simply masked; whereas simulation threatens the difference between the "true" and the "false", between the "real" and the "imaginary".

[. . .]

Had [the Iconoclasts] believed that images only obfuscated or masked the Platonic idea of God, there would have been no reason to destroy them. One can live with the idea of distorted truth. But their metaphysical despair came from the idea that the image didn't conceal anything at all [. . .] What if God himself can be simulated, that is to say, can be reduced to the signs that constitute faith?

[. . .]

Such would be the successive phases of the image: 1. It is the reflection of a profound reality. 2. It masks and denatures a profound reality. 3. It masks the *absence* of a profound reality. 4. It has no relation to any reality whatsoever: it is its own pure simulacrum. In the first case, the image is a *good* appearance: the representation is of the sacramental order. In the second, it is an *evil* appearance: of the order of maleficence. In the third, it *plays at being* an appearance: it is of the order of sorcery. In the fourth, it is no longer in the order of appearances, but of simulation. The transition from signs that dissimulate something to signs which dissimulate that there is nothing marks a decisive turning point. The first reflects a theology of truth and secrecy (to which the notion of ideology still belongs). The second inaugurates an era of simulacra and simulation, in which there is no longer a God to recognize his own, nor any Last Judgment to separate the false from the true, the real from its artificial resurrection, as everything is already dead and resurrected in advance.

When the real is no longer what it used to be, nostalgia assumes its full meaning. There is a plethora of myths of origin and signs of reality a plethora of truth, of secondary objectivity and authenticity. Escalation of the true, of the lived experience, resurrection of the figurative where the object and substance have disappeared. Panic-stricken production of the real and of the referential, parallel to and greater than the panic of material production: this is how simulation appears in the phase that concerns us – a strategy of the real, of the neoreal and the hyperreal, that everywhere is the double of a strategy of deterrence.

[. . .]

Disneyland exists in order to hide that it is the "real" country, all of "real" America that *is* Disneyland. [. . .] Disneyland is presented as imaginary in order to make us believe that the rest is real, whereas all of Los Angeles and the America that surrounds it are no longer real, but belong to the hyperreal and to the order of simulation. . . . saving the reality principle.

[. . .]

It is always the goal of the ideological analysis to restore the objective process; it is always a false problem to wish to restore the truth beneath the simulacrum.

From Gilles Deleuze, *Cinema 2: The Time-Image*

The power of the false exists only from the perspective of a series of powers, always referring to each other and passing into one another. So that investigators, witnesses and innocent or guilty heroes will participate in the same power of the false the degrees of which they will embody, at each stage of the narration. Even 'the truthful man ends up realizing that he has never stopped lying' as Nietzsche said. The forger will thus be inseparable from a chain of forgers into whom he metamorphoses. There is no unique forger, and, if the forger reveals something, it is the existence behind him of another forger, if only the state as in the financial operations in *Stavisky* or in *Le grand escroc*. The truthful man will form part of the chain, at one end like the artist, at the other end, the nth power of the false.

Everywhere it is the metamorphoses of the false which replace the form of the true.
   This is the essential point: how the new regime of the image (the direct time-image) works with pure crystalline optical and sound descriptions, and falsifying, purely chronic narrations. Description stops presupposing a reality and narration stops referring to a form of the true at one and the same time. [. . .] The neo-realist resolution still retained a reference to a form of the true, although it profoundly renewed it, and certain authors were freed from it in their development (Fellini, and even Visconti). But the new wave deliberately broke with the form of the true to replace it by the powers of life, cinematographic powers considered to be more profound.

[. . .]

There is a Nietzscheanism in Welles, as if Welles were retracing the main points of Nietzsche's critique of truth: the 'true world' does not exist, and, if it did, would be inaccessible, impossible to describe, and, if it could be described, would be useless, superfluous. The true world implies a 'truthful man', a man who wants the truth, but such a man has strange motives, as if he were hiding another man in him, a revenge: Othello wants the truth, but out of jealousy, or, worse, out of revenge for being black. [. . .] The truthful man in the end wants nothing other than to judge life; he holds up a superior value, the good, in the name of which he will be able to judge, he is craving to judge, he sees in life an evil, a fault which is to be atoned for: the moral origin of the notion of truth. In the Nietzschean fashion, Welles has constantly battled against the system of judgement: there is no value superior to life, life is not to be judged or justified, it is innocent, it has 'the innocence of becoming', beyond good and evil . . .

[. . .] In Welles, the system of judgement becomes definitively impossible, even and especially for the viewer. [. . .] If the ideal of truth crumbles, the relations of appearance will no longer be sufficient to maintain the possibility of judgement. In Nietzsche's phrase, 'with the real world we have also abolished the apparent world'.

What remains? There remain bodies, which are forces, nothing but forces. But force no longer refers to a centre, any more than it confronts a setting or obstacles.

[. . .]

[. . .] Nietzsche said: behind the truthful man, who judges life, there is the sick man, sick with life itself. And Welles adds: behind the frog, the epitome of the truthful animal, there is the scorpion, the animal sick with itself. The first is an idiot and the second is a bastard. They are, however, complementary as two figures of nihilism, two figures of the will to power.

Does this not amount to restoring a system of judgement? [. . .] Of course there is no more truth in one life than in the other; there is only becoming, and becoming is the power of the false of life, the will to power. But there is good and bad, that is, noble and base. According to physicists, noble energy is the kind which is capable of transforming itself, while the base kind can no longer do so. There is will to power on both sides, but the latter is nothing more than will-to-dominate in the exhausted becoming of life, while the former is artistic will or 'virtue which gives', the creation of new possibilities, in the outpouring becoming.

[. . .]

[. . .] [T]he forger cannot be reduced to a simple copier, nor to a liar, because what is false is not simply a copy, but already the model. Should we not say, then, that the artist, even Vermeer, even Picasso, is a forger, since he makes a model with appearances . . . [. . .] What we can criticize in the forgers, as well as in the truthful man, is their exaggerated taste for *form*: they have neither the sense nor the power of metamorphosis; they reveal an impoverishment of the vital force [*élan vital*], of an already exhausted life. The difference between the forger, the expert and Vermeer is that the first two barely know how to change. Only the creative artist takes the power of the false to a degree which is realized, not in form, but in transformation. There is no longer either truth or appearance. There is no longer either invariable form or variable point of view on to a form. There is a point of view which belongs so much to the thing that the thing is constantly being transformed in a becoming identical to point of view. Metamorphosis of the true. What the artist is, is *creator of truth*, because truth is not to be achieved, formed, or reproduced; it has to be created. There is no other truth than the creation of the New: creativity, emergence, what Melville called 'shape' in contrast to 'form'. Art is the continual production of *shapes*, reliefs and the projections. The truthful man and the forger form part of the same chain, but, in the end, it is not they who are projected, elevated, or excavated; it is the artist, creator of the true, in the very place where the false attains its final power: goodness, generosity. Nietzsche drew up a list of the characters of the 'will to power': the truthful man, then all the forgers who presuppose him and that he presupposes, the long, exhausted cohort of 'superior men', but, still behind, the new man, Zarathustra, the artist or outpouring life.

SUGGESTED READING

Baudrillard, Jean, *Simulacra and Simulations* (Ann Arbor: University of Michigan, 1994).

Baudrillard, Jean, *Selected Writings* (Stanford, CA: Stanford University Press, 2001).

Bourdieu, Pierre, *Language and Symbolic Power* (Cambridge, MA: Harvard University Press, 1991).

Butler, Judith, *Gender Trouble: Feminism and the Subversion of Identity* (New York: Routledge, 1990).

Butler, Judith, *Bodies that Matter: On the Discursive Limits of "Sex"* (New York and London: Routledge, 1993).

Butler, Judith, *Excitable Speech: A Politics of the Performative* (New York and London: Routledge, 1997).

Deleuze, Gilles, *Cinema 2: The Time-Image* (Minneapolis: University of Minnesota Press, 1989).

Dollimore, Jonathan, *Sexual Dissidence: Augustine to Wilde, Freud to Foucault* (Oxford: Oxford University Press, 1991).

Foucault, Michel, *Herculine Barbine* (Brighton: Harvester, 1980).

Irigaray, Luce, "The Power of Discourse and the Subordination of the Feminine," in *The Sex Which is Not One*, trans. Catherine Porter with Carolyn Burke (Ithaca, NY: Cornell University Press, 1985).

Irigaray, Luce, *The Irigaray Reader*, ed. Margaret Whitford (Oxford: Blackwell, 1991).

Ricoeur, Paul, *History and Truth* (Evanston, IL: Northwestern University Press, 1965).

Sedgwick, Eva K., *Epistemology of the Closet* (Berkeley and Los Angeles: University of California Press, 1990).

Žižek, Slavoj, *For They Know Not What They Do: Enjoyment as a Political Factor* (London and New York: Verso, 1991).

Žižek, Slavoj, *The Žižek Reader*, ed. Elizabeth Wright and Edmond Wright (Oxford: Blackwell, 1999).

INDEX